MW01537485

Charles Fillmore

The Infinite Realms of the Spirit

e-artnow 2022

Charles Fillmore

The Infinite Realms of the Spirit

Christian Healing, The Twelve Powers of Man, Prosperity, Jesus Christ Heals, Mysteries of John, Atom-Smashing Power of Mind

e-artnow, 2022
Contact: info@e-artnow.org

ISBN 978-80-273-4520-5

Contents

Christian Healing

Preface

These are not simply lectures; they are, rather, lessons. They are not merely to be read; they are to be studied and applied as one studies and applies mathematical rules.

When the text suggests that the reader "hold a thought," or affirm or deny a certain proposition, the student should stop reading, and both audibly and mentally do as bidden. This will set up new thought currents in mind and body, and will make way for the spiritual illumination that will follow in all who are faithful to these instructions.

The statements following each lesson should be used for mental discipline. Write these statements down and apply them daily while studying the lesson to which they correspond. Anyone can do spiritual healing who will use the simple rules of denial and affirmation here set forth. If you wish to heal another, hold him in mind and mentally repeat the denials and affirmations; this will raise your consciousness to spiritual reality, where all healing power originates. If you wish to heal yourself, talk to your mind and body as you would talk to a patient

Lesson One

The True Character of Being

1. *"There is a spirit in man, and the breath of the Almighty giveth them understanding."* The science that is here set forth is founded upon Spirit. It does not always conform to intellectual standards, but it is, nevertheless, scientific. The facts of Spirit are of a spiritual character and, when understood in their right relation, they are orderly. Orderliness is law, and is the test of true science.

2. The lawful truths of Spirit are more scientific than the constantly shifting opinions based on intellectual standards. The only real science is the science of Spirit. It never changes. It is universally accepted by all who are in Spirit, but one must be *"in the Spirit"* before one can understand this science of Spirit. The mind of Spirit must become active in those who would grasp the orderly science of Being that these lessons proclaim.

3. It is not absolutely necessary that the spiritual part of man's nature be active at the beginning of his study of this science. The primal object of the lessons is to quicken the spiritual realm of consciousness and to bring about the *"breath of the Almighty"* that gives understanding.

4. So let it be understood that we are teaching the science of Spirit, and that those who are receptive to the teaching will be inspired to spiritual consciousness. It is not difficult to accomplish, this receiving the *"breath"* or inspiration of Spirit. We all are inspired by Spirit, in certain states of consciousness. Understanding of the laws governing the realm of Spirit will make it possible to attain this consciousness and to receive this inspiration whenever requirements are met.

5. The starting point in spiritual realization is a right understanding of that One designated as the Almighty. It is strictly logical and scientific to assume that man comes forth from this One, who is named variously, but who, all agree, is the origin of everything. Since man is the offspring of the Almighty, he must have the character of his Parent. If the earthly child resembles his parents, how much more should the heavenly child resemble his Parent. The truth that God is the Father of man does away with the oft proclaimed presumption that it is impossible for the finite to understand the Infinite. God must be in His universe as everywhere intelligent power; otherwise, it would fall to pieces. God is in the universe as its constant *"breath"* or inspiration; hence it is only necessary to find the point of contact in order to understand the One in whom we all *"live, and move, and have our being."*

6. A sense of logic is a fundamental constituent of man's being, and all minds acquiesce in statements of logical sequence. We all see the relation and unity of cause and effect, mentally stated, but, because the realm of forms does not always carry out our premise, we fall away from the true standard and try to convince ourselves that our logic is, somehow, defective. The one important thing that the student of spiritual science must learn is to trust the logic of mind. If appearances are out of harmony with your mental premise, do not let them unseat your logic. *"Judge not according to appearance, but judge righteous judgment."* You would not take the mixed figures of a child working a problem in mathematics as an example of the trueness of the principle; nor could you detect an error in the problem unless you were somewhat familiar with the rules of mathematics. Mental propositions are the standards and governing principles in all sciences developed by man. In the science of creation the same rule holds good. You may rest in the assurance that the principles that you mentally perceive as true of God are inviolate, and that, if there seems to be error in their outworking, it is because of some misapplication on the part of the demonstrator. By holding to the principle and insisting upon its accuracy, you open the way to a fuller understanding of it; you will also be shown the cause of the errors in the demonstration.

7. Then, if you have been in confusion mentally through contemplation of a world both good and evil, and have, in consequence, got into skeptical ways, the only true remedy is to stand by the pure reason of your spiritual perception and let it clear up the proposition for

you. Dismiss all prejudices based upon the mixed perception; make your mind receptive to the clearer understanding that will surely appear when you have taken sides with Spirit, when you look to Spirit alone for the outworking of the problem.

8. This is not blind belief; it is, in the superconsciousness, an acquiescence in the logic of Being. The superconsciousness is man's only sure guide in the mazes of the creative process. By trusting to the infallibility of this guide, man opens himself to the inspiration of the Almighty. Spirituality may be cultivated by, and the deep things of God may be revealed to, anyone who will mentally proclaim and affirm the logical perception of the goodness and the Truth of Being.

9. The central proposition in the inspiration of Spirit is that God, or primal Cause, is good. It does not make any great difference what you name this primal Cause; the important consideration is a right concept of its character. The Hindu calls it Brahma, a being of such stupendous proportions that man shrinks into nothingness in contemplating it. Although this greatness of absolute Being is true, there is also another point of view--the smallness of that same Being as evidenced in the presence of its life in the most insignificant creations. So, in order to get at the very heart of Being, it is necessary to realize that it is manifesting in the least as well as in the greatest, and that, in the bringing forth of a universe, not one idea could be taken away without unbalancing the whole. This brings us to a fuller realization of our importance in the universe and to the necessity of finding our right place. It also puts us into very close touch with the Father of all, the one omnipresent Intelligence pervading everything.

10. The Father within you, so lovingly and familiarly revealed by Jesus, is not a distance, far away in a place called *"heaven."* His abode is in the spiritual realms that underlie all creative forces. As Jesus realized and taught, *"the kingdom of God is within you."* Spirit is the seat of power; its abode is on the invisible side of man's nature.

11. This revelation of God immanent in the universe was clearly set forth by Paul: "over all, and through all, and in all." The inspired ministers of all times have proclaimed the same.

12. The Power that creates and sustains the universe includes in its activity the creating and the sustaining of man. The desire for a fuller understanding of this Power has awakened a great inquiry into the character of the all-pervading One. On every hand men are earnestly seeking to know about God, seeking to come into harmonious relation with Him. Some are succeeding, while others seem to make but little progress. The diversity of results obtained is caused by the variety of ways of approaching the one Mind--for such God is. In mind is the key to the whole situation, and when man clearly discerns the science of mind, he will solve easily all the mysteries of creation.

13. The dictionary definitions of mind and spirit are nearly identical; with this analogy realized, we much more easily get in touch with God. If spirit and mind are synonymous, we readily perceive that there is no great mystery about spiritual things, that they are not far removed from our daily thoughts and experiences. *"Ye are a temple of God, and . . . the Spirit of God dwelleth in you,"* simply means that God dwells in us as our mind dwells in our body. Thus we see that God creates and moves creation through the power of mind. The vehicles of mind are thoughts, and it is through our mind in thought action that we shall find God and do His will.

14. There are mental laws that investigators are discovering, observing, and tabulating as never before in the world's history. Man has the ability to discern and understand the various factors entering into the creative processes of mind, and he is, through the study of mental laws, perceiving and accepting the science of ideas, thoughts, and words. But those who investigate nature and her laws from the intellectual and physical viewpoint fall short of complete understanding, because they fail to trace back to the causing Mind the multitudinous symbols that make up the visible universe. The material forms that we see about us are the chalk marks of a mighty problem being outworked by the one Mind. To comprehend that problem and to catch a slight glimpse of its meaning, we must grasp the ideas that the chalk marks represent; this is what we mean studying Mind back of nature. Man is mind and he is capable of comprehending the plan and the detailed ideas of the supreme Mind.

15. Divine ideas are man's inheritance; they are pregnant with all possibility, because ideas are the foundation and cause of all that man desires. With this understanding as a foundation, we easily perceive how *"all . . . mine are thine."* All the ideas contained in the one Father-Mind are at the mental command of its offspring. Get behind a thing into the mental realm where it exists as an inexhaustible idea, and you can draw upon it perpetually and never deplete the source.

16. With this understanding of the potentiality of primal Cause, we find it a simple matter to work the problem of life--the key to the situation being ideas. Thus life in expression is activity; in Being it is an idea of activity. To make life appear on the visible plane, we have but to open our mind and our thoughts to the divine idea of life and activity, and lo, all visibility is obedient to us. It is through this understanding, and its cultivation in various degrees, that men have acquired the ability to raise dead bodies. Jesus understood this realm of supreme ideas, or, as He termed it, *"the kingdom of God . . . within you."* When He raised Lazarus He invoked this power. When Martha talked about a future resurrection, He said, *"I am the resurrection, and the life: he that believeth on me, though he die, yet shall he live."* One who identifies his whole mind with omnipresent Mind becomes so much at one with it that he can overcome death.

17. The real of the universe is held in the mind of Being as ideas of life, love, substance, intelligence, Truth, and so forth. These ideas may be combined in a multitude of ways, producing infinite variety in the realm of forms. There is a right combination, which constitutes the divine order, the kingdom of heaven on earth. This right relation of ideas and the science of right thought is practical Christianity.

18. The student in the science of Being should start all his investigations and mental activities from the one-Mind foundation. If you are skeptical about the existence of God, or if you are an abstract believer in God without having had any experience or conscious mental awakening that has given you proof, you should be very industrious in prayer, affirmation, and invocation. Remember, God is not a king who can force his presence upon you whether you will or not, but an omnipresent Mind enfolding and interpenetrating all things.

19. There are goodness everlasting and joy beyond expression in a perfect union between your mind and this perfect Mind. The point of contact is a willingness and a seeking on your part. *"Seek, and ye shall find; knock, and it shall be opened unto you."*

20. This question naturally presents itself: If we are offspring of Divine Mind, why are we not naturally conscious of its presence? The answer to this is: In using the privilege of our inheritance--the power to make ideas visible as things--we have created a realm that separates us in consciousness from the Father-Mind. This is the teaching of Jesus in the parable of the prodigal son. When we are weary of the sense consciousness, we have only to turn our face (intelligence) toward our Father's house; there we shall meet a loving welcome.

21. The understanding that God is not in a distant heaven, nor located in any way geographically, gives us a feeling of nearness to and unity with the parent Mind. This intercommunion of the man consciousness with the omnipresent spiritual force of the universe was beautifully exemplified by Jesus. God was closer to Him than hands or feet. He referred all things to this loving Father, who was in constant communion and cooperation with the Son; yet there was, even in His case, the independent personal consciousness that beset Him when He sought to be free from mortal limitations. So we should not be discouraged or cast down if we do not quickly find the kingdom of God within us. Jesus spent whole nights in prayer; we should not be weary with a few moments each day. A daily half hour of meditation will open up the mind to a consciousness of the inner One and will reveal many things that are hidden from the natural man.

22. The fact is, Truth cannot be imparted--it must be individually experienced. The presence of Divine Mind in the soul cannot be told in words; it can be hinted at and referred to in parable and likened to this or to that, but it can never be described as it is. The ability of the individual mind to combine the ideas of Divine Mind in a consciousness of its own makes each of us the *"only begotten Son,"* a particular and special creation. No two individuals in all the universe are

exactly alike, because there is always diversity in the ideas appropriated by each individual from Divine Mind.

23. The truth is, then:

That God is Principle, Law, Being, Mind, Spirit, All-Good, omnipotent, omniscient, omnipresent, unchangeable, Creator, Father, Cause, and source of all that is;

That God is individually formed in consciousness in each of us, and is known to us as "Father" when we recognize Him within us as our Creator, as our mind, as our life, as our very being;

That mind has ideas and that ideas have expression; that all manifestation in our world is the result of the ideas that we are holding in mind and are expressing;

That to bring forth or to manifest the harmony of Divine Mind, or the "*kingdom of heaven,*" all our ideas must be one with divine ideas, and must be expressed in the divine order of Divine Mind.

Statements For The Realization Of Divine Mind
(To be used in connection with Lesson One)

1. There is one Presence, one Intelligence, one Substance, one Life: the good omnipotent.

2. God is the name of the everywhere-present Principle, in whom I live, move, and have my being.

3. God is the name of my good.

4. God almighty, *"Father of all, who is over all, and through all, and in all."*

5. Thy name is Spirit. I know Thee as the one, the all-seeing, Mind.

6. *"Our Father who art in heaven [the everywhere-present inner harmony], Hallowed be thy name [wholeness manifests Thy character]."*

7. Thou art always with me as indwelling wisdom and love.

8. Thy law is now the standard of my life, and I am at peace.

9. *"I in thee . . . and thou in me."*

10. Thou art never absent from me--I now see Thee face to face.

11. I think Thy thoughts after Thee.

12. I dwell in Thee and share Thine omnipotence.

13. In Thee is my perfection.

Lesson Two

Being's Perfect Idea

1 . The foundation of our religion is Spirit, and there must be a science of Truth. The science of Truth is God thinking out creation. God is the original Mind in which all real ideas exist. The one original Mind creates by thought. This is stated in the first chapter of John:

2. In the beginning was the Word [Logos--thought-word], and the Word was with God, and the Word was God. The same was in the beginning with God. All things were made through him; and without him was not anything made that hath been made.

3. Eadie's Biblical Cyclopedia says: *"The term Logos means thought expressed, either as an idea in mind or as vocal speech."*

4. An understanding of the Logos reveals to us the law under which all things are brought forth--the law of mind action. Creation takes place through the operation of the Logos. God is thinking the universe into manifestation right now. Even He cannot create without law. The law of the divine creation is the order and harmony of perfect thought.

5. God-Mind expresses its thoughts so perfectly that there is no occasion for change, hence all prayers and supplications for the change of God's will to conform to human desires are futile. God does not change His mind, or trim His thought, to meet the conflicting opinions of mankind. Understanding the perfection of God thoughts, man must conform to them; so conforming, he will discover that there is never necessity for any change of the will of God in regard to human affairs.

6. A key to God-Mind is with everyone--it is the action of the individual mind. Man is created the *"image"* and *"likeness"* of God; man is therefore a phase of God-Mind, and his mind must act like the original Mind. Study your own mind, and through it you will find God-Mind. In no other way can you get a complete understanding of yourself, of the universe, and of the law under which it is being brought forth. When you see the Creator thinking out His universe as the mathematician thinks out his problem, you will understand the necessity for the very apparent effort that nature makes to express itself; you will also understand why the impulse for higher things keeps welling up within your soul. God-Mind is living, acting thoughts. God-Mind is thinking in you; it is pushing your mind to grasp true ideas and carry them into expression.

7. It is therefore true, in logic and in inspiration, that man and the universe are within God-Mind as living, acting thoughts. God-Mind is giving itself to its creations, and those creations thus are evolving an independence that has the power to cooperate with, or to oppose, the original God will. It is then of vital importance to study the mind and understand its laws, because the starting point of every form in the universe is an idea.

8. Every man asks the question at some time, *"What am I?" God answers: "Spiritually you are My idea of Myself as I see Myself in the ideal; physically you are the law of My mind executing that idea." "Great is the mystery of godliness,"* said Paul. A little learning is a dangerous thing in the study of Being. To separate oneself from the whole and then attempt to find out the great mystery is like dissecting inanimate flesh to find the source of life.

9. If you would know the mystery of Being, see yourself in Being. Know yourself as an integral idea in Divine Mind, and all other ideas will recognize you as their fellow worker. Throw yourself out of the Holy Trinity and you become an onlooker. Throw yourself into the Trinity and you become its avenue of expression. The Trinity is known commonly as Father, Son, and Holy Spirit; metaphysically it is known as mind, idea, expression. These three are one. Each sees itself as including the other two, yet in creation separate. Jesus, the type man, placed Himself in the Godhead, and said: *"He that hath seen me hath seen the Father."* But, recognizing the supremacy of spiritual Principle, which He was demonstrating, He said: *"The Father is greater than I."*

10. Reducing the Trinity to simple numbers takes away much of its mystery. When we say that there is one Being with three attitudes of mind, we have stated in plain terms all that is involved in the intricate theological doctrine of the Trinity. The priesthood has always found it profitable to make complex that which is simple. When religion becomes an industry it has its trade secrets, and to the uninitiated they seem very great. Modern investigation of the character of the mind is taking away all the mysteries of Egyptian, Hindu, Hebrew, and many other religious and mystical systems of the past. Advocates of these systems are attempting to perpetuate their so-called secret knowledge through the occult societies springing up on every side in our day, but they meet with indifferent success. The modern Truth seeker takes very little on trust. Unless the claimant to occult lore can demonstrate his power in the world of affairs, people are suspicious of him. Religious awe for the priesthood, which is prevalent in Oriental countries, is lacking in the majority of Western people. In India, a yellow-robed holy man is regarded with reverence by both adults and children; in this country adults stare and small boys throw stones until he seeks the protection of the police. This seems irreverent, almost heathenish, yet it is the expression of an innate repudiation of everything that seeks to establish itself on any other foundation than that of practical demonstration.

11. The mind of God is Spirit, soul, body; that is, mind, idea, expression. The mind of man is Spirit, soul, body--not separate from God-Mind, but existing in it and making it manifest in an identity peculiar to the individual. Every man is building into his consciousness the three departments of God-Mind, and his success in the process is evidenced by the harmony, in his consciousness, of Spirit, soul, and body. If he is all body, he is but one-third expressed. If to body he has added soul, he is two-thirds man, and if to these two he is adding Spirit, he is on the way to the perfect manhood that God designed. Man has neither Spirit, soul, nor body of his own--he has identity only. He can say, *"I."* He uses God Spirit, God soul, and God body, as his *"I"* elects. If he uses them with the idea that they belong to him, he develops selfishness, which limits his capacity and dwarfs his product.

12. In his right relation, man is the inlet and the outlet of an everywhere-present life, substance, and intelligence. When his *"I"* recognizes this fact and adjusts itself to the invisible expressions of the one Mind, man's mind becomes harmonious; his life, vigorous and perpetual; his body, healthy. It is imperative that the individual understand this relation in order to grow naturally. It must not only be understood as an abstract proposition, but it is necessary that he blend his life consciously with God life, his intelligence with God intelligence, and his body with the *"Lord's body."* Conscious identification must prevail in the whole man before he can be in right relation. This involves not only a recognition of the universal intelligence, life, and substance, but also their various combinations in man's consciousness. These combinations are, in the individual world, dependent for perfect expression upon man's recognition of and his loyalty to his origin--God-Mind. Man is in God-Mind as a perfect idea. God-Mind is constantly trying to express in every man its perfect idea, the real and only man.

13. The perfect-man idea in God-Mind is known under various names in the many religious systems. The Krishna of the Hindu is the same as the Messiah of the Hebrews. All the great religions of the world are founded upon spiritual science, but not all of that science is understood by their followers. The Hebrews had been told again and again, by the spiritually wise, that a Messiah, or Christ man, would be born in their midst, but when He came they did not recognize Him, because of their lack of understanding. They understood only the letter of their religion. A similar lack of understanding prevails generally today. The Christ man, or perfect idea of God-Mind, is now being expressed and demonstrated by men and women as never before in the history of the race. Those who claim to be followers of the true religion should beware of putting the perfect-man idea out of their synagogues as the Jews put out Jesus Christ. The ancient Pharisees asked Jesus: "By what authority doest thou these things?" Modern Pharisees are repeating the same question. The substance of Jesus' answer was: *"By their fruits ye shall know them."* (Read Mt. 21:23-46.)

14. This perfect-idea-of-God man is your true self. God-Mind is, under the law of thought, constantly seeking to release its perfection in you. It is your spirit, and when you ask for its guidance and place yourself, by prayer and affirmation, in mental touch with it, there is a great increase in its manifestation in your life. It has back of it all the powers of Being, and there is nothing that it cannot do if you give it full sway and make your thought strong enough to express the great forces that it is seeking to express in you.

15. A most important part of the law of mind action is the fact of thought-unity. It is absolutely necessary to understand the nature of this fact before one can demonstrate the power of the superconscious mind. Among our associates, we like and are attracted to those who understand and sympathize with our thoughts. The same law holds good in Divine Mind--its thoughts are drawn to and find expression in the minds of those who raise themselves to its thought standard. This means that we must think of ourselves as God thinks of us, in order to appreciate and to receive His thoughts and to bring forth the fruits. If you think of yourself as anything less than the perfect child of the perfect Parent, you lower the thought standard of your mind and cut off the influx of thought from Divine Mind. Jesus referred to this law when He said: *"Ye therefore shall be perfect, as your heavenly Father is perfect."*

16. When we go forth in the understanding of man's perfect nature, we find a new state of consciousness forming in us; we think and do many things not according to the established custom, and the old consciousness rises up and asks: "By what authority?" We have so long looked for man-made authority in religious matters that we feel that we are treading on dangerous ground if we dare to think beyond prescribed doctrines. Right here we should appeal to the supreme reason of Spirit and proclaim what we perceive as the highest truth, regardless of precedent or tradition, mental ignorance or physical limitation: I AM is the "image of God," the "only begotten Son" (the expressed, or pressed out, Mind) of the Most High. This is our true estate, and we shall never realize it until we enter into it in mind, because there it is, and nowhere else.

17. Only through the superconscious mind can we behold and commune with God. "No man hath seen God at any time; the only begotten Son, who is in the bosom of the Father, he hath declared him." It is taught that Jesus was exclusively the "only begotten Son," but He Himself said: "Is it not written in your law, 'I said, Ye are gods'?" He proclaimed the unity of all men in the Father. "I am the light of the world." "Ye are the light of the world." Paul says, "As many as are led by the Spirit of God, these are sons of God." We are "heirs of God, and joint-heirs with Christ."

18. In this matter of sonship is one important point that we should not overlook; that point is the difference between those who perceive their sonship as a possibility, and those who have demonstrated it in their lives. "Ye must be born anew," was the proclamation of Jesus. The first birth is the human--the self-consciousness of man as an intellectual and physical being; the second birth, the being *"born anew"* is the transformation and translation of the human to a higher plane of consciousness as the son of God.

19. The second birth is that in which we *"put on Christ"* It is a process of mental adjustment and body transmutation that takes place right here on earth. *"Have this mind in you, which was also in Christ Jesus"* is an epitome of a mental and physical change that may require years to work out. But all men must go through this change before they can enter into eternal life and be as Jesus Christ is.

20. This being *"born anew,"* or *"born from above,"* is not a miraculous change that takes place in man; it is the establishment in his consciousness of that which has always existed as the perfect-man idea in Divine Mind. God created man in His *"image"* and *"likeness"* God being Spirit, the man that He creates is spiritual. It follows as a logical sequence that man, on the positive, formative, creative side of his nature, is the direct emanation of his Maker; that he is just like his Maker; that he is endowed with creative power, and that his very being is involved in God-Mind which he is releasing by his creative thought. It is to this spiritual man that the Father says: *"All things that are mine are thine."*

21. Understanding of the status of all men in Divine Mind gives us a new light upon the life of Jesus of Nazareth and makes plain many of His seemingly mysterious statements. This spiritual consciousness, or Christ Mind, was quickened in Him, and through it He realized His relation to First Cause. When asked to show the Father, whom He constantly talked to as if He were personally present, He said, *"He that hath seen me hath seen the Father."* His personality had been merged into the universal. The mind of Being and the thought of Being were joined, and there was no consciousness of separation or apartness.

22. Everything about man presages the higher man. Foremost of these prophesies is the almost universal desire for the freedom that spiritual life promises, freedom from material limitations. The immortal perception spurs man on to invent mechanical devices that will carry him above limitations. For example, he flies by means external. In his spiritual nature he is provided with the ability to overcome gravity; when this power is developed, it will be common to see men and women passing to and fro in the air, without wings or mechanical appliances of any description.

23. The human organism has a world of latent energies waiting to be brought into manifestation. Distributed throughout the body are many nerve centers whose offices are as yet but vaguely understood. In the New Testament, which is a work on spiritual physiology, these centers are referred to as "*cities*" and "*rooms*." The "*upper room*" is the very top of the head. Jesus was in this "upper room" of His mind when Nicodemus came to see Him "*by night*"–meaning the ignorance of sense consciousness. It was in this "*upper room*" that the followers of Jesus prayed until the Holy Spirit came upon them. The superconsciousness, or Christ Mind, finds its first entrance into the natural mind through this higher brain center. By thought, speech, and deed this Christ Mind is brought into manifestation. The new birth is symbolically described in the history of Jesus.

24. *"Verily I say unto you, that many prophets and righteous men desired to see the things which ye see, and saw them not; and to hear the things which ye hear, and heard them not."*

Statements For The Realization Of The Son Of God
(To be used in connection with Lesson Two)

1. I am the son of God, and the Spirit of the Most High dwells in me.
2. I am the only begotten son, dwelling in the bosom of the Father.
3. I am the lord of my mind, and the ruler of all its thought people.
4. I am the Christ of God.
5. Through Christ I have dominion over my every thought and word.
6. I am the beloved son in whom the Father is well pleased.
7. Of a truth I am the son of God.
8. All that the Father has is mine.
9. He that hath seen me hath seen the Father.
10. I and my Father are one.
11. My highest ideal is a perfect man.
12. My next highest ideal is that I am that perfect man.
13. I am the image and likeness of God, in whom is my perfection.
14. It is written in the law of the Lord, "*Ye are gods, and . . . sons of the Most High.*"
15. These are written, that ye may believe that Jesus is the Christ, the Son of God; and that believing ye may have life in his name.

Lesson Three

Manifestation

1. As a rule, religious people are not scientific. They think that religion and science are separated by a gulf, and that the scientific mind is spiritually dangerous. Science, to them, is associated with Darwin, Huxley, and other students of natural law who have been skeptical about the accuracy of the Bible from the standpoint of natural science, and whom, because of this skepticism, they brand as infidels. Hence it has come to be almost heresy for a good Christian to think about his religion as having a *"scientific"* side.

2. By science we mean the systematic and orderly arrangement of knowledge. This definition does not confine science to the facts of the material world. There is a science in Christianity, and it is only through the understanding of this science as a fundamental of Christianity that the Christ teachings can be fully demonstrated in the life of man. To fail to understand the science upon which spiritual understanding rests is to fail in nearly every demonstration of its power. Paul says: *"I will pray with the spirit, and I will pray with the understanding also."*

3. There is a gulf between the high spiritual understanding and the material manifestation. It is only by bridging this gulf that science and religion can be reconciled. The bridge needed is the structure that thought builds. When Christians understand the science of thinking, the power of thought to manifest itself, and how the manifestation of thought is accomplished, they will no longer fear material science; when material scientists have fathomed the real nature of the living force that they even now discern as ever active in all nature's structures, they will have more respect for religion.

4. Both the religionist and the physicist incorrectly hold that the Bible is a historical description of man's creation. Beginning with the very first chapter of Genesis, the Bible is an allegory. It is so regarded by the majority of Hebrew scholars, and they certainly ought to know the character of their own Scriptures. Paul was a Hebrew, and thoroughly versed in the occultism of spiritual writings; he said, referring to the story of Abraham and Sarah, *"Which things contain an allegory."* Hebrews almost universally claim that the story of the Garden of Eden, Adam, Eve, and the serpent is symbology.

5. In the face of these facts, it seems strange that orthodox Christianity should insist that the Bible is a literal history. It is this literal viewpoint that has stood in the way of true spiritual understanding. Read in the light of Spirit, the 1st chapter of Genesis is a description, in symbol, of the creative action of universal Mind in the realm of ideas. It does not pertain to the manifest universe any more than the history of the inventor's idea pertains to the machine that he builds to manifest the idea. First the problem is thought out, and afterward the structure is produced. So God builds His universe. This is explained in the 2nd chapter of Genesis, which says that God *"rested . . . from all his work," and yet there were no plants of the field, "and there was not a man to till the ground." "And Jehovah God formed man of the dust of the ground, and breathed into his nostrils the breath of life; and man became a living soul."*

6. Only through perception of the mental law by which ideas manifest from the formless to the formed can we understand and reconcile these two apparently contradictory chapters. In the light of true understanding everything is made plain, and we discern just how Divine Mind is creating man and the universe: first the ideal concept, then the manifestation.

7. The six days of creation, as described in the 1st chapter of Genesis, represent six great ideal projections from Divine Mind, each more comprehensive than its predecessor. The final climax is reached in the sixth degree, when that phase of Being called man appears, having dominion over everything, or every idea, that has gone before. This ideal man, who is made in the *"image"* and *"likeness"* of Elohim, is the epitome and focal center around which all creation revolves; hence the one important study of man is the mind of man. In mind is the key to all mysteries, both religious and material. When we know how mind manifests from the ideal to

the so-called real, we are no longer in the dark, but have that Truth which Jesus said would make us free.

8. There is but one man. On the spiritual side of his being, every man in the universe has access to that man, eternally existing in Divine Mind as a perfect-man idea. When man appreciates this mighty truth and applies it in his conscious thinking, all manifestation becomes harmonious and orderly to him, and he sees God everywhere.

9. A right understanding of the divine law of creation reveals man as a necessary factor in God's great work. Through man, God is forming or manifesting outwardly that which exists in the ideal. In order, then, that the creation shall go on and be fulfilled as God has designed, man must not only understand the law of mind action in his individual thought, but he must also understand his relation to the universal thought. Not only must he understand it, but in his every thought he must consciously cooperate with divine ideals. Jesus understood this law and repeatedly claimed that He was sent of God to carry out the divine will in the world. This commission is given to every man, and man will not have satisfaction in life until he recognizes this universal law; until he becomes an obedient, willing co-worker with Divine Mind.

10. Spiritual man is I AM; manifest man is I will. I AM is the Jehovah God of Scripture, and I will is the Adam. It is the I AM man that forms and breathes into the I will man the *"breath of life."* When we are in the realm of the ideal, we are I AM; when we are expressing ideals in thought or in act, we are I will. When the I will gets so absorbed in its realm of expression that it loses sight of the ideal and centers all its attention in the manifest, it is Adam listening to the serpent and hiding from Jehovah God. This breaks the connection between Spirit and manifestation, and man loses that spiritual consciousness which is his under divine law. In this state of mind the real source of supply is cut off, and there is a drawing upon the reserve forces of the organism, the tree of life. It is in this experience that man is described as being driven out of the Garden of Eden, or the paradise of Being.

11. Every idea projects form. The physical body is the projection of man's idea; we carry the body in the mind. The body is the fruit of the tree of life, which grows in the midst of the garden of mind. If the body-idea is grounded and rooted in Divine Mind, the body will be filled with a perpetual life flow that will repair all its imperfect parts and heal all its diseases.

12. When man realizes that there is but one body-idea and that the conditions in his body express the character of his thought, he has the key to bodily perfection and immortality in the flesh. But *"flesh and blood cannot inherit the kingdom of God."* The "flesh and blood" here referred to is the corruptible-body idea that men carry in mind. When we get the right idea of the origin and character of the body, the corruptible will put on incorruption and our bodies will be raised from the dead, as was the body of Jesus. "Neither was he left unto Hades, nor did his flesh see corruption."

13. The resurrection of our bodies from the dead begins in our minds. We must change our ideas about the body, and hold to the truth of its origin and destiny as conceived of God, in whose mind its real being exists. The spiritual body of man is the conception of Divine Mind, the creation of Spirit for us. Our work is to make this spiritual body manifest.

14. When we have the right understanding of creation, and, with the help of this understanding, begin the redemption of the body, the Spirit of God quickens the inner life of the whole organism, and we know that the promise in Acts 2:17 is being fulfilled in us: "In the last days, saith God, I will pour forth of my Spirit upon all flesh."

15. The problem before man in the present race consciousness is how to get back to the "Father's house," in which is inexhaustible abundance. As it is by an exercise of the free will inherent in us that we separate ourselves from the Father, so it must be through that same faculty that we again make conscious union with Him. We must realize the foolishness of living in that most external realm where only the husks of things are, and upon which we would fain satisfy ourselves, but cannot. Then let us turn our attention within; by traveling for a season in that direction we find the source and substance of life.

16. This turning within, after one has for a long time been looking without, is no easy matter. The mind that has been trained to the standards of the formed universe is often slow to grasp the formless. But there is a state of consciousness in the soul that has, through ages of experience, learned about this formless world and is at home in it. Our dreams, visions, and spiritual experiences, of which we seldom speak, come from this inner realm. So it is found that we have a household waiting for us on the subjective side of our being, and its welcome is worth all the effort of our seeking it. "*We seek a country from which we came forth,*" Paul said in substance.

17. Individualize yourself in the highest degree by affirming that in Spirit and in Truth you are all that God is. This is true of man in his spiritual nature, and he must claim the supreme inheritance before he can enter into the mighty mental and spiritual forces that are released from the kingdom of God within man. No one enters the kingdom of God, and sits upon the throne and abides there, until he has the courage and fearlessness to proclaim himself joint heir with Jesus. Then he must prove his dominion by his purity of motive, an unselfish devotion to Truth universal, and a steady industry and patience in overcoming the limitation of his own sense consciousness.

18. Man's true identity is as the perfect-man idea in Divine Mind. This idea has no mind separate from the one universal realm of ideas. Man must establish himself in the one and only Mind. He came forth from it, and his whole existence depends on it; then why should he not consciously make the mental connection that will establish in himself the harmony and order on which all existence depends?

19. Nearly all religious systems aim to bring about this unity between God and man, and many of them are quite successful in their methods. We owe much to the church, to the education and the help that we have received directly and indirectly through the efforts of spiritual-minded people in all ages. The Truth has pressed upon them, and they have demonstrated it up to their highest understanding of it. We are now in a fuller degree of enlightenment concerning the spiritual laws that govern man and the universe, and consequently we can more definitely and scientifically apply the methods for spiritual development that, in religious systems, are usually followed through faith. To your faith you can now add understanding.

20. One's getting back into the Garden of Eden, or taking possession of the Promised Land, is a conscious entering into the subjective part of one's own being. In divine order the will acts upon the body center from within; in the average person this action is through reflection from without. In practice we live outside our body instead of within it. This gives us a very slender hold upon it, and it is in consequence weak and likely to slip away from us on very slight pretexts.

21. Man should constantly affirm: I AM, and I will manifest, the perfection of the Mind within me. The first part of the statement is abstract Truth; the second part is concrete identification of man with this Truth. We must learn the law of expression from the abstract to the concrete--from the formless to the formed. Every idea makes a structure after its own image and likeness, and all such ideas and structures are grouped and associated according to their offices.

22. All ideas pertaining to power group themselves about structures impregnated with power. Such ideas are not attracted to ideas of love. Love has its group, and it builds its structures in a place apart. We have observed certain of the manifest centers in our body; we have recognized and named them as the seat of emotions, as the expression of characteristics supposed to exist in the soul. Love is universally recognized as expressing itself through the heart, and intelligence as expressing itself through the head.

23. In the study of Mind and Spirit, these inner centers of consciousness are concentrated on until they respond to the I will and become obedient to it. By this method man finds that he can control and direct every body function and perpetuate it.

24. This is the "*regeneration*" of the New Testament, a process of body refinement to the point of physical immortality. Jesus called this estate "the regeneration when the Son of man shall sit on the throne of his glory."

"I AM" REALIZATIONS
(To be used in connection with Lesson Three)

1. *"I AM THAT I AM."*
2. I am identity demonstrated.
3. I AM THAT I AM, and there is no other besides me.
4. I am one with Almightiness.
5. I am the substance of Being made manifest.
6. I am formed in the perfection of the divine-idea man, Christ Jesus.
7. My body is not material; it is spiritual and perfect in all its being.
8. Centered and established in the one Mind, I am not disturbed by the falsities without me.
9. My identity is in God, and my work is to establish His kingdom within me.
10. I can do nothing of myself, *"but the Father abiding in me does his works."*
11. I am striving in all my thoughts and ways to make the image and likeness of God manifest in me.
12. My *"life is hid with Christ in God."*

Lesson Four

The Formative Power of Thought

1. That the body is moved by thought is universally accepted, but that thought is also the builder of the body is not so widely admitted. We know that thought moves the various members of the body, because we have constantly before us manifestations of the close sympathy between thought and act. Before I run, I think that I will run, and my legs begin to move swiftly in imagination before I begin the action outwardly. It was found by a system of experiments made at Harvard University that the thought of running causes the blood to rush into the legs. A man was put flat on his back on a balanced beam, which was adjusted so that the least bit of added weight at head or foot registered on the index. When a perfect balance was attained the man was given a problem in mathematics to solve. Immediately the index showed increased weight at the head, indicating that thought had called the blood there. Then he was told to imagine that he was running, and the index showed added weight shifting to the feet.

2. Here is proof that thought not only moves the external members of the body, but that it controls the fluids flowing within the body. If thought so readily moves the blood from place to place, who shall say that it does not move the nerve fluid, or that still more volatile substance, the magnetic force that pervades all organisms? We affirm that thought controls nerve forces and magnetic force, and that it not only moves them but also forms and organizes their activities in the body.

3. Medical authorities of the highest repute tell us that certain organs of the body are self-renewing; that it is a puzzle to them how these parts ever wear out. If you had a sewing machine that constantly replaced the little particles worn away by friction, would that machine ever be destroyed? In health, man's body has this power of replacing worn parts and when it is in harmony it never wears out. The harmony referred to is self adjustment to the law of Being, to the law of divine nature, to the law of God. It does not matter what you call this fundamental principle underlying all life--the important thing is to understand it, and to put yourself in harmony with it.

4. We have often been told that we should be healthy if we conformed to the laws of nature, but no one has been able to tell us just what those laws are. Some have said that this conformity consists in eating the right kind of food, or in drinking the right kind of water in the right sort of way, or in breathing pure air and wearing suitable clothes. We have done all these things, and there is yet something lacking. It is quite evident that we have not, by observing these external adjustments, gotten at the underlying principle of nature. Nature works intelligently, and we shall never be able to conform to her laws until we approach her as we would a wise and loving mother, who, we know, gladly gives us what we want when we use it wisely. Nature is not a blind force working in darkness and ignorance. All her works indicate intelligence--mind in action. This being true, we perceive that we cannot conform to the laws of nature until we recognize the Mind through which she works.

5. Those who have not thought about this proposition, those who have not tried to know and understand the mental side of life, are like men walking in broad daylight with their eyes closed. The mind has eyes, and we can see (perceive) the inner intelligence when we look with mind. But those who look wholly with the physical eye are really blind--having eyes, they see not. Man's salvation from sin, sickness, pain, and death comes by his understanding and conforming to the orderly Mind back of all existence. *"Ye shall know the truth, and the truth shall make you free."*

6. Man is an epitome of Being. Psychology finds his soul responding to all the emotions, sensations, and vibrations of the sentient world about him, and spiritual science discerns that his superconsciousness is inspired with all the ideas fundamental in Divine Mind. Man, then, is the key to God and the universe, and he may know all things by studying his own constitution.

Supreme in this constitution is mind. Man must base all his researches on mind, because mind is the starting point of every thought and act.

7. Some metaphysicians teach that man makes himself, others teach that God makes him, and still others hold that the creative process is a co-operation between God and man. The latter is proved true by those who have had the deepest spiritual experiences. Jesus recognized this dual creative process, as is shown in many statements relative to His work and the Father's work. *"My Father worketh even until now, and I work."* God creates in the ideal, and man carries out in the manifest what God has idealized. Jesus treats of this relation between the Father and the Son in the 5th chapter of John: *"The Son can do nothing of himself, but what he seeth the Father doing: for what things soever he doeth, these the Son also doeth in like manner."*

8. Thought is the creative power by which man builds a mentality and a body of perfection. Man understandingly uses his creative thought power by mentally perceiving the right relation of ideas, *"what he seeth the Father doing,"* as stated by Jesus. Thus we see the necessity not only for thinking right thoughts, but also for having a right basis for our thinking. We must think according to universal Principle. The successful mathematician bases all his calculations on the rules of mathematical science; so the successful metaphysician bases his creative thinking on the unlimited ideas of the one Mind. Christianity is a science because it is governed by scientific principles of mind action. These principles are really the foundation of all the various sciences, but these sciences are secondary; divine science is primary.

9. The physical scientist deals with the electron, or molecule, or cell, in his analysis of forms. He postulates that atoms exist, but he has never seen one. He assumes that the realm beyond the ken of physical perception is not possible of investigation. The metaphysician, however, delves into the realm where atoms, and molecules, and cells are formed, and he not only sees how they are made, but he acquires the ability to make them. He finds that they all are dependent on ideas, and that by using right ideas he can make manifest any form or shape that he may desire. For example, what externally is named substance has its source in a mental idea of form and shape. What is termed life has its source in an idea of action. What is termed intelligence has its source in an idea of knowing. All the manifestations that we see about us are produced in the same way; they have their source in some idea in mind, and they can be formed and transformed at will by one who understands and uses this mind power.

10. A study of the mind and its innumerable manifestations reveals often a difference between a thing and the mind in which the thing has its original impetus as an idea. Life in Divine Mind is unlimited as an idea back of perpetual, omnipresent action, but by man's thought it may be subjected to many limitations. Substance in Divine Mind is an idea of perfection in form, but man's thought usually caricatures it. Intelligence in Divine Mind is all-knowing, but man's thought has said that there is ignorance, so ignorance has been demonstrated. But we should not assume that all manifestation is good because the originating idea came from Divine Mind. All ideas have their foundation in Divine Mind, but man has put the limitation of his negative thought upon them, and sees them *"in a mirror, darkly."*

11. Applying this reasoning to individual consciousness, we find just how man thinks his body into disease. Instead of basing his thought on what is true in the absolute of Being, he bases it on conditions as they appear in the formed realm about him, and the result is bodily discord in multitudinous shapes. Pervading all nature is a universal thought substance that is more sensitive than the phonographic record. The mechanical record receives and preserves vibrations of sound, but the thought substance does better than this; it transcribes not only all sounds, but even the slightest vibration of thought.

12. The telephone system of a large city is a good illustration of the manner in which thought works on the organism. The nerves are the wires and the nerve fluids are the electricity. The ganglionic aggregations throughout the body are the substations. The presiding intelligence sends its thought from the head; *"Central,"* at the solar plexus, receives the message and makes connection with the part of the body designated. You think of your stomach; instantly the connection is made with that center and the presiding thought stationed there takes your message

and carries it into effect. If the message is, "*You are weak,*" weakness is recorded. If you say, "*You are strong, vigorous, fearless, spiritual intelligence, life, and substance,*" that message is transcribed and carried into action.

13. Every part of the body is connected with the great solar-plexus central station, which is very obedient in carrying out instructions received from the presiding intelligence in the head. There are several great subcenters and innumerable minor centers in the organism. These centers of thought are the formed ideas of mind that have an affinity for one another, based upon the attractive power of love, the binding factor of the organism. Physical science calls this binding energy centripetal force, but all forces of whatever character are fundamentally spiritual, and they must be reduced to ideas, thoughts, and words, in order to be understood.

14. All ideas pertaining to life expression have their center of action in that part of the body called the generative system; whatever thought we think or express in words about life is immediately sent to this generative ganglion and registered there. Not only are these thoughts registered, but man has, by repeated thinking, built up an ego, or identity, at that center. The dominant thought of this identity is life action in its various phases. The life center is divine, and should be thought about and used in the purest, highest way. This will lead to the perfect manifestation of life in the whole body. All thoughts about the loss of life, or the weakness of life, or the impurity of life, should be persistently denied out of mind, and we should make the strongest kind of affirmations of what life is in God. In this way we connect the life center with its spiritual source, and it is restored to divine harmony.

15. A majority of the ills that afflict the body have their origin in erroneous thoughts about life and in misuse of the generative life function. In Genesis the life center is compared to a tree--its roots are in the ground and its branches reach up to the heavens. All the pleasant sensations in the organism are produced by the forces emanating from this center. Along the nerves, or branches, the life center sends its currents of life to the very extremities of the body, and even beyond, into the finer ethers of the soul. The life center is spiritual, but its vibrations are so subtle (serpentlike) that man is tempted to eat its fruits, to consume in its pleasant sensations the reserve forces of his organism. His indulgence unfrocks him--takes away his robe of power and mastery and dominion over the physical forces that environ him. Instead of abiding at the center of his body and consciously ruling it and the world of nature without him, he is cast out "*from the garden of Eden.*"

16. By a right understanding, and by using right thoughts and words, man will regain the kingdom within him and will be reinstated in the Garden of Eden. This process of man's taking up power and dominion again is now being carried out in all those who are seeking the righteousness of the Christ consciousness. In this higher-thought realm, all ideas pertaining to the life of man are in harmonious relation, and when we ask in silent thought for this knowledge, our mind is flooded with its light. We apprehend only according to the receptivity, steadfastness, understanding, and persistent faith of our mind. But we grow in faith and understanding, and no matter how slowly we seem to be progressing we should never be discouraged or give up. Everyone is heir to this higher-thought consciousness, and all must eventually attain it. When the beauty of this spiritual realm is spread before us we should express gratitude--give thanks to the great Soul of the universe. When the astronomer Kepler realized the grandeur of the laws that were revealed to him, he exclaimed: "*O God, I am thinking Thy thoughts after Thee.*"

AFFIRMATIONS FOR RIGHT THINKING
(To be used in connection with Lesson Four)

1. *"As he thinketh within himself, so is he."*

2. My heart is righteous toward God.

3. Where my thoughts are gathered together in my Christ name, there I am in the midst of them.

4. I will think no evil, for Thou art always with me.

5. The thoughts of God are His angels: *"He shall give his angels charge concerning thee."*

6. *"The thought of foolishness is sin."*

7. *"The thoughts of the righteous are just."*

8. *"Commit thy works unto Jehovah, and thy purposes shall be established."*

9. *"I know the thoughts that I think toward you, saith Jehovah, thoughts of peace, and not of evil."*

10. *"How precious also are thy thoughts unto me, O God!"*

11. *"Search me, O God, and know my heart: try me, and know my thoughts."*

12. *"Bringing every thought into captivity to the obedience of Christ."*

13. *"Finally, brethren, whatsoever things are true, whatsoever things are honorable, whatsoever things are just, whatsoever things are pure, whatsoever things are lovely, whatsoever things are of good report; if there be any virtue, and if there be any praise, think on these things."*

Lesson Five

How To Control Thought

1. Each thought of mind is an identity that has a central ego. By this we mean that every thought has a center around which all its elements revolve and to which it is obedient when no higher power is in evidence. Thoughts are capable of expressing themselves--they think. Man thinks, and he thinks into his thoughts all that he is; hence man's thoughts must be endowed with a secondary power of thought.

2. There is, however, a difference between the original thinking and the secondary thought. One has its animating center in Spirit; the other, in thought. One is Son of God; the other is son of man.

3. The one essential fact to understand is that there can be no manifestation without intelligence as a fundamental factor or constituent part. Every form in the universe, every function, all action, all substance--all these have a thinking part that is receptive to and controllable by man. Material science has observed that every molecule has three things: intelligence, substance, and action. It knows where it wants to go, it has form, and it moves.

4. This intelligent principle in all things is the key to the metaphysician's work. He does not concern himself with the action and reaction of the chemistry of matter, nor does he need to know all the intricate laws of electricity and magnetism in order to get the very highest use of them. They are susceptible to thought through the knowing factor in their construction, and to this susceptibility he appeals. It is through this all-pervading intelligence that man exercises his highest dominion. The scriptural statement of man's power and dominion over all things is true only when his power and dominion are estimated mentally and spiritually.

5. It is the testimony of all philosophers that everything is in a state of construction or destruction. These two states are all-pervading, and they are apparently essential in building the universe. The metaphysician discerns the cause of these two movements to be the "*yes*" and the "*no*" of mind. These dual attributes of mind are in evidence everywhere, but they are not understood by those who observe only form instead of Spirit. The positive and negative poles of the magnet are states of mental affirmation and denial. In acid and alkali, in sour and sweet, chemistry is proclaiming "*yes*" and "*no.*" Day and night, heat and cold, sunshine and shadow, intelligence and ignorance, good and evil, saint and sinner, all are the reflections of mental affirmations and denials. The constructive or destructive factor in all manifestation is "*yes*" or "*no.*"

6. It is found that, by the use of these mind forces, man can dissolve things by denying their existence, and that he can build them up by affirming their presence. This is a simple statement, but when it is applied in all the intricate thought forms of the universe it becomes complex. The law of mental denial and affirmation will prove its truth to all those who persistently make use of it.

7. The power of the mind to build or destroy is exemplified most strikingly in the human body. Whatever we affirm as true of us manifests itself in due season somewhere in the organism. Whatever we deny is taken away, when the law has had time to work itself out.

8. The body is made of cells; some in a radiant state, some crystallized into form. The crystallizing of these radiant thought forms is the result of affirmations in man's mind that his body is material instead of spiritual. The affirmative state of mind is a binding, holding process; it involves all thoughts and all thought manifestations that come within its scope. If man affirms his unity with the life, substance, and intelligence of God, he lays hold of these spiritual qualities; if he affirms the reality of matter and of the physical body he forms a material picture that works itself out in flesh.

9. Affirmations do not have to be made in set terms, such as, "*I affirm my body to be spiritual*"; the general trend of the mind, the sum total of thought in all its aspects, aggregates the affirmations that fix and crystallize thoughts into forms. The universal desire and striving of men and women for material possessions is the strongest kind of affirmation, affecting both mind and body in a marked degree. Stomach troubles and constipation seem to be common complaints with those who are financially grasping. The tense state of mind that this affirmation sets up extends throughout the body; all the muscles, nerves, and organs become fixed and almost immovable. This was forcibly illustrated in a certain banker, who was so grasping that his right hand closed rigidly, so that he could not open it. Again, a set ambition and intense desire to excel in some chosen field of work will produce like results. A dominating will fixed in any direction is a form of affirmation, and it affects the life action in the body organism according to its intensity. Congestion, stiffness, rigidity, may all be traced to excessive affirmation.

10. The metaphysical remedy for this selfish state of mind is denial. Jesus said that man must "Deny himself . . . and follow me." The "me" here referred to is the higher self, the Christ, and the "himself" is personality. Denial is a putting away of the mental error and an entering into conscious relaxation of both mind and body. The healer does not tell the patient that constipation is caused by grasping, stingy states of mind. Instead, he mentally denies these habits and holds the patient open and receptive to the great unselfish Mind of the universe. People do not realize how they are bound by their selfishness, and it is not wise to tell them openly, until they understand the difference between their real being and the mortal personality.

11. Where the "no" phase of mind is too much in evidence, the whole consciousness is in relaxation. This excessive negation makes the thought indefinite and vacillating, the body weak and flabby. Prolapsus, dropsy, certain forms of kidney complaints, nearly all relaxations in body and functions, are the result of the "*I can't*" state of mind. For example, if a businessman who for years had been intent on money-making should meet with a large loss and mourn over it, he would have kidney trouble of some kind. He would believe that he had lost his substance, and a void-thought would begin its dissipation of the voiding cells of his body. One who has been very ambitious for the attainment of some office or position, and who has been defeated in that ambition, will usually let go the positive mental pole and drop to the negative. The result is bodily weakness somewhere. We speak of such people as having "*lost their grip.*" This is exactly what they have done--their mental relaxation has loosened their grasp upon the organism, and it is in a condition of dissolution. Physicians have marveled that so many public men have diabetes and heart disease. It is because, through defeat, they have dropped from success to discouragement. The failure state of mind throws the whole organism into a panic, and its functions are weakened in their life action. Instead of the tonic of aspiration and hope, there is the enervation of discouragement and despair.

12. These are conditions that come to those who trust in the arm of flesh. When the mind of man is set on high, he never gives up or allows defeat to thwart his righteous ambitions. His thought is not set on selfish attainment, consequently he does not develop a mental vacuum when he meets with loss. To one in spiritual understanding there is no loss. The going and coming of material and intellectual things are but changes in the panorama of life. Changes are constantly taking place and will continue so long as we live in the consciousness of duality, the "*yes*" and "*no*" state of existence, which is mortality.

13. The object of man's existence is to demonstrate the Truth of Being. This demonstration takes place through experience; but there are two ways of working out experience. The first is by knowing the law of every process, and the second is by blindly testing the process without understanding the law.

14. The human race made a choice when a certain stage of discretion was attained. An illustration of this statement is the allegory of the Garden of Eden. Adam represents generic man. In his early stages he was under the law of divine knowing--the Lord God was his guide and instructor; he made no mistakes, but lived consciously in divine understanding.

15. All experience develops personal identity--the consciousness of the powers of Being in the self. This is the bringing forth of free will, which is inherent in all. In the course of his demonstrations of Being, man arrives at the place where he feels his own ability, and he knows that he can exercise it without restraint. "*Satan*" is the personal mind that tempts man to try experience without knowledge. In divine illumination man does not consciously enter into that dual condition typified by "*the tree of the knowledge of good and evil.*" Good is all; evil is that which might be if man forsook his guiding light. In the serene mind of God there is no duality, no good and bad, no understanding-and-ignorance. The brilliancy of all-knowing Mind dissolves all shadows, all negations.

16. It is man's privilege to abide in the light, to know how to work out the problem of existence as accurately as the mathematician who follows, without deviation, the rules of his science. The Lord admonishes the unfolding Adam not to "*eat*"–not to incorporate into his consciousness the knowledge of duality, good and evil. But, like the child who refuses to take the advice of one who knows, man falls into indulgence of the sense of pleasure and excess. The reaction of sense indulgence is pain. Through these experiences, man comes into a consciousness of an opposite to the good. The dual mentality naturally sets up positive and negative forces in his mind, and these opposing forces are reflected into his body. The commotion is so great that the soul is forced out of its temple--man is put out of the garden, and in time forgets his former Edenic state.

17. Some metaphysicians argue that eating the fruit of the tree of knowledge was a necessary step in man's evolution; that by experience we learn all truth, and that without experience we should always remain infants. Herein is the difference between the practical Christian and other men: the one seeks the guiding light of Spirit in all his ways, while the other ignores that light and works out his character as did Adam, in the sweat of his face. Hard experiences come into our lives because we do not know the law of harmonious thinking. If we think that evil exists as a power in the world, that it is working in our lives and in the lives of those about us, we make it an active force, and it appears to be all that we imagine it. The poet truly discerned that "*there is nothing either good or bad, but thinking makes it so.*"

18. Some metaphysicians claim that it is not wise to make denials; that affirmation includes all the mental movement necessary to man's perfect development. This position would be tenable if we had built up our consciousness according to divine law. The student who has carried his mathematical problem forward without making an error does not find it necessary to erase. But if he sees where he has made a wrong computation, what then? Nothing but an erasure, followed by a right computation, will bring the correct answer. We have all fallen short of divine ideals; we must cross out our errors and insert Truth, until our character is brought up to the Jesus Christ standard.

19. Repentance is a form of denial. The forgiveness of sin is an erasure of mortal thought from consciousness. The joy that comes to the converted Christian results from the inflow of divine love, which occurs after the mind has been cleansed by denial of sin. This is a real experience, which may be repeated again and again by one who understands the law of Holy Spirit baptism, until the whole man is sanctified and freed from sin. Christians think of the joyous exaltation that marked their conversion as a special sign from the Lord in recognition of their change of heart. They look back upon it as an experience that comes but once in a lifetime. But metaphysicians who have studied the law of mind, who have practiced denials and affirmations as a science, find that they can throw themselves into this ecstatic state at will.

20. The personal self is the ego around which revolve all thoughts that bind us to error. We cannot cross all out at once, but little by little we cast out the specific thoughts that have accumulated and built up the false state of consciousness termed Judas. In the life of Jesus, Judas represents the false ego that error thought has generated. This "*son of perdition*" is so interwoven into the consciousness that to kill him at one fell swoop would destroy the mental entity, so he must be counted as one of the twelve, even while we know that he "*hath a devil.*"

21. In the symbology of Jesus' life, Judas is represented as the treasurer; he "had the bag." This means that this ego has possession of the sex, or life, center in the organism and is using it for its own selfish ends. Judas was a "thief." The selfish use of the life and vitality of the organism for the gratification of sense pleasure robs the higher nature, and the spiritual man is not built up. This is the betrayal of Christ, and it is constantly taking place in those who live to fleshly, selfish ends.

22. A time comes, however, when Judas must be eliminated from consciousness. The agony of mind and the final crucifixion of Jesus represent the crossing out wholly of the false ego, Judas.

"*I die daily,*" said Paul. The "*I*" that dies daily is personal consciousness, formed of fear, ignorance, disease, the lust for material possessions, pride, anger, and the legion of demons that cluster about the personal ego. The only Savior of this one is Christ, the spiritual ego, the superconsciousness. We cannot, in our own strength, solve the great, self-purifying problem, but by giving ourselves wholly to Christ and constantly denying the demands of the personal self, we grow into the divine image. This is the process by which we "*awake, with beholding thy form.*"

Cleansing And Purifying Statements
(To be used in connection with Lesson Five)

1. God is good, and God is all, therefore I refuse to believe in the reality of evil in any of its forms.

2. God is life, and God is all; therefore I refuse to believe in the reality of loss of life, or death.

3. God is power and strength, and God is all; therefore I refuse to believe in inefficiency and weakness.

4. I am in authority. I say to this thought, "*Go, and he goeth; and to another, Come, and he cometh.*" *(Read Mt. 8:5-13.)*

5. God is wisdom, and God is all! therefore I refuse to believe in ignorance.

6. God is spiritual substance, and God is all; therefore there is no reality in the limitations of matter.

7. God is inexhaustible resource, and God is all; therefore I refuse to believe in the reality of lack or poverty.

8. God is love, and God is all; therefore I refuse to believe in hate or revenge.

9. "*He that is slow to anger is better than the mighty; and he that ruleth his spirit, than he that taketh a city.*"

Lesson Six

The Word

1. In pure metaphysics there is but one word, the Word of God. This is the original creative Word, or thought, of Being. It is the *"God said"* of Genesis. It is referred to in the 1st chapter of John as the Logos. It cannot be adequately translated into English. In the original it includes wisdom, judgment, power, and, in fact, all the inherent potentialities of Being. This divine Logos was and always is in God; in fact, it is God as creative power. The Divine Mind creates under law; that is, mental law. Man may get a comprehension of the creative process of Being by analyzing the action of his own mind. First is mind, then the idea in mind of what the act shall be, then the act itself. In Divine Mind the idea is referred to as the Word.

2. According to Genesis and all other mystical writings bearing upon creation, Divine Mind expresses its Word, and through the activity of that Word the universe is brought forth. Man is the consummation of the Word, and his spirit has within it the concentration of all that is contained within the Word. Jesus is called the Word of God. *"The Word became flesh, and dwelt among us (and we beheld his glory, glory as of the only begotten from the Father)."* God being perfect, His idea, thought, Word, must be perfect. The perfect Word of God is spiritual man. It is through spiritual man, or the *Word of God, that all things are made, are brought into manifestation." "And without him was not anything made that hath been made."* The Word is the "only begotten" of God, because there is but one idea of man in Divine Mind, and that idea is the perfect pattern of man's character.

3. In the 1st chapter of John it is implied that there are things made that are not after divine ideals, consequently not real. The creations of the Word of God are permanent and incorruptible. As an imitator of Divine Mind, man has power to form and make manifest whatsoever he idealizes; but unless his thought is unified with Divine Mind and guided in its operations by infinite wisdom, his thought forms are perishable.

4. Mental processes enter into all creations. Physical science has discovered that every atom has substance, force, and intelligence; these are the three constituent parts of mind. Mind is the one and only creative power, and all attempts to account for creation from any other standpoint are futile. The creative processes of mind are continuously operative; creation is going on all the time, but the original plan, the design in Divine Mind, is finished.

5. Man cannot know how the thought, or Word, works except through his own consciousness; consequently he must understand, control, and put in order his own word, for through it he comprehends the Word of God. Our most important study, then, is our own consciousness. The old Greeks recognized this and wrote over the door of one of their temples: *"Man, know thyself."* The self of man is spiritual, and when it is in direct conscious unity with the Father-Mind it has permanent formative power. Even in his ignorant use of thought, man's mind is forming conditions, even to the changing of the face of nature itself. Every thought that goes forth from the brain sends vibrations into the surrounding atmosphere and moves the realm of things to action. The effect is in proportion to the ability of the thinker to concentrate his mental forces. The average thought vibration produces but temporary results, but under intense mind activity conditions more or less permanent are impressed upon the sensitive plate of the universal ether, and through this activity they are brought into physical manifestation.

6. Every idea originating in Divine Mind is expressed in the mind of man; through the thought of man the Divine Mind idea is brought to the outer plane of consciousness. In the organism of man are centers that respond to the divinemideas, as a musical instrument sympathetically responds to musical vibrations. Then through another movement on what is termed the conscious, or most outer, plane of action, the thought takes expression as the spoken word.

There is in the formed conscious man, or body, a point of concentration for this word; and through this point the word is expressed in invisible vibrations. For example, at the root of the tongue is a brain center, and through it the mind controls the larynx, the tongue, and all the other organs used in forming words. Following the creative law in its operation from the formless to the formed, we can see how an idea fundamental in Divine Mind is grasped by the man ego, how it takes form in his thought, and how it is later expressed through his spoken word. If in each step of this process he conformed to the divine creative law, man's word would make things instantly, as Jesus made the increase of the loaves and fishes. But since he has lost, in a measure, knowledge of the steps in this creative process from the within to the without, there are many breaks and abnormal conditions, with more failures than successes in the products.

7. However, every word has its effect, though unseen and unrecognized. Jesus said that a man would be held accountable for *"every idle word,"* and a close observation of the power of mind in the affairs of the individual proves this to be true. What we think, we usually express in words; and our words bring about in our life and affairs whatever we put into them. A weak thought is followed by words of weakness. Through the law of expression and form, words of weakness change to weakness the character of everything that receives them.

8. The nerves are the wires that transmit the mind's messages to all parts of the body, and these parts, being thought formations, carry out, in their turn, the word that has been spoken into them. Talking about nervousness and weakness will produce corresponding conditions in the body; on the other hand, sending forth the word of strength and affirming poise will bring about the desired strength and poise. Your talking about a weak stomach will make your stomach weak. Your talking about your bad liver will fix that idea in your liver. The usual conversation among people creates ill health instead of good health, because of wrong words. If the words speak of disease as a reality, disintegrating forces are set in action, and these, in the end, shatter the strongest organism, if not counteracted by constructive forces.

9. As an example of the vibratory power of the spoken word, a vocalist can shatter a wineglass by concentrating upon it certain tones. Every time we speak we cause the atoms of the body to tremble and change their places. Not only do we cause the atoms of our own body to change their position, but we raise or lower the rate of vibration and otherwise affect the bodies of others with whom we come in contact. By telling the little child that he looks sick and tired, the mother produces these conditions in the child's mind and body. If the mother addresses words of health, life, and strength to the child, these will set his bodily functions into activity and they will express the harmony of the dominant thought.

10. Thus every word brings forth after its kind. The *"seed"* is the creative idea inherent in the word, the nature that it inherits from its parent source--God. The enthusiast in floral culture, who hovers over and talks in loving tones to his flowers, always has success with them, while his neighbor, who is cold and indifferent, fails. The mental emanation and the creative word are the forces that stimulate the receptive intelligence of nature, and although the enthusiast may know nothing of the law of mind, he is using it in its most effective mode, the creative word. In like manner the spiritual healer mentally and audibly speaks to the same all-pervading receptacle, and it responds by building up wasted tissues and weakened functions.

11. Mind is everywhere and its avenues of expression, like the ether waves of radio, run in every direction. The wonderful discovery that messages can be sent around the earth without wires should forever silence those who have been incredulous when thought transference through a like ether is claimed. But there is a means by which ideas may be transmitted even more rapidly than by mental vibrations, and that is unity with supreme Mind. This Mind exists as the absolute, the unlimited. In its consciousness there is no apartness, no separation, and whoever puts himself into its consciousness can accomplish things instantly.

12. When the centurion said to Jesus, *"Only say the word, and my servant shall be healed,"* the Master said that He had not found so great faith in all Israel, and His healing word was: *"As thou hast believed, so be it done unto thee."* We must have a certain amount of faith in the substance of the invisible and in its ability to do our will. When Peter recognized in Jesus that inner

principle called Christ, the Son of God, the response was: "*Flesh and blood hath not revealed it unto thee, but my Father who is in heaven.*" The Father must have been present to Peter as He was to Jesus, and the "heaven" in which Jesus said that the Father was must also have been there. The fact is, Being is always present. Mortal ignorance and lack of faith prevent our realization of this truth. The more we believe in the wisdom, power, substance, love, and life of the one Mind, the greater is its activity in us and our affairs. Not only should we have faith in the All-Presence, but we should also develop our understanding to the end that we may know why the All-Presence manifests through us. Physical science is today in advance of religion in its recognition of a universal life substance and intelligence. Religion is looking for this mighty Creator away off in some distant heaven, right in the face of the distinct teaching of Jesus that God is Spirit and that His kingdom is within man.

13. But physical science falls short in that it fails to recognize the unity between omnipresent Intelligence and the knowing principle in man. Science is seeking to know intellectually, or from the plane of forms and shapes, that which is of the mind. Physical science has recognized the presence of the creative forces, but it does not know the power that moves them. Divine metaphysics has discovered the moving power to be the thought and word of man, and is proving the truth of this principle through results in a multitude of directions.

14. The spoken word carries vibrations through the universal ether, and also moves the intelligence inherent in every form, animate or inanimate. It has been discovered that even rocks and all minerals have life. This is proof of the omnipresence of the one animating substance. Man, being the highest emanation of Divine Mind, has great directive power and is really co-operator with God in forming the universe. We should be speaking words of truth to everything, not only to mankind but to the mineral, vegetable, and animal kingdoms. The fine discernment of the poet reveals that "*the very stones cry out*" where a tragedy has occurred. The all-penetrating ether receives our thoughts and words, like the wax cylinder of the phonograph, only a thousand times more accurately; it preserves them and echoes them back to us in continuous vibrations. There are no secrets and no concealments. Jesus said that what you think and speak in the inner chamber is proclaimed from the housetops, and now we know why this is true. The very walls of your room, aye, even the substance of the atmosphere in that room, are proclaiming over and over the words that you have spoken there, whether you are present or not. For example, a woman rented a room in a certain city. Several nights in succession, just as she fell asleep, she heard a man talking incoherently about the grain market. This continued for some time, and she mentioned it to the landlady who informed her that the room had been last occupied by a dealer on the board of trade.

15. The power of the word is given man to use. The better he understands the character of God and his own relation to humanity, the more unselfishly will he exercise this power. Some are using it in selfish ways, but this should not deter others who have a better understanding of the law from using it in righteous ways. "*If ye shall ask anything of the Father, he will give it you in my name,*" is a promise that none should ignore. If we need things and if they are necessary to our happiness, it is not sacrilegious to set into action this higher law in attaining them.

16. The curses of the witch and the blessings of the priest have always been believed in by so-called ignorant and credulous people. In the light of modern revelation, the charge of ignorance should be shifted to the unbelieving. The word of one in authority carries weight and produces far-reaching effects. The fiat of the physician that a certain disease must result disastrously to the patient will, when believed, counteract all the healing forces of nature. A pin scratch has resulted in blood poison, because there was no proper denial that such a result might follow.

17. Man has the power to deny and dissolve all disintegrating, discordant, and disease-forming words. Knowledge of this fact is the greatest discovery of all ages. No other revelation from God to man is to be compared with it. You can make yourself a new creature, and you can build the world about you to your highest ideals. Do not fear, but speak to the law supreme the desires of your heart. If your word is selfish, that which will come to you through its use

will be unsatisfactory, but you will profit by the experience and thus learn to speak words of righteousness only. But it is your duty as expresser of the divine law to speak forth the Logos, the very Word of God, and cause the Garden of Eden, the everywhere-present Mind-Substance, to manifest for you and in you in its innate perfection.

The Power Of Words
(To be used in connection with Lesson Six)

1. *"Death and life are in the power of the tongue."*

2. *"The tongue of the wise is health."*

3. *"He that guardeth his mouth keepeth his life."*

4. *"Whoso keepeth his mouth and his tongue keepeth his soul from troubles."*

5. *"A fool's mouth is his destruction, and his lips are the snare of his soul."*

6. *"Seest thou a man that is hasty in his words? There is more hope of a fool than of him."*

7. *"Pleasant words are as a honeycomb, sweet to the soul, and health to the bones."*

8. *"The lips of the wise shall preserve them."*

9. *"Put away from thee a wayward mouth, and perverse lips put far from thee."*

10. *"Shun profane babblings: for they will proceed further in ungodliness, and their word will eat as doth a gangrene."*

11. *"He that would love life, and see good days, let him refrain his tongue from evil, and his lips that they speak no guile."*

12. *"To him that ordereth his way aright will I show the salvation of God."*

13. *"I will take heed to my ways, that I sin not with my tongue: I will keep my mouth with a bridle, while the wicked is before me."*

14. *"What man is he that desireth life, and loveth many days, that he may see good? Keep thy tongue from evil, and thy lips from speaking guile."*

15. *"Every idle word that men shall speak, they shall give account thereof in the day of judgment."*

Lesson Seven

Spirituality or Prayer and Praise

1. By the employment of many symbols the Bible describes man in his wholeness--Spirit, soul, and body. The symbols used are men, places, tents, temples, and so forth. The name of every person mentioned in the Bible has a meaning representative of that person's character. The twelve sons of Jacob represent the twelve foundation faculties of man. The name of each of these sons, correctly interpreted, gives the development and office of its particular faculty in triune association; that is, its relation to consciousness in Spirit, in soul, and in body. For example, when the sons of Jacob were born, their mothers revealed the character of the faculty which each represented. This is set forth in the twenty-ninth and thirtieth chapters of Genesis.

2. It is written of the birth of Reuben, "*Leah conceived, and bare a son, and she called his name Reuben: for she said, Because Jehovah hath looked upon my affliction.*" The emphasis is upon the word "*looked*," and by referring to the concordance we find that the meaning of the word Reuben is, "*One who sees; vision of the son.*" It is clear that this refers to the bringing forth of sight.

3. "*And she conceived again, and bare a son: and said, Because Jehovah hath heard that I am hated.*" Here the emphasis is upon the word heard, and we find that Simeon means, "*That hears or obeys; that is heard.*" This is the bringing forth of hearing.

4. "*And she conceived again, and bare a son; and said, Now this time will my husband be joined unto me.*" In this case the emphasis is upon the word joined. Levi means "*unity*," which in body is feeling; in soul, sympathy; and in Spirit, love. So each of the twelve faculties in the complete man functions in this threefold degree.

5. What is here described as the birth of the twelve sons of Jacob is the first, or natural, bringing forth of the faculties. A higher expression of the faculties is symbolized in the Twelve Apostles of Jesus Christ. Simon Peter is hearing and faith united. John is feeling and love joined. When we believe what we hear, there is formed in us the substance of the word, which is Peter, a rock, a sure foundation. "*Belief cometh of hearing, and hearing by the word of Christ.*"

6. The Bible is a very wonderful book; as man develops in spiritual understanding it reveals itself to him, and he sees why it has been reverenced and called holy by the people. It is a deep exposition of mental laws, and it is also a treatise on the true physiological estate of the body. It shows that the human organism is mind in action, rather than an aggregation of purely material functions. But above all, the Bible explains the spiritual character of man and the laws governing his relation to God. These are symbolically set forth as states of consciousness, illustrated by parables and allegories. Paul says, referring to the history of Sarah and Abraham, "*Which things contain an allegory." It is written of Jesus, "And without a parable spake he nothing unto them: that it might be fulfilled which was spoken through the prophet, saying, I will open my mouth in parables; I will utter things hidden from the foundation of the world.*" Jesus was Himself a parable. His life was an allegory of the experiences that man passes through in developing from natural to spiritual consciousness; hence the Bible and the prophets can be understood only by those who arrive at that place in consciousness where the writers were when they gave forth their messages. It requires the same inspiration to read the Scriptures with understanding that it required originally to receive and write them.

7. In the 29th chapter of Genesis we read of Jacob's wife, Leah: "*And she conceived again, and bare a son: and she said, This time will I praise Jehovah: therefore she called his name Judah.*" The Hebrew meaning of the word Judah is "*praise.*" In Spirit praise, or prayer, the Judah faculty, accumulates ideas. In sense consciousness this faculty is called acquisitiveness; it accumulates material things and when self is dominant, "*hath a devil.*" This is Judas.

8. Each of the twelve faculties has a center and a definite place of expression in the body. Physiology has designated these faculty locations as brain and nerve centers. Spiritual perception reveals them to be aggregations of ideas, thoughts, and words. Thoughts make cells, and

thoughts of like character are drawn together in the body by the same law that draws people of kindred ideas into assemblies and communities. The intellectual man centers in the head; the affectional man lives in the heart; the sensual man expresses through the abdomen. The activities of these indicated regions are subdivided into a multitude of functions, all of which are necessary to the building up of manifest man as he is idealized in Divine Mind.

9. At the very apex of the brain is a ganglionic center, which we may term the throne of reverence or spirituality. It is here that man holds converse with the knowledge in Divine Mind. This center is the place or "*upper room*" of spiritual consciousness, and is designated in Scripture as Judah. Its office is to pray and praise. The Judah faculty opens the portal of that mysterious realm called the superconsciousness where thought is impregnated with an uplifting, transcendent quality. Every lofty ideal, all the inspiration that elevates and idealizes in religion, poetry, and art, originates here. It is the kingdom of the true and real in all things.

10. The importance of Judah is indicated by his place in the family of Jacob and Leah. Jacob (supplanter) was betrothed to Rachel (ewe). At the time of the espousal the father of Rachel substituted his elder daughter Leah for the covenanted bride. Leah means "*weary.*" The first son of Leah was "*sight*"; weariness saw the light of Spirit. The second son was "*hearing*"; she was able to receive the word. The third son was "*union*"; she merged with the limitless. The fourth son was "*praise.*" After the birth of Judah, Leah "*left off bearing.*" Praise is the complement of sight, hearing, and unity. It is the redemption of weariness, and from it issues Messiah, the anointed One, Savior of the world. Instead of a supplication, prayer should be a jubilant thanksgiving. This method of prayer quickens the mind miraculously, and, like a mighty magnet, draws out the spiritual qualities that transform the whole man when they are given expression in mind, body, and affairs.

11. Spirituality is one of the foundation faculties of the mind. It is the consciousness that relates man directly to the Father-Mind. It is quickened and enlarged through prayer and through other forms of religious thought and worship. When we pray we look up from within, not because God is off in the sky, but because this spiritual center in the top of the head becomes active and our attention is naturally drawn to it.

12. Prayer is natural to man, and it should be cultivated in order to round out his character. Prayer is the language of spirituality; when developed, it makes man master in the realm of creative ideas. In order to get results from the use of this faculty, right thinking should be observed here as well as elsewhere. To pray, believing that the prayer may or may not be answered at the will of God, is to miss the mark. It is a law of mind that every idea is fulfilled as soon as conceived. This law holds true in the spiritual realm. "*All things whatsoever ye pray and ask for, believe that ye receive them, and ye shall have them.*" In the light of our knowledge of mind action, the law expressed in these words is clear. Moreover, the faith implied is absolutely necessary to the unfailing answer to prayer. If we pray asking for future fulfillment, we form that kind of thought structure in consciousness, and our prayers are always waiting for that future fulfillment which we have idealized. If we pray thinking that we do not deserve the things for which we ask, these untrue and indefinite thoughts carry themselves out, and we grow to look upon prayer with doubt and suspicion. This is called the prayer of blind faith, but it is not the kind that Jesus used, because His prayers were answered.

13. It should not be inferred that the will of Divine Mind is to be set aside in prayer; we are to pray that the will of God enter into us and become a moving factor in our life. "*Not my will, but thine, be done,*" prayed Jesus. The Father does not take our will from us; rather, He gives us the utmost freedom in the exercise of the will faculty, and He also imparts an understanding of the law, through the operation of which we can make any condition that we desire. "*Whatsoever ye shall ask in my name, that will I do,*" becomes our assurance.

14. One of the offices of spirituality is to aggregate divine ideas. Through this action man draws absolutely true ideas from the universal Mind. Thus prayer is cumulative. It accumulates spiritual substance, life, intelligence; it accumulates everything necessary to man's highest expression. When we pray in spiritual understanding, this highest realm of man's mind contacts

universal, impersonal Mind; the very mind of God is joined to the mind of man. God answers our prayers in ideas, thoughts, words; these are translated into the outer realms, in time and condition. It is therefore important that we pray with understanding of the law, important that we always give thanks that our prayers have been answered and fulfilled, regardless of appearances. When Jesus multiplied the loaves and fishes, He prayed, blessed, and gave thanks. With understanding and realization of the relation between the idea and the fulfillment of the idea, He quickened the slow processes of nature, and the loaves and fishes were increased quickly. We may not be able to attain at once such speedy operation of the law, but we shall approximate it, and we shall accelerate natural processes as we hold our ideas nearer to the perfection of the realm of divine ideas.

15. Praise is closely related to prayer; it is one of the avenues through which spirituality expresses itself. Through an inherent law of mind, we increase whatever we praise. The whole creation responds to praise, and is glad. Animal trainers pet and reward their charges with delicacies for acts of obedience; children glow with joy and gladness when they are praised. Even vegetation grows best for those who praise it. We can praise our own abilities, and our very brain cells will expand and increase in capacity and intelligence when we speak words of encouragement and appreciation to them.

16. *"What is seen hath not been made out of things which appear."* There is an invisible thought-stuff on which the mind acts, making things through the operation of a law not yet fully understood by man. Every thought moves upon this invisible substance in increasing or diminishing degree. When we praise the richness and opulence of our God, this thought-stuff is tremendously increased in our mental atmosphere; it reflects into everything that our minds and our hands touch. When common things are impregnated with our consciousness of divine substance, they are transformed according to our ideals. Through persistent application of the Judah faculty, a failing business proposition can be praised into a successful one. Even inanimate things seem to receive the word of praise, responding in orderly obedience when, before, they have seemed unmanageable. A woman used the law on her sewing machine, which she had been affirming to be in bad order. It gave her no trouble afterward. A linotype operator received a certain spiritual treatment given him by a healer at a certain hour, and his linotype, which had been acting badly, immediately fell into harmonious ways. A woman living in a country town had a rag carpet on her parlor floor; she had for years hoped that this carpet might be replaced by a better one. She heard of the law and began praising the old carpet. Greatly to her surprise, inside of two weeks she was given a new carpet from an unexpected source. These are a few simple illustrations of the possibilities latent in praise. Whether the changes were in the inanimate things, or in the individuals dealing with them, does not matter so long as the desired end was attained.

17. Turn the power of praise upon whatever you wish to increase. Give thanks that it is now fulfilling your ideal. The faithful law, faithfully observed, will reward you. You can praise yourself from weakness to strength, from ignorance to intelligence, from poverty to affluence, from sickness to health. The little lad with a few loaves and fishes furnished the seed that, through the prayer and thanksgiving of Jesus, increased sufficiently to feed five thousand people.

18. If we do not receive answers to our prayers it is because we have not fully complied with the law. *"Ye ask, and receive not, because ye ask amiss."* This does not mean that we ask of the Lord things that we do not need; it means that we miss the mark in the method of asking, thatour relation to Divine Mind is not in harmony with the law; the failure is not in God, but in us. We should therefore never be discouraged, but, like Elijah praying for rain, we should persevere until our prayers are answered.

19. All causes that bring about permanent results originate in Spirit. Spirituality, faith, and love are God-given faculties, and when we are raised in consciousness to their plane they act naturally under a spiritual law that we may not comprehend. There is a law of prayer, which man will eventually recognize and apply as he now recognizes and applies the laws of mathematics and of music.

20. Jesus said, "*Whatsoever ye shall ask in my name, that will I do.*" We ask in His name when we pray in the Jesus consciousness of universal Spirit. He attained unity with Divine Mind, and realized that His thoughts and words were not from Himself, but from God. When we pray in His name we enter into His unity with the Father, and attain the same consciousness that He attained.

21. God is the always present, indwelling Mind. To realize God we must quiet our outer thoughts and enter into the stillness, peace, and harmony of Spirit. "*When thou prayest, enter into thine inner chamber, and having shut thy door [outer consciousness], pray to thy Father who is in secret, and thy Father who seeth in secret shall recompense thee.*" If we make proper connection with Divine Mind in the kingdom of heaven within us, the Father will surely answer our prayers. No good thing will He withhold from us if we comply with the law of righteous asking. "*Be still, and know that I am God.*"

Living Words To Quicken Spirituality

1. *"It is the spirit that giveth life; the flesh profiteth nothing."*
2. *"The letter killeth, but the spirit giveth life."*
3. *"The words that I have spoken unto you are spirit, and are life."*
4. *"Ye must be born from above."*
5. *"I am the light of the world." "Ye are the light of the world."*
6. *"Let your light shine before men; that they may see your good works, and glorify your Father who is in heaven."*
7. *"I am the light" that "lighteth every man, coming into the world."*
8. My understanding is illumined by Spirit. I am the light of my consciousness.
9. I acknowledge God at all times as the one source of my understanding.
10. *"Arise, shine; for thy light is come, and the glory of Jehovah is risen upon thee."*
11. The glory of the Lord is risen upon me, and I walk in the light of life.
12. My body is the temple of the living God, and the glory of the Lord fills the temple.
13. Christ within me is my glory. The brightness of His presence casts out all the darkness of error, and my whole body is full of light.
14. *"He that loveth his brother abideth in the light, and there is no occasion of stumbling in him."*
15. *"Jehovah is my light and my salvation; whom shall I fear? Jehovah is the strength of my life; of whom shall I be afraid?"*
16. *"Then shall Thy light break forth as the morning, and thy health shall spring forth speedily."*

Establishing The Perfect Substance
(To be used in connection with Lesson Seven)

1. *"And God created man in his own image, in the image of God created he him; male and female created he them."*

2. My perfection is now established in Divine Mind.

3. *"Ye therefore shall be perfect, as your heavenly Father is perfect."*

4. By seeing perfection in all things, I help to make it manifest. "I must be in my Father's house."

5. The corruptible flesh is changed into incorruption when it is seen as perfect and pure in Christ.

6. I see in mind that perfect character which I desire to be, and thus plant the seed thought that brings forth the perfect man.

7. *"But we all, with unveiled face beholding as in a mirror the glory of the Lord, are transformed into the same image from glory to glory, even as from the Lord the Spirit."*

8. *"When Christ, who is our life, shall be manifested, then shall ye also with him be manifested in glory."*

9. My mind is opened anew to the splendor of God's kingdom, and a flood of rich substance now pours itself into my affairs.

Lesson Eight

Faith

1. Now faith is assurance of things hoped for, a conviction of things not seen. . . . By faith we understand that the worlds have been framed by the word of God, so that what is seen hath not been made out of things which appear.

2. In the 11th chapter of Hebrews, we find the achievements of faith piled mountain high:

By faith Enoch was translated that he should not see death. . . . By Faith Noah . . . prepared an ark to the saving of his house. . . . By faith Abraham, being tried, offered up Isaac. . . . By faith Moses, when he was born, was hid three months by his parents. . . . By faith the walls of Jericho fell down. . . . And what shall I more say? for the time will fail me if I tell of Gideon, Barak, Samson, Jephthah; of David and Samuel and the prophets: who through faith subdued kingdoms, wrought righteousness, obtained promises, stopped the mouths of lions, quenched the power of fire, escaped the edge of the sword, from weakness were made strong, waxed mighty in war, turned to flight armies of aliens. Women received their dead by a resurrection.

3. The idea that faith is something that has to do only with one's religious experience is incorrect. Faith is a faculty of the mind that finds its most perfect expression in the spiritual nature, but in order to bring out one's whole character it should be developed in all its phases. That it is a power is self-evident. People who have faith in themselves achieve far more than those who do not believe in their own ability. We call this self-faith innate confidence, but confidence is only a form of faith. Belief is another of the expressions of faith. Jesus apparently made no distinction between faith and belief. He said, "*Believe ye that I am able to do this?*" and "*Whosoever . . . shall not doubt in his heart, but shall believe that what he saith cometh to pass; he shall have it.*" In an analysis of the constituent parts of man's consciousness, we locate belief in the intellect, working in the thought realm without contact with the more interior substance of Spirit, upon which true faith is founded.

4. In Spirit, faith is related to omnipresent substance or assurance. Jesus used the same illustration when He referred to Peter, a type of faith, as a rock upon which He would found His church. Here is proof that faith is closely allied to the enduring, firm, unyielding forms of earth substance. But free faith has power to do, and power to bring about results in the affairs of those who cultivate it.

5. Like the other faculties, faith has a center through which it expresses outwardly its spiritual powers. Physiologists call this center the pineal gland, and they locate it in the upper brain. By meditation man lights up the inner mind, and he receives more than he can put into words. Only those who have strengthened their interior faculties can appreciate the wonderful undeveloped possibilities in man. The physiologist sees the faculties as brain cells, the psychologist views them as thought combinations, but the spiritual-minded beholds them as pure ideas, unrelated, free, all-potential.

6. Faith can be extended in consciousness in every direction. It will accomplish wonderful things if quickened and allowed free expression in its native realm. When Jesus said, "*If ye have faith as a grain of mustard seed, ye shall say unto this mountain, Remove hence to yonder place; and it shall remove; and nothing shall be impossible unto you,*" He referred to faith's working in spiritual substance. Such results are possible only to the faith that co-operates with creative law. Where faith is centered in outer things, the results are not worthy of mention. Men have named them luck, accident, chance, and the like. Such charms seem to work for a little while, then suddenly change, so it is evident that they are not under any enduring law.

7. When faith is exercised in the intellectual realm, the results are usually profitable to the man of brains. If he has faith in his art, or his science, or his philosophy, it answers his purpose, for a time at least, but it never gets beyond the traditions and experiences of precedent. Intellectual people do no miracles through faith, because they always limit its scope to what the

intellect says is law. It is when faith is exercised deep in spiritual consciousness that it finds its right place, and under divine law, without variation or disappointment, it brings results that are seemingly miraculous. 8. Faith has always played a very large part in the experiences of religious people because they have given it free scope, expecting great things through it from the Lord. But nearly all faith demonstrations have been the result of a sort of blind confidence that God would carry out whatever was asked of Him. Sometimes a petitioner has been disappointed, and a series of disappointments has usually led to doubt and to the conclusion that God has in some way changed His law. The early Christians were taught by Jesus and His disciples to have faith in God, and they did wonderful, so-called miraculous, works. As time went on and their attention was more and more drawn to worldly things, the Christians of a later day became separated from the spiritual forces within them, and their faith lost its energy. Then they began teaching that miracles were no longer necessary; that God had given them to the early Christians because they did not have the Bible or an organized church. They also taught that the miracles had been given to prove that Jesus was the Son of God.

9. Now we have a fuller understanding of the law of God, and know that whatever has been done once can be done again under like conditions. If Jesus and His disciples and the early Christians did marvelous things through the prayer of faith, we can do likewise. All that is required is perseverance in our use of faith until we make connection with the higher realms of consciousness, where, as Jesus said, though our faith be as small as the smallest of seeds, it will spring forth and demonstrate its power to carry out every desire into which we infuse it. "*Nothing shall be impossible unto you,*" if your faith is in Spirit, and if your work is in harmony with Divine Mind.

10. The Christian religion has been a great factor in the development of faith in the inner realms of man's being. "*Blessed are they that have not seen, and yet have believed.*" The power to see in Spirit is peculiar to faith. In its outer expression this power is sight; interiorly it is that which perceives the reality of the substance of Spirit. Mental seeing is knowing; when we perceive the truth of a proposition, we say, "*I see, I see,*" meaning that we mentally discern.

11. Faith in the reality of things spiritual develops the faith center in the brain, called the pineal gland. When this mental eye is illuminated with spiritual faith, it sheds a radiance that hovers like a halo around the head and extends in lessening degree throughout the whole body. "*When thine eye is single, thy whole body also is full of light.*" The halo that the early artists painted around the heads of saints was not imaginary, but real. This illuminating power of faith covers the whole constitution of man, making him master of all the forces centering about spiritual consciousness. Faith and prayer go hand in hand.

12. "*The faith which thou hast, have thou to thyself before God. Happy is he that judgeth not himself in that which he approveth.*" Have faith in what you do, and after it is done do not condemn yourself. We all are seeking happiness, contentment, and we know by experience that we are happy when we are in tune with our environment. There is a great variety of ideas that cause us inharmony. We think that if we have money and friends we can be happy; but things do not make happiness. It is our mental attitude toward things that fixes our relation to them, and the better we understand the innate substance of the world about us, the more do we appreciate it.

13. Faith is ever active, and it should be made the truth substance of every idea. We should have faith in our own power, capacity, and ability; if we are to have this faith our thoughts must be centered in the great universal Mind. Success lies in God. Whatsoever is not of faith is sin; then whatsoever is of faith is not sin. This is the new standard of righteousness for the man who would "*put on Christ.*" It is his breastplate, his protection, while he is coming up into knowledge of the absolute good. Sin is a missing of the mark, and we miss the mark by not having faith.

14. Faith in the reality, power, and willingness of the mental and spiritual forces is absolutely essential to success in demonstrating the higher law. Jesus was the herald of a set of laws that will revolutionize the civilization of this world and will produce a new and higher type of man. He spoke of a new condition for the uplift of the race; He called it the "*kingdom of heaven,*" and He said that it must be built upon the foundation typified by Peter (a rock), which is faith. The

development of the faith faculty in the mind is as necessary to the worker in spiritual principles as is the development of the mathematical faculty in the worker in mathematics. Neither of these faculties comes at a bound fully formed into consciousness, but both grow by cultivation. "*Increase our faith,*" said the apostles, and Jesus answered: "*Have faith in God.*"

15. Nearly all readers of Scripture recognize Peter as a type of faith. By studying his experiences we may get suggestions on the development of that faculty in ourselves. The fluctuating allegiance of Peter to Jesus illustrates the growth of faith in one who has had no development of that faculty. Faith and doubt contended for supremacy in Peter, and we wonder why Jesus chose as His chief disciple this vacillating, weak, and cowardly fisherman. But we observe that Peter was enthusiastic, bold at times, receptive and patient under reproof. He had never walked on the water, but when Jesus said, "*Come,*" he boldly went out to meet Him. Doubt entered his mind, and he sank; but the helping hand was extended to him and he was made stronger by the experience. This and many other illustrations in the history of Peter show how faith grows in the mind, and we should not be discouraged if our first efforts fall short of the desired end.

16. A very little faith often produces surprising results. The forces invisible are much closer than we think, and when we turn our attention in their direction the response is usually so pronounced and so swift that we cannot but feel that a miracle has been performed. A more intimate acquaintance with the divine law convinces us that under it all things are possible if we only believe, and if we at the same time conform our thoughts to its principle.

17. Peter (faith), James (judgment), and John (love) were the three apostles who were very close to Jesus, and they are more prominent in His history than any of the others. This indicates that these three faculties are developed in advance of the others, also that they are closely associated. Understanding reveals to us that God is a mind-principle whose foundation is ideas. When this character of the creative principle dawns upon us, we see how easy it is to commune with God. Through this communion we almost unconsciously strengthen faith, and we find that one faculty helps another to grow. But there must be room in which to grow, and room is made by love. Selfishness is limitation; it binds man in a little prison called personality. The only way to enlarge one's character and give play to all the faculties is through love. Love enlarges the field of consciousness by leveling the thoughts of enmity and opposition. Make friends with all your adversaries quickly, whether they be persons, thoughts, or things.

18. We are constantly making conditions through our thoughts. Some people declare that everything is against them. If they miss a car, they say, "*It is always that way,*" and they build up a state of mind in which everything seems contrary to them.

19. In all our experience we should condemn nothing that comes to us and nothing that we do. We know the law; let us keep it, and not set up any adverse conditions by our thoughts of condemnation. Whatever you are doing, be happy in it. If you are getting wrong results, do not believe in an angry God. You are getting the results of your acts, according to your faith. Be wise; pronounce nothing evil, and only good will come. Shall we call everything good? Yes. If the savage knew this law he could lift himself to a higher consciousness by it. We get out of savagery by idealizing the good.

20. Have faith in the innate goodness of all men and all conditions. Do not condemn, no matter how great the provocation. What you think, you create in your own consciousness. Enlarge your range of vision, and you may see good in what now seems evil. God is good and God is all, hence there can be no real condition but the good. Why should we waste our time fighting evil? If we build our character upon faith, understanding, and love, with the great I AM as the focal center, we shall become pillars in the temple of God.

Faith Affirmations
(To be used in connection with Lesson Eight)

1. *"Now faith is assurance of things hoped for, a conviction of things not seen."*

2. Holding continuously to the reality of things spiritual establishes them in mind--they become mental substance.

3. I believe in the presence and power of the one Mind, and it is to me substantial intelligence.

4. *"According to your faith be it done unto you."*

5. My doubts and fears are dissolved and dissipated; in confidence and peace I rest in God's unchangeable law.

6. *"Great is thy faith: be it done unto thee even as thou wilt."*

7. With my mind's eye I see more and more the reality of the true ideas ever existing in divine principle.

8. *"I believe; help thou mine unbelief."*

9. Jesus said: *"Have faith in God."*

10. I am saved from pain and sorrow through my unswerving faith in the protection and care of God.

11. *"Lord, increase our faith."*

12. My faith grows greater day by day, because it is planted in Truth, and through it the mountains of mortal error are moved into the sea of nothingness.

13. The understanding of Spirit clarifies my faith 14. *"I know him whom I have believed." I am persuaded that He is able, that He is willing, that He is eager, to give me whatsoever I ask."*

15. My faith comprehends the beauty of wholeness.

16. My faith is of God and in God.

17. *"Go thy way; thy faith hath made thee whole."*

Lesson Nine

Imagination

1. The teachings about the things of Spirit are said to be mystical. We have thought them so because we have not come into consciousness of the many faculties necessary to comprehend Spirit. Victor Hugo said: "*There are no occult or hidden truths; everything is luminous with mind.*" So we find in the study of Truth that what is called mysterious and occult is simply a range of facts that man has not yet explored. When he expands his mind and takes in a larger horizon, he sees the interrelation of a multitude of hitherto unknown laws which, from his former viewpoint, seemed mysterious.

2. Mind manifests through faculties; if mind is to comprehend increasingly, there must be an increase of these avenues. That man has latent possibilities goes without argument; that there is a limit to the ability of the mind is unthinkable. What a man imagines he can do, that he can do. The doing is a question of adopting the right way. To allow the imagination to drift in daydreams never brings anything to pass. Ideas must be worked up into living, breathing, thinking things. Man can compress his vagrant ideas into visibility as the chemist liquefies and makes visible the invisible atmosphere; but to do this he must, like the chemist, have the necessary machinery.

3. Physiology says that, in order to think, man must have brains. However, thinking is not limited to material brain cells but, like everything else in the universe, has a wide range of expression. There are brains within brains, and cells within cells. All through the body are brain centers, whose offices have not yet been determined. Psychology shows that these nerve centers are acted upon by invisible forces; it teaches that man has what is called a subconscious mind, which transcends the conscious mind in knowledge and in ability. Jesus gives us this still higher teaching concerning our mental powers:

Man has a mind called the Lord, transcending both the conscious and the subconscious minds. Yet the harmonious working together of these three seemingly separate minds is necessary to the bringing forth of the latent possibilities of the man.

4. In truth there is but one Mind; in it all things exist. Accurately speaking, man does not have three minds, nor does he have even one mind; but he expresses the one Mind in a multitude of ways. To believe in the possession of an individual mind, and that it is necessary to store up knowledge in it, makes living burdensome. This is why very intellectual people are often impractical and unsuccessful; they have accumulated more knowledge than they have wisdom and power to apply. Like the miser who starves surrounded by his gold, they perish for lack of real understanding. Through thinking of their stored-up knowledge as a personal possession, they have insulated it from the original fount of wisdom and life, and it has consequently become stale and forceless.

5. There is in man that which, when opened, will place him in direct contact with universal knowledge and enable him instantly and continuously to draw forth anything that he may wish to know. God is our fount of wisdom, even as He is our source of supply. The understanding of the Christ Mind reveals that man of himself knows nothing. Jesus, who developed this higher consciousness, claimed that all His knowledge and power came direct from the Father: "*I can of myself do nothing.*" "*The Father abiding in me doeth his works.*"

6. All that man really needs is the quickening and rounding out of the thinking centers in his consciousness; that having been done, Divine Mind will think through him. This supreme Mind holds man at its center, a perfect instrument through which to express its possibilities. The writer of the first chapter of Genesis says that man is formed in the image and after the likeness of God. He is the I-am-age, or the identical I AM of God-Mind in expression. God looks into the mirror of the universe and sees Himself as man; He gives Himself to man, and man in his highest is God manifest. "*He that hath seen me hath seen the Father.*" Thus God gives

to His image the power to express all that He is. This not only includes man's ability to think, but also the power to shape and form thought. This formative power of thought requires a distinctive faculty, which is called the *"imagination."* The mind makes its forms in a way similar to that in which cooks make biscuits. First is the gathering of the materials, then the mixing, then the biscuit cutting, which gives shape to the substance. In thinking, man accumulates a mass of ideas about substance and life, and with his imagination he makes them into forms.

7. Whatever we mirror in our minds becomes a living, active thing, and through it we are connected with the world about us. Through the work of the imaging faculty, every thought makes a form, and multitudes of thoughts make multitudes of forms. These crowd in upon one another around the central I-am-age, and appear in what is called the body. Physiology says that all the organs of the body are made up of cells, and that every cell contains the essential elements of its particular organ. The liver is made of a multitude of liver elements, the heart of heart elements, and so forth. The starting point is an idea, and through the mechanism of the mind (often erroneously called the mechanism of the body) man forms his organism. With this key anyone can unlock the door of his temple and in mind visit all its various rooms and set the furniture in order.

8. The imagination has its center of action in the front brain; it uses what phrenology calls the perceptive faculties. It is really the author of these faculties; size, weight, form, color, and the like are its children. When it flashes its light into the cells that make up the organs, they at once respond to the thought, and out of substance visible and invisible make forms that correspond to the idea held in imagination. If the idea originates in Spirit, the creation is harmonious and according to law. The nerve centers are so sensitive and receptive to thought that they take impressions from without and make in the ether the forms that correspond to the impressions received. This is an inversion of the creative law, which is that all creations shall have their patterns in the mind. When man allows his imagination to run on in a lawless way, he brings about such discord in mind and body that the flood of error thought submerges his understanding and he is drowned in it. *"And Jehovah saw that the wickedness of man was great in the earth, and that every imagination of the thoughts of his heart was only evil continually." "And I, behold, I do bring the flood of waters upon the earth, to destroy all flesh."*

9. All things, including the mind, work from center to circumference. A knowledge of this fact puts man on his guard and causes him to direct that his imagination shall not create things in his mind that have been impressed upon him from without. This does not imply that the outer world is all error, or that all appearance is the creation of finite mind; it means that the outer is not a safe pattern from which to make the members of the body. When Moses was instructed by the Lord to furnish the tabernacle, the command was, *"See . . . that thou* make all things according to the pattern that was showed thee in the mount." *"The mount"* is the place of high understanding in mind, which Jesus called the kingdom of God within us. The wise metaphysician resolves into ideas each mental picture, each form and shape seen in visions, dreams, and the like. The idea is the foundation, the real; when understood and molded by the power of the word, it creates or recreates the form at the direction of the individual I AM. By working with this simple law, man may become an adept or master. By handling the cause of things he attains mastery over things, and instead of giving up to his emotions and feelings, he controls them. Instead of letting his imagination run riot, conjuring up all sorts of situations, he holds it steadily to a certain set of ideas that he wants brought forth. *"Thou wilt keep him in perfect peace, whose imagination is stayed on thee."* (Is. 26:3, margin.)

10. As man develops in understanding, his imagination is the first of his latent faculties to quicken. Esau represents the natural man. Jacob represents the intellectual man supplanting Esau; hence Jacob is called the *"supplanter."* Historically, he seems a trickster, taking advantage of those of less wisdom, but this incident merely shows how the higher principle appropriates the good everywhere. Imagination was the leading faculty in Jacob's mind. He dreamed of a ladder reaching from earth to heaven, the angels of God ascending and descending upon it. This is prophecy of union between the ideal and its manifestations, between Spirit and body; the

union is made by pure thoughts of the absolute--the angels of Jacob's dream. Farther along in his development Jacob awakened all his faculties, represented by his twelve sons. Joseph was a dreamer and an interpreter of dreams. He was the favorite son of Jacob, the I AM, who gave him a coat of many colors. This is all representative of the imaging faculty, which Joseph typifies.

11. The history of Joseph is the history of man's imagination developed under the divine law. His dreams were messages from God, and God interpreted them for him; his life is one of the most interesting and fascinating romances in the Bible. For a time the way of Joseph was thorny, but through his obedience to Spirit he reached the highest place in the king's domain. This shows that man begins the development of the imagination in the darkness of materiality and in the depths of ignorance, represented by Joseph's being cast into the pit and sold into Egypt. Through spiritual understanding, the *"dreamer"* becomes the most practical son of the family; by following his dream interpretations, multitudes are saved from starvation. The individual application of this is: Having our attention fixed on Spirit, we discern the ebb and flow of the forces in the organism, and we know how to conserve and husband our resources.

12. Instead of treating the visions of the night as idle dreams, we should inquire into them, seeking to know the cause and the meaning of every mental picture. Every dream has origin in thought, and every thought makes a mind picture. The study of dreams and visions is an important one, because it is through these mental pictures that the Lord communicates with man in a certain stage of his unfoldment. Solomon was instructed in dreams. *"In Gibeon Jehovah appeared to Solomon in a dream by night; and God said, Ask what I shall give thee."* In Job 33:15, 16, we read, *"In a dream, in a vision of the night, when deep sleep falleth upon men, in slumberings upon the bed; then he openeth the ears of men, and sealeth their instruction." "Then was the secret revealed unto Daniel in a vision of the night."* Joseph, the husband of Mary, was told in a dream to take the young child Jesus and go down into Egypt. Peter was shown his intolerance in a vision, and Paul was obedient to the *"heavenly vision."* God has instructed all the great and wise in every age in dreams and visions. *"Where there is no vision, the people cast off restraint."*

13. Every form and thing, whether in the ether or on the earth, represents some idea or mental attitude. The idea is first projected into mind substance, and afterward formed in consciousness. The mind of man sees all things through thought forms made by the imagination. The lover idealizes the object of his affection, and is often disappointed on close acquaintance. We are always creating ideals that have existence in our minds alone. A true story is told of a sailor who went on a long voyage and left his affianced behind. He thought of her continuously, and often saw her in his dreams. Finally he began to see and talk to her in his waking state, and she told him many remarkable things. She said that it was her soul that visited him; that her body was in her English home, awaiting his return. After some twenty years he arrived at home, expecting a welcome from his loved one. He was dumfounded to learn that she was married, had a family, and had forgotten him. Out of his own mind substance he had created the object of his affection, which had faithfully reflected all his thoughts about her.

14. Through the power of the imagination we impress upon the body the concepts of the mind. Here are stories of actual occurrences: a woman watched her little daughter pass through a heavy iron gate. The gate swung shut and the mother imagined that it had caught and crushed the little one's fingers. But the child had withdrawn her fingers before the gate struck. The mother felt pain in her own hand, and the next day she found a dark streak across her fingers, in the place where she had imagined that the child's had been crushed. In a secret-society initiation, the candidate was told that the word "coward" was to be branded upon his back with a red-hot iron. A piece of ice was used instead, but the promised brand arose in blistered letters.

15. We could cite cases without number to prove the power of the imagination in forming and transforming the body. Also, one mind can suggest to another and produce any desired condition, if there be mental receptivity. This can be done most effectively through the hypnotic state, but hypnosis is not always necessary. Experiments prove that we are constantly suggesting all sorts of things to one another, and getting results according to the intensity of

the imagination. Thus disease is reflected into susceptible minds by people's merely talking about disease as an awful reality.

16. A man can imagine that he has some evil condition in body or affairs, and through the imaging law build it up until it becomes manifest. On the other hand, he can use the same power to make good appear on every side. The marks of old age can be erased from the body by one's mentally seeing the body as youthful. If you want to be healthy, do not imagine so vain a thing as decrepitude. Make your body perfect by seeing perfection in it. Transient patching up with lotions and external applications is foolish; the work must be an inner transformation. *"Be ye transformed by the renewing of your mind."*

17. The highest and best work of the imagination is the marvelous transformation that it works in character. Imagine that you are one with the Principle of good, and you will become truly good. To imagine oneself perfect fixes the idea of perfection in the invisible mindsubstance, and the mind forces at once begin the work of bringing forth perfection.

18. Paul saw this wonderful law at work in character-forming through imitating Christ: *"But we all, with unveiled face beholding as in a mirror the glory of the Lord, are transformed into the same image from glory, to glory, even as from the Lord the Spirit."*

Perfection In Form Established
(To be used in connection with Lesson Nine)

1. I see my countenance in its divine perfection.
2. *"Thou wilt keep him in perfect peace, whose imagination is stayed on thee."*
3. I see perfection in all forms and shapes.
4. His Son is the brightness of His glory, and the express image of His person.
5. I see the light of the Christ consciousness always.
6. I am formed anew every day in my mind and my body.
7. Be renewed in the spirit of your mind.
8. My spirit is quickened in Christ.
9. *"In a dream, in a vision of the night . . . he openeth the ears of men, and sealeth their instruction."*
10. I know the reality back of the shadows.

Lesson Ten

Will and Understanding

1. *"If any man willeth to do his will, he shall know of the teaching."* Man manifests that which exists eternally in Being. We talk about the faculties of man's mind as if they belonged to the individual and had origin in him. Man exists in the one invisible Mind. He may assume to have a mind of his own, but his origin and destiny are in God-Mind.

2. Primal causes are complete, finished, absolute. All that man manifests has its origin in a cause that we name Divine Mind, Spirit, God. This being true in logic and intuition, it is not a difficult matter to arrive at the conclusion that the manifestation proves the character of the cause. In dealing with the faculties of man, the relation between them and the one Mind should not be lost sight of. There is but one Mind, and that Mind cannot be separated or divided, because, like the principle of mathematics, it is indivisible. All that we can say of the one Mind is that it is absolute and that all its manifestations are in essence like itself. This brings us to the true estimate of man, and when we speak of spiritual man, or Christ man, or the son of God, we refer to this original expression of Divine Mind.

3. In analyzing these faculties and in establishing their relation in the individual consciousness, we should clearly understand that they are never separated from their Principle, the Divine Mind. In the text quoted above, Jesus refers to two of the powers of man and brings out a certain phase of their relation. Will and know designate the faculties of mind that we term will and understanding. Through appropriation, through expansion and growth in consciousness, will and understanding would seem to have their source in individual man. But, however adapted by man, they can never be divorced from the mind of Being, in which they exist as essential members of its wholeness.

4. Individual consciousness is like an eddy in the ocean--all the elements that are found in the ocean are also found in the eddy, and every eddy may, in due course, receive and give forth all that is in the ocean. As the will of God, man represents I AM identity. This is individual consciousness, freedom to act without dictation of any kind, selfhood without consciousness of cause, the power to make or break without limitation, constructive and destructive ability with a universe of workable potentialities. The will is the man. Without absolute freedom of will, man would be an automaton. If his will were restricted in the least degree on any side, he would not be perfectly free. We know that God is the Great Unlimited, and man, His *"image"* and *"likeness,"* must be of the same character; consequently man has the same freedom that God has to act in the fulfillment of desire. God does not dictate man's acts, although He may instruct and draw him through love away from error. The idea that God makes man do certain things cannot be true in a single instance, because, if it were, man would not be a free agent. If God interfered with man's will in some things, it would follow that He could interfere in any and all things. Logic and observation clearly reveal the freedom of man in everything.

5. Creative thought uses the will to build up individual consciousness. The Lord God, or Jehovah, of Genesis, is the original *"I WILL BE THAT I WILL BE."* In mind, both Jehovah and Jesus mean I AM. I AM is man's self-identity. I AM is the center around which man's system revolves. When the I AM is established in a certain understanding of its Principle, it is divinely guided in its acts, and they are in harmony with divine law. This is the union of will and understanding. In the Scripture these two are designated as Ephraim and Manasseh, sons of Joseph. Their allotments in the Promised Land were joined, indicating that these faculties work in the body from a single brain center. The center is in the forehead.

6. The will should never be retarded in its development, but should be strengthened along all lines. The idea of breaking the will of children is wholly erroneous. The perfect man is produced by rounding out the will and joining it to the understanding. The idea of giving up the will to God's will should not include the thought of weakening it, or causing it to become

in any way less; it properly means that the will is being instructed how to act for the best. Do not act until you know how to act. "*Look before you leap.*" This does not imply that one should be inactive and indefinite, waiting for understanding, as do many persons who are afraid to act because they may possibly do the wrong thing; it means that understanding will be quickened and the will strengthened by the confidence that comes as a result of knowledge.

7. To strengthen the will, and at the same time to discipline it along right lines, requires an understanding nothing less than divine. But man can balance his will and his understanding; when he does this he will always do the right thing at the right time. Nearly every mistake is the result of will's acting without the cooperation of its brother, understanding. When the will is permitted to act on its own account, man becomes emotional and willful. These states of consciousness lead to all kinds of bodily discord. Willfullness makes tenseness, and a tense mind ties knots in the nerves, muscles, and tendons of the whole organism. The metaphysician, observing these conditions, treats for relaxation of will and for a general letting go of the whole system. The universal treatment for this condition given by Jesus is, "*Not my will, but thine, be done.*" This surrender causes personal will to "*let go,*" and a unification of man's will with God's will takes place. When this is accomplished, all goes well.

8. Willful persons often complain of a feeling like that produced by a tight band around the head. This feeling results from the pressure of thought substance, which the will has laid hold of and is clinging to with centripetal force. In all such cases, and, in fact, in every sense of pressure, treat against personal willfullness and affirm the divine freedom.

9. Every organ of the body is affected by the action of the will, and when this faculty becomes fixed in a certain attitude, it holds the whole body to its central affirmation. The determination to have one's own way, regardless of the rights of others, tends to stop the free action of the heart; the stomach is then sympathetically affected. Persons affected in these ways seldom realize that they have a set determination as to how things shall be done in their lives, and they are sometimes slow in accepting the higher understanding that is necessary to the untangling of mistakes made by the ignorant will. Contrariness is another name for perverted will. An exaggerated idea of self and its needs takes possession of the mind, and the will is used to carry out this shortsighted policy. The result is a belittling of the whole man. Persons who are contentious for their personal rights place themselves in bondage to material conditions and stop spiritual growth.

10. How shall we bring the divine will to bear? By understanding; by appropriating universal wisdom; by affirming: Not my will, but thine, be done. God is potential, unformed will; man is manifest God will, or goodwill. When man links his will with the principle of divine force he has superior executive capacity. He swiftly brings forth faculties that, under the slow action of human personality, would take ages to develop.

11. There is a knowing quality in Divine Mind. God is supreme knowing. That in man which comprehends is understanding; it knows and compares in wisdom. Its comparisons are not made in the realm of form, but in the realm of ideas. It knows how to accomplish things. We may know without experience. The human family has learned by hard knocks that experience is a severe schoolmaster. In the allegory of Adam and Eve, we see a picture of man's falling under the sway of sensation (serpent) and having to learn by experience. One of the esoteric meanings of serpent is "*experience.*" All the bitter lessons that come through blundering ignorance can be evaded when men declare their divine understanding and in it follow the divine guidance.

12. For all willfullness, the healing treatment should be affirmations of spiritual understanding. The will is not to be broken, but disciplined. The absolute freedom of the individual must be maintained at all hazards. God is the one principle; we are all as free to use God as we are free to use the principles of mathematics or of music. The principle never interferes, but if it is to be rightly applied we must develop understanding. Freedom leads to many errors, but, since it is a part of Being, man must learn to use it properly; he must learn that the freedom of the law means control and conservation, not lust and license.

13. We should be careful not to enter into any healing system that interferes with freedom. Hypnotism is not real healing. Any system that suppresses the will is radically wrong. It is the work of the true healer to instruct the patient, to show cause and remedy from the viewpoint of spiritual understanding. All other methods are temporary. The old states of mind will come again into action unless the causing thought is uncovered and removed. A man may have a paralyzed arm through selfish desire for money, and though he may find temporary relief in mere mental suggestions of health, or hypnotism, he will never get permanent healing until he understands the divine law governing possessions, and conforms thereto.

14. There are people who claim that they are being spiritually developed through mediumship. This is error. If you believe that you are under the control of another's will, if you give up to another will, your own will is gradually weakened. If you continue to submit to the domination of another, you will finally lose control of your own life. The will must be strengthened by being constantly used in divine understanding. Mesmerism weakens the will. Spiritual understanding quickens and makes alive. God never puts anyone to sleep. *"Awake, thou that sleepest . . . and Christ shall shine upon thee."*

15. Never say, *"I don't know," "I don't understand."* Claim your Christ understanding at all times, and declare: I am not under any spell of human ignorance. I am one with infinite understanding. The accumulation of ignorance gathered through association with ignorant minds can be dissolved by using the word. You may know by simply holding the thought that you know. This is not egotism, but spiritual knowing. When you declare divine understanding, you sometimes meet your old line of thought and are disappointed. Right then continue to hold to your declaration for knowing. Judge not by appearances. Do not act until you get the assurance; if you keep close to Spirit by affirmation, the assurance will come. Will it come by voice? No! You will know through the faculty of intuition. Divine knowing is direct fusion of mind of God with mind of man. Sometimes we are taught by symbols, visions, and the like, but this is only one of the ways that Divine Mind has of expressing itself. When the mind deals with God ideals it asks for no symbols, visible or invisible, but rests on pure knowing. It was in this consciousness that Jesus said: *"Father, I thank thee that thou heardest me. And I knew that thou hearest me always."*

16. A very practical application of the truth about the will can be made in the matter of self-control. Those who try to get control through suppressing the personal will fall short. We should be free to express all that we are. If you are afraid of any force within you, your fear leads to suppression. In the true self-control, the will and the understanding both play a part. The feelings and appetites and passions must be disciplined. They are not merely to be held in check by the will, but they are to be lifted up and developed through the Christ Mind.

17. The problem of self-control is never settled until all that man is comes into touch with the divine will and understanding. You must understand all your forces before you can establish them in harmony. This overcoming is easy if you go about it in the right way. But if you try to take dominion through will, force, and suppression, you will find it hard and will never accomplish any permanent results. Get your I AM centered in God, and from that place of Truth speak true words. In this way you will gain real spiritual mastery and raise your will consciousness from the human to the divine.

18. The will plays the leading part in all systems of thought concentration. The simple statement, I will to be well, gathers the forces of mind and body about the central idea of wholeness, and the will holds the center just so long as the I AM continues its affirmation. No one ever died until he let go his will to live, and thousands live on and on through the force of a determined will.

19. The *"devil"* that we are to overcome is the adverse will, which seeks to master man in the without. This *"adversary"* troubles us because we strive to maintain personal freedom instead of submitting to divine guidance. Self-confidence is a virtue when founded on the Truth of Being, but when it arises from the personal consciousness it keeps man from his dominion. Are you trying just from yourself to be free from the traditions of the outer world, or are you

resting in the understanding and assurance that you are a son of God? To know yourself as a son of God is to overcome the *"devil"*–the personal self. The *"devil"* makes you believe that you are the son of the flesh. To overcome, say: I put Satan behind me by the realization that God is my Father. I am centered in Him, and all things are under His dominion. I live in the infinite Power that produces all self-control. I have no necessity for controlling people. Events and people are controlled by divine law. There is an eternal law of justice. I am one with that law and I rest in it.

20. Among the apostles of Jesus, Matthew represents the will, and Thomas the understanding. Matthew was the taxgatherer who sat at the gate, representing the executive part of the government; so the will is the executive faculty of the mind and carries out the edicts of the I AM. All thoughts that go into or out of man's consciousness pass the gate at which sits the will, and if the will understands its office, the character and the value of every thought are inquired into and a certain tribute is exacted for the benefit of the whole man.

21. Thomas, the understanding, is represented as under discipline; that is, not yet in the light of Spirit. The understanding, in its first steps in Truth, wants its lessons and accompanying demonstrations to be couched in terms like those used in the outer world. When Jesus showed Himself to Thomas, the latter said that he would not believe unless he could see the prints of the nails and feel the wound in the side of the Lord. This double proof was given him, and Jesus said: *"Be not faithless, but believing." Thomas was then spiritually awakened and he made the acknowledgment: "My Lord and my God."*

22. The people who are being educated in Truth through the written and the spoken word will finally arrive at that place where the true light from Spirit will dawn upon them, and they will, like Thomas, see with spiritual understanding and have proof of the reality of the Christ Mind.

The Establishment Of Will And Understanding (To be used in connection with Lesson Ten)

1. My understanding is established in Divine Mind.

2. *"Ye shall know the truth, and the truth shall make you free."*

3. The will of God is ever uppermost in my consciousness.

4. *"Not my will, but thine, be done."*

5. I firmly believe the guiding Intelligence that directs all my thoughts.

6. *"There is a spirit in man, and the breath of the Almighty giveth them understanding."*

7. The willfullness and stubborness of the flesh have no power in me. I am obedient to Spirit and receptive to all its secret thoughts.

8. *"Not . . . of the will of flesh, nor of the will of man, but of God."*

9. I am willing to change my mind.

10. *"Be ye transformed by the renewing of your mind."*

11. The Christ of God is born in my consciousness, and I am glorified in my understanding.

Lesson Eleven

Judgment and Justice

1. *"Judge not, that ye be not judged. For with what judgment ye judge, ye shall be judged: and with what measure ye mete, it shall be measured unto you"*.–Mt. 7:1,2.

2. *"And thou shalt put in the breastplate of judgment the Urim and the Thummim; and they shall be upon Aaron's heart, when he goeth in before Jehovah: and Aaron shall bear the judgment of the children of Israel upon his heart before Jehovah continually"*.-Ex. 28:30.

3. The Urim and Thummim (Lights and Perfections). These were the sacred symbols (worn upon the breastplate of the high priest, upon his heart) by which God gave oracular responses for the guidance of His People in temporal matters. What they were is unknown; they are introduced in Exodus without explanation, as if familiar to the Israelites of that day. Modern Egyptology supplies us with a clue; it tells us that Egyptian high priests in every town, who were also its magistrates, wore round their necks a jeweled gem bearing on one side the image of Truth, and on the other sometimes that of Justice, sometimes that of Light. When the accused was acquitted, the judge held out the image of him to kiss. In the final judgment Osiris wears around his neck the jeweled Justice and Truth. The Septuagint translates Urim and Thummim by *"Light and Truth."* Some scholars suppose that they were the twelve stones of the breastplate; others that they were two additional stones concealed in its fold. Josephus adds to these the two sardonyx buttons, worn on the shoulders, which he says emitted luminous rays when the response was favorable; but the precise mode in which the oracles were given is lost in obscurity.–Bible Glossary of Antiquities.

4. The law as given by Moses is for the guidance of man in the evolution of his faculties. The figures, personalities, and symbols represent potentialities developed and undeveloped on various planes of consciousness. The high priest stands for spiritual man, officiating between God and sense man. The breastplate in an armor protects the most vital part, the heart. The heart is love, the affectional consciousness in man; it may be subject to the force of weak sympathy, unless balanced by another power in which is discrimination, or judgment.

5. The breastplate had on it twelve precious stones, representing the twelve tribes of Israel. This clearly means that the twelve faculties of the mind must be massed at the great brain center called the solar plexus. It means that all the intelligence of man's faculties must be brought into play in the final judgments of the mind. The Urim and Thummim (Lights and Perfections; under the Egyptian symbology, *"Truth and Justice"*) are the oracular edicts of Divine Mind that are intuitively expressed as a logical sequence of the divine principles, truth and justice.

6. A modern metaphysician would interpret all this as signifying the omnipresence of Divine Mind in its perfect idea, Christ. Truth is ready at all times to give judgment and justice. As God is love, so God is justice. These qualities are in Divine Mind in unity, but are made manifest in man's consciousness too often in diversity. It is through the Christ Mind in the heart that they are unified. When justice and love meet at the heart center, there are balance, poise, and righteousness. When judgment is divorced from love, and works from the head alone, there goes forth the human cry for justice. In his mere human judgment, man is hard and heartless; he deals out punishment without consideration of motive or cause, and justice goes awry.

7. Good judgment, like all other faculties of the mind, is developed from Principle. In its perfection it is expressed through man's mind, with all its absolute relations uncurtailed. Man has the right concept of judgment, and ideally the judges of our courts have that unbiased and unprejudiced discrimination which ever exists in the Absolute. A prejudiced judge is abhorred, and a judge who allows himself to be moved by his sympathies is not considered safe.

8. The metaphysician finds it necessary to place his judgment in the Absolute in order to demonstrate its supreme power. This is accomplished by one's first declaring that one's judgment is spiritual and not material; that its origin is in God; that all its conclusions are based on

Truth and that they are absolutely free from prejudice, false sympathy, or personal ignorance. This gives a working center from which the ego, or I AM, begins to set in order its own thought world. The habit of judging others, even in the most insignificant matters of daily life, must be discontinued. *"Judge not, that ye be not judged,"* said Jesus. The law of judgment works out in a multitude of directions, and if we do not observe it in small things, we shall find ourselves failing in large.

9. Judging from the plane of the personal leads into condemnation, and condemnation is always followed by the fixing of a penalty. We see faults in others, and pass judgment upon them without considering motives or circumstances. Our judgment is often biased and prejudiced; yet we do not hesitate to think of some form of punishment to be meted out to the guilty one. He may be guilty or not guilty; decision as to his guilt or innocence rests in the divine law, and we have no right to pass judgment. In our ignorance we are creating thought forces that will react upon us. *"With what judgment ye judge, ye shall be judged." "With what measure ye mete, it shall be measured unto you."* Whatever thought you send out will come back to you. This is an unchangeable law of thought action. A man may be just in all his dealings, yet if he condemns others for their injustice, that thought action will bring him into unjust conditions; so it is not safe to judge except in the Absolute. Jesus said that He judged no man on His own account, but in the Father; that is, He judged in the Principle. This is the stand which everyone must take--resting judgment of others in the Absolute. When this is done the tendency to condemn will grow less and less, until man, seeing his fellow man as God sees him, will leave him to the Absolute in all cases where he seems

10. The great judgment day of Scripture indicates a time of separation between the true and the false. There is no warrant for the belief that God sends man to everlasting punishment. Modern interpreters of the Scripture say that the *"hell of fire"* referred to by Jesus means simply a state in which purification is taking place.

11. The word hell is not translated with clearness sufficient to represent the various meanings of the word in the original language. There are three words from which *"hell"* is derived: Sheol, *"the unseen state"*; Hades, *"the unseen world"*; and Gehenna, *"Valley of Hinnom."* These are used in various relations, nearly all of them allegorical. In a sermon Archdeacon Farrar said: *"There would be the proper teaching about hell if we calmly and deliberately erased from our English Bibles the three words, 'damnation,' 'hell,' and 'everlasting.' I say--unhesitatingly I say, claiming the fullest right to speak with the authority of knowledge--that not one of those words ought to stand any longer in our English Bible, for, in our present acceptation of them, they are simply mistranslations."* This corroborates the metaphysical interpretation of Scripture, and sustains the truth that hell is a figure of speech that represents a corrective state of mind. When error has reached its limit, the retroactive law asserts itself, and judgment, being part of that law, brings the penalty upon the transgressor. This penalty is not punishment, but discipline, and if the transgressor.

12. Under our civil law, criminals are confined in penitentiaries where it is intended that order, regular habits, and industry be inculcated, and that what seems punishment may prove to be educational. Men are everywhere calling for broader educational methods in our prisons, and this demand is an acknowledgment of the necessity of purification through discipline and training in morals. This purifying process is the penalty taught by Jesus--the judgment passed on sinners--the *"hell of fire."* When it is received in the right spirit, this fire burns up the dross in character and purifies mind and body.

13. Metaphysicians have discovered that there is a certain relation between the functions and organs of the body and the ideas in the mind. The liver seems to be connected with mental discrimination, and whenever man gets very active along the line of judgment, especially where condemnation enters in, there is disturbance of some kind in that part of the organism. A habit of judging others with severity and fixing in one's mind what the punishment should be causes the liver to become torpid and to cease its natural action; the complexion becomes muddy as a result. *"There is therefore now no condemnation to them that are in Christ Jesus . . . who walk not after the flesh, but after the Spirit."* This statement held in mind, and carried out in thought and

act, will heal liver complaint of that kind. Another form of thought related to judgment is the vacillating of the mind that never seems to know definitely what is the proper thing to do: *"A double-minded man, unstable in all his ways."* There must be singleness of mind and loyalty to true ideas. Everyone should have definite ideas of what is just and right, and stand by them. This stimulates the action of the liver, and often gives so-called bad people good health, because they are not under self-condemnation. Condemnation in any of its forms retards freedom of action in the discriminative faculty. When we hold ourselves in guilt and condemnation, the natural energies of the mind are weakened and the whole body becomes inert.

14. The remedy for all that appears unjust is denial of condemnation of others, or of self, and affirmation of the great universal Spirit of justice, through which all unequal and unrighteous conditions are finally adjusted.

15. Observing the conditions that exist in the world, the just man would have them righted according to what he perceives to be the equitable law. Unless such a one has spiritual understanding, he is very likely to bring upon himself physical disabilities in his efforts to reform men. If his feelings come to a point of "righteous indignation," and he "boils" with anger over the evils of the world, he will cook the corpuscles of his blood. Jesus gave this treatment for such a mental condition: *"For neither doth the Father judge any man, but he hath given all judgment unto the Son."* This Son is the Christ, the Universal cosmos; to its equity, man should commit the justice that he wishes to see brought into human affairs. Put all the burdens of the world upon the one supreme Judge and hold every man, and all the conditions in which men are involved, amenable to the law of God. By so doing, you will set into action mind forces powerful and far-reaching.

16. If you think that you are unjustly treated by your friends, your employers, your government, or those with whom you do business, simply declare the activity of the almighty Mind, and you will set into action mental forces that will find expression in the executors of the law. This is the most lasting reform to which man can apply himself. It is much more effective than legislation or any attempt to control unjust men by human ways.

17. Jealousy is a form of mental bias that blinds the judgment and causes one to act without weighing the consequences. This state of mind causes the liver to act violently one day and to be torpid the next, finally resulting in a "jaundiced eye" and yellow skin. We speak of one *"blinded by jealousy,"* or *"blinded by prejudice."* We do not mean by this that the physical eyes have been put out, but that the understanding has been darkened. Whatever darkens the understanding interferes in some way with the purifying processes of the organism, and the fluids and pigments are congested and the skin becomes darkened in consequence.

18. The remedy for all this is a dismissal of that poor judgment which causes one to be jealous, and a fuller trust in the great all-adjusting justice of God. In this there should be active trust, which is a form of prayer. The disturbing elements that come into life should be definitely placed in the hands of God. This is much more than mere doubtful trust, or negative expectancy that things will be made right. The Spirit of justice should be appealed to and prayed to with the persistency of an Elijah, or of the Gentile woman whose importunity was rewarded. When the metaphysician sits by his patient with closed eyes he is not asleep, but very much awake to the reality and mental visibility of forces that enter into and make the conditions of the body. This spiritual activity is necessary to the demonstration of the law.

19. Success in the world is largely dependent on good judgment. A prominent businessman was once asked what he considered the most valuable trait of mind in an employee, and he replied: "Good judgment." Everywhere businessmen are looking for people who have judgment equal to the making of quick decisions, on the spur of the moment. Years ago a passenger train was wrecked near a little town in Texas. The station agent in the little town showed his good judgment by settling, right on the spot, with the injured. He did this without authority from headquarters, but he showed such excellent judgment that his ability was recognized and he was rapidly advanced until he became president of one of the largest railroad systems in the United States.

20. By clearing your understanding and acknowledging the one supreme Mind in which is all discrimination, you can cultivate the ability of your mind to arrive quickly at right conclusions. Take the stand that it is your inheritance from God to judge wisely and quickly, and do not depart therefrom by statements of inefficiency in matters of judgment. When you are in doubt as to the right thing to do in attaining justice in worldly affairs, ask that the eternal Spirit of justice shall go forth in your behalf and bring about and restore to you that which is your very own. Do not ask for anything but your very own under the righteous law. Some people unconsciously overreach in their desire for possessions. When they put the matter into the care of Spirit, and things do not turn out just as they had expected in their self-seeking way, they are disappointed and rebellious. This will not do under the spiritual law, which requires that man shall be satisfied with justice and accept the results, whatever they may be. "*There is a divinity that shapes our ends*"; it can be co-operated with by one who believes in things spiritual, and he will thereby be made prosperous and happy.

Judgment And Justice Statements
(To be used in connection with Lesson Eleven)

1. *"Teach me thy way, O Jehovah; and lead me in a plain path."*

2. The righteousness of the divine law is active in all my affairs, and I am protected.

3. *"Stand therefore, having girded your loins with truth, and having put on the breastplate of righteousness."*

4. *"The meek will he guide in justice."*

5. *"I will sing of loving kindness and justice."*

6. My judgment is just, because I seek not my own will, but the will of the Father.

7. *"Judge not, that ye be not judged."*

8. *"Behold now, I have set my cause in order; I know that I am righeous."*

9. I believe in the divine law of justice, and I trust it to set right every transaction in my life.

10. *"There is . . . now no condemnation to them that are in Christ Jesus."*

11. I no longer condemn, criticize, censure, or find fault with my associates; neither do I belittle or condemn myself.

Lesson Twelve

Love

1. Behold what manner of love the Father hath bestowed upon us, that we should be called children of God; and such we are.

2. He that abideth in love abideth in God, and God abideth in him.

3. He that hath my commandments, and keepeth them, he it is that loveth me: and he that loveth me shall be loved of my Father, and I will love him, and will manifest myself unto him.

4. Love, in Divine Mind, is the idea of universal unity. In expression, love is the power that joins and binds in divine harmony the universe and everything in it.

5. Among the faculties of the mind, love is pivotal. Its center of mentation in the body is the cardiac plexus. The physical representative of love is the heart, the office of which is to equalize the circulation of the blood in the body. As the heart equalizes the life flow in the body, so love harmonizes the thoughts of the mind.

6. We have found that the twelve sons of Jacob represent the twelve faculties of mind. When Levi (love) was brought forth by the human soul (Leah), his mother said: "*Now this time will my husband be joined unto me.*" We connect our soul forces with whatever we center our love upon. If we love the things of sense or materiality, we are joined or attached to them through a fixed law of being. In the divine order of being, the soul, or thinking part, of man is joined to its spiritual ego. If it allows itself to become joined to the outer or sense consciousness, it makes personal images that are limitations. The Lord commanded Moses to "*make all things according to the pattern that was showed thee in the mount.*" This "*mount*" is the place of high understanding, or spiritual consciousness, whose center of action is in the very apex of the brain.

7. In the regeneration, our love goes through a transformation, which broadens, strengthens, and deepens it. We no longer confine love to family, friends, and personal relations, but expand it to include all things. The denial of human relationships seems at first glance to be a repudiation of the family group, but it is merely a cleansing of the mind from limited ideas of love when this faculty would satisfy itself solely by means of human kinship. If God is the Father of all, then men and women are brothers and sisters in a universal family, and he who sees spiritually should open his heart and cultivate that inclusive love which God has given as the unifying element in the human family. Just to the extent that we separate ourselves into families, cliques, and religious factions we put away God's love. Unless there is specific denial along every line of human-thought bondage, one will still be under the law of sense. Direct affirmation of spiritual unity, based upon obedience, should be made by everyone who desires to realize this true relation. Jesus said: "*Who is my mother? and who are my brethren? And he stretched forth his hand towards his disciples, and said, Behold, my mother and my brethren! For whosoever shall do the will of my Father who is in heaven, he is my brother, and sister, and mother.*"

8. Among the apostles of Jesus, John represents love--he laid his head on the Master's bosom. When this apostle is "*called*," love is quickened in consciousness. The calling of this apostle consists in bringing into one's consciousness a right understanding of the true character of love, also in exercising love in all the relations of life. One should make it a practice to meditate regularly on the love idea in universal Mind, with the prayer, Divine love, manifest thyself in me. Then there should be periods of mental concentration on the love center in the cardiac plexus, near the heart. It is not necessary to know the exact location of this aggregation of love cells. Think about love with the attention drawn within the breast, and a quickening will follow; all the ideas that go to make up love will be set into motion. This produces a positive love current, which, when sent forth with power, will break up opposing thoughts of hate, and render them null and void. The thought of hate will be dissolved, not only in the mind of the thinker but in the minds of those with whom he comes in contact in mind or in body. The love current is not a projection of the will; it is a setting free of a natural, equalizing, harmonizing

force that in most persons has been dammed up by human limitations. The ordinary man is not aware that he possesses this mighty power, which will turn away every shaft of hate that is aimed at him. We know that *"a soft answer turneth away wrath,"* but here is a faculty native to man, existent in every soul, which may be used at all times to bring about harmony and unity among those who have been disunited through misunderstandings, contentions, or selfishness.

9. Henry Drummond says that Paul's 13th chapter of I Corinthians is the greatest love poem ever written. In his book based on this chapter, *"Love, the Supreme Gift,"* Professor Drummond analyzes love and portrays its various activities. We quote:

10. THE SPECTRUM OF LOVE. Love is a compound thing, Paul tells us. It is like light. As you have seen a man of science take a beam of light and pass it through a crystal prism, as you have seen it come out on the other side of the prism broken up into its component colors--red and blue and yellow and orange, and all the colors of the rainbow--so Paul passes this thing, love, through the magnificent prism of his inspired intellect, and it comes out on the other side broken up into its elements. And in these few words we have what one might call the Spectrum of Love, the analysis of love. Will you observe what its elements are? Will you notice that they have common names; that they are virtues which we hear about every day; that they are things that can be practiced by every man in every place in life; and how, by a multitude of small things and ordinary virtues, the supreme thing, the Summum bonum, is made up? The Spectrum of Love has nine ingredients, viz.:

11. Patience--*"Love suffereth long."* Kindness--*"and is kind."* Generosity--*"Love envieth not."* Humility--*"Love vaunteth not itself, is not puffed up."* Courtesy--*"Doth not behave itself unseemly."* Unselfishness--*"Seeketh not her own."* Good Temper--*"Is not easily provoked."* Guilelessness--*"Thinketh no evil."* Sincerity--*"Rejoiceth not in iniquity, but rejoiceth in the truth."*

12. Professor Drummond, in his address on this chapter to Mr. Moody's students gathered at Northfield, Massachusetts, said: *"How many of you will join me in reading this chapter once a week for the next three months? A man did that once and it changed his whole life. Will you do it? Will you?"*

13. Love is more than mere affection, and all our words protesting our love are not of value unless we have this inner current, which is real substance. Though we have the eloquence of men and of angels, and have not this deeper feeling, it profits us nothing. We should deny the mere conventional, surface affection, and should set our mind on the very substance of love.

14. Charity is not love. You may be kindhearted, and give to the poor and needy until you are impoverished, yet not acquire love. You may be a martyr to the cause of Truth and consume your vitality in good works, yet be far from love. Love is a force that runs in the mind and body like molten gold in a furnace. It does not mix with the baser metals--it has no affinity for anything less than itself. Love is patient; it never gets weary or discouraged. Love is always kind and gentle. It does not envy; jealousy has no place in its world. Love never becomes puffed up with human pride, and does not brag about itself. It is love that makes the refinement of the natural gentleman or lady, although he or she may be ignorant of the world's standards of culture. Love does not seek its own--its own comes to it without being sought.

15. Jesus came proclaiming the spiritual inter-relationship of the human family. His teaching was always of gentleness, nonresistance, love. "I say unto you, Love your enemies, and pray for them that persecute you." To do this, one must be established in the consciousness of divine love, and there must be discipline of the mental nature to preserve such a high standard. The divine law is founded in the eternal unity of all things, and *"love therefore is the fulfillment of the law."* Physical science has discovered that everything can be reduced to a few primal elements, and that if the universe were destroyed it could be built up again from a single cell. So this law of harmony, which has its origin in love, is established in the midst of every individual. *"I will put my law in their inward parts, and in their heart will I write it."* But before this fixed inward principle can be brought to the surface, man must open the way by having faith in the power of love to accomplish all that Jesus claimed for it.

16. *"The love of money is a root of all kinds of evil."* The love of money, not money itself, is the root of all kinds of evil. Money is a convenience that saves men many burdens in the exchange of values. Primitive civilization used the cumbersome method of trading products without a money measure of value, while modern progress uses money continually as a medium of exchange. Money is therefore good to the man of sense perception; but when he allows himself to become enamored of it and hoards it, he makes it his god. The erasure of this idea from human consciousness is part of the metaphysician's work. Trusting in God, we have faith in Him as our resource, and He becomes a perpetual spiritual supply and support; but when we put our faith in the power of material riches, we wean our trust from God and establish it in this transitory substance of rust and corruption. This point is not clearly understood by those who are hypnotized by the money idea. When the metaphysician affirms God to be his opulent supply and support and declares that he has money in abundance, the assumption is that he loves money and depends upon it in the same way that the devotees of Mammon do. The difference is that one trusts in the law of God, while the other trusts in the power of Mammon. The man who blindly gives himself up to money getting acquires a love for it and finally becomes its slave. The wise metaphysician deals with the money idea and masters it.

17. When Jesus said, *"I have overcome the world,"* He meant that by the use of certain words He had dissolved all adverse states of consciousness in materiality, appetite, and selfishness. Christ is the Word, the Logos. Because the word is the mind seed from which springs every condition, great stress is laid on the power of the word, both in the Scriptures and in metaphysical interpretations of the Scriptures. The word is the most enduring thing in existence. *"Heaven and earth shall pass away, but my words shall not pass away."* All metaphysicians recognize that certain words, used persistently, mold and transform conditions in mind, body, and affairs. The word love overcomes hate, resistance, opposition, obstinacy, anger, jealousy, and all states of consciousness where there is mental or physical friction. Words make cells, and these cells are adjusted one to the other through associated ideas. When divine love enters into man's thought process, every cell is poised and balanced in space, in right mathematical order as to weight and relative distance. Law and order rule in the molecules of the body with the exactness that characterizes their action in the worlds of a planetary system.

18. Divine love and human love should not be confounded, because one is as broad as the universe and is always governed by undeviating laws, while the other is fickle, selfish, and lawless. It was to this personal aspect of the love center in man that Jesus referred when He said: *"Out of the heart of men, evil thoughts proceed."* But in the regeneration all this is changed; the heart is cleansed and becomes the standard of right relation among all men. "By this shall all men know that ye are my disciples, if ye have love one to another." We cannot enter fully into the Christ consciousness so long as we have a grudge against anyone. The mind is so constituted that a single thought of a discordant character tinges the whole consciousness; so we must cast out all evil and resisting thoughts before we can know the love of God in its fullness. *"If therefore thou art offering thy gift at the altar, and there rememberest that thy brother hath aught against thee, leave there thy gift before the altar, and go thy way, first be reconciled to thy brother, and then come and offer thy gift."*

19. Divine love in the heart establishes one in fearlessness and indomitable courage. *"God gave us not a spirit of fearfulness; but of power and love and discipline."* A woman who understands this law was waylaid by a tramp. She looked him steadily in the eye and said, *"God loves you."* He released his hold upon her and slunk away. Another woman saw a man beating a horse that could not pull a load up a hill. She silently said to the man: *"The love of God fills your heart and you are tender and kind."* He unhitched the horse; the grateful animal walked directly over to the house where the woman was, and put his nose against the window behind which she stood. A young girl sang *"Jesus, Lover of My Soul,"* to a calloused criminal; the man's heart was softened, and he was reformed.

20. The new heaven and the new earth that are now being established among men and nations the world over are based on love. When men understand each other, love increases. This

is true not only among men, but between man and the animal world, and even between man and the vegetable world. In Yellowstone Park, where animals are protected by our government, grizzly bears come to the house doors and eat scraps from the table, and wild animals of all kinds are tame and friendly. "*The wolf shall dwell with the lamb, and the leopard shall lie down with the kid; and the calf and the young lion and the fatling together; and a little child shall lead them. . . . They shall not hurt nor destroy in all my holy mountain; for the earth shall be full of the knowledge of Jehovah, as the waters cover the sea.*"

21. Beloved, let us love one another: for love is of God; and every one that loveth is begotten of God; and knoweth God. He that loveth not knoweth not God; for God is love. Herein was the love of God manifested in us, that God hath sent his only begotten Son into the world that we might live through him. Herein is love, not that we loved God, but that he loved us, and sent his Son to be the propitiation for our sins. Beloved, if God so loved us, we also ought to love one another. No man hath beheld God at any time: if we love one another, God abideth in us, and his love is perfected in us: hereby we know that we abide in him and he in us, because he hath given us of his Spirit. And we have beheld and bear witness that the Father hath sent the Son to be the Savior of the world. Whosoever shall confess that Jesus is the Son of God, God abideth in him, and he in God. And we know and have believed the love which God hath in us. God is love; and he that abideth in love abideth in God, and God abideth in him. Herein is love made perfect with us, that we may have boldness in the day of judgment; because as he is, even so are we in this world. There is no fear in love: but perfect love casteth out fear, because fear hath punishment; and he that feareth is not made perfect in love. We love, because he first loved us. If a man say, I love God, and hateth his brother, he is a liar: for he that loveth not his brother whom he hath seen, cannot love God whom he hath not seen. And this commandment have we from him, that he who loveth God love his brother also.

Love Demonstrated
(To be used in connection with Lesson Twelve)

1. "God is love; and he that abideth in love abideth in God."

2. I dwell consciously in the very presence of infinite love.

3. God is love, and everyone that loves is born of God.

4. I am born of love.

5. "Love . . . is the fulfillment of the law."

6. I love everybody and everything.

7. Faith works by love.

8. I have faith in the supreme power of love.

9. God has not given us the spirit of fear, but of power, and of love, and of a sound mind.

10. I am fearless, powerful, and wise in God's love.

11. "Behold what manner of love the Father hath bestowed upon us, that we should be called children of God."

12. I love the Lord my God with all my heart, and with all my mind, and with all my soul, and with all my strength.

13. "But now abideth faith, hope, love, these three; and the greatest of these is love."

Study Helps and Questions

These study helps and questions have been arranged for the convenience of students, whether they are working in class or in the privacy of their own homes. A careful comparison of the students' answers with the text will show how far they have progressed in their study.

Lesson I--The True Character Of Being

1. Is there anything scientific about Spirit? Give reasons for your answer.

2. Is it necessary for man's spiritual consciousness to be awake in the beginning of his study of spiritual science? In what attitude should one study?

3. What attitude precedes inspiration of spiritual consciousness? May a certain amount of intellectual study help?

4. What is the starting point in spiritual attainment? What is the Almighty? How does man understand the Almighty?

5. What is one of the most important things that a student of spiritual science can learn? Why?

6. What is the way out of confusion? How does it differ from "blind belief"?

7. How does one get at the very heart of Being?

8. Where is the abode of the Father?

9. Explain God as immanent in the universe. How does this understanding differ from the old idea of God?

10. Does the Power that creates and sustains the universe include man? What is the key to the whole situation?

11. Define Spirit, and explain how it dwells in us.

12. What do we mean by studying "Mind back of nature"?

13. What is man's inheritance, and how can he perpetually draw upon it?

14. What is life in Being?

15. What is the real of the universe? What is practical Christianity?

16. Where should the student start his investigations? Why?

17. What is the point of contact between man and the perfect Mind?

18. What does the parable of the prodigal son typify?

19. Why should the student never be discouraged?

20. Can Truth be imparted? Why?

21. Sum up, in a concise manner, the vital points of this chapter.

Lesson II--Being's Perfect Idea

1. What is spiritual Truth? How does the one Mind create? What is the Logos?

2. What is the law of divine creation?

3. Do the supplications of man change the law of God? Explain.

4. What is the key to our understanding of Divine Mind? Can man come to understand himself or the universe in any other way?

5. Is it important to understand mind and its laws? Why?

6. What is man from the viewpoint of Being?

7. Explain the Trinity and man's place in it.

8. What is the demand of the present age regarding spiritual ideals?

9. What are the three essentials to perfect manhood? What determines the degree to which any one or all of these phases may be expressd?

10. What position does man occupy in relation to God? Is it imperative that man understand this relationship?

11. Is the same faculty required to discern the Christ today that was required in the time of Jesus? If so, what is it?

12. Is it possible for man today to be divinely guided? How is divine guidance brought about?

13. Explain the law of attraction, as applied to mind and ideas.

14. What authority does man require for thinking or speaking beyond prescribed standards?

15. Through what phase of mind do we commune with God?

16. Explain the difference between perceiving and demonstrating one's spiritual sonship. What is the first birth?

17. Explain the first birth; the second birth.

18. What is it to be "born from above"?

19. Explain Jesus' relationship to the Father, and how it was developed.

20. Why does man invent mechanical devices? How will he attain the satisfaction that he seeks in these things?

21. How is the Christ Mind brought into manifestation in the individual?

Lesson III-Manifestation

1. What characterizes Christianity as a science?

2. What will bridge the gulf between spiritual and material science?

3. Should the Scriptures be considered allegorical?

4. When read in the light of Spirit, what does the 1st chapter of Genesis portray? What is meant by the words, "and God . . . rested from all his work"?

5. How is the apparent contradiction between the 1st and 2d chapters of Genesis explained?

6. What do the six days of creation mean? How shall we attain the Truth that Jesus said would make us free?

7. How does all creation become harmonious and orderly to man?

8. Describe the difference between the I AM man and the I will man. How was man driven out of Eden?

9. What is the physical body, and how is it formed?

10. What will a right idea of the character and origin of the body do for one?

11. Where does the resurrection begin, and what takes place?

12. How shall we get back to the "Father's house"?

13. Where do our dreams, visions, and spiritual experiences come from?

14. How shall we enter into the dominion of the "kingdom" within us?

15. Explain man's true identity?

16. What have the old and the new religious ideas contributed to the solution of our spiritual problems?

17. How shall we get back into the Garden of Eden?

18. Explain the grouping of ideas.

19. How are centers of consciousness brought to respond to the "I will"?

20. What is regeneration?

Lesson IV--Formative Power Of Thought

1. What is the directive power in man?
2. Explain the relation of thought to the functions of the body.
3. Why have we failed to demonstrate perfect health?
4. Upon what must man base his study of God?
5. What is God's work in the creation of man?
6. What part has man in the creation of himself and his world?
7. How does man build his body and his world?
8. Upon what must we base our thinking?
9. Why has the physical scientist failed to demonstrate wholeness and perfection?
10. Explain the difference between life as expressed by man and life in Divine Mind.
11. Upon what do the thoughts act to produce form?
12. Illustrate in your own words how thought works in the organism.
13. Where do ideas pertaining to life have their center of action?
14. How may we connect the life center with its spiritual source, and what is the result of making such connection?
15. What is the cause of imperfect bodies?
16. How may man regain his spiritual dominion?
17. What attitude of mind is conducive to a higher state of consciousness?

Lesson V--How To Control Thought

1. What is the difference between the original thinker and the secondary thought?
2. What is the essential fact in all manifestation?
3. How may man exercise his highest dominion?
4. What are the two fundamental attitudes of mind?
5. What use can man make of these movements of the mind in building his world?
6. What is the result of letting one's thoughts dwell on the acquiring of wealth?
7. Is excessive affirmation advisable? Explain.
8. What is the remedy for the ill effects in the organism that have come as a result of too much exercise of the affirmative mental attitude?
9. What is the result of excessive denial? What is the remedy for this result?
10. What is the object of man's existence?
11. What is meant by the "Adam" in man?
12. What benefit do we derive from experience?
13. What is "Satan" in man's consciousness?
14. How may man become free from his dual condition?
15. Is experience necessary in man's evolution?
16. What is repentance?
17. What is the meaning of "Deny himself . . . and follow me"?
18. Explain the "Judas" in consciousness.
19. Explain the meaning of Paul's words, "I die daily."
20. What is the result of this process of dying daily?

Lesson VI--The Word

1. What is the word?
2. How may man comprehend the creative process?
3. What is the result when the Word is expressed by Divine Mind?
4. Explain how the Word becomes flesh.
5. How may man make his creation perfect?
6. Explain the original plan of creation in Divine Mind.
7. How may man comprehend the word of God?
8. How are divine ideas brought to the outer plane of consciousness?
9. Explain the creative law, from the formless to the formed.
10. What is the result when man's word conforms to the divine law?
11. Explain how we give an account for "every idle word."
12. What determines the character of the word?
13. What ideas make constructive words?
14. Explain the word as the "seed."
15. What is the result of putting oneself into the consciousness of the supreme Mind?
16. What quality must be included in the word, to accomplish results?
17. Wherein does physical science fall short in explaining the plan of creation?
18. Explain the effect of the spoken word.
19. How must we use the word for sure results?
20. Give an illustration of the power of the word.

Lesson VII--Spirituality,

Or Prayer And Praise

1. What is a symbol?
2. Explain how symbols are used to describe man.
3. What do the twelve sons of Jacob symbolize in man?
4. Explain how a higher expression of the twelve faculties is attained.
5. What is a parable? What is an allegory?
6. How are we able to understand parables and allegories?
7. Is it possible to understand the twelve centers through the intellect?
8. Where is the center of spirituality?
9. What is the work of the Judah faculty?
10. Why should praise be a component part of prayer?
11. Define prayer in your own words.
12. Why do we not receive immediate answer to our prayers?
13. Name some of the benefits to be derived from prayer.
14. What is the effect of praise in prayer?
15. Explain the increasing power of praise.
16. What does it mean to ask "in my name"?
17. Where do we make connection with God, the Father?
18. What is God's will for us?
19. What attitude of mind is most conducive to the effectiveness of prayers?
20. Name five points that you consider essential in prayer.

Lesson VIII--Faith

1. Define faith in your own words.
2. Where does faith find its most perfect expression?
3. Explain the difference between faith and belief.
4. What disciple represents faith? Why?
5. What and where is the center through which faith acts?
6. What is the result of placing faith in outer things?
7. Where must faith be exercised in order to bring the results spoken of by Jesus?
8. What is blind faith? Are the results of blind faith satisfactory?
9. How, in consciousness, is faith increased?
10. What is the inner power of faith? The outer expression?
11. How must faith be used to master the spiritual forces?
12. What fixes our relation to outer things?
13. Where should faith be centered to insure success?
14. Explain, from the experience of Peter on the water, how faith grows.
15. What should be added to faith in order to make it more effective?
16. What two faculties are developed along with faith?
17. Explain how these faculties work with faith.
18. What does it mean to make friends with the "adversary"?
19. Explain how we may have faith in the goodness of all men.
20. Why is faith essential in healing?

Lesson IX--Imagination

1. How does mind manifest?
2. Explain wherein man is the "image" and "likeness" of God.
3. What power has man as the "image" and "likeness"?
4. Define imagination.
5. Explain how the imaging faculty works on substance.
6. What effect does the imaging power have upon thought?
7. Locate the center of imagination.
8. What faculties of mind does the imagination use, and how?
9. Is it possible to impress these faculties from without, and if so, what is the result?
10. What happens when man allows his imagination to run riot, regardless of law?
11. How do the faculties of the mind work?
12. How can one avoid receiving impressions from without?
13. What is meant by the "mount," as spoken of in the Scriptures?
14. What is the power through which the I AM creates or recreates form?
15. How are we to control the things that we create?
16. What does Jacob represent in consciousness?
17. What does the ladder in Jacob's dream represent?
18. What does Joseph represent, and how did he reach the highest place in the king's domain?
19. What are dreams, and how may they be made useful?
20. What power has the imagination in forming the body? Explain.
21. What is the highest work of the imagination?

Lesson X--Will And Understanding

1. To what does Jesus refer in the text at the beginning of this lesson?
2. Explain how will and understanding work in the individual mind.
3. What does man represent as the will of God?
4. Explain man as a free agent.
5. How do we build individual consciousness?
6. What is the I AM? Explain what the I AM means to you.
7. How may we unify will and understanding?
8. How do we produce the perfect man?
9. What results when the will acts independently of the understanding? Explain.
10. Explain the effect, on the body, of a strong personal will.
11. Explain God and man in relation to will.
12. Define understanding, and show how it works in the mind.
13. What treatment do you suggest for willfullness?
14. Explain why the will should not be broken.
15. Should one try to dominate the will of another, in order to develop him spiritually? Explain.
16. How should you proceed in order to let Divine Mind express itself through you?
17. What is true self-control? How may man exercise it?
18. How may we gain spiritual mastery?
19. What apostle represents will? Explain the use of will in consciousness.
20. Upon what must our understanding be based, that we may be willing to do God's will?

Lesson XI--Judgment And Justice

1. Explain the law as given by Moses.
2. Why is judgment necessary in the use of the love faculty?
3. Give the metaphysical meaning of the Urim and Thummim.
4. How may love and justice be balanced in one's life?
5. What is the cause of injustice?
6. Where must judgment be placed, in order to express perfect justice?
7. What is the meaning of "Judge not, that ye be not judged"?
8. Why is man incapable of judging?
9. What is the correct way to judge, as explained by Jesus?
10. What is meant by "the day of judgment"?
11. Explain how and why we are punished.
12. How should we receive punishment?
13. What is the result of the active use of judgment without understanding?
14. What organ of the body is most affected by the active use of judgment, and why?
15. Why should we have definite ideas of justice?
16. What is the result of condemnation?
17. How may we receive perfect justice?
18. Explain the effect of jealousy on the faculty of judgment; give remedy.
19. What is the relation of judgment to success?
20. State the order of procedure in obtaining justice.

Lesson XII--Love

1. Explain love in Divine Mind.
2. What is the work of love in man?
3. What is the result of centering our love on things?
4. How may we realize our true relation to life?
5. Explain the process of love in the regeneration.
6. What apostle represents the faculty of love?
7. Where is the love center?
8. How may thoughts of hatred be overcome in consciousness?
9. What qualities are brought out in man through the activity of the love principle?
10. How shall we make love of real value to ourselves?
11. Explain how love is the fulfilling of the law.
12. What is our relationship to our fellow man when divine love is established in consciousness?
13. When is money really the root of evil?
14. Explain the difference between divine love and human love.
15. How can we know the love of God in its fullness?
16. How shall we proceed to maintain a right relation among all creatures?
17. What is the result when divine love enters into the thought process?
18. Is it possible to approach God while there is aught in the heart against a brother?
19. How may we become established in fearlessness and courage? Give an illustration from your own experience.
20. What is the unfailing antidote for fear?

The Twelve Powers of Man

Introduction

JESUS prophesied the advent of a race of men who would sit with Him on twelve thrones, judging the twelve tribes of Israel. This book explains the meaning of this mystical reference, what and where the twelve thrones are, and what attainments are necessary by man before he can follow Jesus in this phase of his regeneration. Regeneration follows generation in the development of man. Generation sustains and perpetuates the human; regeneration unfolds and glorifies the divine.

It is not expected that beginners in the study of metaphysical Christianity will understand this book. It deals with forces that function below and above the field of the conscious mind. The average religious thinker knows nothing about the subconscious mind and very little about the superconscious; this book presupposes a working knowledge of both.

This book aims to clear up the mystery that ever envelops the advent, life, and death of Jesus. To the superficial reader of the Gospels His life was a tragedy and, so far as concerns the kingly reign that was prophesied, it was a failure. Yet those who understand the subtlety of the soul and supremacy of Spirit see that Jesus was conqueror of a psychic force that was destroying the human race.

Jesus was the star actor in the greatest drama ever played on earth. This drama was developed in the celestial realm, its object being to inject new life into perishing men. The full significance of this great plan of salvation cannot be understood by man until he awakens faculties that relate him to the earth beneath and the heavens above.

It had long been prophesied that the time was ripe for the advent on this planet of a new race, and there had been much speculation as to the character and advent of the superman. Herein is set forth the metaphysical idea of the spiritual quickening of man on the human plane and his transformation into the divine: not by a miracle or the fiat of God, but by the gradual refinement of the man of flesh into the man of Spirit. As Paul taught, "This corruptible must put on incorruption, and this mortal must put on immortality."

Jesus was the "first-fruits" of those who are coming out of the mortal into the immortal. He was the type man, the Way-Shower, and, through following His example and taking on His character as a spiritual-minded man, we shall come into the same consciousness.

Spiritual discernment always precedes demonstration, consequently more is taught in this book as a possibility of attainment by man than has been demonstrated by any man save Jesus. Those who feel that they are ready for the great adventure in the attainment of eternal life in the body here and now should not be deterred because there are no outstanding examples of men who have risen to this most exalted degree. Through mental energy, or the dynamic power of the mind, man can release the life of the electrons secreted in the atoms that compose the cells of his body. Physical science says that if the electronic energy stored in a single drop of water were suddenly released its power would demolish a six-story building. Who can estimate the power stored in the millions of cells that compose the human body? The method of release of this body energy and its control are mystically taught by Jesus. He was transfigured before His apostles, "and his face did shine as the sun, and his garments became white as the light." Before His crucifixion He had attained such mastery over His body cells that He told the Jews that they might destroy His body and "in three days" He would "raise it up." He demonstrated this in the resurrection of His body after it had been pronounced lifeless. When He disappeared in a cloud He simply unloosed the dynamic atoms of His whole body and released their electrical energy. This threw Him into the fourth dimension of substance, which He called the "kingdom of the heavens."

The dynamic energy that man releases through prayer, meditation, and the higher activities of his mind is very great, and if not controlled and raised to the spiritual plane, may prove a source of body destruction; if carried to the extreme, it may even prove a cause of soul destruction. "Be not afraid of them that kill the body, but are not able to kill the soul: but rather fear him who is able to destroy both soul and body in hell." This one who is able to destroy both soul and body in Gehenna is the personal self or selfish ego that is in man.

The electronic energy in man is a form of fire, which is represented by Gehenna. This electronic fire must be used unselfishly. If used to further the selfishness of man it becomes destructive, through the crosscurrents that it sets up in the nervous system.

We do not encourage those who still have worldly ambitions to take up the development of the twelve powers of man. You will be disappointed if you seek to use these superpowers to gain money (turn stones into bread), control others ("the kingdoms of the world . . . All these things will I give thee"), or make a display of your power ("If thou art the Son of God, cast thyself down"). These are the temptations of the selfish ego, as recorded in the 4th chapter of Matthew, which Jesus had to overcome, and which all who follow Him "in the regeneration" have to overcome.

Unspeakable joy, glory, and eternal life are promised to those who with unselfish devotion strive to develop the Son of God consciousness. All the glories of the natural man are as nothing compared with the development of the spiritual man. The things of this world pass away, but the things of Spirit endure forever. In his flesh body man may be compared to the caterpillar that is the embryo of the butterfly. In its undeveloped state the caterpillar is a mere worm of the earth, but it has, infolded within it, a beautiful creature awaiting release from its material envelope. Paul visualized this when he wrote in Romans 8:22, "For we know that the whole creation groaneth and travaileth in pain together until now. And not only so, but ourselves also, who have the first-fruits of the Spirit, even we ourselves groan within ourselves, waiting for our adoption, . . . the redemption of our body."

Jesus, the Great Teacher, gave many lessons for our instruction, the greatest and most mystical being The Revelation of John. Here He showed Himself to John as He is in His redeemed body. He stood in the midst of seven lights, which represent the seven ideas of Divine Mind ruling in the restored earth. "One like unto a son of man, clothed with a garment down to the foot, and girt about at the breasts with a golden girdle. And his head and his hair were white as white wool, white as snow; and his eyes were as a flame of fire; and his feet like unto burnished brass, as if it had been refined in a furnace; and his voice as the voice of many waters. And he had in his right hand seven stars: and out of his mouth proceeded a sharp two-edged sword: and his countenance was as the sun shineth in his strength."

This description of the appearance of Jesus is partly symbolical, because John did not himself understand the full import of the powers that were being exercised by the spiritual man, whose words were so clean-cut that they appeared to John as a two-edged sword; whose eyes were so discerning that they seemed a flame of fire; whose voice was like the rippling of many waters. Language is poor and bare when one seeks to describe the glories of the spiritual state. Comparisons within the comprehension of the reader are necessary, and they but tamely tell of the superhuman man and his powers.

However, this pen picture by John of what he saw when he was lifted up "in the Spirit on the Lord's day" gives us a glimpse of what the redeemed man is like, and what we shall attain when we "awake, with thy likeness."

It should be thoroughly understood that this sight of Jesus that was given to John was not a vision of a man who had died and gone to heaven up in the skies, but it was the opening of John's eyes to existence in what may be termed the fourth-dimension man. We use this term fourth dimension because it is the name given to a state of existence that popular material science says must be, in order to account for the effects that are being expressed on every side. It is also called the interpenetrating ether, which is not to be understood as something material, or as being matter, but as something having properties far more substantial than matter. Through the application of mathematical principles scientific men are proving the existence of the spiritual side of Being. This does not refer to the psychical realm in which undeveloped souls rest while awaiting reincarnation. Many people take it for granted that soul realms and spiritual realms are identical. But these stand to each other as moonshine and sunshine. Jesus called the interpenetrating state of being the kingdom of heaven, or, in the original Greek, "the kingdom of the heavens." He said that it was like a treasure hid in a field, which, when a man discovered it, he would sell all that he had to buy. The majority of Christians believe that they are going to this heaven when they die, but Jesus does not teach that the dead go first to glory. On the contrary, Jesus teaches that death may be overcome. "If a man keep my word he shall never see death." Paul taught that Jesus attained victory over death. "Christ being raised from the dead dieth no more." "Let not sin therefore reign in your mortal body, that ye should obey the lusts thereof: neither present your members unto sin as instruments of unrighteousness; but present yourselves unto God, as alive from the dead, and your members as instruments of righteousness unto God."

The Psalmist writes:

"What is man, that thou art mindful of him? And the son of man, that thou visitest him? For thou hast made him but little lower than God, And crownest him with glory and honor. Thou makest him to have dominion over the works of thy hands; Thou hast put all things under his feet."

With the mind of the seer, Ralph Waldo Emerson says:

"Great hearts send forth steadily the secret forces that incessantly draw great events, and wherever the mind of man goes, nature will accompany him, no matter what the path." Verily I say unto you, that ye who have followed me, in the regeneration when the Son of man shall sit on the throne of his glory, ye also shall sit upon twelve thrones, judging the twelve tribes of Israel. And every one that hath left houses, or brethren, or sisters, or father, or mother, or children, or lands, for my name's sake, shall receive a hundredfold, and shall inherit eternal life. -Jesus

Chapter I

The Twelve Powers of Man

THE SUBCONSCIOUS realm in man has twelve great centers of action, with twelve presiding egos or identities. When Jesus had attained a certain soul development, He called His twelve apostles to Him. This means that when man is developing out of mere personal consciousness into spiritual consciousness, he begins to train deeper and larger powers; he sends his thought down into the inner centers of his organism, and through his word quickens them to life. Where before his powers have worked in the personal, now they begin to expand and work in the universal. This is the first and the second coming of Christ, spoken of in the Scriptures. The first coming is the receiving of Truth into the conscious mind, and the Second Coming is the awakening and the regeneration of the subconscious mind through the superconscious or Christ Mind.

Man expands and grows under divine evolution as an industrial plant grows. As the business expands, it is found that system is necessary. Instead of one man's being able to do the work with the assistance of a few helpers, he requires many helpers. Instead of a few helpers, he needs hundreds; and in order to promote efficiency he must have heads for the various departments of the work. Scripture symbology calls the heads of departments in man's consciousness the twelve apostles.

Each of these twelve department heads has control of a certain function in soul or body. Each of these heads works through an aggregation of cells that physiology calls a "ganglionic center." Jesus, the I AM or central entity, has His throne in the top head, where phrenology locates spirituality. This is the mountain where He so often went to pray. The following outline gives a list of the Twelve, the faculties that they represent, and the nerve centers at which they preside:

Faith — Peter – center of brain.

Strength--Andrew –loins.

Discrimination or Judgment--James, son of Zebedee--pit of stomach.

Love--John--back of heart.

Power--Philip--root of tongue.

Imagination--Bartholomew--between the eyes.

Understanding—Thomas--front brain.

Will—Matthew--center front brain.

Order—James, son of Alphaeus--navel.

Zeal— Simon the Cananaean--back head, medulla.

Renunciation or Elimination –Thaddaeus-abdominal region.

Life Conserver--Judas--generative function.

The physiological designations of these faculties are not arbitrary--the names can be expanded or changed to suit a broader understanding of their full nature. For example, Philip, at the root of the tongue, governs taste; he also controls the action of the larynx, as well as all vibrations of power throughout the organism. So the term "power" expresses but a small part of his official capacity.

The first apostle that Jesus called was Peter. Peter represents faith in things spiritual, faith in God. We begin our religious experience, our unity with Divine Mind, by having faith in that mind as omnipresent, all-wise, all-loving, all-powerful Spirit.

Faith in the spiritual man quickens spiritual understanding. Peter believed that Jesus was the Messiah; his faith opened his spiritual discernment, and he saw the living Christ back of the personal mask worn by Jesus. When asked, "Who do men say that the Son of man is?" the apostles, looking upon personality as the real, said: "Some say John the Baptist; some, Elijah; and others, Jeremiah, or one of the prophets." Then Jesus appealed to their own inner spiritual understanding and He said: "But who say ye that I am?" Only Simon Peter answered: "Thou art the Christ, the Son of the living God." And Jesus answered, "Thou art Peter, and upon this rock I will build my church, and the gates of Hades [the grave] shall not prevail against it. I will give unto thee the keys of the kingdom of heaven."

Spiritual discernment of the reality of man's origin and being is the only enduring foundation of character. It was to this faith in the understanding of the real being of man that Jesus gave power in earth and heaven. It was not to the personal Peter that Jesus gave the keys to His kingdom, but to all who through faith apply the binding (affirming) and loosing (denying) power of Spirit in the earth (substance consciousness). Right here and now the great work of character-building is to be done, and whoever neglects present opportunities, looking forward to a future heaven for better conditions, is pulling right away from the kingdom of heaven within himself.

People who live wholly in the intellect deny that man can know anything about God, because they do not have quickened faith. The way to bring forth the God presence, to make oneself conscious of God, is to say: I have faith in God; I have faith in Spirit; I have faith in things invisible. Such affirmations of faith, such praise to the invisible God, the unknown God, will make God visible to the mind and will strengthen the faith faculty. Thus faith (Peter) is called and instructed spiritually.

When a center loses its power it should be baptized by the word of Spirit. We are told in the Scriptures that Philip went down to Gaza ("the same is desert"), and there baptized a eunuch. Gaza means a "citadel of strength." It refers to the nerve center in the loins, where Andrew (strength) reigns. "Lo now, his strength is in his loins." Gaza is the physical throne of strength, as Jerusalem is the throne of love.

The back grows weak under the burden of material thought. If you are given to pains in your back, if you become exhausted easily, you may know at once that you need treatment for freedom from material burdens. Eliminate from your mind all thought of the burdens of the world, the burdens of your life, and all seeming labors. Take your burdens to Christ. "Come unto me, all ye that labor and are heavy laden, and I will give you rest."

We are pressed upon by ideas of materiality. Thoughts make things, and the material ideas that are pressing upon us are just as substantial in the realm of mind as material things are substantial in the realm of matter. Everything has origin in thought, and material thoughts will bring forth material things. So you should baptize and cleanse with your spiritual word every center, as Philip baptized the eunuch of Gaza. Baptism is cleansing. It always represents the erasing power of the mind.

When the baptizing power of the word is poured upon a center, it cleanses all material thought; impotence is vitalized with new life, and the whole subconsciousness is awakened and quickened. The word of the Lord is there sown in the body, and once the word of the Lord is sown in any of these centers--the cells of which are like blank phonograph records--they take the thought that is given them, and send it through the whole organism. The baptism of strength goes to the uttermost parts of the body, and every one of the twelve powers, under the divine law, feels the new strength.

James, the son of Zebedee, represents discrimination and good judgment in dealing with substantial things. James is the faculty in man that wisely chooses and determines. It may be in the matter of food; it may be in the matter of judgment about the relation of external forces; it may be in the choosing of a wife or a husband--in a thousand different ways this faculty is developed in man. The spiritual side of the James faculty is intuition, quick knowing.

James and John are brothers, and Jesus called them "sons of thunder." These brothers preside over the great body brain called the solar plexus, or sun center. James has his throne at the pit of the stomach; and John, just back of the heart. They are unified by bundles of nerves and are metaphysically closely related. Whatever affects the stomach will sympathetically affect the heart. People with weak stomachs nearly always think they have heart trouble.

Jesus called those two apostles "sons of thunder." Tremendous vibrations or emotions that go forth from the solar plexus. When your sympathies are aroused, you will find that you begin to breathe deeply and strongly, and if you are very sympathetic you can feel the vibrations as they go out to the person or thing to which you are directing your thoughts. All fervor, all the high energy that comes from soul, passes through these centers.

Bartholomew represents the imagination. The imagination has its center of action directly between the eyes. This is the point of expression for a set of tissues that extend back into the brain and connect with an imaging or picture-making function near the root of the optic nerve. Through this faculty you can project an image of things that are without, or ideas that are within. For instance, you can project the image of jealousy to any part of your body and, by the chemistry of thought combined with function, make your complexion yellow, or you can image and project beauty by thinking goodness and perfection for everybody. Bartholomew is connected directly with the soul, and has great power in the pictures of the mind. Jesus saw him under a fig tree, a long way off, before he was visible to the natural eye. Do not imagine anything but good, because under the law of thought combined with substance it will sooner or later come into expression, unless you head it off, eliminate it by denial.

Man has faculties of elimination, as well as of appropriation. If you know how to handle them you can expel error from your thought body. The denial apostle is Thaddaeus, presiding in the abdominal region, the great renunciator of the mind and the body. All the faculties are necessary to the perfect expression of the man. None is despised or unclean. Some have been misunderstood; through ignorance man has called them mean, until they act in that way and cause him pain and sorrow. The elimination, by Thaddaeus, of the waste of the system through the bowels is a very necessary function.

Thomas represents the understanding power of man. He is called the doubter because he wants to know about everything. Thomas is in the front brain, and his collaborator, Matthew, the will, occupies the same brain area. These two faculties are jointly in occupation of this part of the "promised land." Like the land of Ephraim and Manasseh, their inheritance in undivided.

James, the son of Alphaeus, represents divine order. His center is at the navel.

Simon, the Cananaean, represents zeal; his center is at the medulla, at the base of the brain. When you burn with zeal and are anxious to accomplish great things, you generate heat at the base of your brain. If this condition is not balanced by the co-operation of the supplying faculties, you will burn up the cells and impede the growth of the soul. "For the zeal of thy house hath eaten me up."

Judas, who betrayed Jesus, has his throne in the generative center. Judas governs the life consciousness in the body, and without his wise co-operation the organism loses its essential substance, and dies. Judas is selfish; greed is his "devil." Judas governs the most subtle of the "beasts of the field"–sensation; but Judas can be redeemed. The Judas function generates the life of the body. We need life, but life must be guided in divine ways. There must be a righteous expression of life. Judas, the betrayer of Jesus, must in the end be cleansed of the devil, selfishness; having been cleansed, he will allow the life force to flow to every part of the organism. Instead of being a thief (drawing to the sex center the vital forces necessary to the substance of the whole man) Judas will become a supplier; he will give his life to every faculty. In the prevailing race consciousness Judas drains the whole man, and the body dies as a result of his selfish thievery.

It is through Judas (the desire to appropriate and to experience the pleasure of sensation) that the soul (Eve) is led into sin. Through the sins of the sex life (casting away of the precious substance), the body is robbed of its essential fluids and eventually disintegrates. The result is called death, which is the great and last enemy to be overcome by man. Immortality in the body is possible to man only when he has overcome the weaknesses of sensation, and conserves his life substance. When we awaken to the realization that all indulgence for pleasure alone is followed by pain, then we shall know the meaning of eating of the tree of the knowledge of good and evil, or pleasure and pain.

If you would build up your faculties under the divine law, redeem Judas. First have faith in the power of Spirit, and then speak to Judas the word of purity. Speak to him the word of unselfishness; baptize him with the whole Spirit--Holy Spirit. If there is in you a selfish desire to exercise sensation, to experience the pleasures of sense in any of its avenues, give that desire to the Lord; in no other way can you come into eternal life.

These twelve powers are all expressed and developed under the guidance of Divine Mind. "Not by might, nor by power, but by my Spirit, saith Jehovah of hosts." You must keep the equipoise; you must, in all the bringing forth of the twelve powers of man, realize that they come from God: that they are directed by the Word of God, and that man (Jesus) is their head.

Chapter II

The Development of Faith

FAITH has an abiding place in man's consciousness. This place of abiding is described in the Scriptures as the "house of Simon and Andrew." A house is a structure that some person has built for a home. A man's house is his castle. Perhaps generation after generation is born and reared in the same house. The house where a great genius was born is preserved with care, and it is visited year after year by those who are devotees of the one who expressed some great thought, art, or discovery. If the barn cave at Bethlehem, where Jesus was born, were found, it would become the most famous shrine in the world. The importance that we give to the places where great men and women were born is founded on the centralizing power of thought. All structures are thought concentrations. Constructive thinking ultimates in the construction of places of abode. Savages do not build houses or cities, because they do not think constructively.

In the time of David the Children of Israel were nomads. The consciousness of indwelling Spirit had not been born in their minds, and could not, in consequence, be formed in their bodies. That the time was ripe for a more constructive state of mind is set forth in these words of Jehovah, in II Samuel 7:5, 6:

Shalt thou build me a house for me to dwell in? for I have not dwelt in a house since the day that I brought up the children of Israel out of Egypt, even to this day, but have walked in a tent and in a tabernacle.

After receiving this message, David, the drawing power of love, began gathering material for Solomon's Temple. Jehovah told David that he could not build the Temple because he was a man of war. The temple of God is man's body ("Your body is a temple of the Holy Spirit"), but if man has not complied with the law of permanent body building, he is like the nomadic Children of Israel; he goes from body to body and from tabernacle to tabernacle.

Except Jehovah build the house. They labor in vain that build it.

The tents and the tabernacles that the Children of Israel built for Jehovah represent the transitory bodies of flesh. The Lord has merely "walked" in these flimsy temples; they have not afforded an abiding place for Spirit, because of their unsubstantial character. The underlying weakness of the tent body was its lack of faith in the inhabiting soul. A new consciousness of the indwelling spiritual substance and life was necessary, and a man was chosen to bring it forth. This man, named Abraham, represents obedience and faith. His original name was Abram, which means "exalted father." The name is identified with the highest cosmic principle, the all-pervading, self-existent spiritual substance, which is the primary source of the universe.

Abraham was tested again and again, to the end that he might be strong in faith. His great test of faith was his willingness to sacrifice his beloved son Isaac in the mountain of the Lord. "And Abraham called the name of that place Jehovah-jireh: as it is said to this day, In the mount of Jehovah it shall be provided."

This incident is intended to show the necessity of a man's giving up that which he considers his dearest possession before he can realize the divine providence. The incident takes place in the mount of the Lord; that is, in a high spiritual understanding.

The law of giving and receiving pertains to the realm of ideas; one must give up personal attachments before one can receive the universal. If a parent idealizes a child, loves it so dearly that its pleasure is first in his consciousness, the spiritual development of the parent is impeded. Then, before the love of God (which is the supreme thing) can fill the heart, there must be a sacrifice of human love. If like Abraham one is faithful and obedient and willing to give to the Lord his most precious possession, there is always a receiving or providing equivalent.

When Abraham was willing to sacrifice his beloved Isaac, the Lord stayed his hand; his attention was directed to a ram in a thicket nearby, and he was directed to sacrifice the animal upon the altar, in place of the child. Here is illustrated an often misunderstood law of sacrifice or renunciation. We do not have to give up our cherished things, if they are real, but the error that prevents their full expression must be destroyed. The ram (which represents the resistance and opposition of personality to the complete expression of Truth) must be sacrificed.

"Give, and it shall be given unto you" is the statement of a law that operates in every thought and act of man. This law is the foundation of all barter and financial exchange. Men scheme to get something for nothing; but the law, in one of its many forms, overtakes them in the end. Even metaphysicians, who above all people should understand the law, often act as if they expected God to provide abundantly for them before they have earned abundance. It is an error to think that God gives anybody anything that has not been earned. The Holy Spirit comes upon those who pray in the "upper room." The "upper room" corresponds to the "mount of Jehovah." It is the high place in consciousness where man realizes the presence of Divine Mind. The greatest work that one can do is to strive to know God and to keep His law. God pays liberally for this service and the reward is sure. Faith is built up in consciousness under this law.

"Faith is assurance of things hoped for." When there has been an aspiration and a reaching out for the spiritual life, the faith faculty becomes active in consciousness. The prayer of supplication is impotent--the prayer of affirmation is immediately effective.

Intellectual faith admits doubt, and hope of fulfillment in the future; spiritual faith includes unfailing assurance and immediate response. These two attitudes of faith are often observed acting and reacting upon each other. Peter started to walk on the water in spiritual faith, but when he saw the effects of the wind he was afraid, and began to sink. Then the I AM (Jesus) gave its hand of spiritual power, the wind ceased, and there was no longer any doubt of faith's ability to rise above the negative consciousness.

The first and greatest disciple of Jesus was Peter, who has been universally accepted by the followers of Jesus the Christ as a type representing faith. Before he met Jesus, Peter was called Simon. Simon means "hearing," which represents receptivity. We understand from this that listening to Truth in a receptive state of mind opens the way for receiving the next degree in the divine order, which is faith. Jesus gave Peter his new name and also its meaning: "Thou art Peter, and upon this rock I will build my church."

Faith in the reality of the invisible builds a real, abiding substance in mind and in body. All kinds of ideas grow quickly when planted in this rich substance of the mind. Jesus also called this substance of faith the "earth," and He said to Peter, "Whatsoever thou shalt bind [affirm] on earth shall be bound in heaven; and whatsoever thou shalt loose [deny] on earth shall be loosed in heaven." In all His teaching Jesus emphasized that the ruling forces of both heaven and earth are in man. "The kingdom of God is within you." "All authority hath been given unto me in heaven and on earth." "Is it not written in your law, I said, Ye are gods?" When we understand the omnipresence of Spirit (God) we quickly see how simple and true this beautiful doctrine of Jesus is.

There is but one real faith; the avenue of expression determines the character and power of faith. Trust is a cheaper brand of faith, but trust is better than mistrust. As a rule, people who merely trust in the Lord do not understand all the law. If they had understanding they would affirm the presence and power of God until the very substance of Spirit would appear in consciousness--and this is faith established on a rock.

Faith words should be expressed both silently and audibly. The power of the spoken word is but slightly understood, because the law of the Word is not rightly observed. The Word is the creative idea in Divine Mind, which may be expressed by man when he has fulfilled the law of expression. All words are formative but not all words are creative. The creative word lays hold of Spirit substance and power. Physical science hints at this inner substance and energy, in its description of the almost inconceivable power inherent in the universal ether. We are told that the manifest forces, such as heat, light, and electricity, are but faint manifestations of an omnipresent element which is thousands of times greater than these weak expressions.

Radio is opening up a new field of activity in the use of the spoken word. A newspaper article on the wireless telephone says:

Do You happen to know that a single word spoken in lower Broadway, New York, among the skyscrapers, could break every pane of glass in adjacent buildings and create a disturbance that would be felt for a mile in every direction?

The human voice, transformed into electrical energy for wireless transmission, develops 270 hp. The power of 10 men equal to 1 hp. The human voice electrified for wireless purposes is equivalent to the power of 2,700 men. in the various processes that stuff up a voice for radio transmission across the Atlantic Ocean, it becomes 135,000 times more powerful than when uttered by a person sending the message.

Thus, starting with an initial energy of 1/1000 of an electrical watt, the voices boosted by powerful station until it is intensified 100 million times.

If the spoken word can mean mechanically intensified 100 million times, how much greater will be its power when energized by Spirit! when Jesus said with a loud voice to Lazarus "come forth," He must've had contact with the creative word referred to in the 1st chapter of John, because the results showed its life-giving character. When he healed the centurion's servant by His word sent forth on invisible currents, He said that the work was done through faith. So faith must boost the spoken word even more than 100 million times, as evidenced by its marvelous results. That the word of faith has an inner force, and that this force rushes forth and produces remarkable transformations in the phenomenal world, is the testimony of thousands who have witnessed its results.

Jesus said: " if ye have faith as a grain of mustard seed, ye shall say unto this mountain, Remove hence to yonder place; and it shall remove; and nothing shall be impossible unto you." He knew about the great spiritual machinery that the word of faith sets into action. He illustrated how man spiritually developed could by faith control the elements, quell storms, walk on water, retard or increase the growth of life and substance in grains, trees, animals, and men.

The ponderous dynamos that generate electricity to light a city are set going by a touch on a button. There is a button in the mind of man that connects him, through faith, with almighty energy. When the word of faith is spoken to large tumors and they melt away, is not the transformation equal to the removal of mountains? When a paralyzed limb, or a lifeless organ, is quickened and restored to natural functioning, is not that quickening a raising of the dead?

It is not necessary that the one who touches the button of faith shall understand all the intricate machinery with which he makes contact; he knows, like one who turns the electric switch, that the light or power will spring forth. The faith center, the pineal gland, opens the mind of man to spiritual faith. Merely affirming the activity of this superpower will quicken it in consciousness. Jesus said, "I speak not from myself: but the Father [faith] abiding in me doeth his works."

The transformers of electricity are paralleled by the transforming power of mind. That if a man sanely believes he can do a thing he will eventually find a way to do it is an accepted axiom of psychology. The mind generates an energy that contacts the universal energy, and causes circumstances and events to fall into line for the attainment of the latent ideal. John came crying in the wilderness of mortal thought, "Repent ye"; that is, change your mind. Paul discerned a like necessity, hence his call: "Be ye transformed by the renewing of your mind."

When people see the possibilities that follow a right change of mind, they will crowd the halls of metaphysical teachers as they now crowd moving-picture shows. When it is clearly understood that doubt, fear, poverty, disease, and death--every thought, good or bad, that men have expressed--have existence through mind we shall see a shifting of consciousness and a radical change in thought and word by everybody of sane mind. Then we shall ask for the true source and find it, as did Paul, who said: "Have this mind in you, which was also in Christ Jesus." It was not Jesus but the mind in Jesus that did the great works. He was the center of faith that transformed the mighty creative forces of Being (which are active in the universe through the mind and brain of man) into a form of force usable in His environment. Tap this inner reservoir of faith, and you can do what Jesus did. That was His promise; its fulfillment is the test of a true follower.

"By faith Enoch was translated that he should not see death . . . By faith Noah . . . prepared a ark to the saving of his house . . . By faith Abraham, being tried, offered up Isaac . . . By faith Moses, when he was born, was hid three months by his parents . . . By faith the walls of Jericho fell down . . . And what shall I more say? for the time will fail me if I tell of Gideon, Barak, Samson, Jephthah; of David and Samuel and the prophets: who through faith subdued kingdoms, wrought righteousness, obtained promises, stopped the mouths of lions, quenched the power of fire, escaped the edge of the sword, from weakness were made strong, waxed mighty in war, turned to flight armies of aliens. Women received their dead by a resurrection."

Chapter III

Strength, Stability, Steadfastness

WHEN the strong man fully armed guardeth his own court, his goods are in peace: but when a stronger than he shall come upon him, and overcome him, he taketh from him his whole armor wherein he trusted, and divideth his spoils.

Jesus gave the foregoing illustration of a strong man's being overcome by a stronger. The incident is mentioned in three of the Gospels, those of Matthew, Mark, and Luke. It is usually interpreted as illustrating in a general way the overcoming of evil, but the peculiar identification of the strong man in his court (or house), and the necessity of overcoming him, hint at a deeper significance. One who has studied man as an aggregation of personalities readily identifies the "strong man" as one of the twelve foundation powers that make up the manifest man. Among the apostles of Jesus the strong man is designated as Andrew, brother of Peter. The Greek meaning of Andrew is "strong man."

The development of the natural world from coarser to finer types in vegetable life and in animal life is paralleled in many respects in the unfoldment of man. The source of everything is in the realm of ideas; a knowledge of this fact, coupled with faith in the working power of the unseen, makes man greater than all other expressions of Divine Mind. However, knowledge of the law of mind evolution does not relieve man of the necessity of refining and transmuting the various types of man that he has brought forth, and of which he is the epitome.

The Jehovah man is constantly making the Adam man and breathing into his nostrils the breath of life. The Adam man exists in the subconsciousness as a multitude of men: The wise man and the foolish man, the kind man and the cruel man, the loving man and the hateful man, the stingy man and the generous man, the hungry man and the full man, the happy man and the troubled man, the weak man and the strong man, the good man and the bad man, the live man and the dead man, the poor man and the rich man, the timid man and the courageous man, the sick man and the healthy man, the old man and the young man, the erratic man and the sane man--these, and a thousand other types of man as active personalities, occupy the consciousness of every human being. Every male has within him the female and every female has within her the male. This fact is admitted by physiology, substantiating the Genesis record of the ideal creation of man as "male and female," and his expression in Adam and Eve as the male and female in one man. The fact was corroborated by the Great Teacher when He said, "Have ye not read, that he who made them from the beginning made them male and female?"

The "strong man fully armed," referred to by Jesus, is the strength and stability in man. In the natural man he is manifest as physical strength, but in the regeneration he is overcome and his possessions are divided or given to the other faculties as a nucleus around which the higher forces gather. The "stronger than he" who takes away the "whole armor" in which the strong man trusted is spiritual strength. The overcoming of Goliath by David illustrates the mastery of the spiritual over the material. Goliath trusted in his armor, which represents the protective power of matter and material conditions. David, spiritual strength, had no armor or material protection. David's power was gained by trust in divine intelligence, through which he saw the weak place in Goliath's armor. Direct to this weak place, with the sling of his concentrated will, he sent a thought that shattered the forehead of the giant. This incident shows how easy it is to overcome the seemingly strong personal and material conditions when the mind of Spirit is brought into action.

David was sure of himself, because he had slain the lion that had killed his sheep. The lion is the beast in man; when overcome, or, rather, transmuted to finer energy, this lion becomes a mighty soul strength.

The life of Samson, as set forth in Judges, shows the different movements of strength in human consciousness, and its betrayal and end. Samson did all kinds of athletic stunts, but was finally robbed of his strength by Delilah, a Philistine woman, who had his head shaved while he slept on her knees. Hair represents vitality. When the vital principle is taken away the strength goes with it. The body is weakened by this devitalization and finally perishes. Eve took away the strength of Adam in like manner, and every man who gives up the vital essence of his body for the pleasure of sensation blindly pulls down the pillar of his temple, as did Samson.

Supreme strength as demonstrated by Jesus can be attained by one who trusts in Spirit and conserves his vital substance. The strength of Spirit is necessary to the perpetuation of soul and body and to the overcoming of death. "For there are eunuchs, that were so born from their mother's womb: and there are eunuchs, that were made eunuchs by men: and there are eunuchs, that made themselves eunuchs for the kingdom of heaven's sake."

The body has many "brain" and nerve centers, through which the mind acts. Consciously we use only the brain in the head. We should think through every cell in the organism, and consciously direct every function in building up the body. When one has attained the mastery of these various bodily functions through thinking in the brain center that stores the vital energy of each particular faculty, then all deterioration ceases and the body is perpetually renewed.

The strength here discussed is not physical strength alone, but mental and spiritual strength. All strength originates in Spirit; and the thought and the word spiritually expressed bring the manifestation. "The name of Jehovah is a strong tower."

We grow to be like that which we idealize. Affirming or naming a mighty spiritual principle identifies the mind with that principle; then all that the principle stands for in the realm of ideas is poured out upon the one who affirms.

"Be strong in the Lord, and in the strength of his might" is a great strengthening affirmation for ourselves and for others. Be steadfast, strong, and steady in thought, and you will establish strength in mind and in body. Never let the thought of weakness enter your consciousness, but always ignore the suggestion and affirm yourself to be a tower of strength, within and without.

The development of man is under law. Creative Mind is not only law, but it is governed by the action of the law that it sets up. We have thought that man was brought forth under the fiat or edict of a great creative Mind that could make or unmake at will, or change its mind and declare a new law at any time; but a clear understanding of ourselves and of the unchangeableness of Divine Mind makes us realize that everything has its foundation in a rule of action, a law, that must be observed by both creator and created.

Man's development is not primarily under the physical law, because the physical law is secondary. There is a law of Spirit, and the earthly is but the showing forth of some of the results of that law. We begin our existence as ideas in Divine Mind; those ideas are expressed and developed and brought to fruitage, and the expression is the important part of the soul's growth.

Evolution is the result of the development of ideas in mind. What we are is the result of the evolution of our consciousness, and that consciousness is the result of seed ideas sown in our mind. When Froebel, the great teacher of children, began his primary school, he thought a long time before he gave it a name. One day the name came to him, "a children's garden"; so he called his school a "kindergarten." Froebel may not have seen the connection, but in naming his system of educating the children of men, he was true to the plan given in Genesis 2:8. Humanity is the garden of God, of which the soil is the omnipresent thought substance.

Jesus says that the seed is the word; He gives illustrations of the various places in which the seed is sown, and the results of the sowing. The seed, or Word of God, is sown in the minds of men; these seed ideas go through many changes, and they bring forth a harvest according to the capacity of the receiving soil. If you will to do the will of God, the exercise of your will in God-Mind strengthens your will power. If you have faith in things invisible, the faith seed is growing in your mind and your faith will be increased. Every word or idea in Divine Mind is sown by man in his mind, and is then brought forth--according to man's receptivity. "Whatsoever a man soweth, that shall he also reap." So all the faculties that exist in Divine Mind (the twelve pillars of the temple of God) are in this way expressed through the mind and the body of man.

Some have claimed that the Bible is a work on physiology. So it is, but it is far more; it treats of spirit, soul, and body as a unit. That is the reason why those who have studied the Bible from a merely physiological standpoint have not understood it. They have looked for descriptions of flesh and bones. In truth those things have no active existence without accompanying life and intelligence; and the Bible sets forth this fact in many symbols.

Jesus, the Great Teacher, who knew what was in man, began His evolution with Spirit. He is the "only begotten Son of God"; He is the type that you should strive to follow, not only in spiritual culture and in soul culture, but in physical culture. If you would bring forth the very best that is in you, study the methods of Jesus. Study them in all their details, get at the spirit of everything that is written about this wonderful man, and you will find the key to the true development of your soul and your body. If you will carry out His system, there will be revealed to you a new man, a man of whom you never dreamed, existing in the hidden realms of your own subconsciousness.

Chapter IV

Wisdom, Judgment

WHICH is the greater, wisdom or love? After long study of the analysis of love given by Paul in the 13th chapter of I Corinthians, Henry Drummond pronounced love to be "the greatest thing in the world." His conclusion is based on Paul's setting forth of the virtues of love. Had wisdom been as well championed as love was, the author of "The Greatest Thing in the World" might not have been so sure of his ground. It goes without argument that love wins when everything else fails, but, notwithstanding her mightiness, she makes many blunders. Love will make any and every sacrifice for the thing that she loves; on the other hand, she is enticed into trap after trap in her blind search for pleasure. It was this kind of love that caused Eve to fall under the spell of sensation, the serpent. She saw that the fruit of the tree was "pleasant to the eyes." She followed the pleasure of life instead of the wisdom that would have shown her how to use life. Ever since we have had pleasure and pain, or good and evil, as the result of Eve's blind love.

What kind of people would we be if Eve and Adam had been obedient to the Lord of wisdom, instead of obeying the sense of love? This is one of the biggest questions that anyone can ask. It has been debated for many, many centuries. It has a double answer. Those who get the first answer will claim that it is correct, and those who get the second answer will assure you that there can be no other conclusion. The question hinges on one point, and that is: Must one experience evil in order to appreciate good? If it were possible for man to know all the wisdom and joy of the Infinite, he would have no necessity for experience with the opposite. But do we have to have pain before we can enjoy pleasure? Does the child that burns its hand on a hot stove have a larger consciousness of health when the hand is healed? Has it learned more about stoves? Unnumbered illustrations of this kind might be given to show that by experimentation we learn the relations existing between things in the phenomenal world. But if we apply this rule to sciences that are governed by absolute rules, it becomes evident that there is no necessity for knowing the negative. To become proficient in mathematics it is not necessary that one make errors. The more closely one follows the rules in exact sciences, the more easily and successfully one makes the demonstrations. This goes to prove that the nearer one comes to the absolute or cause side of existence, the greater is one's understanding that wisdom and order rule, and that he who joins wisdom and order rules with them.

God knows that there is a great negative, which is a reflection of His positive, but He is not conscious of its existence. We know that there is an underworld of evil, in which all the rules of civilized life are broken, but we are not conscious of that world because we do not enter into it. It is one thing to view error as a thing apart from us, and quite another to enter into consciousness of it. In the allegory of Adam and Eve, the man and the woman were told by wisdom not to "eat" (not to enter into consciousness of the fruit of the tree of knowledge of good and evil). But the pleasure of sensation (serpent) tempted them, and they ate.

Sensation, feeling, affection, and love are closely allied. Sensation is personified in the Edenic allegory as the serpent, the most subtle of the beasts of the field (animal forces alive in substance). The subtlety of sensation in its various guises is in its pleasure, the thrill that comes when mind and matter join in the ecstasy of life. When the desire for the pleasures of sensation is indulged and the guiding wisdom ignored, a realm of consciousness is established that regards the material universe as the only reality. The Lord, the knowing side of man, talks to him in the "cool of the day." In the heat of passion and the joy of pleasure, man does not listen to the "still, small voice," but in the "cool of the day," that is, when he cools off, he reflects, and he hears the voice of wisdom and judgment saying: "Where art thou, Adam?"

The "great day of judgment"–which has been located at some fateful time in the future when we all shall be called before the judge of the world and have punishment meted out to us for our sins--in every day. The translators of the Authorized Version and of the American Standard

Version of the New Testament are responsible for the "great judgment day" bugaboo. In every instance where judgment was mentioned by Jesus, He said "in a day of judgment," but the translators changed a to the, making the time of judgment appear a definite point in the future, instead of the repeated consummations of causes that occur in the lives of individuals and nations. We know that we are constantly being brought to judgment for transgressing the laws moral and physical. Yet back of these is the spiritual law, which the whole race has broken and for which we suffer. It was to mend the results of this law breaking that Jesus was incarnated.

When we awaken to the reality of our being, the light begins to break upon us from within and we know the truth; this is the quickening of our James or judgment faculty. When this quickening occurs, we find ourselves discriminating between the good and the evil. We no longer accept the race standards or the teachings of the worldly wise, but we "judge righteous judgment"; we know with an inner intuition, and we judge men and events from a new viewpoint. "Knowledge comes but wisdom lingers," sings the poet. This pertains to intellectual development only. When man kindles the inner light, he speaks the word of authority to his subjective faculties. Jesus represents the Son-of-God consciousness in man, to whom was given dominion over all the earth. The Son-of-God man is wholly spiritual, and he uses spiritual thoughts, words, and laws in all that he does.

When Jesus called the Twelve, He spoke silently to the faculties that preside over and direct the functions of mind and body. When He called Peter, James, and John, there was in His consciousness a quickening of faith, judgment, and love. These three apostles are mentioned more often than His other apostles because they are most essential in the expression of a well-balanced man. Andrew (strength) was also among the first few called; he represents the stability that lies at the foundation of every true character.

"James the Just" was the title bestowed by historians upon the first bishop of Jerusalem. There were many Jameses among the early followers of Jesus, and there is some doubt as to whether James the Just and James the apostle are identical.

An analysis of man in his threefold nature reveals that on every plane there is a certain reflective and discerning power of the mind and its thoughts. In the body, conclusions are reached through experience; in intellect, reason is the assumed arbiter of every question; in Spirit, intuition and inspiration bring the quick and sure answer to all the problems of life. Jesus was the greatest of the teachers of men, because He knew all knowledge from the highest to the lowest. He did not blight the senses by calling them "error" (because they are limited in their range of vision), but He lifted them up. He took Peter, James, and John up into the mountain, and was transfigured before them. When we realize the spiritual possibilities with which we are indued by omnipotent Mind, we are lifted up, and all the faculties that we have "called" are lifted up with us. "I, if I be raised on high from the earth, will draw all to myself" (Diaglott).

Wisdom, justice, judgment, are grouped under one head in spiritual consciousness. Webster says in effect that the ground of reason in judgment, which makes conclusions knowledge, is found in the connecting link that binds the conceptions together. In religion there is the postulate of a judgment through direct perception of the divine law.

Solomon (Sol-o-mon), the sun man, or solar plexus man, when asked by the Lord what He should give him, chose wisdom above riches and honor; then all the other things were added. Solomon was also a great judge. He had a rare intuition, and he used it freely in arriving at his judgments. He did not rest his investigations on mere facts, but sought out the inner motives. In the case of the two women who claimed the same infant, he commanded an attendant to bring a sword and cut the child in twain and give a half to each woman. Of course the real mother begged him not to do this, and he knew at once that she was the mother.

The appeal of the affectional nature in man for judgment in its highest is in harmony with divine law. We have thought that we were not safe in trusting our feelings to guide us in important issues. But spiritual discernment shows that the "quick-knowing" power of man has its seat of action in the breast. The breastplates worn by Jewish high priests had twelve stones, representing the twelve great powers of the mind. Ready insight into the divine law was the glory of the high priest. Jesus is called the high priest of God, and every man's name is the name Jesus, written large or small, according to his perception of his Son-of-God nature.

Intuition, judgment, wisdom, justice, discernment, pure knowing, and profound understanding are natural to man. All these qualities, and many more, belong to every one of us by and through his divine sonship. "I said, Ye are gods, and all of you sons of the Most High!" the Christ proclaims in us all. Paul saw Christ waiting at the door of every soul, when he wrote: "Awake, thou that sleepest, and arise from the dead, and Christ shall shine upon thee."

A quickening of our divine judgment arouses in us the judge of all the world. "The wisdom that is from above is first pure, then peaceable." When we call this righteous judge into action, we may find our standards of right and wrong undergoing rapid changes, but if we hold steadily to the Lord as our supreme guide, we shall be led into all righteousness.

Many persons doubt that there is an infinite law of justice working in all things; let them now take heart and know that this law has not worked in their affairs previously because they have not "called" it into activity in the creative center of the soul. When we call our inner forces into action, the universal law begins its great work in us, and all the laws both great and small fall into line and work for us. We do not make the law; the law is, and it was established for our benefit before the world was formed. Jesus did not make the law of health when He healed the multitudes; He simply called it into expression by getting it recognized by those who had disregarded its existence. Back of the judge is the law out of which he reads. This fact is recognized even by those who are intrusted with the carrying out of man-made laws. Blackstone says that the judgment, though pronounced and awarded by the judges, is not their determination or sentence, but the determination and sentence of the law. So we who are carrying forward the fulfillment of the law as inaugurated by Jesus should be wise in recognizing that the law in all its fullness already exists right here, waiting for us to identify ourselves with it and thus allow it to fulfill its righteousness in us and in all the world.

"I am the vine, ye are the branches." In this symbol Jesus illustrated a law universal to organisms. The vine-building law holds good in man's body. The center of identity is in the head and its activities are distributed through the nerves and the nerve fluids to the various parts of the body. The Twelve Apostles of Jesus Christ represent the twelve primal subcenters in man's organism. A study of man's mind and body reveals this law.

Even physiologists, who regard the body as a mere physical organism, find certain aggregations of cells which they have concluded are for no other purpose than for the distribution of intelligence. To one who studies man as mind, these aggregations of cells are regarded as the avenues through which certain fundamental ideas are manifested. We name these ideas the twelve powers of man, identified in man's consciousness as the Twelve Apostles of Jesus, having twelve houses, villages, cities, or centers in the body through which they act.

Wisdom includes judgment, discrimination, intuition, and all the departments of mind that come under the head of knowing. The house or throne of this wise judge is at the nerve center called the solar plexus. The natural man refers to it as the pit of the stomach. The presiding intelligence at this center knows what is going on, especially in the domain of consciousness pertaining to the body and its needs. Chemistry is its specialty; it also knows all that pertains to the sensations of soul and body. In its highest phase it makes union with the white light of Spirit functioning in the top brain. At the solar plexus also takes place the union between love and wisdom. The apostle who has charge of this center is called James. Volumes might be written describing the activities by which this power builds and preserves man's body. Every bit of food that we take into our stomachs must be intelligently and chemically treated at this center before it can be distributed to the many members waiting for this center's wise judgment to supply them with material to build bone, muscle, nerve, eye, ear, hair, nails--in fact every part of the organism. When we study the body and its manifold functions we see how much depends on the intelligence and ability of James, who functions through the solar plexus.

When man begins to follow Jesus in the regeneration he finds that he must co-operate with the work of his disciples or faculties. Heretofore they have been under the natural law; they have been fishers in the natural world. Through his recognition of his relation as the Son of God, man co-operates in the original creative law. He calls his faculties out of their materiality into their spirituality. This process is symbolized by Jesus' calling His apostles.

To call a disciple is mentally to recognize that power; it is to identify oneself with the intelligence working at a center--for example, judgment, at the solar plexus. To make this identification, one must realize one's unity with God through Christ, Christ being the Son-of-God idea always existing in man's higher consciousness. This recognition of one's sonship and unity with God is fundamental in all true growth. Christ is the door into the kingdom of God. Jesus once spoke of the kingdom as a sheepfold. If man tries to get into this kingdom except through the door of the Christ, he is a thief and a robber. We can call our twelve powers into spiritual activity only through Christ. If we try to effect this end by any other means, we shall have an abnormal, chaotic, and unlawful soul unfoldment.

Having identified oneself with God through Christ, one should center one's attention at the pit of the stomach and affirm:

The wisdom of the Christ Mind here active is through my recognition of Christ identified and unified with God. Wisdom, judgment, discrimination, purity, and power are here now expressing themselves in the beauty of holiness. The justice, righteousness, and peace of the Christ Mind now harmonize, wisely direct, and surely establish the kingdom of God in His temple, my body. There are no more warring, contentious thoughts in me, for the peace of God is here established, and the lion and the lamb (courage and innocence), sit on the throne of dominion with wisdom and love

Chapter V

Regenerating Love

WE CANNOT get a right understanding of the relation that the manifest bears to the unmanifest, until we set clearly before ourselves the character of original Being. So long as we think of God in terms of personality, just so long shall we fail to understand the relation existing between man and God.

Then let us dismiss the thought that God is a man, or even a man exalted far above human characteristics. So long as the concept of a man-God exists in consciousness, there will be lack of room for the true concept, which is that God is First Cause, the Principle from which flow all manifestations. To understand the complex conditions under which the human family exists, we must analyze Being and its creative processes.

Inherent in the Mind of Being are twelve fundamental ideas, which in action appear as primal creative forces. It is possible for man to ally himself with and to use these original forces, and thereby co-operate with the creative law, but in order to do this he must detach himself from the forces and enter into the consciousness of the idea lying back of them.

In Scripture the primal ideas in the Mind of Being are called the "sons of God." That the masculine "son" is intended to include both masculine and feminine is borne out by the context, and, in fact, the whole history of the race. Being itself must be masculine and feminine, in order to make man in its image and likeness, "male and female."

Analyzing these divine ideas, or sons of God, we find that they manifest characteristics that we readily identify as masculine or feminine. For example, life is a son of God, while love is a daughter of God. Intelligence is a son of God, and imagination is a daughter of God. The evidence that sex exists in the vegetable and animal worlds is so clear that it is never questioned, but we have not so clearly discerned that ideas are also male and female. The union of the masculine and feminine forces in man is most potent in the affectional nature, and that these forces should endure and never be separated by external causes was laid down as a law by Jesus. He said, as recorded in Mark 10:6-9

From the beginning of the creation, Male and female made he them. For this cause shall a man leave his father and mother, and shall cleave to his wife; and the two shallbecome one flesh; so that they are no more two, but one flesh. What therefore God hath joined together, let no man put asunder.

We should clearly understand that each of the various ideas, or sons and daughters of God, has identity and in creation is striving with divine might to bring forth its inherent attributes. It is to these ideas, or sons and daughters, that Being, or Elohim, says: "Let us make man in our image, after our likeness" (Gen. 1:26) Spiritual man is the sum total of the attributes or perfect ideas of Being, identified and individualized. This man is the "only begotten" of Elohim. Jehovah, or I AM THAT I AM, is the name of this divine man. He was manifest as the higher self of Jesus, and in the Scriptures is called the Christ. Jesus named Him the "Father in me"; in the book of Matthew, He called Him "Father" more than forty times. Christ is our Father; through Him, Elohim or original Being brings forth all human beings. It was Jehovah, or I AM, that formed Adam out of the dust of the ground and breathed into his nostrils the breath of life. Breathing is the symbol of inspiration. Jesus breathed upon His disciples, and said to them: "Receive ye the Holy Spirit."

Three primal forces of Being are manifest in the simplest protoplastic cell. Science says that every atom has substance, life, and intelligence. This corresponds with the symbolical creative process of Jehovah, as described in Genesis 2:7. The "dust of the ground" is substance; "breathed" refers to the impartation of intelligence; and the "living soul" is the quickening life. These three constitute the trinity of the natural world, in which the body of man is cast. When one understands the creative processes to be the working of the various principles of Being in the development of man, many inexplicable situations are cleared up. God cannot bring forth without law and order. To produce a man, there must be a combination of forces that at some stages of soul evolution may seem to work against one another; but when one understands that the great creative Mind brings forth under law, reconciliation and consistency are found where in-harmony and contradiction seemed dominant.

Of all the daughters of God, love is undoubtedly the most beautiful, enticing, and fascinating. She is by nature exceedingly timid and modest, but when roused she is bold and fearless in the extreme. Mother love is as strong as life and will make every sacrifice to protect offspring. This whole-hearted, self-sacrificing aspect of love indicates a spirit deeper and stronger than the animal or the human, and we are forced to admit that it is divine. For this reason mother love is exalted to first place in our analysis of the great passion. But mothers should take heed lest they incorporate human selfishness into the divine love that is expressed in and through them.

The most popular expression of love in the world is the love between men and women. Here also love is misunderstood, and for that reason she has been forced to act in ways that are unnatural to her. She has also been compelled to do things that are abhorrent to her, yet under the compelling power of man's will she could not do otherwise. Right here is a crying need for a purer judgment of love and her right adjustment in the most sacred relation existing between men and women. Love is from God, and it is given to man in its virgin purity. It is the pure essence of Being that binds together the whole human family. Without love we should lose contact with out mother earth, and, losing that, we should fly off into space and be lost in the star dust of unborn worlds. "Gravity" is mortal man's name for love. By the invisible arms of love we are held tight to earth's prolific bosom, and there we find the sweetest home in all the universe. All love of home is founded on man's innate love for this planet. When John Howard Payne wrote "Home, Sweet Home," he was inspired by mother love to sing of the only abiding place of this race--our dear mother earth.

The original Eden of the human family was planted by God on earth, and it is still here. Its prototype is within the human soul, but we have not entered it, because we have not understood the relation that love bears to the original substance of Being, out of which all things are formed.

It is no great task to tell of the higher aspects of love, but who will champion love submerged in human consciousness and smothered with selfishness? You say: "This is not love, but passion and lust." But we should remember that we have laid down, as a foundation principle, that God is love, and, as there is but one God, there can be but one love. This being true, we must find place in the creative law for every manifestation, regardless of its apparent contradictions of the righteousness of First Cause.

Love is submerged or cast down to sense consciousness between men and women in the marriage relation, and great misery floods the world in consequence. This marriage should be a perpetual feast of love, and so it would be if the laws of love were observed. Courtship is usually the most joyous experience that comes to men and women, because love is kept free from lust.

If the laws of conjugality were better understood, the bliss of courtship would continue throughout all the years of married life and divorces would be unknown. It is a fact well known to psychologists that the majority of estrangements between husbands and wives result from the breaking of sex law. This sin that ends in feebleness and final disintegration of the physical organism is symbolically pictured in the so-called fall of man, in the early chapters of Genesis. Adam and Eve represent the innocent and uneducated powers of the masculine and feminine in every individual. The serpent symbolizes sensation, which combines with life and substance in all living organisms. The desire for pleasure, and for a seemingly short and easy way to get wisdom, tempts the feminine, and she eats, or appropriates. The masculine also eats. In the "cool of the day" (after the heat of passion has cooled off) they both find that they are naked. They have had pleasure with pleasure as the only object, which is contrary to the law of Being. All things should be done with a purpose, with pleasure as a concomitant only. Pleasure lends zest to all action, but it should never be exalted to the high place in consciousness.

Sex indulgence for mere pleasure is an eating or appropriating of the pure substance that pervades the whole nervous system, which is appropriately compared to a tree. This excess of pleasure is sooner or later followed by equal reaction, which is destructive, and the body cries out in pain. The pleasure we call "good," and the pain we call "evil." Here, in a nutshell, is an explanation of eating of the tree of the "knowledge of good and evil."

When the substance in the organism is conserved and retained, the nerves are charged with a spiritual energy, which runs like lightning through an organism filled with the virgin substance of the soul. When in the ignorance of sensation men and women deplete their substance, the rose of the cheek and the sparkle of the eye fade away. Then the kiss and the touch that were once so satisfying become cold and lifeless.

In the conservation of this pure substance of life is hidden the secret of body rejuvenation, physical resurrection, and the final perpetuation of the whole organism in its transmuted purity. (John saw Jesus in this state of purity, as described in Revelation 1:12-16.) No man can in his own might attain this exalted estate, but through the love of God, demonstrated by Jesus, it is attainable by everyone. "For God so loved the world, that he gave his only begotten Son, that whosoever believeth on him should not perish, but have eternal life."

Regeneration is not possible without love. As through the union of the male and female elements the new body of the infant is brought forth, so through the joining of the creative forces of Spirit by souls attuned in love the new body in Christ is speedily formed. The work can be done through individual effort, and there must always be continuous constructive action between the masculine and feminine faculties of soul and body; but the anointing with the precious love of the divine feminine is necessary to the great demonstration. The woman who anointed the head and feet of Jesus "loved much," and Jesus said that which she did would be remembered wherever the Gospel should be preached in the whole world. This symbolical representation of pouring into the masculine the pure love of the feminine is a guide for all women. All over the world the submerged love of the feminine is crying for release from the sensual dominance of the masculine. The remedy is: Anoint man's head (will) and his feet (understanding) with the Christ love, and he will be purified and satisfied. Not a word need be spoken to bring about the change. If in quietness and confidence the presence and the power of divine love are affirmed, the law will be fulfilled.

Love submerged in sense still retains the remembrance of her virginity, and repels and resists the onslaughts of lust. Some of the most terrible ills are brought upon the body by the misuse of love. This is not the way of freedom; through a steady and firm holding to the one Presence and one Power will the son of man be lifted up, as Moses lifted up the serpent in the wilderness.

Wisdom and love combined are symbolically described in Scripture as the "Lamb slain from the foundation of the world" (A.V.). But now men and women are studying the laws of Being, and in some degree are striving to observe them in the marriage relation. Instead of submerging love in lust, the children of light retain their virgin purity and go hand in hand toward the dawn of a new order, in which there will be a bringing forth of the multitude of waiting souls in a way which is now hidden, but which will be revealed when love is lifted up.

Call it not love, for love to heaven is fled
Since sweating lust on earth usurp'd his name;
Under whose simple semblance he hath fed
Upon fresh beauty, blotting it with blame;
Which the hot tyrant stains and soon bereaves,
As caterpillars do the tender leaves.
Love comforteth like sunshine after rain,
But lust's effect is tempest after sun;
Love's gentle spring doth always fresh remain,
Lust's winter comes ere summer half be done;
Love surfeits not, lust like a glutton dies;
Love is all truth, lust full of forged lies.

–Shakespeare--

Chapter VI

Power, Dominion, Mastery

MAN DOES not exercise the power of his spiritual nature, because he lacks understanding of its character and of his relation to the originating Mind in which he exists. From Divine Mind man inherits power over the forces of his mind--in truth, power over all ideas. A quickening from on high must precede man's realization of his innate control of thought and feeling. The baptism of the Holy Spirit is a quickening of the spiritual nature, which is reflected in intellect and in body. When one understands the science of Being, one is prepared to receive this baptism and to utilize it along deeper lines of thought. Jesus had taught His apostles and followers, and they were prepared for the baptism that they received on the day of Pentecost.

"Ye shall receive power, when the Holy Spirit is come upon you." Power is essential to the work that Jesus Christ expects His followers to do in the great field of humanity. The command is: Go to every nation and preach the gospel. Man should apply the power of the word to his individual redemption, and he should speak the redeeming word of Spirit to the multitudinous thought people of his own soul and body.

Among the apostles of Jesus, Philip represents the power faculty of the mind. The word "Philip" means "a lover of horses." In physical activity the horse represents power; the ox, strength. Each of the twelve fundamental faculties of man has an ego that reflects, in a measure, the original man idea in God. In the body consciousness the twelve apostles, as egos, have twelve centers, or thrones, from which they exercise their power. The will expresses its dominion from the head; love, from the breast; and power (the ego whose character we are analyzing in this writing), from the throat. Power is one branch of the great tree; in Genesis it is named "life." The body of the life tree is the spinal cord, over which the motor system, with branches to every part of the organism, exercises its nervous energy.

The power center in the throat controls all the vibratory energies of the organism. It is the open door between the formless and the formed worlds of vibrations pertaining to the expression of sound. Every word that goes forth receives its specific character from the power faculty. When Jesus said, "The words that I have spoken unto you are spirit, and are life," He meant that through the spoken word He conveyed an inner spiritual quickening quality that would enter the mind of the recipient and awaken the inactive spirit and life. When the voice has united with the life of the soul, it takes on a sweetness and a depth that one feels and remembers; the voice that lacks this union is metallic and superficial. Voice culture may give one tone brilliancy, but every great singer has the soul contact. But higher and deeper still is the voice of one who has made union with Spirit and who can say with Jesus: "Heaven and earth shall pass away, but my words shall not pass away."

When we understand this power of the word, we have the key to the perpetuity of sacred writings. According to tradition, all the writings of the Bible were destroyed but they were restored by Esdras, who, "remembered in his heart" and rewrote them. Modern discoveries in the realm of mind in a measure explain this mystical statement. We know now that every word that man utters makes an imprint in the astral ethers, and that, when there is consciousness of God life in the mind of the speaker, all his words become living identities and are perpetuated. Anyone who develops sufficient spiritual power may enter this book of life within the cosmic mind and read out of its pages.

The mind and the body of man have the power of transforming energy from one plane of consciousness to another. This is the power and dominion implanted in man from the beginning. According to Scripture, "God said, Let us make man in our image, after our likeness; and they shall have dominion over the fish of the sea, and over the fowl of the heaven, and over the cattle, and over all the earth, and over every creeping thing that creepeth upon the earth" (Gen. 1:26; Lesser translation). Paul corroborates this statement by calling attention to the glory of man's inheritance:

Having the eyes of your heart enlightened, that ye may know what is the hope of his calling, what the riches of the glory of his inheritance in the saints, and what the exceeding greatness of his power towards who believe, according to that working of the strength of his mightwhich he wrought in Christ, when he raised him from the dead, and made him to sit at his right hand in the heavenly places, far above all rule, and authority, and power, and dominion, and every name that is named, not only in this world, but also in that which is to come.

In the kingdom of God within man's consciousness, the power faculty plays an important part in controlling the expression of the many emotions, inspirations, and thoughts. The voice is the most direct avenue of this expression, when man has dominion over the emotions and feelings from which the original impulse arises. The power of love makes the voice rich, warm, and mellow. Man can set love free in his soul by cultivating a loving attitude toward everybody and everything; he may add strength by silently speaking words of strength to each of the apostles sitting upon the twelve thrones within. Power swings open all the doors of mind and body. When one feels vital and energetic, the voice is strong and vibrant and brilliant. When one is sorrowful, the body weakens and the voice betrays its lack by its mournful intonation. Through the vibrations of power in the throat, one can feel the power of unity with the higher self more quickly than in any other way. This reveals that ideas rule the man, Jesus affirmed: "All power is given unto me in heaven [mind] and in earth [body]" (A.V.). When Jesus made this affirmation He undoubtedly realized His innate spiritual dominion, and when He consciously attuned His spiritual identity to mind and body, there was a conscious influx of power, and His hearers said that He "taught them as having authority, and not as the scribes."

In the process of regeneration the consciousness of power ebbs and flows, because the old and the new tides of thought act and react in the conscious and the subconscious realms of mind. However, when a disciple realizes his unity with Omnipotence, he is but little disturbed by the changes that go on in his mind and his body; he knows that his spiritual dominion is established, and that firm conviction expresses itself in firm words. Jesus said: "Heaven and earth shall pass away, but my words shall not pass away." Here is the evidence of spiritual power united with the idea of eternity. This union destroys the thought of years and declining power, and when awakened in those who have believed in age it will transform them and make all things new for them.

Every great vocalist has had inner spiritual power as an abiding conviction. This is strikingly illustrated in the indomitable persistency and power with which the famous singer, Galli-Curci, overcame obstacles. In the early stages of her career she was discouraged by opera critics. They told her that she could never make a success, but she persevered; and so she finally mastered every defect of her voice. This is a wonderful lesson to those who are apparently meeting with discouragements, who are tempted to succumb to circumstances and conditions in body and in environment. Take the words of Paul, "None of these things move me" (A.V.), and make unqualified affirmations of your spiritual supremacy.

Some metaphysical schools warn their students against the development of power, because they fear that it will be used in selfish, ambitious ways. It doubtless is true that the personal ego sometimes lays hold of the power faculty and uses it for selfish aggrandizement; we can readily see how what is called the Devil had origin. To be successful in the use of the power of Being, one must be obedient in exercising all the ideas that make man. If there is an assumption of personal power, Lucifer falls like "lightning from heaven," and the adverse or carnal mind goes to and fro in the earth. The casting out of these demons of personality formed a large part of the work of Jesus, and those who follow Him in the regeneration are confronted with similar states of mind and find it necessary to cast out the great demon selfishness, which claims to have power but is a liar and the father of lies.

No disciple can do any great overcoming work without a certain realization of spiritual power, dominion, mastery. Without power, one easily gives up to temporal laws, man-made. The psychic atmosphere is filled with thoughts that are not in harmony with Divine Mind. These psychic thoughts are legion, and to overcome them one must be on one's guard. Jesus said, "Watch." This means that we should quicken our discernment and our ability to choose between the good and the evil. "And why even of yourselves judge ye not what is right?" This wisdom of Spirit is man's through the all-knowing and all-discerning power of Spirit within him, and he need never fear going wrong if he listens to his divine intuition. "Ye shall know the truth, and the truth shall make you free." But man can never be free until he declares his freedom. Jesus said "I am from above." It is the prerogative of every man to make this declaration and thereby rise above the psychisms of mortal thought. Then do not fear to develop your power and mastery. They are not to be exercised on other people, but on yourself. "He that ruleth his spirit, [is more powerful] than he that taketh a city." Alexander cried because there were no more worlds to conquer, yet he had not conquered his own appetite, and died a drunkard at the age of thirty-three. Today men are striving to acquire power through money, legislation, and man-made government, and falling short because they have not mastered themselves.

Jesus said, "My kingdom is not of this world," yet He set up a kingdom in the world greater than all other kingdoms. In its beginning His kingdom was a very small affair, and the wise and the mighty laughed to scorn the proclamation that He was a king. Yet He was every inch a king. His people have been slow to follow the laws that He promulgated for His kingdom, but men in every walk of life are beginning to comprehend the vital integrity of His edicts, they are seeing that there can be no permanent peace or even civilization on earth until the Golden Rule, laid down by Him, is adopted by nations in commercial and in all other relationships. Businessmen are teaching the precept of Jesus, "All things therefore whatsoever ye would that men should do unto you, even so do ye also unto them," as fundamental in commercial success. Everywhere we hear them talking co-operation instead of competition. Commercial seers are discerning the dawn of a new day, in which good service instead of big profits will be the goal. Here we see the coming of the Christ "as a thief in the night." The night of ignorance and destructive competition is being burned out.

It follows that every kind of human industry must be carried forward by a power that recognizes the divine law. Man is the power of God in action. To man is given the highest power in the universe, the conscious power of thought. There is a universal creative force that urges man forward to a recognition of the creative power of his individual thought. This force is elemental, and all its attributes come under the dominion of man. When he co-operates with divine principle, man sits on the throne of his authority and the elemental force is subject to him.

But the power and the authority that are to rule in the kingdom of heaven are dependent on man's authority and his rule in the earth. Jesus said to Peter: "Whatsoever thou shalt bind on earth shall be bound in heaven; and whatsoever thou shalt loose on earth shall be loosed in heaven." If man binds or controls the appetites, passions, and emotions in the body (earth), he establishes ability and power to control the same forces in the realms universal, out of which the heavens are formed. When he attains a freedom in the expression of the qualities inherent in soul and body, he expands in power and can set free the elements universal and restore equilibrium between heaven and earth, or Spirit and matter.

When enough people have attained this power, the "new heaven and . . . new earth" (described in the 21st chapter of Revelation) will appear. It will not be necessary for anyone to wait for the full complement of overcomers, the mystical 144,000 who are to rule the new world, but each individual who complies with the overcoming law may enter into power with Jesus. It should not be overlooked by the elect that the Scripture reads: "He that overcometh shall inherit these things." To overcome and sit with Jesus on His throne means that man must overcome as He overcame. Jesus overcame the world, the flesh, and the Devil. To overcome the world one must be proof against all its allurements of riches and honor. To overcome the flesh one must spiritualize the five-sense man until material consciousness is raised to spiritual consciousness in feeling, tasting, seeing, hearing, and smelling. This change will ultimate in man's complete mastery of the body and in its final redemption from death.

The Devil is the personal ego who has in his freedom formed a state of consciousness peculiarly his own. When man lives wholly in the consciousness that personality has built up, he is ruled by the carnal mind, which is the Adversary, or Satan. In the mystery of the cross is hidden the overcoming of Satan. The crucifixion of Jesus is the symbolical representation of the crossing out (destruction) of the carnal mind (Satan) in the redeemed man's consciousness. Christ was not killed on the cross, neither was the body of Jesus destroyed. The "ghost" that Jesus gave up with His last breath was mortality. It was the personal, mortal consciousness that cried, "My God, my God, why hast thou forsaken me?" (The god should be spelled with a small g.) The personal-concept God fails to save its worshiper.

When the I AM identity, which is man, becomes so involved in its personal affairs that it ignores God, I AM lays hold of the body and rules all the bodily functions. When this rule is broken by the power of the Christ or supermind, there is a crucifixion. It may seem that Jesus is being crucified, but this is seeming only. Death comes to the Judas consciousness, which "hath a devil" (A.V.), but the body, being closely connected with this usurping mind, passes through suffering and apparent death. This is no more than appearance, because the higher principle, the Christ, resurrects the body and transmutes it into higher spiritual substance, where it enters into harmony or heaven. The climax of man's power and dominion is set forth in the resurrection and ascension of the type man, Jesus.

Chapter VII

The Work of the Imagination in Regeneration

WHEN THE faculties of the mind are understood in their threefold relation--spirit, soul, body--it will be found that every form and shape originated in the imagination. It is through the imagination that the formless takes form. It is well known that the artist sees in mind every picture that he puts on canvas. Man and the universe are a series of pictures in the Mind of Being. God made man in His image and likeness. Man, in his turn, is continually making and sending forth into his mind, his body, and the world about him living thought forms embodied and indued with his whole character. These images are formed in the front brain, and clothed with substance and life drawn from subcenters in the body.

Very intellectual people, concentrating the intensity of their thought in the head, fail to connect with the substance, life, and love centers in the body, and their work, although it may be very brilliant, lacks what we term "soul." The thought creations of this type seldom live long. Where the thought form and its substance are evenly balanced, the projected idea endures indefinitely. Jesus was a man thoroughly conversant with this law, and every idea that He clothed has lived and grown in wisdom and power in the minds of those who make union with Him in faith and spiritual understanding. He said: "Heaven and earth shall pass away: but my words shall not pass away."

Among the apostles, Bartholomew represents the imagination. He is called Nathanael in the 1st chapter of John, where it is recorded that Jesus saw him under the fig tree--the inference being that Jesus discerned Nathanael's presence before the latter came into visibility. This would indicate that images of people and things are projected into the imaging chamber of the mind and that by giving them attention one can understand their relation to outer things. Mind readers, clairvoyants, and dreamers have developed this capacity to varying degree. Where consciousness is primary in soul unfoldment there is confusion, because of lack of understanding of the fundamental law of mind action. Forms are always manifestations of ideas. One who understands this can interpret the symbols shown to him in dreams and visions, but lack of understanding of this law makes one a psychic without power. Joseph was an interpreter because he sought the one creative Mind for guidance. "And Joseph answered Pharaoh, saying, It is not in me: God will give Pharaoh an answer of peace." When Pharaoh told him the dream about the fat kine and the lean kine, Joseph at once gave the real meaning of the dream; he understood the metaphysical law. The early Christians had understanding of this law. The same law is in existence today and can be used more effectually by us, the reincarnated followers of Jesus, because mind and its modes of action are now better understood.

The Spirit of truth projects into the chamber of imagery pictures that, rightly understood, will be a sure guide for all people who believe in the omnipresence of mind. Everybody dreams, but the great majority do not attempt to interpret the handwriting on the wall of the mind, or they take their dreams literally and, because the dreams do not come true, consider them foolish. Through ignorance of the law with which imagination works, man has made imagination a byword. We look upon imaginary things as trivial, yet we know that through the imagination we can produce wonderful changes in the body. Studying this law, we find that the character of both soul and body is determined by the imagination and its associated faculties. Paul referred to this power of the imagination when he wrote:

But we all, with unveiled face beholding as in a mirror the glory of the Lord, are transformed into the same image from glory to glory, even as from the Lord the Spirit.

There has been much speculation about the method that Jesus used to impart spiritual understanding to His apostles and other early Christians, who were wonderfully illumined. It is true that the Twelve apostles had His personal instruction, but it was apparently preparatory only; the thorough training was to follow. Jesus promised that the Spirit of truth would, in

His name, come as teacher, guide, and instructor. He did not say how Spirit would guide and teach those who believed in Him; we gain this conclusion from their experiences in the new school of life to which He introduced them.

It is possible to impart Truth through direct inspiration, but this requires a student with a development of mind superior to the average, and Jesus sought converts in every walk of life. So we find that the simple and universally intelligible avenue of visions and dreams, the work of the imagination, was adopted as an important means by which the believers were instructed and called together. In fact, a large part of the work of the early church was carried forward by this means.

Saul was converted by a vision. Jesus appeared to him in person and rebuked him for his persecution of the Christians, told him that He had a work for him to do, and gave him directions as to his future movements.

And as he [Saul] journeyed, it came to pass that he drew nigh unto Damascus: and suddenly there shone round about him a light out of heaven: and he fell upon the earth, and heard a voice saying unto him, Saul, Saul, why persecutest thou me? And he said, Who art thou, Lord? And he said, I am Jesus whom thou persecutest; but rise, and enter into the city, and it shall be told thee what thou must do. And the men that journeyed with him stood speechless, hearing the voice, but beholding no man. And Saul arose from the earth; and when his eyes were opened, he saw nothing; and they led him by the hand, and brought him into Damascus. And he was three days without sight, and did neither eat nor drink.

Those who look to the Holy Spirit for guidance find that its instruction is given to all who believe in Christ, and they are often drawn together by direction of the inner voice, or by a dream, or by a vision. Saul, after beholding the blinding light of the spiritual realms, needed to have his sight restored. The brightness, or high potency, of Jesus' glorified presence had confused his intellectual consciousness, and this had brought about blindness. He needed the harmonious, peace-giving power of one who understood the inner life, and this was found in a certain disciple named Ananias. The Lord said to Ananias in a vision:

Arise, and go to the street which is called Straight, and inquire in the house of Judas for one named Saul, a man of Tarsus: for behold, he prayeth; and he hath seen a man named Ananias coming in, and laying his hands on him, that he might receive his sight. But Ananias answered, Lord, I have heard from many of this man, how much evil he did to thy saints at Jerusalem: and here he hath authority from the chief priests to bind all that call upon thy name. But the Lord said unto him, Go thy way: for he is a chosen vessel unto me, to bear my name before the Gentiles and kings, and the children of Israel: for I will show him how many things he must suffer for my name's sake. And Ananias departed, and entered into the house; and laying his hands on him said, Brother Saul, the Lord, even Jesus, who appeared unto thee in the way which thou camest, hath sent me, that thou mayest receive thy sight, and be filled with the Holy Spirit. And straightway there fell from his eyes as it were scales, and he received his sight; and he arose and was baptized; and he took food and was strengthened.

The Lord's appearing to Saul, with the conversion of the latter, is considered one of the great miracles of the Bible, but the experience of Ananias is seldom mentioned. Yet we are told in this text that the Lord appeared to Ananias and talked to him, just as He had appeared and talked to Saul, and there was apparently no difference in the real character of the incidents, except such be found in the mental attitude of the participants. Saul was antagonistic and full of fight. Ananias was receptive and obedient; he doubtless had received this sort of guidance many times. From the text we readily discern his spiritual harmony. He knew the reputation of Saul and protested against meeting him, but the Lord explained the situation and Ananias obeyed.

Today disciples of Jesus who are obedient and receptive and believe in the presence and the power of the Master and the Holy Spirit, are everywhere receiving visions and dreams. They are being drawn together and are helping one another to recover from the discords and inharmonies of life. Never before in the history of the race has there been so great a need for spiritual instruction as there is now, and this need is being met by Jesus and His aids in a renaissance of early Christianity and of its methods of instruction.

Spirit imparts its ideas through a universal language. Instead of being explained by words and phrases as used in ordinary language, the idea is formed and projected in its original character. This system of transferring intelligence is called symbolism. It is the only universal and correct means of communicating ideas. For example, if one wished to tell about a procession that he had seen, and could mentally picture it so that others could see it, how much more complete the communication than descriptive words! The mind formulates into thought images every idea that arises in it, and then tries to express it in language, which is nearly always inadequate. The French say: "Words are employed to conceal ideas." As the early disciples of Jesus had to learn that the symbol represents the idea rather than the thing, so modern disciples, following the same line of instruction, should not allow the intellect to materialize their dreams and visions; although they may be puzzled, like Peter, subsequent events will bring to them a clearer understanding of the lesson.

In the 10th chapter of Acts, we read:

Peter went up upon the housetop to pray, about the sixth hour: and he became hungry, and desired to eat: but while they made ready, he fell into a trance; and he beholdeth the heaven opened, and a certain vessel descending, as it were a great sheet, let down by four corners upon the earth: wherein were all manner of fourfooted beasts and creeping things of the earth and birds of the heaven. And there came a voice to him, Rise, Peter; kill and eat. But Peter said, Not so, Lord; for I have never eaten anything that is common and unclean. And avoice came unto him again a second time, What God hath cleansed, make not thou common. And this was done thrice: and straightway the vessel was received up into heaven.

Now while Peter was much perplexed in himself what the vision which he had seen might mean, behold, the men that were sent by Cornelius, having made inquiry for Simon's house, stood before the gate, and called and asked whether Simon, who was surnamed Peter, were lodging there. And while Peter thought on the vision, the Spirit said unto him, Behold, three men seek thee.

Peter was still bound by the Jewish teaching that there was no salvation for any except those of his faith, and this vision was to break the bondage of such narrowness and show him that the gospel of Jesus Christ is for all people. In a vision the Lord had already instructed Cornelius, the Roman soldier, that he should send certain of his servants to Joppa and fetch Peter to Caesarea.

Some advocates of flesh eating make the mistake of giving a literal interpretation to Peter's vision, holding that the Lord commanded him to kill and eat "all manner of fourfooted beasts and creeping things of the earth and birds of the heaven," and that God has cleansed them and thus prepared them for food for man. If this view of the vision should be carried out literally, we should eat all fourfooted animals, including skunks, all the creeping things, and all birds of the air, including vultures. We know, however, that the vision is to be taken in its symbolizing meaning. Peter was to appropriate and harmonize in his inner consciousness all thoughts of separation, all uncleanliness and impurity, narrowness, selfishness--the thoughts that bring diversity and separation.

We have within us, bound in the cage of the subconsciousness, all the propensities and the savagery of the animals. In the regeneration these are brought forth and a great reconciliation takes place. We find that there is really nothing unclean, except to human consciousness. In the original creative idealism of Divine Mind, everything was made perfect and sanctified and pronounced "very good." But God did not tell man to eat everything because it was good in its place.

And God said, Behold, I have given you every herb yielding seed, which is upon the face of all the earth, and every tree, in which is the fruit of a tree yielding seed; to you it shall be for food.

When man has regenerated and lifted up the beasts of the field, he will carry out the injunction given to the original Adam and name them "good."

Man's body represents the sum total of the animal world, because in its evolution it has had experience in nearly every type of elemental form. These memories are part of the soul, and in the unregenerate they come to the surface sporadically. Sometimes whole nations seem to revert from culture to savagery without apparent cause, but there is always a cause. These reversions are the result of some violent wrenching of the soul, or of concentration, to the exclusion of everything else, on a line of thought out of harmony with divine law. When the soul is ready for its next step in the upward way, a great change takes place, known as regeneration. Jesus referred to this when He said to Nicodemus: "Ye must be born anew." In one of its phases the new birth is a resurrection. All that man has passed through has left its image in the subconsciousness, wrought in mind and matter. These images are set free in the regeneration, and man sees them as part of himself. In his "Journal," George Fox, the spiritual-minded Quaker, says:

I was under great temptations sometimes, and my inward sufferings were heavy; but I could find none to open my condition to but the Lord alone, unto whom I cried night and day. I went back into Nottinghamshire, where the Lord shewed me that the natures of those things which were hurtful without, were within the hearts and minds of wicked men. The natures of dogs, swine, vipers, of Sodom and Egypt, Pharaoh, Cain, Ishmael, Esau, etc. The natures of these I saw within, though people had been looking without. I cried to the Lord saying, "Why should I be thus, seeing I was never addicted to commit those evils?" And the Lord answered, "It was needful I should have a sense of all conditions, how else should I speak of all conditions?" In this I saw the infinite love of God. I saw also, that there was an ocean of darkness and death; but an infinite ocean of light and love, which flowed over the ocean of darkness. In that also I saw the infinite love of God, and I had great openings. As I was walking by the steeple-house side in the town of Mansfield, the Lord said unto me, "That which people trample upon must be thy food." And as the Lord spake he opened to me that people and professors trampled upon the life, even the life of Christ was trampled upon; they fed upon words, and fed one another with words; but trampled under foot the blood of the son of God, which blood was my life: and they lived in their airy notions talking of him. It seemed strange to me at the first, that I should feed on that which the high professors trampled upon; but the Lord opened it clearly tome by his eternal Spirit and power.

In the regeneration man finds that he has, in the part of his soul called the natural man, animal propensities corresponding to the animals in the outer world. In the pictures of the mind, these take form as lions, horses, oxen, dogs, cats, snakes, and the birds of the air. The visions of Joseph, Daniel, John, and other Bible seers were of this character. When man understands that these animals represent thoughts, working in the subconsciousness, he has a key to the many causes of bodily conditions. It is clear to him that the prophets of old were using symbols to express ideas, and he sees that to interpret these symbols he must learn what each represents, in order to get the original meaning.

According to Genesis, the original creation was ideal, and through man the ideal was given character and form. Adam gave character to all the beasts of the field: "and whatever the man called every living creature, that was the name thereof." To the spiritually wise it is revealed that, when man is fully redeemed, he redeems and purifies and uplifts the animals in himself. The animal world will go through a complete transformation when the race is redeemed. As Isaiah says, "the wolf and the lamb shall feed together, and the lion shall eat straw like the ox." Some even go farther than this, and say that in the millennium there will be no necessity for animals; that they are, in reality, the dissipated forces of the human family and that when those forces are finally gathered into the original fount in the subjective, there will be no more animals in the objective; that in this way man will be immensely strengthened and a certain connection will be made between the so-called material and the spiritual.

Chapter VIII

Understanding

REFERENCE to the dictionary shows the words wisdom, understanding, knowledge, and intelligence to be so closely related that their definitions overlap in a most confusing way. The words differ in meaning, but various writers on the mind and its faculties have given definitions of these words in terms that directly oppose the definitions of other writers. There are two schools of writers on metaphysical subjects, and their definitions are likely to confuse a student unless he knows to which class the writer belongs. First are those who handle the mind and its faculties from an intellectual standpoint, among whom may be mentioned Kant, Hegel, Mill, Schopenhauer, and Sir William Hamilton. The other school includes all the great company of religious authors who have discerned that Spirit and soul are the causing factors of the mind. Compilers of dictionaries have consulted the former class for their definitions, and we have in consequence an inadequate set of terms to express the deep things of the mind. Even Christian metaphysicians who belong in the second classification have no clear understanding of the two great realms of mind; first, that in which pure ideas and pure logic rule; and second, the realm in which the thoughts and the actions of the mind are concerned with reason and the relation of ideas in the outer world. It is only in the last half century that large numbers of Christians have discerned that Jesus taught a metaphysical science.

Poets are natural mystics and metaphysicians, and in their writings we find the safest definitions of the names used to represent the actions of the mind. Poets nearly always make the proper distinction between wisdom and understanding. Tennyson says, "Knowledge comes, but wisdom lingers." Spiritual discernment always places wisdom above the other faculties of mind and reveals that knowledge and intelligence are auxiliary to understanding. Intellectual understanding comes first in the soul's development, then a deeper understanding of principles follows, until the whole man ripens into wisdom.

'Tis the sunset of life gives me mystical lore, And coming events cast their shadows before'.

The writings of the Hebrew prophets are good examples of original inspiration, which is wisdom. Solomon was famous for his wisdom. Jehovah appeared to him in a dream and said: "Ask what I shall give thee." Solomon replied: "Give thy servant therefore an understanding heart to judge thy people, that I may discern between good and evil." Pleased because Solomon had asked for wisdom instead of riches and honor, the Lord said:

Behold, I have done according to thy word; lo I have given thee a wise and an understanding heart . . . And I have also given thee that which thou hast not asked, both riches and honor . . . And Solomon awoke; and, behold, it was a dream.

It was after this occurrence that two women appealed to Solomon to decide which of them really was the mother of the child that they both claimed.

And the king said, Fetch me a sword. . . .And the kingsaid, Divide the living child in two, and give half to the one, and half to the other. Then spake the woman whose the living child was unto the king, for her heart yearned over her son, and she said, Oh, my lord, give her the living child, and in no wise slay it. But the other said, It shall be neither mine nor thine; divide it. Then the king answered and said, Give her the living child, and in no wise slay it: she is the mother thereof. And all Israel heard of the judgment which the king had judged; and they feared the king: for they saw that the wisdom of God was in him, to do justice.

The foregoing is a fine example of intuitive knowing. Instead of indulging in the usual taking of testimony and the various methods of proving the case by witnesses, Solomon appealed directly to the heart and got the truth quickly. No amount of exoteric testimony would have accomplished what the appeal to love brought forth at once.

Although it is sometimes difficult to determine between pure knowing and the quick perception of the intellect, the decision can always be made truly, based on the presence of the affectional nature.

Great philosophers in every age have testified to the activity of a supermind quality, which they have variously named. Socrates had it. He called it his daemon. Plato named it pure reason. Jesus called it the kingdom of the heavens.

In an article by M. K. Wisehart, printed in the American Magazine for June, 1930, entitled "A Close Look at the World's Greatest Thinker," Professor Albert Einstein is quoted as saying:

"'Every man knows that in his work he does best and accomplishes most when he has attained a proficiency that enables him to work intuitively. That is, there are things which we come to know so well that we do not know how we know them. So it seems to me in matters of principle. Perhaps we live best and do things best when we are not too conscious of how and why we do them.'

"He spoke of the great extent to which intuition figures in his work, and gave me to understand that the ability to work by intuition is one that can be acquired in any walk of life. It comes as the result of prolonged effort and reflection and application and failures and trying again. Then, in the end, one knows things without knowing how one knows them! And I gathered that the Professor meant to say that no man knows anything until he knows it in this thorough, instinctive way.

"People frequently ask Professor Einstein whether, as a scientist, he believes in God. Usually he answers: 'I do not believe in a God who maliciously or arbitrarily interferes in the personal affairs of mankind. My religion consists of an humble admiration for the vast power which manifests itself in that small part of the universe which our poor, weak minds can grasp!'

"In a discussion, when the Professor is impressed by the correctness of his own views or those of another, he will suddenly exclaim: 'Yes! So it is! It is just! It must be so! I am quite sure that God could not have made it different!' For him, God is as valid as a scientific argument.

"At one time, after prolonged concentration upon a single problem (it lasted for nearly four years), the Professor suffered a complete physical collapse. With it came severe stomach trouble. A celebrated specialist said: 'You must not get out of bed! You cannot stand on your feet for a long time to come.'

"'Is this the will of God?' queried the Professor instantly. 'I think not! The voice of God is from within us. Something within me tells me that every day I must get up at least once. I must go to the piano and play! The rest of the day I will spend in bed! This I am prepared to accept as the will of God!'

"And with the will of God, as set forth by Einstein, the specialist had to be content. Every day the Professor got up, put his bathrobe over his night-shirt, and went to the piano to play.

"I asked many questions to elicit the lessons of his experience that might be of most use to the rest of us. I learned that he reads little. 'Much reading after a certain age,' he says, 'diverts the mind from its creative pursuits. Any man who reads too much and uses his own brain too little falls into lazy habits of thinking, just as the man who spends too much time in the theaters is apt to be content with living vicariously instead of living his own life.

"'I have only two rules which I regard as principles of conduct. The first is: Have no rules. The second is: Be independent of the opinion of others.'"

So we find that there is in man a knowing capacity transcending intellectual knowledge. Nearly everyone has at some time touched this hidden wisdom and has been more or less astonished at its revelations. It certainly is a most startling experience to find ourselves giving forth logical thoughts and words without preparation or forethought, because we nearly always arrive at our conclusions through a process of reasoning. However, the reasoning process is often so swift that we are likely to think that it is true inspiration, especially when we have received either the reflected uplift of other wise ones or the baptism of the Holy Spirit. This quickening of the intellect is the John-the-Baptist or intellectual illumination that precedes the awakening of the ideal, the Christ understanding. Some Truth students become so enamored of the revelations that they receive through the head that they fail to go on to the unfoldment of the One who baptizes in "Holy Spirit and in fire." The Old Testament writers had a certain understanding of the first and the second opening of the mind to spiritual Truth; Isaiah said:

The voice of one that crieth, Prepare ye in the wilderness the way of Jehovah; make level in the desert a high way for our God.

Elijah had intellectual illumination, and the Israelites were taught that he would come again as a forerunner of the Messiah, Jesus said that Elijah had come again in the personality of John the Baptist:

I say unto you, that Elijah is come already, and they knew him not . . . Then understood the disciples that he spake unto them of John the Baptist.

The history of the Israelites is a sort of moving picture of man's soul and body development. When we understand the psychology of the different scenes, we know what we have passed through or will pass through in our journey from sense to Spirit.

Intellectual understanding of Truth, as given in the first baptism, is a tremendous step in advance of sense consciousness, and its possession brings a temptation to use for selfish ends the wisdom and the power thereby revealed. When Jesus received this baptism He was "led up of the Spirit into the wilderness to be tempted of the devil" (personal ego) before he could take the next degree in Son-of-God consciousness.

But Jesus knew that the illumination of the personal is not the fulfillment of the law, and He rejected every temptation to use His understanding for selfish ends.

Unless the disciple is very meek he will find the mortal ego strongly asserting its arguments for the application of the power of Spirit to personal needs. The god of mammon is bidding high for men that have received the baptism of Spirit, and many sell out, but their end is dust and ashes. No man can serve two masters; one cannot serve both God and Mammon.

When we discover in ourselves a flow of thought that seems to have been evolved independently of the reasoning process, we are often puzzled about its origin and its safety as a guide. In its beginnings this seemingly strange source of knowledge is often turned aside as a daydream; again it seems a distant voice, an echo of something that we have heard and forgotten. One should give attention to this unusual and usually faint whispering of Spirit in man. It is not of the intellect and it does not originate in the skull. It is the development, in man, of a greater capacity to know himself and to understand the purpose of creation. The Bible gives many examples of the awakening of this brain of the heart, in seers, in lawgivers, and in prophets. It is accredited as coming from the heart. The nature of the process is not explained; one who is in the devotional stage of unfoldment need not know all the complex movements of the mind in order to get the message of the Lord. It is enough to know that the understanding is opened in both head and heart when man gives himself wholly to the Lord.

This relation of head and heart is illustrated in the lives of John the Baptist and Jesus. They were cousins; the understanding of the head bears a close relation to the wisdom of the heart. They both received the baptism of Spirit, John preceding Jesus and baptizing Him. Here the natural order of spiritual illumination is illustrated. Man receives first an intellectual understanding of Truth which he transmits to his heart, where love is awakened. The Lord reveals to him that the faculty of love is the greatest of all the powers of man and that head knowledge must decrease as heart understanding increases.

However, we should remember that none of the faculties is eliminated in the regeneration. Among the apostles of Jesus, Thomas typifies the head, representing reason and intellectual perception. Jesus did not ignore Thomas's demand for physical evidence of His identity, but respected it. He convinced Thomas by corporal evidence that there had been a body resurrection; that He was living, not in a physical or ghost body, but in the same body that had been crucified.

Jesus plainly taught that He had attained control of the life in the body and could take it up or lay it down. We may construe the death and the resurrection of Jesus in various ways, many of them fanciful and allegorically far removed from practical life, but the fact remains that there is good historical evidence of the physical reality of the Resurrection in its minutest detail.

Spiritual understanding shows us that the resurrection of the body from death is not to be confined to Jesus, but is for all men who comprehend Truth and apply it as Jesus applied it. He had the consciousness of the new flood of life that comes to all who open their minds and their bodies to the living

Word of God, and He knew that it would raise the atomic vibration of His organism above the disintegrating thought currents of the earth and thus would save His flesh from corruption.

When Jesus told the Jews what He discerned, they said that He was crazy ("hath a demon"). One who teaches and practices the higher understanding and reality of man's relation to the creative law is not sane--from the viewpoint of mortal man.

When the higher understanding in Jesus proclaimed, "Verily, verily, I say unto you, If a man keep my word, he shall never see death," they took up stones to cast at Him. This startling claim of the power of the word of Truth to save one from death is beyond all human reason, and it is resented by the material thoughts, which are as hard as rocks.

Jesus did not let the limited race thought about man keep Him from doing the works of Spirit. He knew that the light of Truth had arisen in His consciousness and He was not afraid to affirm it. He went right ahead healing the sick and teaching the Truth as He saw it, regardless of the traditions of the Hebrew fathers, Abraham, Isaac, and Jacob. He kept the light shining in His consciousness by being loyal to it and by making for Himself the highest statements of Truth that He could conceive. The Christ Mind speaking in Him said: "I am the light of the world."

Spiritual understanding is developed in a multitude of ways; no two persons have exactly the same experience. One may be a Saul, to whom the light comes in a blinding flash, while to another the light may come gently and harmoniously. The sudden breaking forth of the light indicates the existence of stored-up reservoirs of spiritual experience, gained from previous lives. Jesus saw that Saul had a spiritual capacity that, turned into right channels, would do great good; so He took some pains to awaken in Saul the true light and thereby restrain the destructive zeal that possessed him. "He is a chosen vessel unto me, to bear my name before the Gentiles and kings, and the children of Israel."

The spiritual nature develops in man as the other attributes of his character develop. "As he thinketh within himself, so is he" is a statement of the law that has no exception. Man develops the capacity to do that which he sets out to do. If one makes no start one never goes.

In idle wishes fools supinely stay;
Be there a will, then wisdom finds a way.

No one ever attained spiritual consciousness without striving for it. The first step is to ask. "Ask, and it shall be given you; seek, and ye shall find; knock, and it shall be opened unto you." Prayer is one form of asking, seeking, and knocking. Then make your mind receptive to the higher understanding, through silent meditations and affirmations of Truth. The earnest desire to understand spiritual things will open the way and revelation within and without will follow. In Daniel 10:12 it is written:

Fear not, Daniel; for from the first day that thou didst set thy heart to understand, and to humble thyself before thy God, thy words were heard: and I am come for thy words' sake.

Daniel humbled himself in the presence of the universal Mind, and thereby opened his understanding and made himself receptive to the cosmic consciousness. Daniel and his companions were superior in wisdom and understanding to all the native magicians and seers in the whole Babylonian realm. The Scriptures say that God gave Daniel knowledge and skill in all learning and wisdom, and "Daniel had understanding in all visions and dreams." Cultivate purity of mind and body, and you will open the way for the higher thoughts, as did Daniel. He "purposed in his heart that he would not defile himself with the king's dainties, nor with the wine which he drank: therefore he requested of the prince of the eunuchs that he might not defile himself."

Spiritual understanding is developed in the feminine realm of the soul. This development is pictured in Acts 16:14: "And a certain woman named Lydia, a seller of purple, of the city of Thyatira, one that worshipped God, heard us: whose heart the Lord opened."

Thyatira means "burning incense"; it represents the intense desire of man for the higher expressions of life. When this inner urge comes forth with power (seller of purple), the Lord opens the heart and we receive the heavenly message, like the disciples who said one to another: "Was not our heart burning within us, while he spake to us in the way, while he opened to us the scriptures?"

Wisdom consisteth not in knowing many things, nor even in knowing them thoroughly; but in choosing and in following what conduces the most certainly to our lasting happiness and true glory.–Landor

Knowledge dwells in heads replete with thoughts of other men, wisdom in minds attentive to their own.–Cowper

She [knowledge] is earthly of the mind, but wisdom heavenly of the soul.–Tennyson

Create in me a clean heart, O God; And renew a right spirit within me. –Psalms 51:10.

For wisdom shall enter into thy heart, And knowledge shall be pleasant unto thy soul.–Proverbs 2:10.

But the path of the righteous is as the dawning light. That shineth more and more unto the perfect day.–Proverbs 4:18.

A tranquil heart is the life of the flesh; But envy is the rottenness of the bones.–Proverbs 14:30.

My son, forget not my law; But let thy heart keep my commandments.–Proverbs 3:1.

Trust in Jehovah with all thy heart, And lean not upon thine own understanding: In all thy ways acknowledge him, And he will direct thy paths. –Proverbs 3:5, 6

Happy is the man that findeth wisdom, And the man that getteth understanding. For the gaining of it is better than the gaining of silver, And the profit thereof than fine gold. She is more precious than rubies: And none of the things thou canst desire art to be compared unto her. Length of days is in her right hand; In her left hand are riches and honor. Her ways are ways of pleasantness, And all her paths are peace. She is a tree of life to them that lay hold upon her: And happy is every one that retaineth her. Jehovah by wisdom founded the earth; By understanding he established the heavens.–Proverbs 3:13-19.–

Chapter IX

The Will Is the Man

OUR CAPTION is quoted from an ancient metaphysical teaching, the origin of which is lost in antiquity. The idea is that the development of the will is possible only through the development of the mind as a whole, and as man is mind, "the will is the man." This conclusion is reached because the will moves to action all the other faculties of the mind and seems to be the whole process.

However, a careful analysis of the various factors entering into an action reveals other equally important attributes of man, and we cannot wholly admit that "the will is the man." The will is undoubtedly the focal point around which all action centers, when there is harmony of mind; but the rule has been accepted by schools of philosophy from most ancient times down to the present that the will and the understanding are very closely related--the understanding comprehending all our speculative, the will all our active, powers. This close relationship is symbolically taught in the Bible, and it appeals to man's reason and is confirmed by his observation.

Jacob, representing the I AM (I will be what I will to be), had twelve sons, one of whom was Joseph, "the dreamer." Joseph represents the imagination, by which all forms and shapes are brought into manifestation. In the development of the mind, certain faculties are given prominence. After they run their race, other faculties that have been held in reserve come forward. When the period of rest comes, the Scriptures recite that a certain one "died, old and full of days." As man goes forward in his unfoldment, there is sometimes a tendency toward the surface of consciousness, or the phenomenal, and a gradual loss of interest in the original sources of action. The ph enomenal phase of creation is so interesting that man sometimes becomes bewildered in its study or its pleasure, and the originating cause may be ignored to the point of forgetfulness. This cessation of creative activity by the imagination (Joseph) is described in these words: "So Joseph died, being a hundred and ten years old: and they embalmed him, and he was put in a coffin in Egypt." This means metaphysically that when the imagination in a life span has fulfilled its mission as a creative power it falls asleep, but it is preserved in the realms of darkness (Egypt).

Joseph's number is eleven. He was the eleventh son, and his age when he stopped active work and fell asleep (110) represents the completeness of the dispensation of that faculty's activity; the cipher indicates an endless capacity for expression. The figure given as the age of a Biblical character usually represents the subject's place in his evolution. Joseph completed his evolution to the eleventh degree plus. The cipher means that he has more to demonstrate.

Jesus' number is twelve. He was wise at the age of twelve.

Adam was third in the Godhead (God, Christ, man). He lived 930 years, according to scriptural chronology. This number tells us that he is third in the trinity, has the capacity of the twelvefold man, but has unfolded only three of the twelve faculties. The order of the numbers indicates the harmony of his unfoldment. In this instance it was orderly--the naught denotes future progress uninterrupted.

Seth, the son whom Adam begat "in his own likeness, after his image," represents the awakening of spiritual consciousness. "Then began men to call upon the name of Jehovah." Seth's years were 912. Here the trinity and the twelvefold man are eptiomized, and we see that Seth was the birth, in Adam, of Adam's own original character, even the image and likeness of Elohim. In the figure nine the trinity is repeated three times, once for each of its identities, God, Christ, man; then the twelve powers of man are added. Again the total of the digits is twelve, the number of divine man demonstrated.

We have called attention to the metaphysical meaning of the chronology of these Biblical characters in order to illustrate more fully the manner in which the faculties are developed. It will be seen that in man is implanted the likeness of God, which man develops in a long series of personalities. The process of forming a soul may be compared to the development, in a photographic negative, of the image that has been imprinted upon the sensitive plate but cannot be seen until it has been put through a regular developing process. When Adam had a spiritual awakening he perceived the truth of his identity in God, and thereby begat Seth, the original image and likeness of spiritual man, imprinted upon him by the Word of creative Mind. Then the worship of Jehovah was restored in man's whole consciousness, for a time at least.

Coming down the chronological stream, we find that Joseph's place was taken by two sons. "And Joseph called the name of the first-born Manasseh: For, said he, God hath made me forget all my toil, and all my father's house. And the name of the second called he Ephraim: For God hath made me fruitful in the land of my affliction." The mother of these sons was Asenath, daughter of Potiphera, Egyptian priest of On. Asenath means "peril." She represents the feminine or love side of the natural man. From this intricate symbology we discern that two faculties of the mind were given birth. The eldest son, Manasseh, had power to forget, to erase by denial, through an understanding of Truth, all the accumulated burden of thoughts, even to that of heredity, "all my father's house." The other son, Ephraim, could add to by affirmation and make fruitful the land that seemed to be a place of affliction. These two sons of Joseph inherited his allotment in the Promised Land, which symbolizes the perfected body. The front brain is the field of operation for these closely related faculties--imagination, understanding, and will. When man's will is working strongly he corrugates his brow, and his quick understanding causes his eyes to flash.

When the imagination is subjective and spiritual and the will and the understanding are objective and alert, we have the creative artist. Then the understanding develops its greatest freedom and originality. It is no longer bound by the traditions of the past in literature, art, music, drama, science, or religion, but launches out into the deep and brings up the "pearl of great price," original creative genius and life. Then the energetic will makes fruitful by its activity all the inspirations of the awakened man.

These two closely related forces of the mind are dominant in the race because their practicality is necessary in man's free development. If the imagination were wholly in command, it would eventually run into a riot of daydreams or fanciful schemes that could not be worked out successfully in a world where natural law is inexorable. It is this "peril" (Asenath) that the mind considers, and brings forth, in sequence, will and understanding. "The highest and most excellent thing in man," says Goethe, "is formless, and we must guard against giving it shape in anything save noble deeds."

Man is a free agent in the possession and the use of the faculty of will. Freedom of will has been variously regarded and defined. It is the subject of volumes of theological literature and also the rock on which religionists have split. The theory of predestination relieves man of all responsibility. If God has fixed every act of man's existence, then there can be no mental or moral freedom. If man cannot determine the character of his acts, he has neither understanding nor will--he is a puppet.

The understanding and the will should be especially active in one who would master the sensations of the body. Potiphar's wife represents the sense consciousness that tempts us to meet its desires, and, when we deny it, has us imprisoned. This means that when a certain habit in the sense consciousness is refused expression, it reacts and for a time seems to prevent our expressing even the good. But let us patiently bide our time; the higher will yet show its God-given power.

The several visits of Joseph's brothers to Egypt for corn, and the final reconciliation, are symbolical representations of the manner in which we make connection with the obscured vitality within the organism and finally bring all our faculties into conjunction with it.

Volumes might be written with Joseph as a text. In his history, as given in Genesis, some of the most interesting processes of regeneration are symbolized. This hidden realm within the subconsciousness is in an Egyptian, or obscured, state to most of us. Yet it is a great kingdom, and its king is Pharaoh, ruler of the sun, or the "brain" and nerve center, which physiology names the solar plexus. This is the brain of the physical man, and it directs the circulation, digestion, assimilation, and so forth. Students of mind have discovered that the solar plexus is the organ through which a ruling thought in the head is carried into the body. He of the "hard heart," who would not let the people go, is human will, acting through the solar plexus, or city of the sun.

The spiritual life in the subconsciousness (Children of Israel in Egypt) is often prevented from expressing itself by the opposition of the will. If the understanding decides that what it conceives to be the natural law shall be the limit of expression, there is further bondage and there are harder tasks. Any hard, dictatorial, or willful state of mind will harden the heart. This state of mind acts through the solar plexus (the distributing station for building forces of the body), and thereby brings its limitations upon the whole system. Hardened arteries are the result of hard thoughts, this hardness originates in the will. Jehovah represents the law of the I AM in action.

The ambiguity in the term "motive" has caused much of the controversy that has raged over free will. The champions of free will commonly suppose that before performing an act a man is affected by various motives, none of which necessarily determines his act. Their opponents, on the other hand, argue that there is no such thing as this unmotivated choice. Some hold that free will proper consists of choice only as between higher and lower good. Some regard it as consisting in the power to do as one pleases or chooses. Others define it as the power to do or to choose as one should.

According to some academic metaphysicians, the freedom of the will includes the power to act contrary to all of one's own motives or inclinations or tendencies, this power being inherent in the will. It is readily seen that this thing called "motive" is another name for understanding, and that it is a necessary adjunct to that faculty. But not all people use understanding as the headlight for both motive and will. The undisciplined mind feels the impulse that lies behind motive, and acts without considering either cause or effect. This is partaking of the knowledge of good and evil without heeding the voice of wisdom--the sin of Adam, undeveloped man. Understanding may be illumined by the Christ Mind, and thus receive the light that "lighteth every man, coming into the world." Without this light man breaks the law in nearly every act. The divorcement of understanding from will has led to endless controversies between those who have written and debated about the necessity for man's having free will, and those who, because of the evils that have come upon man through ignorant willing, have advocated the utter effacement of the will.

We do not need less will; we need more understanding. Jesus (spiritual light) showed Thomas (intellectual understanding) the wounds that ignorance had inflicted upon the innocent body. Jesus' apostles represented His own faculties of mind. When He called them they were ignorant and undisciplined children of the natural world. But the image and likeness of the creative Mind was on them, to discipline them in the wisdom of the Christ (spiritual I AM).

As the executive power of the mind, human will is the negative pole of spiritual decision. Right here is where those who study man from a personal viewpoint fail in their estimate of his power and his accountability. As mortal, living in a material world, he seems circumscribed and limited in capacity and destiny. Philosophers have studied man in this cage of the mind, and their conclusions have been that he is little better than a reasoning animal.

But there is a higher and truer estimate of man, and that estimate is made from what the academic school of philosophy would call the purely speculative side of existence. Failing to discern his spiritual origin, they fail in estimating his real character. As a product of the natural man, will is often a destructive force. Nearly all our systems of training children have been based on breaking the will in order to gain authority over the child and obedience from him. We should remember that the right to exercise freedom of will was given to man in the beginning, according to Genesis, and that will should always be given its original power and liberty.

It is possible, however, for man so to identify his consciousness with Divine Mind that he is moved in every thought and act by that Mind. Jesus attained this unity; when He realized that He was willing not in the personal but in the divine, He said: "Not my will, but thine, be done."

Many sincere Christians have tried to follow in the way of Jesus, and they have negatively submitted their will to God. But they have not attained the power or the authority of Jesus by so doing. The reason is that they have not raised their will to the positive spiritual degree. Jesus was not negative in any of His faculties, and He did not teach a doctrine of submission. He gave, to those who went forth preaching the Gospel, the power and authority of the Holy Spirit. In Mark 16:16-18 it is recorded that Jesus says: "He that believeth and is baptized shall be saved; but he that disbelieveth shall be condemned. And these signs shall accompany them that believe: in my name shall they cast out demons; they shall speak with new tongues; they shall take up serpents, and if they drink any deadly thing, it shall in no wise hurt them; they shall lay hands on the sick, and they shall recover." We must believe in the higher powers and be immersed in the omnipresent water of life. If we fail to exercise faith in things spiritual, we are condemned to the prison of materiality.

Some Christians believe that God's will toward men varies, that His will changes, that He chastises the disobedient and punishes the wicked. This view of God's character is gained from the Old Testament. Jehovah was the tribal God of the Israelites as Baal was of the Philistines. Men's concepts of God are measured by their spiritual understanding. The Jehovah, of Moses, is quite different from the Father, of Jesus, yet they are spiritually one and the same. "It is not the will of your Father who is in heaven, that one of these little ones should perish," is the teaching of Jesus. He bore witness that the will of God is that men should not suffer--that through Him they should have complete escape from sin, sickness, and even death. "God so loved the world, that he gave his only begotten Son, that whosoever believeth on him should not perish, but have eternal life." The sin, sickness, suffering, and death that men experience are not punishment willed by God; they are results of broken law. The law is good; men have joy, satisfaction, and life in everlasting harmony, when they keep the law. Creation would not be possible without rules governing the created.

It is error for anyone to submit his will to the control of any personality. The personal exercise of will by personal understanding is short-sighted and selfish; hence it is never safe to allow oneself to be led by the direction or advice of another. Practice the presence of God until you open your consciousness to the inflow of the omnipresent, all-knowing mind, then affirm your unity with that mind until you know and fully realize, through the many avenues of wisdom, just what you should do. This acquirement of a knowledge of the divine will is not the work of an instant; it results from patient and persistent spiritual study, prayer, and meditation. Even Jesus, with His exalted understanding, found it necessary to pray all night. All who have found the peace and the power of God have testified to the necessity of using prayer in the soul's victory.

One should not intellectually will to bring about results for oneself or for another. The difference between the personal will and the universal will can be known by one who practices thought control in the silence.

Affirmations made in the head alone are followed by a feeling of tension, as if bands were drawn across the forehead. When this state of mind sinks back into the subconsciousness, the nerves become tense; if the practice is continued, nervous prostration follows.

Stubborn, willful, resistant states of mind congest the life flow; they are followed by cramps and congestion. The will often compels the use of the various organs of the body beyond their normal capacity, and the results are found in strained nerves and strained muscles and in impaired sight and impaired hearing. Disobedient children have earache, showing the direct result that self-will has on the nerves of the ear. Deaf persons should be treated for freedom from willfulness and obstinacy. In the present state of race consciousness, all people use the intellectual will to excess. The remedy is daily relaxation, meditation, prayer.

Will, as exercised by man, is the negative pole of the great executive force of the universe. The recognition of this in silent meditation opens the will to the inflow of this mighty, moving principle, and the power that moves to action the members of the body reaches into the invisible realm of ideas and controls the elements. It was comprehension of the will universal that enabled Jesus to say to the wind and the waves, "Peace, be still." Life, liberty, and the pursuit of happiness are the inalienable rights of man, and they should never be interferred with. Hypnotism, mesmerism, and mediumship are based on the submission of one will to another. The one who desires control demands another's submission in mind and body to his own willed thoughts and words of directive power. The effect on the one who submits is always weakening, and, if continued, results in a mental negation that makes him the victim of evil influences too numerous to mention.

"Not my will, but thine, be done" is one of the most far-reaching affirmations of Jesus, and those who follow Him and keep His sayings are finding great peace and relaxation of mind and body.

Jesus, the mighty helper, is always present with those who are earnestly seeking to be Christians and to keep the divine law.

Chapter X

Spiritual Law and Order

THE 23d chapter of Matthew is a philippic against ritualism. Jesus arraigns the scribes and the Pharisees before the bar of the divine law and charges them with a long list of crimes committed in the name of religion. He makes charge after charge of delinquency in spiritual observance of the law and warns His disciples and the multitudes to beware of the works of these blind leaders of the blind. Among other accusations He says:

Yea, they bind heavy burdens and grievous to be borne, and lay them on men's shoulders . . . all their works they do to be seen of men . . . they . . . love the chief place at feasts, and the chief seats in the synagogues . . . and to be called of men, Rabbi. But be not ye called Rabbi: for one is your teacher, and all ye are brethren. And call no man your father on the earth: for one is your Father, even he who is in heaven. Neither be ye called masters: for one is your master, even the Christ. But he that is greatest among you shall be your servant. And whosoever shall exalt himself shall be humbled; and whosoever shall humble himself shall be exalted.

But woe unto you, scribes and Pharisees, hypocrites! because ye shut the kingdom of heaven against men: for ye enter not in yourselves, neither suffer ye them that are entering in to enter.

Woe unto you, scribes and Pharisees, hypocrites! for ye compass sea and land to make one proselyte; and when he is become so, ye make him twofold more a son of hell than yourselves. . . .

Woe unto you, scribes and Pharisees, hypocrites! for ye tithe mint and anise and cummin, and have left undone the weightier matters of the law, justice, and mercy, and faith: but these ye ought to have done, and not to have left the other undone. Ye blind guides, that strain out the gnat, and swallow the camel!

Woe unto you, scribes and Pharisees, hypocrites! for ye cleanse the outside of the cup and of the platter, but within they are full from extortion and excess. Thou blind Pharisee, cleanse first the inside of the cup and of the platter, that the outside thereof may become clean also. . . .

Woe unto you, scribes and Pharisees, hypocrites! for ye build the sepulchers of the prophets, and garnish the tombs of the righteous, and say, If we had been in the days of our fathers, we should not have been partakers with them in the blood of the prophets.

All these "woes" are to those who are living in the letter instead of in the spirit of the law. But Jesus did not condemn religion, nor religious organizations. His denunciations were aimed at those who profess to teach and to follow the law but fall short in carrying it out in their lives.

Right here, however, religious teachers should be on their guard in framing tenets for religious organizations. Do not dogmatize in creed, or statement of Being, as a governing rule of thought and action for those who join your organization. These things are limitations, and they often prevent free development because of foolish insistence on consistency. The creed that you write today may not fit the viewpoint of tomorrow; hence the safe and sure religious foundation for all men is that laid down by Jesus, "The Spirit of truth . . . shall guide you into all the truth." A statement setting forth the teaching of a religious institution is essential, but compelling clauses should be omitted.

The Mosaic law had been framed for the benefit of the Hebrews, but their priesthood made it a hindrance to spiritual progress. Jesus was an iconoclast, and He made it His special business to break nearly every rule of action that the priests had evolved. For example, they had thirty-nine prohibitions in regard to the observance of the Sabbath. These were nearly all trivial, such as preparing food, riding on a beast, drawing water, carrying a burden, going on a journey; yet death was the penalty for transgression. Labor of any kind on the Sabbath was punishable by death. To roll grains of wheat in the hand was considered labor, so when the apostles of Jesus plucked the ears of grain the Pharisees said to Him: "Behold, why do they on the sabbath day that which is not lawful?" Then Jesus gave them a sermon on freedom from their narrow rules governing the Sabbath day; He ended with, "The Sabbath was made for man, and not man for the sabbath."

The fact is that the Sabbath as an institution was established by man. God does not rest from His works every seventh day, and there is no evidence that there has ever been a moment's cessation in the activity of the universe. Those who stickle most for Sabbath-day observance are met on every hand by the evidence of perpetual activity on the part of Him whom they claim to champion.

We are told that trees, flowers, planets, suns, stars, and sidereal systems are the work of God; that it is God who sustains and governs, controls and directs them. Yet trees, flowers, planets, suns, and stars are active the first day and the seventh day of the week, just the same as on other days.

It would seem proper that, if God ordained a certain day of rest and rested on that day Himself, as is claimed, He should give some evidence of it in His creations; but He has not done this, so far as anybody knows. The truth is that Divine Mind rests in a perpetual Sabbath, and that which seems work is not work at all. When man becomes so at-one with the Father-Mind as to feel it consciously, he also recognizes this eternal peace, in which all things are accomplished. He then knows that he is not subject to any condition whatsoever and that he is "lord even of the sabbath."

Man can never exercise dominion until he knows who and what he is and, knowing, brings forth that knowledge into the external by exercising it in divine order, which is mind, idea, and manifestation. Jesus horrified the Jews by healing the sick, plucking grain, and performing other acts, which to them were sacrilegious, on the Sabbath day. The Jews manufactured these sacred days and observances, just as our Puritan fathers made life a burden by their rigid and absurd laws governing the religious acts of the people. For centuries the Jews had been binding themselves to the wheel of religious bigotry, and the Puritans accomplished a like task in a shorter time. The length of time was the only difference.

But Jesus knew all the exacting ecclesiastical rules to be man-made. "He himself knew what was in man" and He attempted to disabuse those benighted minds of their error. He tried to make them understand that the Sabbath was made for man, not man for the Sabbath. They had wound themselves up in religious ceremonies until their ecclesiastical machinery dominated every act of their lives. Not only were they subjects of their sacred law, but they were its absolute slaves.

It was the mission of Jesus to break down this mental structure which had been reared through ages of blind servitude to form and ritual. The Mosaic law had been made so rigid that it held the Jews in its icy bonds to the exclusion of all reason and common sense. Jesus saw this, and He purposely overstepped the bounds of religious propriety in order that He might more effectively impress on them the fact that the old Mosaic dispensation was at an end. He told them that He did not come to break the law, but to fulfill it. He was speaking of the true law of God, and not their external rules of sacrifice, penance, Sabbath observance, and the like. He knew that these rules were of the letter--purely perfunctory; that they were in reality hindrances to the expression of the inner spiritual life.

Man cannot grow into the understanding of Spirit, nor be obedient to its leading, if he is hampered by external rules of action. No man-made law is strong enough, or true enough, or exact enough, to be a permanent guide for anyone.

If in your path toward the light you have fixed a point of achievement that attainment of which you think will satisfy you, you have made a limitation that you must eventually destroy. There is no stopping place for God; there is no stopping place for man.

If the church goes back to Moses and the old dispensation, ignoring the lessons of Jesus, it is no guide for you. If you want to be His disciple, you must unite your spirit with His.

Paul, with his dominant beliefs in the efficiency of the old way, at times loaded those beliefs upon the free doctrine of Jesus, but that is no reason why you should be burdened with them. You can never be what the Father wants you to be until you recognize that you stand alone, with Him as your sole and original guide, just as much alone as if you were the first and only man. You can hear His Word when you have erased from your mind all tradition and authority of men, and His Word will never sound clearly in your mind until you have done this.

It is not necessary that you despise the scriptures of the Jews, of the Hindus, or of any people, but you are to take them for what they are--the records of men as to what their experiences have been in communing with the omnipresent God. As Jesus said to the Pharisees: "Ye preach the scriptures, because ye think that in them ye have eternal life; and these are they which bear witness of me; and ye will not come to me, that ye may have life." From all sacred writings you can get many wonderfully helpful hints as to the work of God in the minds of men. You should treasure all pure words of Truth that have been written by brothers in the Spirit, yet they are not authority for you nor should you be moved to do anything simply because it is written in the Scriptures as a law of God for the specific guidance of man.

Mortal man loves to be dominated and whipped into line by rituals and masters, but divine man, the man of God, oversteps all such childish circumscribings and goes direct to the Father for all instruction.

It is your privilege to be as free as the birds, the trees, the flowers. "They toil not, neither do they spin," but are always obedient to the divine instinct, and their every day is a Sabbath. They stand in no fear of an angry God, though they build a nest, spread a leaf, or open a petal, on the first day or on the seventh day. All days are holy days to them. They live in the holy Omnipresence, always doing the will of Him who sent them. It is our duty to do likewise. That which is instinct in them is conscious, loving obedience in us. When we have resolved to be attentive to the voice of the Father and to do His will at any cost, we are freed from the bondage of all man-made laws. Our bonds--in the form of some fear of transgressing the divine law--slip away into the sea of nothingness, and we sit on the shore and praise the loving All-Good that we are never more to be frightened by an accusing conscience or by the possibility of misunderstanding His law.

But we are not to quarrel with our brother over observance of the Sabbath. If he insists that the Lord should be worshiped on the seventh day, we shall joyfully join him on that day; and if he holds that the first day is the holy day, we again acquiesce. Not only do we do God's service in praise, song, and thanksgiving on the seventh day and the first day, but also on every day. Our minds are open to God every moment. We are ever ready to acknowledge His holy presence in our hearts; it is a perpetual Sunday with us. We are not satisfied with one day out of the seven set aside for religious observance, but, like the birds, the trees, and the flowers, we join in a glad refrain of thanksgiving in and out of season. When we work and when we sleep we are ever praising the holy Omnipresence that burns its lamp of love perpetually in our hearts and keeps forever the light of life before us.

This is the observance of God's holy day that the divinely wise forever recognize. It is not in churches nor in temples reared by man in any form, that he finds communion with the Father. He has found the true church, the heaven within himself. There he meets the Father face to face; he does not greet Him as one removed to a distant place, to whom he communicates his wishes through some prophet or priest, but each for himself goes to the Father in closest fellowship.

"God so loved the world, that he gave his only begotten Son, that whosoever believeth on him should not perish, but have eternal life." This does not mean that a personal man, named Jesus of Nazareth, was sent forth as a special propitiation for the sins of the world, or that the only available route into the Father's presence lies through such a person. It simply means that God has provided a way by which all men may come consciously into His presence in their own souls. That way is through the only begotten Son of God, the Christ consciousness, which Jesus demonstrated. This consciousness is the always present Son of the Father, dwelling as a spiritual seed in each of us and ready to germinate and grow at our will. The Son of God is in essence the life, the love, and the wisdom of the Father himself; through us the Son is made manifest as a living individuality. He cannot be killed out entirely; He ever grows at the center of our being as the "light which lighteth every man, coming into the world."

To believe on the Son is to come to His terms of expression. It is the simplest thing in the world. Just believe that He is the only begotten Son of the Father. Do not believe that there are other sons wiser than He is, and that from them you can get wisdom, guidance, and understanding, but know that He is indeed the only begotten Son.

This distinction is a vital point for you to apprehend, and when you have once apprehended it your journey back to the Father's house is easy. "No one cometh unto the Father, but by me," the only Son is constantly saying in your heart, and you must not ignore His presence if you would know the sweets of the heavenly home where the love of God forever burns its incense of peace, plenty, and contentment. Let Christ be formed in you, was Paul's admonition. This is not hyperbole or an abstraction, but a statement of a definite rule of procedure, which you can discover and prove by making terms with this indwelling Son of the Father. His terms are not severe. They are simply obedience, obedience.

Jesus of Nazareth found this inner flame and let it burn all through His body. It so lighted Him up that His presence warms all sin-sick men to this very day.

But no one lives by reflection. You could not live a moment if it were not for this only begotten Son of the Father within you. So you cannot live and grow on the reflected light of Jesus of Nazareth. The only begotten Son of God must come forth in you as it did in Jesus. Then your life will be permanent, and the discords of the flesh will drop away forever; then will your Sabbath be revealed to you.

The redemptive, restorative, and regenerative work that the Christ of God did through Jesus is not ignored by Christian metaphysicians. However, the salvation of men from the sins of mortality was not accomplished by the man Jesus alone; it was through the power of the Christ in Jesus that God provided purified life and substance for the corruptible bodies of men. Jesus' body was used as the vehicle through which a fresh and pure life stream and a regenerative substance were made available to all those who will accept them. The redeemed substance of the body of the Lord is just as essential to full salvation as His blood. Also, this is a salvation that is to be attained here in the earth, and not after death. Jesus' body was metamorphosed or changed from the corruptible flesh of the average man to the incorruptible substance of divine man. When we eat and drink of His body we shall become like Him in body perfection. This process of restoration of the body of man to its original purity is the basis of divine or spiritual healing. The complete redemption of the body may not be accomplished in one incarnation, but whoever accepts the Christ as life and substance, and conforms to righteous living as taught by the Spirit of truth, will finally sit with Jesus on the throne of dominion over disease and death.

There is a law of spiritual and mental growth constantly at work in the mind, a law that is raising man from sense consciousness, or Egypt, to spiritual consciousness, or Canaan. Moses means "drawn out," and represents in Scripture symbology this progressive or drawing-out process, which works from within out. As applied to the universe, this upward trend of all things is called by material science the evolutionary law. In our spiritual interpretation we observe the working of the law in the individual, because by that method we can bring home the lesson.

Through intelligent use of the hints given, we apply the lesson to ourselves with great profit.

Involution always precedes evolution. That which is involved in mind evolves through matter. Joseph down in Egypt portrays the involution in matter of a high spiritual idea. The spiritual idea attracted other ideas like it (Joseph's relatives), and they greatly multiplied in the land of Egypt. It is estimated that the Children of Israel increased from a few score to at least two millions. This illustrates the fact that spiritual thoughts grow with tremendous rapidity in consciousness when they have Truth as a nucleus.

Yet these true thoughts, which have so greatly multiplied are in slavery to the Egyptians (sense nature), and a special effort has to be made to free them. We have our high ideals, but because the temporal life seems so important those ideals are made to work in the most menial ways to carry on this passing show. A time comes, however, when we rebel at this tyranny; we rise up in so-called righteous indignation, and in violent ways we kill out the opposing sense nature, as Moses killed the Egyptian. But this is not the right way. We are not to be liberated by suppression of sense, or by violent overcoming, but by a steady step-by-step demonstration over every error. The Lord recognizes the rights of the physical man, and He hardens Pharaoh's heart that he may sustain for a season his rightful place in consciousness.

The fleeing of Moses to the wilderness represents the discipline that we must undergo when we seek the exalted One. Horeb means "solitude"; that is, we have to go into the solitude of the within and lead our flock of thoughts to the back of the wilderness, where dwells the exalted One, the I AM, whose kingdom is good judgment. There we are in training forty years, or until we arrive at a four-sided or balanced state of mind. Then the light of intuition or flame of fire burns in our hearts, yet it is not consumed--there is no loss of substance. In brain thinking there is a vibratory process that uses up nerve tissue, but in the wisdom that comes from the heart the "bush" or tissue is not consumed. This thinking in wisdom is "holy ground," or substance in its spiritual wholeness; that is, the idea of substance in Divine Mind. When this holy ground is approached by man he must take off from his understanding all limited thoughts of the Absolute--he must put his shoes off his feet.

It is at this wisdom center within us that God proclaims Himself to be the Father of fathers, the God of Abraham, Isaac, and Jacob; thus our real Father is revealed to us as Spirit.

In our communion in the silence with the light within us, the bondage of the higher to the lower is made clear to us, and the true way of release is indicated. We see the possibilities of man and the goodness of the "promised land," to which we can raise every thought. But Moses was very meek--we feel our inability, and we say, "Who am I, that I should go unto Pharaoh, and that I should bring forth the children of Israel out of Egypt?" Then we have the assurance that God's power is with us--"Certainly I will be with thee." It is in the recognition of the power and the presence of God that all our strength and all our ability lie. Jesus, the great spiritual master, said, "The Father abiding in me doeth his works."

All great structures are erected on firm foundations. Anyone whom the Lord calls to a work will succeed in the end, if he lays his foundation deep and strong in spiritual understanding. This understanding is attained through meditation and study in the silence. Moses was forty years separated from the busy haunts of men, learning to know God "face to face."

In our silent meditations and prayers we must infuse into the inner mind realms the same energy that, used without, would make us notable in some worldly achievement. But unless we do this inner work and lay the foundation of strength and power in the subjective mind, we shall find ourselves in failing health when called upon for extra exertion in some great effort.

The angel of the Lord, the flame of fire, and the bush, are all within the consciousness of man, becoming manifest through interior concentration. The bush is a nerve center through which the universal life energy runs like electricity over a wire, making a light but not consuming. The angel is the presiding intelligence that is always present in every life action or function.

Man is first attracted by the phenomenal side of spiritual things; then, when he gives his attention for the purpose of knowing the cause, the Lord reveals Himself. When Moses turned aside and began to investigate, he found that he was on holy ground. The forces of Spirit at the center of man's body are so intense that the outer consciousness cannot stand the current and hold itself together; absolutely pure in essence, this inner fire must be approached by the pure spiritual thought. Removing the sandals is symbolical of taking all material concepts from the understanding.

The Spirit of the Lord has been evolving in the subconsciousness, incarnation after incarnation. This I AM was the moving factor in Abraham, Isaac, and Jacob--the Lord is present in all.

Egypt is strictly material consciousness. It pertains to the physical sense of life, the corporeal organism. Canaan is life and substance in a radiant state; here Spirit finds its natural expression. The thoughts that belong in the radiant body have become slaves of material sense, and the higher self, the Lord, would set them free. But to do this the higher understanding must become part of their consciousness. All things are created by and through certain states of mind or consciousness. The higher spiritual consciousness is infused into the mortal or personal consciousness. Personal I must take on supreme I AM. When this is first experienced there is a feeling of inefficiency. But the Lord's promise to be present under all circumstances is a mighty inner assurance of spiritual law and order.

Christian metaphysicians have learned by experience the power of words and thoughts sent forth in the name of the supreme I AM. The word of the Lord spoken by naturally weak men has produced marvelous results, because they set their minds not on their own weak ideas of man and his abilities, but upon the mightiness of the great I AM. The Lord God, speaking through them, does the work of the Master. "I speak not from myself: but the Father abiding in me [supreme I AM] doeth his works."

Moses and Pharaoh represent two forces at work in the consciousness--especially that part of it pertaining to the body. Moses represents the evolutionary force of new ideas that have grown in the subconsciousness; these forces struggle with the old states of limitation and material ignorance, trying to rise out of their depths into a higher life expression. The rising into a higher life is symbolized by the man Moses, whose name means "drawn out." As a child he was drawn out of the water, a negative yet universal condition of life evolution. Pharaoh represents the force that rules the body under the material regime. The Lord is the universal law, whose impulse is always upward and onward. It is found, by those who are undergoing the regenerative process that in the story of Moses the Scriptures symbolically describe, that these two forces are constantly at work in consciousness, one holding to old ideas and striving to perpetuate them in form, and the other idealizing the new and bending every effort to break away from material bondage and rise above its limitations. Paul says, "The flesh lusteth against the Spirit, and the Spirit against the flesh." Looking at it from the personal standpoint, we are likely to cry out in this struggle, "Who shall deliver me out of the body of this death?" But as philosophers, with an understanding of the law of change, we balance ourselves between these two forces and let them work out under the equilibrium of the universal preserver of all forms, the Lord.

Here is consolation for those who chafe under the whips and cords of the regenerative law. Because of their many defeats and the snail's pace at which they progress, they think that they are off the track. However, they are not. They will attain their good if they persevere and patiently wait upon the Lord. If the energy of Spirit were instantly poured into the body it would destroy the organism because of the impurities of the flesh, but, by and through the evolutionary adjustment of the natural man, the Spirit not only preserves but raises up the substance and life of the organism. The purpose of our spiritual thoughts (the Children of Israel) down in the body (Egypt) is to raise up the body--gradually to infuse into it a more enduring life and substance. At the same time our spiritual thoughts get the substance (corn) that is to sustain their existence in the world of phenomena.

When you affirm the spirituality of the body and yearn for release from its bondage, you are making demands on Pharaoh. In fear that he will all at once lose his hold on life, he hardens his heart, and sometimes the Lord, the universal law of equilibrium, hardens it for him. Then there seems a failure to attain that which you have tried to demonstrate. But a step has been taken in the evolution of the body, and you will find that you are gradually becoming stronger, both physically and spiritually.

There are climaxes in this refining trend of the consciousness, and in these we make a signal effort and realize a great uplift. "Jewels of silver, and jewels of gold" represent wisdom and love in an external sense, which are to be asked or demanded by the Children of Israel. (The word "borrow" in the Authorized Version is an error.) The meaning is that we are to affirm that all wisdom and all love, even in their most external manifestations, are spiritual. By so affirming we put Spirit into control both within and without ourselves, and do away with the external ruling power, which is the "first-born in the land of Egypt." The first-born of every state of consciousness is the personal I. When the flood of light from the universal is let in through our declaration of the one wisdom and one love, this I of every mortal state of consciousness is slain, and there is a "great cry throughout all the land of Egypt."

We may mentally have made our truest statements and seemingly complied with all the law, yet Pharaoh does not let our people go--there is no realization of freedom in the body consciousness. Another step toward freedom is necessary, which is typified in the feast of the Passover.

In every change of consciousness on the physical plane, there is a breaking down of some cells and a building up of other cells to take their place. Mentally this is denial and affirmation, and this process in the body is the result of these two movements in the mind which have occurred at some previous period. We let go of the animal life and take hold of the spiritual by giving up consciously to this "passing over" process, which takes place when the old cells are replaced by the new. The lamb that is killed and eaten in the night represents giving up the animal life in the obscurity of the mortal body. The command is that the lamb shall be without spot or blemish, and be wholly eaten after being roasted with fire. This refers to the complete transmutation and surrender of the human life after it has been purified by the fires of regeneration. Fire represents the positive, affirmative state of mind, as opposed to the negative or watery state. The Children of Israel were commanded not to let the lamb be "sodden." "Sodden" is an Old English past participle of "seethe." We are not to allow the life in our organism to simmer and stew with the worries and negative words of mortality, but we must set it afire with strong words of absolute Truth.

This is to show us that there must be a physical as well as a mental sacrifice, and that "the whole congregation of the children of Israel" will join in it; that is, the whole consciousness of spiritual desire will acquiesce. Many metaphysicians think that it is not necessary to change the habits of the sense man--that one has only to keep one's thoughts right and the flesh will thereby be wholly regulated. But the Scripture teaches that there must be a conscious physical change before the complete demonstration in mind and body is manifest. Thoughts work themselves out in things, and we get the full result of their work only when we follow them consciously every step of the way and help them along. Watch your thoughts as they work their way through your organism, and, if you find that some pure thought of spiritual life is striving to free the life in the appetites and passions of your physical Egypt, help it by consciously elevating that life to the open door of your mind. This is typified by putting the blood of the lamb on the two side posts and on the lintel of the door of the house. Do not be afraid to express your inner life to the Lord, for only in perfect candor and childlike innocence can man come under the protection of the divine law.

So long as there is a hidden, secret use of God's life in our habits and ways that we are not willing that all should know, just so long will the bondage of Egypt's Pharaoh hold us in its clutches. The whole man must be pure, and his inner life must be made so open and free that he will not be afraid to blazon it upon the very doors of his house where all who pass may read. Then the Lord will execute His judgment, and those who have purified the life of the lamb of the body will escape the messenger or thought of death.

Chapter XI

Zeal- Enthusiasm

THE EGO, the free I, the imperishable and unchangeable essence of Spirit, which man is, chooses every state of consciousness and every condition in which it functions. It does not create the basic substances that enter into these mental structures, for these substances have been provided from the beginning, but it gives form and character to them in consciousness, as men build houses of lumber, stone, or whatever material they may choose in the manifest.

These mental states are all constructed under the dynamic power of the great universal impulse that lies back of all action--enthusiasm or zeal. Zeal is the mighty force that incites the winds, the tides, the storms; it urges the planet on its course, and spurs the ant to great exertion. To be without zeal is to be without the zest of living. Zeal and enthusiasm incite to glorious achievement in every aim and ideal that the mind conceives. Zeal is the impulse to go forward, the urge behind all things. Without zeal stagnation, inertia, death would prevail throughout the universe. The man without zeal is like an engine without steam or an electric motor without a current. Energy is zeal in motion, and energy is the forerunner of every effect.

If you desire a thing, you set in motion the machinery of the universe to gain possession of it, but you must be zealous in the pursuit in order to attain the object of your desire. Desire goes before every act of your life, hence it is good. It is the very essence of good; it is God Himself in a phase of life. When they called Jesus good, He said: “Why callest thou me good? none is good save one, even God.” So the universal desire for achievement, giving its mighty impulse to all things, is divinely good. Divine enthusiasm is no respecter of persons or things. It makes no distinctions. It moves to new forms of expression even that which appears corrupt. It tints the cheek of the innocent babe, gleams from the eye of the treacherous savage, and lights in purity the face of the saint.

Some have named this universal life impulse God, and have left the impression that it is all of God and that all the attributes of God-Mind are therefore involved as a conscious entity in every situation where life is manifest. In this they lack discrimination. God’s Spirit goes forth in mighty streams of life, love, substance, and intelligence. Each of these attributes is conscious only of the principle involved in it and in the work that it has to do. Though it is man’s mission to combine these inexhaustible potentialities under divine law, man is free to do as he wills. But the divine law cannot be broken, and it holds man responsible for the result of his labors. Man cannot corrupt the inherent purity of any of God’s attributes, but he can unwisely combine them in states of consciousness that bring dissatisfaction and incompleteness to him. It is his privilege to learn the harmonious relations of all the chords of life and to arrange them on the staff of existence with such masterly art that no discord can be detected. Then life becomes to him a song of joy, and he absolutely knows that in its ultimate all is good.

Never repress the impulse, the force, the zeal welling up within you. Commune with it in spirit and praise it for its great energy and efficiency in action. At the same time analyze and direct its course. As zeal alone, it is without intelligence or discretion as to results. As Jesus taught His disciples and combined their various talents, so every man must grow in wisdom and zeal. You are not to repress but to guide the spirit of enthusiasm, which in co-operation with wisdom will bring you happiness and satisfaction.

Zeal is the affirmative impulse of existence; its command is “Go forward!” Through this impulse man forms many states of consciousness that he ultimately tires of. They may have served a good purpose in their day in the grand scheme of creation, but as man catches sight of higher things zeal urges him forward to their attainment.

Let your zeal be tempered with wisdom. “The zeal of thy house hath eaten me up” means that the zeal faculty has become so active intellectually that it has consumed the vitality and left nothing for spiritual growth. One may even become so zealous for the spread of Truth as to bring on nervous prostration. "Take time to be holy." Turn a portion of your zeal to do God's will to the establishing of His kingdom within you. Do not put all your enthusiasm into teaching, preaching, healing, and helping others; help yourself. Many enthusiastic spiritual workers have let their zeal to demonstrate Truth to others rob them of the power to demonstrate Truth for themselves. Do not let your zeal run away with your judgment. Some persons get so fired with zeal when they first tackle a job that they quickly grow tired, and eventually get "fired" from every job that they tackle.

Watch the first pull of a giant locomotive; note how it slowly but steadily moves forward, almost by inches at first but gradually increasing, until its mile-long train swiftly disappears in the distance.

Man is a dynamo of pent-up power, but he needs judgment in its use. Even love (John), the "greatest thing in the world," is linked in the twelve-power integration of Jesus with James (judgment). Jesus called these two brothers "Sons of thunder," comparing the effect of their combined power to the tremendous vibrations set up by unrestrained electrical energy. Judgment says to Love, "Look before you leap." Do not let unselfish zeal and enthusiasm for the loved one run away with your judgment. Remember that these two are brothers and that you should sit on the throne of your I AM dominion, with love on the right hand and judgment on the left, judging the twelve tribes of Israel. In these symbols we see portrayed the poise and mastery of regenerated man, directing and disciplining all his thought-people in wisdom and in love.

Even doctors are beginning to take notice of the emotional contests that take place between love and wisdom in our nervous system. Some of them say that indigestion may be caused by the disturbance that our emotions cause in the delicate nerve aggregations at the solar plexus, and that permanent stomach troubles may result. Metaphysicians have always taught that the contending vibrations or "thunder" between love and wisdom cause not only acute but chronic diseases of stomach and heart.

Heart says, "I love," and Wisdom says, "But you can't have what you love"; contention follows, and night and day the nerves are pounded by the warring emotions.

Love disappointed may lower the vitality to the vanishing point, while some physical disease is blamed.

Innumerable combinations of thoughts and their attendant emotions are constantly sending their vibrations or "thundering" to various parts of the body through the nerve cables that lead out from the many ganglionic centers.

Jesus had two apostles named Simon, but they represent different talents or faculties of man's mind. Simon Peter represents receptivity from above, and Simon the Cananaean represents receptivity from below. Simon means "hearing" and Canaan means "zeal." The Canaanites dwelt in the lowlands, so we know that the faculty designated by Simon the Cananaean has its origin in the body consciousness.

But the receptivity to, and the zeal for, the truth that were manifested by Simon the Cananaean were lifting him to spiritual consciousness. This is symbolized in Acts 1:13, where it is written,"And whenthey were come in, they went up into the upper chamber, where they were abiding." Among them is mentioned "Simon the Zealot."

To grow spiritually we should always be careful to exercise our zeal in spiritual ways, since Christians are apt to fall into commercial ways in carrying forward the Lord's work. We should remember that Jesus said, "God is spirit: and they that worship him must worship in spirit and truth." When Jesus cast the money-changers out of the Temple His disciples remembered that it was written, "Zeal for thy house shall eat me up." In this act Jesus was casting the commercial bargaining thoughts out of His body temple. This is explained in the context, John 2:18. The Jews said, "What sign showest thou unto us, seeing that thou doest these things? Jesus answered and said unto them, Destroy this temple, and in three days I will raise it up . . . But he spake of the temple of his body."

Whatever takes place in the world about us has its counterpart in some thought process in our body.

Every invention of man is a duplication of some activity in the human body. The explosion of gasoline in an automobile cylinder is copied from the explosion of nerve substance in the cell centers of the body. The nerve fluid is conducted to a nerve chamber, corresponding to an automobile combustion chamber, where it is electrified and the energy liberated. In the human body spiritual zeal, that is, enthusiasm, electrifies the nerve substance, which breaks forth into energy. Thoughts build nerve and brain centers that serve as distributors of the vital substance manufactured in the body. The vitamins in the food that we eat are stored up by the body chemistry and liberated in thought and action.

Every thought and emanation of mind liberates some of this stored substance. We, the controlling intelligence, with our conscious mind direct these processes in a manner quite similar to that employed by the driver of an automobile.

An automobile driver should be familiar with the mechanism of his car. But in the great majority of cases the driver knows merely enough to perform a few mechanical motions, and the car does the rest.

So the mass of humans know but little about the delicate mind-and-body interaction. They perform a few necessary superficial acts, call in the doctor when anything goes wrong, and in the end dump the old "boat" at the junk pile.

Extraordinary zeal in the accomplishment of some ideal develops what is called genius. Jesus of Nazareth was undoubtedly the greatest genius that this earth has ever developed. He is not usually named among the geniuses of the earth, because He was a genius of such transcendental character that He is classed with the gods. He did manifest the mind of God as no other has ever done, yet He was a man, and herein lies His genius:

In His humanity He developed extraordinary ability in spiritual wisdom, love, and power. There have been men who have told us about God, but none who have demonstrated the wisdom and power of God as Jesus did. His zeal in doing the will of God made Him a spiritual genius in human form.

Like others who manifest original genius, Jesus got His genius from within. He was not known to have been taught in the theological schools of His day, yet He exhibited a mental acumen and understanding of religion that astonished His associates. They exclaimed in effect, "Where did this man get wisdom, never having studied."

Genius is the accumulated zeal of the individual in some chosen field of life action. The idea that God has arbitrarily endowed some persons with abilities superior to others is not good logic, and makes God a partisan. God has no favorites, notwithstanding the fact that the Scriptures sometimes so interpret Him. "God is no respecter of persons." "This is my beloved Son, in whom I am well pleased," is the ideal or spiritual man, the Messiah, the Christ man, who is the pattern given to every man to follow.

However, we see on every hand evidences of pronounced diversity in human character, and, looking at life superficially, we think that God has given advantages in mind, body, and affairs to some men that He has not given to others. But what we see with the eye of flesh is only the physical manifestation of man. Spirit and mind must be taken into consideration and become factors in our reasoning before we can know a man and properly estimate the whole man.

The body represents but one third of man's being. Man is spirit, soul, and body. The spirit is that in man which says I AM, and has existed from eternity. Spirit is potential man--soul is demonstrated man. Soul is man's memory, conscious and subconscious. We have carried along in our subconscious mind the memory of every experience that we have had since we began to think and act for ourselves. The soul is the mind, and the mind is the man.

The race to which we belong on this planet began thinking and acting in self-consciousness many millions of years ago. God alone knows the exact age of every man. Jesus said, "The very hairs of your head are all numbered."

Every experience, every achievement, every failure, and every success is remembered and stored up in the subconscious mind. A new soul is not created with every physical birth. A physical birth simply means that a soul is taking on another body. Every man inhabiting this earth and the psychic realms immediately surrounding it has gone through this process of dying and being reincarnated many times. You who read these lines have had experience as a thinking, free-acting soul for millions of years, instead of the score or three score that mortal man usually counts. Emerson said, "Be not deceived by dimples and curls; that child is a thousand years old."

Then the question arises, "Do we always get the fruit of our earthly acts in some future earthly life?" Certainly, "Whatsoever a man soweth, that shall he also reap." Here in this earth is the place of harvest. When a man relinquishes his hold on brain and nervous system, he gives up the only avenue through which he can adequately express himself.

So death is the great enemy to be overcome, as taught in Scripture. Death came into the world through Adamic ignorance, and it must go out through Christ understanding.

Genius is the breaking forth of the accumulated achievements of a man in that field of activity for which he has been very zealous in many incarnations. Mozart at the age of four played the organ without instruction. Where did he get such marvelous musical ability? A history of his soul would show that he had cultivated music for ages, carrying from one incarnation to another his zeal for the harmony of sound, until he became the very soul of music.

The genius of Shakespeare was the accumulated experience of a man who had been poet and philosopher since the "morning stars sang together."

Let no man think that he can retire from living. Do not shirk the responsibilities of life. You have made them and you can unmake them. A way of escape has been provided for every one of us. That way is to overcome mistakes by incorporating into mind and heart the attributes of the Christ Mind. your attention for a moment at the base of your brain and quietly affirm that infinite energy and intelligence are pouring forth in zeal--enthusiasm. Then follow in imagination a set of motor nerves that lead out from the medulla to the eyes, affirming all the time the presence and power of energy and intelligence now manifesting in your eyes.

For the ears affirm energy and intelligence, adding, "Be you open."

For the nose affirm energy and intelligence, adding, "The purity of Spirit infolds you."

For the mouth carry the life current to the root of the tongue, with the thought of freedom.

At the root of the tongue is situated the throne of another disciple, Philip. When you carry the zeal current from its medulla center and connect it with the throne of Philip, a mighty vibration is set up that affects the whole sympathetic nervous system. In this treatment you will strengthen your voice, revitalize your teeth, and indirectly impart energy to your digestion.

It was at Cana of Galilee, the nerve center in the throat, that Jesus turned water into wine. Metaphysically this miracle is accomplished when we in spirit realize that the union (wedding) of the fluid life of the body with the spiritual life at this power center makes a new element, symbolized by wine.

When the chemistry of the body and the dynamics of the mind are united, a third element is brought forth, and man feels that, "in Christ, he is a new creature."

Chapter XII

Renunciation

ALL CHRISTIANS who have had experiences variously described as "change of heart," "salvation," "conversion," and "sanctification" will admit that, before they experienced the great change of consciousness represented by these names, they had been "convicted of sin" or had determined to give up the ways of the world and do the will of God. The sinners most open to reform are those who sin in the flesh. The hardest to reach are the self-satisfied moralists or religionists. Jesus said to such, "Verily I say unto you, that the publicans and the harlots go into the kingdom of God before you." One who is living up to man-made morals or religious standards is not repentant, and he makes no room in his mind for new and higher ideals of life and Truth. Unless our repentance is accompanied by sacrifice we are still in our sins. "Apart from shedding of blood there is no remission." The blood represents the life, and when the life of the flesh is given up, the beasts of the body are literally killed and their blood or life carries away the dead cells. This was symbolically illustrated by Jesus when He sent the demons or evils into the swine (Matt. 8:32).

A change of mind effects a corresponding change in the body. If the thoughts are lifted up, the whole organism is raised to higher rates of vibration. If the system has been burdened with congestion of any kind, a higher life energy will set it into universal freedom. But there must be a renunciation or letting go of old thoughts before the new can find place in the consciousness. This is a psychological law, which has its outer expression in the intricate eliminative functions of the body.

As the physiologist studies the body, so the metaphysician studies the mind. It is true that some metaphysicians are not careful students. They often jump to conclusions, just as the ancient physiologists made wild guesses about the character of the bodily organs; but the majority of those who work with the inner forces get an understanding that conforms in fundamentals to the discoveries of other metaphysicians in the same field of work. The careful modern metaphysician does not arrive at his conclusions through speculation; he analyzes and experiments with the operations of his own mind until he discovers laws that govern mind action universally.

All those who go deep enough into the study of the mind agree perfectly on fundamentals, one of which is that the universe originated in mind, was projected into action by thought, and is being sustained by mind power. Self-analysis reveals the manner in which the individual mind acts, and this action is the key to all action in the small and the great, in the microcosm and the macrocosm, in man and in God. Another point of agreement is that thoughts are things, that they are ideas projected into form, partaking of the nature of the thinker.

Metaphysicians make a sharp distinction between the realm of ideas, which is Spirit, and the realm of thought, which is mind. Thoughts act in a realm just above, around, and within the material. They have but one degree more of freedom than matter. Thoughts have a four-dimensional capacity, while things have but three. Yet thoughts are limited to the realm in which they function, and man's consciousness, being made up of thoughts, is of like character. Thus it is possible to overload the mind, as one overloads the stomach. Thoughts must be digested in a manner similar to the way in which food is digested. An eagerness to gain knowledge without proper digestion and assimilation ends in mental congestion. The mind, like the bowels, should be open and free. It is reported that Lyman Beecher said to a friend, whom he was bidding good-by, "Worship God, be even-tempered, and keep your bowels open." It is found by metaphysicians that praise and thanksgiving are laxatives of efficiency and that their cleansing work not only frees the mind of egotism but also cleanses the body of effete matter.

Thoughts are things; they occupy space in the mental field. A healthy state of mind is attained and continued when the thinker willingly lets go the old thoughts and takes on the new. This is illustrated by the inlet and the outlet of a pool of water. Stop the inlet, and the pool goes dry. Close the natural outlet, and the pool stagnates, or, like the Dead Sea, it crystallizes its salts until they preserve everything that they touch.

The action of the mind on the body is, in some of its aspects, similar to that of water on the earth. Living old thoughts over and over keeps the inlet of the new thoughts closed. Then begins crystallization--which materia medica has named arteriosclerosis. The cause is supposed to be some other disease, such as syphilis, which is classed as one of the most important of the primal causes of arteriosclerosis. Metaphysicians recognize syphilis as secondary in the realm of effects, and they ask, "What causes syphilis?" The cause is the uncontrolled enjoyment of sex sensation without asking or caring to know the object of that function in human consciousness. It would seem that in this respect the animals were under better discipline than men and women.

The enjoyment of the pleasures of sensation without wisdom's control may be compared to riding in a runaway automobile for the pleasure of the swift pace, wholly disregarding the crash that is sure to follow. But to take away man's freedom would delay his attaining the "son of God" degree, which is open to him when he learns to make a lawful use of the attributes of Being; consequently he must acquire more wisdom and self-control. Tuberculosis, syphilis, cancers, tumors, and the many other ills of the flesh are evidences that nature has been outraged and is protesting and striving to free itself from its unhappy condition.

Every cell of the body is enveloped in soul or thought, and its initial impulse is to conform to the divine-natural law. When this law is not observed by the will of man and cells are reduced to the slavery of lust, they combine with other cells of like condition, and, rather than submit longer to the debased condition, they destroy the organism. But the destruction of the cell as matter does not destroy it on the mental plane; the mental entity survives, and again seeks to carry out the great law of soul evolution that was implanted in it from the beginning. Thus the repeated incarnations of the soul--not only of the soul cell but of the great aggregation of cells known as man--are found to be a fact that explains the continuity of traits of mind and body handed down from generation to generation. It is not in the flesh that we inherit, but in the thoughts of the flesh. The flesh has returned to dust, but its memories endure until a higher mind power cleanses and lifts them to purer states of consciousness.

It is related in Genesis that when fleeing from the cities of Sodom and Gomorrah, which God was destroying, Lot's wife looked back, and "became a pillar of salt." Salt is a preservative, corresponding to memory. When we remember the pleasures of the senses and long for their return, we preserve or "salt" the sense desire. This desire will manifest somewhere, sometime, unless the memory is dissolved through renunciation. The desire for sensation in the flesh in one incarnation may be expressed in the next in a strong desire for personal love. Having become subconscious, it works in the subcenters of the organism in a fever of anxiety to attain its object, and it may be named consumption, or some other cell-consuming disease.

Modern medical science has traced nearly all the ills of the body to micro-organisms. The popular remedy is to introduce into the body germs much like the disease germs but of weakened power. The body, thereupon, in self-defense generates in the blood stream that which counteracts or neutralizes the disease, and renders the body immune to severe attack. If the patient is to continue to be immune, it logically follows that he must continue to have the disease germs in his system, because if they should desert him he would again be open to attack. Typhoid fever is quieted, or forestalled, by turning loose in the system good-natured typhoid germs. But the cause is not removed, and some who follow up such cases say that serums are spreading various forms of disease, and in various ways making the human family less virile. The writer knows of one instance where a healthy boy was vaccinated. A few months later he was attacked by tuberculosis of the hip, which the doctors said was caused by impure blood. All of this goes to show that the right kind of serum has not yet been discovered by medical science and that diseases are not cured by serums but are merely diverted, and eventually break out in other forms.

We see that such bacteriologists as Koch and Pasteur have merely a clue to the real serum, which is the new life stream opened to man by Jesus Christ. It is true that the bodies of men are being destroyed by disease germs and that the palliative methods of bacteriology may enable us to live a little longer in the body, but until the Christ remedy is applied no real healing has been done. Destructive germs are the creations of destructive thoughts, and until the specific thought is found, physicists will continue to search for the healing serum. Their search is evidence that such a serum exists.

Destructive thinking separates soul and body, and, when the separation is complete, bacteria take up the work and distribute the body wreckage over the earth. If the body were left intact, this planet would soon become the abode of mummies, and the dead would crowd out the living. Then, so long as people continue to die, it is well that microbes make their bodies of some use.

Imperious Caesar, dead and turn'd to clay,
Might stop a hole to keep the wind away.

When the body becomes locally infested with bacterial thoughts and separates from the higher self, a forced removal of the adverse colony, by surgery, sometimes gives at least temporary relief. Man is the dominant thinking and character-giving force of the earth, and he has made it a place of desolation when it should be a paradise. Because of his lust, anger, arrogance, and ignorance, man has been tormented by pests, storms, and earthquakes.

Tradition says that in the dim past this planet's mental atmosphere was charged with the thoughts of men and women who exercised the power of mind in lust, arrogance, and ambition until extreme measures had to be restored to by the planetary God.

This story (which is merely a legend) relates that perversion of nature and her innocent life energies began cycles ago, when man in the first exuberance of psychic power built up a priestly hierarchy in the ancient continent of Atlantis. These masters of black magic dominated the world and dispossessed the cosmic mind. Extraordinary measures of safety for the whole race became necessary, and the higher powers planned and carried out the destruction of the continent Atlantis and all its people. The very soil of the continent which these occultists occupied had become saturated with lust and selfishness, and it was condemned as unfit to remain a part of the parent planet. The corrupted soil was scooped out of what is now the Atlantic Ocean and thrown off into space, where it became the lifeless mass known as the moon. The earth reeled like a drunkard under this terrible surgical operation, and still wabbles out of true perpendicular, the result of the shock and of the removal of so large a part of its body. Before this catastrophe occurred, a tropical climate extended to the very poles. The remains of tropical plants and animals are found in the frigid zones today, mute evidences that a great and sudden change has at some time taken place in the planet's relation to the sun. The withdrawal of warmth from the poles resulted in an unnatural coldness that congealed rain into snow and ice, which slowly piled up at the poles until they capped the earth to a great depth. This brought about the great glacial period, which lasted thousands of years, a reminder of which we get in icy blasts from the north, with months of cold and snow. However, the earth is slowly regaining its equilibrium and will in due season be restored to its pristine golden age, and all the desert places will bloom as the rose. So runs the tradition.

But how about the states of consciousness that man has built up and from which he would be free? No one can play fast and loose with God. What one builds one must care for. What man forms that is evil he must unform before he can take the coveted step up the mountain of the ideal. Here enters the factor that dissolves the structures that are no longer useful; this factor in metaphysics is known as denial. Denial is not, strictly speaking, an attribute of Being as principle, but it is simply the absence of the impulse that constructs and sustains. When the ego consciously lets go and willingly gives up its cherished ideals and loves, it has fulfilled the law of denial and is again restored to the Father's house.

As all desire is fulfilled through the formative word, so all denial must be accomplished in word or conscious thought. This is the mental cleansing symbolized by water baptism. In a certain stage of his problem man makes for himself a state of consciousness in which selfishness dominates. Personal selfishness is merely an excess of self-identity. This inflation of the ego must cease, that a higher field of action may appear. One who has caught sight of higher things is desirous of making unity with them. That unity must be orderly and according to the divine procession of mind. One who is housed in the intellect through desire may be ushered into the realm of Spirit by zeal. The first step is a willingness to let go of every thought that holds the ego on the plane of sense. This willingness to let go is symbolical of John the Baptist's crying in the wilderness, denying himself the luxuries of life, living on locusts and wild honey, and wearing skins for clothing.

The personalities of Scripture represent mental attitudes in the individual. John the Baptist and the Pharisees symbolize different phases of the intellect. John is willing to give up the old and is advocating a general denial through water baptism-mental cleansing. The Pharisees cling to tradition, custom, and Scripture, and refuse to let go. John represents the intellect in its transition from the natural to the spiritual plane. The Pharisees have not entered this transition, but cling to the old and defend it by arguments and Scripture quotations. Jesus, who represents the spiritual consciousness, does not take the Pharisees into account as a link in His chain, but of John He says: "Among them that are born of women there hath not arisen a greater than John the Baptist: yet he that is but little in the kingdom of heaven is greater than he." Jesus recognizes that the mental attitude represented by John is a prophecy of greater things, in fact the most desirable mental condition for the intellect on its way to attainment, yet not to be compared with the mental state of those who have actually come into the consciousness of Spirit.

Every man who cries out for God is John the Baptist crying in the wilderness. You who are satiated with the ways of the flesh man, and are willing to give up his possessions and pleasures, are John. The willingness to sacrifice the things of sense starts you on the road to the higher life, but you do not begin to taste its sweets until you actually give up consciously the sense things that your heart has greatly desired.

There are many phases of this passing over from John to Jesus, and some involve unnecessary hardships. The ascetic takes the route of denial so energetically that he starves his powers instead of transforming them. Some Oriental suppliants for divine favor castigate their flesh in many ways, starve their bodies, slash their flesh, and then salt it; they maltreat the body until it becomes a piece of inanimate clay that the soul can vacate until the birds build their nests in the hair of its head. This is Oriental denial, atrophy of the senses. Some Occidental metaphysicians are trying to imitate these agonizing methods of discipline, but in the mind rather than in the body.

John the Baptist stands for the mental attitude that believes that because the senses have fallen into ignorant ways they are bad and should be killed out. There is a cause for every mental tangent, and that which would kill the sense man, root and branch, has the thought of condemnation as its point of departure from the line of harmony. In John it seemed a virtue, in that he condemned his own errors, but this led to his condemnation of Herod, through which he lost his head. We learn from this that condemnation is a dangerous practice from any angle.

The intellect is the Adam man that eats of the tree of good and evil. Its range of observation is limited, and it arrives at its conclusions by comparison. It juggles with two forces, two factors--positive and negative, good and evil, God and Devil. Its conclusions are the result of reasoning based on comparison, hence limited. The intellect, judging by appearances, concludes that existence is a thing to be avoided. The intellect, beholding the disaster and the misery wrought by the misuse of men's passions, decides that they should be crushed out by starvation. This is the origin of asceticism, the killing out, root and branch, of every appetite and passion, because in the zeal of action they have gone to excess.

Yet John the Baptist has a very important office in the development of man from intellectual to spiritual consciousness. As Jesus said:

"This is he, of whom it is written, Behold, I send my messenger before thy face, Who shall prepare thy way before thee."

Thus John the Baptist is the forerunner of Spirit. He stands for the perception of Truth which prepares the way for Spirit through a letting go of narrow beliefs, and a laying hold of divine ideas.

The beliefs that you and your ancestors have held in mind have become thought currents so strong that their course in you can be changed only by your resolute decision to entertain them no longer. They will not be turned out unless the ego through whose domain they run decides positively to adopt means of casting them out of his consciousness, and at the same time erects gates that will prevent their inflow from external sources. This is done by denial and affirmation; the denial always comes first. The John the Baptist attitude must begin the reformation. Man must be willing to receive the cleansing of Spirit before the Holy Ghost will descend upon him. Whoever is not meek and lowly in the presence of Spirit is not yet ready to receive its instruction.

This obedient, receptive state means much to him who wants to be led into the ways of the supreme good. It means that he must have but one source of life, one source of truth, and one source of instruction; he must be ready to give up every thought that he has imbibed in this life, and must be willing to begin anew, as if he had just been born into the world a little, ignorant, innocent babe. This means so much more than people usually conceive that it dawns on the mind very slowly.

All who sincerely desire the leading of Spirit acquiesce readily in the theoretical statement of the necessity of humility and childlikeness, but when it comes to the detailed demonstration many are non-plused. This is just as true among metaphysicians as among orthodox Christians. Spirit will find a way to lead you when you have freely and fully dedicated yourself to God, and you will be led in a path just a little different from that of anyone else. Your teaching has been in generalities, so when Spirit in its office as an individual guide shows you Truth different from that which you have been taught, you may object. If, for instance, you have been taught to ignore the body with all its passions and appetites, and Spirit in its instruction shows you that you are to recognize these appetites and passions as your misdirected powers, what are you going to do about it?

There can be but one course for the obedient devotee. If you have surrendered all to omnipresent wisdom, you must take as final what it tells you. You will find that its guidance is that right course for you and, in the end, that it was the only course that you could possibly have taken.

All things are manifestations of the good. Man in his spiritual identity is the very essence of good, and he can do no wrong. He can in his experience misuse the powers placed at his disposal by the Father, but he can do no permanent evil. He always has recourse to Spirit, which forgives all his transgressions and places him on the right road, a new man, when he willingly gives up his own way and as a little child asks to be led. Then comes the redemption of the appetites and passions, which the ignorant intellect has pronounced evil and has attempted to kill out by starvation and repression. This does not mean that the indulgence of appetites and passions is to be allowed in the old, demoralizing way, but it means that they are to be trained anew under the direction of Spirit.

John the Baptist represents the attitude of spiritual receptivity that awaits the higher way as a little child awaits the helping hand of a parent. It is not the arbitrary disciplinarian, but the loving, tender kindergarten teacher, that illustrates in visible life the intricate problems that perplex the mind. When man is receptive and obedient, giving himself unreservedly up to Spirit and to receiving its guidance without antagonism, he is delighted with the possibilities that are disclosed to him in the cleansing of mind and body. He then begins to realize what Jesus meant when He said: "If any man would come after me, let him deny himself, and take up his cross, and follow me."

The cross is not a burden, as commonly understood, but is a symbol of the forces in man adjusted in their right relation. The body of Jesus was lifted up and nailed to the cross, which indicates that the physical man must be lifted into the harmony of Spirit and adjusted to its four-dimensional plane, represented by the four branches of the crosstree.

Man thinks in the fourth dimension, but his body, in its present fleshly consciousness, can express in three dimensions only. Hence we must cleanse our thoughts by denying materiality. Then the flesh will become radiant ether with power to penetrate all so-called material substance. But before this can be done the mind of the man must become John the Baptist--it must be cleansed by the waters of denial, and the old material ideas must be put away forever.

If you are clinging to any idea that in any way prevents your eyes from seeing the millennium here and now, you are a Pharisee; you are crying, "Beelzebub," whenever you say "crank" of the one who has caught sight of the spiritual mountaintops now glistening in the sun of the new age.

John the Baptist is now moving swiftly among the children of men. His cry is heard in many hearts today, and they are following him in the wilderness of sense. But the bright light of the Christ still shines in Galilee, and they who are earnest and faithful shall see it and be glad.

Those who attempt to heal the body by injecting into it a new life stream from without are attempting to do in a material way what Jesus attained spiritually. The vitality of the race was at a low ebb at His advent; He saw the necessity of a larger consciousness of life, and He knew how to inoculate the mind of everyone who would accept His method. In John 5:26 it is written, "For as the Father hath life in himself, even so gave he to the Son also to have life in himself." Life is spiritual, as everyone admits who has tried to find it in a physical laboratory. No one has even seen life in food or drink, but it is there in small degree, and it is through eating and drinking that the body absorbs the invisible life elements that physical science has named vitamins. The vitamin is the essential life within all forms and, being spiritual in character, must be spiritually discerned. We feel life's thrill in our body; by raising this consciousness of life to Christ enthusiasm, we may come to such fullness of energy that the whole life stream will be quickened and the congestions in arteries and glands swept away. "I came that they may have life, and may have it abundantly."

All spiritual metaphysicians know that the body and the blood of Jesus were purified and that each cell was energized with original spiritual substance and life, until all materiality was purged away and only the pure essence remained. This vitamin, or essence of life and substance, was sown as seed in the whole race consciousness, and whoever through faith in Christ draws to himself one of these life germs becomes inoculated to that degree with Jesus Christ quality, and not only the mind but also the body is cleansed.

"He that soweth the good seed is the Son of man; and the field is the world." Like a seed planted in soil, the word or thought germ will multiply and bring forth after its kind. "He that abideth in me, and I in him, the same beareth much fruit: for apart from me ye can do nothing."

The apostle Thaddaeus, called also Lebbaeus, carries forward the work of elimination of error thoughts from the mind and of waste food from the body.

The nerve center from which the eliminative function directs the emptying of the intestines is located deep in the lower bowels.

This center is very sensitive to thoughts about substance and all materiality. A gripping mental hold on material things will cause constipation. A relaxation of the mind and a loosening of the grip on material possessions will bring about freedom in bowel action.

The prevailing ills of the abdominal region, constipation, tumors, and the like, are caused by constriction of the whole body energy.

The faculties centering in the head are responsible for this slowing down of the life forces. The will, operating through the front brain, controls the circulation of the life force in the whole organism. A tense will, set to accomplish some personal end, keys everything to that end and puts a limitation on the activity of every other function.

The set determination to succeed in some chosen field of action, study, profession, business, or personal ambition calls most of the body energy to the head and starves the other centers.

In our schools the minds of our children are crammed with worldly wisdom, and they are spurred on to make their grades, thus constantly forcing the blood to the head and depleting its flow to the abdomen.

This overflow to the will center causes enlarged adenoids, inflamed tonsils, sinus trouble, and other ills of the head, while the abdominal region suffers with constipation and general lack of vital action.

Some persons relax in sleep and thus give the body an opportunity to recoup its depleted energy. But if the eager pace is kept up night and day, the end is nervous prostration. The remedy is relaxation of will, the letting go of personal objectives.

The strife to get on in the world is responsible for most of the ills of the flesh. Worry or anxiety about temporal needs disturbs in the body the even flow of nature's all-providing elements. Jesus warned against the tension of anxiety when He said, "Be not anxious for your life, what ye shall eat, or what ye shall drink; nor yet for your body, what ye shall put on. Is not the life more than the food, and the body than the raiment?"

A divine law has been provided for man that will meet every need when it is observed. "Seek ye first his kingdom, and his righteousness; and all these things shall be added unto you."

So we find that relaxation of the tense abdomen depends on relaxation of the tense will.

Give up your willfulness and ask that the divine will be done in you and in all your affairs. Jesus set aside His will that God's will might be done in Him. "Not my will, but thine, be done."

Chapter XIII

Generative Life

THE LAW of generation is undoubtedly the mystery of mysteries in human consciousness. Men have probed, with more or less success, nearly every secret of nature, but of the origin of life they know comparatively nothing. It is true that they have with chemical combinations simulated life, but the activity has been temporary only.

In the phenomenal world, life is the energy that propels all forms to action. Life in the body is like electricity in a motor. As the engineer directs and regulates the electricity in a motor, so the life in the body has its engineer. Life is not in itself intelligent--it requires the directive power of an entity that knows where and how to apply its force, in order to get the best results. The engineer of the life force in the body of man is the life ego; this is the consciousness of life in the organism.

The life ego is the most subtle and most variable of all the powers of man. It is an animal force, and is designated in the Bible allegory as one of the "beasts of the field." It presides over the life and generative function of the body, and because of its tendency to separate and segregate itself from the other bodily functions, it is called the "adversary." It is not essentially evil, but because of its place as the central pole of all bodily activity, its tendency is to centralize all action around its consciousness.

In its divine-natural relation, the life ego has its positive pole in the top head, which is the "heaven" of man's consciousness. When the personality gets active and begins to exercise in the higher or spiritual forces, the life ego becomes inflated with its own importance and falls from heaven (top head) to earth, or front brain. When the seventy whom Jesus had indued with spiritual power returned, they proclaimed that even the demons were subject to them. Then Jesus said, "I beheld Satan as lightning fall from heaven." Jesus was evidently quoting Isaiah, who wrote in the 14th chapter of his book (King James Version):

How art thou fallen from heaven, O Lucifer, son of the morning; how art thou cut down to the ground, which didst weaken the nations!

For thou hast said in thine heart, I will ascend into heaven, I will exalt my throne above the stars of God: I will sit upon the mount of the congregation, in the sides of the north:

I will ascend above the heights of the clouds; I will be like the Most High.

Yet thou shalt be brought down to hell, to the sides of the pit.

Jesus warned the seventy not to rejoice over their spiritual power, and added, "but rejoice that your names are written in heaven."

In order to give man a body having life in itself, God had to endow him with a focal life center, located in the generative organs. This center of activity in the organism is also the seat of sensation, which is the most subtle and enticing of all factors that enter into being. But these qualities (sensation and generation) were necessary to man's character, and without them he would not have been the complete representative, or image and likeness, of God.

God does not tempt man to break His law, but a great creative plan is being worked out in which the Deity is incarnating itself in its creation. This incarnation is called the Son of man; in man a wonderful being is in process of creation. This being is spiritual man, who will be equal with God, when he overcomes, or handles with wisdom and power, the faculties of the body. The body is the Garden of Eden.

What metaphysicians most need is a comprehension of the factors that go to make up consciousness. This requires discrimination, judgment, and self-analysis.

We talk glibly about God as life, love, intelligence, and substance, and about man as His manifestation, but when we come to describe that manifestation we "lump it off" as the product of thought.

What we now need to know is how thought groups the different attributes of Being, for on this combination depends the bringing forth of the ideal man.

We must learn to watch our consciousness, its impulses and desires, as the chemist watches his solutions. Man forms his own consciousness from the elements of God, and he alone is responsible for the results.

Consciousness is a deep subject, and to go into it exhaustively would require the writing of many books. Concisely stated, three great factors enter into every consciousness--intelligence, life, substance. The harmonious combination of these factors requires the most careful attention of the ego, because it is here that all the discords of existence arise.

In Scripture the divine life combined with divine substance is termed "the Lamb of God." This phrase carries the symbology of the Lamb's purity, innocence, and guilelessness. Its nature is to vivify with perpetual life all things that it touches. It knows only to give, give unceasingly and eternally, without restraint. It does not carry wisdom; that is another quality of Being, which man comprehends from a different part of his consciousness.

The pure life of God flows into man's consciousness through the spiritual body, and is sensed by the physical at a point in the loins. This is the "river of water of life, bright as crystal, proceeding out of the throne of God and of the Lamb," referred to in the 22d chapter of Revelation.

Only those who have come into consciousness of the spiritual body can feel this holy stream of life. When the ego has found it, and laved in its cleansing currents, the ecstasy of Elysian realms is experienced. It cannot be described, because all the sensations of the mortal consciousness are coarse, compared with its transcendent sweetness and purity.

Many feel its thrills in part in silent meditation or in religious enthusiasm, and are temporarily stimulated by its exquisite vibrations. Just here is where the danger lies for those who have not brought out the other pole of Being--intelligence.

The ego, through its recognition of this life stream, sets it flowing to every faculty. Being by nature formless, the life stream takes the mold and character of that into which it is poured. It is the servant of the ego, the I, which man is, and through his failure to recognize the divine intelligence, which should show him how to use it in the right way, he blunders ahead in his ignorance, and the Lamb of God is slain from the foundation of the world.

The greatest danger of perversion lies in the direction of the carnal thought of sex, because it is there that this pure stream has been most foully polluted by ignorance. Sex sensation has made a broken cistern of man's consciousness; for generations the life stream has been turned into this receptacle, and lust has robbed the bodies of the whole race, making them mere shells, void of life. The failing eye, the deaf ear, the festering of withering flesh, all bear testimony to this perversion of God's life.

Yet men and women, otherwise applying good reason, continue their lustful practices and at the same time wonder why God does not give them more life.

They run here and there, seeking a restoring elixir for their failing powers; they call on God for help, while they continue to squander His energy in lust.

Man is male and female, which are qualities of mind--love and wisdom. Every attempt to lower these divine attributes to the physical plane meets with disaster. It has been tried again and again in every age, and its votaries have always gone into demoralization if they persisted in trying to carry out their theories.

Yet it is not unlawful to have bodily sensations in regeneration. A change in ideas must necessarily produce a change in the body, and there is a perfect response in every center of consciousness when Spirit has been welcomed as the rightful inhabitant of the body. The marriage mystically spoken of in Scripture, and in other sacred books, takes place in the consciousness; it is a soul communion of the two-in-one, more sweet than that between the most harmoniously mated man and woman. This eliminates sex in its outer manifestation.

Persistently deny the carnal belief in sex, and realize that the life stream, which has been turned outward and named sex, is not of that character in its original purity, but is pure spiritual life.

You must cleanse this pure stream in its outward flow by destroying the carnal sense of sex. This can be done only by the power of your word. Do not kill out the life manifesting through your body by denying it away entirely; deny away the sense of impurity with which the animal ego has clothed it.

"To the pure all things are pure" does not mean that lasciviousness is pure, nor that the deifying of sexuality is pure. The purity is in knowing that behind and interior to these shadows is a pure substance that is of God, that must be seen by the eye of the pure. So long as your eye sees sex and the indulgence thereof, on any of its planes, you are not pure. You must become so mentally translucent that you see men and women as sexless beings--which they are in the spiritual consciousness.

Sex lust is the father of death. James, in the 1st chapter of his epistle, gives its history in these words: "Then the lust, which it hath conceived, beareth sin: and the sin, when it is full-grown, bringeth forth death."

Paul says, "to be carnally minded is death" (A.V.), and Jesus, in the 12th chapter of Mark, sums up the whole question in these words: "For when they shall rise from the dead [come out of the carnal consciousness], they neither marry, nor are given in marriage; but are as angels in heaven."

To desire to be instructed by God is the first step in exalting the inner life force. The sincere desire of the heart is always fulfilled by the divine law. All the woes of humanity have their root in disregard of law. Man has to deal with many factors in his "garden." The most "subtle" is the "serpent," or sense consciousness. It is not evil, as we have been taught to believe. The allegory given in the 3d chapter of Genesis plainly teaches that sensation (serpent) is a blind force, which should not be regarded as a source of wisdom. In its right relation the serpent stands upright on its tail, and forms the connecting link between the swift vibratory forces of Spirit and the slow vibrations of the flesh. "As Moses lifted up the serpent in the wilderness, even so must the Son of man be lifted up." In the body the spinal cord is the main cable of sensation, "the tree . . . in the midst of the garden," and its branches extend to all parts of the system. The "fruit" of this "tree," which the desire for sensation (serpent) urges man to eat, is the seminal fluid, which flows throughout the nervous system and is the connecting link between the mind and the body. When desire for sensation leads man to dissipate (eat) this precious "fruit" of the "tree" in his earthly garden, the whole nervous system is drained of its vitality and the spinal cord loses its capacity to conduct the higher life into the consciousness. Man feels a lack; he is "naked." Sensation is no longer a heavenly ecstasy but a fleshly sex vibration. It crawls on its "belly" and eats "dust" all the days of its life; that is, it functions in the driest, most lifeless part of man's being.

Yet sensation is a divine creation; it is part of the Lord God's formation and must find expression somewhere in the consciousness. This brings us to the root cause of that appetite which craves stimulants and goes to excess in seeking satisfaction in eating and in drinking. The cause is plainly to be seen when we understand the anatomy of mind and body. Sensation is seeking satisfaction through the appetites. By listening to this serpent of sense, man becomes sexually insane, a glutton and a drunkard.

The remedy is this: Turn away from the lusts of the flesh and seek God. Take up the problem from its spiritual standpoint. Sensation is a mental quality. It can be satisfied only by cultivation of the spiritual side of the nature. If you are a sexual drunkard, deny the power of this ungodly lust over you. Pray for the help to overcome, then affirm your own power and spiritual dominion over all the "beasts of the field" in your "garden." When you have obtained mastery over sexual intemperance, you will find the conquest of appetite easy. Simply deny all desire for material stimulants and affirm that you are satisfied with the stimulant of Spirit. Whenever the desire for the material stimulant manifests itself, say to it: You are nothing. You have no power over me or over anybody else. I am Spirit, and I am wholly satisfied by the great flood of spiritual life that now fills my being.

The result of sin is death; the truth of these words has been proven for ages. But when he was tempting her to disobey the divine law, the "adversary" said to Eve, "Ye shall not surely die." The tragedy of Eden is being enacted every day in every individual of the race, and death reigns in consequence. We may call it by any other name, but the breaking up of consciousness and the separation of spirit, soul, and body take place just the same. As Emerson said, "Behold a god in ruins." In face of the facts that God pronounced death to be the wages of sin and that the experience of the race has proved His words true, many people have listened to the "adversary" and have believed his lie. We hear them on every side saying, "Ye shall not surely die."

As the result of sin the whole human race is already "dead in trespasses and sins"; that is, the race is in a dying condition, which ends in the loss of the body. Death is not annihilation, because a resurrection has been promised.

To be "dead in trespasses and sins" is to lack realization of God, to be ignorant of His law and disobedient to it. When Jesus said, "I am the resurrection, and the life," He was telling of the power of the Christ Mind to enter the mind and the body of man as quickening Spirit to awaken the whole consciousness to the knowledge of God. This resurrecting process is now going on in many people. It is a gradual change that brings about a complete transformation of the body through renewal of the mind. Spirit, soul, and body become unified with Christ Mind, and body and soul become immortal and incorruptible. In this way death is overcome.

Those who insist that men do not die as a result of sin are building up a false hope of finding life after death. Those who understand that eternal life has been lost to the race through sin, and can be regained only through the resurrecting power of the Christ Mind in the individual, are building on the eternal foundation of Truth. Everyone must at some time come to understand that this statement is absolutely true: "He that hath the Son [consciousness of Christ] hath the life; he that hath not the Son of God hath not the life."

The belief that all the entities that speak through mediums are the spirits of dead people is not proved. The communications are so fragmentary, and usually so inferior to the natural ability of the supposed egos delivering them, that those of wide investigation doubt the authenticity of the authorship. No great literary production, great scientific discovery, or great sermon has ever come from spirits, yet the country in which it is claimed that they exist should contain all the wise people who have lived on the earth.

This theory of continuous progressive life after death contradicts the teachings of the Bible. God did not create man to die; death is the result of a transgression of law. Christianity teaches that man was created to live in his body, refining it as his thoughts unfold, and that the work of the Christ--the supermind in man--is to restore this state; that is, unite spirit, soul, and body here on earth. This must be fulfilled in the whole race, and every thought of death, or the possibility of leaving the body, must be put out of the mind.

Practical Christians object to thoughts that tend to separate soul and body, because by such thoughts is built up a consciousness that finally brings about that dissolution. It is a fact, well known to those who have deeply studied the law of Being, that death does separate spirit, soul, and body; that the communications received by spiritualists are but echoes of the soul, without its animating, inspiring, spiritual I AM; that this mentality that communicates falls in its turn into a sleep, or coma, even as the body does, until the law again brings about a union with its I AM or higher self, and the building of another physical organism takes place. This process of repeated body building by the ego continues until the man, through Christ, makes a complete union of spirit, soul, and body here on earth. This union brings all of man's powers into conjunction, and what is mystically known as the Jesus Christ man, or redeemed man, appears.

We can easily see how illogical, unwise, and futile it is to teach that man can lay off his body as a worn-out garment and, by weakly giving up and dying, go on to higher attainment. We know whereof we speak, and we must proclaim this great truth that Jesus taught: "Whosoever liveth and believeth on me [spiritual I AM] shall never die."

If God created man to die and go on to a spirit land to get his education, then it would be better for him to die in infancy and escape the hardships of life. Also, if death is part of God's law, we are defeating the law every time we attempt to escape death by trying to heal the body.

If man's birth as an infant a few years ago was the beginning of his existence, then God has performed a miracle and made an exception of man in the progressive law of development that is evident in all His other works.

The fact is--and it is well known to initiates--that spiritualists are in communication with the mentality of humanity, that is, the personal consciousness. Not having developed the superconscious mind, they do not understand the creative law. They function mentally and physically in a thought psychism that is mixed and uncertain. Their communications can all be explained in the action of the subconscious minds of the living, and the majority of mediums are uncertain as to whether they are moved by their own or some other mentality.

When man has brought his higher self into action he will see clearly the relation of spirit, soul, and body, in all phases of their action.

If you want to know all the mysteries of life, study life and put out of your mind every thought about death or the condition of the dead. Then through the law of thought formation you will build up in yourself such a strong consciousness of life that its negative (or absence) will ever be to you nonexistent. Jesus meant this when He said, "If a man keep my word, he shall never see death."

The desire to live does not cease when the body dies. The mind lives on, not in heaven or hell, but in the states of consciousness that it has cultivated in life. Mind does not change with a change of environment. Those who leave the body of matter find themselves in a body of ether, which does not respond to their desire for coarse sensations. Jesus taught in Luke 16:23 that the rich man who died was in "torment" in Hades. In the original language in which the Bible was written Hades was a term used to represent the unseen world. Those who have cultivated spiritual thoughts find themselves at death in an environment and in an ether body corresponding to their prevailing thoughts. But the very fact that they died proves that they gave up to the "adversary," that they did not attain the dominion, power, and authority of spiritual man. Consequently after a period of recreation and rest they will again take up active, overcoming life in a flesh body through reincarnation. So this process of life and death will continue until the ego overcomes sin, sickness, and death, and raises the body of flesh to the body of Spirit without the tragedy of death. "This corruptible must put on incorruption; this mortal must put on immortality."

Our theologians have not discerned man's life in its entirety--they have attempted to crowd into one physical incarnation the character that it has taken aeons to develop. As taught by Jesus, and by all spiritual teachers, the goal of man is the attainment of eternal life; the overcoming of physical death. The human race on this planet will continue to die and be reborn until it learns the law of right living, which will ultimate in a body so healthy that it will never die. Jesus demonstrated this, and He promised those who should follow Him in the regeneration that they would never see death if they should keep His words. Many Christians are getting this understanding--that they have not attained eternal life so long as they allow the body to continue in the corruption that ends in death, and they are earnestly beginning the appropriation, or eating and drinking, of the life and substance of the Lord's body, until He appears again in their regeneration organism.

The End

Prosperity

Foreword

It is perfectly logical to assume that a wise and competent Creator would provide for the needs of His creatures in their various stages of growth. The supply would be given as required and as the necessary effort for its appropriation was made by the creature. Temporal needs would be met by temporal things, mental needs by things of like character, and spiritual needs by spiritual elements. For simplification of distribution all would be composed of one primal spiritual substance, which under proper direction could be transformed into all products at the will of the operator. This is a crude yet true illustration of the underlying principles on which the human family is supplied on this earth. The Father has provided a universal seed substance that responds with magical power to the active mind of man. Faith in the increasing capacity of this seed substance, whether wrapped in visible husks or latent in invisible electrical units, always rewards man with the fruits of his labor.

The farmer may seem to get his supply from the seeds he plants, but he would never plant a seed unless he had faith in its innate capacity to increase, and that seed would never multiply without the quickening life of Spirit. Thus we see that all increase of substance depends on the quickening life of Spirit, and this fact gives us the key to mental processes that when used spiritually will greatly increase and at the same time simplify our appropriation of that inexhaustible substance which creative Mind has so generously provided.

In the following lessons we have attempted to explain man's lawful appropriation of the supplies spiritually and electrically provided by God. When we understand and adjust our mind to the realm or kingdom where these rich ideas and their electrical thought forms exist we shall experience in our temporal affairs what is called "prosperity."

We said "their electrical thought forms." Let us explain that all creative processes involve a realm of ideas and a realm of patterns or expressions of those ideas. The patterns arrest or "bottle up" the free electric units that sustain the visible thing. Thus creation is in its processes a trinity, and back of the visible universe are both the original creative idea and the cosmic rays that crystallize into earthly things. When we understand this trinity in its various activities we shall be able to reconcile the discoveries of modern science with the fundamentals of religion.

Modern science teaches us that space is heavily charged with energies that would transform the earth if they could be controlled. Sir Oliver Lodge says that a single cubic inch of the ether contains energy enough to run a forty-horse-power engine forty million years. The divergence of opinion among physicists as to the reality of the ether does not nullify the existence in space of tremendous potentialities. Sir Arthur Eddington says that about half the leading physicists assert that the ether exists and the other half deny its existence, but, in his words, of that inexhaustible substance which creative Mind has so generously provided.

In the following lessons we have attempted to explain man's lawful appropriation of the supplies spiritually and electrically provided by God. When we understand and adjust our mind to the realm or kingdom where these rich ideas and their electrical thought forms exist we shall experience in our temporal affairs what is called "prosperity."

We said "their electrical thought forms." Let us explain that all creative processes involve a realm of ideas and a realm of patterns or expressions of those ideas. The patterns arrest or "bottle up" the free electric units that sustain the visible thing. Thus creation is in its processes a trinity, and back of the visible universe are both the original creative idea and the cosmic rays that crystallize into earthly things. When we understand this trinity in its various activities we shall be able to reconcile the discoveries of modern science with the fundamentals of religion.

Modern science teaches us that space is heavily charged with energies that would transform the earth if they could be controlled. Sir Oliver Lodge says that a single cubic inch of the ether contains energy enough to run a forty-horse-power engine forty million years. The divergence of opinion among physicists as to the reality of the ether does not nullify the existence in space of tremendous potentialities. Sir Arthur Eddington says that about half the leading physicists assert that the ether exists and the other half deny its existence, but, in his words, him. Instead of a universe of blind mechanical forces Jesus showed the universe to be persuaded and directed by intelligence.

What we need to realize above all else is that God has provided for the most minute needs of our daily life and that if we lack anything it is because we have not used our mind in making the right contact with the supermind and the cosmic ray that automatically flows from it.

Chapter I

Spiritual Substance, the Fundamental Basis of the Universe

DIVINE MIND is the one and only reality. When we incorporate the ideas that form this Mind into our mind and persevere in those ideas, a mighty strength wells up within us. Then we have a foundation for the spiritual body, the body not made with hands, eternal in the heavens. When the spiritual body is established in consciousness, its strength and power is transmitted to the visible body and to all the things that we touch in the world about us.

Spiritual discernment reveals that we are now in the dawn of a new era, that the old methods of supply and support are fast passing away, and that new methods are waiting to be brought forth. In the coming commerce man will not be a slave to money. Humanity's daily needs will be met in ways that are not now thought practical. We shall serve for the joy of serving, and prosperity will flow to us and through us in streams of plenty. The supply and support that love and zeal will set in motion are not as yet largely used by man, but those who have tested their providing power are loud in their praise.

The dynamic power of the supermind in man has been sporadically displayed by men and women of every nation. It is usually connected with some religious rite in which mystery and priestly authority prevail. The so-called "common herd" are kept in darkness with respect to the source of the superhuman power of occult adepts and holy men. But we have seen a "great light" in the discovery by physical scientists that the atom conceals electronic energies whose mathematical arrangement determines the character of all the fundamental elements of nature. This discovery has disrupted the science based on the old mechanical atomic theory, but has also given Christian metaphysicians a new understanding of the dynamics back of Spirit.

Science now postulates space rather than matter as the source of life. It says that the very air is alive with dynamic forces that await man's grasp and utilization and that these invisible, omnipresent energies possess potentialities far beyond our most exalted conception. What we have been taught about the glories of heaven pales into insignificance compared with the glories of the radiant rays--popularly referred to as the "ether." We are told by science that we have utilized very meagerly this mighty ocean of ether in producing from it the light and power of electricity. The seemingly tremendous force generated by the whirl of our dynamos is but a weak dribble from a universe of energy. The invisible waves that carry radio programs everywhere are but a mere hint of an intelligent power that penetrates and permeates every germ of life, visible and invisible. Scientific minds the world over have been tremendously moved by these revolutionary discoveries, and they have not found language adequate to explain their magnitude. Although a number of books have been written by scentists, setting forth guardedly the far-reaching effects that will inevitably follow man's appropriation of the easily accessible ether, none has dared to tell the whole story. The fact is that the greatest discovery of all ages is that of physical science that all things apparently have their source in the invisible, intangible ether. What Jesus taught so profoundly in symbols about the riches of the kingdom of the heavens has now been proved true.

According to the Greek, the language in which the New Testament has come down to us, Jesus did not use the word heaven but the word heavens in His teaching. He was not telling us of the glories of some faraway place called "heaven" but was revealing the properties of the "heavens" all around us, called both "space" and "ether" by physicists. He taught not only its dynamic but also its intelligent character, and said that the entity that rules it is within man: "The kingdom of God is within you." He not only described this kingdom of the heavens in numerous parables but made its attainment by man the greatest object of human existence. He not only set this as man's goal but attained it Himself, thereby demonstrating that His teaching is practical as well as true.

The scientists tell us that the ether is charged with electricity, magnetism, light rays, X rays, cosmic rays, and other dynamic radiations; that it is the source of all life, light, heat, energy, gravitation, attraction, repulsion; in short, that it is the interpenetrating essence of everything that exists on the earth. In other words, science gives to the ether all the attractions of heaven without directly saying so. Jesus epitomized the subject when He told His followers that it was the kingdom from which God clothed and fed all His children. "Seek ye first his kingdom, and his righteousness; and all these things shall be added unto you." Science says that the electrical particles that break into light in our earth's atmosphere are also a source of all substance and matter. Jesus said that He was the substance and bread that came from the heavens. When will our civilization begin really to appropriate and use this mighty ocean of substance and life spiritually as well as physically?

This inexhaustible mind substance is available at all times and in all places to those who have learned to lay hold of it in consciousness. The simplest, shortest, and most direct way of doing this was explained when Jesus said, "Whosoever ... shall not doubt in his heart, but shall believe that what he saith cometh to pass, he shall have it." When we know that certain potent ideas exist in the invisible mind expressions, named by science both "ether" and "space" and that we have been provided with the mind to lay hold of them, it is easy to put the law into action through thought and word and deed.

"There is a tide in the affairs of men,

Which, taken at the flood, leads on to fortune," said Shakespeare. That flood tide awaits us in the cosmic spaces, the paradise of God.

The spiritual substance from which comes all visible wealth is never depleted. It is right with you all the time and responds to your faith in it and your demands on it. It is not affected by our ignorant talk of hard times, though we are affected because our thoughts and words govern our demonstration. The unfailing resource is always ready to give. It has no choice in the matter; it must give, for that is its nature. Pour your living words of faith into the omnipresent substance, and you will be prospered though all the banks in the world close their doors. Turn the great energy of your thinking toward "plenty" ideas, and you will have plenty regardless of what men about you are saying or doing.

God is substance, but if by this statement we mean that God is matter, a thing of time or condition, then we should say that God is substanceless. God is not confined to that form of substance which we term matter. God is the intangible essence of that which man has formed into and named matter. Matter is a mental limitation of that divine substance whose vital and inherent character is manifest in all life expression.

God substance may be conceived as God energy, or Spirit light, and "God said, let there be light, and there was light." This is in harmony with the conclusions of some of the most advanced physicists. Sir James Jeans says, in "The Mysterious Universe," "The tendency of modern physics is to resolve the whole material universe into waves, and nothing but waves. These waves are of two kinds: bottled-up waves, which we call matter, and unbottled waves, which we call radiation, or light. The process of annihilation of matter is merely unbottling imprisoned wave energy, and setting it free to travel through space."

Spirit is not matter. Spirit is not person. In order to perceive the essence of Being we must drop from our mind all thought that God is in any way circumscribed or has any of the limitations that we associate with things or persons having form or shape. "Thou shalt not make unto thee a graven image, nor any likeness of any thing that is in heaven above, or that is in the earth beneath."

God is substance, not matter, because matter is formed, while God is the formless. God substance lies back of matter and form. It is the basis of all form yet does not enter into any form as a finality. Substance cannot be seen, touched, tasted, or smelled, yet it is more substantial than matter, for it is the only substantiality in the universe. Its nature is to "sub-stand" or "stand under" or behind matter as its support and only reality.

Job says, "The Almighty shall be thy defence, and thou shalt have plenty of silver." This refers to universal substance, for silver and gold are manifestations of an everywhere present substance and are used as symbols for it. Lew Wallace, in "Ben-Hur," refers to the kingdom as "beaten gold." You have doubtless in your own experience caught sight of this everywhere present substance in your silence, when it seemed like golden snowflakes falling all about you. This was the first manifestation from the overflow of the universal substance in your consciousness.

Substance is first given form in the mind, and as it becomes manifest it goes through a threefold activity. In laying hold of substance in the mind and bringing it into manifestation, we play a most important part. We do it according to our decree. "Thou shalt decree a thing, and it shall be established unto thee." We are always decreeing, sometimes consciously, often unconsciously, and with every thought and word we are increasing or diminishing the threefold activity of substance. The resulting manifestation conforms to our thought, "As he thinketh within himself, so is he."

There is no scarcity of the air you breathe. There is plenty of air, all you will ever need, but if you close your lungs and refuse to breathe, you will not get it and may suffocate for lack of air. When you recognize the presence of abundance of air and open your lungs to breathe it deeply, you get a larger inspiration. This is exactly what you should do with your mind in regard to substance. There is an all-sufficiency of all things, just as there is an all-sufficiency of air. The only lack is our own lack of appropriation. We must seek the kingdom of God and appropriate it aright before things will be added to us in fullness.

There is a kingdom of abundance of all things, and it may be found by those who seek it and are willing to comply with its laws. Jesus said that it is hard for a rich man to enter into the kingdom of heaven. This does not mean that it is hard because of his wealth, for the poor man gets in no faster and no easier. It is not money but the thoughts men hold about money, its source, its ownership, and its use, that keep them out of the kingdom. Men's thoughts about money are like their thoughts about all possessions; they believe that things coming out of the earth are theirs to claim and control as individual property, and may be hoarded away and depended on, regardless of how much other men may be in need of them. The same belief is prevalent among both rich and poor, and even if the two classes were suddenly to change places, the inequalities of wealth would not be remedied. Only a fundamental change in the thoughts of wealth could do that.

Before there is any fundamental social or economic change men must begin to understand their relationship to God and to one another as common heirs to the universal resource that is sufficient for all. They must give up some of their erroneous ideas about their "rights." They must learn that they cannot possess and lock up that which belongs to God without themselves suffering the effects of that sequestration. The poor man is not the greatest sufferer in this concentration of wealth, for he has not concentrated his faith in material things and chained his soul to them. Those who are rich in the things of this world are by their dependence on those things binding themselves to material things and are in material darkness.

Every thought of personal possession must be dropped out of mind before men can come into the realization of the invisible supply. They cannot possess money, houses, or land selfishly, because they cannot possess the universal ideas for which these symbols stand. No man can possess any idea as his own permanently. He may possess its material symbol for a little time on the plane of phenomena, but it is such riches that "moth and rust consume, and where thieves break through and steal."

Men possess as valuables their education, trade, ability, or intellectual talent. Ministers of the gospel possess scholarship or eloquence, and take pride in these spiritual possessions. Yet even these are burdens that must be unloaded before they may enter the kingdom of the heavens. The saint who is puffed up with his saintly goodness must unload his vanity before he gets in. Whoever is ambitious to do good, to excel his fellow men in righteousness, must lose his ambition and desire before he beholds the face of the all-providing Father.

The realm of causes may be compared to steam in a glass boiler. If the glass is clear one may look right at it and see nothing at all. Yet when an escape valve is touched the steam rushes out, condenses and becomes visible. But in this process it has also lost its power. Substance exists in a realm of ideas and is powerful when handled by one who is familiar with its characteristics. The ignorant open the valves of the mind and let ideas flow out into a realm with which they have nothing in common. The powerful ideas of substance are condensed into thoughts of time and space, which ignorance conceives as being necessary to their fruition. Thus their power is lost, and a weary round of seedtime and harvest is inaugurated to fulfill the demands of the world.

It is the mind that believes in personal possessions that limits the full idea. God's world is a world of results that sequentially follow demands. It is in this kingdom that man finds his true home. Labor has ceased for him who has found this inner kingdom. Divine supply is brought forth without laborious struggle: to desire is to have fulfillment.

This is the second step in demonstration for the one who has fully dedicated himself to the divine guidance. He immediately enters into easier experiences and more happiness than the world affords, when he covenants to follow only the good. There is an advanced degree along the same line of initiation into the mysteries of the divine. Before this step may be taken, a deeper and more thorough mental cleansing must be undergone. A higher set of faculties is then awakened within the body, and new avenues of expression are opened for the powers of the Spirit, not only in the body but also in the affairs of the individual. As he proceeds to exercise these faculties he may find some of them clogged by the crystals of dead thought that some selfish ideas have deposited, which makes him go through a fresh cleansing. If he is obedient to the Spirit and willing to follow without cavil or protest, the way is easy for him. If however he questions and argues, as did Job, he will meet many obstructions and his journey will be long and tedious.

Again, he who seeks the kingdom of substance for the sake of the loaves and fishes he may get out of it will surely be disappointed in the end. He may get the loaves and fishes, that is quite possible; but if there remains in his soul any desire to use them for selfish ends, the ultimate result will be disastrous.

Many people are seeking the aid of Spirit to heal them of their physical ills. They have no desire for the higher life, but having found their lusts and passions curtailed by physical infirmities, they want these erased in order that they may continue in their fleshly way. It is the experience of all who have dealt with Spirit that it is a vigorous bodily stimulant. It restores the vitality of the body until it is even more sensitive to pleasure or pain than it was before the spiritual quickening. This supersensitiveness makes it more susceptible and liable to more rapid waste if further indulgence is gratified.

That is why those who receive spiritual treatment should be fully instructed in the Truth of Being. They should be shown that the indulgence of bodily passions is a sin against their success in every walk of life and especially in the way of finances and prosperity. If substance is dissipated, every kind of lack begins to be felt. Retribution always follows the indulgence of appetite and passion for mere sensation. Both sinners and saints suffer in this valley of folly. The alternative is to dedicate yourself to the Father's business. Make a definite and detailed covenant with the Father, lay your desires, appetites, and passions at His feet and agree to use all your substance in the most exalted way. Then you are seeking the kingdom, and all things else shall be added unto you.

We want to make this substance that faith has brought to our mind enduring and abiding, so that we do not lose it when banks fail or men talk of "hard times." We must have in our finances a consciousness of the permanency of the omnipresent substance as it abides in us. Some wealthy families succeed in holding their wealth while others dissipate it in one generation because they do not have the consciousness of abiding substance. For many of us there is either a feast or a famine in the matter of money and we need the abiding consciousness. There is no reason why we should not have a continuous even flow of substance both in income and outgo. If we have freely received we must also freely give and keep substance going, confident in our understanding that our supply is unlimited and that it is always right at hand in the omnipresent Mind of God.

In this understanding we can stand "the slings and arrows of outrageous fortune," depressions, losses, and financial failures and still see God as abundant substance waiting to come into manifestation. That is what Paul meant by taking up "the whole armor of God that ye may be able to withstand in the evil day." The substance that has in the past been manifest in our affairs is still here. It is the same substance and it cannot be taken away. Even though there seems to be material lack, there is plenty of substance for all. We are standing in the very midst of it. Like the fish we might ask, "Where is the water," when we live and move and have our being in it. It is in the water, in the air everywhere, abounding, glorious spiritual substance. Take that thought and hold it. Refuse to be shaken from your spiritual stand in the very midst of God's prosperity and plenty, and supply will begin to come forth from the ether and plenty will become more and more manifest in your affairs.

Jesus was so charged with spiritual substance that when the woman touched His garment the healing virtue went out from it and she was healed. There were thousands of people in the crowd, but only the woman who had faith in that substance got it. It was already established in her consciousness, and she knew that her needs would be met if she could make the contact. In this there is a lesson for us. We know that strength is manifest everywhere, for we see it in the mechanical world. A great locomotive starts from the depot, moving slowly at first, but when it gains momentum it speeds down the track like a streak. Thus it is with spiritual strength. Beginning sometimes with a very small thought, it takes on momentum and eventually becomes a powerful idea. Every one of us can strengthen his hold on the thought of divine substance until it becomes a powerful idea, filling the consciousness and manifesting itself as plenty in all our affairs.

As you lay hold of substance with your mind, make it permanent and enduring. Realize your oneness with it. You are unified with the one living substance, which is God, your all-sufficiency. From this substance you were created; in it you live and move and have your being; by it you are fed and prospered.

The spiritual substance is steadfast and immovable, enduring. It does not fluctuate with market reports. It does not decrease in "hard times" nor increase in "good times." It cannot be hoarded away to cause a deficiency in supply and a higher price. It cannot be exhausted in doles to meet the needs of privation. It is ever the same, constant, abundant, freely circulating and available.

The spiritual substance is a living thing, not an inanimate accumulation of bread that does not satisfy hunger nor water that fails to quench thirst. It is living bread and living water, and he that feeds on God's substance shall never hunger and never thirst. The substance is an abiding thing, not a bank deposit that can be withdrawn nor a fortune that can be lost. It is an unfailing principle that is as sure in its workings as the laws of mathematics. Man can no more be separated from his supply of substance than life can be separated from its source. As God permeates the universe and life permeates every cell of the body, so does substance flow freely through man, free from all limit or qualification.

In the new era that is even now at its dawn we shall have a spirit of prosperity. This principle of the universal substance will be known and acted on, and there will be no place for lack. Supply will be more equalized. There will not be millions of bushels of wheat stored in musty warehouses while people go hungry. There will be no overproduction or underconsumption or other inequalities of supply, for God's substance will be recognized and used by all people. Men will not pile up fortunes one day and lose them the next, for they will no longer fear the integrity of their neighbors nor try to keep their neighbor's share from him.

Is this an impractical utopia? The answer depends on you. Just as soon as you individually recognize the omnipresent substance and put your faith in it, you can look for others around you to do the same. "A little leaven leaveneth the whole lump," and even one life that bears witness to the truth of the prosperity law will quicken the consciousness of the whole community.

Whoever you are and whatever your immediate need, you can demonstrate the law. If your thoughts are confused, become still and know. Be still and know that you are one with the substance and with the law of its manifestation. Say with conviction: I am strong, immovable Spirit substance.

This will open the door of your mind to an inflow of substance-filled ideas. As they come, use them freely. Do not hesitate or doubt that they will bring results. They are God's ideas given to you in answer to your prayer and in order to supply your needs. They are substance, intelligent, loving, eager to manifest themselves to meet your need.

God is the source of a mighty stream of substance, and you are a tributary of that stream, a channel of expression. Blessing the substance increases its flow. If your money supply is low or your purse seems empty, take it in your hands and bless it. See it filled with the living substance ready to become manifest. As you prepare your meals bless the food with the thought of spiritual substance. When you dress, bless your garments and realize that you are being constantly clothed with God's substance. Do not center your thought on yourself, your interests, your gains or losses, but realize the universal nature of substance. The more conscious you become of the presence of the living substance the more it will manifest itself for you and the richer will be the common good of all.

Do not take anyone's word for it, but try the law for yourself. The other fellow's realization of substance will not guarantee your supply. You must become conscious of it for yourself. Identify yourself with substance until you make it yours; it will change your finances, destroy your fears, stop your worries, and you will soon begin to rejoice in the ever-present bounty of God.

Be still and turn within to the great source. See with the eye of faith that the whole world is filled with substance. See it falling all about you as snowflakes of gold and silver and affirm with assurance: Jesus Christ is now here raising me to His consciousness of the omnipresent, all-providing God substance, and my prosperity is assured.

I have unbounded faith in the all-present spiritual substance increasing and multiplying at my word.

Chapter II

Spiritual Mind, the Omnipresent Directive Principle of Prosperity

EVERYTHING that appears in the universe had its origin in mind. Mind evolves ideas, and ideas express themselves through thoughts and words. Understanding that ideas have a permanent existence and that they evolve thoughts and words, we see how futile is any attempted reform that does not take them into consideration. This is why legislation and external rules of action are so weak and transient as reforms.

Ideas generate thought currents, as a fire under a boiler generates steam. The idea is the most important factor in every act and must be given first place in our attention if we would bring about any results of a permanent character. Men formulate thoughts and thoughts move the world.

Ideas are centers of consciousness. They have a positive and a negative pole and generate thoughts of every conceivable kind. Hence a man's body, health, intelligence, finances, in fact everything about him, are derived from the ideas to which he gives his attention.

Man has never had a desire that could not somewhere, in the providence of God, be fulfilled. If this were not true, the universe would be weak at its most vital point. Desire is the onward impulse of the ever-evolving soul. It builds from within outward and carries its fulfillment with it as a necessary corollary.

All is mind. Then the things that appear must be expressions of mind. Thus mind is reality, and it also appears as phenomena. The is-ness of mind is but one side of it. Being is not limited to the level of is-ness; it has all possibilities, including that of breaking forth from its inherencies into the realm of appearances. Mind has these two sides, being and appearance, the visible and the invisible. To say that mind is all and yet deny that things do appear to have any place in the allness is to state but half the truth.

An idea is capable of statement as a proposition. The statement is made in response to a desire to know experimentally whether the proposition is capable of proof. A number of elements are involved in the statement of a proposition that are not integral parts of the proposition itself but necessary to its working out. In the simplest mathematical problem processes are used that are not preserved after the problem is solved yet that are necessary to its solution. The figures by the use of which we arrived at the solution are immediately forgotten, but they could not be dispensed with and it is to them we owe the outcome. The exact outcome of each step in the solution is a matter of experiment. The intermediate steps may be changed or retracted many times, but ultimately the problem is solved and the fulfillment of the desired result attained. If this is true of the simplest problem in arithmetic it is equally true of the creation of the universe. "As above, so below." Here is where many who have caught sight of the perfection and wholeness of the ideal fail to demonstrate. They deny the appearance because it does not express perfection in its wholeness.

The student in the depths of a mathematical problem who should judge thus would erase all his figures because the answer was not at once apparent, though he may have already completed a good part of the process leading up to the desired answer. We would not say that a farmer is wise who cuts down his corn in the tassel because it does not show the ripened ears. Do not jump to conclusions. Study a situation carefully in its various aspects before you decide. Consider both sides, the visible and the invisible, the within and the without.

The very fact that you have an ideal condition or world in your mind carries with it the possibility of its fulfillment in expression. Being cannot shirk expression. To think is to express yourself, and you are constantly thinking. You may deny that the things of the outer world have existence, yet as long as you live in contact with them you are recognizing them. When you affirm being and deny the expression of being, you are a "house divided against itself."

We have all wondered why we do not understand more truth than we do or why it is necessary to understand at all, since God is all-wise and all-present. Understanding is one of the essential parts of your I AM identity. Man is a focal point in God consciousness and expresses God. Therefore he must understand the processes that bring about that expression. Infinite Mind is here with all its ideas as a resource for man, and what we are or become is the result of our efforts to accumulate in our own consciousness all the attributes of infinite Mind. We have learned that we can accumulate ideas of power, strength, life, love, and plenty. How should we use these ideas or bring them into outer expression without understanding? Where shall we get this understanding save from the source of all ideas, the one Mind? "But if any of you lacketh wisdom, let him ask of God, who giveth to all liberally and upbraideth not; and it shall be given him."

In following the principles of mathematics we use rules. There is a rule of addition that we must observe when we add; other rules that must be followed when we subtract or multiply. The ideas of Divine Mind can only be expressed when we follow the rules or laws of mind, and these rules require understanding if we would follow them intelligently and achieve results. Man is given all power and authority over all the ideas of infinite Mind, and the idea of wisdom is one of them.

Closely associated with the idea of wisdom in Divine Mind is the idea of love. These ideas are the positive and the negative pole of the creative Principle. "Male and female created he them." The ideas of God-Mind are expressed through the conjunction of wisdom and love. God commanded that these two ideas should be fruitful and multiply and replenish the whole earth with thoughts in expression.

We have access to the divine realm from which all thoughts are projected into the world. We are constantly taking ideas from the spiritual world and forming them into our own conception of the things we desire. Sometimes the finished product does not satisfy or please us. That is because we have taken the idea away from its true parents, wisdom and love, and let it grow to maturity in an atmosphere of error and ignorance.

In the matter of money or riches we have taken the idea of pure substance from the spiritual realm, then have forgotten the substance idea and tried to work it out in a material atmosphere of thought. It was a wonderful idea, but when we took it away from its spiritual parents wisdom and love, it became an unruly and disappointing child. Even if without love and understanding of substance you accumulate gold and silver, your store will not be stable or permanent. It will fluctuate and cause you worry and grief. There are many people who "don't know the value of a dollar," with whom money comes and goes, who are rich today and poor tomorrow. They have no understanding of the substance that is the underlying reality of all wealth.

To have adequate supply at all times, an even flow that is never enough to become a burden yet always enough to meet every demand, we must make union with the Spirit that knows how to handle ideas as substance. Men have the idea that material substance is limited, and they engage in competition trying to grab one another's money. Divine Mind has ideas of substance as unlimited and everywhere present, equally available to all. Since man's work is to express substance ideas in material form, we must find a way to connect ideas of substance with ideas of material expression, to adjust the ideas of man's mind with the ideas of Divine Mind. This is accomplished by faith through prayer.

That part of the Lord's Prayer which reads, "Give us this day our daily bread," is more correctly translated, "Give us today the substance of tomorrow's bread." By prayer we accumulate in our mind ideas of God as the substance of our supply and support. There is no lack of this substance in infinite Mind. Regardless of how much God gives, there is always an abundance left. God does not give us material things, but Mind substance--not money but ideas--ideas that set spiritual forces in motion so that things begin to come to us by the application of the law.

It may be that you solve your financial problem in your dreams. Men often think over their problems just before going to sleep and get a solution in their dreams or immediately upon awakening. This is because their minds were so active on the intellectual plane that they could not make contact with the silent inner plane where ideas work. When the conscious mind is stilled and one makes contact with the superconsciousness, it begins to show us how our affairs will work out or how we can help to bring about the desired prosperity.

This is the law of mind. The principle is within each one of us, but we must be spiritually quickened in life and in understanding before we can successfully work in accord with it. However we must not discount the understanding of the natural man. The mind in us that reasons and looks to the physical side of things has also the ability to look within. It is the door through which divine ideas must come. Jesus, the Son of man, called Himself "the door" and "the way." It is the divine plan that all expression or demonstration shall come through this gateway of man's mind. But above all this are the ideas that exist in the primal state of Being, and this is the truth of which we must become conscious. We must become aware of the source of our substance. Then we can diminish or increase the appearance of our supply or our finances, for their appearance depends entirely on our understanding and handling of the ideas of substance.

The time is coming when we shall not have to work for things, for our physical needs in the way of food and clothing, because they will come to us through the accumulation of the right ideas in our mind. We will begin to understand that clothing represents one idea of substance, food another, and that every manifest thing is representative of an idea.

In the 2d chapter of Genesis this living substance is called "dust of the ground" in the Hebrew, and Adam was formed from it. We find that the elemental substance is in our body. The kingdom of the heavens or the kingdom of God is within man. It is a kingdom of substance and of Mind. This Mind interpenetrates our mind and our mind interpenetrates and pervades our body. Its substance pervades every atom of our body. Are you giving it your attention, or do you still look to outer sources for supply? Are you meditating and praying for an understanding of this omnipresent substance? If you are, it will come, and it will demonstrate prosperity for you. When it does, you are secure, for nothing can take that true prosperity from you. It is the law that does not and cannot fail to operate when once set in operation in the right way.

This law of prosperity has been proved time and time again. All men who have prospered have used the law, for there is no other way. Perhaps they were not conscious of following definite spiritual methods, yet they have in some way set the law in operation and reaped the benefit of its unfailing action. Others have had to struggle to accomplish the same things. Remember that Elijah had to keep praying and affirming for a long time before he demonstrated the rain. He sent his servant out the first time, and there was no sign of a cloud. He prayed and sent him out again and again with the same result, but at last, after repeated efforts, the servant said he saw a little cloud. Then Elijah told them to prepare for rain, and the rain came. This shows a continuity of effort that is sometimes necessary. If your prosperity does not become manifest as soon as you pray and affirm God as your substance, your supply, and your support, refuse to give up. Show your faith by keeping up the work. You have plenty of Scripture to back you up. Jesus taught it from the beginning to the end of His ministry and demonstrated it on many occasions. Many have done the same thing in His name.

Jesus called the attention of His followers to the inner realm of mind, the kingdom of God substance. He pointed out that the lilies of the field were gloriously clothed, even finer than Solomon in all his glory. We do not have to work laboriously in the outer to accomplish what the lily does so silently and beautifully. Most of us rush around trying to work out our problems for ourselves and in our own way, with one idea, one vision: the material thing we seek. We need to devote more time to silent meditation and like the lilies of the field simply be patient and grow into our demonstrations. We should remember always that these substance ideas with which we are working are eternal ideas that have always existed and will continue to exist, the same ideas that formed this planet in the first place and that sustain it now.

A great German astronomer had worked the greater part of his life with a desire to know more about the stars. One night, quite suddenly and strangely enough--for he had given but little thought to the spiritual side of things--he broke right out into a prayer of thanksgiving because of the perfect order and harmony of the heavens. His prayer was "O God, I am thinking Thy thoughts after Thee." The soul of this man had at that moment made the contact and union with infinite Mind. But though this contact seemed to be made suddenly, it was the result of long study and the preparation of his mind and thought. Jesus expressed the same at-one-ment with God at the moment of His supreme miracle, the raising of Lazarus. His words were "Father, I thank thee that thou heardest me. And I knew that thou hearest me always."

This gives us another side of the prosperity law. We open the way for great demonstrations by recognizing the Presence and praising it, by thanking the Father for Spiritual quickening. We quicken our life by affirming that we are alive with the life of Spirit; our intelligence by affirming our oneness with divine intelligence; and we quicken the indwelling, interpenetrating substance by recognizing and claiming it as our own. We should meditate in this understanding and give sincere thanks to the God of this omnipresent realm of ideas because we can think His thoughts after Him. We can thank the Father that His thoughts are our thoughts and that our natural mind is illumined by Spirit. We can illumine our mind any time by affirming this thought:

I thank Thee, Father, that I think Thy thoughts after Thee and that my understanding is illumined by Spirit.

Spiritual thoughts are infinite in their potentiality, each one being measured by the life, intelligence, and substance with which it is expressed. The thought is brought into expression and activity by the word. Every word is a thought in activity, and when spoken it goes out as a vibratory force that is registered in the all-providing substance.

The mightiest vibration is set up by speaking the name Jesus Christ. This is the name that is named "far above all rule, and authority," the name above all names, holding in itself all power in heaven and in earth. It is the name that has power to mold the universal substance. It is at one with the Father-Mother substance, and when spoken it sets forces into activity that bring results. "Whatsoever ye shall ask of the Father in my name, he may give it to you." "If ye shall ask anything in my name, that will I do." There could be nothing simpler, easier, or freer from conditions in demonstrating supply. "Hitherto [before the name Jesus Christ was given to the world] have ye asked nothing in my name: ask, and ye shall receive, that your joy may be made full."

The sayings of Jesus were of tremendous power because of His consciousness of God. They raised the God ideal far above what had ever before been conceived. These ideas so far transcended the thought plane of the people that even some of the disciples of Jesus would not accept them, and they "walked no more with him." Until fairly recent times most men have failed to grasp the lesson of the power of the spoken word expressing spiritual ideas. Jesus has never been taken literally, else men would have sought to overcome death by keeping His sayings. Few have taken His words in full faith, not only believing them but so saturating their minds with them that they become flesh of their flesh and bone of their bone, being incarnated in their very bodies, as Jesus intended.

The secret of demonstration is to conceive what is true in Being and to carry out the concept in thought, word, and act. If I can conceive a truth, there must be a way by which I can make that truth apparent. If I can conceive of an inexhaustible supply existing in the omnipresent ethers, then there is a way by which I can make that supply manifest. Once your mind accepts this as an axiomatic truth it has arrived at the place where the question of processes begins to be considered.

No one ever fully sees the steps that he must take in reaching a certain end. He may see in a general way that he must proceed from one point to another, but all the details are not definite unless he has gone over the same ground before. So in the demonstration of spiritual powers as they are expressed through man, we must be willing to follow the directions of someone who has proved his understanding of the law by his demonstrations.

We all know intuitively that there is something wrong in a world where poverty prevails and we would not knowingly create a world in which a condition of poverty exists. Lack of any kind is not possible in all God's universe. So when there is an appearance of poverty anywhere, it is our duty to deny it. Sorrow and suffering accompany poverty, and we wish to see them all blotted out. This desire is an index pointing the way to their disappearance. As the consciousness of the kingdom of heaven with its abundant life and substance becomes more and more common among men, these negative conditions will fade out of seeming existence.

Jesus said that all things should be added to those who seek the kingdom of heaven. We do not have to wait until we have fully entered the kingdom or attained a complete understanding of Spirit before prosperity begins to be manifest, but we do have to seek, to turn the attention in that direction. Then things begin to be added unto us. Thousands of people are proving the law in this age. They accept the promise of the Scriptures and are looking to God to supply their every need. In the beginning of their seeking they may have little to encourage them to believe that they will be provided for or helped along any particular line. But they carry out the command to seek and in faith act just as though they were receiving, and gradually there opens up to them new ways of making a living. Sometimes avenues are opened to them to which they are strangers, but they find pleasant experience and are encouraged to continue seeking the kingdom of God and rejoicing in its ever increasing bounty.

Many such people today are wisely using their one talent. They may not have seen the holy of holies in the inner sanctuary, but they are getting closer to it. This is the step we must all take: begin to seek this kingdom of God's substance. Trust in the promise and see the result in the mental currents that are set in motion all about us. You may not be able to see at just what point success began, or what separate word of allegiance to the Father first took effect, but as the weeks or months go by you will observe many changes taking place in your mind, your body, and your affairs. You will find that your ideas have broadened immensely, that your little limited world has been transformed into a big world. You will find your mind more alert and you will see clearly where you were in doubt before, because you have begun thinking about realities instead of appearances. The consciousness of an omnipotent hand guiding all your affairs will establish you in confidence and security, which will extend to the body welfare and surroundings. There will be a lessening or entire absence of prejudice and faultfinding in you. You will be more forgiving and more generous and will not judge harshly. Other people will feel that there has been a change in you and will appreciate you more, showing it in many ways. Things will be coming your way, being added unto you indeed according to the promise.

All this is true not only of your own affairs. The effects extend also to those with whom you come in contact. They will also become more prosperous and happy. They may not in any way connect their improvement with you or your thoughts, but that does not affect the truth about it. All causes are essentially mental, and whoever comes into daily contact with a high order of thinking must take on some of it. Ideas are catching, and no one can live in an atmosphere of true thinking, where high ideas are held, without becoming more or less inoculated with them.

Do not expect miracles to be performed for you, but do expect the law with which you have identified yourself to work out your problem by means of the latent possibilities in and around you. Above all, be yourself. Let the God within you express Himself through you in the world without.

"Ye are gods,
And all of you sons of the Most High."

The idea of God covers a multitude of creative forces. In this case you are working to bring prosperity into your affairs. Hence you should fill your mind with images and thoughts of an all-providing all-supplying Father. The ancient Hebrews understood this. They had seven sacred names for Jehovah, each one of which represented some specific idea of God. They used the name Jehovah-jireh when they wished to concentrate on the aspect of substance. It means "Jehovah will provide," the mighty One whose presence and power provides, regardless of any opposing circumstance. To quicken the consciousness of the presence of God the Hebrews used the name Jehovah-shammah which means "Jehovah is there," "the Lord is present." Realize the Lord present as creative mind, throbbing in the ether as living productiveness.

Charge your mind with statements that express plenty. No particular affirmation will raise anyone from poverty to affluence, yet all affirmations that carry ideas of abundance will lead one into the consciousness that fulfills the law. Deny that lack has any place or reality in your thought or your affairs and affirm plenty as the only appearance. Praise what you have, be it ever so little, and insist that it is constantly growing larger.

Daily concentration of mind on Spirit and its attributes will reveal that the elemental forces that make all material things are here in the ether awaiting our recognition and appropriation. It is not necessary to know all the details of the scientific law in order to demonstrate prosperity. Go into the silence daily at a stated time and concentrate on the substance of Spirit prepared for you from the foundation of the world. This opens up a current of thought that will bring prosperity into your affairs. A good thought to hold in this meditation is this: The invisible substance is plastic to my abundant thought, and I am rich in mind and in manifestation

Chapter III

Faith in the Invisible Substance, the Key to Demonstration

IN THIS LESSON we are considering the subject of faith especially as it applies to the demonstration of prosperity. In this study, as in all others, we must start in the one Mind. God had faith when He imaged man and the universe and through His faith brought all things into being. Man, being like God, must also base his creations on faith as the only foundation. Here then is our starting point in building a prosperity consciousness and making our world as we would have it. We all have faith, for it is innate in every man. Our question is how we may put it to work in our affairs.

Jesus gave us our best understanding of faith when He described Peter as a "rock" and asserted that His church, the ecclesia or "called-out ones," was to be built up with this rock or faith as its sure foundation. In this sense faith represents substance, the underlying, basic principle of all manifestation. "Now faith is assurance of things hoped for, a conviction of things not seen."

It is quite possible to possess a reality that cannot be seen, touched, or comprehended by any of the outer senses. It is faith when we are fully conscious of "things not seen" and have the "assurance of things" not yet manifest. In other words, faith is that consciousness in us of the reality of the invisible substance and of the attributes of mind by which we lay hold of it. We must realize that the mind makes real things. "Just a thought" or "just a mere idea," we sometimes lightly say, little thinking that these thoughts and ideas are the eternal realities from which we build our life and our world.

Faith is the perceiving power of the mind linked with a power to shape substance. You hear of a certain proposition that appeals to you and you say, "I have faith in that proposition." Some man whose character seems right is described to you and you say, "I have faith in that man." What do you mean by having faith? You mean that certain characteristics of men or things appeal to you, and these immediately begin a constructive work in your mind. What is that work? It is the work of making the proposition or man real to your consciousness. The character and attributes of the things in your mind become substantial to you because of your faith. The office of faith is to take abstract ideas and give them definite form in substance. Ideas are abstract and formless to us until they become substance, the substance of faith.

A very important work in soul culture is the establishment of a faith substance. Once we discern this law of soul building by faith, we find the Hebrew Scriptures full of illustrations of it. The 1st chapter of Luke's Gospel tells us how Elisabeth and Zacharias were told by an angel that they would have a son and that his name would be John. Zacharias was burning incense at the altar in the exercise of his duties as a priest. This means that when the mind is looking toward Spirit, even if it be in a blind way, and is seeking spiritual things, it will become spiritualized. The burning of incense typifies spiritualization. Zacharias represents the perceptive and Elisabeth the receptive qualities of the soul. When these two work in conjunction in prayer, meditation, and aspiration, the soul is open to the higher thoughts or angels that bring the promise of a new and definite state of consciousness. Zacharias doubted the promise of a son because his wife was past the age of childbearing, and because of his doubts he was stricken dumb. This means that when we perceive spiritual Truth and doubt it, we retard its outer expression; it cannot be spoken into manifestation through us because of our doubt. All the growth is then thrown upon the soul. Elisabeth "hid herself five months," but when the soul begins to feel the presence of the new ego or new state of consciousness, then we again come into faith expression: the speech of Zacharias is restored.

It was the same way in the bringing forth of Jesus. A promise was first made to Mary, and Joseph was assured that the child was the offspring of the Holy Spirit. This represents a still higher step in the work of faith. The bringing forth of John the Baptist is the intellectual perception of Truth. The intellect grasps Truth first. The next step is the bringing forth of substance and life in the subconsciousness. When we have given ourselves entirely to Spirit, we may do things without knowing exactly why. That is because faith is at work in us, and even if we do not know the law and cannot explain faith to the outer consciousness, it continues to do its perfect work and eventually brings forth the demonstration.

Do not fear the power that works out things in the invisible. When you get a strong perception of something that your inner mind tells you is true and good, act on it and your demonstration will come. That is the way a living faith works, and it is the law of your creative word.

Faith can also have understanding added to it. We call our spiritual faculties out of our subconsciousness. When Jesus did some of His most remarkable works He had with Him Peter, James, and John; Peter represents faith, James wisdom or judgment, and John love. These three faculties when expressed together in mind accomplish apparent miracles. You have called out faith in things spiritual, you have faith in God, and you have cultivated your unity with the one Mind; if you then use spiritual judgment and do your work in love, you have become "a teacher in Israel."

In order to have understanding of the law through which we gain or lose in the use of the invisible substance, we must use discrimination or judgment. There is a guiding intelligence always present that we can lay hold of and make our own. It is ours. It belongs to us and it is our birthright both to know it and to use it. Some metaphysicians mistakenly think that they must have hard experiences in order to appreciate the better things of life. They think poverty is a blessing because it educates people to the appreciation of plenty when they get it. They say that it is God's will for us to have some hard times and some good times, feasts and famines. This is not logically true when you consider God as principle. If you think of God as a man who arbitrarily gives or withholds by the exercise of His personal will, you might reach such a conclusion. But God is changeless, and if He gives one moment He will continue to give eternally. It is His nature to give, and His nature is eternally the same. When you talk of hard times, famines, lack, you are talking of something that has no place in the Mind of God. You are not acknowledging God in all your ways but are acknowledging error and affirming that the world has its source in outer things. You must turn around and get into this consciousness, that in Mind, in Spirit, there is abundance.

We often wonder how Jesus could multiply the five loaves and two fishes to meet the hunger of five thousand persons. It was done through a thorough understanding of this law. The five loaves represent the five-sense application of divine substance.

The two fishes represent the yeast or multiplying power put into the substance, the source of the increase. We are told that if the yeast of a single setting of bread were allowed to increase, it would fill a space larger than this planet. This shows that there is no limit to the increasing power of elemental substance. It is for us to use as Jesus used this power. It was not a miracle but something that we all have within us as an unawakened ability and that we can learn to develop and use as Jesus did.

Jesus entered into the silence; prayed and blessed the substance at hand. If we would multiply and increase the power, substance, and life in us and at our command, we must get very still and realize that our resource is Spirit, that it is God, and that it is here in all its fullness. We must make contact with it in faith. Then we shall find it welling up within us. Some of you have no doubt had that experience. But if you just let it ooze away without understanding it, you get no benefit. Here is the key to this life and substance you feel when you sit in the silence. You must begin to speak these words with power and authority.

When there is world-wide belief in financial depression, lack of circulation, stagnation, things do not go as we expect and we develop fear, a belief in lack of circulation of money. But if we know the law, we do not come under this fear thought. At any time many persons make money; they use this law and take advantage of opportunity. We should bless everything that we have, for we can increase and multiply what we have by speaking words. Jesus said that His words were spirit and life. Did you ever think that your word is charged with great spiritual life force? It is. Be careful of your words. Man shall be held accountable for his lightest word. If you talk about substance in a negative way, your finances will be decreased, but if you talk about it in an appreciative, large way, you will be prospered.

If we could release the energy in the atoms the scientists tell us about, we could supply the world. This power lies within every one of us. We can begin by freeing the little ideas we have and making them fill the world with thoughts of plenty. We must realize that all power is given to us in heaven and in earth, as Jesus said. He told His apostles that they should receive power when the Holy Spirit had come upon them. They were told to go up into that upper room, in the crown of the head, where spiritual forces begin the formation of new ideas. After you get into the spiritual consciousness and receive the quickening, speak the word with authority and power, concentrating the attention at the power center in the throat. We find it effective to speak the words aloud and then sink back to "the other side" (Galilee), as Jesus often did, to rest and speak them again silently. You can send forth this vibratory energy of Spirit and break down the inertia caused by thoughts of fear and lack, carve out ways, open new avenues to the demonstration of your good.

To bring forth these undeveloped spiritual qualities we must believe in them. "For he that cometh to God must believe that he is." Lord, keep us from unbelief, from leaning on the things we see, from judging according to appearances. You can conjure up in your mind a thousand imaginary things that will seem real to you. This shows that the mind creates by forming things according to its ideas. The world is awakening in a wonderful way to the truth about the creative power of the mind. Everywhere people are studying psychology or soul culture. The imagination builds things out of the one substance. If you will associate faith with it in its creative work, the things you make will be just as real as those that God makes. Whatever you make in mind and really put faith in will become substantial. Then you must be constantly on your guard as to what you believe, in order that you may bring what is for your good into manifestation.

In what do you have faith? In outer things? If so, you are building shadows without substance, shadows that cease as soon as your supporting thought is withdrawn from them, forms that will pass away and leave you nothing. If you would demonstrate true prosperity, you must turn from things and, as Jesus told His disciples, "have faith in God." Do not have faith in anything less than God, in anything other than the one Mind, for when your faith is centered there, you are building for eternity. Mind and the ideas of Mind will never pass away. There will never be an end to God. There will never be an end to Truth, which God is. There will never be an end to substance, which God is. Build with the divine substance, cultivate faith in realities and "lay up for yourselves treasures in heaven."

The foundation of every work is an idea. Faith is that quality of mind which makes the idea stand out as real, not only to ourselves but to others. When others have faith in the thing you are doing, making, or selling, they see it as real and worth while. Then your success and your prosperity are assured. Only that exists in whose becoming really visible or valuable you have great faith. If you say and believe, "I have faith in the substance of God working in and through me to increase and bring abundance into my world," your faith will start to work mightily in the mind substance and make you prosperous. Whatever you put into substance along with faith will work out in manifestation in your world. We have seen it done and we have proved the law too many times to have any doubt.

The Scriptures are filled with illustrations of this activity of bringing things to pass through faith in substance. The characters of whom we read in the Scriptures represent ideas carrying forward their work in human souls. If we think that they existed only as people of thousands of years ago, we put our faith back thousands of years, instead of letting it work for us this minute in our everyday affairs of life. To demonstrate as Jesus did we must put our faith in the one substance and say, "I have faith in God."

You demonstrate prosperity by an understanding of the prosperity law and by having faith in it, not by appealing to the sympathy of others, trying to get them to do something for you or give you something.

Faithfulness and earnestness in the application of the prosperity law will assure you of success.

"Every good gift and every perfect gift is from above, coming down from the Father of lights, with whom can be no variation, neither shadow that is cast by turning."

"In all thy ways acknowledge him, And he will direct thy paths."

Let us all know that just now we are in the very presence of creative Mind, the Mind that made the universe and everything in it. This Mind is here and at work right now as much as it ever was or ever will be. When we fully realize this, we increase the activity of Mind in us immeasurably. You must realize that God is Spirit and that Spirit is very real and powerful, and by far the most substantial thing in all the world.

It may be hard for those who have become attached to material things to realize that there is an invisible real life and substance that is much more substantial and real than the material. The men of science tell us that the invisible forces have a power that is millions of times more real and substantial than all the material world. When we read statements about some of the recent discoveries of science, which everyone accepts and talks about, we are truly amazed. Such statements made by religionists would be called preposterous and unbelievable. Yet religion has been making the same statements in different ways for thousands of years. Now science is helping religion by proving them.

In comparing substance and matter as regards their relative reality one scientific writer says that matter is merely a crack in the universal substance. It is universal substance that man is handling all the time with his spiritual mind. Through your thoughts you deal with the wonderful spiritual substance, and it takes form in your consciousness according to your thought about it. That is why we must hold the thought of divine wisdom and understanding: so that we may use these creative mind powers righteously. We use them all the time either consciously or unconsciously and we should use them to our advantage and blessing.

Every time you say, "I am a little short of funds," "I haven't as much money as I need," you are putting a limit on the substance in your own consciousness. Is that wisdom? You want a larger supply, not a limited supply of substance. Therefore it is important to watch your thoughts so that the larger supply may come through your mind and into your affairs. Say to yourself, "I am God's offspring, and I must think as God thinks. Therefore I cannot think of any lack or limitation." It is impossible that in this universal Mind that fills everything there can be any such thing as absence. There is no lack of anything anywhere in reality. The only lack is the fear of lack in the mind of man. We do not need to overcome any lack, but we must overcome the fear of lack.

This fear of lack led men to speculate in order to accumulate substance and have a lot of it stored up. This caused a still greater fear of lack in other men, and the situation grew worse and worse until it became generally believed that we must pile up the material symbols of substance for a possible lack in the future. We have tried that system and found that it fails us every time. We must learn to understand the divine law of supply and the original plan, which is that we have each day our daily bread. That is all we really want, just the amount of things we need for today's use, plus the absolute assurance that the supply for tomorrow's needs will be there when tomorrow comes. This assurance cannot be found in hoarding or piling up, as we have learned by experience. It can be had if we have faith and understand the truth about omnipresent, always available substance. Anything less than today's needs is not enough. Anything more than we need for today is a burden. Let us start with the fundamental proposition that there is plenty for you and for me and that the substance is here all the time, supplying us with every needful thing, according to our thought and word.

In the morning, immediately upon awakening, take a quiet meditative thought. A good foundation statement to hold in the silence is:

"Let the words of my mouth and the meditation of my heart Be acceptable in Thy sight, O Jehovah, my rock, and my redeemer."

Think of the meaning of these words as you meditate on them. The words of your mouth and the thoughts of your heart are now and always molding the spiritual substance and bringing it into manifestation. They will not be acceptable to the Lord unless they bring into manifestation things that are true, lovely, and altogether good. After your morning meditation, when you have declared the omnipresence and the allness of the good, receive it as true and go forth to the day's activities with faith that all things needful are provided and your good must come. The soil and substance omnipresent has many names.

Jesus called it the kingdom of the heavens. Moses in Genesis named it the Garden of Eden. Science says it is the ether. We live in it as fishes live in the sea, and it lives in us and supplies us with all things according to our thoughts. When you start to your work, pause a moment and declare: "I set God before me this day, to guide and guard, to protect and prosper me." Or: "The Spirit of the Lord goes before me this day and makes my way successful and prosperous." Make this your proclamation for the day. Decree it to be so, and the Lord will bring it to pass. During the day, if a thought of lack or limitation should for a moment disturb you, banish it at once with the statement: "Jehovah is my shepherd; I shall not want."

When your mind comes around again to the subject of prosperity, realize most strongly that your prosperity comes from God. It came with you from God, from your contact with God-Mind in your silence, and your prosperity is right with you wherever you are. Supply may seem to come through outer channels, but your real success depends on your inner hold on the prosperity realization. Be thankful for supply that comes through outer channels, but do not limit God's giving to any one channel. Look unto Him and be prospered.

Some Prosperity Prayers

I am always provided for because I have faith in Thee as my omnipresent abundance.

I have faith in Thee as my almighty resource and I trust Thee to preserve me in my prosperity.

I trust the universal Spirit of prosperity in all my affairs. I come to God because I believe that He is and that He is a rewarder of them that seek alter Him.

Chapter IV

Man, the Inlet and Outlet of Divine Mind

THE POSSESSIONS of the Father are not in stocks and bonds but in the divine possibilities implanted in the mind and soul of every man. Through the mind of man ideas are brought into being. Through the soul of man God's wealth of love finds its expression.

It is well said that the mind is the crucible in which the ideal is transmuted into the real. This process of transformation is the spiritual chemistry we must learn before we are ready to work intelligently in the great laboratory of the Father's substance. There is no lack of material there to form what we will, and we can all draw on it as a resource according to our purpose. Wealth of consciousness will express itself in wealth of manifestation.

One who knows Principle has a certain inner security given him by the understanding of God-Mind. Our affirmations are for the purpose of establishing in our consciousness a broad understanding of the principles on which all life and existence depend. Our religion is based on a science in which ideas are related to Principle and to other ideas in a great universal Mind that works under mental laws. It is not a new religion nor a religious fad but points out the real and the true in any religion. If you know Principle, you are able to know at once whether a religion is founded on facts or has a basis of man-made ideas.

In order to demonstrate Principle we must keep establishing ourselves in certain statements of the law. The more often you present to your mind a proposition that is logical and true the stronger becomes that inner feeling of security to you. The mind of man is built on Truth and the clearer your understanding of Truth is the more substantial your mind becomes. There is a definite and intimate relation between what we call Truth and this universal substance of Being. When the one Mind is called into action in your mind by your thinking about it, it lays hold of the substance by the law of attraction or sympathy of thought. Thus the more you know about God the more successful you will be in handling your body and all your affairs. The more you know about God the healthier you will be, and of course the healthier you are the happier, more beautiful, and better you will be in every way. If you know how to take hold of the universal substance and mold it to your uses, you will be prosperous. Mind substance enters into every little detail of your daily life whether you realize the Truth or not. However, to establish yourself in a certain security in the possession and use of universal life, love, intelligence, and substance, you must get a consciousness of it by first mentally seeing the Truth.

All true action is governed by law. Nothing just happens. There are no miracles. There is no such thing as luck. Nothing comes by chance. All happenings are the result of cause and can be explained under the law of cause and effect. This is a teaching that appeals to the innate logic of our mind, yet we sometimes feel like doubting it when we see things happen that have no apparent cause. These happenings that seem miraculous are controlled by laws that we have not yet learned and result from causes that we have not been able to understand. Man does not demonstrate according to the law but according to his knowledge of the law, and that is why we must seek to learn more of it. God is law and God is changeless. If we would bring forth the perfect creation, we must conform to law and unfold in our mind, body, and affairs as a flower unfolds by the principle of innate life, intelligence, and substance.

The United States Congress establishes laws that rule the acts of all American citizens. Those who keep the laws are rewarded by the protection of the law. Congress does not see to it that men obey the laws. That is left to the executive department of the government. The same thing is true of the universal law. God has ordained the law but does not compel us to follow it. We have free will, and the manner of our doing is left entirely to us. When we know the law and work with it, we are rewarded by its protection and use it to our good. If we break the universal law, we suffer limitations, just as a convicted lawbreaker is limited to a cell or prison. The Holy Spirit is the executive official through whom Divine Mind enforces its laws.

You can see from this consideration that God has bestowed the power of Divine Mind on every man. You are using your organism, body, mind, and soul, to carry out a law that God established as a guide for all creation. If you righteously fulfill this mission, you cannot fail to get the righteous results. If you fail to live in accordance with the law--well, that is your affair. God cannot help it if you are not following the law and by it demonstrating health, happiness, prosperity, and all good. Blackstone said that law is a rule of action. So with God's law: if you follow the rules of action, you will demonstrate Truth. You will have all that God has prepared for you from the foundation of the world.

What are the rules of the law? First, God is good and all His creations are good. When you get that firmly fixed in your mind, you are bound to demonstrate good and nothing but good can come into your world. If you let in the thought that there is such a thing as evil and that you are as liable to evil as to good, then you may have conditions that conform to your idea of evil. But remember, evil and evil conditions are not recognized by Divine Mind. If you have thought of evil as a reality or as having any power over you, change your thought at once and begin to build up good brain cells that never heard about anything but good.

Pray thus: I am a child of the absolute good. God is good, and I am good. Everything that comes into my life is good, and I am going to have only the good. Establish this consciousness and only the good will be attracted to you and your life will be a perpetual joy. I cannot tell you why this is true but I know that it is and that you can prove it for yourself to your satisfaction.

If you will start right now with the idea of universal and eternal goodness uppermost in your mind, talk only about the good, and see with the mind's eye everything and everybody as good, then you will soon be demonstrating all kinds of good. Good thoughts will become a habit, and good will manifest itself to you. You will see it everywhere. And people will be saying of you, "I know that that man is good and true. I have confidence in him. He makes me feel the innate goodness of all men." That is the way in which the one Mind expresses itself through man. It is the law. Those who live in accordance with the law will get the desired results. Those who fail to do so will get the opposite results.

The law also applies to our demonstrations of prosperity. We cannot be very happy if we are poor, and nobody needs to be poor. It is a sin to be poor. You may ask whether Jesus cited any example of poverty's being a sin? Yes. You will find it in the story of the prodigal son. That is often used as a text to preach to moral sinners, but a close study of it shows that Jesus was teaching the sin of lack and how to gain plenty. It is a wonderful prosperity lesson.

The prodigal son took his inheritance and went into a far country, where he spent it in riotous living and came to want. When he returned to his father's house he was not accused of moral shortcoming, as we should expect. Instead the father said, "Bring forth quickly the best robe and put it on him." That was a lesson in good apparel. It is a sin to wear poor clothes. This may seem to some to be rather a sordid way of looking at the teaching of Jesus, but we must be honest. We must interpret it as He gave it, not as we think it ought to be.

The next act of the father was to put a gold ring on the prodigal's finger, another evidence of prosperity. The Father's desire for us is unlimited good, not merely the means of a meager existence. The ring symbolizes the unlimited, that to which there is no end. It also represents omnipresence and omnipotence in the manifest world. When the father gave that ring to the son, he gave him the key to all life activity. It was the symbol of his being a son and heir to all that the father had. "All that is mine is thine." The Father gives us all that He has and is, omnipotence, omniscience, all love, and all substance when we return to the consciousness of His house of plenty.

"Put ... shoes on his feet" was the father's next command to the servants. Feet represent that part of our understanding that comes into contact with earthly conditions. In the head or "upper room" we have the understanding that contacts spiritual conditions, but when we read in Scripture anything about the feet, we may know that it refers to our understanding of things of the material world.

The next thing the father did for his returned son was to proclaim a feast for him. That is not the way we treat moral sinners. We decree punishment for them; we send them to jail. But the Father gives a feast to those who come to Him for supply. He does not dole out only a necessary ration but serves the "fatted calf," universal substance and life in its fullness and richness.

The parable is a great lesson on prosperity, for it shows us that people who are dissipating their substance in sense ways are sinners and eventually fall into a consciousness of lack. It also proves that they may become lawful and prosperous again by returning to the Father-Mind. When there are so many lessons in the Bible for moral delinquents, there is no need to twist the meaning of this parable to that purpose. It is so plainly a lesson on the cause of lack and want. Jesus expressly states that the youth wasted his substance in a "far country," a place where the divine law of plenty was not realized. There is a very close relation between riotous living and want. Persons who waste their substance in sensation come to want in both physical and financial ways. If we would make the right use of the divine substance and the divine law, we must come back to the consciousness of the Father and conserve our body substance. Then health and prosperity will become naturally manifest. If we are not resourceful or secure in our use of the one divine substance, we are not secure in anything. Substance is a very important thing in our world, in fact the foundation of it. Therefore we should be secure in our understanding of it and use it according to God's law.

Then let us enter into the very Truth of Being and observe the divine law. Let us realize that our Father is always here and that we are in a "far country" only when we forget His presence. He is constantly giving us just what we will acknowledge and accept under His law. We can take our inheritance and divorce ourselves in consciousness from the Father, but we shall suffer the results, for then we shall not do things in divine wisdom and divine order, and there will be a "famine" in that land. Let us rather seek the divine wisdom to know how to handle our substance and the law of prosperity will be revealed to us. To come into this realization, declare with faith and all assurance: The all-providing Mind is my resource, and I am secure in my prosperity.

Primitive men did not contend for the products of nature so long as they could easily pick the fruits from the trees and sleep beneath the branches. When they began to live in caves contention arose over the best places, and the strongest were usually the victors. "Success leads to success." Those who were able to take the best did so and proved the law that "whosoever hath, to him shall be given, and he shall have abundance." This seems at first thought to be an unjust law, but it has always prevailed in the affairs of the world. Jesus, the greatest of metaphysicians, taught it as a divine law and gave it His commendation. He could not have done otherwise, for it is a righteous law that man shall have what he earns, that industry, effort, and ability be rewarded and laziness discouraged.

This law operates in every department of being. Those who seek the things that the material realm has to offer usually find them. Those who strive for moral excellence usually attain that goal. Those who aspire to spiritual rewards are also rewarded. The law is that we get what we want and work for, and all experience and history have proved it a good law. If this law were removed, world progress would cease and the race become extinct. Where there is no reward for effort, there will be no effort and society will degenerate. We may talk wisely about the inner urge, but when it has no outer field of action it eventually becomes discouraged and ceases to act.

When men evolve spiritually to a certain degree, they open up inner faculties that connect them with cosmic Mind, and attain results that are sometimes so startling that they seem to be miracle workers. What seems miraculous is the action of forces on planes of consciousness not previously understood. When a man releases the powers of his soul, he does marvels in the sight of the material-minded, but he has not departed from the law. He is merely functioning in a consciousness that has been sporadically manifested by great men in all ages. Man is greater than all the other creations of God-Mind because he has the ability to perceive and to lay hold of the ideas inherent in God-Mind and through faith bring them into manifestation. Thus evolution proceeds by man's laying hold of primal spiritual ideas and expressing them in and through his consciousness.

In the exercise of his I AM identity man needs to develop certain stabilizing ideas. One of them is continuity or loyalty to Truth. In the Scriptures and in life we have many examples of how love sticks to the thing on which it has set its mind. Nothing so tends to stabilize and unify all the other faculties of mind as love. That is why Jesus gave as the greatest commandment that we love God.

When you first begin to think of God as everywhere present substance, your mind will not adhere continuously to the idea. You will drop your attention after a while and think, "I haven't enough to meet all our bills." There you have made a break and have lost momentum in your ongoing, and you must patch it up quickly. Affirm, "I am not going to be led astray. The old ideas are error and they are nothing. They have no power over me. I am going to stick to this proposition. God is love, the substance of my supply."

Ruth, the Moabitish woman, became so attached to Naomi (spiritual thought) that she would not leave her but accompanied her back to Palestine. She was loyal and steadfast because of her love. What was the result of her stick-to-itiveness? She was at first a gleaner; then became the wife of a very rich man and was immortalized as one of the ancestresses of David. This lesson of abiding in our highest ideals is one that we must understand. Nothing is so important as sticking to the ideal and never giving up the work we have set out to accomplish. Affirm the law continuously and be loyal to it and you will become successful in its demonstration.

You have doubtless found that there is a spiritual law that brings into manifestation the thoughts we concentrate our attention on, a divine universal law of mind activity that is unfailing. Some adverse condition of your own thought has prevented a full demonstration. Do not let this swerve you from your loyalty to the law. You may seem to attain results very slowly, but that is the best reason for sticking closely to your ideal and not changing your mind. Be loyal to Principle and the adverse condition will break up. Then the true light will come and the invisible substance you have been faithfully affirming will begin to reveal itself to you in all its fullness of good.

Jesus stressed the idea that God has made abundant provision for all His children, even to the birds of the air and the lilies of the field. The Lord has clothed you with soul substance as gloriously as He did Solomon. But you must have faith in this all-providing substance of good and by your continuity of imagination set it to forming the things you desire. If you are persistent in working this idea in your conscious mind, it will eventually drop down into your subconscious mind and continue to work there where things take form and become manifest. Invisible substance, when your subconsciousness becomes filled with it to the overflowing point, will ooze out, as it were, into all your affairs. You will become more prosperous and successful so gradually, simply, and naturally that you will not realize that it derives from a divine source and in answer to your prayers. We must realize all the while however that whatever we put as seed into the subconscious soil will eventually bring forth after its kind and we must exercise the greatest caution so that we do not think or talk about insufficiency or allow others to talk to us about it. As we sow in mind so shall we reap in manifestation.

Some of our well-meaning friends have a way of loading us up with "hard-times" ideas that disperse this prosperity substance that we have accumulated. Sometimes even one adverse thought will cause it to escape; then we must go back and patch up the broken reservoir of substance thinking. We have to hold it in our mind in all its fullness and we should not let go of it for a minute lest the work of demonstration be delayed. When you retire at night, let your last thought be about the abundance of spiritual substance. See it filling all the house and the minds of all the people in the house. That potent thought will then sink into your subconsciousness and continue to work whether you are asleep or awake.

The law of supply is a divine law. This means that it is a law of mind and must work through mind. God will not go to the grocery and bring food to your table. But when you continue to think about God as your real supply, everything in your mind begins to awaken and to contact the divine substance, and as you mold it in your consciousness, ideas begin to come which will connect you with the visible manifestation. You first get the ideas in consciousness direct from their divine source, and then you begin to demonstrate in the outer. It is an exact law and it is scientific and unfailing. "First the blade, then the ear, then the full grain in the ear."

When you work in harmony with this universal law, every needed thing is abundantly supplied. Your part is simply to fulfill the law; that is, to keep your mind filled with mind substance, to store up spiritual substance until the mind is filled with it and it cannot help but manifest in your affairs in obedience to the law "Whosoever hath, to him shall be given." But you are not fulfilling the law when you allow poverty-stricken thoughts to dwell in your mind. They draw other like thoughts, and your consciousness will have no room for the truth that prosperity is for you. Poverty or prosperity, it all depends on you. All that the Father has is yours, but you alone are responsible for the relationship of the Father's good to your life. Through conscious recognition of your oneness with the Father and His abundance you draw the living substance into visible supply.

Do not hesitate to think that prosperity is for you. Do not feel unworthy. Banish all thoughts of being a martyr to poverty. No one enjoys poverty, but some people seem to enjoy the sympathy and compassion they can excite because of it. Overcome any leaning in that direction and every belief that you were meant to be poor. No one is ever hopeless until he is resigned to his imagined fate. Think prosperity, talk prosperity, not in general but in specific terms, not as something for the other fellow but as your very own right. Deny every appearance of failure. Stand by your guns and affirm supply, support, and success in the very face of question and doubt, then give thanks for plenty in all your affairs, knowing for a certainty that your good is now being fulfilled in Spirit, in mind, and in manifestation.

A Prosperity Treatment Twenty-Third Psalm (Revised)

The Lord is my banker; my credit is good. He maketh me to lie down in the consciousness of omnipresent abundance; He giveth me the key to His strongbox. He restoreth my faith in His riches; He guideth me in the paths of prosperity for His name's sake.

Yea, though I walk in the very shadow of debt, I shall fear no evil, for Thou art with me; Thy silver and Thy gold, they secure me. Thou preparest a way for me in the presence of the collector; Thou fillest my wallet with plenty; my measure runneth over. Surely goodness and plenty will follow me all the days of my life, And I shall do business in the name of the Lord forever.

Chapter V

The Law That Governs the Manifestation of Supply

IT IS SAFE to say that all men are striving to fulfill the law of their being, but few have understood the law. The law is one of the most important things we can study, because only as we come to understand it and in proportion as we understand it can we comply with its requirements and demonstrate our divine possibilities through it.

In reading the Scriptures we gradually raise our consciousness of them as mere history and begin to apprehend them as setting forth the principle or law of life. We find the great Bible characters fitting into the pattern of our own consciousness, where they represent ideas. This makes the Bible a divine Book of Life rather than merely the history of a people. The idea of the law is symbolized by Moses. In our individual consciousness he is denial, the negative side of the law that precedes its affirmative expression.

Moses gave the law as "Thou shalt not." Jesus represents the law in its affirmative expression "Thou shalt love the Lord thy God."

Moses could not go into the Promised Land, the four-dimensional state of consciousness, for there can be no negation there. Joshua, whose name has the same meaning as that of Jesus, entered the Promised Land and opened the way for the Children of Israel. He represents the first step in mind toward that full consciousness of the omnipresence and omnipotence of God that was attained in Jesus. Moses was the lawgiver, and Jesus was, in His own words, the fulfillment of the law.

We must begin to see this four-dimensional world within, with its innate capacity for all things. Everything is right here, all that ever was or ever could be, simply waiting to be brought forth into manifestation. The Lord has prepared a great feast and invited all of us to it, just as Jesus explained in parable. We have right here within and all around us this substance ready for our appropriation or eating. Eating is the outer symbol of mental appropriation. We begin to break bread by breaking the substance of mind, everywhere abundantly provided.

We have discovered that there is within us a life force that can be quickened into greater activity by thinking. Everyone has at some time demonstrated that he could overcome the negative condition of weakness by holding the thought of strength. Sometimes the strength follows the thought immediately, sometimes the thought must be persistently held for days or weeks. In demonstrating the law of ever-present abundance we should and do expect the same results. If the demonstration seems slow in coming, patience and persistence will win. That may be because the poverty consciousness has a tenacious hold and takes effort to be got rid of.

There is a law that governs the manifestation of supply, and we may learn that law and apply it by mental determination and faith in the logical sequences of spiritual realities. We have thought that the laws of God were mysterious and sacred, far removed from the ordinary individual, and that we had better try first to learn the laws of food, of medicine, of a thousand other secondary things. A strict metaphysician looks on all these temporal laws as secondary to the one law of God. That one law, we are told, is to be written in our heart, our inward parts. Then there is something within us that naturally responds to the law of God. If we accept this as true, that we know the one law by an inner intelligence and that all other laws are secondary to it, we are in a position to get results, to demonstrate prosperity.

In the natural world about us we see that everything is governed by law. We are told that the whole animal kingdom is guided by instinct. Many theories have been advanced to explain instinct in terms of material thought. Some philosophers have stated that it is something handed down from one generation to the next, incorporated in germ cells. Whether this is true or not, there is every evidence that there is a law either in or around the cells that controls their formation and duplicates the pattern laid down ages ago in Mother Eve and Father Adam. This is the law written in our inward parts, which is not a figure of speech but a recognized fact. We must look within for the law and not without. The laws we find in the outer are the secondary laws. The infinite, creative Mind has given to every one of us a key to the workings of this unfailing inner law. It is that everything we touch mentally or physically represents substance and that it is limited only by ourselves in our thought capacity. We cannot ask God for more substance, for the universe is full of it. We can and should ask for understanding to lay hold of it with our mind; that is, for an increase in our capacity. Back of the substance is the substance idea, and man is related to the cause side of this idea through his oneness with God.

You may think that you could live better and do more good if you had lots of money. Things would not be a bit better with you if you had a million dollars, unless you also had the understanding to use it for the good of yourself and others. Would you give a child a million dollars to go buy candy and ice cream for himself? We must evolve with our possessions until we get the ability to handle them. Then the law is fulfilled. The supply unfolds at the same rate as the need or ability to use substance is developed. Let us realize this law of unfolding substance and get busy to fulfill it in ourselves by developing our understanding and appreciation of it. We should pray for just as much each day as we need or can handle. "Give us this day our daily bread" is a prayer that conforms to the divine law and answers itself.

Infinite Mind has a lawful way for providing its children with supply for all their needs. Nothing is left to chance. God feeds the birds of the air and clothes the lilies of the field, and He will feed and clothe us unless we make it impossible by our refusal to accept His bounty. Paul said that the fulfilling of the law is love. That is exactly what we must do, love the Lord and love our neighbor as ourselves, and love our work. The law is there, in our inward parts, in our very heart. We know what to do. We don't have to pray or beg for God to give us anything. All we need do is to meditate quietly and affirm the presence and power of the great Giver of all, and then accept the gifts. To be true to the law is to stop looking to the without and to look within for supply. Looking to the within means fixing the mind on God as an ever-present Spirit that is also substance and power. Wrapped up within each of us is a great richness of thoughts. These thoughts are prisoners in the subconsciousness only waiting to be set free to go to work for us. They are waiting for the coming of the Son of God, who releases the prisoners and sets the captives free. This Son is now seeking expression in you; is you. Release your rich thoughts, set free your innate powers, and take from the rich substance of the Father what you will.

Through faith in the overcoming power of Jesus Christ, the sense mind will be overcome and the spiritual mind brought into control of your life and affairs. The sense mind is filled with lacks and limitations; the spiritual mind knows only limitless abundance.

You are linked with the universal spiritual mind through the Christ Mind. It is through the Christ Mind that all things come to you; it is the channel to the all-mind of the Father. Make the unity of wholeness with the Christ Mind. Hold that you are master with the Master, one with the all-providing substance and that your prosperity runneth over. As you begin this process of unifying yourself consciously with the inner life and substance, it will begin to well up within you and to overflow into your affairs, so that you will be prosperous. Remain true to this inner life no matter what the outer appearance may be, and you cannot help but bring the good things of life into manifestation.

All manifest substance flows from a realm of light waves, according to the findings of modern physical science. James says, "Every good gift and every perfect gift is from above, coming down from the Father of lights." This is an exact statement of a scientific law, even to the use of the plural form of the word "lights," for as science states, one or more light particles, electrons, form the atom that is the basis of all material manifestation. God ideas then are the source of all that appears. Accept this as an absolute truth, an all-productive truth, and consciously connect your mind with the Father-Mind. Then you will begin to realize a never-failing prosperity that comes from Being itself.

The German philosopher and poet Goethe says, "The highest and most excellent thing in man is formless, and we should guard against giving it shape in anything less than noble dress." This is a recognition of the truth that man has the capacity within himself to give form to the formless substance. Jesus expressed the law by saying, "Whatsoever thou shalt bind on earth shall be bound in heaven; and whatsoever thou shalt loose on earth shall be loosed in heaven." This heaven is the realm of pure ideas in Mind. We are constantly incorporating these ideas into our mind and giving them form and shape according to our loyalty to Truth.

To every metaphysician this is a very important and very delicate process, because it is through this that we develop our soul. This soul development is often compared to the development of a photographic plate. The light puts the image on the sensitive plate in the first place, or as James says, it is a gift from "the Father of lights." There is then an image on the plate, but it is invisible and unmanifest until it goes through a developing process. Infinite Mind has imaged all its attributes in the soul of every man. But man must develop this image into the clear picture, and much of that work must be done in the dark with perfect faith in the law of manifestation. The photographer works in the darkroom, putting the plate through many processes. Sometimes the developer may make an error in some of the operations and the plate will come out with an imperfect image. So the human manifestation sometimes seems distorted, but the image of perfection imprinted by creative Mind is there. This perfect image is "Christ in you, the hope of glory."

Our body and affairs are first proofs of the development of the picture, but floating in our mind are the higher ideas, the real image to be developed. Our mind is engaged more or less in a chemical process. It is hard to find a line of demarcation between physical and mental chemistry, for they follow the same law. However what has been imaged can be brought out by the proper method of development. Whatever you image yourself as doing, you can do.

In our human understanding we have divorced this imaging power of the mind from the executive power. Now let us bring them together and unify them, for when imagination and will work together all things are possible to man. The will is symbolized in Scripture by the king. King Solomon was probably the world's richest man, and in so far as the world is concerned he was a great success. He demonstrated prosperity. He did not ask God for riches. Let us note that carefully. He asked God for wisdom, for ideas. God is mind and His gifts are not material but spiritual, not things but ideas. Solomon asked for and received the ideas and then developed them himself. Because he was wise all the world came to his court seeking wisdom and bringing riches in exchange for it. The King of Tyre brought the material he needed to build the Temple. The Queen of Sheba brought him great quantities of gold. From this we should get our cue: ask God for rich ideas (substance) and then put them to work in our affairs.

Do not hesitate to use the divine ideas that come to you, but do not forget their source or foundation. There are many people who are very active executives. The moment they get an idea they make use of it, but oftentimes they do not get far, because they forget the foundation on which such ideas rest and from which we must start to build. With a foundation of Truth, of spiritual ideas and substance we can build an enduring structure of prosperity. It will not be based on a false premise. It will stand when the rains descend and the floods come and the winds blow and beat upon it. We do not desire prosperity today and poverty tomorrow. We should seek for the steady, day-by-day realization of abundant supply.

Jesus understood and used this law of forming the formless substance by the power of imagination and will. When the woman touched the hem of His garment, some of this substance, of which He was vividly conscious, flowed from Him and healed her. He immediately remarked that someone had touched Him. Many had touched Him in the throng and no substance had left His body from those contacts, but the woman of faith was open to receive the healing substance and consciously appropriate it. This proved her faith, and Jesus told her to be of good cheer, for her faith had made her whole. The same substance was available to others who crowded against Him, but only the one who recognized it and laid hold of it received. Even so you and I shall receive no benefit, although substance is everywhere around us and in us, unless we recognize its presence by faith and lay hold of it by the hem of its garment (outer expression).

Jesus recognized the omnipresence of substance when He laid hold of it to multiply the loaves and the fishes. He dwelt in a consciousness of it at all times. Once He told the apostles when they asked Him to eat, "I have meat to eat that ye know not of." He built this divine substance into His body, cell by cell, replacing the mortal flesh with the spiritual substance, until His whole body was immortalized. He demonstrated it and told us how it was done. He said, "He that believeth on me, the works that I do shall he do also; and greater works than these shall he do." Then why are so many people poor, distressed, ill, or troubled? There is a way, a law, and a wisdom to apply the law, and there is an abundance of substance waiting to be formed by each of us into whatsoever we will, when we apply that law as a son of God.

There is an inherent faculty that instinctively lays hold of what it calls its own. Even little children like to have their own toys and to keep them separate from those of other children. There is nothing to be condemned in this, for it is the natural outworking of a divine law. It proves that we know, somewhere in our deepest being, that we have been provided for from the foundation of the world and are entitled to our own portion without question. The power of the mind to draw to us those things to which we are divinely entitled is a power that can be cultivated and should be.

We are now on the verge of a new state of mind in matters financial. Let us do away with the erroneous idea that men must be poor to be righteous. Money is man's instrument, not his master. Money was made for man, not man for money. Only those who put money above man and give it power in their minds by worshiping it, are the "rich" men to whom Jesus referred in His story about the camel and the needle's eye. It is not money that controls men, but the ideas they have about money. Ideas of poverty are just as powerful to enslave men as are ideas of wealth. Every man should be taught how to handle ideas, rather than money, so that they serve him rather than have dominion over him.

Some physical scientists are telling us that the time is near when men will manufacture from the ether, right at hand, everything that they need or desire. Man will not have to wait for seedtime and harvest when he learns to use the power of his mind. When we have that consciousness in which our ideas are tangible, all our demands will be quickly fulfilled by the higher law. Throw into your ideas all the life and power of your concentrated thought, and they will be clothed with reality.

When Jesus went into the wilderness of His (then) untried mental powers He was tempted to turn stones into bread. We all have had this temptation, and most of us have succumbed to it. We get our bread out of material things (stones) instead of out of the words that proceed from the mouth of God. It is the word, the idea, that feeds the soul of man. That is admitted. But we must realize that it is the word, the idea, that feeds the body and the affairs of man also, for unless the word is recognized and appropriated, there is a lack of the true substance and there is no satisfaction in the food. Fortunately the "Father knoweth that we have need of all these things," and in His compassion and mercy He feeds us with the substance even while we still try to assimilate the stones. If we would seek first the kingdom of God, the substance, the "things" would be added and we should consciously enjoy the fullness of living, the abundant life of Jesus Christ.

There is a universal law of increase. It is not confined to bank accounts but operates on every plane of manifestation. The conscious co-operation of man is necessary to the fullest results in the working of this law. You must use your talent, whatever it may be, in order to increase it. Have faith in the law. Do not reason too much but forge ahead in faith and boldness. If you let yourself think of any person or any outer condition as hindering your increase, this becomes a hindrance to you, for you have applied the law of increase to it. Fear of it may cause you to become timid and bury your talent, which defeats the law. Keep your eyes on the abundant inner reality and do not let the outer appearance cause you to falter.

Do not give too close study to yourself or your present condition. To dwell in mind upon your seeming limitations only prolongs their stay and makes your progress slow. A child loses sight of everything but his increase in size. The boy sees himself as a larger boy, even as a man. It is the childlike mind that finds the kingdom. Then look ahead to the perfect man you are to be in the Spirit and behold yourself as the beloved son in whom the Father is well pleased.

God gives the increase, we are told in the Scripture. This is to be remembered, for we so often think that increase is the result of our personal efforts. Increase comes by the operation of a universal law, and our part is to keep that law. Use the talent of life, and it will expand wonderfully. You do this by talking about life, praising it, and giving God thanks for it. Act as though you were alive and glad to be alive and you will gain a new realization of life, an increase in life itself.

Never allow yourself to come under the control of the "I can't" man. He believes in limitations, wraps his talent in them, and hides it away in the negative earth, and no increase is possible to him. Be positive in Spirit and you will succeed. All the negative talents that are buried away in the depths of material thought can be resurrected by Spirit and made positive, put to the right use, contributing to the increase of your good. Appetite and passion, which are decreasing and destructive in the material can be made increasing and constructive when directed to the things of Spirit. "Blessed are they that hunger and thirst after righteousness: for they shall be filled."

If there is any lack apparent in man's world it is because the requirements of the law of manifestation have not been met.

This law is based on mind and its operation through thoughts and words. The key to the operation of mind is symbolically set forth in the Genesis account of the six days of creation. Man's mind goes through the identical steps in bringing an idea into manifestation. Between the perception of an idea and its manifestation there are six definite, positive movements, followed by a (seventh) "day" of rest, in which the mind relaxes and sees its work in process of fulfillment.

In bringing forth a manifestation of God's abundant supply, take the first step by saying, "Let there be light"; that is, let there be understanding. You must have a clear perception of the principle back of the proposition "God will provide." The one universal, eternal, substance of God, which is the source of all, must be discerned and relied on, while dependence on material things must be eliminated from thought. So long as you depend on money alone you are worshiping a false god and have not discerned the light. You must first enter into the understanding that God, omnipresent, omnipotent, and omniscient, is the source and that you can draw on this source without limit. If you have established that light, you have begun your demonstration and can go to the second step. A "firmament" must be established; that is, a firm place in the mind, a dividing of the true from the apparent. This is done through affirmation. As you affirm God as your supply and support, your words will in due season become substance to you, the substance of faith.

The third step is the forming of this substance into tangibility. "Let the dry land appear." Out of the omnipresent substance your mind forms whatever it wants by the power of imagination. If it is food you need, see yourself as bountifully supplied with food. If you have already taken the other steps, you can picture in mind the things you desire and bring them into your manifest world. If the other steps of understanding and faith have not been taken first, there will of course be no demonstration, for above all the creative law is orderly and works by progressive steps. Many people have tried to demonstrate by visualizing and concentrating and have failed because they have put the third step first. They have not developed understanding or faith. If you work according to the law, conforming to its orderly operation as revealed in the degrees of creation, you cannot fail, because when you have fulfilled the law you have found the kingdom.

Jesus recognized order as a fundamental factor in the law of increase. When He fed the multitude He made them sit down in companies. If you study the story carefully you will see that there was a great deal of preliminary preparation before the demonstration was made. There was a recognition of the seed ideas, the loaves and fishes carried by the small boy. There was a prayer of thanks for that supply and then it was blessed. All this preceded the actual appearing and appropriation of the supply. Every demonstration is based on the same law of increase and goes through the same orderly steps.

Pray, but let your prayer be affirmative, for that is the prayer of faith. A begging prayer filled with ifs is a prayer of doubt. Keep praying until affirmations become a habit of mind. The race thought of lack must be penetrated and so charged with the truth of God's omnipresent abundance that all consciousness of lack and poverty disappears from the face of the earth. The more we trust to the simplicity and infallibility of the law the better will be our individual demonstration and the more we shall contribute to the transformation of the race thought that causes lack and famine. Those who make the greatest spiritual demonstrations are not the wise of the world but the obedient children of the law on the bosom of infinite love.

See what you need as already manifest and as yours. Do not put it off to some uncertain future time. God wants you to have it now. Remember always God's omnipresence, and if doubts come in, do not entertain them. Say: "I trust Omnipotence." "I refuse to be anxious about tomorrow or even the next minute. I know that God does provide for the fulfillment of His divine idea, and I am that divine idea." This divine idea is the son, the perfect man, the Christ, brought forth on the sixth day. If you would have your inheritance, you must not omit this sixth-day realization. God expresses Himself as man and works through man to bring perfection into expression.

To give up all anxiety and trust in the Lord does not mean to sit down and do nothing. "My Father worketh even until now, and I work." We are to work as God works; to work with God, as a son follows the occupation of his father. We are to form what God has created. In the 1st chapter of Genesis we see how the Father works. The various steps in His method are clearly pointed out, and we shall have results only as we faithfully follow them.

Some people think of prosperity as something separate from their spiritual experience, "outside the pale" of religion. They live in two worlds: in one for six days of the week when man runs things, and in the other on the seventh day when God is given a chance to show what He can do. It is personality's demonstration when people find themselves complaining of hard times and depression, but it is not the way to demonstrate God in the fullness of all things. Do all things to the glory of God seven days a week rather than one. Take God into all your affairs. Use this thought in the silence and bring God and His law of prosperity into your affairs: I trust Thy universal law of prosperity in all my affairs.

Chapter VI

Wealth of Mind Expresses Itself in Riches

PROSPERITY, according to Webster, is an advance or gain in anything good or desirable, successful progress toward, or attainment of a desired object. Prosperity does not mean the same thing to any two persons. To the wage earner an increase of a few dollars in the weekly income may seem like wonderful prosperity, for it means an increase in the comfort and welfare of his family. The man who engages in vast enterprises reckons prosperity in larger terms, and does not consider himself prosperous unless things are coming to him in a big way. Between these extremes are many ideas of prosperity, which shows quite plainly that prosperity is not in the possession of things but in the recognition of supply and in the knowledge of free and open access to an inexhaustible storehouse of all that is good or desirable.

In the great Mind of God there is no thought of lack, and such a thought has no rightful place in your mind. It is your birthright to be prosperous, regardless of who you are or where you may be. Jesus said to all men, "Seek ye first his kingdom, and his righteousness; and all these things shall be added unto you." This does not mean that if you belong to a certain church you will be prospered, for "righteousness" is not conforming to some particular religious belief but to the law of right thinking, regardless of creed, dogma, or religious form. Get into the prosperity thought and you will demonstrate prosperity. Cultivate the habit of thinking about abundance everywhere present, not only in the forms of imagination but in forms without. Jesus did not make a separation between the two as though they were at enmity. He said, "Render therefore unto Caesar the things that are Caesar's; and unto God the things that are God's." Put things in their right relation, the spiritual first and the material following, each where it belongs, and render to each its own.

Realize first of all that prosperity is not wholly a matter of capital or environment but a condition brought about by certain ideas that have been allowed to rule in the consciousness. When these ideas are changed the conditions are changed in spite of environment and all appearances, which must also change to conform to the new ideas. People who come into riches suddenly without building up a consciousness of prosperity soon part from their money. Those who are born and bred to riches usually have plenty all their life even though they never make the effort to earn a dollar for themselves. This is because the ideas of plenty are so interwoven into their thought atmosphere that they are a very part of themselves. They have the prosperity consciousness, in which there is no idea of any condition under which the necessities of life could be lacking.

We are sometimes asked whether we advocate the accumulation of riches. No. The accumulation of riches, as has been explained, is futile unless it is the outgrowth of a rich consciousness. We advocate the accumulation rather of rich ideas, ideas that are useful, constructive, and of service to the well-being of all mankind. The outer manifestation of riches may follow or it may not, but the supply for every need will be forthcoming because the man of rich ideas has confidence in an all-providing power that never fails. He may not have an extra dollar, but his ideas have merit and he has confidence, a combination that cannot fail to attract the money to carry him forward. This is true riches, not an accumulation of money, but access to an inexhaustible resource that can be drawn on at any time to meet any righteous demand. When a person has this rich consciousness there is no necessity for laying up gold or accumulating stocks and bonds or other property to ensure future supply. Such a one may be most generous with his wealth without fear of depletion, because his rich ideas will keep him in constant touch with abundance. Those who have the thought of accumulating material wealth, a thought that is dominant in the world today, are unbalanced. They have a fear of the loss of riches that makes their tenure insecure. Their prosperity is based on a wrong idea of the source of riches and eventually means disaster. The sin of riches is not in the possession but in the love of money, a material selfishness that leads to soul starvation.

It is not a crime to be rich nor a virtue to be poor, as certain reformers would have us think. The sin lies in hoarding wealth and keeping it from circulating freely to all who need it. Those who put wealth into useful work that contributes to the welfare of the masses are the salvation of the country. Fortunately, there are many in this country who have the prosperity consciousness. If we were all in a poverty consciousness, famines would be as common here as they are in India or China. Millions in those lands are held in the perpetual thought of poverty and they suffer want in all its forms from the cradle to the grave. The burden of the poverty thought reacts on the earth so that year after year it withholds its products and many people starve.

Universal Mind controls all nature and is in possession of all its products. "The earth is the Lord's, and the fulness thereof" is a great Truth. Puny, personal man uses all his craft to get control of the products of nature but is always defeated in the end. Only the universal man of Spirit is in indisputed possession, and to him the Father says, "All that is mine is thine." Jesus did not have title to a foot of land and evidently had no money, for the apostles carried whatever funds the company had. He did not even burden Himself with a tub, as did Diogenes, and "had not where to lay his head." Yet He was always provided with entertainment of the best. He took it for granted that whatever He needed was His. The fish carried His pocketbook, and the invisible ethers furnished the sideboard from which He handed out food for thousands. He was rich in every way for He had the prosperity consciousness and proved that the earth with all its fullness does belong to the Lord, whose righteous sons are heirs to and in possession of all things.

The anxious thought must be eliminated and the perfect abandon of the child of nature assumed, and when to this attitude you add the realization of unlimited resources, you have fulfilled the divine law of prosperity.

The imagination is a wonderful creative power. It builds all things out of the one substance. When you associate it with faith, you make things just as real as those that God makes, for man is a co-creator with God. Whatever you form in the mind and have faith in will become substantial. Then you should be on guard as regards what you put your faith in. If it is material forms, shadows that cease to be as soon as your supporting thought is withdrawn from them, you are building temporary substance that will pass away and leave you nothing. Put your faith in the real or, as Jesus told His disciples, "have faith in God."

The real search of all people is for God. They may think they are looking for other things, but they must eventually admit that it is God they seek. Having once felt His presence within them, they are keenly conscious that only God can satisfy. The place where we meet God should be made so sure and so pure that we can never mistake His voice or be hidden from His face. This place we know as the mind, the inmost recess of the soul, the kingdom of the heavens within us.

It is not sufficient however to sit down and hold thoughts of abundance without further effort. That is limiting the law to thought alone, and we want it to be fulfilled in manifestation as well. Cultivating ideas of abundance is the first step in the process. The ideas that come must be used. Be alert in doing whatever comes to you to do, cheerful and competent in the doing, sure of the results, for it is the second step in the fulfilling of the law.

You can do anything with the thoughts of your mind. They are yours and under your control. You can direct them, coerce them, hush them, or crush them. You can dissolve one thought and put another in its stead. There is no other place in the universe where you are the absolute master. The dominion given you as your divine right is over your own thoughts only. When you fully apprehend this and begin to exercise your God-given dominion, you begin to find the way to God, the only door to God, the door of mind and thought.

If you are fearful that you will not be provided with the necessities of life for tomorrow, next week, or next year, or for your old age, or that your children will be left in want, deny the thought. Do not allow yourself for a moment to think of something that must be outside the realm of all-careful, all-providing good. You know even from your outer experience that the universe is self-sustaining and that its equilibrium is established by law. The same law that sustains all sustains you as a part. Claim your identity under that law, your oneness with the all, and rest in the everlasting arms of Cause, which knows nothing of lack. If you are in a condition of poverty, this attitude of mind will attract to you opportunities to better your condition. Insulate your mind from the destructive thoughts of all those who labor under the belief in hard times. If your associates talk about the financial stringency, affirm all the more persistently your dependence on the abundance of God.

By doing this you place yourself under a divine law of demand and supply that is never influenced by the fluctuations of the market or the opinions of men. Every time you send out a thought of wholehearted faith in the I AM part of yourself, you set in motion a chain of causes that must bring the results you seek. Ask whatsoever you will in the name of the Christ, the I AM, the divine within, and your demands will be fulfilled; both heaven and earth will hasten to do your bidding. But when you have asked for something, be on the alert to receive it when it comes. People complain that their prayers are not answered when, if we knew the truth, they are not awake to receive the answer when it comes.

If you ask for money, do not look for an angel from the skies to bring it on a golden platter, but keep your eyes open for some fresh opportunity to make money, an opportunity that will come as sure as you live.

These are some tangible steps along the way to the larger manifestation you desire. No one is ever given the keys to the Father's storehouse of wealth until he has proved his faith and his reliability. Then he may go in and pass out the goods freely. If the men of the world, with their selfish ideas of "mine and thine," were given the power, without a thorough mental cleansing, of instantly producing whatever they desire, they would undoubtedly practice still greater oppressions on their fellows, and existing conditions would not be improved.

A stonecutter sees a block of marble as so many hours work, while Michelangelo sees it as an angel that it is his privilege to bring forth. This is the difference between those who see the material world as so much matter and those who look on it with the eyes of mind and the imagination that works toward perfection. One who paints a picture or makes a piece of sculpture first sees it in his mind. He first imagines or images it. If he wants a strong picture he makes force one of the elements of his image. If he wants beauty and character, he puts love into it. He may not see the perfect picture until all these elements are combined, then it requires but little effort to transfer it from his mind to the canvas or to the marble.

On the sixth day of creation, we are told, God "imaged" His man, made him in His image and likeness. This does not mean that God looks like man, a personal being with manlike form. We make a thing in our own image, the image we have in mind for the thing, and our creation does not resemble us in any way. God is without form, for He is Spirit. God is an idea that man has tried to objectify in various forms. He is the universal substance, the life that animates the substance, and the love that binds it together. Man just naturally gives some form to every idea he has, even the idea of God, for the formative faculty of the mind is always at work whether we are awake or asleep. We get material for forming mental pictures from without and from within.

This imaging or formative power of the mind could not make anything unless it had the substance out of which to form it. One could not make a loaf of bread without the flour and other ingredients. Yet with all the ingredients at hand one could not make a loaf unless one had the power of imaging the loaf in one's mind. This seems simple, but the fact is that the power to form the loaf is less common than the available material for the loaf. Flour and water are abundant, but only certain people can use them in the right way to form a palatable loaf of bread. So with this subject of prosperity. Substance is everywhere, filling all the universe. There is no lack. If we have not been successful in forming it into the things we have needed and wished for, it is not because of lack of substance but of lack of understanding how to use our imaging power.

The world goes through periods of seeming lack because the people have refused to build their prosperity on the inner, omnipresent, enduring substance, and on the contrary have tried to base it on the substance that they see in the outer. This outer substance, formed by the imaging power of men in past ages, seems to be limited, and men struggle for it, forgetting their own divine power to form their own substance from the limitless supply within. The lesson for all of us should be to build our prosperity on the inner substance.

Those who do demonstrate prosperity through the law of men have nothing permanent. All their possessions may be swept away in a moment. They have not built on the orderly law of God, and without the rich thoughts of God's bounteousness no one can have an enduring consciousness of supply.

No disease, poverty, or any other negative condition can enter into our domain unless we invite it. Nor can it remain with us unless we entertain it. Conscious power over all such conditions is one of our greatest delights and a part of our divine inheritance, but we must learn the law and apply the power in the right way.

Men have a consciousness of lack because they let Satan, the serpent of sense, tempt them. The Garden of Eden is within us here and now, and the subtle temptation to eat of the tree of sensation is also still with us. We have been given dominion over the animal forces of the body, the "beasts of the field," and must tame them, making them servants instead of masters of the body. Instead of feeding them we must make them feed us. When we overcome the animals within, it will be easy to train them in the without. This truth of overcoming is taught all through the Scriptures, and we can demonstrate it in our life, for God has endowed us with the power to overcome. We must lay hold of that inherent power and begin to use it constructively.

The whole human family seems to be sensation mad. All our economic and social troubles can be traced right back to the selfishness of the sense man. We can never overcome these conditions in the outer until we overcome their causes in the inner soul of ourselves. There is sure to be repetition of war and peace, plenty and famine, good times and depressions until we take the control of mind substance away from the sense man and give it to the spiritual man. We know that there is a spiritual man and we look forward in some ideal way to his coming, but he will never come until we bring him. We hope and pray for the coming of better things; but as Mark Twain said about the weather, "no one does anything about it." We can do something about the matter of self-control and each of us must if we are ever to improve our condition physically and financially as well as morally and spiritually.

We must lift up this serpent of sense, as Moses lifted up the serpent in the wilderness, and control it in the name of Christ.

Eliminate all negative thoughts that come into your mind. Yet do not spend all your time in denials but give much of it to the clear realization of the everywhere present and waiting substance and life. Some of us have in a measure inherited "hard times" by entertaining the race thought so prevalent around us. Do not allow yourself to do this. Remember your identity, that you are a son of God and that your inheritance is from Him. You are the heir to all that the Father has. Let the I AM save you from every negative thought. The arrows that fly by day and the pestilence that threatens are these negative race thoughts in the mental atmosphere. The I AM consciousness, your Saviour, will lead you out of the desert of negation and into the Promised Land of plenty that flows with milk and honey.

Deny that you can lose anything. Let go of negative thoughts of financial loss or any other kind of loss and realize that nothing is ever lost in all the universe. There are opportunities everywhere, just as there have always been, to produce all that you need financially, or otherwise. God wants you to be a producer of new ideas. New ideas come to you from within. Do not think for a moment that you are limited to the ideas that come from without. Many of those ideas are outgrown anyway and have outlived their usefulness. That is why we go through periods of change; so that old outworn ideas can be discarded and replaced with new and better ones. There have been more inventions since the beginning of the so-called depression than in any previous similar period of American history. This shows that new ideas are within man, just waiting to be called out and put into expression. We can find new ways of living and new methods of work; we are not confined to the ways and methods of the past. When we commune with the Spirit within and ask for new ideas, they are always forthcoming. When these ideas from within us are recognized, they go to work and come to the surface. Then all the thoughts we have ever had, as well as the thoughts of other people, are added to them and new things are quickly produced. Let us quit slavishly depending on someone else for everything and become producers, for only in that direction lies happiness and success. Let us begin to concentrate on this inner man, this powerful man who produces things, who gets his ideas from a higher-dimensional realm, who brings ideas from a new territory, the land of Canaan.

What kind of character are you giving to this inner substance by your thoughts? Change your thought and increase your substance in the mind, as Elisha increased the oil for the widow. Get larger receptacles and plenty of them. Even a very small idea of substance may be added to and increased. The widow had a very small amount of oil, but as the prophet blessed it it increased until it filled every vessel she could borrow from the neighbors. We should form the habit of blessing everything that we have. It may seem foolish to some persons that we bless our nickels, dimes, and dollars, but we know that we are setting the law of increase into operation. All substance is one and connected, whether in the visible or the invisible. The mind likes something that is already formed and tangible for a suggestion to take hold of. With this image the mind sets to work to draw like substance from the invisible realm and thus increase what we have in hand. Jesus used the small quantity of loaves and fishes to produce a great quantity of--loaves and fishes. Elisha used a small amount of oil to produce a great amount of--oil. So when we bless our money or other goods, we are complying with a divine law of increase that has been demonstrated many times.

Another step in the demonstration of prosperity is the preparation of the consciousness to receive the increase. If we pray for rain, we should be sure that we have our umbrellas with us. You read in the 3d chapter of II Kings how Elisha caused the water to come from the invisible and fill trenches in the desert. But first the trenches had to be dug in the dry ground. That required faith, but the kings had it, and they dug trenches all over a large valley, just as Elisha had commanded. It was through the understanding of Elisha, who knew the truth about the invisible substance, that this seeming miracle was accomplished. Yet the trenches had to be prepared, and you must prepare your consciousness for the inflow of the universal substance. It obeys the law of nature, just as does water or any other visible thing, and flows into the place prepared for it. It fills everything you hold in your mind, whether vessels, trenches, or your purse.

It is not advisable to hold for too specific a demand. You might visualize a hundred dollars and get it when a thousand was coming your way. Do not limit the substance, to what you think you need or want; rather broaden your consciousness and give infinite Mind freedom to work, and every good and needful thing will be provided you. Make your statements broad and comprehensive so that your mind may expand to the Infinite rather than trying to cram the Infinite into your mind.

Statements To Broaden The Mind And Fill It With The Richness Of Substance

Infinite wisdom guides me, divine love prospers me, and I am successful in everything I undertake.

In quietness and confidence I affirm the drawing power of divine love as my magnet of constantly increasing supply.

I have unbounded faith in the omnipresent substance increasing and multiplying at my word of plenty, plenty, plenty.

Father, I thank Thee for unlimited increase in mind, money, and affairs.

Chapter VII

God Has Provided Prosperity for Every Home

THE HOME is the heart of the nation. The heart is the love center. Love is the world's greatest attractive power. The electromagnet that lifts the ingots of steel must first be charged with the electric current, for without the current it is powerless. So the heart of man, or the home that is the heart of the nation, must be aglow with God's love; then it becomes a magnet drawing all good from every direction. God has amply provided for every home, but the provision is in universal substance, which responds only to law. Through the application of the law the substance is drawn to us and begins to work for us.

It is the law of love that we have whatsoever we desire. As a father gives his children gifts so the Lord gives to us, because of love. When we desire aright, we put our thoughts into the supermind realm; we contact God-Mind and from it draw the invisible substance that is manifest in temporal things. The substance thus becomes a part of our mind and through it of our affairs. We draw spiritual substance to ourselves just as the magnet draws the iron. When we think about the love of God drawing to us the substance necessary for support and supply, that substance begins to accumulate all around us, and as we abide in the consciousness of it, it begins to manifest itself in all our affairs.

"Perfect love casteth out fear." Fear is a great breeder of poverty, for it breaks down positive thoughts. Negative thoughts bring negative conditions in their train. The first thing to do in making a demonstration of prosperity in the home is to discard all negative thoughts and words. Build up a positive thought atmosphere in the home, an atmosphere that is free from fear and filled with love. Do not allow any words of poverty or lack to limit the attractive power of love in the home. Select carefully only those words that charge the home atmosphere with the idea of plenty, for like attracts like in the unseen as well as the seen. Never make an assertion in the home, no matter how true it may look on the surface, that you would not want to see persist in the home. By talking poverty and lack you are making a comfortable place for these unwelcome guests by your fireside, and they will want to stay. Rather fill the home with thoughts and words of plenty, of love, and of God's substance; then the unwelcome guests will soon leave you.

Do not say that money is scarce; the very statement will scare money away from you. Do not say that times are hard with you; the very words will tighten your purse strings until Omnipotence itself cannot slip a dime into it. Begin now to talk plenty, think plenty, and give thanks for plenty. Enlist all the members of the home in the same work. Make it a game. It's lots of fun, and, better than that, it actually works.

Every home can be prosperous, and there should be no poverty-stricken homes, for they are caused only by inharmony, fear, negative thinking and speaking. Every visible item of wealth can be traced to an invisible source. Food comes from grain, which was planted in the earth; but who sees or knows the quickening love that touches the seed and makes it bear a hundredfold? An unseen force from an invisible source acts on the tiny seeds, and supply for the multitude springs forth.

The physical substance that we name earth is the visible form of a superabundant mind substance, everywhere present, pervading all things, and inspiring all things to action. When the grain or seed is put into the earth, the quickening thought of the universe causes the little life germ to lay hold of the spiritual substance all about it and what we call matter proves to be a form of mind. "There is no matter; all is mind."

Words are also seeds, and when dropped into the invisible spiritual substance, they grow and bring forth after their kind.

"Do men gather grapes of thorns, or figs of thistles?" Farmers and gardeners choose their seed with the greatest care. They reject every defective seed they find and in this way make sure of the coming crop. To have prosperity in your home you will have to exercise the same intelligent discrimination in the choice of your seed words.

You should expect prosperity when you keep the prosperity law. Therefore, be thankful for every blessing that you gain and as deeply grateful for every demonstration as for an unexpected treasure dropped into your lap. This will keep your heart fresh; for true thanksgiving may be likened to rain falling upon ready soil, refreshing it and increasing its productiveness. When Jesus had only a small supply He gave thanks for the little He had. This increased that little into such an abundance that a multitude was satisfied with food and much was left over. Blessing has not lost its power since the time Jesus used it. Try it and you will prove its efficacy. The same power of multiplication is in it today. Praise and thanksgiving impart the quickening spiritual power that produces growth and increase in all things.

You should never condemn anything in your home. If you want new articles of furniture or new clothes to take the place of those you now have, do not talk about your present things as old or shabby. Watch your words. See yourself clothed as befits a child of the King and see your house furnished just as pleases your ideal. Thus plant in the home atmosphere the seed of richness and abundance. It will all come to you. Use the patience, the wisdom, and the assiduity that the farmer employs in planting and cultivating, and your crop will be sure.

Your words of Truth are energized and vitalized by the living Spirit. Your mind is now open and receptive to an influx of divine ideas that will inspire you with the understanding of the potency of your own thoughts and words. You are prospered. Your home is a magnet of love, drawing to it all good from the unfailing and inexhaustible reservoir of supply. Your increase comes because of your righteous application of God's law in your home.

"The blessing of Jehovah, it maketh rich; And he addeth no sorrow therewith."

Jesus showed men how to live in rest and peace, a simple life. Where the simplicity of His teaching is received and appreciated the people change their manner of living, doing away with ostentation and getting down to the simplicity and beauty of the things that are worth while. Every summer those who feel that they can, plan to go away for a vacation and many of them enjoy a small cabin in the woods where they can live a simple and natural life close to nature. This shows that they long to let go of the burdens of conventionality and rest in touch with the real of things. The soul wearies of the wear and tear of the artificial world, and now and then it must have a season of rest. Jesus invites, "Come unto me, all ye that labor and are heavy laden, and I will give you rest."

There is a great difference between the simple life and poverty. The two have been associated in the minds of some people, and this is the reason they shun the idea of the simple life. Even those who have come into some degree of spiritual understanding sometimes put out of mind all thought of a simple manner of living, because they fear that others will think they are failing to demonstrate prosperity. In such cases those who judge should remember to "judge not according to appearance," and those who are judged should be satisfied with the praise of God rather than with the praise of men. All those who base their prosperity on possessions alone have a purely material prosperity which, though it may seem great for a time, will vanish, because it is founded on the changing of the external and has no root within the consciousness.

There is a great similarity in the homes of nearly all people who have about the same-sized incomes. Each one uhconsciously follows suggestion and furnishes his home with the same sort of things as his neighbors. Here and there are exceptions. Someone is expressing his or her individuality, overcoming mass suggestion and buying the kind of furniture he really wants or that is really comfortable and useful. This free, independent spirit has much in its favor in making a prosperity demonstration. The delusion that it is necessary to be just like other people or to have as much as other people have, causes a spirit of anxiety that hinders the exercise of faith in demonstration.

The simple life does not imply poverty and it is not ascetic. It is as different from the austere as it is from wanton luxury. It is the natural, free, childlike, mode of living, and one never really knows what true prosperity is until one comes into this simplicity and independence of spirit. The simple life is a state of consciousness. It is peace, contentment, and satisfaction in the joy of living and loving, and it is attained through thinking about God and worshiping Him in spirit and in truth.

You want to learn how to demonstrate prosperity in your home by the righteous exercise of powers and faculties that God has given you. Realize in the very beginning that you do have these powers and faculties. You are in possession of everything necessary for the demonstration of prosperity and can undertake it with the utmost confidence and faith. You can draw on the omnipresent substance throughout all eternity, yet it will never grow less, for it consists of ideas. Through thinking you take some of these ideas into your mind and they begin to become manifest in your affairs.

Love is one of the ideas that provide a key to the infinite storehouse of abundance. It opens up generosity in us. It opens up generosity in others when we begin to love and bless them. Will it also open up a spirit of generosity in God? It certainly will and does. If you consciously love and bless God, you will soon find that things are coming your way. It will surprise you that just thinking about God will draw to you the things you want and expect, and bring many other blessings that you had not even thought about. Thousands of persons have proved this law to their entire satisfaction, and we have many records that illustrate how people have demonstrated abundance in the very face of apparent lack, simply by thinking about the love of God and thanking Him for what they have. This law will demonstrate itself for you or for anyone who applies it faithfully, for "love never faileth."

Men in business and industry have demonstrated great amounts of money through love. They did not love God, but the love of money attracted the money to them. It drew the substance right to them and enabled them to accumulate money, but merely as material, without the divine idea that assures permanence. We hear about men in high finance going bankrupt quite as often as we hear about men making great fortunes. When we develop a spiritual consciousness, we transfer this personal love to a higher and more stable plane, from the love of money and material things to the love of God, and thus conceived it will attract to us all the resources of infinite Mind forever and ever. Once make a connection with the universal bank of God and you have a permanent source of wealth.

Jesus said that when we come to the altar to make an offering, we should have nothing in our heart against our brother. He said that before we can make contact with the love and power of God we must first make peace with our brother. This means that we must cultivate a love for our fellows in order to set the attractive force of love into operation. All we need do is quicken our love for others by thinking about love and casting out of our mind all hate and fear that would weaken the perfect working of that mighty magnet. As love attracts, hate dissipates. Before you approach God's altar of plenty, go and make friends with your brother men. Make friends even with the money powers. Do not envy the rich. Never condemn those who have money merely because they have it and you do not. Do not question how they got their money and wonder whether or not they are honest. All that is none of your business. Your business is to get what belongs to you, and you do that by thinking about the omnipresent substance of God and how you can lay hold of it through love. Get in touch with God riches in spirit, lay hold of them by love, and you will have sufficient for every day. "Love therefore is the fulfillment of the law."

The eternal law of Spirit goes right on operating regardless of what you may think, say, or do. It is ordained that love will bring you prosperity, and you need not wonder whether it will or how it will. "Be not therefore anxious, saying, What shall we eat? or, What shall we drink? or, Wherewithal shall we be clothed?" Do not worry. Worry is a thief and a robber, for it keeps your good from you. It breaks the drawing law of love, the law that says, "Perfect love casteth out fear." Banish worry by quietly and confidently affirming the drawing power of divine love as the constantly active magnet that attracts your unfailing supply. A good affirmation to rout worry is one like this: Divine love bountifully supplies and increases substance to meet my every need.

Nearly all books or articles that deal with success or prosperity stress the well-known virtues of honesty, industry, system and order, faithfulness, hard work. These make an excellent foundation and can be developed. Anyone with determination and will can overcome habits of laziness, carelessness, and weakness. The use of the will is very important in the demonstration of prosperity. If there is disorder or lack of system in your home, overcome it. Affirm: I will to be orderly. I will be orderly. I will be systematic in all my work and affairs. I am systematic. I am orderly. I am efficient.

It takes the use of the will to be persistent, and we must be persistent in making demonstrations. Spasmodic efforts count for little, and many people give up too easily. If things don't come out just right the first time they try, they say the law is wrong and make no further effort. Anything so much worth while as prosperity in the home, and especially a permanent and unfailing supply that continues to meet the daily needs year after year, is worth any effort that we can make. Then be patient but be persistent. Declare: I am not discouraged. I am persistent. I go forward.

When success fails to crown our very first efforts we become discouraged and quit. Then we try to console ourselves with the old thought that it is God's will for us to be poor. Poverty is not God's will, but man lays it to the charge of God to excuse his own feeling of inadequacy and defeat. God's will is health, happiness, and prosperity for every man; and to have all that is good and beautiful in the home is to express God's will for us. God's will is not expressed in a hovel, nor in any home where discord, lack, and unhappiness are entertained. Even a human guest would not stay long in such a home. To have a prosperous home prepare it as the abiding place of God, who gives prosperity to all His children and adds no sorrow therewith. Determine to know God's will and do it. Affirm: I am determined to achieve success through doing God's will. That sums up the whole law. God is more willing to give than we are to receive.

What we need to do is to determine what is His will, what He is trying to give, and open ourselves to receive His bounty. We do that by willing to do His will. You can be and have anything that you will to be and to have. Will to be healthy. Will to be happy. Will to be prosperous.

There are many persons who will to be prosperous and who have made up their minds, as they think, very determinedly. But they have not overcome all doubts, and when their demonstration is delayed, as it is in such cases, the doubt increases until they lose faith altogether. What they need is more persistence and determination. The word determined is a good word, a strong, substantial word with power in it. Jesus said that His words were spirit and life and would never pass away. Emerson says that words are alive and if you cut one it will bleed. Use the word determined and emphasize it in your affirmations. If things do not seem to come fast enough, determine that you will be patient. If negative thoughts creep in, determine to be positive. If you feel worried about the results, determine to be optimistic. In response to every thought of lack or need determine to be prosperous. The Lord has prosperity to give, and those who are determined go after their share. Jesus was quite positive and very determined in all His affirmations. He made big claims for God, and demonstrated them. Without the slightest doubt that the money would be there, He told Peter to put his hand into the fish's mouth and take out the wanted money. His prayers were made of one strong affirmation after another. The Lord's Prayer is a series of determined affirmations. We claim the will of God is for us to be rich, prosperous, and successful. Make up your mind that such is God's will for you and your home and you will make your demonstration.

In the Old Testament, in the 4th chapter of II Kings, there is a fine prosperity lesson for any home. The widow represents one who has lost his consciousness of God's supply and support. That divine idea of God as all-abundance is our true support. The two children of this home represent the thoughts of debt, what the family owes, and what someone owes the family. The prophet is divine understanding. The house is the body consciousness. The pot of oil is faith in spiritual substance. The neighbors are outside thoughts, and their "empty vessels" are thoughts of lack. To go in "and shut the door," as the widow was told to do, is to enter the inner consciousness and shut out the thoughts of lack. This is followed by strong words of affirmation: "pouring" the substance into all the places that seem to be empty or to lack, until all are full.

In conclusion it is affirmed that every obligation is met, every debt paid, and there is so much left over that there are no vessels left to hold it.

This compares with the promise of God "I will ... open you the windows of heaven, and pour you out a blessing, that there shall not be room enough to receive it." "Heaven" represents the mind. All this is done in the mind, and you can do it. Carry each step forward in your imagination exactly as if it were occurring in the without. Form your prosperity demonstration in your mind, then hold to the divine law of fulfillment. "And, having done all ... stand." You may not be able to fill all the vessels with oil on your first attempt, but as you practice the method day by day your faith will increase and your results will be in proportion to your increasing faith.

Work at the problem until you prove it. Apply the principle and the solution is sure. If it does not come at once, check over your methods carefully and see wherein your work has not been true. Do not allow one empty thought to exist in your mind but fill every nook and corner of it with the word plenty, plenty, plenty.

If your purse seems empty, deny the lack and say, "You are filled even now, with the bounty of God, my Father, who supplies all my wants." If your rooms are empty, deny the appearance and determine that prosperity is manifest in every part of every room. Never think of yourself as poor or needy. Do not talk about hard times or the necessity for strict economy. Even "the walls have ears" and, unfortunately, memories too. Do not think how little you have but how much you have. Turn the telescope of your imagination around and look through the other end. "Revile not the king, no, not in thy thought; and revile not the rich in thy bedchamber: for a bird of the heavens shall carry the voice, and that which hath wings shall tell the matter."

"Blessed is the man that walketh not in the counsel of the wicked, Nor standeth in the way of sinners, Nor sitteth in the seat of scoffers: But his delight is in the law of Jehovah; And on his law doth he meditate day and night. And he shall be like a tree planted by the streams of water. That bringeth forth its fruit in its season, Whose leaf also doth not wither; And whatsoever he doeth shall prosper." "Through wisdom is a house builded; And by understanding it is established; And by knowledge are the chambers filled With all precious and pleasant riches."

"Jehovah will open unto thee his good treasure." "And the Almighty will be thy treasure, And precious silver unto thee." "Jehovah is my shepherd; I shall not want." "Trust in Jehovah, and do good; Dwell in the land, and feed on his faithfulness." "Jehovah will give grace and glory; No good thing will he withhold from them that walk uprightly." "That I may cause those that love me to inherit substance, And that I may fill their treasuries." "If ye be willing and obedient, ye shall eat the good of the land."

Chapter VIII

God Will Pay Your Debts

FORGIVE US our debts, as we also have forgiven our debtors." In these words Jesus expressed an infallible law of mind, the law that one idea must be dissolved before another can take its place. If you have in your mind any thought that someone has wronged you, you cannot let in the cleansing power of Spirit and the richness of spiritual substance until you have cast out the thought of the wrong, have forgiven it fully. You may be wondering why you have failed to get spiritual illumination or to find the consciousness of spiritual substance. Perhaps the reason is here: a lack of room for the true thoughts because other thoughts fill your mind. If you are not receiving the spiritual understanding you feel you should have, you should search your mind carefully for unforgiving thoughts.

"Thoughts are things" and occupy space in the mind realm. They have substance and form and may easily be taken as permanent by one not endowed with spiritual discernment. They bring forth fruit according to the seed planted in the mind, but they are not enduring unless founded in Spirit. Thoughts are alive and are endowed by the thinker with a secondary thinking power; that is, the thought entity that the I AM forms assumes an ego and begins to think on its own account. Thoughts also think but only with the power you give to them.

Tell me what kind of thoughts you are holding about yourself and your neighbors, and I can tell you just what you may expect in the way of health, finances, and harmony in your home. Are you suspicious of your neighbors? You cannot love and trust in God if you hate and distrust men. The two ideas love and hate, or trust and mistrust, simply cannot both be present in your mind at one time, and when you are entertaining one, you may be sure the other is absent. Trust other people and use the power that you accumulate from that act to trust God. There is magic in it: it works wonders; love and trust are dynamic, vital powers. Are you accusing men of being thieves, and fear that they are going to take away from you something that is your own? With such a thought generating fear and even terror in your mind and filling your consciousness with darkness, where is there room for the Father's light of protection? Rather build walls of love and substance around yourself. Send out swift, invisible messengers of love and trust for your protection. They are better guards than policemen or detectives.

Do not judge others as regards their guilt or innocence. Consider yourself and how you stand in the sight of the Father for having thoughts about another's guilt. Begin your reform with yourself. That means much to one who enjoys an understanding of mind and its laws, though it may mean little to the ordinary individual. He who knows himself superficially, just his external personality, thinks he has reformed when he has conformed to the moral and governmental laws. He may even be filled with his own self-righteousness and daily lift up his voice to praise God that he is not as other men are, that he has forgiven men their transgressions. He looks on all men who do not conform to his ideas of morality and religion as being sinners and transgressors and thanks God for his own insight and keenness. But he is not at peace. Something seems lacking. God does not talk to him "face to face," because the mind, where God and man meet, is darkened by the murky thought that other men are sinners. Our first work in any demonstration is to contact God, therefore we must forgive all men their transgressions. Through this forgiveness we cleanse our mind so that the Father can forgive us our own transgressions.

Our forgiving "all men" includes ourselves. You must also forgive yourself. Let the finger of denial erase every sin or "falling short" that you have charged up against yourself. Pay your debt by saying to that part of yourself which you think has fallen short: "Thou art made whole: sin no more, lest a worse thing befall thee." Then "loose him, and let him go." Treat sin as a mental transgression, instead of considering it as a moral deflection. Deny in thought all tendency to the error way and hold yourself firmly to the Christ Spirit, which is your divine self. Part company forever with "accusing conscience." Those who have resolved to sin no more have nothing in common with guilt.

"Shall I be in debt as long as I hold debts against others?" We find this to be the law of mind: a thought of debt will produce debt. So long as you believe in debt you will go into debt and accumulate the burdens that follow that thought. Whoever has not forgiven all men their debts is likely to fall into debt himself. Does this mean that you should give receipted bills to all those who owe you? No. That would not be erasing the thought of debt from your mind. First deny in mind that any man or woman owes you anything. If necessary, go over your list of names separately and sincerely forgive the thought of debt which you have been attaching to each person named. More bills may be collected in this way than in any other, for many of these people will pay what they owe when you send them this forgiving thought.

Debt is a contradiction of the universal equilibrium, and there is no such thing as lack of equilibrium in all the universe. Therefore in Spirit and in Truth there is no debt. However, men hold on to a thought of debt, and this thought is responsible for a great deal of sorrow and hardship. The true disciple realizes his supply in the consciousness of omnipresent, universally possessed abundance. Spirit substance is impartial and owned in common, and no thought of debt can enter into it. Debts exist in the mind, and in the mind is the proper place to begin liquidating them. These thought entities must be abolished in mind before their outer manifestations will pass away and stay away. The world can never be free from the bondage of financial obligations until men erase from their minds the thoughts of "mine and thine" that generates debts and interest. Analyze the thought of debt and you will see that it involves a thought of lack. Debt is a thought of lack with absence at both ends; the creditor thinks he lacks what is owed him and the debtor thinks he lacks what is necessary to pay it, else he would discharge the obligation rather than continue it. There is error at both ends of the proposition and nothing in the middle. This being true, it should be easy to dissolve the whole thought that anyone owes us or that we owe anyone anything. We should fill our mind with thoughts of all-sufficiency, and where there is no lack there can be no debts. Thus we find that the way to pay our debts is by filling our mind with the substance of ideas that are the direct opposite of the thoughts of lack that caused the debts.

Ideas of abundance will more quickly and surely bring what is yours to you than any thoughts you can hold about debtors discharging their obligations to you. See substance everywhere and affirm it, not only for yourself but for everyone else. Especially affirm abundance for those whom you have held in the thought of owing you. Thus you will help them pay their debts more easily than if you merely erased their names from your book of accounts receivable. Help pay the other fellow's debts by forgiving him his debts and declaring for him the abundance that is his already in Spirit. The idea of abundance will also bring its fruits into your own life. Let the law of plenty work itself out in you and in your affairs. This is the way the Father forgives your debts: not by canceling them on His books but by erasing them from His mind. He remembers them no more against you when you deny their reality. The Father is the everywhere present Spirit in which all that appears has its origin. God's love sees you always well, happy, and abundantly provided for; but God's wisdom demands that order and right relation exist in your mind before it may become manifest in your affairs as abundance. His love would give you your every desire, but His wisdom ordains that you forgive your debtors before your debts are forgiven.

To remedy any state of limited finances or ill-health that has been brought about by worry one must begin by eliminating the worry that is the original cause. One must free one's mind from the burden of debt before the debt can be paid. Many people have found that the statement "I owe no man anything but love" has helped them greatly to counteract this thought of debt. As they used the words their minds were opened to an inflow of divine love and they faithfully co-operated with the divine law of forgiveness in thought, word, and deed. They built up such a strong consciousness of the healing and enriching power of God's love that they could live and work peacefully and profitably with their associates. Thus renewed constantly in health, in faith, and in integrity, they were able to meet every obligation that came to them.

The statement "I owe no man anything but love" does not mean that we can disclaim owing our creditors money or try to evade the payment of obligations we have incurred. The thing denied is the burdensome thought of debt or of lack. The work of paying debts is an inner work having nothing to do with the debts already owed but with the wrong thoughts that produced them. When one holds to the right ideas, burdensome debts will not be contracted. Debts are produced by thoughts of lack, impatient desire, and covetousness. When these thoughts are overcome, debts are overcome, forgiven, and paid in full, and we are free from them for all time.

Your thoughts should at all times be worthy of your highest self, your fellow man, and God. The thoughts that most frequently work ill to you and your associates are thoughts of criticism and condemnation. Free your mind of them by holding the thought "There is now no condemnation in Christ Jesus." Fill your mind with thoughts of divine love, justice, peace, and forgiveness. This will pay your debts of love, which are the only debts you really owe. Then see how quickly and easily and naturally all your outer debts will be paid and all inharmonies of mind, body, and affairs smoothed out at the same time. Nothing will so quickly enrich your mind and free it from every thought of lack as the realization of divine love. Divine love will quickly and perfectly free you from the burden of debt and heal you of your physical infirmities, often caused by depression, worry, and financial fear. Love will bring your own to you, adjust all misunderstandings, and make your life and affairs healthy, happy, harmonious, and free, as they should be. Love indeed is the "fulfillment of the law."

The way is now open for you to pay your debts. Surrender them to God along with all your doubts and fears. Follow the light that is flooding into your mind. God's power, love, and wisdom, are here, for His kingdom is within you. Give Him full dominion in your life and affairs. Give Him your business, your family affairs, your finances, and let Him pay your debts. He is even now doing it, for it is His righteous desire to free you from every burden, and He is leading you out of the burden of debt, whether of owing or being owed. Meet every insidious thought, such as "I can't," "I don't know how," "I can't see the way," with the declaration "Jehovah is my shepherd; I shall not want." You "shall not want" the wisdom, the courage to do, or the substance to do with when you have once fully realized the scope of the vast truth that Almightiness is leading you into "green pastures ... beside still waters."

In the kingdom of Truth and reality ideas are the coin of the realm. You can use the new ideas that divine wisdom is now quickening in your mind and start this very moment to pay your debts. Begin by thanking God for your freedom from the debt-burden thought. This is an important step in breaking the shackles of debt. The funds to pay all your bills may not suddenly appear in a lump sum; but as you watch and work and pray, holding yourself in the consciousness of God's leadership and His abundance, you will notice your funds beginning to grow "here a little, there a little," and increasing more and more rapidly as your faith increases and your anxious thoughts are stilled. For with the increase will come added good judgment and wisdom in the management of your affairs. Debt is soon vanquished when wisdom and good judgment are in control.

Do not yield to the temptation of "easy-payment plans." Any payment that drains your pay envelope before you receive it is not an easy payment. Do not allow false pride to tempt you to put on a thousand-dollar front on a hundred-dollar salary. There may be times when you are tempted to miss paying a bill in order to indulge a desire for some thing. This easily leads one into the habit of putting off paying, which fastens the incubus of debt on people before they realize it. It is the innocent-appearing forerunner of the debt habit and debt thought that may rob you of peace, contentment, freedom, integrity, and prosperity for years to come. The Divine Mind within you is much stronger than this desire mind of the body. Turn to it in a time like this, and affirm: "Jehovah is my shepherd; I shall not want" this thing until it comes to me in divine order.

Bless your creditors with the thought of abundance as you begin to accumulate the wherewithal to pay off your obligations. Keep the faith they had in you by including them in your prayer for increase. Begin to free yourself at once by doing all that is possible with the means you have and as you proceed in this spirit the way will open for you to do more; for through the avenues of Spirit more means will come to you and every obligation will be met.

If you are a creditor, be careful of the kind of thoughts you hold over your debtor. Avoid the thought that he is unwilling to pay you or that he is unable to pay you. One thought holds him in dishonesty, and the other holds him subject to lack, and either of them tends to close the door to the possibility of his paying you soon. Think well and speak well of all those who owe you. If you talk about them to others avoid calling them names that you would not apply to yourself. Cultivate a genuine feeling of love for them and respect their integrity in spite of all appearances. Declare abundant supply for them and thus help them to prosper. Pray and work for their good as well as for your own, for yours is inseparable from theirs. You owe your debtor quite as much as he owes you and yours is a debt of love. Pay your debt to him and he will pay his to you. This rule of action never fails.

Far-seeing Christians look forward to an early resumption of the economic system inaugurated by the early followers of Jesus. They had all things in common, and no man lacked anything. But before we can have a truly Christian community founded on a spiritual basis we must be educated into a right way of thinking about finances. If we should all get together and divide all our possessions, it would be but a short time until those who have the prevailing financial ideas would manipulate our finances, and plethora on one hand and lack on the other would again be established.

The world cannot be free from the bondage of debt and interest until men start to work in their minds to erase those things from consciousness. If the United States forgave the nations of Europe all their debts and wiped the slate clean, the law would not necessarily be fulfilled; for there would probably remain a thought that they still owed us and that we had made a sacrifice in canceling the obligations. We should not feel very friendly about it and would not truly forgive them, and in that case the error thought would be carried on. We must first forgive the error thought that they owe us money and that we would be losing money by canceling the debts. The man who is forced to forgive a debt does not forgive it.

Above all we should fill our mind with the consciousness of that divine abundance which is so manifest everywhere in the world today. There is as much substance as there ever was, but its free flow has been interfered with through selfishness. We must rid our mind of the selfish acquisitiveness that is so dominant in the race thought, and in that way do our part in the great work of freeing the world from avarice. It is the duty of every Christian metaphysician to help in the solution of this problem by affirming that the universal Spirit of supply is now becoming manifest as a distributing energy the world over; that all stored-up, hoarded, vicious thoughts are being dissolved; that all people have things in common. that no one anywhere lacks anything; and that the divine law of distribution of infinite supply that Jesus demonstrated is now being made manifest throughout the world. "The earth is the Lord's, and the fulness thereof."

There is a legitimate commerce that is carried on by means of what is called credit. Credit is a convenience to be used by those who appreciate its value and are careful not to abuse it, for to do so would be to ruin it. However, many persons are not equipped to use the credit system to advantage and are likely to abuse it. In the first place, few individuals are familiar with the intricacies of sound credit systems and often assume obligations without being certain of their ability to meet them, especially should some unforeseen complication arise. Frequently an individual loses all that he invests and finds himself involved in a burden of debt in addition. Such things are not in divine order and are largely responsible for retarding prosperity.

No one should assume an obligation unless he is prepared to meet it promptly and willingly when it comes due. One who knows God as his unfailing resource can be assured of his supply when it is needed. Then why should he plunge into debt when he is confident of his daily supply without debt? There are no creditors or debtors in God's kingdom. If you are in that kingdom, you need no longer be burdened with the thought of debt either as debtor or creditor. Under divine law there is no reaching out for things that are beyond one's present means. There is an ever-increasing richness of consciousness coming from the certain knowledge that God is infinite and unfailing supply. Outer things conform to the inner pattern, and riches are attracted to the one who lives close to the unselfish heart of God. His environment is made beautiful by the glory of the Presence, and there is satisfying and lasting prosperity in his affairs.

There is but one way to be free from debt. That is the desire to be free, followed by the realization that debt has no legitimate place in God's kingdom and that you are determined to erase it entirely from your mind. As you work toward your freedom you will find it helpful to have daily periods for meditation and prayer. Do not concentrate on debts or spoil your prayers by constantly thinking of debts. Think of that which you want to demonstrate, not that from which you seek freedom. When you pray, thank the Father for His care and guidance, for His provision and plenty, for His love and wisdom, for His infinite abundance and your privilege to enjoy it.

Here are a few prosperity prayers that may help establish you in the truth of plenty and erase the error thought of debt. They are offered as suggestions for forming your own prayers but may be used as given with excellent results.

I am no longer anxious about finances; Thou art my all-sufficiency in all things.

The Spirit of honesty, promptness, efficiency, and order is now expressed in me and in all that I do.

I am free from all limitations of mortal thought about quantities and values. The superabundance of riches of the

Christ Mind are now mine, and I am prospered in all my ways.

The 23d Psalm A Treatment To Free The Mind Of The Debt Idea

Jehovah is my shepherd; I shall not want He maketh me to lie down in green pastures: He leadeth me beside still waters. He restoreth my soul: He guideth me in the paths of righteousness for his name's sake. Yea, though I walk through the valley of the shadow of death, I will fear no evil; for thou art with me; Thy rod and thy staff, they comfort me. Thou preparest a table before me in the presence of mine enemies: Thou hast anointed my head with oil; My cup runneth over. Surely goodness and lovingkindness shall follow me all the days of my life: And I shall dwell in the house of Jehovah for ever.

Chapter IX

Tithing, the Road to Prosperity

AS YE abound in everything, in faith, and utterance, and knowledge, and in all earnestness, and in your love to us, see that ye abound in this grace also."

"Honor Jehovah with thy substance, And with the first-fruits of all thine increase: So shall thy barns be filled with plenty, And thy vats shall overflow with new wine."

Under the Mosaic law a tithe (or tenth) was required as the Lord's portion. Throughout the Old Testament the tithe or tenth is mentioned as a reasonable and just return to the Lord by way of acknowledging Him as the source of supply. After Jacob had seen the vision of the ladder with angels ascending and descending on it he set up a pillar and made a vow to the Lord, saying, "Of all that thou shalt give me I will surely give the tenth unto thee." In the 3d chapter of Malachi we find God's blessing directly connected with faithfulness in giving to the Lord's treasury, but gifts should be made because it is right and because one loves to give, not from a sense of duty or for the sake of reward.

That there will be a reward following the giving we are also assured by Jesus in a direct promise "Give, and it shall be given unto you; good measure, pressed down, shaken together, running over, shall they give unto your bosom. For with what measure ye mete it shall be measured to you again."

Promises of spiritual benefits and increase of God's bounty through the keeping of this divine law of giving and receiving, abound in all the Scriptures.

"There is that scattereth, and increaseth yet more; And there is that withholdeth more than is meet, but it tendeth only to want. The liberal soul shall be made fat; And he that watereth shall be watered also himself." "He that hath a bountiful eye shall be blessed; For he giveth of his bread to the poor." "He that soweth bountifully shall reap also bountifully." "Blessed are ye that sow beside all waters."

We are living now under larger and fuller blessings from God than man has ever known. It is meet therefore that we give accordingly and remember the law of the tithe, for if a tenth was required under the law in those olden times, it is certainly no less fitting that we should give it cheerfully now. One of the greatest incentives to generous giving is a keen appreciation of the blessings secured to us through the redemptive work of Jesus Christ. "He that spared not His own Son, but delivered him up for us all, how shall he not also with him freely give us all things?" "Freely ye received, freely give." True giving is the love and generosity of the Spirit-quickened heart responding to the love and generosity of the Father's heart.

In his second letter Paul made a stirring appeal to the Corinthians for a generous gift to their poorer brethren in Jerusalem. He suggests some principles of giving that are always applicable, for giving is a grace that adds to the spiritual growth of all men in all times. Without giving the soul shrivels, but when giving is practiced as a part of Christian living, the soul expands and becomes Godlike in the grace of liberality and generosity. No restoration to the likeness of God can be complete unless mind, heart, and soul are daily opening out into that large, free, bestowing spirit which so characterizes our God and Father. Therefore it is not surprising that Paul classes the grace of giving with faith, knowledge, and love.

A very simple yet practical plan for exercising this grace of giving had been suggested by Paul in his first letter to the Corinthian church. "Upon the first day of the week," he said, "let each one of you lay by him in store, as he may prosper"; that is, each member was asked to contribute to the establishing of a treasury. This was to be the Lord's storehouse, into which each one was to put his offerings regularly and in proportion to his means. In adopting this plan the offerer became a steward of the Lord's goods and entered upon a course of training and discipline needed to make a good steward, for it takes wisdom to know how rightly to dispense the bounty of God. Perhaps no simpler way to begin one's growth in the grace of giving can be suggested for our own day. Those who have followed this method have usually found that they had more money to give than they had thought possible.

In order that the plan of giving may be successful there are several things that must be observed. First there must be a willing mind. "If the readiness is there, it is acceptable according as a man hath, not according as he hath not." "God loveth a cheerful giver." Secondly, the giving must be done in faith, and there must be no withholding because the offering seems small. Many of the instances of giving that are recorded in the Bible as worthy of special mention, commendation, and blessing are instances where the gift itself was small. The widow who fed Elijah in his time of famine gave him a cake made with her last handful of meal. For her faith and her generous spirit she was rewarded with a plentiful daily supply of food for herself and her sons, as well as for Elijah. "The jar of meal shall not waste, neither shall the cruse of oil fail."

This same truth is set forth beautifully in the New Testament, where it is clearly shown that not the amount of the offering but the spirit in which it is given determines its value and power. "And he [Jesus] sat down over against the treasury, and beheld how the multitude cast money into the treasury: and many that were rich cast in much. And there came a poor widow, and she cast in two mites, which make a farthing. And he called unto him his disciples, and said unto them, Verily I say unto you, This poor widow cast in more than all they that are casting into the treasury: for they all did cast in of their superfluity; but she of her want did cast in all that she had, even all her living."

This poor widow exemplified what it is to give in faith; and were ever two mites so great a gift as when they brought forth such praise from the Master Himself! The results of giving in faith are just as sure in this age as in the time of Jesus, for the law is unfailing in all ages.

A third requisite for keeping the law of giving and receiving is that the offering shall be a just and fair proportion of all that one receives. The amount was settled by Paul and the measure he gave was: "as he may prosper." There is a certain definiteness about this, and yet it admits of freedom for the giver to exercise his individual faith, judgment, and will.

The question of wise distribution is closely related to the matter of filling God's treasury. To whom shall we give and when are questions quite important. There are several truths that may be considered in this connection, but then each individual finds it necessary to trust to the Spirit of wisdom manifest in his own heart, since there are no rules or precedents that one can follow in detail. This is as it should be, for it keeps the individual judgment, faith, love, sympathy, and will alive and active. Yet a careful study of the underlying laws of spiritual giving will help one to exercise these divine faculties as they should be exercised. If we follow the Spirit of wisdom we shall not give to anything that is contrary to the teaching of Jesus, but spend every penny in the furtherance of the good news of life that He proclaims and in the promotion of the brotherhood of man that it is His mission to establish on earth among all those who become sons through Him.

True spiritual giving rewards with a double joy: first that which comes with the laying of the gift upon the altar or in the Lord's treasury; then the joy of sharing our part of God's bounty with others. One of the blessings is the satisfying knowledge that we are meeting the law and paying our debt of love and justice to the Lord. The other is the joy of sharing the Lord's bounty. Justice comes first; then generosity.

Even the so-called heathen recognize giving as a part of worship, for we find them coming with offerings when they worship their idols. All ages and all religious dispensations have stressed giving as a vital part of their worship. In this age, when we have so much, more is required of us, even to the giving of ourselves with all that we are and have. This privilege carries immeasurable benefits with it, for it looses us from the personal life, unifies us with the universal, and so opens our inner and outer life to the inflow and the outflow of the life, love, bounty and grace of God. This is the blessed result of faithful obedience to the law and exercise of the grace of giving.

The people were amazed when the prophet Malachi told them that they had been robbing God and desired to know wherein they had failed when they thought they had been serving the Lord so faithfully. People are as much amazed today to learn that they have been untrue to God's law, for the message of Malachi is for us quite as much as for the ancients. The Spirit of God gave this message through the prophet: "Bring ye the whole tithe into the store-house, that there may be food in my house, and prove me now herewith, saith Jehovah of hosts, if I will not open you the windows of heaven, and pour you out a blessing, that there shall not be room enough to receive it. And I will rebuke the devourer for your sakes, and he shall not destroy the fruits of your ground; neither shall your vine cast its fruit before the time in the field, saith Jehovah of hosts. And all nations shall call you happy; for ye shall be a delightsome land, saith Jehovah of hosts."

Study this 3d chapter of Malachi carefully if you would know the happy solution of the problem of giving and receiving. See how practical it is for people in every walk of life and for nations as well. It offers the solution to the problems of the farmer. It sets forth clearly a law of prosperity for all classes of people; for those who need protection for their crops from frosts, droughts, floods; for those who would escape the plagues, pestilences, and manifold things that would destroy their supply and support. It is a simple law but so effective: simply give a tithe or tenth or the "first-fruits" or their equivalent to the Lord. God should not be expected to meet all man's requirements in the matter of giving this protection and increase unless man fulfills the requirements of God. The act of giving complies with the divine law, because it involves the recognition of God as the giver of all increase; and unless we have a recognition of the source of our supply we have no assurance of continuing in its use.

Many people have doubts as to whether it will really do any good to ask the Lord for protection and for plenty in regard to crops or other supply. Many who are employed in cities or who are in business think it strange that they should believe in omnipresent prosperity. Thus unbelief is present with them at the very time when an unwavering faith is most necessary.

There is a psychological reason why people should obey spiritual law. When a person obeys the law of God along any line, his faith immediately becomes strengthened in proportion and his doubts disappear. When anyone puts God first in his finances, not only in thought but in every act, by releasing his first fruits (a tenth part of his increase or income) to the Lord, his faith in omnipresent supply becomes a hundredfold stronger and he prospers accordingly. Obeying this law gives him an inner knowing that he is building his finances on a sure foundation that will not fail him.

Everything in the universe belongs to God, and though all things are for the use and enjoyment of man, he can possess nothing selfishly. When man learns that a higher law than human custom and desire is working in the earth to bring about justice, righteousness, and equalization, he will begin to obey that law by tithing, loving his neighbor, and doing unto others as he would have them do unto him. Then man will reach the end of all the troubles brought upon himself by his selfishness and greed, and will become healthy, prosperous, and happy.

The pastor of a small church in Georgia suggested to his congregation, composed largely of cotton farmers, that they dedicate a tenth part of their land to the Lord and ask Him for protection against the ravages of the boll weevil, which had devastated the crops in that vicinity for several years. Seven farmers in the congregation decided to do this. They took no measures to protect their crop on these dedicated acres, yet the pest did not attack the cotton there. The quality of the fiber was better on those acres than on any that adjoined them. The experiment was so successful in fact that practically all the farmers in that community have decided to follow the plan in the future.

Many experiences such as this are awakening men to respect our relation to the infinite principle of life, everywhere present, that we know as God. This divine element of life that manifests itself as growth and substance resides within the factors that combine to produce cotton, wheat, and all other forms of vegetation. Then certainly if the farmer works in acknowledged sympathy with this life principle, it will work in sympathy with him and for his good. Each contributing in love and understanding to the other, a larger crop will be the result, and a larger measure of prosperity for the farmer. Not only the farmer but the banker, the tradesman, the professional man can work in sympathy and harmony with this principle of growth and increase. The infinite life principle is as responsive in one field as another, and it is everywhere present. Even so-called inanimate objects are filled to the full with this infinite life, and even coined gold is tense with the desire to expand and to grow. The materials handled by the tradesman are made of the same substance that makes the universe and contain within themselves the germ of growth and increase. All men are therefore daily associated with life, and through rendering it the reverent acknowledgment that is its due and through witnessing this acknowledgment by dedicating a part of their increase they are prospered.

The tithe is the equivalent of the increased fertility of the land. If by acknowledging God as the giver of all life the farmer raises two or six or twenty bushels more on his field, that extra portion, which he would not have had otherwise, is the Lord's portion. In trade the tithe is the equivalent of the increased quality of goods. In professional life the tithe is the increased ability or the increased appreciation. The tithing principle can be applied in all of our industrial and social relationships. In every case where it has been applied and followed for a time, the tither has been. remarkably blessed; quite as much so as in the case of the cotton farmers and their tithe acres.

There are many people who wish to give but seem at a loss as to how to go about it or where to begin. They do not know how much they should give, or when or how often to offer their gifts, and there are a host of related questions. To answer these questions there must be found a definite basis for their giving, a rule to which they can conform. This is where the law of tithing fits beautifully, for it is a basis and a sound one, tested and proved for thousands of years. The tithe may be a tenth part of one's salary, wage, or allowance, of the net profits of business, or of money received from the sale of goods. It is based on every form of supply, no matter through what channel it may come, for there are many channels through which man is prospered. The tenth should be set apart for the upkeep of some spiritual work or workers. It should be set apart first even before one's personal expenses are taken out, for in the right relation of things God comes first always. Then everything else follows in divine order and falls into its proper place.

The great promise of prosperity is that if men seek God and His righteousness first, then all shall be added unto them. One of the most practical and sensible ways of seeking God's kingdom first is to be a tither, to put God first in finances. It is the promise of God, the logical thing to do, and the experience of all who have tried it, that all things necessary to their comfort, welfare, and happiness have been added to them in an overflowing measure. Tithing establishes method in giving and brings into the consciousness a sense of order and fitness that will be manifested in one's outer life and affairs as increased efficiency and greater prosperity.

Another blessing that follows the practice of tithing is the continual "letting go" of what one receives, which keeps one's mind open to the good and free from covetousness. Making an occasional large gift and then permitting a lapse of time before another is made will not give this lasting benefit, for one's mind channel may in the meantime become clogged with material thoughts of fear, lack, or selfishness. When a person tithes he is giving continuously, so that no spirit of grasping, no fear, and no thought of limitations gets a hold on him. There is nothing that keeps a person's mind so fearless and so free to receive the good constantly coming to him as the practice of tithing. Each day, week, pay day, whenever it is, the tither gives one tenth.

When an increase of prosperity comes to him, as come it will and does, his first thought is to give God the thanks and the tenth of the new amount. The free, open mind thus stayed on God is certain to bring forth joy, real satisfaction in living, and true prosperity. Tithing is based on a law that cannot fail, and it is the surest way ever found to demonstrate plenty, for it is God's own law and way of giving.

"And all the tithe of the land, whether of the seed of the land, or of the fruit of the tree, is Jehovah's: it is holy unto Jehovah."

Let us give as God gives, unreservedly, and with no thought of return, making no mental demands for recompense on those who have received from us. A gift with reservations is not a gift; it is a bribe. There is no promise of increase unless we give freely, let go of the gift entirely, and recognize the universal scope of the law. Then the gift has a chance to go out and to come back multiplied. There is no telling how far the blessing may travel before it comes back, but it is a beautiful and encouraging fact that the longer it is in returning, the more hands it is passing through and the more hearts it is blessing. All these hands and hearts add something to it in substance, and it is increased all the more when it does return.

We must not try to fix the avenues through which our good is to come. There is no reason for thinking that what you give will come back through the one to whom you gave it. All men are one in Christ and form a universal brotherhood. We must put away any personal claim, such as "I gave to you, now you give to me," and supplant it with "Inasmuch as ye did it unto one of these my brethren, even these least, ye did it unto me." The law will bring each of us just what is his own, the reaping of the seeds he has sown. The return will come, for it cannot escape the law, though it may quite possibly come through a very different channel from what we expect. Trying to fix the channel through which his good must come to him is one of the ways in which the personal man shuts off his own supply.

The spiritual-minded man does not make selfish use of the law but gives because he loves to give. Because he gives with no thought of reward and no other motive than love, he is thrown more completely into the inevitable operation of the law and his return is all the more certain. He is inevitably enriched and cannot escape it. Jesus said, "Give, and it shall be given unto you; good measure, pressed down, shaken together, running over." He was not merely making a promise but stating a law that never fails to function.

So inexhaustible is the bounty of the Giver of all good that to him who has eyes to see it and faith to receive it God is an unfailing source of supply. The munificent Giver withholds nothing from him who comes in the name of a son and heir and lays claim to his portion. It is the Father's good pleasure to give us the kingdom, and all that the Father has is ours. But we must have the faith and the courage to claim it.

Men who accomplish great things in the industrial world are the ones who have faith in the money-producing power of their ideas. Those who would accomplish great things in the demonstration of spiritual resources must have faith to lay hold of the divine ideas and the courage to speak them into expression. The conception must be followed by the affirmation that the law is instantly fulfilled. Then the supply will follow in manifestation.

Chapter X

Right Giving, the Key to Abundant Receiving

THERE IS a law of giving and receiving and it requires careful study if we would use it in our prosperity demonstrations. It is a law of mind action, and it can be learned and applied the same as any other law. The teaching of Jesus stands out prominently, because it can be practically applied to the affairs of everyday life. It is not alone a religion in the sense that word is usually taken but is a rule of thinking, doing, living, and being. It is not only ethical but practical, and men have never yet sounded the depths of the simple but all-inclusive words of Jesus. To some people it is unthinkable to connect the teaching of Jesus with the countinghouse and the market place, but a deeper insight into their meaning and purpose, which the Spirit of Truth is now revealing to the world, shows that these lofty teachings are the most practical rules for daily living in all departments of life. They are vital to modern civilization and the very foundation of business stability. The law of giving and receiving that Jesus taught, "Give, and it shall be given unto you," is found to be applicable to all our commercial as well as our social relationships.

We have not been more successful in making this doctrine of Jesus a practical standard for everyday guidance because we have not understood the law on which it is based. Jesus would not have put forth a doctrine that was not true and not based on unchanging law, and we can be sure that this doctrine of giving and receiving is powerful enough to support all the affairs of civilization. We have not gone deeply enough into the teaching but have thought we understood it from a mere surface study. "Ye look at the things that are before your face," says Paul, and Jesus also warned us to "judge not according to appearance." We should form no conclusions until we have gone thoroughly into the causes and the underlying laws. The things we see outwardly are the effects that have arisen from causes that are invisible to us. There is an inner and an outer to everything: both the mental and the material conditions pervade the universe. Man slides at will up and down the whole gamut of cause and effect. The whole race slides into an effect almost unconsciously and so identifies the senses with the effect that the causes are lost sight of for thousands of years.

An awakening comes in time and the cause side of existence is again brought to the attention of men, as set forth, for example, in the doctrine of Jesus Christ. But men cannot grasp the great truth in a moment and cling to what is plainly visible to them, the effect side. The truth that things have a spiritual as well as a material identity and that the spiritual is the cause side and of greatest value, is a revelation that may be slow in coming to most people. In this instance it is the material side that they cling to, thinking it to be all and refusing to let go. Men have taken the letter or appearance side of the Jesus Christ doctrine and materialized it to fit their beliefs and customs. That is the reason why the Christ message has not purified commerce, society, and government. But it should be made spiritually operative in those fields. It will easily do the work desired when its mental side is studied and when it is understood and applied from the spiritual viewpoint.

There is need for reform in economics more than in any other department of everyday life. Money has been manipulated by greed until greed itself is sick and secretly asks for a panacea. But it does not look to the religion of Jesus Christ for healing. In fact that is the very last place it would apply for aid, because many of the advocates of the Jesus Christ doctrine are themselves economic dependents and have no solution for the economic problem--not understanding the power of their own religion. Yet no permanent remedy will ever be found for the economic ills of the world outside a practical application of the laws on which the doctrine of Jesus Christ is based.

The correctness of the solution of any problem is assured by the right relation of its elements. All true reform begins with the individual. Jesus began there. He did not clamor for legislation to control men or their actions. He called His twelve apostles and through them individually instituted that reform which has as its basis an appeal to the innate intelligence, honesty, and goodness in every man. He told them, "Go ye into all the world, and preach the gospel to the whole creation."

As people learn more definitely about the dynamic effect of thought and how ideas pass from mind to mind, they see more and more the wisdom of the Christ teaching. They are beginning to understand that there is one undeviating law of mind action and that all thinking and all speaking is amenable to it. Thus when Jesus said, "By thy words thou shalt be justified, and by thy words thou shalt be condemned," He taught the power of thoughts and words to bring results in accordance with the ideas back of them.

Following the metaphysical side of the teaching of Jesus, we have found that certain thoughts held in the minds of the people are causing widespread misery, disease, and death. We have also found that these thoughts can be dissolved or transformed and the whole man made over through his conscious volition. Paul well understood this process. He said, "Be ye transformed by the renewing of your mind."

Among the destructive thoughts that men indulge in and exercise are those forms of selfishness which we know as avarice, covetousness, money getting, the desire for financial gain and for possessing the things of the world. These thoughts threaten seriously to disturb the civilization of the world and the stability of the whole race. The sole thought of money getting is being allowed by men and women to generate its cold vapor in their souls until it shuts out all the sunlight of love and even of life. The remedy for the misery caused by destructive thoughts is not far to seek. It lies in constructive thinking along the lines that Jesus laid down. Indeed the remedy for all the ills to which flesh is heir lies in conformity to the divine law that Jesus revealed to His true followers. It is said of these true followers (Acts 4:32) that they were "of one heart and soul: and not one of them said that aught of the things which he possessed was his own; but they had all things common."

Many true Christians have observed this righteous law and sought to conform to it in community life. Such efforts have not always been successful, because there was not the necessary recognition of the mental factor and the discipline of ideas. So long as the idea of covetousness is lodged in the human mind as its dominant generating factor, there can be no successful community life. That idea must be eliminated from the mental plane first; the next step, the outer practice, will then be safe and successful.

Everywhere true metaphysicians are preparing themselves to be members in the great colony that Jesus is to set up, by working to eliminate from their mind all selfish ideas, along with all other discordant vibrations that produce inharmony among members of the same group. A step in this direction is the gradual introduction of the "freewill offering" plan to replace the world's commercial standard of reward for services. We are striving to educate the people on this question of giving and receiving and to let their own experience prove to them that there is a divine law of equilibrium in financial matters that corresponds to the law of balance and poise that holds the suns and the planets in place. In order to make a success of this great effort we must have the loving co-operation of everyone to whom we minister. The law is based on love and justice, and it equitably and harmoniously adjusts all the affairs of men. It goes even further, for it restores a harmony and balance in both mind and body that results in happiness and health as well as prosperity. Love and justice are mighty powers, and all things must eventually come under their influence, because even a few men and women of right motive can, by right thinking and consequent just action, introduce these ideas into the race consciousness and pave the way for their universal adoption.

The movement has already begun and is rapidly gaining headway. Every student and reader is asked to give it impetus by resolving to be unselfish and just without compulsion.

The race consciousness is formed of thought currents and the dominant beliefs of all the people. A few men and women rise above these currents of thought and become independent thinkers. The dominating race idea of money getting as the goal of success is now being replaced by the idea of usefulness and good works. This idea must be carried out by individuals who have resolved to think and to act in the Jesus Christ way. To be one of these individuals and to contribute to the change in the race consciousness, first dedicate yourself in Spirit to the ministry of Jesus and resolve to carry forward the great work He has commissioned you to do. This does not mean that you must preach like Paul or necessarily carry on any extensive work in the outer. In the silence of your "inner chamber" you can do a mighty work of power by daily denying the beliefs in avarice and covetousness and affirming the universal sway of divine love and justice. You can make the idea of exact equity and justice between man and man the central theme of all your saying and doing. When you see examples of greed and avarice or when thoughts of these seek a place in your mind, remember the words of the Master: "What is that to thee? follow thou me."

Never for a moment allow yourself to entertain any scheme for getting the better of your fellows in any trade or bargain. Hold steadily to the law of equity and justice that is working in and through you, knowing for a certainty that you are supplied with everything necessary to fulfill all your requirements. Give full value for everything you get. Demand the same for everything you give, but do not try to enforce that demand by human methods. There is a better way: think of yourself as Spirit working with powerful spiritual forces, and know that the demands of Spirit must and will be met.

Do not plan to lay up for the future; let the future take care of itself. To entertain any fears or doubts on that point saps your strength and depletes your spiritual power. Hold steadily to the thought of the omnipresence of universal supply, its perfect equilibrium and its swift action in filling every apparent vacuum or place of lack. If you have been in the habit of hoarding or of practicing stringent economy, change your thought currents to generosity. Practice giving, even though it may be in a small way. Give in a spirit of love and give when you cannot see any possibility of return. Put real substance into your gift by giving the substance of the heart with the token of money or whatever it is. Through the power of your word you can bless and spiritually multiply everything that you give. See yourself as the steward of God handing out His inexhaustible supplies. In this manner you are setting into action mental and spiritual forces that eventually bring large results into visibility. Be happy in your giving. God loves a cheerful giver because his mind and heart are open to the flow of the pure substance of Being that balances all things.

Do not give with any idea that you are bestowing charity. The idea of charity has infested the race consciousness for thousands of years and is responsible for the great army of human dependents. Do all you can to annul this mental error. There is no such thing as charity as popularly understood. Everything belongs to God and all His children are equally entitled to it. The fact that one has a surplus and gives some of it to another does not make the one a benefactor and the other a dependent. The one with the surplus is simply a steward of God and is merely discharging the work of his stewardship. When one asks for divine wisdom and understanding about giving it becomes a joy both to the giver and the recipient.

Followers of Jesus who are doing His work of teaching and healing should, like Him, receive free-will offerings for their ministry to the people. The majority of those who apply to teachers and healers recognize this law of giving and receiving, but there are quite a number who do not understand it. First there are those who are in bondage to the idea of avarice, and secondly, there are those who still are in bondage to the idea of charity. Both these classes need education and treatment to release them from mental limitation and mental disease. The avaricious suffer most in body and are the most difficult to heal, because of the mental bias that prompts them to get everything as cheaply as possible, including the kingdom of heaven. They must be patiently educated to be just because it is right, and to learn to "let go" of the acquisitive spirit and replace it with the spirit of generosity. They will do this readily enough as a mental drill but are not so willing to let go of the money symbol. However, continued treatments in the silence, supplemented with oral and written instruction, will eventually prevail and heal them.

There are many examples that could be given to prove the outworking of the law. The covetous idea has a great power over the body. It would avail little to treat the outer manifestation before first removing the inner cause from the mind. The salvation of such people is to learn to give generously and freely, not from compulsion or for the sake of reward but from a love of the giving. Some metaphysicians think to cure their patients of the hold of avaricious thoughts by charging them a good round price for their treatments. By the same token the medical doctor who charges the most is surest to heal his patients, and any service for which an exhorbitant price is charged is the best! Surely this would be a foolish idea. Metaphysical healing has become so popular that hundreds have gone into it as a business and are making of it an industry founded on the old commercial idea, just as cold and calculating, as hard and unyielding as the idea is in the ranks of the money-changers of mammon.

Surely there is a "more excellent way," one more in harmony with divine law, a way that permits the heart as well as the head and hand to be used in the grace of giving and receiving. Those who are using the freewill offering method meet with some criticism and opposition from those who hold to the commercial method and say that charging a definite sum is the legitimate way. They accuse Unity of fostering charity and poverty and keeping alive the spirit of getting something for nothing that is manifested by so many people. Our reply is that we are pursuing the only course that could ever effectually eradicate these erroneous states of consciousness and bring people into an understanding of the spiritual law of prosperity through giving in love.

Everyone should give as he receives; in fact, it is only through giving that he can receive. Until the heart is quickened at the center and the mind is opened up to Truth there is no permanent healing. Everyone can make a fair return for everything he gets. We aim to show moneyless paupers that they can give something in return for the good that has been done them. It may be to pass the true word to some other needy one, or merely to lift up their voice in thanksgiving and praise where before they were dumb. We recognize the necessity of some action of the mammon-bound mind. It must be made to let go somewhere before it can receive the light and the power of Spirit.

Our work is to bring men and women to the place of true and lasting dominion where they are superior to both riches and poverty. We can do this by showing them that they are spiritual beings, that they live in a spiritual world here and now, and that through the apprehension of the Truth of their being and their relation to God this dominion is to be realized.

The central and most vital fact that they must come to realize is that an idea has the power of building thought structures, which in turn materialize in the outer environment and affairs and determine every detail of their existence. Every man is a king ruling his own subjects. These subjects are the ideas existing in his mind, the "subjects" of his thought. Each man's ideas are as varied and show as many traits of character as the inhabitants of any empire. But they can all be brought into subjection and made to obey through the I AM power that is the ruler of the kingdom. In your domain of mind there may be colonies of alien ideas--the Philistines, Canaanites, and other foreign tribes, that the Children of Israel found in their Promised Land when they attempted to take possession of it. The story of the Children of Israel and how they gained the possession of that land is a symbolical representation of the experience of everyone who seeks to reclaim his own consciousness in the name of the Lord. The meaning in Hebrew of the name Canaanite is "merchant" or "trader"; in other words, a set of ideas that has to do with the commercial phase of life. Study the Children of Israel (spiritual ideas) in their experiences with these Canaanites and you will get many valuable hints on subduing and handling your own money-getting ideas.

You may allow avariciousness and stinginess to develop in your mind domain until the very blood in your body starts to dry up and your nerves are shaken and palsied with the fear of future poverty. If so, it is time these ideas were driven out and a new set of ideas settled in your domain to become active in building up a new state of consciousness (nation). Begin at once to let go of your all-consuming thoughts of gain. Think about generosity and begin to be generous for your own sake. "It is more blessed to give than to receive" will prove itself to you as the law, for you will be blessed by a new influx of ideas of life, health, and prosperity when you start giving.

Instead of being grasping and avaricious, perhaps you have gone to the other extreme and have cultivated ideas of small things financially. You may have been fostering poverty by holding ideas of pennies instead of dollars or of hundreds instead of thousands. You may be thinking that you cannot give because your income is small or your supply is limited. Your remedy is to cultivate ideas of abundance. Claim God as your inexhaustible resource; that all things are yours. But in order to set in motion the accumulated energy of your thought you must also begin to give. You may be able to give only pennies at first, but give them in the name and the spirit of your opulent God.

Send them forth with all the love of your heart and say to them as they go, "Divine love through me blesses and multiplies you."

Your consciousness is like a stream of water. If the stream is in any way dammed up, the water settles in all the low places and becomes stagnant. The quickest way to purify and reclaim the low, "swampy" places in your consciousness is to let in the flood from above by opening the dam. Many people try to demonstrate God as their supply by repeating affirmations of abundance now present, but fail to deny and thus to let go of the old condition and old belief in lack by beginning to give as generously as possible. It is not the amount you give measured by standards of the world, it is the good will you send forth with the gift; which can be measured only by spiritual standards.

"God loveth a cheerful giver." The Greek word here translated cheerful is hilarion, which means really "hilarious, joyful." The gift may be measured in dollars and cents but God looks not on such standards, He looks on and loves the "joyful" giver. We read in Deuteronomy 28:47, 48, "Because thou servedst not Jehovah thy God with joyfulness, and with gladness of heart, by reason of the abundance of all things; therefore shalt thou serve thine enemies ... in hunger, and in thirst, and in nakedness, and in want of all things." This shows that there is a definite relation between the cheerfulness or joyfulness of our giving and our prosperity. Whether we make a large or a small gift, let us make it with largeness of cheer and joy, even of hilarity, remembering that God loveth a "hilarious" giver. "Keep therefore the words of this covenant, and do them, that ye may prosper in all that ye do."

Blessings That May Be Placed On Our Gifts

Divine love, through me, blesses and multiplies this offering.

The Father gives abundantly; I receive thankfully, and give again generously.

This is the bounty of God, and I send it forth with wisdom and joy.

Divine love bountifully supplies and increases this offering.

I give freely and fearlessly, fulfilling the law of giving and receiving.

Chapter XI

Laying Up Treasures

AFTER the multitude had been fed by the increase of the loaves and fishes, Jesus commanded that they gather up the fragments so that nothing might be lost. "And they all ate, and were filled: and they took up that which remained over of the broken pieces, twelve baskets full." Any form of waste is a violation of the divine law of conservation. Everywhere in nature there is evidence of stored-up energy substance, ready for use when needed.

This reserve force is not material but spiritual. It is ready to be called into expression to meet any need. But when it is not put to use or called into expression, there is a manifestation of inharmony or lack either in the body of man or in its outer supply.

It is in his wrong conception of this spiritual force that man makes the mistake of falling into the habit of hoarding instead of conserving. He tries to gather things together in the external in a vain effort to avert an imagined shortage in the future and he counts himself rich by the amount of his material possessions.

Spiritually awakened people are coming to know that all riches are spiritual and within the reach of all as divine ideas. They study the law of conservation as it pertains to the spiritual and seek to build up a large reserve consciousness of substance, life, strength, and power, rather than laying up material treasures that "moth and rust consume" and "thieves break through and steal."

Men and women scatter their energies to the four winds in the effort to satisfy the desires of the flesh, and then wonder why they do not demonstrate prosperity. If they only realized the truth that this same thought force can be conserved and controlled to express itself in constructive channels, they would soon be prosperous. Spirit must have substance to work on and there must be substance in the ideas of your mind. If your substance is going here, there, and everywhere, being spent in riotous thinking, how can it accumulate to the point of demonstration? Such a waste of substance is a violation of the law of conservation, a law that all should know. When you overcome your desire for dissipation, not the overt acts only but the inner desire, then you will begin to accumulate substance that must manifest itself as prosperity according to the law.

One of the fundamental principles in the study of Christianity is that God's great objective is the making of a perfect man. Man is the apex of creation, made in God's image and likeness, and endowed with full authority and dominion over his elemental thoughts. We sometimes think that we must succeed in some business or occupation before we can become rich or famous. This is a missing of the mark of "the high calling of God in Christ Jesus," which is to demonstrate the divine idea of a perfect man. The real object of life is not making money or becoming famous but the building of character, the bringing forth of the potentialities that exist in every one of us. A part of the divine plan is substantial provision by the Creator for all the mental and physical needs of His creation. We are not studying prosperity to become rich but to bring out those characteristics that are fundamental to prosperity. We must learn to develop the faculty that will bring prosperity and the character that is not spoiled by prosperity.

Faith is the faculty of mind that deals with the universal-substance idea. Faith is the substance of things hoped for. Everything in God is ideal, without form or shape but with all possibilities. He is omnipresent in our mind and in our body. It is in our body that we bring God into visible manifestation. Faith is the faculty that does this. It lays hold of the substance idea and makes it visible.

The scramble for wealth seems to be the only object of existence for certain minds. Writers of Biblical times were incessantly preaching against the evils of money. Yet Jehovah was always promising riches and honor to all those who kept His commandments. The gold and silver that God promised were spiritual rather than material. God is mind, and mind can give only ideas.

These ideas can be translated into terms of gold or of anything else we desire, according to our thought. The only treasures that are worth saving are those we lay up in the heavens of the mind. The only gold that can be trusted to bring happiness is the gold of Spirit. Jesus says, "I counsel thee to buy of me gold refined by fire, that thou mayest become rich; and white garments, that thou mayest clothe thyself, that the shame of thy nakedness be not made manifest."

Paul tells us that "the love of money is a root of all kinds of evil." That means of course that by loving money man has in some way limited it. He has not loved the true source of money but has loved the thing rather than the Spirit that it expresses. He has broken the law by trying to grasp the thing and failing to acknowledge the idea that lies back of it. We must know this law, observing it in the handling of money, and make love the magnet of supply instead of becoming entangled in that selfishness and greed which is causing so much inharmony and suffering in the world today. We should know that there is a universal money substance and that it belongs to all of us in all its fullness.

In the parable of the sower Jesus uses a most striking phrase. Part of the good seed was choked out by thorns and the thorns represent the "deceitfulness of riches." Money is indeed a cheat. It promises ease and brings cares; it promises pleasures and pays with pain; it promises influence and returns envy and jealousy; it promises happiness and gives sorrow; it promises permanence and then flies away.

Metaphysically, it is better or at least safer to be poor than to be rich. Jesus taught this in the parable of the rich man and Lazarus. The rich man is pictured in torment, crying for the poor man to give him a drink of water. But if the rich are miserable, the poor who greatly desire to be rich are equally so. Poverty and riches are the two poles of a magnet whose pivot is a belief that the possession of matter will bring joy to the possessor. This belief is a delusion, and those who are attracted by this belief and allow their minds to be hypnotized by the desire for material possessions are to be pitied whether their desire is realized or not.

The real possessor of wealth is the one who feels that all things are his to use and to enjoy yet does not burden himself with the personal possession of anything. Diogenes was a most happy man though he lived in a tub. His philosophy has outlived the influence of the rich and powerful people who were his contemporaries. He walked around with a lantern at midday looking for an honest man, so they seem to have been as rare in his day as in ours.

However, the widespread desire for material possessions indicates that there is somewhere some good in it. The natural man is from the soil, formed of the dust of the ground, and loves his native element. The spiritual man is from above, originating in the heavens of the mind. He is given first place and like Jacob supplants the natural man. Men should not condemn the earth because of this, yet they should not love it to the exclusion of the heavens. They should understand that substance is the day from which the Father makes the body of His people. "Your heavenly Father knoweth that ye have need of all these things ... But seek ye first his kingdom, and his righteousness; and all these things shall be added unto you."

The divine law holds that the earth is the Lord's and the fullness thereof. If this truth were thoroughly understood, men would begin at once to make all property public, available for the use and enjoyment of all the people. The early disciples of Jesus understood this and their religion required them to bring all their possessions and lay them at the feet of their leaders, to be distributed and used according to the needs of all. Paul's companion Barnabas gave his field. Ananias and Sapphira sold their land and brought part of the price to Peter but held back part of it. They had not overcome the fear of future lack and had not put their faith fully in the teaching and promises of the Master.

When we have recognized the truth of the omnipresence of God as substance and supply for every need, there will be no occasion for holding back part as Ananias and Sapphira did. We cannot hoard money in its material phase without breaking the law, which is that we have all the substance necessary for our supply. We ask the Lord for our "daily" bread and expect to have it but we do not get an accumulation that will spoil on our hands or that will deny the proper supply to any other man. The metaphysical idea of this part of the Lord's Prayer is "Give us this day the substance of tomorrow's bread." We ask not for bread but for the substance that Spirit arranges to manifest as bread, clothing, shelter, or the supply for any need we may have.

Substance in the form of money is given to us for constructive uses. It is given for use and to meet an immediate need, not to be hoarded away or be foolishly wasted. When you have found freedom from the binding thought of hoarding money, do not go to the opposite extreme of extravagant spending. Money is to be used, not abused. It is good to keep one's obligations paid. It is good to have some money on hand for good uses, such as hospitality, education, for developing industries that will contribute to the good of numbers of people, for the furtherance of spiritual work, for helping others to build useful and constructive lives, and for many other purposes and activities. But in such conservation of money one should keep ever in mind the necessity of a constructive motive back of the action. Money accumulated for a definite and definitely constructive purpose is quite a different thing from money hoarded with the fearful thought of a "rainy day" or a prolonged season of lack and suffering. Money saved for "rainy days" is always used for just that, for fear attracts that which is feared unfailingly. "The thing which I fear cometh upon me."

Money saved as "an opportunity fund" brings an increase of good, but money hoarded from fear as a motive or with any miserly thought in mind cannot possibly bring any blessing. Those who hold the thought of accumulation so dominant in the world today are inviting trouble and even disaster, because right along with this thought goes a strong affirmation of the fear of loss of riches. Their actions bespeak fear, and the loss they dread is certain to be manifested sooner or later. The worldly idea of prosperity is based on the wrong idea of supply. One may have the right idea about the source of riches as spiritual and yet have the wrong idea about the constancy of supply as an ever-present, freely flowing spiritual substance. God does not clothe the lilies in a moment and then leave them to the mercy of lack; He gives them the continuous supply necessary to their growth. We can rest assured that He will much more clothe us and keep us clothed from day to day according to our need. When we doubt this and place our dependence on stored-up money instead, we shut off the stream of divine supply. Then when our little accumulation is spent, stolen, or lost, we are like the prodigal son and we begin to be in want.

Jesus did not own a foot of land. Yet never did He lack for anything needed. Without laying up treasures on earth He was rich in His consciousness of the treasures of heaven within Himself, treasures ready to be manifested in the outer whenever He needed them.

We know perfectly well that sooner or later we shall have to let go of our earthly possessions. Does this bring the thought of death and of leaving the world behind? Then it shows what a powerful hold this race belief of worldly wealth has taken in your mind. Men can think of letting go of their material possessions only in connection with death. They seem to prefer death to giving up their idea of wealth. When they make such a choice they decree what shall come to pass for them. That is why it is hard for a "rich man" to enter into the kingdom of heaven. He has laid up treasures on earth and not enough in heaven. He has not made it possible for his mind to lay hold of the positive pole of wealth, the true idea of wealth. He is holding to the negative side of the wealth idea, and that side is always changing. Material things pass away unless they are firmly connected with the unchanging, positive Source.

True riches and real prosperity are in the understanding that there is an omnipresent substance from which all things come and that by the action of our mind we can unify ourselves with that substance so that the manifestations that come from it will be in line with our desires and needs. Instead of realizing the inexhaustible, eternal, and omnipresent nature of that substance, we have limited it in our thought. We have thought that there is only about so much of it and that we had better hurry to get our share. We have thought that we must be careful how we spend it and put some of it away for a time when there won't be any more. In building up this consciousness of a limited supply we have concluded that it is necessary to be economical and more and more saving. We begin to pinch in our mind, and then our money becomes pinched, for as we think in our mind, so we manifest in our affairs. This attitude pinches the channel through which our substance comes to manifestation and slows down the even flow of our supply. Then comes depression, hard times, shortage, and we wonder why, looking for some way to lay the blame on the government, or on war, or on industry, or even on the Lord, but never by any chance do we put the blame where it belongs: on ourselves.

The "pinching attitude" of mind does even worse than bring people into want. If people would relax in mind, they would loosen up the nerves and muscles of the body. They must learn the cause of their strained, pinching mental attitude and let go of that first. Then the relief of the outer condition will become manifest as the condition itself did.

Nearly all of us have been brought up in the belief that economy is an important thing, even a virtue. We should save our money and have a bank account. Saving money is the recipe for success given by many of our wealthy men. It is not a bad idea. There must be money available in banks to carry on business and industry. By having a bank account we contribute to the welfare of the community, if we have the right idea; which is that the Lord is our banker.

The word miser is from the Latin root from which also comes "miserable." It describes the condition of those who love and hoard money, lands, or other material things. The stories that are told about misers are almost beyond credence, but nearly every day the press recounts the story of the pitiable straits to which misers have reduced themselves in order to add to their riches. They sometimes starve themselves to add a few dollars or even a few pennies to their hoarded store. The papers recently carried an item about a miser in New York worth eleven million dollars. He goes from office to office in one of his great office buildings and picks up the waste paper from the baskets, which he sells for a few cents. Another almost as wealthy will not buy an overcoat but keeps his body warm by pinning newspapers under his house coat. Such men are not only themselves miserable but they make miserable all those around them. A New York paper tells of a miser worth millions when he died. Once burglars broke into his home, but they succeeded in getting out again without losing anything.

You do not need to lay up treasures for the future when you know that the law of omnipresent good is providing for you from within. As you evolve into this inner law of mind, you draw to yourself more and more of the good things of life.

In your mind see plenty everywhere. Yes, it is hard sometimes to overcome the thought that there is not enough, for it is an insidious thought that has been in consciousness for a long time. But it can be done. It has been done and is being done by others. The prosperity law is not a theory but a demonstrated fact, as thousands can testify. Now is the time to open your mind and to see plenty. As you do so you will find that there is an increase in your supply. Deny out of mind every thought of lack and affirm the abundance of all good. The infinite substance that infinite Mind has given to you is all about you now, but you must lay hold of it. It is like the air, but you must breathe the air to get it. It is yours for the taking, but you must take it. You should cultivate this wonderful power of the mind to know that everything is bountiful and this power to lay hold of invisible substance in the mind and by faith bring it forth into manifestation. Know with Job that we have as much now, in reality and in Truth, as we ever had. There is no shortage, lack, or depression with God.

Do not be fearful, regardless of how outer appearances may affect others. Keep your head when all about you are losing theirs. Refuse to load up your mind with the old material thoughts of economy to the point of denial of what you really need. Eliminate the old limiting ideas. Assert your freedom and your faith as a child of God. Do not spend foolishly or save foolishly. The farmer does not throw away his wheat when he sows a field. He knows how much he must sow per acre and does not stint, for he knows that a stinted sowing will bring a stinted harvest. He sows bountifully but not extravagantly and he reaps bountifully as he has sown. "Whatsoever a man soweth, that shall he also reap." "He that soweth sparingly shall reap also sparingly; and he that soweth bountifully shall reap also bountifully."

We cannot help but see that apparent lack and hard times are the result of states of mind. We have such things in the manifest world because men have not squared their action with divine Principle. They have not used spiritual judgment. When they invest in stocks and property, they get the opinions of other men, sometimes those who call themselves experts. Then comes the crash, and even the experts prove how little they understand the real laws of wealth. We can go to an expert who really knows the law because He ordained it in the first place. And He is not far away, but right within ourselves. We can go within and meditate on these things in the silence, and the Lord will direct our personal finances. He will show us just how to get the most and give the most with our money and He will see to it that we have the supply that we need so that we may not be in want of anything needful to our good. This may not mean riches piled up or "saved for a rainy day," but it will insure our supply for today, the only day there is in Truth.

As we continue to grow in the consciousness of God as omnipresent life and substance we no longer have to put our trust in accumulations of money or other goods. We are sure that each day's need will be met, and we do not deprive ourselves of today's enjoyment and peace in order to provide for some future and wholly imaginary need. In this consciousness our life becomes divinely ordered, and there is a balance in supply and finances as in everything else. We do not deprive ourselves of what we need today; neither do we waste our substance in foolish ways nor deplete it uselessly. We do not expect or prepare for adversity of any kind, for to do so is not only to invite it but to show a doubt of God and all His promises. Many people bear burdens and deny themselves sufficient for their present needs in order to prepare for dark days that never come. When we look back over the past we find that most of our fears were groundless, and most of the things we dreaded so much never happened. However the things we prepared for probably did happen and found us not fully prepared even after all our efforts in that direction. This should enable us to trust God now and rest in the positive assurance that He will supply every need as it arises.

Things are never so bad as you think. Never allow yourself to be burdened with the thought that you are having a hard time. You do not want a soul structure of that kind and should not build it with those thoughts. You are living in a new age. Yesterday is gone forever; today is here forever. Something grander for man is now unfolding. Put yourself in line with the progress of thought in the new age and go forward.

Chapter XII

Overcoming the Thought of Lack

THE KINGDOM of heaven is like unto a net, that was cast into the sea, and gathered of every kind; which, when it was filled, they drew up on the beach; and they sat down, and gathered the good into vessels, but the bad they cast away."

The mind of man is like the net catching every kind of idea, and it is man's privilege and duty under the divine law to separate those that are good from those which are not good. In this process the currents of unselfish, spiritual love flowing through the soul act as great eliminators, freeing the consciousness of thoughts of hate, lack, and poverty, and giving the substance of Spirit free access into the consciousness and affairs.

In another parable Jesus explained the same process as a separation of the sheep from the goats. When this divine current of love and spiritual understanding begins its work, we must make this separation. We put the sheep, the good and obedient and profitable thoughts, on the right, and we put the goats, the stubborn, selfish, useless thoughts, on the left. Each must handle his own thoughts and overcome them by aligning them with the harmony and order of the divine thought. There is an infinite, omnipresent wisdom within us that will deal with these thoughts and guide us in making the discrimination between the right and the wrong when we trust ourselves fully to its intelligence. We can establish a connection between the conscious mind and the superconscious mind within us by meditation, by silence, and by speaking the word.

The superconscious mind within you discriminates among the kinds of food you assimilate, controls your digestion, your breathing, and the beating of your heart. It "doeth all things well," and it will help you do this important work of directing you in the thoughts you should hold and the ones you should cast out. As you develop this mind within yourself you will find that you can gradually turn over more and more of your affairs to its perfect discrimination. Nothing is too great for it to accomplish, nor is anything too trivial for it to handle with perfection and dispatch. This mind of the Spirit will guide you in perfect ways, even in the minute details of your life, if you will let it do so. But you must will to do its will and trust it in all your ways. It will lead you unfailingly into health, happiness, and prosperity, as it has done and is doing for thousands, if and when you follow it.

It is just as necessary that one should let go of old thoughts and conditions after they have served their purpose as it is that one should lay hold of new ideas and create new conditions to meet one's requirements. In fact we cannot lay hold of the new ideas and make the new conditions until we have made room for them by eliminating the old. If we feel that we cannot part with the goats, we shall have to do with fewer sheep. If we insist on filling the vessels with the bad fish, we shall have to do without the good. We are learning that thoughts are things and occupy "space" in mind. We cannot have new or better ones in a place already crowded with old, weak, inefficient thoughts. A mental house cleaning is even more necessary than a material one, for the without is but a reflection of the within. Clean the inside of the platter, where the food is kept as well as the outside that people see, taught Jesus.

Old thoughts must be denied and the mind cleansed in preparation before the affirmative Christ consciousness can come in. Our mind and even our body is loaded with error thoughts. Every cell is clothed with thought: every cell has a mind of its own. By the use of denial we break through the outer crust, the material thought that has enveloped the cells, and get down into the substance and the life within them. Then we make contact with that substance and life which our denials have exposed, and by it express the positive, constructive side of the law. When we consistently deny the limitations of the material, we begin to reveal the spiritual law that waits within ourselves to be fulfilled. When this law is revealed to our consciousness, we begin to use it to demonstrate all things that are good. That is the state of consciousness that Jesus had, the Christ consciousness.

Every man has a definite work to do in the carrying forward of the divine law of spiritual evolution. The law is set into action by our thinking and is continually supported by our thought as it develops our soul. Within us are the great potentialities of Spirit that, put into action, enable us to be, do, or have anything we will. Science tells us that each of us has enough energy within himself to run a universe, if we knew how to release and control it. We do this releasing by a process of letting go and taking hold: letting go of the old or that which has done its part and is no longer useful, and taking hold of the new ideas and inspirations that come from the superconscious mind. Jesus told Peter that what he should bind in earth would be bound in heaven and what he should loose in earth would be loosed in heaven. He was not talking about a geographical earth or a definite place in the skies called heaven. He was explaining to Peter the law of mind. The conscious mind is but the negative pole of a very positive realm of thought. That positive realm of thought, Jesus called "the kingdom of the heavens." It is not a place at all but is the free activity of the superconscious mind of man. Whatever we bind or limit in earth, in the conscious mind, shall be bound or limited in the ideal or heavenly realm, and whatever we loose and set free in the conscious mind (earth) shall be loosed and set free in the ideal, the heavenly. In other words, whatever you affirm or deny in your conscious mind determines the character of the supermind activities. All power is given unto you both in heaven and in earth through your thought.

We must carefully choose what thoughts we are going to loose in the mind and what thoughts we are going to bind, for they will come into manifestation in our affairs. "As he [man] thinketh within himself, so is he" and "whatsoever a man soweth [in the mind], that shall he also reap [in the manifestation]." We must loose all thoughts of lack and insufficiency in the mind and let them go, just as Jesus commanded be done with the wrappings that held Lazarus: "Loose him, and let him go." Loose all thoughts of lack and lay hold of thoughts of plenty. See the abundance of all good things, prepared for you and for all of us from the foundation of the world. We live in a very sea of inexhaustible substance, ready to come into manifestation when molded by our thought.

Some persons are like fish in the sea, saying, "Where is the water?" in the presence of spiritual abundance they cry, "Where will I get the money? How will I pay my bills? Will we have food or clothes or the necessities?" Plenty is here, all around, and when you have opened the eyes of Spirit in yourself, you will see it and rejoice.

We mold omnipresent substance with our mind and make from it all the things that our mind conceives. If we conceive lack and poverty we mold that. If we visualize with a bountiful eye we mold plenty from the ever-present substance. There is perhaps no step in spiritual unfoldment more important than the one we are taking here. We must learn to let go, to give up, to make room for the things we have prayed for and desired. This is called renunciation or elimination, sacrifice it may even seem to some people. It is simply the giving up and casting away of old thoughts that have put us where we are, and putting in their place new ideas that promise to improve our condition. If the new ideas fail to keep this promise, we cast them away in their turn for others, confident that we shall eventually find the right ideas that will bring that which we desire. We always want something better than we have. It is the urge of progress, of development and growth. As children outgrow their clothes we outgrow our ideals and ambitions, broadening our horizon of life as we advance. There must be a constant elimination of the old to keep pace with this growth. When we cling to the old ideals we hinder our advance or stop it altogether.

Metaphysicians speak of this eliminative work as denial. Denial usually comes first. It sweeps out the debris and makes room for the new tenant that is brought into the mind by the affirmation. It would not be wise to eliminate the old thoughts unless you knew that there are higher and better ones to take their place. But we need not fear this, because we know the divine truth that God is the source of all good and that all good things can be ours through the love and grace of Jesus Christ.

None of us has attained that supreme place in consciousness where he wholly gives up the material man and lives in the Spirit, as Jesus did, but we have a concept of such a life and His example showing that it can be attained. We shall attain it when we escape the mortal. This does not mean that we must die to get free from mortality, for mortality is but a state of consciousness. We die daily and are reborn by the process of eliminating the thought that we are material and replacing it with the truth that we are spiritual. One of the great discoveries of modern science is that every atom in this so-called material universe has within it superabundant life elements. God is life and Spirit, and He is in every atom. We release this spiritual life quality by denying the crust of materiality that surrounds the cells and affirming that they are Spirit and life. This is the new birth, which takes place first as a conception in the mind, followed by an outworking in body and affairs. We all want better financial conditions. Here is the way to obtain them: Deny the old thoughts of lack of money and affirm the new thought of spiritual abundance everywhere manifest.

Every lesson of Scripture illustrates some phase of mental action and can be applied to each individual life according to the need that is most pressing at the time of its perception. If you do not look for the mental lesson when reading Scripture, you get but the mere outer shell of Truth. If however you have the proper understanding of the characters in the narrative, knowing that they represent ideas in your own mind, you can follow them in their various movements and find the way to solve all the problems of your life. This does not mean that a study of the written Scriptures will itself solve your problems unless you come into the apprehension of the real Scriptures, the Bible of the ages, the Book of Life within your own consciousness. But a study of the outer symbols as given in the written Scriptures can and should lead you into the understanding of the Truth of Being.

In every person we find the conflicting ideas represented by the Children of Israel and the Philistines. They are pitted against each other in a conflict that goes on night and day. We call these warring thoughts Truth and error. When we are awakened spiritually we stand on the side of Truth, knowing that Truth thoughts are the chosen of the Lord, the Children of Israel. But the error thoughts sometimes seem so real and so formidable that we quake and cringe with fear in their presence.

We know that Truth will eventually prevail, but we put the victory off somewhere in the future and say that the error is so large and strong that we cannot cope with it now--we will wait until we have gathered more strength. Then we need to stand still and affirm the salvation of the Lord.

Ideas are not all of the same importance. Some are large and strong; some are small and weak. There are aggressive, dominating ideas that parade themselves, and brag about their power, and with threats of disaster keep us frightened into submission to their wicked reign. These domineering ideas of error have one argument that they always use to impress us, that of the fear of results if we should dare to come out and meet them in open opposition. This fear of opposing ideas, even when we know them to be wrong, seems to be woven into our very mental fabric. This fear is symbolized by the spear of Goliath which, as the story relates, "was like a weaver's beam."

What is the most fearful thought in the minds of men today? Is it not the power of money? Is not mammon the greatest Philistine, the Goliath in your consciousness? It is the same whether you are siding with the Philistines and are successful in your finances from a material viewpoint, or whether you are with the Israelites and tremble in your poverty. The daily appearance of this giant Goliath, the power of money, is something greatly feared. Neither the Philistines nor the Israelites are in possession of the Promised Land, neither side at peace or happy in any security, so long as this domineering giant parades his strength and shouts his boasts. This error idea claims he is stronger than the Lord of Israel. He must be killed before all the other error thoughts will be driven out of your consciousness and you can come into the consciousness of plenty, the Promised Land of milk and honey.

The whole world today trembles before this giant error idea, the belief that money is the ruling power. The nations of the world are under this dominion because men think that money is power. The rich and the poor alike are slaves to the idea. Kings and great men of the earth bow and cringe before the money kings. This is because man has given this power to money by his erroneous thinking. He has made the golden calf and now he falls before it in worship. Instead of making it his servant he has called it master and become its slave. The rule of this mad giant has been disastrous, and the end of it is rapidly approaching.

The first step in getting your mind free from this giant bugaboo is to get a clear perception of your right as a child of God. You know that you should put no other gods or powers before the true God. You know also that you should not be under the dominion of anything in the heavens above or the earth beneath, for you have been given dominion over all. You will never find a better time to come into the realization of the truth of who and what you are and what your rights are. Never was a more propitious time to seek a new and better state of consciousness. If you are in fear of the boasting Philistine giant, as so many around you are, begin now to seek a way, as did David, to give his "flesh unto the birds of the heavens." There is a way, a righteous way, that cannot fail, and it is your duty to find it. Follow each step of the way that is symbolically and beautifully set forth in the 17th chapter of I Samuel.

The name David means "the Lord's beloved," and David represents your righteous perception of your privileges as the child of God. You are not a slave to anything or to anybody in the universe. The threat of this Goliath, the power of money, holds no terrors for you in this consciousness. You have a smooth perception of Truth and you sling it straight to the center of his carnal thinking, his forehead. The weight of his shield and his armor does not intimidate you, for you see them for what they are, empty and meaningless show, vulnerable in many places to the true ideas with which you are armed.

Even the most ardent defenders of the money power will admit that it is a tyrant and that they would not have it rule their world if they could help it. It nearly always destroys its friends in the end. Any man who becomes a slave to money is eventually crushed by it. On the other side are whole armies of righteous people, Christians, who like the army of Israel think that this giant cannot be overcome. They are waiting for reinforcements, something larger and stronger in a physical way, with which to overcome this enemy. They forget that "the battle is Jehovah's."

Do you cringe before this giant when he comes out daily to impress you with his boastings and threats? It does not have to be so. You need not continue to fear. There is a little idea in your mind that can slay him. You perhaps have not considered this little idea of much importance. Perhaps you have kept it off on a lonely mountainside of your spiritual consciousness, herding the sheep, which are your innocent thoughts. Now let this David come forth, this perception of your rightful place in Divine Mind. Get a clear idea of where you really belong in creation and what your privileges are. Do you think for a moment that God has so ordained that men cannot escape from the terrible servitude of hard conditions? Of course not. That would be injustice, and God is above all just.

It is your privilege to step out at any time and accept the challenge of this boaster. The Lord has been with you in the slaying of the fear of sin and sickness (the bear and the lion), and He will still be with you in slaying the fear of poverty, which Goliath symbolizes. "The battle is Jehovah's," and He is with us to deliver us "out of the hand of the Philistines."

The weapons of the Lord's man are not carnal. He does not wage war after the manner of the world. He does not use armor of steel or brass, the protection of selfishness and the weapons of oppression. He goes forth in the simplicity of justice, knowing that his innocence is his defense. He uses only his shepherd's sling and smooth stones, words of Truth. This is the will and the words of Truth that it sends forth. They are disdained by the Philistines and many people laugh at the idea of using words to overcome conditions. But words do their work, the work whereto they are sent, and the great mass of materiality goes down before their sure aim.

We know that money was made for man and not man for money. No man needs to be a slave to his brother man or cringe before him to obtain money, which is the servant of all alike. We are not bound to the wheel of work, of ceaseless toil day after day, in order to appease the god of mammon on his own terms. We are children of the living God, who as a loving Father is right here in our midst, where we may claim Him as our support and our resource on such conditions as He lovingly reveals when we have acknowledged Him and denied mammon. This day has Jehovah delivered this proud Philistine into our hands, and the victory is ours. Praise God.

The five smooth stones chosen by David from the brook represent five irrefutable statements of Truth. These statements sent forth from a mind confident of itself, its cause, and its spiritual strength will crush the forehead of Goliath, error's giant. The statements are the following:

I am the beloved of the Lord. He is with me in all my righteous words, and they do accomplish that whereto I send them forth.

My cause is just, for it is my divine right to be supplied with all things whatsoever that the Father has placed at the disposal of His children.

I dissolve in my own mind and the minds of all others any thought that my own can be withheld from me. What is mine comes to me by the sure law of God, and in my clear perception of Truth I welcome it.

I am not fearful of poverty, and I am under obligations to no one. My opulent Father has poured out to me all resources, and I am a mighty channel of abundance.

I selfishly own nothing, yet all things in existence are mine to use and in divine wisdom to bestow upon others.

Do not hold yourself in poverty by the fear of lack and by practicing a pinching economy. If you believe that all that the Father has is yours, then there is surely no reason for skimping. Nothing will so broaden your mind and your world as the realization that all is yours. When you realize the boundlessness of your spiritual inheritance, nothing shall be lacking in all your world. See with the bountiful eye; for "he that hath a bountiful eye shall be blessed." This passage states an exact law, the law of increase.

Religious leaders in the past have spread the belief that it is a Christian duty to be poor and that poverty is a virtue. This is by no means the doctrine of Jesus. He accepted the proposition fully, without reservation or qualification, that God is our resource and that the Father has provided all things for His children. He is often described as being poor, without a place to lay His head, yet He had a parental home at Nazareth and was welcomed gladly into the homes of both the rich and the poor all over Palestine. He dressed as a rabbi, and His clothing was so rich and valuable that the Roman soldiers coveted the seamless robe He wore and cast lots for it. He found abundance in the kingdom of God where everything needful becomes manifest not through hard labor but through the realization of Truth.

Jesus seldom had need for money, because He went back of money to the idea it represents and dealt with money in the idea realm. Our government is back of all our paper dollars, else they would have no value. God is back of every material symbol, and it is in God rather than in the symbol that we should put our faith. He is back of our call for food and raiment and everything that we could need or desire. Jesus says all we need do is ask in faith and in His name, believing that we receive, and we shall have. And we should not hesitate to ask largely, for God can give much as easily as He can give a little.

Question Helps

Lesson I
Spiritual Substance, The Fundamental Basis Of The Universe

1. What is Divine Mind?
2. What is man, and how is he connected with divine ideas?
3. What great change in methods of production and distribution seems about to be made? How will it affect our prosperity?
4. What is the ether of science and metaphysics? To what extent has man drawn on it, and what are its possibilities?
5. What did Jesus demonstrate regarding the kingdom of the ether?
6. What is the source of all material, according to science? According to Jesus?
7. What is the simplest and surest way to lay hold of substance?
8. Explain from this viewpoint how substance can never be depleted.
9. Why does God give to just and unjust alike, to all equally?
10. How does this truth of the ether help us better to understand the nature of God as pure being or Spirit?
11. What is symbolized by gold and silver? Why are they precious?
12. What is the threefold activity through which substance must go on its way to becoming manifest as material?
13. If substance is omnipresent and man can control its manifestation, why does man suffer from lack and limitation?
14. Explain the teaching of Jesus that it is hard for a rich man to enter the kingdom of the heavens.
15. What is meant by "property rights" and the right to wealth? What error is implied in this doctrine? To whom do ideas belong?
16. What are some of the "great possessions" that must be unloaded before we can enter the kingdom of consciousness?
17. After recognizing the existence, potentiality, and availability of universal substance, what is the next step in demonstration?
18. Can the kingdom be found by one with selfish motives? Why should we desire healing and prosperity?
19. What is the prosperity consciousness? Give examples. How can it be cultivated wisely?
20. What will be the social and economic results of a widespread prosperity consciousness in the whole race?

Lesson II
Spiritual Mind, The Omnipresent Directive Principle Of Prosperity

1. Why are ideas the most important things in life?

2. What is desire in origin, purpose, and result?

3. What is the difference between "is-ness" and "existence"?

4. What is the difference between "being" and "appearance"?

5. What is the relation of figures to the problem they help solve? How does this illustrate spiritual reality and material phenomena?

6. What is implied in the fact that man can conceive of an ideal world?

7. Should we deny the existence of material things? Can we do so successfully? What should we deny about the things of the outer?

8. What is the "I AM identity"? How does it differ from Divine Mind?

9. Why is spiritual understanding important? How is it gained?

10. What connection exists between ideas in Divine Mind?

11. What divine idea is back of riches? What ideas are the "parents" of this idea? How can this knowledge help us in demonstrating?

12. Are all men equally entitled to wealth? What ideas should accompany the acquiring, using, and spending of wealth?

13. Do we expect God to give us actual loaves of bread when we pray the Lord's Prayer? What does He give instead of material things?

14. Why do people have dreams? Do dreams help men with their problems?

15. What is the value of relaxation and the silence when we seek God's gifts?

16. What relation has prosperity demonstration to the kingdom-of-the-heavens consciousness?

17. What is the physical, psychological, and spiritual reason for preparing the way for the prosperity demonstration?

18. What does the parable of the lilies teach us about substance?

19. What effect does the attitude of thanksgiving and praise have upon our prosperity?

20. Why is asking in the name of Jesus Christ more effective than any other prayer?

Lesson III
Faith In The Invisible Substance, The Key To Demonstration

1. What is the starting point in building a prosperity consciousness?
2. What is the relation between faith and substance?
3. What does it mean to "have" faith?
4. What is a "seeking" faith? For what does it seek?
5. Explain how doubt retards manifestation.
6. What is the difference between the conception of John the Baptist and that of Jesus?
7. How do love and understanding assist faith in its accomplishments?
8. Are difficult experiences necessary in life? Why do we have them?
9. Show that it is sinful to think and talk hard times, lack, and other limitations.
10. Explain the symbology of the five loaves and two fishes.
11. How does fear produce a stagnation in financial circulation? How does confidence or faith restore normal conditions?
12. How can we go into "the upper room" to wait for the power from on high?
13. How does your mind create? Are its creations always real?
14. Why should our faith be in Spirit rather than in material things?
15. Show how faith is essential to success in the professions, in manufacturing, in sales, and in other lines of activity.
16. What do the Bible characters represent to us today? What Bible personage represents faith?
17. Is science antagonistic to religion or helpful to its cause?
18. What is the relation between material and substance?
19. Is there any lack of anything anywhere? What are we to overcome?
20. What affirmations help most to banish fear and abide in the consciousness of plenty?

Lesson IV
Man, The Inlet And Outlet Of Divine Mind

1. What is meant by Principle as applied to prosperity?

2. How do we establish a consciousness of Principle as related to us?

3. How can the study of Truth make one happier, healthier, more beautiful, more prosperous?

4. What is a miracle? Is prosperity miraculous?

5. How are the keepers of divine law rewarded, and its breakers punished?

6. What are the legislative, judicial, and executive phases of the divine law?

7. What is the first rule of the divine law?

8. What is the effect of thinking and speaking of everything as good?

9. Is there any virtue in poverty?

10. What is meant by the "far country," and what is the homeland of the prodigal son?

11. What is the psychological and spiritual effect of old clothes?

12. What is symbolized by the putting on of new shoes.

13. How is true substance wasted, and what is the connection between waste and want?

14. What is our best insurance of financial security?

15. How does the law "Seek and ye shall find" apply to prosperity?

16. Should one who works harder or has more ability receive a greater reward than another?

17. What power has love in helping one to demonstrate prosperity?

18. How does the subconscious mind help or hinder in demonstration?

19. What form does God's answer to prayer take? How do we know when a prayer is answered?

20. Must one be morally worthy to become prosperous?

Lesson V
The Law That Governs The Manifestation Of Supply

1. What in our consciousness is represented by Moses? By Joshua? By Jesus?

2. What is the metaphysical significance of eating? How do we break bread in the four-dimensional world?

3. What retards manifestation when we work to attain the consciousness of abundance?

4. What do we mean by the "one law"? How may we know it? How keep it?

5. Explain how our ability to use wealth wisely to a large degree determines our prosperity.

6. Is it necessary to beseech God for prosperity? To ask? To thank?

7. How do we look or go "within"?

8. Compare the sense mind with the spiritual mind and show how true prosperity depends on the latter.

9. What is the light theory of matter formation, and how does it agree with the teaching of the New Testament?

10. Where and what is heaven? How is the soul formed?

11. How did King Solomon demonstrate great prosperity?

12. What is meant by "laying hold of" the substance?

13. How did Jesus develop His consciousness of omnipresent substance and what did that consciousness ultimately do for Him?

14. What is the true interpretation of "rich man" in the famous parable of the camel and the needle's eye?

15. How do we constantly "turn stones into bread," and what results?

16. What does the parable of the talents teach us regarding prosperity?

17. What six steps necessary to manifestation may be discerned in the story of creation?

18. What do we contribute to the world by raising our own consciousness to the prosperity level?

19. Analyze and explain the statement "I trust Thy universal law of prosperity in all my affairs."

Lesson VI
Wealth Of Mind Expresses Itself In Riches

1. What is prosperity?
2. Explain the prosperity law that Jesus gave.
3. What relation has a prosperity consciousness to wealth in the outer?
4. What is the "sin of riches"?
5. What causes crop failure and famine in some countries?
6. Why did Jesus carry no money and own no property?
7. What is the only thing that can satisfy human longing, and where is it found?
8. Is the law of prosperity limited to thought? What else is needful?
9. Over what is man given dominion by his Creator?
10. How can man master his fear of financial lack?
11. Why are prosperity prayers sometimes unanswered?
12. What is the true idea of God, and how does man give it form?
13. What causes "depressions" in the affairs of men and nations?
14. What part does self-control in the matter of sensation play in prosperity demonstration?
15. What is the relative importance of denial and affirmation in the demonstration of prosperity?
16. Who are the real producers of wealth in the nation?
17. What is the law of increase as applied to Mind substance?
18. How should we prepare for an increased prosperity?
19. Should we be specific and definite in our prayers for increase?
20. Write a prosperity affirmation of your own embodying the four essential steps of recognition, love, faith, and praise.

Lesson VII
God Has Provided Prosperity For Every Home

1. Of what great spiritual power is the home the symbol?

2. What has the "atmosphere" of a home to do with its prosperity? How may an atmosphere of worry and fear be changed?

3. Explain the importance of speaking true words in the home.

4. Aside from the feeling of religious duty, why should we be thankful for what we have and express our thanks often?

5. Is it good policy to condemn the furnishings in the home or to be apologetic about them?

6. Should our homes be ostentatious and rich looking to attract prosperity?

7. Why should we be individual in furnishing the home rather than following the "accepted" or "in-the-mode" style only?

8. How will a deep and sincere love for God attract prosperity?

9. Why must there be love and understanding between members of the family to insure a prosperous home?

10. Explain the law of "Love thy neighbor" as applied to home prosperity.

11. What is God's will for the home, and how does the home express it?

12. Explain how trying to live and do as others live and do may hold back our prosperity demonstration.

13. How can we use our will to help the demonstration of home prosperity?

14. Why should the individual express his own ideas in order to demonstrate?

15. Where and how is the prosperity demonstration started?

16. Do we have any personal claim on God's substance?

17. How do we "pour" substance into the "empty" places of the home?

18. Why is it necessary to have determination in order to demonstrate?

19. Does the possession of material things give satisfaction?

Lesson VIII
God Will Pay Your Debts

1. What law of mind is observed in true forgiveness?

2. Why should we trust rather than distrust people?

3. Is there any such thing as debt in Truth? Why?

4. Where must we start in forgiving our debtors and creditors?

5. How can we forgive ourselves for holding others in our debt?

6. What is the only sure way of getting out and staying out of debt?

7. Explain forgiveness as a good method of bill collecting.

8. How does God forgive our debts? How does His love pay our debts?

9. How do debt and worry about debt affect health? What is the remedy?

10. Does God have a place in modern business?

11. What are the merits and the dangers of installment buying?

12. What is the importance of paying all obligations promptly?

13. What kind of thoughts should one hold toward creditors? Debtors?

14. What dominant belief has caused world depression, and how must it be overcome? What is our part in its overcoming?

15. Is the credit system responsible for widespread debt?

16. Does our faith in supply justify us in assuming obligations and trusting that we shall be able to pay when the time comes?

17. What is the value of prayer in gaining freedom from debt?

Lesson IX
Tithing, The Road To Prosperity

1. What is a "tithe," and how was tithing started?

2. What benefits accrue to the tither, according to the promises of the Bible?

3. Should one regard one's tithe as an investment that pays rewards?

4. In what way is giving a divine grace?

5. What was the practical plan that Paul suggested to the Corinthians?

6. What effect does a willing and cheerful spirit have on the giver, the gift, and the receiver?

7. How can faith be exercised in giving?

8. How should wisdom be employed in giving?

9. How can one who is puzzled about giving--as regards how much, when, and where--be helped by the decision to tithe?

10. What should tithing mean to the farmer? Businessman? Professional man? Mechanic? Laborer?

11. How does tithing help fulfill "the first and greatest commandment" about loving God and the neighbor?

12. Aside from Bible promises, do we have direct evidence that tithing increases prosperity? Cite instances.

13. Should the tithe have a definite place in the personal or family budget? Should we keep a record of our giving, as we do of other disbursements?

14. Why is the regular tithe, though it may be small, better than the occasional giving of a larger gift in a lump sum?

15. What is the psychological basis and effect of tithing?

16. What attitude should one assume toward a seemingly delayed demonstration?

17. Should we look for our good to come through the channel of those to whom we give or serve?

18. Why is it better to give without thought or expectation of return?

19. What must we do about receiving what God has and desires for us?

20. Discuss giving as a form of affirmation.

Lesson X
Right Giving, The Key To Abundant Receiving

1. In what ways is the religion of Jesus applicable to the problems of daily living?

2. State briefly the law of giving and receiving that Jesus taught.

3. Why has the teaching of Jesus not been more effective in changing conditions in the world and in individual life?

4. Why is economic reform so much needed at the present time?

5. Can any effective reform be based on the material phase of the economic problem? Why?

6. Why do men who direct finance and business fail to seek any advice or assistance from the church?

7. Why is individual reform necessary before national or world changes can be made?

8. What do metaphysical teaching and study contribute toward world betterment?

9. How does the desire for the accumulation of money and goods affect the finer nature and sensibilities of people?

10. Does avarice or greed have any effect on the health of men?

11. What is the chief cause of stagnation in money circulation and its attendant evils?

12. What rule did Jesus give us for freeing ourselves from financial lack?

13. Is the method practiced by the early Christians practicable in the world as it is today?

14. What substitute is now being advocated for the commercial standard of payments for goods and service?

15. What is the divine law of equilibrium? Why does it not seem to operate in financial matters?

16. Is there any direct connection between poverty and ill-health? How may this problem be approached? Is there a problem at the other extreme--great wealth? How may it be solved?

17. What is meant by the "race consciousness"? Can we escape its effects? How can we help to change it for the better?

18. What should we do about saving money for the future?

19. What attitude should we take toward charity?

Lesson XI
Laying Up Treasures

1. What is the law of conservation as applied to spiritual substance?
2. What is the difference between hoarding and conserving?
3. Is accumulation of substance necessary to demonstration?
4. How is spiritual substance accumulated? How dissipated?
5. What is the true objective of man's life?
6. Explain why character development must be a part of our study of the demonstration of prosperity.
7. Is the ambition for wealth commendable or reprehensible?
8. Of what is gold the symbol, metaphysically understood?
9. What is the deceitfulness of riches? What is money?
10. Does great wealth bring happiness? Does extreme poverty make one any better than the rich? What is the truth about riches?
11. What is the only true deed or title to possessions?
12. What do we want when we ask for "our daily bread"?
13. How does the hoarding of money injure society?
14. Should we prepare for that "rainy day" by saving part of our money?
15. Was Jesus poor? Was He ever in want? What does it mean to turn stones into bread?
16. Explain the meaning of the rich man and the eye of the needle.
17. What are some of the financial and bodily results of the pinching attitude toward money?
18. What attitude toward hard times and lack is most helpful to us?
19. How shall we learn to get the most and give the most with the means we have at our disposal?

Lesson XII
Overcoming The Thought Of Lack

1. Why must we constantly examine our thoughts and separate them?
2. By what standard do we judge our thoughts?
3. What is the work of the superconscious mind in the body?
4. How may we use this superconscious mind in our outer affairs?
5. What is the importance of thought elimination or mental clean-up?
6. How do we go about this work of eliminating error thoughts?
7. What further benefits accrue from the use of denial words?
8. Where or what is the "kingdom of the heavens," and what is it like?
9. What is meant by "loosing in heaven"? What should we loose and what should we guard against loosing?
10. Where and what is "substance"? How do we contact it?
11. What is the result of clinging to past ideas and methods?
12. What is mortality? Do we escape it by dying? How otherwise?
13. Explain the new birth and the relation of denial to it.
14. What do Bible characters mean to us? What can they do for us?
15. What do David and Goliath stand for in consciousness?
16. What is the modern "golden calf" that most men worship?
17. Name some of the evil results of the error of money worship.
18. Would the doing away with money entirely solve the problem? What is the solution?
19. What "little but mighty" idea in consciousness is symbolized by David?
20. What are the weapons of this David that slay the giant fear?

Jesus Christ Heals

Foreword

Much has been written and said about the healing methods that Jesus used in His very striking cures of physical ills. The generally accepted theory is that they were miracles, but to this there have been many objections, among them Jesus' promise "He that believeth on me, the works that I do shall he do also." So many millions have claimed that they believed on Jesus, yet not only have they failed to heal others but they have gloried in sickness and finally death under the assumption that it was the will of God.

Few have dared even to suggest that Jesus applied universal law in His restorative methods; for on the one hand it would annul the miracle theory and on the other it would be sacrilegious to inquire into the miracles of God. So it has been generally accepted that Jesus' great works were miracles and that the power to do miracles was delegated to His immediate followers only. But in recent years a considerable number of Jesus' followers have had the temerity to inquire into His healing methods, and they have found that they were based on universal mental and spiritual laws that anyone can utilize who will comply with the conditions involved in these laws. This inquiry has led to the conclusion that man and the universe are founded on mind and that all changes for good or ill are changes of mind.

Ages of thought upon the reality and solidarity of things have evolved a mental atmosphere that has produced the present material universe. These and millions of other concepts are the work of men and not God, as is popularly supposed. However they all rest on the original God-Mind and can be restored to the perfect law and order of that Mind by those who free themselves from their mental entanglements with materiality and identify their thinking with that of the Mind that is Spirit. "Ye shall know the truth, and the truth shall make you free."

It is taught in the Bible that Jesus was born into the human family to save its people from extinction; that, according to Paul, as in Adam all died so in Christ shall all be made alive. A psychological study of the whole situation proves this to be virtually true. Millions have accepted Christianity on faith and have found peace of mind and spiritual satisfaction without understanding the fundamental mind principles on which the redemptive system rests. This is proof that there is more to Christianity than the surface acceptation of Jesus as mediator between God and man.

We are all in mind related to a great creative Spirit that infuses its very life into our minds and bodies when we turn our attention to it. We have mentally wandered away from this creative Spirit or Father-Mind and lost contact with its life-giving currents. Jesus made connection for us, and through Him we again begin to draw vitality from the great fountainhead.

Ability to pick up the life current and through it perpetually to vitalize the body is based on the right relation of ideas, thoughts, and words. These mental impulses start currents of energy that form and also stimulate molecules and cells already formed, producing life, strength, and animation where inertia and impotence was the dominant appearance. This was and is the healing method of Jesus.

Although the Bible repeatedly refers to the creative power of the Word, men have not dared to think that the creative law is universal and could be taught to any man who would discipline his thoughts and words and center them on God-Mind. Jesus gave His whole attention to God, so much so that He claimed He did not even originate the words that He spoke: they came from the Father. By careful thinking and wholehearted concentration on God, Jesus made such complete union with creative Mind that His body was transformed in the presence of His disciples. He taught that men would eventually reap the reward of every word they uttered. "For by thy words thou shalt be justified, and by thy words thou shalt be condemned."

Perfect health is natural, and the work of the spiritual healer is to restore this perfect health, which is innate and can be spoken into expression. Our ills are the result of our sins or failure to adjust our minds to Divine Mind. "Man hath authority on earth to forgive sins." When the sinning state of mind is forgiven and the right state of mind established, man is restored to his primal and natural wholeness. This is wholly a mental process, and so all conditions of man are the result of his thinking. "As he [man] thinketh in his heart, so is he." No book, not even the Bible, covers all phases of human thought. Therefore the mental panacea for every ill is beyond the description of words, but Jesus Christ epitomized in His own consciousness all the thought processes necessary to man's complete restoration. So it is taught that Jesus Christ is the Word or Divine Logos in which is contained all the original creative essence.

The truth that divine man is manifest God is the great mystery hid for ages and generations and now revealed in Jesus Christ.

Chapter I - Be Thou Made Whole

JESUS saw in Himself the perfect pattern of the God-Mind. He lived so close to that pattern that He became its perfect expression. As He continued to live closer and ever closer to God He beheld all men as living inventions of God, and through His spiritualized mentality awakened the image of the perfect pattern of the God-Mind in those who came to Him for help. Thus by arousing their souls' energy to such an extent that the physical became immersed in the healing life He enabled the perfect man to come into manifestation.

For example, when Jesus said in a loud voice to the spiritual man in the sleeping Lazarus who had been in the tomb four days, "Lazarus, come forth," the power of the Word in His voice aroused the spiritual man in Lazarus, who in turn awakened his soul to activity. Then the soul life in Lazarus resurrected and restored the seeming dead body, and Lazarus arose and walked out of the tomb.

The more enlightened man becomes the greater is his desire for perfect health. This is logical, for to be healthy is natural. It is a state of being sound or whole in mind, body, and soul. To heal then is to bring forth the perfect Christ man that exists within each of us.

There is quite a bit of misunderstanding on the part of both Christians and non-Christians with regard to the meaning of the words Christ and Jesus, and their use as applied to Jesus of Nazareth. Christ, meaning "messiah" or "anointed," designates one who had received a spiritual quickening from God, while Jesus is the name of the personality. To the metaphysical Christian--that is, to him who studies the spiritual man--Christ is the name of the supermind and Jesus is the name of the personal consciousness. The spiritual man is God's Son; the personal man is man's son. In the unregenerate God's Son is a mere potentiality. But in those who have begun the regenerative process Jesus, the Son of man, is in a state of becoming the Son of God; that is, man is being born again. At the time Jesus told Nicodemus, "Except one be born anew, he cannot see the kingdom of God," He Himself was undergoing that mysterious unfoldment of the soul called the "new birth." He promised great power to those who followed Him in soul development. "Ye who have followed me, in the regeneration . . . shall sit upon twelve thrones."

The Christ or Son-of-God evolution of man's soul is plainly taught in the New Testament as the supreme attainment of every man. "For the earnest expectation of the creation waiteth for the revealing of the sons of God."

Without some evidence in us of the Christ man we are little better than animals. When through faith in the reality of things spiritual we begin soul evolution there is great rejoicing; "we rejoice in hope of the glory of God."

Christ existed long before Jesus. It was the Christ Mind in Jesus that exclaimed, "And now, Father, glorify thou me with thine own self with the glory which I had with thee before the world was."

We should clearly understand that the Christ, the spiritual man, spoke often through Jesus, the natural man; and then again the natural man, Jesus, spoke on His own account. Spiritual understanding reveals to us when it was that Christ spoke and when it was that Jesus spoke. We know that Christ, the spiritual man, could not have experienced death, burial, and resurrection. The experiences were possible only to the mortal man, who was passing from the natural to the spiritual plane of consciousness. The Christ was present with Jesus, quickening and healing His body and finally raising it to the ethereal realm, where He exists to this day.

As Christ the Son of God became manifest in Jesus so He becomes manifest in us when we follow Him in the regeneration. "The Spirit of him that raised up Jesus from the dead . . . shall give life also to your mortal bodies."

But we must have faith in Spirit and through our thinking build it into our consciousness; then our bodies will be restored to harmony, health, and eternal life.

Jesus still lives in the spiritual ethers of this world and is in constant contact with those who raise their thoughts to Him in prayer. The promise was not an idle one that He would be with those who have faith in Him. "Let not your heart be troubled, neither let it be fearful. Ye heard how I said to you, I go away, and I come unto you."

His body disappeared from our fleshly eyes because He raised it to its true place in the ether; but He can make His presence felt to anyone who looks to Him for help. "For where two or three are gathered together in my name, there am I in the midst of them."

If but two persons agree in their prayers and thoughts about Jesus Christ and His power to help, by sympathetic soul unity He instantly responds. "Again I say unto you, that if two of you shall agree on earth as touching anything that they shall ask, it shall be done for them of my Father who is in heaven."

Jesus did not go to a faraway heaven, there to abide to the great day of His "Second Coming." He explained again and again, in language that anyone who has even a slight understanding of the interrelation of spirit, soul, and body may comprehend, that He would continue to exist in the etheric realm that He called "the heavens." He appeared after His crucifixion to five hundred at one time, and to many others: notably Paul, whom He converted by talking to him out of the ether. This all confirms His promise "Lo, I am with you always, even unto the end of the world."

Paul says that we are all dead or asleep in trespasses and sins and that Jesus was the "firstfruits of them that are asleep." Physiology teaches that the body is alive to the degree that the cells are alive; that we are carrying around many dead cells. Jesus knew how to quicken with new life the cells of His organism, and He promised that all who follow Him will do likewise.

So both Scripture and science agree that there must be a resurrection of the body from the dead; that is, the dead substance that our minds have organized into cells, tissues, flesh, and blood. The all-important task for everyone is how to get the mastery of the negative life or microbe that is reducing our bodies to corruption and final dissolution.

Paul says, "This corruptible must put on incorruption, and this mortal must put on immortality." Here is a concise statement of where resurrection is to take place. Other writings of Paul's have seemingly prophesied a great day on which all the dead are to come forth from their graves, but this would involve situations complex and contradictory beyond reconciliation. That we have all lived hundreds, even thousands, of times and have left our bodies in many lands is being accepted by logical persons everywhere. If our old bodies are to be resurrected, which of these discarded ones shall we repossess? Chemistry says that our flesh becomes again the dust of the ground:

> "Imperious Caesar, dead and turned to clay,
> Might stop a hole to keep the wind away."

Jesus spent whole nights in prayer according to the Gospels, and it is quite evident that He was resurrecting His body by realizing, as we do in our prayers, that God was His indwelling life. His affirmation for more life was "I am the resurrection, and the life." I AM is the spiritual name of Jehovah, the everliving one. When we affirm, "I am," with our thoughts centered on Spirit, we quicken the life flow in the body and awaken the sleepy cells. Such affirmations clear up congested areas of the organism and restore the circulation to its normal state, health.

A prominent scientist recently stated that man's body is composed of trillions of cells, every one an electric battery. A battery emits electrical impulses of various kinds, transformable into light, power, heat. The human body is undoubtedly the most powerful dynamo in existence for the carrying on of life. The presiding ego or I AM in each organism determines the particular kind of impulse that the cells shall radiate. The field of dynamic energy is limitless. God is Spirit, and Spirit is the very essence of the ether in which we live, move, and have our being.

Affirmations of health by Christian healers right in the face of sickness often result in marvelous restorations that are sometimes called miracles of healing. But when one understands the power of words spoken in spiritual consciousness the results are in fulfillment of divine law. Jesus stated the essence of this law when He said, "Whosoever . . . shall not doubt in his heart, but shall believe that what he saith cometh to pass; he shall have it."

Every word has within it the power to make manifest whatever man decrees, but especially spiritual words have this power. God creates by the power of the word. "God said, Let there be light: and there was light." Every act of creation was preceded by "God said." Man, the apex of God's creation, was created in His image and likeness; that is, exactly like Him in the power of his word to bring forth what he says.

In order to create as God creates man must have undoubting faith in God-Mind and the obedience of the creative electrons hidden in the atoms of all substance. In Hebrews it is written, "By faith we understand that the worlds have been framed by the word of God." In the 1st chapter of John the Word or Logos is given as the source of all things, and this Word is said to become flesh and be glorified as the only-begotten from the Father. "As many as received him, to them gave he the right to become children of God, even to them that believe on his name." Jesus said that every man would be justified or condemned by his word. He demonstrated the power of the word of faith in His mastery of natural laws and in His many marvelous healings.

Although we all get definite results in body and affairs from the words we utter, those results would be infinitely greater if we understood the power of words and had undoubting faith in their creative power. Jesus said, "The words that I have spoken unto you are spirit, and are life."

We all want to be like Jesus, and millions have made and are making Him the pattern for their life. So among His faithful followers of the past twenty centuries we should expect to find a world of glorified men and women. Why have we not brought forth more of the fruits of Spirit that He so generously promised? The answer is that we have emphasized the negative qualities as portrayed by the human side of His character. We have sought to imitate Him in our acts instead of our thoughts and words.

We are now realizing that as a man "thinketh within himself, so is he." The outer acts are secondary; the primal world of causes is within, and it is to this inner realm that we must look for the transforming power of man and of the world about him as well. "Be ye transformed by the renewing of your mind." Hence the quick and lawful way to attain health is to put your creative words to work and bring into swift action the superman Christ.

There can be no logical doubt that an all-wise and all-powerful Creator would plan perfection for His creations and also endow them with the ability to bring His plan into manifestation. That is the status of the world and its people. We are God's ideal conception of His perfect man, and He has given us the power of thought and word through which to make that ideal manifest.

It is written in John 5:21 (King James Version): "For as the Father raiseth up the dead, and quickeneth them; even so the Son quickeneth whom he will."

The American Standard Version says that the Father raises up the dead and gives them life, and that even so the Son gives life to whom He will. To quicken means to vivify, vitalize, energize, hence to make alive.

Jesus made this assertion of the life-giving power of the Son of God immediately after He had healed a man at the Pool of Bethesda who had been infirm and helpless for thirty-eight years. Jesus said to him, "Behold, thou art made whole: sin no more, lest a worse thing befall thee."

Here Jesus again emphasizes sin as the cause of infirmity. All the ills of humanity are the effect of broken law, of sin. That word "sin" covers more ground than we have usually granted it. There are sins of omission and commission. If we fail to cultivate the consciousness of the indwelling spiritual life, we commit a sin of omission that eventually devitalizes the organism. To be continuously healthy we must draw on the one and only source of life, God. God is Spirit, and Spirit pours its quickening life into mind and body when we turn our attention to it and make ourself receptive by trusting Spirit to restore us to harmony and health.

As for all the marvelous works that Jesus did, He never claimed His personality as their author. "The Son can do nothing of himself, but what he seeth the Father doing: for what things soever he doeth, these the Son also doeth in like manner." We all have access to the Son of God (the Christ) implanted in us by the Father-Mind if we will give it a chance to quicken us with creative ideas.

Let us remember that in declaring Jesus to be present with us we are placing ourselves in a thought atmosphere that will help us to quicken our own supermind or Christ Mind. Jesus raised His mind and body to His supermind level, permitting a life radiation without crosscurrents or discords of any kind. He preceded us, and as He said, He had prepared a "place" for us. This "place" is a spiritual current in the cosmic ether, in which we live, and we can feel it when we direct our attention to Christ in prayer and meditation. "The kingdom of God is come nigh unto you."

Jesus called attention to the fact that the creative Mind, which He lovingly called Father, had provided for the subsistence of the birds and flowers, and that man was of more value than these; and would it not be reasonable, He argued, that the Father would also provide for man? His logic is unanswerable, and we must all admit that judging from our human ideas about providing for our children, we should expect God to have done even better for His progeny.

When we understand the nature of the creative Mind--that it is Spirit-mind, that all things come out of ideas, and that there are unlimited ideas right at the door of the mind--it dawns on us that God has provided for us beyond our fondest dreams.

We have been so persistently taught that nature heals that we do not as a rule give the question of the origin of her healing power any serious thought. But we should, because our thought calls into action in our consciousness the mind principle to which we give our attention. If we center our attention on nature as the healing principle, we stir up natural activities that are secondary to the one cause of all action, that is, infinite Mind. But it is our privilege as creations of supreme Mind to bring into action all its forces, primary and secondary. By our thought and the mighty mind energy back of thought we can stir to action all the powers of Being and get the results of their concentrated healing currents instead of the weakened, segregated seepage from one.

Just here is a good opportunity to urge Truth students to shape their spiritual unfoldment on one system of development instead of chasing after every spectacular scheme that pops up. All signs both spiritual and secular point to Jesus Christ as the appointed head of our race. Through Him we have received a philosophy of life that has been tested in the past, that is now being tested as never before, and that is proving to have no peer as a revealer of Truth and as a remedy for all the ills of humanity.

This being obvious and so many of us having received special revelations confirming it, why should we feel the lack of another or listen to the many "Lo, there! Lo, here!" proclamations of those who discern superficial things only? Concentrate your I AM attention on God as the one and only supreme Spirit and Jesus Christ as the Son of God through whom we all have access to the Father. Then you will lift your consciousness into a sphere of spiritual clarity and power superior to anything in the heavens above or the earth beneath.

Certain persons called "masters" have forged ahead of the race in their understanding and use of some of the powers of mind and have in personal egotism set up little kingdoms and put themselves on thrones.

These so-called "masters" and members of occult brotherhoods are attracting susceptible minds away from the "straight and narrow path" and leading them to believe that there is a short cut into the kingdom. Jesus described the situation forcibly and clearly in Matthew 24:24:

"For there shall arise false Christs, and false prophets, and shall show great signs and wonders; so as to lead astray, if possible, even the elect."

Read the whole 24th chapter of Matthew. In it Jesus describes in symbols and facts what is taking place today in all parts of the world. It may be argued that these conditions have been present in every generation, and so they have; but never have so many of the signs stood out so forcibly as now. All this indicates the end of a world dispensation, a climax in race development. The end of the world of matter came with the discovery that the atom is electrical, and all the things that revolved about that material supposition are coming to an end with it. This means the end of our old ideas that God is a big man sitting on a throne in a heaven with streets of shining gold, with Jesus at His right hand writing in the book of life, as well as the end also of our ideas of Satan and his fiery hell, of the divine right of kings and the prestige of royalty and other established institutions. These crude ideas about God and man having lost the sustaining thoughts of the race, old religions and governments dissolve and the world seems a chaos. However the wise see in all this the passing away of old ideas and old things to make room for the new. "Behold, I make all things new."

The only safety from chaos is unity with God and His Son Jesus Christ, the head of every man. If we are not anchored to this supreme and immovable reality, we shall be exposed to the storms of mortal thought and shipwrecked on the rocks of materiality. "Have this mind in you, which was also in Christ Jesus."

Jesus taught that His mission was to establish the kingdom of heaven on earth. The first step in His great work was the awakening of men to certain fundamental truths of being. He taught the power of mind, thoughts, words. He cast out the demons (errors) and healed the sick with a word. He planted the seed thoughts in our race mind that will, when properly used, grow into the kingdom of the heavens here on earth. But peace, harmony, and love must first be planted in the minds of men.

Jesus gave us the consciousness of peace. "My peace I give unto you." The mind of peace precedes bodily healing. Cast out enmity and anger and affirm the peace of Jesus Christ, and your healing will be swift and sure.

Chapter II - God Presence

I AM NOW in the presence of pure Being and immersed in the Holy Spirit of life, love, and wisdom.

I acknowledge Thy presence and power, O blessed Spirit. In Thy divine wisdom now erase my mortal limitations, and from Thy pure substance of love bring into manifestation my world, according to Thy perfect law.

Man knows intuitively that he is God's supreme creation and that dominion and power are his, though he does not understand fully. The I AM of him ever recognizes the one divine source from which he sprang, and he turns to it endeavoring to fathom its wonderful secrets. Even children grope after the truths of Being.

No man knows the beginning of the query, Who, what, and where is God? It is dropped from the lips of the little child when he first begins to lisp the name of father and of mother, and it is repeated throughout the years.

Who made you? Who made me? Who made the earth, the moon, and the sun? God.

Then who made God?

Thus back to the cause beyond the cause ever runs the questioning mind of man. He would understand the omnipresence that caused him to be.

Does an answer ever come to these questionings? Does man ever receive satisfactory returns from this mental delving in the unfathomable? Each man and each woman must answer individually; for only the mind of God can know God. If you have found God in your own mind you have found the source of health, of freedom, and of the wisdom that answers all questions.

Language is the limitation of mind; therefore do not expect the unlimited to leap forth into full expression through the limited.

Words never express that which God is. To the inner ear of the mind awakened to its depths words may carry the impulses of divine energy and health that make it conscious of what God is, but in their formulations such words can never bind the unbindable.

So let us remember that by describing God with words in our human way we are but stating in the lisping syllables of the child that which in its maturity the mind still only faintly grasps. Yet man may know God and become the vehicle and expression of God, the unlimited fount of life, health, light, and love.

God is the health of His people.

Man recognizes that health is fundamental in Being and that health is his own divine birthright. It is the orderly state of existence, but man must learn to use the knowledge of this truth to sustain the consciousness of health.

Health is from the Anglo-Saxon word meaning "whole," "hale," "well." The one who uses the word really implies that he has an understanding of the law of the perfect harmony of Being. Health is the normal condition of man and of all creation. We find that there is an omnipresent principle of health pervading all living things. Health, real health, is from within and does not have to be manufactured in the without. Health is the very essence of Being. It is as universal and enduring as God.

Being is the consciousness of the one Presence and the one Power, of the one intelligence, and man stands in the Godhead as I will. When man perceives his place in the great scheme of creation and recognizes his I AM power, he declares, "I discern that I will be that which I will to be."

Man is the vessel of God and expresses God. But there is a mighty difference between the inanimate marble, chiseled by the sculptor into a prancing steed, and the living, breathing horse consciously willing to be guided by the master's rein.

So there is a wide gap between the intelligence that moves to an appointed end under the impulse of divine energy and that which knows the thoughts and desires of Divine Mind and co-operates with it in bringing about the ends of a perfect and healthy creation.

"No longer do I call you servants; for the servant knoweth not what his Lord doeth; but I have called you friends; for all things that I have heard from my Father I have made known unto you."

It must be true that there is in man a capacity for knowing God consciously and communing with Him. This alone insures health and joy and satisfaction. It is unthinkable that the Creator could cause anything to be that is so inferior to Himself as to remove it beyond the pale of fellowship with Him.

It is our exalted ideas of God and our little ideas of ourselves that built the mental wall that separates us from Him. We have been taught that God is a mighty monarch with certain domineering characteristics, who wills us to be sick or healthy; that He is of such majesty that man cannot conceive of Him.

Even in metaphysical concepts of God the impression left us is of a Creator great in power, wisdom, and love. In one sense this is true, but the standard by which man compares and judges these qualities in his mind determines his concept of God.

If I say that God is the almighty power of the universe and have in mind power as we see it expressed in physical energy and force, I have not set up the right standard of comparison. It is true that all power comes from God, but it does not follow that the character of the thing we term power is the same in the unexpressed as in the expressed.

God is power; man is powerful. God is that indescribable reservoir of stored-up energy that manifests no potency whatever until set in motion through the consciousness of man yet possesses an inexhaustible capacity that is beyond words to express. When that power is manifested by man it becomes conditioned. It is described as powerful, more powerful, most powerful, and it has its various degrees of expansion, pressure, velocity, force, and the like.

This power is used by men to oppress one another, and there has come to be a belief that God is power in the sense of great oppressing capacity. It is an ancient belief that He can and does exercise His power in punishing His creations, pouring out upon them His vengeance.

But this is not the character of divine power. If by power we mean force, energy, action, oppression, then we should say that God has no power, that God is powerless; because His power is not like the so-called power that is represented by these human activities.

God is wisdom--intelligence--but if we mean by this that God is "intelligent," that His knowledge consists of the judgments and inferences that are made in a universe of things, then we should say that God is nonintelligent.

God is substance; but if we mean by this that God is matter, a thing of time, space, condition, we should say that God is substanceless.

God is love; but if we mean by this that God is the love that loves a particular child better than all children, or that loves some particular father or mother better than all fathers and mothers, or that loves one person better than some other person, or that has a chosen people whom He loves better than some other people who are not chosen, then we should say that God is unloving.

God does not exercise power. God is that all-present and all-quiet powerlessness from which man "generates" that which he calls power.

God does not manifest intelligence. God is that unobtrusive knowing in everyone which, when acknowledged, flashes forth into intelligence.

God is not matter nor confined in any way to the idea of substance termed matter. God is that intangible essence which man has "formed" and called matter. Thus matter is a limitation of the divine substance whose vital and inherent character is above all else limitless.

God is not loving. God is love, the great heart of the universe and of man, from which is drawn forth all feeling, sympathy, emotion, and all that goes to make up the joys of existence.

Yet God does not love anybody or anything. God is the love in everybody and everything. God is love; man becomes loving by permitting that which God is to find expression in word and act.

The point to be clearly established is that God exercises none of His attributes except through the inner consciousness of the universe and man.

God is the "still small voice" in every soul that heals and blesses and uplifts, and it is only through the soul that He is made manifest as perfect wholeness.

Drop from your mind the idea that God is a being of majesty and power in the sense that you now interpret majesty and power.

Drop from your mind the belief that God is in any way separated from you or that He can be manifested to you in any way except through your own consciousness.

We look at the universe with its myriad forms and stupendous evidences of wisdom and power and we say: All this must be the work of one mighty in strength and understanding; I should stand in awe of such a one and realize my own insignificance in His presence. Yet when we behold the towering oak with its wide-spreading branches, we say it grew from a tiny acorn. A little stream of life and intelligence flowed into that small seed and gradually formed the giant tree. It was not created in the sense that it was made full-orbed by a single fiat of will, but it grew from the tiny slip into the towering tree through the inherent potentialities of the little seed, the acorn.

So God is in us the little seed through which is brought forth the strong, healthy Christ man.

That "still small voice" at the center of our being does not command what we shall be or what we shall do or not do. It is so gentle and still in its work that in the hurly-burly of life we overlook it entirely. We look out, and beholding the largeness of the world of things, we begin to cast about for a god corresponding in character with this world.

But we do not find such a god on the outside. We must drop the complex and find the simplicity of "the most simple One" before we can know God. We must become as a little child.

Jesus said, "God is Spirit," not "a Spirit," as in the King James Version. According to Webster, the generates" that which he calls power.

word spirit means life or living substance considered independently of corporeal existence; an intelligence conceived of apart from any physical organization or embodiment; vital essence, force, or energy as distinct from matter; the intelligent, immaterial, and immortal part of man; the spirit, in distinction from the body in which it resides.

Paul says, "In him we live, and move, and have our being." If we accept Scripture as our source of information there can be no higher authority than that of Jesus and Paul. They say that God is Spirit.

Spirit is not matter, and Spirit is not person. In order to perceive the essence of Being we must drop from mind the idea that God is circumscribed in any way or has any of the limitations usually ascribed to persons, things, or anything having form or shape. "Thou shalt not make unto thee a graven image, nor any likeness of any thing that is in heaven above, or that is in the earth beneath."

God is life. Life is a principle that is made manifest in the living. Life cannot be analyzed by the senses. It is beyond their grasp, hence it must be cognized by Spirit.

God is substance; but this does not mean matter, because matter is formed while God is the formless. This substance which God is lies back of all matter and all forms. It is that which is the basis of all form yet enters not into any form as finality. It cannot be seen, tasted, or touched. Yet it is the only "substantial" substance in the universe.

God is love: that from which all loving springs.

God is Truth: the eternal verity of the universe and man.

God is mind. Here we touch the connecting link between God and man. The essential being of God as principle cannot be comprehended by any of the senses or faculties, but the mind of man is limitless, and through it he may come in touch with divine Principle.

It is the study of mind that reveals God. God may be inferentially known by studying the creations that spring from Him, but to speak to God face to face and mouth to mouth, to know Him as a child knows his father, man must come consciously into the place in mind that is common to both man and God.

Men have sought to find God by studying nature, but they have always fallen short. This seeking to know God by analyzing things made is especially noticeable in this age. Materialistic science has sought to know the cause of things by dissecting them. By this mode they have come to say: We must admit that there is a cause, but we have not found it; so we assume that God is unknowable.

To know God as health one must take up the study of the healthy mind and make it and not physical appearance the basis of every calculation. To study mind and its ideas as health is a departure so unusual that the world, both religious and secular, looks upon it as somehow impracticable. The man who lives in his senses cannot comprehend how anything can be got out of the study of something apparently so intangible.

"The man of affairs cannot see what mind or its study has to do with matters pertaining to his department of life, and the religionist who worships God in forms and ceremonies makes no connection between the study of mind and finding out the real nature of God.

> Behold, I go forward, but he is not there;
> And backward, but I cannot perceive him;
> On the left hand, when he doth work,
> but I cannot behold him;
> He hideth himself on the right hand,
> that I cannot see him.

Thus ever cries the man who looks for God in the external; for health from an outside source.

In mathematics the unit enters into every problem; and in existence mind is common to all, above and below, within and without. The secret of existence will never be disclosed before man takes up and masters the science of his own mind.

Man's consciousness is formed of mind and its ideas, and these determine whether he is healthy or sick. Thus to know the mysteries of his own being he must study mind and its laws.

Many people in every age have come into partial consciousness of God in their souls and have communed with Him in that inner sanctuary until their faces shone with heavenly light; yet the mysteries of creative law were not revealed to them, because they did not get an understanding of its key, which is mind.

Mind is the common meeting ground of God and man, and only through its study and the observation of all the conditions and factors that enter into its operation can we come into the realization of God as abiding health and sustenance.

God is mind; and we cannot describe God with human language, so we cannot describe mind. To describe is to limit, to circumscribe. To describe mind is to limit it to the meanings of sense. In our talk about mind we are thus forced to leave the plane of things formed and enter the realm of pure knowing.

We can only say: I am mind; I know. God is mind; He knows. Thus knowing is the language I use in my intercourse with God.

If you ask me about the language I use in communicating with God, I am not able to tell you; because you are talking from the standpoint of using words to convey ideas, while in the language of God ideas in their original purity are the vehicles of communication.

But ideas are the original and natural agents of communication; and everyone is in possession of this easy way of speaking to God and man. Thus we may learn to use this divine and only true way consciously if we will but recognize it and use it on the plane of mind.

But we must recognize it. This is the one truth that we have to reveal to you: How to recognize this divine language in your own consciousness and how through recognition to bring it forth into visibility. It is a truth however that we cannot reveal to you by a series of eloquent essays on the majesty, power, and wisdom of God and on the everlasting joy that follows when you have found Him; but only by showing you in the simplest way how to come into conscious relations with the source of omnipresent wisdom, life, and love, by taking with you in the silent inner realms the first steps in the language of the soul.

Compared with audible language, communion in mind can be said to be without sound. It is the "still small voice," the voice that is not a voice, the voice using words that are not words. Yet its language is more definite and certain than that of words and sounds, because it has none of their limitations. Words and sounds are attempts to convey a description of emotions and feelings, while by the language of mind emotions and feelings are conveyed direct. But again you must transcend what you understand as emotion and feeling in order to interpret the language of God. This is not hard. It is your natural language, and you need only return to your pristine state of purity to achieve it entirely.

You are mind. Your consciousness is formed of thoughts. Thoughts form barriers about the thinker, and when contended for as true they are impregnable to other thoughts. So you are compassed about with thought barriers, the result of your heredity, your education, and your own thinking. Likewise your degree of health is determined by your thoughts, past and present.

These thoughts may be true or false, depending on your understanding and use of divine law. You must open the walls of your mental house by a willingness to receive and weigh these thoughts in the balance of good judgment and to drop out of your mind everything except the one idea:

I want to know Truth, I am willing to learn. I want to express radiant health.

If there is not in your consciousness a demonstration that mind has a language on its own silent plane and that it can manifest itself in your mind, body, and affairs, then you can go back to your old convictions.

The fundamental basis and starting point of practical Christianity is that God is principle. By principle is meant definite, exact, and unchangeable rules of action. That the word principle is used by materialistic schools of thought to describe what they term the "blind forces of nature" is no reason why it should convey to our minds the idea of an unloving and unfeeling God. It is used because it best describes the unchangeableness that is an inherent law of Being.

From the teaching that the Deity is a person we have come to believe that God is changeable; that He gets angry with His people and condemns them; that some are chosen or favored above others; that in His sight good and evil are verities, and that He defends the one and deplores the other. We must relieve our minds of these ideas of a personal God ruling over us in an arbitrary, manlike manner.

God is mind. Mind evolves ideas. These ideas are evolved in an orderly way. The laws of mind are just as exact and undeviating as the laws of mathematics or music. To recognize this is the starting point in finding God.

God loves spiritual man, and that love is expressed according to exact law. It is not emotional or variable, nor is there any taint of partiality in it. You are primarily a spiritual being, the expression of God's perfection, the receptacle of His love; and when you think and act in the consciousness of perfection and love, you cannot help being open to the influx of God's love and to the fulfillment of His divine purpose. This is the exact and undeviating law that inheres in the principle that God is.

God is wisdom; and wisdom is made manifest in an orderly manner through your consciousness.

God is substance--unchangeable incorruptible, imperishable--to the spiritual mind and body of man.

This substance of mind--faith--does not happen to be here today and there tomorrow, but it is moved upon by ideas which are as unchanging as Spirit.

In Spirit you never had a beginning, and your I AM will never have an ending. The world never had a beginning and will never have an ending. All things that are always were and always will be, yesterday, today, and forever the same.

But things formed have a beginning and may have an ending.

But God does not form things. God calls from the depths of His own being the ideas that are already there, and they move forth and clothe themselves with the habiliments of time and circumstance in man's consciousness. We must have firmly fixed in our understanding the verity that we shall have to square all the acts of life.

God is never absent from His creations, and His creations are never absent from their habiliments; hence wherever you see the evidences of life, there you may know that God is.

If you are manifesting health, that health has a source that is perpetually giving itself forth. A perpetual giving forth implies a perpetual presence.

There is no absence or separation in God. His omnipresence is your omnipresence, because there can be no absence in Mind. If God were for one instant separated from His creations, they would immediately fall into dissolution. But absence in Mind is unthinkable. Mind is far removed from the realm where time and distance prevail. Mind is without metes or bounds; it is within all metes and bounds; it does not exist but inheres in all that is. Hence in spirit and in truth you can never for one instant be separated from the life activity of God even though you may not externally feel or know of His presence.

God lives in you, and you depend on Him for every breath you draw. The understanding you have, be it ever so meager, is from Him, and you could not think a thought or speak a word or make a movement were He not in it. Your body is the soil in which God's life is planted. Your mind is the light for which He supplies the oil. "I am the light of the world," said Jesus. "Ye are the light of the world."

Intelligence is the light of the world. "Let your light shine." How? By increasing the supply of oil, by increasing your consciousness of life, and by learning how to draw upon the omnipresent God for every need.

A good healing drill is to deny the mental cause first, then the physical appearance. The mental condition should first be healed. Then the secondary state, which it has produced in the body, must be wiped out and the perfect state affirmed.

Deny:

I deny that I inherit any belief that in any way limits me in health, virtue, intelligence, or power to do good.

Those with whom I associate can no longer make me believe that I am a poor worm of the dust. The race belief that "nature dominates man" no longer holds me in bondage, and I am now free from every belief that might in any way interfere with my perfect expression of health, wealth, peace, prosperity, and perfect satisfaction in every department of life.

By my all-powerful word, in the sight and presence of almighty God, I now unformulate and destroy every foolish and ignorant assumption that might impede my march to perfection. My word is the measure of my power. I have spoken, and it shall be so.

Affirm:

I am unlimited in my power, and I have increasing health, strength, life, love, wisdom, boldness, freedom, charity, and meekhess, now and forever.

I am now in harmony with the Father, and stronger than any mortal law. I know my birthright in pure Being, and I boldly assert my perfect freedom. In this knowledge I am enduring, pure, peaceful, and happy.

I am dignified and definite, yet meek and lowly, in all that I think and do.

I am one with and I now fully manifest vigorous life, wisdom, and spiritual understanding.

I am one with and I now fully manifest love, charity, justice, kindness, and generosity.

I am one with and I now fully manifest infinite goodness and mercy.

Peace floweth like a river through my mind, and I thank Thee, O God, that I am one with Thee!

Chapter III - Realization Precedes Manifestation

GOD'S MAN is hale, whole, hearty. This is Truth. A spiritual realization is a realization of Truth. A spiritual realization of health is the result of holding in consciousness a statement of health until the logic of the mind is satisfied and man receives the assurance that the fulfillment in the physical must follow. In other words, by realizing a healing prayer man lays hold of the principle of health itself and the whole consciousness is illumined; he perceives principle working out his health problems for him.

However when man lays hold of the principle of wholeness, he finds that he is automatically working with God and that much new power is added. He realizes: "My Father worketh even until now, and I work." After man has applied his mind diligently for a season, he exhausts his resources or powers of realization for the time being and rests from all his work; but his accumulated thought energy is completed or fulfilled in a higher realm, and he has a double assurance that health must become manifest.

Jesus understood and demonstrated this law perfectly. He was so much at one with the principle of health that He needed only to say, "Thy faith hath made thee whole" or "Lazarus, come forth," in order to bring into evidence the perfect demonstration.

Realization means at-one-ment, completion, perfection, wholeness, repose, resting in God. A realization of health brings to the consciousness an inner knowing that the divine law has been fulfilled in thought and act. Then as man lays hold of the in-dwelling Christ he is raised out of the Adam or dark consciousness into the Christ consciousness. This at-one-ment with God brings a lasting joy that cannot be taken away.

God-Mind rests in a perpetual realization of health, and that which seems to be sickness does not exist in Truth. When man becomes so much at one with God-Mind that he abides in the consciousness of health he enters the eternal peace in which he knows that "it is finished."

In order to understand God-Mind we need to study our own mind. The more we analyze the processes of the mind the more plainly the mind with its mental "compounds" appears as the source of health and of all other things. In the realms of dense matter intelligence may be so faint as to have lost all contact with Mind. Yet the poet sings about there being "sermons in stones." Again science announces that life is present in and is disintegrating the solid rocks and the whole earth groans and creaks in her struggle with inertia. So if we want to know the secrets of health and how right thinking forms the perfect body, we must go to the mind and trace step by step the movements that transform ideas of health into light, electrons, atoms, molecules, cells, tissues, and finally into the perfect physical organism.

Although there is almost universal skepticism with reference to the mind's ability to know consciously how relative substance is formed, there are those who have made contact with the thought processes and can apply them in transforming the cells and tissues of their own body. The almost insurmountable obstacle to explaining to others how this is accomplished is the paucity of language. The mind functions in ways that are so strange and unbelievable that the pioneers on this frontier of metaphysics choose as a rule to remain silent.

Jesus is the outstanding pioneer in this realm where the health-producing processes of cells are released and imbued with supermind vitality.

He spent years in becoming acquainted with His body and freeing its cells from the material bondage to which the race thought had bound them.

Yet He gave no scientific explanation of the purifying through which He put His body to transform it before Peter, James, and John, as stated in Luke 9:29: "And as he was praying, the fashion of his countenance was altered, and his raiment became white and dazzling." Modern metaphysicians do not excuse their ignorance by claiming that this and many other instances in which Jesus showed mastery over His body were miracles. Scientific Christians regard as mortal superstition the prevalent view that miracles are the abrogation by God of His laws and are performed as a sort of legerdemain to attract and astonish the people. The marvelous things that Jesus did we can do when we understand the law. "The works that I do shall he do also; and greater" still holds good.

Much that is attributed to the subconscious, strictly speaking, springs from the all-knowing or spiritual Mind. When we cannot intellectually account for our knowledge we assume the subconscious to be its source. Yet we should know that the subconscious is the storehouse of past knowledge and past experiences. So it knows only what has filtered through the conscious mind. It cannot therefore be the source of knowledge except through reflection or memory. This memory of what man has passed through in the aeons of his experience is often called intuition; it is the instinct of the animal soul.

The world today looks up to science; that is, it does not accept or believe anything unless it can be demonstrated by well-known universal laws. There are no known laws governing religion that can be scientifically explained; hence it is not acceptable to the scientific mind. But there is a technique for molding thought stuff by means of the mind, and metaphysicians follow it in their scientific thinking and in healing. The metaphysician handles omnipresent Spirit life and substance very much as the electrician handles electricity. Energy is locked up in all this life and substance and its release enables the metaphysician to utilize it in demonstrating health and in achieving success. All the chemical elements adhere to their particular form and endeavor to retain it. Electricity is supposed to be a universal invisible energy whose unity can be broken up by the whirl of a dynamo. The electronic units exert all the force of their nature in a pull to regain their original status. Thus the power generated by a dynamo is gained from the force exerted by the electrical units in their rush to establish their primal equipoise.

Only a certain percentage of this energy is utilized because of the pull of the electrical units to get back home to their mother principle. The dissipation of energy is one of the great problems of the engineer. The loss of electricity in transmission is so great that only a small part of the original current reaches its destination.

We exist right in the midst of forces that would yield us power to do all our work if we knew how to conserve and properly utilize their energies. This is not only true of our use of the many elements in the natural world all about us but especially of our utilization of the energy generated by our minds. If we could utilize this dissipated energy constructively it would restore the body, illumine the mind, and establish us in a lasting consciousness of dominion and mastery.

With every thought there is a radiation of energy. If a person is untrained in thinking and lets his mind express all kinds of thoughts without control, he not only uses up his thought stuff but fails also to accomplish any helpful result.

Conservation of thought stuff is essential to right thinking. Right thinking is using the mind to bring about right ends idealized by the thinker. All the elements necessary to the restoration of health exist in the higher dimensions of the mind. Through concentration and conservation of thought force man regains the consciousness of health in his mind, and health then becomes manifest in his body.

Laws fixed by infinite Mind automatically accomplish whatever man desires when he becomes obedient to the inner guide. Concentration, one-pointed attention, forms a mental magnet in the mind to which thought substance rushes like iron filings to a loadstone. Then follows confidence or faith in one's ability to accomplish the desired end. According to the Scriptures this is the law by which the universe was brought into manifestation. In the 11th chapter of Hebrews it is written: "By faith we understand that the worlds have been framed by the word of God."

Modern science by its most daring proponents is launching out into the deeps of the invisible and describing in detail the electrical processes that ultimate in the atom and its aggregations in visible things. In substance they tell us that when points of light gather about a certain nucleus an atom is created, and from this a cell, and cell aggregations make tissues and these merge into the realm of things.

Here we have the scientific explanation and the Christian metaphysician's formula for making the invisible visible. The greatest of all physicists cannot tell what electricity is. Even Edison said he was ignorant of its real nature. Some find it sometimes acting very much like mind and have so stated. The head of the General Electric research department was asked by a reporter to give him a definition of electricity. The professor replied that to his mind electricity was like what the Christians describe as faith.

The scientific metaphysician fixes his attention powerfully on the consummation of a certain idea until he has a realization, which means that the idea has nucleated a certain amount of thought substance. When this realization is had the metaphysician rests "from all his work." Through faith and work he has fulfilled the law of mind and he rests in the conviction that his ideal of health will appear in manifestation in due season.

To a metaphysician realization is the conviction that a person gets when he has persistently concentrated his attention on an ideal until he feels assured of the fulfillment of that ideal. Elohim God pronounced His spiritual creation "very good"; then rested from all His work. There was as yet no manifestation, "no herb of the field had yet sprung up," and "there was not a man to till the ground"; yet the planning Mind had the realization that the spiritual law had been fulfilled and that it should rest from all its works.

That all things visible are held in place by a force invisible is the conviction of the majority of logical thinkers. In other words, everything is ensouled.When we understand that the soul has consciousness, that it thinks, we have the explanation of many mysterious phenomena. Some 150 years ago Franz Mesmer announced in Germany that under certain conditions he could induce a magnetic sleep in persons and control their minds. His demonstrations attracted the attention of doctors and mental scientists the world over. In this day the system is practiced under the name of hypnotism. It is full of pitfalls for both operator and patient because its tendency is to weaken the positive control that the mind should always exercise over its own brain structure. However it is one of the many proofs that the mind can produce conditions in the mental world that ultimate in the material world. A great physical scientist stated recently that it may be that the gods that determine our fates are our own minds working on our brain cells and through them on the world about us. This is very close to the Truth.

Every Christian metaphysician knows that back of the personal mind there is a great creative Mind that also recreates. This creative Mind has been named and described by men all down the ages. God-Mind not only can restore and heal but can establish us in the consciousness of permanent health. Do not allow your conception of God to be handicapped by what men have said about Him.

"There is a spirit in man,
And the breath of the Almighty giveth them understanding."

Let the Spirit of God in you reveal to you His true character. God was never sick a day; He is the source of life and health and joy. God wills that we express His "image" and "likeness," in which we were created.

The prayer for realization attains its consummation when with concentrated spiritual attention one has affirmed that God Spirit is present, that with all His power He is bringing to pass the perfect health desired, and that all is well. When your thoughts radiate with the speed of spiritual light, they blend with creative Mind (called by Jesus "heaven"), and the thing you have asked for will be done. Jesus told Peter that whatever he bound (affirmed) in earth would be bound in heaven and whatever he loosed (denied) in earth would be loosed in heaven. Peter had unbounded faith in Jesus (who represents spiritual man). When any man has unbounded faith in spiritual power his words, uttered in the limitations of matter, are flashed to heaven (creative Mind) and they accomplish whatever he puts into them. The fulfillment of this spoken word in the world of activities may take moments, hours, days, years, centuries; Jesus said that the Father only knew when these things would come to pass. Do not think because you do not get an instant response to your prayers that they are not answered. Every sincere desire and every effectual prayer for health that has ascended to heaven (creative Mind) is fulfilled, and will be made manifest whenever material limitations permit. Shakespeare had an inkling of this law of the relation of thoughts and words when he wrote,

"My words fly up, my thoughts remain below:
Words without thoughts never to heaven go."

The kingdom of heaven (the heavens) so often referred to by Jesus and described by Him as very near to us is far more accessible and is more often contacted by us than we imagine. Not only those who pray but those who persistently concentrate their thoughts on mathematics, music, or philosophies based in principle, are often rewarded with the marvelous intuitions of genius. These persons apparently break into a realm where no effort is required to gain the answer to their questions. The mathematical genius is called a prodigy. He solves instantly the most complex mathematical problem, yet cannot explain how he does it. He simply knows the answer, often before the statement of the problem has been completed.

Henri Poincare in his book "Science and Method" says that his discoveries in mathematics came to him in flashes after he had spent long periods of study and concentration on the subject. Concentrated attention of the mind on an idea of any kind is equal to prayer and will make available the spiritual principle that is its source in proportion to the intensity and continuity of the mental effort. Anyone can attain spiritual understanding and bec ome conscious of the light who will persistently pray for it. "He that cometh to God must believe that he is, and that he is a rewarder of them that diligently seek him." The emphasis here is on the word "diligently."

The mind is the seat of perfection, not only of health but also of talents like music, art, writing, and the like. The idea of health and the idea of music are interblended, for instance. Music is a great aid to the healing force. Musical and health ideas interblend, and their establishment in order produces this kingdom of the heavens.

Our spiritual realizations produce that silent shuttle of thought which, working in and through cell and nerve, weaves into one harmonious whole mind and body and is expressed as health and wealth and genius.

The musical genius says he hears the music in a flash and is often at his wit's end to transcribe it fast enough. Many an immortal poem and prose work as well has been flashed from the mind of the author without any apparent effort on his part. But if all the prayers and mind efforts of literary geniuses were inquired into, it would be found that there had been heroic mental effort somewhere at some time. So it is with healing. The realization of perfection takes root in the soul and may come forth in a flash as perfect health. We should not confine ourselves to the present life of the individual but go into previous incarnations in which the work was done that made the genius in this incarnation.

Professor Einstein was considered the greatest mathematical genius of our time. The scientific world does not connect his insight into scientific principles with his religious life, but he freely stated that he worshiped God. He said: "The voice of God is from within. Something within me tells me what I must do every day." For him God is as valid as a scientific argument. On the subject of spiritual realization he once said:

"Every man knows that in his work he does best and accomplishes most when he has attained a proficiency that enables him to work intuitively. That is, there are things that we come to know so well that we do not know how we know them. Perhaps we live best and do things best when we are not too conscious of how and why we do them."

The supreme realization of man is his unity with God. Jesus had this realization and proclaimed it before there was any manifestation. When He told His followers, "I and the Father are one" and "He that hath seen me hath seen the Father," they demanded that He show them the Father. They could not then understand that He had spiritually united with creative Mind. Men in our day are having this realization in a more universal way than ever before in the history of the race, and they are affirming it in the face of ridicule and condemnation. When this inner consciousness is attained by any man the foundation has been laid of the Peter church or temple that is man's immortal body, which will never pass away.

Metaphysically realization is expectancy objectified. The mind conceives a proposition and then marshals all its forces to make that conception a reality in the objective world. All things material are first thought pictures, carved by the imagination from omnipresent thought substance. Shakespeare in "Much Ado about Nothing" brings out the idea as follows:

> The idea of her life shall sweetly creep
> Into his study of imagination,
> And every lovely organ of her life,
> Shall come appareled in more precious habit,
> More moving-delicate and full of life
> Into the eye and prospect of his soul.

This realm of realization is so real to the mind that it requires a trained metaphysician to detect the difference between its creations and the manifest realm of things. We all have a body in the ether that is the counterpart of the physical. It is through this psychic body that we have sensation in the physical. It is possible to think of the psychic body and cultivate its sensations until it appears as real as the physical. Many persons have done this until they have formed a psychic world consciousness and they are often unable to separate it from the physical. They search materially for the treasures they see psychically. To them the realm of thought forms is the finality of creation instead of the mental pictures of that which is about to appear.

The trained metaphysician is no stranger to this picture gallery of the mind and he is not deceived into believing that it is any more than a mental reflection. One who enters the realm of spiritual ideas does not allow his consciousness to become confused with the mind pictures that flash into psychic sight. They are part of the process of making ideas manifest. When a Christian healer realizes that his treatment has firmly formed the picture of health, he relaxes his decrees and statements of Truth and trusts the divine law to make health manifest.

Paul urges in many of his writings that we have the Mind of Christ: that we let Christ be formed in us. This has usually been taken to mean that we are to imitate Christ. This is good as far as it goes, but it does not go far enough. To follow Jesus Christ in the regeneration or new birth we must fulfill the law of body building, which is a reconstruction of the corrupt cells: "This corruptible must put on in-corruption." To accomplish this and make the body conform to His perfect body we must see Him as He is in His perfect body. This perfect body exists as an ideal body in us all. By mentally concentrating on this perfect body and focusing all our powers on it as the vital life of the physical a transformation will begin that will finally raise the physical to divine stature. Paul points the way in II Corinthians:

"But we all, with unveiled face beholding as in a mirror the glory of the Lord, are transformed into the same image from glory to glory, even as from the Lord the Spirit."

Chapter IV - Producing Results

IT IS A striking fact that even back in the time of Moses the health of the people was considered of great importance and was always mentioned in connection with their spiritual welfare. If they were obedient to the law, they kept in health; if disobedient, they fell sick. The same law that brought about these results has always been operative and is active in our midst today. Faith in God as the health of His people and obedience to the law of Being bring health. Distrust and disobedience produce ill-health.

It has been proved again and again that there is a definite relation between the thoughts of man and the conditions in his body. Scientists of the world are experimenting with mental processes and are discovering that the old Scripture writers knew whereof they spoke when they taught that sin produces sickness and righteousness health. It is known that infants have been poisoned by the milk from the breasts of angry mothers. Persons under the stress of fear suffer a loss of appetite. Many other illustrations of the effect of discordant mental states come to those who study mind and its manifestations. Job understood the relation between a mental concept and its result. He said: "The thing which I fear cometh upon me."

In the past century there has been a general awakening among people to the realization of the relation between righteousness and health, and men everywhere are seeking the knowledge of God and His healing power. God becomes to them their "all-sufficiency in everything." This all-sufficiency manifests itself to them according to their needs. To one it is health, to another it is freedom from bondage to some habit, to a third person it is illumination.

Jesus was the great teacher and example of obedience to the law of constructive thinking. All His commandments and sayings tend toward the enhancement of life and health and harmony. The reforms that man in mortal consciousness tries to make are all based on destructive ideas set to work in the external. The reform of Jesus is an inner transformation: "I am not come to destroy, but to fulfill." He came not to tear down but to build up. If we follow Him we shall give our strength and substance and thought force to constructive activity.

In order to understand the Scriptures and especially the portion of them that gives the life and experiences of Jesus it is necessary to study the action of the mind. The movement of every mind in bringing forth the simplest thought is a key to the great creative process of universal Mind. In every act is involved mind, idea, and manifestation. The mind is neither seen nor felt; the idea is not seen, but it is felt; and the manifestation appears.

The history of mankind in the majority of its aspects shows a steady growth or ascent from a lower to a higher estate. In the forms of nature external to man the same law of development is seen. Jesus' statement that "the earth beareth fruit of herself; first the blade, then the ear, then the full grain in the ear" is a recognition of the truth that evolution in the earth is universal.

The progress of man through the aid of uplifting influences has been especially marked in the education of the mind. In the field of mathematics alone almost unbelievable increase in the understanding of abstract truth has been gained over a period that began with the crude though systematic work of the Egyptians, about 2500 B.C., and extended to include the seventeenth-century research of Leibnitz, who developed the branch of higher mathematics known as the infinitesimal calculus.

Steady progress has been the rule also in that phase of life which deals with a man's relations to his fellow men. The various activities of social service have led to improved working conditions, better homes, and more helpful environments for those whose condition of life has called for the help of their brothers. Sociology has thus resulted in many movements for the uplift of mankind.

In the field of religion the upward march has been especially remarkable. There is a wide range of religious experience between the blindly groping faith that caused men to pass their children through the fire as sacrifices to their deities and the divine consciousness of Jesus Christ, who submitted His body to the purifying fire of the Spirit and came forth alive with a life that never dies.

The healing of the body of man must follow the law of evolution, in common with the education of his mind and the adjustment of his social relations. Jesus did His healing spiritually. When He was told of the "great fever" of Simon's mother-in-law, He administered no drug to reduce her temperature. Instead He "stood over her, and rebuked the fever; and it left her." Jesus knew the law that "without any dispute the less is blessed by the better." He knew that the blessing of health comes through the exercise of faith on the part of the man who seeks it, that faith opens the mind to the influx of power from on high, and that the power of the Highest heals all diseases both of soul and of body.

When faith is sufficiently strong to dissolve all adverse conditions and to open the mind fully to the power of God, healing is instantaneous. In the natural course of events the patient who survives a fever goes through a long, slow convalescence; hence perhaps the name "patient." Jesus had no "patients" although He healed many who were "sick with divers diseases." Simon's mother-in-law rose up immediately and went about her work when Jesus denied the power of the fever to hold her.

After a busy day of teaching in the synagogue in the course of which Jesus restored to his right mind a man who "had a spirit of an unclean demon," He ended the evening by healing, without exception, "every one of them" that were brought to Him. He had spent no time in the study of pathology prior to this work. Shortly before that time He had spent forty days in the wilderness in communion with God and in setting His own purposes in order by the light of the divine understanding that He had gained there. After each season of healing and intensive teaching He again withdrew into a desert place or to a mountain, either alone or in company with His apostles, and there obtained a new influx of power from the Father. So the healing work went on. There is no record of incurables.

Further there is no record that Jesus took any precautions to avoid infection when He was engaged in healing the sick. He was without fear of evil because He acknowledged only the power of the Highest, which is good. He put His hand on the leper to prove to him that He was fearless and confident. He spoke six short, decisive words, "I will; be thou made clean"; and we are told that "straightway his leprosy was cleansed" although the Scripture shows that he was in the last stage of the disease ("full of leprosy"). There were no long explanations, no instructions given. Jesus simply turned His super-will upon the leper, and the power of the Highest flowed through Him instantly to do its perfect work. Then only did an instruction follow. The leper was told to offer the usual praise and sacrifice to God and to ascribe his healing to the Highest rather than to the power of personality.

Jesus always connected sin and sickness as cause and effect. When the man sick of the palsy was let down through the roof of a house that he might be brought before Jesus for healing, there were those present who expected the healing to be done in some mysterious way; and when Jesus spoke of forgiving the man's sins in order to heal him they said: "Who is this that speaketh blasphemies? Who can forgive sins, but God alone?" These men lived in a material world and saw everything from a material viewpoint. They did not understand that the man's sins caused his palsy. As a proof of man's power to forgive sin and thus heal the effects of sin Jesus said when the man was brought for healing:

"But that ye may know that the Son of man hath authority on earth to forgive sins (he said unto him that was palsied), I say unto thee, Arise, and take up thy couch, and go unto thy house. And immediately he rose up before them, and took up that whereon he lay, and departed to his house, glorifying God."

Jesus taught plainly that the mind was the place of origin of every act. He said that if there was lust in the heart, it was sin even though no overt act were committed. All thinking people in this day accept without question the fact that the body is moved by the mind; and those who have made a study of mental processes have found that all the conditions of the body are brought about by the mind; also that there is a law of right thought and that a departure from that law is sin or "missing one's aim," which is the original Hebrew conception of sin.

Forgiveness really means the giving up of something. When you forgive yourself, you cease doing the thing that you ought not to do. Jesus was correct in assuming that man has power to forgive sin. Sin is a falling short of the divine law, and repentance and forgiveness are the only means that man has of getting out of sin and its effect and coming into harmony with the law. But who can tell what the law is? Only those who study man as a spiritual and mental being. Study of manifestation alone is futile; it leads nowhere. We must get at it from the cause side. All sin is first in the mind; and the forgiveness is a change of mind or repentance. Some mental attitude, some train of mental energy, must be transformed. We forgive sin in ourselves every time we resolve to think and act according to the divine law. The mind must change from a material to a spiritual base. The law is already fixed; there is nothing in it to be changed, because God is the lawgiver and does not change. The change must all be on the part of man and within him. The moment man changes his thoughts of sickness to thoughts of health the divine law rushes in and begins the healing work.

The law is Truth, and the Truth is that all is good. There is no power and no reality in sin. If sin were real and enduring, like goodness and Truth, it could not be forgiven but would hold its victim forever. When we enter into the understanding of the real and the unreal, a great light dawns upon us and we see what Jesus meant when He said, "The Son of man hath authority on earth to forgive sins." The Son of man is that in us which discerns the difference between Truth and error. When we get this understanding, we are in a position to free our soul from sin and our body from disease, which is the effect of sin. Sin is the result of desire manifesting itself in erroneous ways and may be compared to the errors of the child working a problem in mathematics. When the error is discovered and there is a willingness to correct it, under the law of forgiveness man erases it as easily as the child rubs out the false figures in his exercise. Thus in spiritual understanding, the I AM of man forgives or "gives" Truth "for" error; the mind is set in order and the body healed. The moment man realizes this he puts himself in harmony with the Truth of Being, and the law wipes out all his transgressions.

In denying the reality of sin send out your freeing thought to others as well as to yourself. Do not hold anyone in bondage to the thought of sin. If you do, it will pile up and increase in power according to the laws of mental action.

No one can understand how forgiveness sets free the sin-bound soul and the sick body unless he studies mind and has some understanding of its laws. There is a universal thought substance in which thought builds whatever man wills.

The right images become active through the power of thought. Man has unlimited power through thought, and he can give his power to things or withhold it. If he thinks about the power of sin, he builds up and gives force to that belief until it engulfs him in its whirlpool of thought substance. He forgets his spiritual origin and sees only the human.

He thinks of himself as a sinner "born in sin and conceived in iniquity" rather than as the image and likeness of God.

Man also sees the law of sowing and reaping, and he fears his sins and their results. Then fear of the divine law is added to his burdens. The way out of this maze of ignorance, sin, and sickness is through man's understanding of his real being, and then the forgiving or the giving up of all thoughts of the reality of sin and its effects in the body.

But we must recognize the unity of the race in Christ and include all people in our forgiving. A good freeing statement is:

"I do not believe in the power of sin in myself or in others."

If anyone tries to free himself while holding others in the thought of sin, he will not demonstrate his freedom. No man can rise except as he lifts the race with him in his thought: "and I, if I be lifted up from the earth, will draw all men unto myself." As by one man sin came into the world so by one man it is taken away. As all were included in the sin of one so all are included in the righteousness of one, and every man stands sinless before God in Christ. Recognition of this will make men free, and the greater the number of men that recognize and declare the Truth the sooner will all men know that they are free from sin in Christ.

You must build upon faith in the reality of the spiritual. The next step is to put your selfishness away. There cannot be two in this kingdom. It is the kingdom of God, and man must give up. The John the Baptist must recognize the Son of God that is in you and that this Son must be always active in you in love, life, and power. The kingdom is for the larger man. The personal man must be eliminated.

The next step is love, universal love: not the love of earthly possessions but the love of spiritual things. We must give up the flesh man and all his possessions and at the same time lay hold of the spiritual man. Then we have everything although apparently we may have nothing. This is a difficult proposition to those who think in terms of material ideas. You must be able to get away from all thought of material things. "Love . . . seeketh not its own"; "is not puffed up." Love is not selfish. We cannot have selfishness and love at the same time. We cannot have this universal brotherhood unless we love everybody. We must love all because we are all one. There must be in our consciousness a recognition of the universal right of all to all the possessions of the world.

Then there must be this inner growth that is a fuller consciousness of the new life which comes with the entering into this kingdom of Christ.

The fact is that there is a foundation for this world-wide movement in behalf of purer men and better things for all. There is something back of it all, and the old conditions, diseases, and limitations must pass away; and the time is now ripe for entering into this kingdom, this attainment of the spiritual side of life, this growing of a new body; and every one of us can enter in if we only will to do so.

True, in all actual transformation of mind and body a dissolving, breaking-up process necessarily takes place, because thought force and substance have been built into the errors that appear. In each individual these errors have the power that man has given to them by his thought concerning them. These thought structures must be broken up and eliminated from consciousness. The simplest, most direct, and most effective method is to withdraw from them the life and substance that have been going to feed them, and to let them shrivel away into their own nothingness. This withdrawal is best accomplished by denial of the power and reality of evil and affirmation of the allness of Spirit. Nothing is destroyed, because "nothing" can't be destroyed. The change that takes place is merely a transference of power from an error belief to faith in the Truth, through the recognition that God is good and is all that in reality exists.

The doctrine of the Trinity is often a stumbling block, because we find it difficult to understand how three persons can be one. Three persons cannot be one, and theology will always be a mystery until theologians become metaphysicians. It is necessary to understand the Trinity in order to be healed in soul and body.

God is the name of the all-encompassing Mind. Christ is the name of the all-loving Mind. Holy Spirit is the all-active manifestation. These three are one fundamental Mind in its three creative aspects.

We have to be healed physically, mentally, and spiritually. Often people think they are sick physically when they are just sick in soul. It is easy to understand how the idea of perfect health may exist in the great Father-Mind; also how that idea may become active in the individual and manifest in his life. This simple comparison clears up the mystery of the Trinity. Here are the Scripture symbols compared with modern metaphysical terms:

God-Christ-man.
Mind--idea--manifestation.
Father--Son--Holy Spirit.
Thinker--thought--action.
Spirit--soul--body.
I AM--I AM conscious--I appear.

We want the actual overcoming power of Christ. To get this we must appreciate life and enter into it thankfully and heartily. "I came that they may have life, and may have it abundantly."

This abundant life is always present. When we recognize it and open our consciousness to it, it comes flowing into mind and body with its mighty quickening, healing power, and they are renewed and transformed.

The following affirmations are for the purpose of establishing the whole man in the consciousness of unity and health. They are given as they came into mind without any attempt at classification:

My body does not starve for my love and appreciation of it. I recognize it, honor it, and love it as the body temple of the living God.

I have now the only body I ever had. Though I were reincarnated a thousand times, yet is my body the same. It is I. Its appearance depends on my beliefs and thoughts and changes accordingly, but it is always the same body, even as my soul and spirit are always the same. My body is as much a part of my individuality as my soul. It is eternal, like any other part of my I. It is I, even as my soul is I.

I cannot disown my body and say that I borrowed it from my parents. This is not the truth. I may have taken up some of my parents' error beliefs and built them into my body; but my body came from no one but God. It came from Him with my spirit and soul and has ever coexisted with them. These three are one, inseparable. It is the belief in man that his body is separate from him and is something that he merely owns that makes the appearance of separation. I do not own my body: I am body. I do not own my soul: I am soul. I do not own my spirit: I am spirit. And these three are one.

The redemption of the body depends on my having the right idea of body. It must be the divine idea, and there must be no other. The eye must be single.

My body (or I manifested as body) is not filled with error, sin, discord. Beholding myself free from these keeps me manifesting thus. The law of growth is in beholding. While I behold the body as anything else but its divine idea I hold it there. It can never change before the belief of it changes.

I am. I am in every cell of my body. I am every cell of my body. I do not disown my body. I do not withdraw my I, but I take possession--full possession--of every part in the name of the Lord.

I now fully identify myself with my body even as with my soul and spirit, thus making the at-one-ment.

Since my body is I, if there appears resistance in it, that resistance is my own; it comes only from me. It comes from my failure properly to identify myself with my body. The way to get control is to take it. This I do, not by will power, by personal force, or by anything that recognizes my body as separate from me, but by my consciousness of oneness with it. This unifies all of me and stops all resistance.

My body is life, purity, wholeness, sinlessness. In my flesh I see God. What I see, what I behold, becomes manifest.

"Beloved, believe not every spirit, but prove the spirits, whether they are of God; because many false prophets are gone out into the world. Hereby know ye the Spirit of God: every spirit that confesseth that Jesus Christ is come in the flesh is of God: and every spirit that confesseth not Jesus is not of God."

I confess that Jesus Christ is come in the flesh, even in my flesh.

"Not for that we would be unclothed, but that we would be clothed upon, that what is mortal may be swallowed up of life."

The idea of the body as an earthly house is now dissolved, and I am now clothed upon with the heavenly house, even the divine idea of man complete. In this idea I am one with the immortal, incorruptible flesh of Jesus Christ, and I have eternal life. I do confess that Jesus Christ is come in the flesh.

Chapter V - The Omnipotence of Prayer

TO A PERSON in the understanding of Truth prayer should be an affirmation of that which is in Being.

What is the necessity of the prayer of affirmation if Being already is? In order that the creative law of the Word may be fulfilled. All things are in God as potentialities. It is man's office under the divine law to bring into manifestation that which has been created or planned by the unmanifest. Everybody should pray. Through prayer we develop the highest phase of character. Prayer softens and refines the whole man. A prominent skeptic once said that the most unattractive thing in existence was a prayerless woman.

Prayer is not supplication or begging but a simple asking for that which we know is waiting for us at the hands of our Father and an affirmation of its existence. The prayer that Jesus gave as a model is simplicity itself. There is none of that awe-inspiring "O Thou" that ministers often affect in public prayer but only the ordinary informal request of a son to his Father for things needed.

"Father . . . Hallowed be thy name." Here in the Lord's Prayer is a recognition of the all-inclusiveness and completeness of Divine Mind. Everything has its sustenance from this one source; therefore "the earth is the Lord's, and the fulness thereof."

We need supplies for the day only. Hoarding for future necessity breeds selfishness. The Children of Israel tried to save the manna, but it spoiled on their hands.

The law "Whatsoever a man soweth, that shall he also reap" is here shorn of its terrors. If we forgive others we shall be forgiven, and the penalty of suffering for sins will be eliminated.

It does not seem possible that God would lead us into temptation. The statement about temptation follows closely that regarding the forgiveness of sin, and it is evidently a part of it. "Let not temptation lead us" is a permissible interpretation.

Jesus advised asking for what we want and being persistent in our demands. People ignorant of the relation in which man stands to God wonder why we should ask and even importune a Father who has provided all things for us. This is explained when we perceive that God is a great mind reservoir that has to be tapped by man's mind and poured into visibility through man's thought or word. If the mind of man is clogged with doubt, lethargy, or fear, he must open the way by persistent knocking and asking. "Pray without ceasing," "continuing instant in prayer." Acquire in prayer a facility in asking equal to the mathematician's expertness in handling numbers and you will get responses in proportion.

We give our children what we consider good gifts from our limited and transitory store, but when the gifts of God are put into our minds we have possessions that are eternal and will go on being productive for all time.

Undoubtedly the one thing that stands out prominently in the teaching of Jesus is the necessity of prayer. He prayed on the slightest pretext, or in some such manner invoked the presence of God. He prayed over situations that most men would deal with without the intervention of God. If He was verily God incarnate, the skeptic often asks, why did He so often appeal to an apparently higher God. To answer this doubt intelligently and truly one must understand the constitution of man.

There are always two men in each individual. The man without is the picture that the man within paints with his mind. This mind is the open door to the unlimited principle of Being. When Jesus prayed He was setting into action the various powers of His individuality in order to bring about certain results. Within His identity was of God; without He was human personality.

The various mental attitudes denoted by the word prayer are not comprehended by those unfamiliar with the spiritual constitution of man. When the trained metaphysician speaks of his demonstrations through prayer, he does not explain all the movements of his spirit and mind, because the outer consciousness has not the capacity to receive it.

When we read of Jesus spending whole nights in prayer, the first thought is that He was asking and begging God for something. But we find prayer to be many-sided; it is not only asking but receiving also. We must pray believing that we shall receive. Prayer is both invocation and affirmation. Meditation, concentration, denial, and affirmation in the silence are all forms of what is loosely termed prayer.

Thus Jesus was demonstrating at night over the error thoughts of mind. He was lifting the mortal mind up to the plane of Spirit through some prayerful thought. The Son of man must be lifted up, and there is no way to do this except through prayer.

One who exercises his thought powers discovers that there is a steady growth with proper use. The powers of the mind are developed in much the same way that the muscles of the body are. Persistent affirmation of a certain desire in the silence concentrates the mental energies and beats down all barriers.

Jesus illustrates the power of such affirmative prayer, of repeated silent demands for justice, for instance, by the case of the widow bereft of worldly protection and power. To the widow's persistence even the ungodly judge succumbs. The unceasing prayer of faith is commanded in the Scriptures in various places.

If a man's prayers are based on the thought of his own righteousness and the sinfulness of others, he does not fulfill the law of true prayer. Self-righteousness is an exclusory thought and closes the door to the great Father love that we all want. We are not to justify ourselves in the sight of God but let the Spirit of justice and righteousness do its perfect work through us.

That God and angels and heaven exist is accepted by all who believe the Scriptures, but there is wide diversity of thought about their character and abode. Those who read the Bible after the letter have invented all kinds of imaginary notions as to the conditions under which God and His angels live and as to the location of heaven. Their minds being fixed on things, they have not conceived of the realm of ideas, and they are therefore totally ignorant of the true teaching of the Scriptures. To understand the Bible one must know about the constitution of man. This is the key to all mysteries, the knowledge of man's true self. "Know thyself."

Man is spirit, soul, body. These are coexistent. God is the principle of being as an axiom is a principle of mathematics. God is not confined to locality. Is a mathematical principle confined to a particular place and not found elsewhere? "The kingdom of God is within you." God is the real of man's being. It follows that all the powers that are attributed to God may become operative in man. Then we live right in the presence of God and angels and heaven. What seems a desert place is filled with angelic messengers, and like Jacob we know it not.

Man sets into action any of the three realms of his being, spirit, soul, and body, by concentrating his thought on them. If he thinks only of the body, the physical senses encompass all his existence. If mind and emotion are cultivated he adds soul to his consciousness. If he rises to the Absolute and comprehends Spirit, he rounds out the God-man.

Spirit is the source of soul and body, hence the ruling power. Its works are so swift and so transcend the limitations of matter that the natural man cannot comprehend them and hence calls them "miracles." But all things are done under law. "Prayer was made earnestly of the church unto God for him," and Peter was delivered from prison by an angel. The earnest prayers of the devout believers in the power of supreme Spirit brought about the result. The history of Christianity is full of instances of so-called miracles wrought through prayer. The hour-long prayer of Luther by what was supposed to be the deathbed of his friend Melanchthon is a famous instance of importunate pleadings. It was Luther's firm belief that Melanchthon's years of continued life were the direct answer to his prayers.

Mighty things have been wrought in the past by those who had mere blind faith to guide them. To faith we now add understanding of the law, and our achievements will be a fulfillment of the promise of Jesus "He that believeth on me, the works that I do shall he do also; and greater works than these shall he do." The prayer of Luther and its results are now being duplicated every day. As we go on in the exercise of the spiritual faculties we shall strengthen them and understand them better, and we shall cease to talk about anything miraculous. All things are possible to man when he exercises his spiritual power under the divine law.

When man directs the power of exalted ideas into his body, he exalts the cells, releases their innate spiritual energy, and causes them finally to disappear from physical sight into the omnipresent luminous ether. This is what Jesus accomplished at His ascension. The promise was that all who follow Him in the regeneration of the body would do likewise. It is true that even the followers of Jesus have not always understood the scientific import of His doctrine. They have mentally absorbed His exalted ideas and looked to their fulfillment in a faraway heaven in the skies. By thus projecting their ideas toward a fulfillment outside of the body they have separated their soul or mind consciousness from its companion, the body, and the deserted cells have been resolved into their mother principle, the earth.

The mind of man is constantly projecting thought energies or waves through brain cells into the ether or space element in which we live. Every person lives in an environment of radiant energy that circulates through the cells of his organism like bees in a hive. Ordinarily we cannot see the radiations of the mind, but we almost universally feel them. When a discordant mind impinges upon our mind radiations we instinctively shrink away. But we are radiantly happy in the presence of an exalted mind.

"No man hath beheld God at any time." Seers, prophets, preachers, and holy men and women in all ages are a unit in saying that they have become acquainted with God through prayer, expressed in the spirit of their minds.

This testimony to God's spiritual presence is so unanimous that no one seeks His help in any way other than through the spirit of the mind; and the fact that we know God with our minds and not with our senses proves that God is Spirit.

In its higher functioning the mind of man deals with spiritual ideas, and we can truthfully say that man is a spiritual being. This fact explains the almost universal worship of God by men and makes possible the conjunction of the heaven and the earth by those who understand the underlying laws of prayer. Jesus stated this emphatically in John 4:24 (margin): "God is Spirit; and they that worship him must worship in spirit and truth."

Then the real foundation of all effective prayer is the understanding that God is Spirit and that man, His offspring, is His image and likeness, hence spiritual.

Such a concept of God gives man a point of contact that is never absent; in all places and under all conditions he has the assurance of the attention and help of God when he realizes the Father's spiritual presence and comradeship.

When it has a spiritually poised mind to work through, Spirit is not limited in its power by any material environment. "With God all things are possible." To make this strong statement of Jesus come true we must study the laws of God and strive to carry them out through a quickened consciousness.

The Bible is replete with situations where men and women seemed beyond any material help, but through faith and prayer they triumphed right in the face of seemingly insurmountable obstacles. The author of the 11th chapter of Hebrews builds pyramids of faith demonstrations. Hear the climax:

"And what shall I more say? for the time will fail me if I tell of Gideon, Barak, Samson, Jephthah; of David and Samuel and the prophets who through faith subdued kingdoms, wrought righteousness, obtained promises, stopped the mouths of lions, quenched the power of fire, escaped the edge of the sword, from weakness were made strong, waxed mighty in war, turned to flight armies of aliens."

Paul might have added to his pyramid of faith the long list of miraculous healings of diseases and many superhuman works recorded in the Bible, among which are the restoration of the leper Naaman and the resurrection of the Shunammite's son by Elisha; the control of the elements by Elijah; the overcoming of gravity in the floating of the workman's axhead from the bottom of the Jordan by Elisha, and Moses' causing the water to gush from the rock.

The majority of people think that great spiritual faith is necessary to get marvelous results. But Jesus taught differently. "The apostles said unto the Lord, Increase our faith. And the

Lord said, If ye had faith as a grain of mustard seed, ye would say unto this sycamine tree, Be thou rooted up, and be thou planted in the sea; and it would obey you."

The mustard is among the smallest of seeds, and the comparison would indicate what a tiny bit of real faith is necessary to cause motion in material things. Paul and Silas in the Roman jail prayed and sang until their bonds fell off, the doors flew open, and they walked out, both free men. On the day of Pentecost the followers of Jesus prayed and sang until the ethers were so accelerated that tongues of fire flashed from the bodies of the worshipers, and they were miraculously quickened in mental ability.

Prayer liberates the energies pent up in mind and body. Those who pray much create a spiritual aura that eventually envelops the whole body. The bands of light painted by artists around the heads of saints are not imaginary; they actually exist and are visible to the sharp eye of the painter. The Scriptures testify in Luke 9:29 that when Jesus was praying "his countenance was altered, and his raiment became white and dazzling." After Moses had been praying on the mountain his face shone so brightly that the people could not look on it, and he had to wear a veil.

Thus prayer is obviously dynamic and actuates the spiritual ethers that interpenetrate all substance. Prayer is related directly to the creative laws of God, and when man adjusts his mind and body in harmony with those laws, his prayers will always be effective and far-reaching. The activity of the mind that is named the understanding is essential in righteous prayer. Spirit is omnipresent, but the individual consciousness gives it a local habitation and a name.

If in thinking about God we locate Him in a faraway heaven and direct our thoughts outward in the hope of reaching Him, all our force will be driven from us to that imaginary place and we shall become devitalized.

"The kingdom of God is within you." The pivotal point around which Spirit creates is within the structure of consciousness. This is true of the primal cell as well as of the most complex organ. The throne on which the divine will sits is within man's consciousness, and it is to this inner center that he should direct his attention when praying or meditating. David called this spiritual center of the soul "the secret place of the Most High," and all the defense and power of the 91st Psalm is promised to the one who dwells in the consciousness of the Almighty within. Paul says, "Know ye not that ye are a temple of God, and that the Spirit of God dwelleth in you?"

In the 6th chapter of Matthew, in giving His disciples directions for prayer, Jesus called attention to the God center in man in these words: "But thou, when thou prayest, enter into thine inner chamber, and having shut the door, pray to thy Father who is in secret, and thy Father who seeth in secret shall recompense thee." He also told them not to use vain repetitions: "For your Father knoweth what things ye have need of, before ye ask him."

If Divine Mind knows our needs, why should we have to ask to have them supplied? We do not ask expecting God to hand us the things we want, but we realize that He has made provision in the very nature of things for our every need to be fulfilled. When we realize this and go about our work in perfect confidence, the fulfillment of the divine law of support and supply is often demonstrated in ways we had not dreamed of.

Do not supplicate or beg God to give you what you need, but get still and think about the inexhaustible resources of infinite Mind, its presence in all its fullness, and its constant readiness to manifest itself when its laws are complied with. This is what Jesus meant when He said, "Seek ye first his kingdom, and his righteousness; and all these things shall be added unto you."

We all need a better understanding of the nature of God if we are to comply with the laws under which He creates. We must begin by knowing that "God is Spirit." Spirit is not located in a big man called God but is everywhere the breath of life and the knowing quality of mind active in and through all bodies, "over all, and through all, and in all." The highest form of prayer is to open our minds and quietly realize that the one omnipresent intelligence knows our thoughts and instantly answers, even before we have audibly expressed our desires.

This being true, we should ask and at the same time give thanks that we have already received. Jesus expressed this idea in Mark 11:24: "Therefore I say unto you, All things whatsoever ye pray and ask for, believe that ye receive them, and ye shall have them." Before He broke the miraculously multiplied loaves and fishes and fed the five thousand He looked up to heaven and gave thanks. When He raised Lazarus He first said: "Father, I thank thee that thou heardest me. And I knew that thou hearest me always." Then He commanded Lazarus to come forth.

We observe that all things come out of the formless, but our knowledge of the formless is so limited that we do not conceive of its infinite possibilities. When we think or silently speak in the all-potential ethers of Spirit, there is always an unfailing effect. "Whatsoever ye have said in the darkness shall be heard in the light; and what ye have spoken in the ear in the inner chambers shall be proclaimed upon the housetops."

Silent prayer is more effective than audible, because by silent prayer the mind comes into closer touch with the creative Spirit. James says, "The prayer of faith shall save him that is sick, and the Lord shall raise him up." Countless thousands are applying this faith prayer today and are being healed as men were in the time of Jesus.

The strange thing is that this very important proof of the Spirit's work in Christian healing should have been neglected for so many hundred years when Jesus gave it as one of the signs of a believer: "These signs shall accompany them that believe; in my name shall they cast out demons; they shall speak with new tongues; they shall take up serpents, and if they drink any deadly thing, it shall in no wise hurt them; they shall lay hands on the sick, and they shall recover."

The history of the Christian church records that during its first three hundred years the followers of Jesus healed the sick by prayer and that healing was gradually dropped as the church became prosperous and worldly. A layman from a rural district was being shown, by a bishop, the riches of a cathedral. The bishop said, "The church can no longer say, 'Silver and gold have I none.'" "No," said the layman. "Neither can it say, 'Take up thy bed, and walk.'"

It is found by those who have faith in the power of God that the prayer for health is the most quickly answered. The reason for this is that the natural laws that create and sustain the body are really divine laws, and when man silently asks for the intervention of God in restoring health, he is calling into action the natural forces of his being. Doctors agree that the object of using their remedies is to quicken the natural functions of the body. But medicine does not appeal to the intelligent principle that directs all the activities of the organism, hence it fails to give permanent healing.

However a conscious union with the natural life forces lying within and back of all the complex activities of man gets right to the fountainhead, and the results are unfailing if the proper connection has been made.

The first step in prayer for health is to get still. "Be still, and know that I am God." To get still the body must be relaxed and the mind quieted. Center the attention within. There is a quiet place within us all, and by silently saying over and over, "Peace, be still," we shall enter that quiet place and a great stillness will pervade our whole being. Jesus Christ said, "Peace be unto you. . . . Receive ye the Holy Spirit." That is, He spoke to the within. He said also, "whatsoever ye shall ask in my name, that will I do, that the Father may be glorified in the Son."

"For my thoughts are not your thoughts, neither are your ways my ways, saith Jehovah. For as the heavens are higher than the earth, so are my ways higher than your ways, and my thoughts than your thoughts." This verse from Isaiah gives us an insight into the difference between the mortal thinker and the divine. Divine Mind is serene, orderly, placid, while sense mind is turbulent, discordant, and violent. We can readily understand from this comparison why we do not get divine guidance even though we strive ever so hard for it. The best of us are subject to crosscurrents of worry that interfere with the even flow of God's thoughts into our consciousness. Jesus warned His followers not to be anxious about what they should eat, drink, or wear. In all literature there is no finer comparison than that given by Jesus when He pointed to the flowers and said: "Consider the lilies of the field, how they grow; they toil not, neither do they spin; yet I say unto you, that even Solomon in all his glory was not arrayed like one of these."

If God so clothes the lilies, shall He not much more clothe His children? This argument holds good with reference to all human needs. There is a natural law whose chief purpose is to take care of the human family. But the divine order of creative Mind must be observed by man before he can receive the benefits of his natural inheritance.

Metaphysicians, who study the mind and its many modes of action, find that when they refuse to let thoughts of worry, anxiety, or other distraction act in their minds, they gradually establish an inner quietness that finally merges into a great peace. This is the "peace of God, which passeth all understanding." When this peace is attained, the individual gets inspirations and revelations direct from infinite Mind.

Any method that will hush the external thought clamor will achieve unity with the inner peace. When we are in peaceful sleep, the outer clamor of thought is stilled and the great Spirit of the universe communicates its higher vision to the inner consciousness of man.

The ancient peoples seem to have been more open than moderns to revelations in sleep. Long ago Job wrote in the 33d chapter of his book:

"In a dream, in a vision of the night, When deep sleep falleth upon men, In slumberings upon the bed; Then he openeth the ears of men, And sealeth their instruction."

It is written in I Kings, chapter 3, that the Lord appeared to Solomon in a dream and said, "Ask what I shall give thee." Solomon did not ask for riches, for honor, or for the glory that kings usually seek, but in meekness he asked the Lord to give him an "understanding heart" so that he might discriminate between good and evil and be a wise judge of his people. Riches and honor followed of course, as they always do when a man is earnestly striving to be honest and just in all ways.

We get our most vivid revelations when in a meditative state of mind. This proves that when we make the mind trustful and confident, we put it in harmony with creative Mind; then its force flows to us in accordance with the law of like attracting like.

The agonizing, supplicating, begging prayer is not answered, because the thoughts are so turbulent that Divine Mind cannot reach the pleader. Jesus prayed with a confident assurance that what He wanted would be granted, and He established a mode of prayer for His followers that never fails when the same conditions and relations are attained and maintained with reference to the Father-Mind.

Through His spiritual attainments Jesus formed a spiritual zone in the earth's mental atmosphere; His followers make connection with that zone when they pray in His "name." He stated this fact in John 14:2: "I go to prepare a place for you." Simon Peter said, "Lord, whither goest thou?" Jesus answered him, "Whither I go, thou canst not follow me now; but thou shalt follow afterwards."

When Jesus had purified His body sufficiently, He ascended into this "place" in the spiritual ethers of our planet. In our high spiritual realizations we make temporary contact with Him and His spiritual character, represented by His "name." But we, like the apostles, are not yet able to go there and abide, because we have not overcome earthly attachments. We shall however attain the same freedom and spiritual power that He attained if we follow Him in the regeneration. But we should clearly understand that we cannot go to Jesus' "place" through death. We must overcome death as He did before we can be glorified with Him in the "heavens," the higher realms of the mind.

We should not cease to pray to the Father in the name of Christ Jesus; He said that man should "pray always." Prayer lifts our thoughts on high and sets us free from the narrow limits of matter, just as the electromagnetic impulse is lifted and carried by the ether and caught by any receptive station. Spiritual-minded people are being united today, as in the past, by zones of spiritual force that will eventually become the permanent thought atmosphere of the planet. In Revelation this is typified as the New Jerusalem descending out of the heavens into the earth.

Jesus said we could ask whatsoever we wished in His name and it should be done unto us: "Verily, verily, I say unto you, If ye shall ask anything of the Father, he will give it you in my name. Hitherto have ye asked nothing in my name: ask, and ye shall receive, that your joy may be made full."

Jesus taught in parables because the people did not understand that spiritual forces, acting through mind, make race conditions. But He told them: "The hour cometh, when I shall no more speak unto you in dark sayings, but shall tell you plainly of the Father."

The time prophesied by Jesus--when we should plainly understand the character of the Father--is now at hand, and it behooves all Christians to come out of parables and to realize that scientific laws govern the material, mental, and spiritual realms of Being.

"Pray without ceasing; in everything give thanks," wrote Paul to the Thessalonians. The idea is that we should be persistent in prayer. We know it is always the will of the air to give us all that we can breathe into our lungs. Jesus compared the Spirit to the air in describing the new birth to Nicodemus. It requires lung capacity to breathe deeply of the oceans of air; so it requires spiritual capacity to realize how accessible and ready omnipresent Spirit is to fill us full of itself. The lack is in us. God is more willing to give than we are to receive.

To acquire the mind that is always open to Spirit we must be persistent in prayer. It is written in the 18th chapter of Luke: "And he spake a parable unto them to the end that they ought always to pray, and not to faint." He then told of the judge who feared not God nor man yet who was worn out by the persistency of a woman who demanded justice.

By experimentation modern metaphysical healers have discovered a large number of laws that rule in the realm of mind, and they all agree that no two cases are exactly alike. Therefore one who prays for the health of another should understand that it is not the fault of the healing principle that his patient is not instantly restored. The fault may be in his own lack of persistency or understanding; or it may be due to the patient's dogged clinging to discordant thoughts. In any case the one who prays must persist in this prayer until the walls of resistance are broken down and the healing currents are tuned in. Metaphysicians often pray over a critical case all night, as history says Luther prayed for the dying Melanchthon and brought about his recovery.

Persistency in prayer awakens the spiritual consciousness and sets into perpetual glow the core of the soul. When this has been accomplished, one is in a constant state of thanksgiving and praising, and the joy of a conscious union with creative Mind is realized.

Chapter VI - God Said, and It Was So

EMERSON said that the utterance of true ideas by one with a mission causes kings to totter on their thrones. Words of Truth from a zealous man possess dynamic power to heal and bless because the spiritual man enters into them. This is why they move multitudes and are not stayed by conditions or time. When the zone of Spirit, from which healing words emanate, is unobstructed, they feed the souls of men and are creative as well as re-creative. This is why the sayings of the prophets and mystics have such enduring qualities. They are attached by invisible currents of life to the one Great Spirit, and they have within them the germ of perfect wholeness that keeps them perpetually increasing.

The scriptures of the different races are examples of the outward expression of this inner germ. The Book of Job is a dateless work that has been preserved through great changes, including the rise and fall of nations. Who wrote it no one knows, but it was not lost with the loss of its custodians. They were wiped out, their lands taken from them, and they are no longer known among the nations of the earth, but the mystic word of Job was not consumed. If they had applied in their own lives the power of the germ word, the fate of these people would have been very different. But the history of the Book of Job is that of nearly all the sacred writings of all peoples. Secular histories and records of the exploits of men and the affairs of nations have disappeared and been forgotten because they told the tale of the passing world of flesh; but the records of those who had to do with the spiritual are preserved, and they are living today as they have lived ever since they were given forth: through the power derived from Spirit. The true prophet of God does not even have to write his words down. He may speak them to the ethers, and through their own inherent power of perpetuation and growth they will find their way into the minds of men to uplift and to heal. Jesus did not write a line except in the sand, yet His words are treasured today as the most precious that we have.

We know by these many examples that the word of Truth has life in it, that it has power to restore and make whole, and that it cannot perish or grow less with the changes that come with the fleeting years. The more spiritual the individual is who gives forth the words the more enduring they are, and the more powerfully the words move men the more surely they awaken them to their divine nature.

The words of Jesus Christ were given to common people--according to the world's standard--by a carpenter in a remote corner of the earth. Yet these words have moved men for more than nineteen hundred years to realize, to dare, and to do as no other words that were ever uttered.

When Jesus said, "The words that I have spoken unto you are spirit, and are life," He was speaking in terms of that inner Word which creates all things. He knew that His words were vivified with a life essence and a moving power that would demonstrate the truth of His statement.

These words have rung through the souls of men and set them afire with God's Spirit throughout the ages. This is because they are spiritual words, words that have within them the seeds of a divine life, of a perfect wholeness. They grow in the minds of all who give them place, just as a beautiful flower or a great tree grows from the seed germ planted in the ground.

Jesus knew that the consciousness of man was submerged in the things of sense, that it could not perceive Truth in the abstract, and that it must, under these conditions, be stirred into activity through some stimulating force dropped into it from without. Hence He sent forth His powerful words of Truth to the thirsty men, and said unto them, "Keep my word."

To "keep" a word is to resolve it in the mind, to go over it in all its aspects, to believe in it as a truth, and to treasure it as a saving, healing balm in time of need.

All peoples have in all ages known about the saving power of words and have used them to the best of their understanding to cast out demons and to heal the sick. The Hebrews bound upon their foreheads and wrists parchments with words of Scripture written upon them. The Hindus, Japanese, Chinese, and nearly all other nations have their various methods for applying sacred words to the alleviation of their ills, and for invoking the invisible powers to aid them in both their material and their spiritual needs. Although these methods are faulty in that they tend to use the letter of the word instead of its spirit, they are significant as indicators of the universal belief in the power of the sacred word.

We know that words express ideas, and to get at their substantial part we must move into the realm of ideas. Ideas are in the mind, and it is there we must go if we want to get the force of our words. The Hebrew's phylacteries and the Buddhist's prayer wheels are suggestive of the wordy prayers of the Christian; but this is not keeping the words of Jesus, nor reading the inner substance of the mystical words. This can be done only by those who believe in the omnipresent Spirit of God and in faith keep in mind the words that express His goodness, wisdom, power, and wholeness.

Jesus voiced this nearness of God to man more fully than any of the prophets, and His words are correspondingly vivified with the divine inner fire and life and wholeness. He said that those who keep His words will even escape death, so potent is the energy attached to them. This is a startling promise, but when we understand that it was not the personal man Jesus making it but the Father speaking through Him, then we know that it was not an idle one; for He said, "The word which ye hear is not mine, but the Father's who sent me." This is why these words of Jesus endure and why more and more they are attracting the attention of men as the years go by. That is the reason why Jesus' words heal.

Whoever takes Jesus' words into his mind should first consecrate himself to the Truth that they represent. That Truth is not the formulated doctrine of any church nor the creed of any sect; not even of Christianity. That truth is written in the inner sanctuary of every heart, and all men know it without external formulas. It is the intuitive perception of what is right in the sight of God and man. It is this Truth and justice which every man recognizes as the foundation of true living. Whoever consecrates himself to follow the inner monitor, the Spirit of truth, and lives up to its promptings regardless of social or commercial customs has consecrated himself to do God's will, and he is fitted to take Jesus' words and make them his own. His words are then spirit and life.

It is no idle experiment, this keeping in the mind the words of Jesus. It is a very momentous undertaking, which may mark the most important period in the life of the individual. There must be sincerity and earnestness and right motive, and withal a determination to understand its spiritual import. This requires attention, time, and patience in the application of the mind to solving the deeper meanings of the sayings that we are urged to "keep."

People have a way of dealing with sacred words that is too superficial to bring results. They juggle words. They toss them into the air with the heavenly tone or the oratorical ring and count that a compliance with divine requirements. But this is only another form of the prayer wheel and the phylactery. It is that lip service which Jesus condemned, because the purpose is to be "heard of men."

To keep the words of Jesus means much more than this. It has peculiar significance for the inner life, and it is only after this inner life is awakened that the true sense of the spiritual word is understood. But through his devotions the sincere keeper of Jesus' sayings will awaken this inner life or Spirit, and the Lord will come to him and minister to him as carefully as to the adept mystic.

Jesus said, "The words that I have spoken unto you are spirit, and are life." Spirit is that indescribable invisible cause that produces all reality. He who lives in the consciousness of effects alone can know nothing about Spirit, because he has not made himself acquainted with the realm in which it operates. But no one is barred from becoming acquainted with Spirit and residing in its domain. It is just as accessible as the material and far more attractive. If you want to know about Spirit, you will have to take up spiritual ways. You cannot go to the realm of Spirit by traveling the lower road. The road to the realm of Spirit does not lie on the map of the earth, and no man has found it in his physical geography. That spiritual things "are spiritually discerned" was the discovery of someone long ago, but he had no copyright on it. To him it was a revelation, just as it will be to you and to everyone when it dawns on the consciousness. It is a great advantage to the spiritual seeker to make this discovery. Millions of persons in every age have tried to find Spirit through matter and material ways, but they have returned unsuccessful to the dust. "For verily I say unto you, that many prophets and righteous men desired to see the things which ye see, and saw them not; and to hear the things which ye hear, and heard them not." They did not fulfill the promise of Jesus, because they saw death and succumbed to its dissolving hand. They missed the goal because they did not keep the words of Jesus. They kept the letter instead of the spirit. They applied in an abstract way what was intended for everyday practical use.

Jesus tells us that His words are spirit, and then says to keep them. How can we keep a thing that we know nothing about? How can we keep the words and sayings of Jesus unless we get right where He was and grasp them with our minds?

Surely there is no other way to keep His words. Those who are trying to do so from any other standpoint are missing the mark. They may be honest and they may be good, sincere people, living what the world calls a pure Christian life, but they are not going to get the fruits of Jesus' words unless they comply with the requirements.

"There's no getting blood out of a turnip" is a trite saying. Neither can you get Spirit and life out of matter and death. Unless you perceive that there is something more in the doctrine of Jesus than keeping up a worldly moral standard as preparation for salvation after death, you will fall far short of being a real Christian.

Jesus did not depreciate moral living; neither did He promise that it would fulfill the law of God. Very negative persons are frequently trustworthy and moral. But that does not make them Christians after the Jesus Christ plan. Jesus' Christianity had a living God in it, a God that lived in Him and spoke through Him. It was a religion of fire and water, of life as well as purity. Men are to be alive: not merely exist in a half-dead way for a few years and then go out with a splutter like a tallow dip. Jesus Christ's men are to be electric lights that glow and gleam with perpetual current from the one omnipresent energy. The connection with that current is to be made through the mind by setting up sympathetic energies.

The mind reacts to ideas, and ideas are made visible in words. Hence the holding of right words in the mind will set the mind going at a rate proportioned to the dynamic power of the idea back of the words. A word with a lazy idea back of it will not stimulate the mind or heal the body. The words must represent swift, strong spiritual ideas if they are to infuse the white energy of God into the mind. This is the kind of words that Jesus reveled in. He delighted in making great and mighty claims for His God, for Himself, for His words, and for all men: "I and the Father are one." "All authority hath been given unto me in heaven and on earth." "My Father . . . is greater than all." "Is it not written in your law, I said, ye are gods?" "He that believeth on me, the works that I do shall he do also; and greater works than these shall he do." These were some of the claims with which He stimulated His mind, and He produced the results: He fulfilled His words. He even raised the dead.

But He did not copyright His words or forbid anyone else to use them. He importuned you and me to keep them as He kept them--right in His heart--to realize that this is no idle repetition of words but the setting up of a living fire in the soul that will never go out. This is what the words of Jesus will do for everybody who keeps them in the inner sanctuary of the mind. They will kindle a fire there that will burn higher and higher until it licks the very canopy of heaven and burns a hole in the blue vault of Truth, revealing the wonders of God to the astonished eyes of man.

Jesus' words are varied, but all are food for the minds of His disciples. None of them is too hard for him who would be a disciple, nor is it too far from his present power of realization. What you now comprehend is not the ultimate of your ability in any direction. Your not consciously feeling that you and the Father are one does not militate against its being true. Men in high states of civilization lived for centuries on this planet without knowing that it was a globe and that just across the seas were other continents inhabited like their own. The race today is in the same position as regards the spiritual world. We look with longing eyes across a sea of doubts, fears, and delusions, trying to catch sight of the "Promised Land," but there seems to be no one to pilot us over. But here comes one who is to us a Columbus and who has given us a ship and compass. He has sailed the sea and found the other shore. He asks us to follow Him, and keep His words. His words are the ship and compass.

In about twenty places in the New Testament Jesus is recorded as saying in substance, "Follow me." When we inquire into Jesus' teaching, it is evident that He meant for us to follow His example of being receptive to God's wisdom, peace, power, and health. For instance, let us consider His healing of the man at the Pool of Bethesda who had been afflicted with an infirmity for thirty-eight years.

Now there is in Jerusalem by the sheep gate a pool, which is called in Hebrew Bethesda, having five porches. In these lay a multitude of them that were sick, blind, halt, withered. And a certain man was there, who had been thirty and eight years in his infirmity. When Jesus saw him lying, and knew that he had been now a long time in that case, he saith unto him, Wouldest thou be made whole? The sick man answered him, Sir, I have no man, when the water is troubled, to put me into the pool; but while I am coming, another steppeth down before me. Jesus saith unto him, Arise, take up thy bed, and walk. And straightway the man was made whole, and took up his bed and walked.

This healing of the man at the pool represents the power of the Christ (typified by Jesus) to restore the equilibrium of the organism through the activity of spiritual ideas in consciousness, independently of the healing methods utilized by the sense man. The true spiritual healing method employs the word of authority, as spoken by Jesus, which must be set into activity. Through the power of the word the "infirmity" gives place to perfect equalization and strength.

To the rich young man who desired to enter into eternal life Jesus recommended the keeping of the commandments, but in addition there was the inevitable "Sell that which thou hast, and give to the poor . . . and come, follow me." Faithfulness to law alone will never make you a follower of Jesus in the regeneration. You must go deeper than this; you must know the inner secrets of the universe. These are revealed in Spirit, and Spirit is found only by those who go about looking for it in an orderly way. People who have for years been students of the science of Christ and who have a clear intellectual perception of its truths are yet outside the kingdom of Spirit. They anxiously ask, "Why is it that I do not realize the presence of Spirit?"

Have you kept the "words" of Jesus? Have you said to yourself in silence and aloud until the very ethers vibrated with its truth, "I and the Father are one"? Have you opened your mind by mentally repeating the one solvent of crystallized conditions, "Even as thou, Father, art in me, and I in thee"? This means mental discipline day after day and night after night until the inertia of the mind is overcome and the way opened for the descent of Spirit.

The personal consciousness is like a house with all the doors and windows barred. He who lives within may hear voices without, but the doors and windows unlock from within, and it is left to him to unfasten them. The doors and windows of the mind are solidified thoughts, and they swing loose when the right word is spoken to them. Jesus voiced a whole army of right words, and if you will take up His words and make them yours, they will open all the doors of your mind, the light and air will come in, and in due time you will be able to step forth.

No one can do this for you. You do not really want another to do it although you sometimes think how nice it would be if some master of spiritual ideas would suddenly help you right into his understanding. But this is a childish dream of the moment. You want to be yourself, and you can be yourself only by living out your own life and finding its issues at the Fountainhead. If it were possible for one person to reveal the Truth to another, we should have heaven cornered by cunning manipulators of mind and its glories stored up in warehouses awaiting a higher market. Let us be thankful that God is no respecter of persons; that Truth cannot be revealed by one mortal to another. God is a special, personal Father to every one of His children, and from no other source can we get Truth.

Jesus, who has clearly revealed the Father in His consciousness, tells all men how it came about. He points out the way. He says, "I am the way, and the truth, and the life"; but there is always a condition attached to its realization by the seeker. He must "believe," he must "keep my words," "follow me." Summed up, the condition is that by adopting Jesus' methods you will find the same place in the Father that He found. But the Father is Spirit and spiritual understanding is the open sesame to His kingdom. The secrets of Jesus' words may be said to be in sealed packages to be opened by those only to whom is given "the mystery of the kingdom of God."

But Jesus did not peddle His doctrine. He did not copyright His "words." He claimed to hold converse with the Father, and He demonstrated extraordinary abilities in many ways in substantiation of this claim. He did not found a sect or in any way fence off His doctrine. He opened wide the way: "Whosoever believeth on me" and "keepeth" My words--shall do thus and so; shall do as I do and do greater things. He made a special prayer to the Father that all who kept His word might be made one with the Father as He was one with Him.

The mighty "words" of Jesus are handed down to us. By using them in the silent corridors of our own consciousness we may come into the place where He now is.

Chapter VII - Indispensable Assurance

MAN CAN be what he determines to be. He can be master or he can be serf. It rests with him whether he shall fill the high places in life or the low, whether he shall serve or be served, lead or be led, or be sickly or healthy. Of course we understand that these distinctions are relative only; in the sight of the Most High the servant may be prized more than his master, but there is within every one an inherent desire to be at the top, which desire has its root deep down in our very nature and is consequently legitimate. That it is frequently misdirected and used toward base ends is no reason why it should be depreciated. We all desire to excel. This desire is the inspiration of Spirit, which ever forces us up through earth toward heaven, and it should be encouraged and cultivated in the right direction.

A man without ambition is like a ship afloat on the waves without sails or power. Such a man simply drifts: if he reaches port safely it is by chance.

But a ship under full sail or power needs one other important thing and that is a rudder. Then it needs a man to handle that rudder, and that man needs faith.

In considering the character of faith we must start, as we do with everything else, in the one Mind. God must have had faith in order to ideate the universe before it was created; and man, being like God, must base his creations on faith. Faith is innate in man. A favorite definition of faith is that of Paul: "Faith is the assurance of things hoped for, a conviction of things not seen." It is by works of faith that we develop our consciousness and heal ourselves. The important question with everyone of us is, How does faith work?

It is possible to have a reality and yet neither touch it nor smell it nor see it nor in any way come into consciousness of it in the outer realm. That is what faith is. It is the consciousness in us of the realities of the attributes of mind. Before we can have the substance of faith we must realize that the mind creates realities. How do we create realities without seeing them, or feeling them, or smelling them, or tasting them, or in any way coming into outer consciousness of them? Faith is the wonderful power that builds these eternally real things.

Faith is a power of the spiritual mind, but in all the realms of existence we find faith. The foundation of faith is in the spiritual, but wherever you find the mind at work you find faith. Faith in its highest form is an exalted idea. And what is the most exalted idea that man can have? That he is spiritual; that he is related directly to the one great Spirit, and that through that Spirit he can do mighty works by faith.

Jesus laid great stress on faith. He always tried to direct the attention of the people to the invisible, the spiritual, by statements like these: "Believe ye that I am able to do this?" "According to your faith be it done unto you." "Thy faith hath made thee whole." All through His works there runs a golden thread of faith. Jesus did not advocate faith in material forces of any character. Through faith He healed thousands. His command was "Have faith in God."

We would not destroy anyone's faith in the lesser things, but would give him a sure foundation for all faith by directing his attention to the one and only source of faith, Divine Mind. The question for us is how to increase our faith in Spirit. You will find that you have plenty of faith. All men have faith, but it is scattered here and there and everywhere by being placed in lesser things, and those lesser things finally fail us.

If you get a good strong perception of something that your inner mind tells you is true, act upon it, and you will find that it will come true.

In developing His apostles Jesus took Peter as the representative of faith, and proclaimed that upon this foundation (of faith) He would build the new man, His "church" or aggregation of spiritual ideas. The faith demonstrated by Peter in the beginning of his career was not of a very high type. When Truth (represented by Christ) was being tried, Peter denied Jesus: said that he did not know Him and swore at Him, showing that Peter's faith must have been at a very low ebb when put to the test. At the very last Jesus tried Peter again and again, asking three times, "Lovest thou me?" Faith and love are very closely related. You must love the Lord, and then you must have faith in His spiritual power and continuity. Peter finally unfolded a mighty healing power. Even his shadow healed.

Now this faith that we are all cultivating and striving for is built up through continuous affirmations of its loyalty to the divine idea, the higher self. You must have faith in your spiritual capacity.

Many have learned how to hold the truth about health steadily in faith even in the midst of the most adverse appearances, and they clearly understand that they are not telling falsehoods when they deny sickness right in the face of the appearance of it. In the same way we achieve our victory over sin. When ill temper, vanity, greed, selfishness, and other sins of greater and lesser degree come up, they should be denied; and the unselfishness, the purity, the uprightness, and the integrity of the higher self should be affirmed. Persons who are quickened spiritually can do very much greater works through the law of faith than those who are still in the material consciousness; and once having discerned the power of Spirit, we should be on our guard and send forth on every occasion exalted ideas of the spiritual.

"I am the living bread which came down out of heaven: if any man eat of this bread, he shall live for ever." Jesus Christ raised people who had let go of the life idea and brought them into such a consciousness of omnipresent life that they came out of the tomb.

This life consciousness that Jesus Christ quickens is as greatly needed in our day as it was in the time when He first worked in the souls of men. If you go to a medical doctor and ask him the cause of your ills, he will tell you that most of them come from lack of vitality, which means lack of life. We all need vitalizing. The question is, How shall we get life? What is the source of life? Those who teach the use of material remedies point us to various things as the source--food, air, water, and so forth; but those who depend on these remedies are fast losing faith in drugs and are reaching out to electricity and similar means of gaining more abundant life. They are thus getting a little closer to the healing system of Jesus, but they still lack the all-important truth that God is life and that they who worship Him must worship Him in the life consciousness, that is, in Spirit. When we worship God in His way, we are vitalized all at once; there is no other way to get real, permanent life. We cannot get life from the outer man or from anything external; we must touch the inner current.

The life source is spiritual energy. It is deeper and finer than electricity or human magnetism. It is composed of ideas, and man can turn on its current by making mental contact with it.

When Jesus came teaching the gospel of Spirit, people did not understand Him. They did not know that universal Spirit is Principle and that we demonstrate it or fail to demonstrate it according to the character of our thinking. It has taken the race two thousand years to find that we turn on the life current by means of thoughts and words. We can have fullness of life by realizing that we live in a sea of abundant, omnipresent, eternal life, and by refusing to allow any thought to come in that stops the consciousness of the universal life flow. We live and move and have our being in life, Mind life. You can think of your life as mental; every faculty will begin to buzz with new life. Your life will never wane if you keep in the consciousness of it as Mind or Spirit; it will increase and attain full expression in your body. If you have faith in the life idea in your consciousness, your body will never be run down but will become more and more alive with spiritual life until it shows forth the glory of Christ.

We must think life, talk life, and see ourselves filled with the fullness of life. When we are not manifesting life as we desire, it is because our thoughts and our conversation are not in accord with the life idea. Every time we think life, speak life, rejoice in life, we are setting free, and bringing into expression in ourselves more and more of the life idea. Here is the place of abundant life, and we can fill both mind and body, both our surroundings and our affairs, with glad, free, buoyant life by exercising faith in it. "According to your faith be it done unto you."

In this way we enter into the same consciousness of abundant, enduring, unfailing, eternal life that Jesus had, and we can readily understand His proclamation that those who believe in the indwelling Christ life will never die. If we are wise, we shall cultivate faith in and understanding of omnipresent life.

I know a man who is a natural pessimist, and if anyone mentions something that is not to be emulated he will say, "Now, let us be careful about that." If you speak of someone who has been doing a good work for the community, he will always throw in a little depreciation. His whole life has been like sodden bread. Everything falls flat in his affairs, and he does not understand why it is. He says, "I have been studying this Truth for years, and I do not understand why I do not succeed." Intellectually he is a Truth seeker, but it has not taken hold of his faith substance. He doubts, and down he goes. When Peter tried to walk on the water to meet Jesus, he went down in the sea of doubt. He saw too much wetness in the water. He saw the negative side of the proposition, and it weakened his demonstration. If you want to demonstrate, never consider the negative side. If mountains seem to oppose the carrying out of your plans, say with Napoleon that there shall be no Alps. The man who is grounded in faith does not measure his thoughts or his acts by the world's standard of facts. "Faith is blind," say people who are not acquainted with the real thing; but those who are in spiritual understanding know that faith has open eyes, that certain things do exist in Spirit and become substantial and real to the one who dwells and thinks and lives in faith. Such a one knows.

Many Christians are like the woman who was on a ship during a great storm. She went to the captain and said, "Now I want to know just how bad it is." He told her plainly that they were in a very desperate and helpless condition and finished by saying, "We shall have to trust in God." She exclaimed, "Oh, dear! has it come to that?"

A close analysis shows that faith is the foundation of all that man does. The doctor knows that the patient's faith in him and his method is essential to his success. I remember a story told me by a lawyer: A certain attorney was subject to periodical headaches. He had some capsules prescribed by his physician that would cure these headaches almost instantly. For emergencies he carried one of the capsules in his vest pocket, and immediately upon swallowing it the pain would disappear. Once when pleading a case he was seized with a headache. He reached into his pocket, secured the little antidote and swallowed it, and immediately the headache left him. He went on with his argument, and after he sat down he wished to make some corrections in his notes, and felt in his pocket for a little rubber pencil tip that he carried for that purpose. Instead of the rubber tip he brought out a capsule, thus discovering that he had swallowed his pencil tip instead of the capsule.

This was an exhibition of faith asserting itself unawares. Suppose we should concentrate such faith on the invisible, the real things, the things of Spirit, how wonderful would be our demonstrations! How effective we should become in using the mighty working power of Spirit!

Jesus told His followers (and we are all His followers) to go forth and do His works--raise the dead and the like--and that we should do even greater works than He did. How? By exercising spiritual faith, by increasing our power through exalted ideas. We must raise our faith to the very highest in us and rest in the "assurance" or substance of its reality.

Jesus had faith in God, and this gave Him faith in all men. Spiritual understanding reveals the universality of all things. When they brought to Him the lame man on the couch, letting him down through the ceiling, "Jesus seeing their faith," healed him, not because of the faith of the man himself but because of the faith of those who brought him. The faith of his neighbors in the power of Spirit did the work for the sick man.

We believe that doctors are doing the very best they know; but if they would only approach a little closer to the spiritual, what a wonderful work they might do! They are giving less and less medicine every year. They recognize more and more that there is something back of medicine that they call the healing power of nature.

Nearly every doctor of large experience will tell you that he can get the same result with a little sweetened water that he can with drugs if he has the confidence of the patient. If the patient can be made to believe that the drug is going to work in a certain way, he will carry out this belief to the letter. Thus the word, the imagination, and faith work together.

Jesus had this high spiritual realization, and He healed through the word. He is the Great Physician. He is the one whom we are to follow, whom we are seeking to emulate; and we do it through laying hold of Spirit. I would say to you that if you want to do the works of God, you must follow Christ. If you want to elevate yourself out of the physical, you must have faith in God and must cultivate that faith through affirmation of your spiritual power and faith. The Lord's Prayer is continual affirmation from beginning to end.

It has been our experience in developing the faculties of mind that the more we affirm a certain thing the stronger it becomes. But we must have the understanding that our relation to God is that of a son to his father; that we exist in the one Mind as an idea, and that this idea does work in us as in a superman, even Christ.

It is a metaphysical law that there are three steps in every demonstration; the recognition of Truth as it is in principle; holding the idea; and acknowledging fulfillment. Pray believing that you have received, and you shall receive.

From the teaching of Jesus it is clear that He accepted fully the proposition that God is our resource and that all things are provided for us by our Father. It is necessary to cultivate these ideas by considering them daily in all that we do.

It is recorded that a pupil of Socrates' once said to him: "Master, when we read what you have inscribed we are inspired; when we come into your presence we are moved to love; when we hear your words we are charmed, and when we touch your hand we are thrilled."

Socrates was a great soul, a master mind, and his soul radiation was very powerful. But Jesus was still greater in His soul radiation; He had through ages of discipline and thought projection in word and deed made Himself a master scientist in the mental and spiritual worlds. His soul radiation or aura was so powerful that it perpetually stimulates to greater achievement and thrills with new life all who enter its sphere of influence. Thought transference is an accepted fact to many persons, and it is sustained by the recent tests in measuring the force projected in the process of human thinking. Machines have been invented so sensitive that they respond to the thoughts of men and women under various emotions. The results are reported to be so pronounced in their order and regularity as to constitute a universal law in mind activity.

This power of the mind to project the results of thinking gives us the key to the work of Jesus in resurrecting His body and making it perpetually radiant in our mental and spiritual atmosphere.

As there are dimensions above that in which we live so there are levels of mind activity above and beyond the intellectual. Jesus said, "In my Father's house are many mansions"; that is, dwelling places in mind or consciousness: states of consciousness.

"I go to prepare a place for you. . . . that where I am, there ye may be also."

The assertions by physical scientists that we have no assurance of any power that will increase our moral stature or save us from suffering and degeneracy is beyond comprehension to one who has gone deeply into the study of psychology and spiritual dynamics.

We may receive spiritual inspiration from within. By prayer and meditation on words of Truth in the silence we may so open our consciousness to the inner divine presence that the necessary understanding, love, and power may be given us to enable us to bring forth in our own lives the good results that we wish to see manifest. This is much better than waiting to see the demonstrations of others before believing and before attempting to bring forth demonstrations of our own.

After Thomas was shown the evidence he believed. After the outer reason sees the works accomplished by the I AM by means of faith and the word it accepts Truth. But there is a quicker way to grow in faith and in spiritual understanding, a way that has nothing to do with intellectual reasoning and belief. Jesus said, "Blessed are they that have not seen, and yet have believed." That way is the quickening of our innate spiritual faith.

True faith in God separates itself from all negative belief in the body as material, impure, transient.

With the growth of faith in the mind of the individual there comes a quickening of all his thoughts by the influx of Truth. "The word of God" increases.

God is never absent from you. He is constantly taking form in your life according to the exact pattern of your words, thoughts, and actions. Just as soon as you really bring your words and your expectations up to the measure of God's love for you, just that soon you will demonstrate.

Thoughts are seeds that, when dropped or planted in the subconscious mind, germinate, grow, and bring forth their fruit in due season. The more clearly we understand this truth the greater will be our ability to plant the seeds that bring forth desirable fruits. After sowing the plants must be tended. After using the law we must hold to its fulfillment. This is our part, but God gives the increase. You must work in divine order and not expect the harvest before the soil has been prepared or the seed sown. You have now the fruits of previous sowings. Change your thought seeds and reap what you desire. Some bring forth very quickly, others more slowly, but all in divine order.

The law of spiritual healing involves full receptivity on the part of the one under treatment. God does not do things in us against our will, as will acts in both the conscious and subconscious realms of mind. However much it may appear that the word is thwarted in its original intent, this is never true; it goes on, and it enters where reception is given it. In this way men are quickened, and whether we see the result with our physical vision or not, the process is as sure as God Himself.

In treating others we are told to see our patients as perfect. So in actualizing our ideals we must see them as if they were part of our phenomenal life. We often hear it said that the genius lives in a world of his own, separate and apart from common minds. From the metaphysical standpoint we see that the genius is merely one who has caught onto the law of believing his dreams of health, perfection, and success to be true, and whose dreams have therefore become true.

A genius is one who lets the full Spirit within him speak out, regardless of how different its utterances may be from those of people who have posed as authority. He has absolute faith in his spiritual revelations and fearlessly proclaims them. He is a pioneer and a leader. He listens to his own inherent genius and has faith in his God-given ability. Not only must he listen but he must act. The world is filled with original dreamers. They have ideas brilliant beyond expression, but they do not clothe them in the habiliments of action.

You must not only perceive and idea; you must also give it form by infusing into it the substance of your living faith. Daydreamers may be found by the score in physics and metaphysics. They all fall short in failing to realize that there are two sides to every proposition, the image and the expression: and that the Lord God formed man out of the ground and breathed into his nostrils the breath of life.

So each one of us must not only see the image of his desires as a theory, but he must also form it into a living, breathing thing through every motive and act of his life. That is, if we have an idea, we must act just as if it were part of our life. We must be formed from the substance of our world, whether it be the dust of the ground or the ethers of the invisible. There must be an actual imaging of them in our consciousness before we shall ever see our ideas realized.

Here is where the dreamer and the divine scientist part company. One says, "I admire your theories greatly, but they can never be realized on this earth. Things are as they are, and they cannot be changed. We are here, and we shall just have to make the best of it."

He who has learned the meaning of man--who and what man is--never allows himself to make any such admissions. He knows that there is a way provided by which he not only can lift himself out of the swamp of belief in sin, sickness, and death but also through his efforts open the way for many others to find the way to perfection. No man ever demonstrated his God-given powers in even a small way who did not help many others to do likewise. Preaching is good, but practice is better. "I, if I be lifted up from the earth, will draw all men unto myself."

There is a work for everyone who will listen and obey the Spirit. That work is important, because it is eternal and brings results eternal in their nature.

If you have heard the voice of the Lord and are obedient to it at any cost, you are chosen. Your life is hid with Christ in God, and the way into the kingdom is assured you.

This is no fanciful sketch, nor does it refer to a theoretical place or condition to be reached in some future state or under circumstances more propitious. This kingdom of God is now existing right here in our midst. It is being externalized little by little.

Whoever has a high, pure thought and affirms his allegiance to it as a part of his daily life is adding to the externality of that kingdom among men. Whoever says, "I will be upright and honest in all that I think and do," is laying the foundation stones for one of the buildings of the New Jerusalem.

Whoever affirms his allegiance to the good, regardless of all appearance of evil, and in dealing with his brother declares by word and act that only the good exists, is building white spires to the one and only true God.

Whoever lays up in his mental storehouse the resolve "I will do unto others as I would have them do unto me" is paving the highways with pure gold in a heavenly city of equity and justice.

There will be no need of the sun or the moon in the city of the kingdom of God, because God, the good, will be the light thereof.

We are the temples of God, of good, and through us is this light to shine, which is so bright as to dim the rays of those shining orbs of the night and the day. Herein is God glorified that we love one another. Herein does the true light shine that we let love and peace and kindness shine forth forever and always. We are to be the very light itself and we can only be the light by becoming so pure that it cannot help but shine through us. This is possible to the highest and lowest in the world's roster of respectability. We are all the chosen of the Lord and we make the covenant that carries us into His visible presence by laying down the personal man and taking up the universal man. He it is that thunders in the depths of our soul. "Who say ye that I am?"

Chapter VIII - The Fullness of Time

ALL SANE persons acknowledge the necessity of observing the laws of health in their daily living, but the great majority have a human standard. Now that the whole race is awakening to the knowledge of a higher source of existence more people every day are giving attention to the law of Spirit in their life.

"Order is heaven's first law." If we desire to demonstrate health when we receive more spiritual life, we must order this life rightly, for if it is not so ordered, mental and physical discord will ensue. This applies to all that we think and do. Everything must be brought into order. If we affirm prosperity, that too must be brought into orderly relations to the rest of our thinking. We may be declaring life and prosperity and at the same time be holding some disorganizing thought. This will produce inharmony and discord in body and affairs. Lack of orderly arrangement of thoughts is responsible for many delayed demonstrations of healing.

We find in the Scriptures constant reference, in symbols and also in direct language, to order as a fundamental law of the universe and of man. There must be order in the spiritual life as well as the material life. All peoples have observed this, and especially the people of God. Paul said, "Let all things be done decently and in order."

Suggestion is systematically used in the business world, and unless you are strong in your own convictions as to what your needs are, you will be loaded up with many things for which you have no use. The remedy is to establish yourself in the spiritual law. You will come under one or the other of these laws, the man-made or the spiritual, and it is for you to choose which is best.

You want to know then the metaphysics of order as a means of demonstrating health. How can you order your life by the divine plan? By accepting it as a truth that there is such a plan and by making this plan yours through affirming your oneness with the omnipresent Mind in which this plan exists in its righteousness. Say, "I am the offspring of God, and I am one with His perfect wisdom, which is now ordering my life in divine harmony and health." Ask for wisdom; then affirm divine order. Put yourself in unity with Spirit. Then you will come into the consciousness of a new world of thought and act and find yourself doing many things differently because the orderly Mind that directs the universe is working through you. A harmonious relation will be established in all your ways. Whatever there was in mind, body, or affairs that was out of harmony will easily be adjusted when you open the way in your mind for the manifestation of divine order.

The bringing forth of man even in the material sense is an orderly process. The birth of Jesus is an example. His coming was foretold and arranged beforehand. It was not left to chance. His mother "magnified" the Lord before He was born. This illustrates the truth that it is necessary to have order from the very beginning. The bringing forth of John the Baptist is an example of the coming of another state of consciousness and of the necessity of law and order in prenatal culture.

The same law holds good in our body and our affairs. The power of the word should be expressed in our homes. We should surround ourselves with words suggestive of spiritual things. If words count, and we know they do, we should be careful of every idea taken into consciousness through the eye as well as through the ear.

From their inception to their expression words are important. The law is fulfilled not only in mind but in manifestation also. Every suggestion that enters the mind brings forth like expression in act. The time is coming when it will be unlawful to print in the daily papers any record of crime or of anything that will bring discord into the minds of readers. Recently I read of a man who committed a crime, and in his pocket was found a newspaper clipping describing almost identically the same criminal act. His crime was the fruit of suggestion. How many such suggestions does one large daily paper carry to its thousands of readers in its recital of the daily horrors that make up the news?

As the world comes more and more under the spiritual law editors and publishers will not ask their readers what they want, but will give them what they should have for mental food. And as the people are raised to higher planes of consciousness they will demand reading of an uplifting character. They will be just as careful as regards what they read as they are now beginning to be in reference to food. There will be the same demand for pure reading as for pure food. If it is against the law of the land to adulterate food, how much more is it against the law of right thinking to adulterate the truth. We can see the necessity of order and law according to Spirit. If we would demonstrate health, every deleterious thought should be kept out of our mental atmosphere even more carefully than harmful elements are kept out of our material food.

This spiritual law is operative in food and clothing. If we think about order and harmony our taste in material things will change. We shall desire the purest foods, and there will be more harmony in the colors we choose to wear. "If God doth so clothe the grass of the field . . . shall he not much more clothe you?" Some people think it is impossible for man to be clothed like the lilies. But if man stands above all creation, has he not power to clothe himself in the richness and glory of Spirit? Out of the air we may manufacture the things we eat and wear. This is not a flight of fancy. Chemists are already considering the possibility. It is not an assumption of theoretical metaphysics that we may be able to make our food and clothing from the air, but a logical conclusion that follows the understanding of God as the omnipresent source of all that appears. So long as we believe in the slow processes of what we call nature we shall place ourselves under a law of slowness. But if we know the spiritual law of health and the power of the word, we shall bring into operation in our lives an entirely different law. Where is the limit to the power of thought?

So let us begin anew and lay down the law of order in all that we do. If there is a tendency to hurry, let us stop and affirm divine order and rest ourselves in its poise. Geologists tell us that our world has been whirling around the sun for over five hundred million years. So you see there is no need to hurry. Remember that you live in eternity now. This thought of omnipresent eternity will alleviate nervous tension. Put every thought and act under the divine law. Even if you think you are going to miss a car, do not hurry. Another car will be right along, and if your mind is in divine order, it will be your car.

If you are disorderly and indefinite along any line, put yourself at once under the order of Divine Mind by affirming daily that the same law that swings the stars in the cushioned ethers is operative in and through your life and all your affairs.

All people who have studied metaphysics and understand somewhat the action of the mind recognize that there is one underlying law and that through this law all things come into expression; also that there is one universal Mind, the source and sole origin of all real intelligence. First is mind, then mind expresses itself in ideas, then the ideas make themselves manifest. This is a metaphysical statement of the divine Trinity, Father, Son, and Holy Spirit. The trinity Mind, the expression of Mind, and the manifestations of Mind are found in simple numbers and complex combinations everywhere.

The metaphysics of the Hebrew Scriptures are based on this law of the Trinity. They were written far ahead of the race thought, and it is probable that those who wrote them did not understand all that was involved in the word of the Spirit. It is seldom that great writings are fully understood. Not many years after Shakespeare's demise a book aiming to give the names of all the English poets was published in London, and Shakespeare's name was left out. It is said that a great man must be dead five hundred years before his work will be appreciated.

In the King James Bible the Hebrew "Jehovah" has been translated "Lord." Lord means an external ruler. Bible students say that Jehovah means the self-existent One, the I AM. Then instead of reading "Lord" we should read I AM. It makes a great difference whether we think of I AM, self-existence within, or "Lord," master without. All Scripture shows that Jehovah means just what God told Moses it meant: I AM. "This is my name for ever, and this is my memorial unto all generations." So instead of "Lord" say I AM whenever you read it and you will get a clearer understanding and realization of what Jehovah is. God was known to the Israelites as Jehovah-shalom: "I am peace." You can demonstrate peace of mind by holding the words "I am peace."

If we start any such demonstration and try to apply the I AM to personality, we fall short. This is frequently the cause of lack of results in carrying out the laws that all metaphysicians recognize as fundamentally true. The mind does not always comprehend the I AM in its highest, neither does it discern that the all-knowing, omnipotent One is within man. This recognition must be cultivated, and everyone should become conscious of the I AM presence. This consciousness will come through prayer and meditation upon Truth. In Truth there is but one I AM, Jehovah, the omnipotent I AM that is eternally whole and perfect. If you take Jehovah-shalom into your mind and hold it with the thought of a mighty peace, you will feel a consciousness, a harmonizing stillness, that no man can understand. This consciousness is healing in itself. It must be felt, realized, and acknowledged by your individual I AM before the supreme I AM can pour out its power. Then you will know that you have touched something; but you cannot explain to another just what it is, because you have gone beyond the realm of words and made union with the divine cause. It is the quickening of your divinity through the power of the word. This divine nature is in us all, waiting to be brought into expression through our recognition of the power and might of the I AM; so Jehovah-rapha is "I am he that healeth thee."

We should not fail to think always of the spiritual law under which the I AM moves. It is possible for man to take I AM power and apply it in external ways and leave out the true spiritual law. In our day we are proclaiming that man can use I AM power to restore health and bring increased happiness; in fact, that through righteous, lawful use of the I AM he can have everything that he desires. But some people are using this power in a material way, neglecting soul culture, building up the external without taking the intermediate step between the supreme Mind and its manifestation in the outer. We should remember that the soul must grow as well as the body. For example, a man was overtaken with physical disability and loss of eyesight some years ago. In his extremity he turned to the spiritual law for help and was very faithful in its mental application. I saw him not long since; his physical condition was unchanged, but there was a great change in his mind. He had found the light and he was filled with inward rejoicing. He had become blind that he might see. However his family thought all his dependence upon Truth had been a failure because his physical sight had not been restored. During all these years however he has managed his business, and it has prospered, and his family has been well provided for. He was himself for a time disappointed and rebellious because his eyes were not healed; but now he is glad, because through the prayers and meditations he has found the inner light. His physical sight will be restored when he has made the complete connection between mind and body.

So if you find yourself disappointed because you do not at once demonstrate health or success, be at peace and know that your earnest prayers and meditations are working out in you a soul growth that will yet become manifest beyond your greatest hopes.

It is easier to seek the Truth willingly and be watchful and obedient than it is to be forced by some severe experience. Hard experiences are not necessary if we are obedient to the Truth that saves us from them. Time should be given to prayer and meditation daily. We cannot grow without them, and no man who neglects them will successfully develop his spiritual powers.

The great I AM is not far away from man. Spirit is closely connected with the little things of daily life. "The kingdom of God is come nigh unto you." This means that the mighty One is with us in all ways. We are all in touch, heart with heart, and a real sympathy makes us one. In reality we all love the simple life. The pomp and parade and pageantry of the external world do not satisfy the soul. It is the small things that touch the heart and appeal to us. We want realities. Even in the drama we demand the realistic. I once read of a playwright who tried to give all his scenes the touch of realism, and in one place he had electric fans so placed that they would blow to the audience the odors of the viands that the actors were eating, thus convincing the people that the food was real.

While one of his plays was being given a cat strayed in, stretched before the fireplace, lay down and went to sleep. The audience applauded. This added a touch of naturalness that the playwright was anxious to introduce as a permanent feature of the play. But it is hard to get a cat to do things when you want it to do them. However the playwright set himself to studying how he could induce the cat to go through with its part, and he hit upon this plan: About noon each day he shut the cat up in a very small box so that it had no room to stretch; then he let it out just at the time its appearance on the stage was desired. Of course the first thing it did was to stretch, then drink from a saucer of milk set ready for it; then it would lie down before the fireplace and go to sleep. So he solved the problem, and this little touch of commonplace realism became the hit of the play.

It is on such little things as these that success hinges in the play called "life." The I AM might is not in the storm nor in the earthquake nor in the fire but in the "still small voice," according to Elijah.

We are receiving new truth in all fields, and if we are to use it, it seems most important that our religion be progressive, that we get new and higher concepts, and that we see deeper and more scientific relations in the lessons and experiences of those who have preceded us in study and demonstration of spiritual Truth.

If there is science in the universe, there must be science in the Mind that projected the universe. If there is mathematical accuracy and order in the material world, there is a like accuracy and order in the mental world. If there is science in the relation of atom to atom, if there is science in the current that flows over the wire and sets in motion the electric fan, there must be science in the Mind back of all these manifestations.

God created all things by His mind, by His thought, by the power of His word. The divine fiat went forth, "Let there be," and there was. The one Mind is still projecting itself into the universe, and its law of health is expressed by man through thought rightly directed. The highest expression of divine thought is man. God created man in His image, in the image of perfect health. How important then that man should study the science of mind and in every way seek to find the law lying back of the harmonious universe in which he functions.

If we make living cells through the power of thought, we should know something of the law underlying the process. On every hand thoughtful men are searching for the scientific cause of things. Here is an illustration that came to my attention. The woman in the case, an ardent Unity student, had a husband who thought Truth was all foolishness. She did not urge it upon him directly, but she would call his attention to various healings. He paid no attention until his mother was healed of a mole on her face. This woman said to her husband: "Your mother's healing was due to the withdrawal of her nourishing thought. That mole is gone." "How did it go?" he asked, showing some interest for the first time. His mother said: "I withdrew the nourishing thought. Before that I had mourned over it and wished it were not there, and that nourished it and sent vital forces into it and it kept growing." "I suggested that she quit thinking about it," said the wife; "that she quit nourishing it, and it gradually withered and disappeared." The husband said: "I can see how through our thought we do nourish these conditions in our bodies. If there is such power behind this healing system I am willing to think about it. There is something satisfactory in knowing that one may learn how healing works. I can see as a reasonable proposition that mind acts on the body through nerves and that the conditions are nourished by thought. When Mother stopped thinking about that mole, it was no longer nourished and consequently disappeared. That appeals to my reason. I thought this was a religion, a sect; but if it is something that a logical mind can understand, I want to know more about it." You will find persons like that everywhere. They think this is some new religion, and when they come to understand that it is absolute science they are willing to look into it. This man saw the truth when it was explained to him.

We may nourish a good thing by thinking how good it is--a beautiful face, a beautiful form, whatever it may be that is good; but suppose we take the negative side, shall we then get results also? Yes, absolutely. We shall get just what we think about. The thought of nourishing is a very good thought, because it shows us just what we do. Our mind draws upon the vital forces, and according to physiological laws we alter our tissues. Either we tear down our bodies or we build them up.

Is that all that is necessary? No, that is only one phase of mind activity. Withdraw the error; then build in the good. Some people leave out this second step. When you get into this understanding of the mind it is always good to use both the denial and the affirmation. Sometimes the denial will produce wonderful results. But this law of the mind working on the body is applicable to both the inner and the outer.

You will get suggestions from newspapers. You may read about some healing drug and a description of how your cold is going to develop into pneumonia and then into consumption if you do not buy some of it. You read the advertisement, which describes in minute detail how terrible you feel, and you say, "Yes, that's my case exactly." If you do this, you will nourish that sick thought. Is it wise then to let this law of mind operate in this way? No. Avoid these things. Don't give yourself up to them.

The universe was not created through illogical assumptions of law. Law is its foundation. There are no miracles in science. Jesus did no miracles. All His marvelous works were done under laws that we may learn and use as He did. As the body is moved by mind, so the mind is moved by ideas; and right here in the mind we find the secret of the universe. This is where Jesus differed from ordinary men: He knew He was the Son of God; He knew the power of spiritual ideas to do mighty works: "The Father abiding in me doeth his works."

Before you can realize the mighty power of ideas you must unify them. All must pull together. Get your ideas in divine order, and a mighty mind force will begin to work for you right away. This divine order is necessary to the upbuilding of both mind and body. This divine order is the "kingdom of heaven" so often referred to by Jesus. To attain this unity and harmony of mind it is necessary to have perfect statements of Truth and to adhere to them in thought and word. States of mind can be set into activity just as through the manipulation of gases, electricity, and so forth we may purify or impart certain potencies to the atmosphere. In a far larger degree ideas change the race thought atmosphere. Jesus had a grasp of divine ideas, and if we believe in and follow Him we shall come into the Christ state of mind. We become like-minded by entering into the absolute Mind. In the absolute Mind there is only harmony.

Spirit is a vigorous stimulant. It uplifts the whole consciousness, vitalizes the organs, and gives us courage and endurance. It also tends to make one supersensitive. In this state one is liable to more rapid waste, especially if fleshly indulgence of any kind is gratified. Failing to restrain one's passions and appetites quickly burns up the cells, and then the collapse is even more complete than before the healing. In order to guard against this students should be instructed carefully in the truths of Being. They must learn that "the wages of sin is death," that they must master their appetites and passions.

As man unifies his own mind forces in the one Mind his body is lifted up into a new state of harmony. If he is not demonstrating this principle, it is because he is not unified with the one great harmonious Mind. He is not expressing this Mind as he should because he is not realizing his oneness with it. Resolve to become one with God through Christ. Harmonize yourself with Him and all your world will be in harmony. Be on the alert to see harmony everywhere. Do not magnify seeming differences. Do not keep up any petty divisions but continually declare the one universal harmony. This will insure perfect order and wholeness. The Christ Mind is here as the unifying principle of this race, and we must believe in this mind working in us and through us and know that through it we are joined to the Father-Mind. That is the Father's house to which, like the prodigal son, we have all so long been seeking to return. In the consciousness of the Father-Mind the unity of God and man is demonstrated.

The fact that you can always return to the Father's house, the ideal world, carries with it the possibility of fulfillment in your life expression. In Being you cannot shirk expression. To think is to express, and you are doing that without cessation. You may deny that these things of the world have existence, yet so long as you live in contact with them you are recognizing their place. A wholesale denial of their existence keeps you even as a house divided against itself. A reconciliation must take place before you can demonstrate the power of the Christ man over death. Jesus did not say that His body was nothing, but He did say, "I have power to lay it down, and I have power to take it again." He laid it down in corruption and raised it up in incorruption. He found that His ideal was not being expressed in the body, which was subject to decay; so He let the corruptible be crossed out and from the ruins raised the body of light, which appeared and disappeared at will. This was the fulfillment of His ministry and the demonstration of the power of the Spirit to overcome the last enemy, death.

All men desire to overcome disease and death. The fulfillment of this desire would be the perpetuation of existence in form. So in the last analysis we see that we all want to continue our chain of expression indefinitely, without break. This has always been the desire of mankind, and the whole world is today and ever has been fighting this monster death. Oceans of medicine are swallowed daily, millions of doctors are exerting all their energies, and prayers unnumbered are uttered in a blind struggle to vanquish this dreaded enemy of mankind. This indicates a most powerful desire to be fulfilled. Jesus showed how it might be done and gave the recipe. He said, "Verily, verily, I say unto you, If a man keep my word, he shall never see death." He also said: "The word which ye hear is not mine, but the Father's who sent me" and "The words that I have spoken unto you are spirit, and are life."

There is a chain of mind action connecting cause and effect in all the activities of life. This chain is forged by man, and its links are thoughts, words. Jesus laid great stress upon the power of the word. Yet He was wise in the injunction that His words should be kept; that is, men were to keep before them the ideal that He had. This realm of the ideal is the realm from which the word draws its substance, and its character determines the result.

The "sayings" of Jesus were charged with tremendous significance. They raised the idea of man and God far above what had ever before been conceived. They so far transcended the thought plane of the people that even His followers could not accept them, and many "walked no more with him." It is but a few years since the followers of Jesus began to grasp the power of the word as taught by Him. Who in the past has taken Jesus literally and sought to overcome death by keeping His sayings? Many have believed in His doctrine, and a great ecclesiastical industry has been built upon it as a foundation; but who has taken in full faith the words of Jesus and made them flesh of his flesh and bone of his bone by not only believing in them but by saturating his mind with them until they reincarnated themselves in his body? This achievement is the secret of every spiritual demonstration; it is not only a concept of what is true of Being but a carrying out in thought, word, and act of that concept.

If I can conceive a truth, it follows that there is a way by which I can make it manifest. If I can conceive of omnipresent life as existing in the omnipresent ethers, there is a way by which I can make that life appear in my body. When once the mind has accepted this as an axiomatic truth, it has arrived at the point where the question of procedure arises. No one ever fully sees the steps he is to take in reaching a goal. He may see in a general way that he is to go on from one point to another, but the details are not definitely clear to him unless he has gone over the ground before. The architect tells the builder to follow the plans. So in this demonstration of the spiritual powers that are ready to find expression through man he must be willing to follow the directions of one who has proved his efficiency by demonstration.

We all intuitively know that there is something wrong in a world where poverty, suffering, and sorrow prevail. We would not, any of us, create such a world. We all want to see these things blotted out in this world. This is the index pointing the way to the possibility of doing so. Whatever we see as wrong is for us to right. Lack of health is not prevalent in God's universe, and if such lack appears anywhere it is the work of man, and it is our duty to do away with it.

There is a way, the "highway of the Lord." Will you take that way? It is a broad way, and there is room for everybody. Jesus called it the kingdom of the heavens and said that "all these things" should be added to those who sought it. This implies that you do not have fully to enter this kingdom in order to have the things added, but you do have to "seek." You must turn your attention in the right direction; then they begin to come to you.

This is being proved by many thousands in this age who have accepted the promises of Scripture literally and are looking to God for every need, health included. They may not in the beginning of the seeking have a single thing to encourage them. They just accept the promise, proceed to carry it out in faith, and act as if it were true, and all at once new life and new strength are theirs. This encourages them to go on still further in seeking this kingdom of God, and eventually they will demonstrate the perfection of Christ.

These are they who have wisely used their one talent. They may not have caught sight of the holy of holies in the inner sanctuary, but they are gradually getting closer and closer to it. This is the step that everybody is commanded to take. Trust God in all things, and see the result made apparent by the mental currents that you set going all about you. You may not be able to point out just how each separate word of allegiance to the Father took effect, but as the months go by you will gradually observe the various changes that are taking place in your mind, body, and affairs. You will find that your ideas have broadened immensely to begin with. The little world has been transformed into a big world. You have begun to think about realities instead of appearances. Your mind is more alert, and you can discern when before you were in doubt. Your body is vital, and you are free from inharmony and weakness. You are not so fearful. The consciousness that there is a divine hand guiding the universe and you has given you a feeling of security. This has extended to your body and your affairs. There is an absence of prejudice and faultfinding in you. You do not judge so harshly. You are more generous, and others respond by being more generous too. Things are coming your way now where you once thought they were blocked.

This is not only true of your own particular life and affairs, but if you are observing you will notice its effect in a measure upon those with whom you come in contact. They are getting more substantially healthy and happy. They may not in the remotest way connect it with you or your thoughts, but that does not affect the truth about it. All things have their cause, and every cause is mental. Whoever comes in daily contact with a high order of thinking cannot help but take on some of it. His mind takes it on unconsciously just as his lungs breathe the air of the room. Ideas are catching, and no man can live where true ideas of wholeness and abundance and peace are being held without becoming more or less infected with them. "For none of us liveth to himself." Health is the divine heritage of every human being.

Chapter IX - Healing through Praise and Thanksgiving

I PRAISE and give thanks that the strength and power of Thy Spirit now restores me to harmony and health.

"Always praise the cooking of the cook" is the instruction of the veteran hobo to the novice. Experience has taught the gentlemen of the road that praise and thanks melt the hardest heart and often open the door to amazing hospitality. Tradespeople have found that "Thank you" has commercial value.

Metaphysicians have discovered that words which express thanks, gratitude, and praise release mind energy of mind and Soul; and their use is usually followed by effects so pronounced that they are quickly identified with the words that provoke them.

Let your words of praise and thanksgiving be to Spirit, and the increase will be even greater than when they are addressed to man. The resources of Spirit are beyond our highest flight of imagination. You can praise a weak body into strength, a fearful heart into peace and trust, shattered nerves into poise and power.

I give thanks for the Christ life now apparent in my mind and body.

It is an easy matter to give thanks for what we have already received, but it is not so easy to give thanks for what we hope to receive. However giving thanks in advance brings to pass a present expectation. Remember what Jesus said about one's mental attitude in demonstrating spirituality: "All things, whatsoever ye shall ask in prayer, believing, ye shall receive." This may be rephrased in this wise: Pray believing that you have received, and you shall receive.

Christians who have discovered the hidden laws of the mind make it a practice to give thanks for health, for peace of mind, for all things that they desire, believing that God has given in Spirit that which is to appear in the visible.

I daily praise and thank the Spirit of life and health for constantly restoring me to perfection of body.

Praising and giving thanks liberate the finer essence of soul and body when we center our attention upon Spirit. Spirit is the dynamic force that releases the pent-up energies within man. The energies have been imprisoned in the cells, and when released are again restored to action in the body by the chemistry of creative Mind. The perfection of this restoration is in proportion to the understanding and industry of the individual.

Every thought we loose in our mind carries with it a certain substance, life, and intelligence. So we might call our thoughts our "thought people." Whenever praise is bestowed on these thought people, who are intelligent, it is carried to every part of the body and through the ether to a large area of our soul aura, and our whole consciousness and everything about us is tinctured with praise. Thus we prove what Jesus proclaimed, that when we seek His kingdom and His righteousness all things are added to us.

The prophets of old knew the power of increase inherent in thanksgiving. "Praise ye Jehovah" is repeated again and again in the Psalms, because the Psalmist knew that praise and thanksgiving divinely directed tap the mighty reservoirs of infinite Mind.

Jehovah-shalom gives me peace of mind, and I am harmonized and healed.

The Bible contains more high mysticism than all other books. But it requires study of certain fundamental spiritual principles to discern it. Spiritual things are spiritually discerned. Unless you call on your own innate spiritual light you cannot appreciate spiritual insight of those who wrote the books of the Bible.

The idea that all the Bible writers were equally inspired is fallacious. They were from every walk of life, and their inspirations were modified by their own mental bias as well as their surroundings. Moreover some of the most important revelations of fundamental principles are undoubtedly the result of borrowing. Although Moses was a trained mystic and inspirational writer, he did not originate all the allegories found in the books that bear his name. It is obvious from the testimony of religious records antedating the Hebrew Scriptures by thousands of years that Moses complied and edited for the benefit of the Israelites.

This discovery does not detract from the truth or importance of the writings but greatly enhances them. The very fact that these sacred writings have been preserved for untold ages points to them as possessing unusual value and as conservers of worthwhile knowledge.

Studying the Bible in the light of the discoveries of modern science, we are amazed at the scientific accuracy of the statements in the early chapters of Genesis. Have men in past ages been wiser than those of the present or were they inspired beyond their understanding? For example, in the 3d verse of the 1st chapter of Genesis, God created the light on the first day, yet the sun, the supposed source of light, was not created until the fourth day. This supposed error in the orderly creative process often has been cited as evidence of crudity by Bible critics. But the very modern scientific discovery that the sun is not the source of light, that the sun merely radiates the light that originates in universal etheric waves proves that Moses was right. So what we call light is not the real light, but a luminous effect produced in our earthly atmosphere. So also all life originates in the ether, and not in the earth, where scientists have vainly sought it. When science admits, as it eventually will, that the ether is moved by omnipresent Mind, we shall have in the Bible a complete spiritual cosmogony.

The Bible is a perpetual revelation to Truth seekers on account of its allegorical character. This is especially outstanding in Genesis, which veils in names and ordinary incidents some of the great truths of creation. The names of the Divinity are not all the same in the Hebrew. Elohim God represents the original Mind in creative action. El means the strong and ever-sustaining one, and alah, to swear or formulate by the power of the word. Here also is implied plurality of attributes in addition to masculine and feminine qualities. Elohim thus represents the universal principle of Being designing all of creation. In the 2d chapter another name for God is used-Jehovah God-metaphysically representing the executive power Elohim. This name is also rich in occult significance. Yahweh is the original form, and its meaning is "the self-existent one" at work or becoming known or revealing Himself to His creation and through His creation. Yahweh revealed Himself to Moses as "I AM THAT I AM." He reveals Himself to every one of us according to our needs when we call upon Him. He revealed Himself to Jesus as the Father within.

The Hebrew teachers gave compound names to Jehovah to meet every situation. That is, they invoked His I AM presence as a creative factor in producing the thing needed. When they needed supply, they invoked Jehovah-jireh, "Jehovah will provide." Jehovah-rapha is "the Lord that healeth thee." Jehovah-shalom is "Jehovah is peace" or "the Lord send peace." The whole world needs peace today as never before, and peace will not be ushered in until men call on the name of Jehovah.

It may sound foolish in the sight of men for a small group of people to call on Jehovah-shalom to make peace in the midst of war, but great miracles have resulted from such action. Jehovah-shalom will save us from personal worry and fear of future ills. It was the Jehovah-shalom in Jesus that proclaimed, "My peace I give unto you: not as the world giveth, give I unto you. Let not your heart be troubled, neither let it be fearful" (John 14:27).

I am a tower of strength and stability in the realization that God is my health."

It is the conclusion of the followers of Jesus that a new and original interpretation of His teaching has sprung up in the last half century. The adherents of this new religion, for such it seems to be, claim that they have a revelation of Christianity that far transcends the old in spiritual understanding and power. The new religion makes Jesus a demonstrator of scientific mind laws that any industrious student can understand and apply as Jesus applied them. In addition to this the new Christianity elevates man to a realm in which seeming miracles of healing become possible to those who train their mind to think spiritually, carrying out the admonition of Paul "Be ye transformed by the renewing of your mind" (Rom.12:2).

As all the physical science books have to be re-written since the discovery that electricity is the mother of matter, so all books of religion that ignore psychology will have to be rewritten.

The new Christianity claims that Jesus Christ understood the real character of space and ether as taught by science and that it is the home of a great and mighty life and intelligence that brought man and the universe into manifestation.

Instead of fighting modern science the new Christianity welcomes its discoveries as proofs of the veritable existence of the kingdom of the heavens that Jesus taught so persistently.

Instead of a heaven after death the new Christianity teaches a kingdom of the heavens existing now as a righteous state of mind. It teaches that man makes his heaven here and now by the formative power of his thought.

It is by way of this emphatic and constant emphasis on the formative power of thought that the new Christianity launches out into the deep. Instead of God's creating man with a mighty word fiat and arbitrarily following it up with vengeance and punishments, God is discerned to be a mind principle that requires the co-operation of its creations, because they are formed of it and in it and are so like it that there is virtual action and reaction between Creator and creation. This places the responsibility for conditions on both God and man. When we think and work in unity with the Father the results are universally good. When we work without reference to the inspiring Mind within our work is usually unsatisfactory. "My Father worketh even until now, and I work," said Jesus.

Then the carping critic cries, "Your religion is psychology instead of Christianity." Our answer is that the new Christianity includes an understanding of psychology but does not stop with an analysis of the mind. It goes on to the highest phase of mind's possibilities, unity with Spirit.

When it dawns upon man that he has within him the primal spiritual spark of God, the living Word or Logos, and that through the Word he is identified with the original Mind, he has the key to infinite soul unfoldment.

Even though a person does not at first have this higher revelation of his sonship and unity with creative Mind, the assumption helps him to bring it to realization. Jesus developed in faith and power as He used His word. According to the text, He did not know that He could do absent healing by the power of His word before the centurion suggested it.

Never dampen your faith or the faith of another in you. Jesus exalted faith to first place in His healing work. "Be of good cheer; thy faith hath made thee whole." "When they cast thee down, thou shalt say, There is lifting up," said Eliphaz to Job. If there is appearance of sickness or weakness, affirm with all your faith the healing thought.

Through the Spirit of truth I now partake of Christ substance and Christ life in holy communion, and I am made whole.

At the Last Supper Jesus taught that the bread and wine that He consecrated were His body and His blood, and He told His followers to partake of them in remembrance of Him. He did not say that these elements were symbols of His blood and body but that they were essentially the same substance and life as His body. This also has been the teaching of the church, as interpreted by the Council of Trent: "Under each species and under each particle of each species Christ is contained whole and entire." This is the doctrine of transubstantiation, that the consecration by the minister of bread and wine changes the material elements to Christ elements, without affecting their appearance.

This doctrine has been attacked both within and without the church, the majority of ministers and laymen accepting it on faith as in some way related to the miraculous. But the discoveries of the elemental character of matter by modern science are revealing the universal unity of substance and the possibility of its transformation from one thing to another by changing the number and arrangement of the electrons in the atom.

According to modern science this whole universe of forms can be dissolved into energy, from which it may again be formed. Science does not say that the directive and formative power is man, but the Bible so teaches and especially Jesus. Jesus said that all power was given unto Him in heaven and in earth. He manifested His power in a small way by multiplying a few loaves and fishes to feed more than five thousand persons. In various other instances He demonstrated that He had an understanding of the transmutation of substance. He raised His flesh body to an energy level far higher in potential life and substance than any reached before.

As a race we have for ages been deprived in our consciousness of union with our creative source, and the result has been a gradual decrease in vitality until the body has lost the ability to hold its atoms together and consequently has disintegrated. Thus death has come to be accepted as in some mysterious way a part of the divine plan. Here again certain biological experiments with cells prove them to be possessed of an ability to reproduce themselves, which at least hints at physical immortality.

There are in the world today men and women who have followed the teaching of Jesus and have developed in their bodies a superenergy or life that not only permeates the physical structure but envelops it in a luminous aura that can be and is felt by both themselves and others. Spirit reveals that spiritual thinking breaks open the physical cells and atoms and releases their imprisoned life, which originally came from Divine Mind. Jesus carried this process so far that His whole body was transformed and became a conscious part of the Father life and intelligence.

In this way the substance and life of Jesus' body became a connecting link between our bodies and the body of God. Jesus merged His consciousness with the race consciousness and made Himself subject to our shortcomings in order to lift us up to spiritual life. This is the secret of His great sacrifice and sin offering.

When we understand that man has the power to release the divine life imprisoned in the cells of his body and project it as spiritual energy, we have the key that unlocks many mysteries of personal influence. The vast difference between mediocre and great speakers and singers is not in voice and words but in invisible soul energies. We feel the presence before a word is uttered. For example, a music critic says of Toscanini, the great orchestra leader: "He brings a charge of electricity into the hall that cannot and does not enter in at any other time. If only certain persons felt this galvanization of the atmosphere one might be accused of romanticism or hero worship for mentioning it. But everybody feels it."

Thousands of great and near-great religious leaders have developed this "soul body," for that is what it is, but none has reached the high development of Jesus, who made it possible for us all to take advantage of His achievement and through Him attain eternal life.

All things and all conditions of body and affairs have their origin in mind, and it is in our minds that we make contact with the Christ Mind. The mind of Jesus Christ penetrates and permeates our race consciousness like the etheric waves from a mighty broadcasting station, and we can tune in at any time by simply concentrating mentally on the Christ life and Christ substance.

God and man, heaven and earth, and all the healing powers that be now unite in healing me.

Socrates, the wise man of Athens, once prayed that "Jove and all the gods that be" hear his prayer.

His idea was to invoke all the higher forces, counting them all worth while. All great men recognize the breadth, height, and depth of Being, that it is not comprehended in one name, but may be expressed in many. Paul preaching to the Athenians on Mars' Hill did not disdain their many shrines, said to be two thousand in number, but complimented them on their piety, at the same time proclaiming that he came as the representative of the "UNKNOWN GOD" to whom they had erected an altar.

So we recognize that there is but one source of Being but that He is expressed in His Son Christ and manifest in His personal representative, Holy Spirit. The ancient Israelites had several outstanding names for Jehovah, each representing some special agency, as supplier, peace giver, guide, and the like. Some sects in our day pray to saints to execute the will of God in their behalf.

These all point to the fact that God is made manifest in a universe of executive powers, upon whom man can call as principle or as some form of personal agency.

This healing statement is recommended particularly to those who have depended upon temporal remedies or persons for their healing. It will amplify and energize the healing idea to the point of omnipotence, because it recognizes all the healing potencies that faith has made substantial in the past and brings them all to a focal center in wholeness.

It is universally recognized that the whole human family has broken loose from the usual stabilized thoughts, that we are afloat in an atmosphere of doubt, that we are walking question marks asking one another at every turn: What next? What will be the outcome?

The world of materiality is ending. Science says that what we thought was a material atom was really the shadow of an amazing aggregation of protons and electrons pulsating with potential life, energy, and power. We have been perpetuating the world of materiality by our material thoughts. Now our dominant thinkers are letting go, and they are telling us that matter is merely the smoke screen of a universe of energy. As an eminent scientist says, "We live in a universe of waves, and nothing but waves."

Christian metaphysicians see the truth that our minds have been jarred loose from their material concepts and that they have not yet laid hold of the true concepts. We are mentally afloat in the cosmic ether, waiting for someone to show us how to lay hold of real, stable ideas. When men's minds lose their stability, chaos reigns in their affairs. Emerson said that when a man of ideas is born into the world kings totter on their thrones.

Jesus said that He came to fulfill the Law and the Prophets; that is, to demonstrate that natural and spiritual law are one. He foresaw this very period when the "powers of the heavens shall be shaken"–that is, the mental realms be broken up--and He attributed this phenomenon to the coming of the Christ as "lightning."

The 24th chapter of Matthew describes in symbols what is taking place in this century. Christ Mind is quickening the cosmic light, which science is interpreting as natural law. Those who see spiritually announce that the next great revelation will be that of the "prophets," those who discern spiritually that the cosmic ether and the Christ Mind are one and that the character and the manner of the coming of the Christ--as a mighty, all-infolding, spiritually quickening mind--is referred to in the very modern metaphor of lightning: "For as the lightning cometh forth from the east, and is seen even unto the west; so shall be the coming of the Son of man."

Jesus answers the flood of queries as to what we shall do when we are caught in a whirlpool of thought: "Seek ye first his kingdom, and his righteousness; and all these things shall be added unto you."

The present panaceas for the ills of the world are all lacking in principle and will eventually be discarded, to be followed by the Christ plan, which will make all the products of the earth directly available to all the people of the earth. Before this Christ plan can be established governments must petition God for His intervention in their affairs; then the divine plan will be revealed.

I press forward with courage and boldness in the power of God, and I am healed.

In the 6th chapter of Revelation it is written: "And I saw when the Lamb opened one of the seven seals, and I heard one of the four living creatures saying as with a voice of thunder, Come. And I saw, and behold, a white horse, and he that sat thereon had a bow; and there was given unto him a crown: and he came forth conquering, and to conquer."

The "four living creatures" represent the four dominant factors in manifest life, which has its original source in the Lamb, which represents the pure, nonresistant life of Being.

The four horses and their riders are, first, "a white horse," representing the power of the Christ; secondly, "a red horse [war]: and to him that sat thereon it was given to take peace from the earth"; thirdly, "a black horse" (commercialism): "a measure of wheat for a shilling, and three measures of barely for a shilling"; and fourthly, "a pale horse: and he that sat upon him, his name was Death."

At no time in the history of the world has there ever been such activity in the riders of the three dark horses as right now. The prodigious preparations for war by nations, incited by the greed for gain will soon lead them to "let slip the dogs of war" unless the rider of the white horse comes forth "conquering, and to conquer."

Although all Truth students are praying for harmony in the settlement of earth's tribulations, they cannot help seeing the effect of thoughts of selfishness. The last section of this chapter in Revelation gives a symbolic description of the chaos to come among those who are not seeking to conquer under the banner of the rider of the white horse, Christ.

We hold that those who have had revealed to them the peace-giving power of the Christ mind should be unusually energetic in declaring it to be the dominant quality in the minds of men everywhere. Do not argue or contend with error but silently (and aloud if the occasion seems propitious) declare the presence and power of the Christ.

In the 7th chapter of Revelation is a symbolical description of four angels protecting the earth until the servants of God are sealed on their foreheads.

The forehead is the center of consciousness, which the understanding of Truth seals; that is, it secretly unites the consciousness with Christ. The number sealed is twelve thousand out of the twelve tribes. This is all symbolical and should not be taken literally. Man has twelve faculties, represented by the twelve tribes of Israel. When the consciousness in the forehead is illumined by Spirit, all twelve centers in the body automatically respond. "These are they that come out of the great tribulation, and they washed their robes, and made them white in the blood of the Lamb."

The "blood of the Lamb" represents the primal life of Being, which Jesus made accessible to all those who believe in Him as the revealer of the pure life of God the Father. This consciousness of spiritual life is mentioned in the 22d chapter: "And he showed me a river of water of life, bright as crystal, proceeding out of the throne of God and of the Lamb."

The concluding verses of the 7th chapter of Revelation reveal the joys of the faithful. Every member of Unity should study chapters 6 and 7.

It will require more than mortal fortitude and courage to cope successfully with the conditions that are imminent in human affairs, and we shall all need the help of a higher power. This higher power we shall find in the Christ Mind.

Cast out fear as far as the tribulations of the world are concerned. Affirm:

"I press forward with courage and boldness in the power of God, and I am healed."

JEHOVAH GOD restores me to health and wholeness. Words are quickened by those who speak them and they pick up and carry the ideas of the speaker, weak or strong, ignorant or wise, good or ill. Thus words descriptive of deity have been personalized in the thought stuff of the race and those who invoke them in prayer and meditation are given a spiritual impetus far beyond what they would receive from common words. It is a fact that the name Jehovah came to be held in such reverence by the rabbis that they never spoke the word aloud. Jesus said that His words were so charged with spirit and life that they would endure longer even than heaven and earth.

Next to Spirit the word of Spirit is the most powerful thing in existence. The author of the Book of Hebrews says "that the worlds have been framed by the word of God." We read in Genesis that "God said" and it came to pass. And God said, "Let us make man in our own image, after our likeness." Thus we see that man is the incarnate word of God, and it logically follows that our words bring forth whatever we put into them. Study the 1st chapter of John. Jesus said that a man will be held accountable for his lightest word.

Spiritually classified, the Jehovah of the Old Testament is identical with the Christ in the New. One who heals by the power of the word should become familiar with the inner meaning of all words and use those that appeal to him as possessing the greatest healing potency. Jesus promised that He would unite with the Holy Spirit in helping those who called upon Him. Unity healers have found that this promise is fulfilled when they concentrate in prayer and positive affirmation on the presence of the Holy Spirit and Jesus Christ. A new and strong contact is felt with spiritual life, as if it were a mighty battery, when the name Jehovah God or Jehovah-rapha ("the Lord that healeth thee") is spoken silently and audibly; then the ethers quicken with the name and shower spiritual life on both patient and healer. The word Jehovah or Yahweh is charged with spiritual power far above and beyond any other word in human language.

I am raised to perfection in mind and body by the healing power of Jesus Christ.

Quite a few Truth students ask why we emphasize Jesus Christ so strongly in our writings and statements of Truth. Spiritual psychology proves that the name of a great character carries his mind potency and that wherever his name is repeated silently or audibly his attributes become manifest. Jesus knew this and commanded His disciples to go forth in His name. The marvelous works they did prove that they exercised power far beyond anything warranted by their education or previous ability, power springing directly from Spirit.

Every thinker who studies the life and teachings of Jesus readily admits that He attained an understanding of spiritual things far beyond that of any other man that ever lived. His mind touched heights far beyond those of other advanced searchers for Truth. As we unfold spiritually we see more and more that Jesus understood the finer shades of metaphysical reasoning and related His mind and body to both ideas and their manifestation.

Jesus demonstrated that He understood the healing power stored up in the body, which He said is released through faith. "Thy faith hath made thee whole." Jesus identified Himself and His name with the sacred name of the Hebrew dispensation, Jehovah, and added another link to that long chain of names and events that brought forth the perfect man ideated by God-Mind, Jesus Christ.

As a directive head is essential in any army, militant or spiritual, so in every forward movement of the human family there must be a leader. The leader is chosen because of his ability as a demonstrator of the principles adopted by the group he represents. The religious principles taught and demonstrated by Jesus were not originated by Him, nor did He claim them as a "discovery." He said that Moses wrote of Him, and He often quoted Moses, but with an interpretation quite different from that of the popular religious leaders. He told them that they studied the Scriptures expecting through them to attain eternal life when the only way to attain that life was through Him, and they would not come to Him. Right here Jesus emphasized the spiritual man, the I AM in man, as the only way by which man can enter the kingdom of God.

Jesus was undoubtedly the greatest of all exponents of the impersonal I AM, which is revealed to man when he opens up the supermind within his own soul. Jesus Christ's real name is Jehovah, I AM. The personal man Jesus is merely the veil or mask worn by the spiritual man Christ or Jehovah. We are all, in our personality, wearing the mask that conceals the real, the spiritual, I AM. Jesus shattered that mask and revealed the spiritual man. He also taught the way by which we may all do what He did and thus fulfill the destiny implanted in us by the parent Mind.

There are many distractions to keep us from finding the one door into the inner kingdom and many voices calling to us that they will show us the easy way, but Jesus Christ is the only one that appeals to those who are grounded in principle.

Any declaration man may make in which the name Jesus Christ is used reverently will contact the spiritual ether in which the Christ I AM lives and will open the mind and body to the inflow of spiritual healing rays. These healing rays are very much superior to the ultraviolet rays that come from the sun or our best medical appliances, because they minister to the mind as well as the body.

Thy vitalizing energy floods my whole being, and I am healed.

The most inclusive name for Being is Jehovah God. Jehovah represents the individual I AM and God (Elohim) the universal Principle. When man thinks or says "I am" he is potentially giving freedom to the seed ideas that contains in its spiritual capacity all of Being. The natural man in his narrowed mental comprehension barely touches the seed ideas that expand in the Christ man to infinite power. The more we dwell upon and expand our I AM the greater looms its originating capacity before us. When Jesus proclaimed, "Before Abraham was born, I am," He realized that the I AM preceded all manifestation, however great, and was capable of infinite expression.

The proposition that the seemingly insignificant individual I AM contains infinite creative capacity appears absurd to the thoughtless, but we have numerous examples of extraordinary capacity for expansion in the little seeds that bring forth gigantic trees. The Scriptures plainly teach that men may become gods. Adam was expelled from the Garden of Eden because Jehovah realized that he might appropriate eternal life and live forever in his ignorance.

When man realizes that "death and life are in the power of the tongue" and begins to use his "I am" statements wisely, he has the key that unlocks the secret chambers of existence in heaven and earth.

The Christ substance (body) and the Christ life (blood) are accessible at all times and in all places to the one who awakens his soul to spiritual omnipresence. The table of the Lord is spread everywhere for those who believe on Him as Spirit and in their Spirit affirmation eat of His body and blood. The appropriation by His followers of His life and substance is the very foundation of salvation through Jesus Christ. The mere acceptance intellectually of the teaching that we are saved by the blood of the Lord Jesus and the partaking of the bread and wine in a perfunctory manner will save neither mind nor body. The only thing that will do it is the understanding that Jesus raised His body life and substance out of the race consciousness into Spirit consciousness and that with our minds poised in that consciousness we can lay hold of the Spirit elements that will save us to the uttermost.

Nearly everyone needs both mind and body healing, and those who give faithful attention to the law as it operates in man are rewarded by demonstrations of healing. Jesus healed "all manner of disease," the same Jesus has broadcast that healing Spirit to the uttermost ends of the earth, and today all who will may be made whole.

The Christ life quickens and heals me.

Although millions have testified that they have felt the quickening life of Christ, other millions doubt if such a thing as the Christ life exists.

The unseen forces have always been an enigma to the masses, and even those who are expecting the unseen to spring forth suddenly into some marvelous manifestation do not recognize it when it comes to pass. It is said that when Marconi demonstrated to a group of scientists in Paris the power of radio waves, they doubted his claims and sought in various ways to discover the concealed wires, which they were sure were being used. So every unseen force man uses has had to prove its existence by some visible manifestation that can be mechanically demonstrated. But are there unseen forces that cannot be mechanically demonstrated? The answer is that all unseen forces can be mechanically demonstrated and that they are being demonstrated every day the world over, but scientists have not yet recognized as mechanical all the devices through which man brings unseen forces into manifestation; for example, his own brain and the radio. These with many other unseen forces come under the head of mechanism.

Brain cells are the only material things that will transmit mind, and man has never yet been able to invent so fine a piece of mechanism outside his own organism. But brains are mechanical, and man does build and use them in expressing his intelligence.

The fact is that each of us builds a brain especially designed and fitted for our individual use and for no one else's. All attempts to turn our brains over to others in hypnosis or mediumship will prove abortive in the end.

In radio terms your brain cells correspond to the tubes in a combined broadcasting and receiving set, and you have tuned them to certain wave lengths and turned on the power. If you have not been informed of your innate ability to turn on or off the mind waves, you are functioning in the established race programs of personality: what your ancestors have thought, what other people think, and what little thought you can conjure up yourself. Unless your mind has been quickened by the light of spiritual understanding, you are living in a little three-dimensional world whose beginning and end is sin or a falling short of the divine ideal.

"If a man keep my word, he shall never see death.""I am the resurrection, and the life."

Jesus stressed the power of words, especially His words. In the parable of the sower He said, "When anyone heareth the word of the kingdom." Here He referred to the Logos, the creative Word, which framed the worlds, according to John. The creative Word or Logos is also identified as Holy Spirit, which is carrying forward the ideas of God as they unfold in the manifest universe.

As the Word of God, the Logos, is creating in the universe (body of God) so man's word is creating in his universe (man's body). That is why Jesus said that we should be judged by our words. We are creating a little universe in which the cells of the body correspond to the planets of the solar system. "And I say unto you, that every idle word that men shall speak, they shall give account thereof in the day of judgment."

The "day of judgment" to us is any day that we get the fruit in body and affairs of some thought or word that we have expressed.

The creative power of man's word is in proportion to his understanding of God-Mind and his unity with its law. The creative power of most men does not get beyond their own body consciousness, because they know very little about Spirit and their relation to its laws. The better we realize our spiritual relationship to creative Mind and conform our thoughts and words to its laws the greater is the power of our words. Jesus "tuned in" to Divine Mind until that Mind reinforced His mind and raised it to superhuman capacity. It was in one of His moments of mental exaltation that He declared, "The words that I have spoken unto you are spirit, and are life."

We have thought that we were to be saved by Jesus' making personal petitions and sacrifices for us, but now we see that we are to be saved by using the creative principles that He developed in Himself, and that He is ever ready to co-operate with us in developing in ourselves by observing the law as He observed it. "I in them, and thou in me, that they may be perfected into one."

Thus we see that when Jesus said, "If a man keep my word, he shall never see death," He meant that we should realize the life-giving properties of the creative words of God as He had realized them, that we should have no consciousness of death.

I have new life in Christ and I am healed.

To attain this realization of the word of life we must create currents of life in our bodies as Jesus did in His. Of all man's possessions the most valuable is life. "For what shall a man be profited, if he shall gain the whole world, and forfeit his life? or what shall a man give in exchange for his life?"

When Jesus uttered these words He was explaining to His disciples that He was about to pass through a transformation in which He would give up His physical life, though He would continue His manifestation in a spiritual life. They did not understand Him, and Peter "began to rebuke him." Jesus told them they did not understand the things of God "but the things of men." Up to this day the passing over of the natural life into the spiritual life is not fully understood by Christians. It is almost universally interpreted as something that takes place after the death of the body, while in fact it is a transformation of the issues of life while the body is intact. Paul said, "I die daily." So Jesus could not have appeared after His crucifixion in the same body if He had not daily given up the physical life and daily put on the Christ life. It is a step-by-step or cell-by-cell transformation.

What did Jesus mean when He said, "If a man keep my word, he shall never see death"? Did He mean death of the soul? There is nothing in His teaching to warrant such a conclusion. He meant that we shall escape physical death if we identify ourselves with the creative Word in Him, the Logos.

Then to understand the new life in Christ we must give attention to that mystical Word or Logos, because in it are wrapped the principles that, planted in our minds, will spring into new life in mind and body.

Eternal life and strength are here, and I am made whole through Jesus Christ.

Among the seven sacred names given to Jehovah by the Hebrew priesthood is "Jehovah-shammah," meaning "Jehovah is there." Jehovah is the name of the ever-living I AM. When the mystic desired to commune with the omnipresent life he did not speak the name aloud but silently intoned, "Jehovah-shammah!" This pervasion of his I AM with the ever-living I AM harmonized the spiritual man with his source, and the individual was merged with the universal.

A certain mystery has always accompanied the use of the sacred name, and the priesthood gained their ascendancy over the people by performing marvelous works through the silent and audible intoning of words charged with thoughts of spiritual power.

However a priest must undergo discipline to acquire mastery of the elemental forces that function in mind and body. A cursory reading of Exodus conveys the idea that for forty years Moses was a shepherd, tending the flocks of his father-in-law Jethro, priest of Midian. But his mastery of nature, as evidenced by his works in Egypt, plainly shows that he understood the control of matter by mind better than did the magicians of Egypt, although he was versed in their magic.

The followers of Jesus did marvelous works in His name, but that name was also used by those who were not His immediate disciples, and they succeeded in casting out demons so well that John complained about it. Jesus said, "Forbid him not: for he that is not against you is for you." So we find that a person's name identifies him with his character. If that character is mighty in spirituality and power, he who invokes it in his prayers is automatically raised into a like sphere of power and what he says comes to pass. "And whatsoever ye shall ask in my name, that will I do, that the Father may be glorified in the Son."

Salvation through Jesus Christ is not accomplished by looking forward to freedom but by realizing that we are now free through His freeing power, which we are using to cut the bonds with which our thoughts have bound us. Then we have only to establish ourselves in real life and strength by understanding that these attributes of Being are omnipresent and that our affirmations of that presence, will cause us to become conscious that we do now and here live, move, and have our being in eternal life and strength.

In the name and by the power and authority of Jesus Christ I am made every whit whole.

Man gives a name--that is, "character"–to every idea that comes into consciousness, and whatever he conceives a thing to be, that it becomes to him. So it is written in Genesis: "Whatsoever the man called every living creature, that was the name thereof."

Jesus taught and demonstrated that man is master of a kingdom far beyond the consciousness of the natural man, but accessible to those who open their mind to its laws and observe those laws in thought and act.

The official declarations of a representative of a country are recognized by all as worthy of credence. Jesus represented the kingdom of the heavens, and we, His agents, take possession of that kingdom in His name and declare that we are vested with authority to bring spiritual forces to bear that will restore man to his primal perfection.

In the 3d chapter of Acts is recorded the healing by Peter of a man lame from his birth; and Peter says, "In the name of Jesus Christ of Nazareth, walk. . . . and immediately his feet and ankle-bones received strength. And leaping up, he stood, and began to walk; and he entered with them into the temple, walking, and leaping, and praising God."

When the people were greatly astonished at this marvelous healing and gathered around Peter and John, Peter explained, "Ye men of Israel, why marvel ye at this man? or why fasten ye your eyes on us, as though by our own power or godliness we had made him to walk? . . . And by faith in his name hath his name made this man strong."

Shakespeare says, "Good name in man and woman . . . is the immediate jewel of their souls." But even Shakespeare, with his psychological insight, never realized how good a name would be or to what heights of power it could lift one who applies the laws of Spirit in its use.

Those who have searched diligently to know God and His Son Jesus and have prayed for the light of Spirit find that they possess a certain confidence and faith in the very name Jesus Christ and that to the one who speaks it the name draws creative forces far beyond mental comprehension. Hence we should have confidence in the promises of Jesus that those who in faith use His name shall do the marvelous wonders that He did and even greater works of a spiritual character.

Read in the 16th chapter of Mark what are the signs of a real follower of Christ and see if you are measuring up to them: "And these signs shall accompany them that believe: in my name shall they cast out demons; they shall speak with new tongues; they shall take up serpents, and if they drink any deadly thing, it shall in no wise hurt them; they shall lay hands on the sick, and they shall recover."

By the grace of God through Christ Jesus I am made whole.

Jesus knew what He had accomplished in breaking the mortal mesmerism of the race, and He boldly proclaimed His ability to help all those who join Him in seeking to effect a direct union with creative Mind.

As Jesus healed in Galilee so He is healing in the same spiritual realm of radiant health today. "To him that overcometh, to him will I give to eat of the tree of life, which is in the Paradise of God." "I am the way, and the truth, and the life."

Chapter XI - Healing Power of Joy

I REJOICE and am glad because Thy harmonizing love makes me every whit whole. All healing systems recognize joy as a beneficent factor in the restoration of health to the sick. "The joy of Jehovah is your strength." This statement is based on a principle recognized by all who help to bring about strength of mind and health of body. An old country doctor used to tell how he healed a woman of a large cyst by telling her a funny story: at which she laughed so heartily that the fluid broke loose and passed away.

The mind puts kinks in the nerves in ways beyond description. A thought of fear will stop the even flow of life in some nerve center deep down in the body, forming a nucleus where other fears may accumulate and finally congest the blood concerned in some important function. The impast of energy of some kind is necessary to break the dam. Physical exercise will sometimes do it, or massage, or electricity; but these are temporary remedies. None of them has touched the cause, which is mental: fear.

There are various methods of erasing fear from the mind and preventing its congestions in the body. One of the most direct and effective shatterers of fear is laughter. Laugh your fears away. See how ridiculous they are when traced to their source. Nearly all persons have some pet fear, and they give up to it without trying to find its source.

The nerves surrounding the heart are most sensitive to thoughts of fear, and when mind and body are strenuously excited the fearfully charged nerve cells grab the heart and hold it like a vise. Businessmen who live in a world of sharp competition and constant risk of loss with few exceptions are subject to this kind of fear.

Christian metaphysicians of course know that the only permanent cure for the ailment is a heartfelt trust in God as the one and only source of good to man. A daily prayer for wisdom and divine guidance in the conduct of one's affairs will restore peace and harmony to mind and body, and health must of necessity follow.

I will sing unto the Lord a new song of harmony and health.

That there is an intimate relation between happiness and health goes without question. When you feel good you sing either audibly or silently. Singing promotes health because it increases the circulation, and a good circulation is a sign and promoter of health. If the blood stream were never congested and all the nerves and pores were open and free and were swiftly carrying forward their appointed work, there would never be an abnormal or false growth in the body. It follows logically then that we should cultivate those mind activities which stimulate naturally the currents of life in the body. One of these, and a very important one, is joy.

No one likes to take medicine even when sugar-coated, because there is an instinctive feeling that it will do no good. Besides it usually tastes bad. But nearly anyone can sing a little song, and those who have tried it right in the face of suffering will tell you that it is a marvelous health restorer.

The reason that singing restores harmony to tense nerves is that its vibrations stir them to action, thus making it possible for the ever-waiting healing Spirit to get in. The organ of the human voice is located right between the thyroid glands, the accelerators of certain important body functions. To a greater or less degree every word you speak vibrates the cells up and down the body, from front brain to abdomen.

The Spirit of health, or as the doctors call it, the restorative power of nature, is always right at hand awaiting an opportunity to enter in to make whole and to harmonize all discords in the body. Back of every true song is a thought of joy. It is the thought that counts in the end, because it is the thought that invites the healing Spirit. Consequently we should sing with the thought that the Lord is right with us and that His joy is giving our words the healing unction; as Jesus said, "that my joy may be in you, and that your joy may be made full."

When men think a great deal about spiritual things and especially about God as an indwelling spiritual presence, both mind and body are thrilled with joy, a feeling of satisfaction, and a tendency to break out in songs of gladness. This is not confined to Christians; persons everywhere, in every age, have told of an inner glory and happiness when they got into the habit of concentrating their mind on God. The great philosopher Spinoza wrote so much about God that he was known as the "God-intoxicated man."

Pythagoras taught that the universe is God's symphony and that all the suns and planets sing as they swing their way through the heavens. All nature has a language and a song for those who listen. Shakespeare says:

"And this our life, exempt from public haunt,
Finds tongues in trees, books in the running brooks,
Sermons in stones, and good in everything."

Shakespeare often quoted from the Bible, and he may have got his idea that trees have tongues from I Chronicles 16:33: "Then shall the trees of the wood sing for joy before Jehovah."

"My mind is cleansed by Christ;
My life flows swift and strong;
The peace of God wells up within,
My soul bursts forth in song."

Some people think it almost a sacrilege to sing when they feel bad. They think that that is the time to groan, and they usually do. That is the way the mortal looks at it, and that is the way you may happen to feel, but you can quickly be released from the prison of pain or grief if you will sing and praise and pray.

First sing in your soul--you can sing 'way down inside of yourself--then you will soon be singing with your voice. So we lay down the metaphysical law that everybody should know how to sing. Everybody can sing. It does not make any difference what your previous thoughts have been about your ability to sing, it does not make any difference what you think about it at present, and it does not make any difference whether you can sing or not; cultivate the singing soul and you will some day break forth into a singing voice.

This is a creative law, and it is a law that everyone should know and use, because through the vibrations of the voice joined with high thinking every cell in the body is set into action, and not only in the body but out into the environing thought atmosphere the vibrations go and break up all crystallized conditions.

The whole universe is in vibration, and that vibration is under law. Chaos would result if the law were not supreme. Each particular thing has its rate of vibration. Heat, light, and color are different rates of vibration in one field of primal energy. Different colors are caused by the different frequencies of the vibrations as they strike the eye. But what causes vibration? We answer Mind.

The cells of the body are centers of force in a field of universal energy. There are no solids. That which appears solid is in reality the scene of constant activity. The eye is not keyed to the pulsations of this universal energy and is therefore deceived into believing that things are solid. All energy and life are governed by laws of spiritual harmony. If the mind that receives sound vibrations is in spiritual consciousness, the body responds to the higher activity. If our mind were trained to think thoughts that harmonized with Divine Mind, we could hear the music of the spheres.

You can drive away the gloom of disappointment by resolutely singing a sunshine song. I believe that we could cultivate the power of music in connection with the understanding of Truth and thus rend all the bonds of sin, sickness, and death. The world needs a new hymnal, with words of Truth only and music so strong and powerful that it will penetrate to the very center of the soul.

Our body is now tuned to the divine harmony; we shall find the keynote by listening in the silence to the singing soul.

The new life in Christ fills me with zeal to live, and I am healed.

In putting on Christ--that is, developing the supermind--every faculty has to be raised to supermind proportions. The exact mathematical degree of power necessary to "synchronize" oneself with the "kingdom of the heavens" in which the supermind functions has not been revealed to human consciousness, if indeed it can be. An eminent British astronomer says that he has discovered that God is a great mathematician, and the logical conclusion of all wise philosophers is that everything in the universe both seen and unseen is under mathematical law. "The very hairs of your head are all numbered," said Jesus.

Jesus also said that He came to bring more life to slow-moving humanity. More vital force now is and always has been the crying need of people everywhere. Disease germs run riot in anemic persons. The cause of such conditions is mental: there is a lack of vital interest in life and a disinclination to assume its responsibilities.

Ralph Waldo Emerson once said that no great work was ever accomplished without enthusiasm. Enthusiasm is another word for zeal, and zeal is a great stimulator of man. You cannot think of or repeat the word zeal without evoking a certain mental thrill that spurs you to action in some direction if you repeat it over and over. This brings us back to the point we mentioned about everything having a mathematical infusion; that is, everything is impregnated with mathematics. Every word we speak goes forth from our mouth charged with atomic energies that vibrate at a definite numerical rate. According to science every atom is composed of protons and electrons, the number of electronic elements in an atom determining the character of the substance. Now we see that modern science is proving the truth of Jesus' statement that we shall be held accountable for every word we speak. Our minds determine the character of our words and what the mind determines the mouth obediently utters, its words loaded with constructive or destructive electrons all mathematically arranged to build up or blow up both ourselves and our aims and ideals. We are perfectly aware that some persons are overzealous, that they consume their vitality by talking and acting without wisdom: "The zeal of thy house hath eaten me up." Such persons are so enthusiastic in externals that they lose contact with the source of things, the inner mind, and they destroy the body, the temple of the living God. However these are the minority. The great majority lack zeal in doing even the most ordinary things, and even the overzealous would find a much-coveted and needed poise by linking their minds with the Christ.

The beginning of the culture of the mind that enables it to make contact with the realm of creative ideas is faith, and faith is superenthusiasm. You must have such confidence in your ability to make union with creative Mind that you fuse the two and the invisible elements melt and fall into the mold you have made for them.

When we know that every word is mathematically linked with certain creative ideas and that Divine Mind has made it possible for every one of us to draw upon these ideas mentally, we have the key to all creative processes. "Whosoever . . . shall not doubt in his heart, but shall believe that what he saith cometh to pass; he shall have it." Here in a nutshell Jesus has stated the law and its fulfillment. The one and only reason that we do not always succeed in our demonstrations is that we do not persist in our mental work. If we have never tested our faith in God and His mathematical laws, we must begin to discipline our minds and raise our thoughts to the point where they abandon the slow inertia of the natural man for the speed and spring of the spiritual man. This is accomplished by prayer, meditation, and the repetition of true words. It is not the vain repetition of words over and over, parrot like, but the quiet realization that there is a listening Mind and a ready host of great ideas at all times waiting for us.

I am at peace because I trust divine justice to regulate my mind, body, and affairs.

The mind may be compared to the sea, which is calm or stormy according to the wind that moves it. Thought utilizes the substance of the mind and forms that which man ideates.

A restful state of mind is greatly to be desired because of its constructive character. When the mind is lashed by a brain storm the cells of the whole organism are shattered and exhaustion ensues. Nervous prostration is the result of exhausted nerve force.

Man's whole character is determined by the thoughts for which he allows a place in his mind. A strong man or a weak man is what he is because of repeated thoughts of strength or weakness.

Steadfast affirmations of peace will harmonize the whole body structure and open the way to attainment of healthy conditions in mind and body. The reason that prayers and treatments for health are not more successful is that the mind has not been put in a receptive state by affirmations of peace.

The Mind of Spirit is harmonious and peaceful, and it must have a like manner of expression in man's consciousness. When a body of water is choppy with fitful currents of air it cannot reflect objects clearly. Neither can man reflect the steady strong glow of Omnipotence when his mind is disturbed by anxious thoughts, fearful thoughts, or angry thoughts.

Be at peace and your unity with God-Mind will bring you health and happiness.

We all should practice delightful, happy, joyous states of mind. It is such thoughts that open the way for the ever-present Father-Mind to pour out its splendid resources into our mind and through us into all our affairs.

Thou art my life unfailing, and I rejoice in Thy abundant, buoyant health.

No one can understand the real character of God without a metaphysical study and analysis of mind and its properties. To think of God as an enormously enlarged man, as most persons do, entangles one in a maze of wrong conclusions concerning the nature and creative processes of Being.

Think of Being as an aggregation of ideas with potential creative capacity but governed in its creative processes by unalterable laws. Mentally see those ideas projected into action in a universe evolving a self-conscious creature possessed of free will called man. As man develops through the combination of those original ideas, behold him arriving at a place in his evolution where he realizes his power of self-determination and consciously begins to choose as his own field of action the many pleasant activities of the universe and to combine them in his own way.

This phase of man's development is symbolized in the Edenic allegory as Adam and Eve eating of the fruit of the tree of the knowledge of good and evil. The tree that bears the fruit of pleasure in the midst of man's body garden is the sympathetic nervous system. Satan, sensation, tempts Adam and Eve –man-- to appropriate or eat of this tree without listening to the voice of wisdom, Jehovah God. The result is unbridled and unlawful development of the sympathetic nervous system with excess of pleasure (good) followed by a corresponding reaction of pain (evil).

Jesus regained this lost Eden and showed us how to regain it by likewise identifying our minds with God-Mind. His prayer was "Not my will, but thine, be done."

Christ is the name of the God-Mind imaged in everyone. When we identify ourselves with that image, we rise superior to the Adamic man and become unified with the spiritual man. It is in the strength of this supermind that we can say to the man of flesh, "I will; be thou made clean." This is the decree of the Christ in you to your conscious mind and its visible body; it is the exercise of the authority given to every child of God. "Decree a thing, and it shall be established unto thee."

And manifest substance flows from a realm of light, according to the most modern conclusions of physical science. James says, "Every good gift and every perfect gift is from above, coming down from the Father of lights." God ideas are the source of all that appears. Accept this mighty and all-productive truth and consciously connect your mind with the Father-Mind, and you will realize abundant health and true joy.

The Holy Spirit life heals me, and I radiate health to everybody and everything.

Some persons think that when they quit lying they are demonstrating Truth. To quit lying is commendable but falls short of fulfilling the complete reformation of the Spirit of truth. In chapter after chapter of the Gospel of John, Jesus repeats the promise that He will send a Comforter, whom He names "the Spirit of truth," to those who believe on Him. In the 15th chapter we read, "But when the Comforter is come, whom I will send unto you from the Father, even the Spirit of truth, which proceedeth from the Father, he shall bear witness of me." In the 16th chapter we find these words: "I have yet many things to say unto you, but ye cannot bear them now. Howbeit when he, the Spirit of truth, is come, he shall guide you into all the truth." "And I will pray the Father, and he shall give you another Comforter, that he may be with you for ever, even the Spirit of truth . . . for he abideth with you, and shall be in you."

The Spirit of truth is the mind of God in its executive capacity: it carries out the divine plan of the originating Spirit. It proceeds from the Father and bears witness of the Son. We have in the operation of our own minds an illustration of how Divine Mind works. When an idea is fully formulated in our minds and we decide to carry it out, our thoughts change their character from contemplative to executive. We no longer plan but proceed to execute what we have already planned. So God-Mind sends forth its Spirit to carry out in man the divine idea imaged in the Son.

It is very comforting to know that Spirit is cooperating with us in our efforts to manifest God's law. God in His divine perfection has seemed so far removed from our human frailties that we have lost heart. But now we see that Jesus taught that God is intimately associated with us in all our life's problems and that we need only ask in His name in order to have all needs fulfilled.

The Spirit of truth is God's thought projecting into our minds ideas that will build a spiritual consciousness like that of Jesus. The Spirit of truth watches every detail of our lives, and when we ask and by affirmation proclaim its presence, it brings new life into our bodies.

Again the Spirit of truth opens our minds to God's law of supply and support, to the existence of a universal etheric thought substance prepared for man's body sustenance by infinite Mind. We have thought that in answer to our prayers God in some mysterious manner brought about the marvelous demonstrations that we had. Now we see that there has been prepared from the beginning an interpenetrating substance that, like a tenuous bread of heaven, showers us with its abundance.

But we must not only ask but bring the Spirit into our consciousness by affirming its abundance to be the source of all our good. Then perfection will begin to be manifested right in the face of apparent negation. Remember the invitation of the Master "Hitherto have ye asked nothing in my name: ask, and ye shall receive, that your joy may be made full."

Chapter XII - Holy Spirit Fulfills the Law

THE SPIRIT of wholeness quickens and heals me. The Spirit of wholeness is called the Holy Spirit in the New Testament. In classical mythology it is called Hygeia. Modern medical men refer to it as the restorative power of nature. It has been recognized by savage and civilized in every land and age. It has many names, and they all identify it as a universal urge toward perfection in man and the universe and toward keeping things going regardless of any interfering force.

We may look on this restorative power as merely the tendency of the cells in an organism to retain their homogeneity, and when we look at it in this light our consciousness robs it of any of the divine qualities it may possess. This is the way the scientific world regards what we call the Holy Spirit. To such a view the Holy Spirit has no warm heart. To persons holding such a view the Holy Spirit is not the Comforter referred to by Jesus but merely an abstract principle that works just the same way whether it is praised or blamed.

But to the Christian metaphysician the Holy Spirit is just what the name implies, the whole Spirit of God in action. In the Hebrew Jehovah is written Yahweh, Yah being masculine and weh feminine.In the New Testament Christ stands for Jehovah. Jesus talked a great deal about the Holy Spirit: that it would bear witness of Him, come with Him, and help Him to the end of the age.

Do not be misled by the personality of the Holy Spirit and the reference to it as "he." This was the bias of the Oriental mind, making God and all forms of the Deity masculine.

Holy Spirit is the love of Jehovah taking care of the human family, and love is always feminine. Love is the great harmonizer and healer, and whoever calls upon God as Holy Spirit for healing is calling upon the divine love.

Just here, in connection with the Holy Spirit is an important point for a good Christian healer to consider. Do not regard the Holy Spirit altogether as a restorative principle without feeling, sympathy, or love. This reduces your healing method to intellectual logic and the slow process of mental science. Under this method the patient must always be educated in Truth principles before he can be healed. No instantaneous healing ever takes place under this method.

The Holy Spirit is sympathetic, comforting, loving, forgiving, and instantly healing.

"Who forgiveth all thine iniquities;
Who healeth all thy diseases."

Do not fear to call mightily upon the Holy Spirit, who has all compassion and healing power at His command.

Thy perfect plan of bodily perfection is now made manifest in me.

That Mind, which designed the universe, must have planned for man, its leading citizen, a body in harmony with the universe is good logic. This conclusion does not require inspiration but merely common sense.

The religions of every race have taught this perfection of the body but have usually assumed that it was to be given to God's elect in some heavenly place after death. They have not thought it possible that the body of flesh with its many apparent defects could be transformed into an ideal body. In consequence man has put the stamp of inferiority upon his body, and through the creative power of thought he has built into the race mind a consciousness of corruptible flesh instead of the inherent incorruptible substance of God-Mind.

This race thought of man's body as impure and perishable in time became so dense that no human thought could penetrate it. It was gradually consuming the little life left in human bodies and would have ended with their total destruction if it had not been for Jesus, who was incarnated as demonstrator of the perfection and immortality of man's body.

That the body of flesh had within it life elements that could be released and incorporated into a much finer body has always been beyond the comprehension of the sense mind, and it required a physical demonstration to convince men that it could be done.

Jesus made that demonstration, and some of His followers were convinced that the body with which He appeared to them after the Crucifixion was the identical body that suffered on the cross. Thomas, for example, was allowed critically to examine that body for the marks and wounds of the cross, and he found them and was convinced.

But the majority still doubted and do so to this day. Not understanding that the body that Jesus occupied for the thirty-three years of His earthly incarnation could be transformed into an imperishable body, they have assumed that Jesus really died on the cross and went to heaven where God gave Him a glorious body. There is no foundation for this in the facts given in the New Testament.

"God is Spirit," said Jesus. "Know ye not that your body is a temple of the Holy Spirit which is in you, which ye have from God?" wrote Paul. Here are two statements by accepted authorities on fundamental Christian principles. If God is Spirit and He dwells in man's body, that body must have within it certain spiritual principles. Here modern science comes to the rescue of primitive Christianity, telling us that the atoms that compose the cells of our body have within them electrical units that, released, can change the whole character of the organism. Jesus had attained an understanding of the law that releases these electrical units, and He knew before the Crucifixion that He could thus make His body unkillable; which He did.

When Elohim God created man in His likeness, first chapter of the Bible with God's command that the dry land appear. Then in the second chapter Jehovah God formed man out of the dust of the ground. Not only here in the beginning do we find mind molding matter; all through the Bible runs the same story. Jesus said of His body that He could raise it up.

When the truth dawns on man that mind rules matter in both the great and the small, he has the explanation of myriad mysteries, strange episodes, reputed miracles. This great truth that mind is the source and moving factor in all creation would, if studied and practiced, prove of tremendous worth to religion, science, and art. Jesus taught the supremacy of mind in many illustrations, but His followers have not understood the metaphysical significance because they have not analyzed the mind or directly applied its spiritual powers. When Jesus said that the Father was within Him and that the words He spoke were not His but the Father's, He must have referred to God as an interpenetrating mind.

Everything in this universe has both its mental and its physical side. Heaven and earth are parallel everywhere. Even the so-called elemental forces of nature are dual. Our men of science are puzzled because light sometimes appears as waves in space and again as particles. To a metaphysician the waves express the mind and the particles the matter. When Jesus walked on the water He blended His mind with the mind of the water and it obeyed His concentrated will.

Nature's mind is always the servant of man's mind when man lifts his thoughts to Spirit. Nature will even obey a determined will on an inferior plane of consciousness. Concentration of will as practiced by metaphysicians of the Orient, African witch doctors, and a horde of occult adepts bears testimony to the power of the mind to manipulate matter visible and invisible.

"I sow no seeds of care and strife;
But those of love, and joy, and life."

It is reported that a great philosopher, Herbert Spencer, once said substantially that he would gladly turn his life over to any creative force that would plan and carry it forward without his having to take any responsibility.

Because of the many blunders that the natural man makes in his life, such a shifting of responsibility would be popular on the part of many who have ideals that they are unable to fulfill because they are bound by material limitations. Also in the secret recesses of all of us there lurks the conviction that there is a power somewhere that may be invoked to show us a hidden way into the city of success. We think we should willingly follow any path in life if we were sure that we were being led by the hand of supreme wisdom.

In his famous soliloquy Hamlet heaps up the measure of the burdens of life with the subtle argument that they could be shifted by death:

For who would bear the whips and scorns of time
The oppressor's wrong, the proud man's contumely,
The pangs of despised love, the law's delay,
The insolence of office and the spurns
That patient merit of the unworthy takes,
When he himself might his quietus make
With a bare bodkin? who would fardels bear,
To grunt and sweat under a weary life,
But that the dread of something after death,
The undiscovered country from whose bourn
No traveler returns, puzzles the will
And makes us rather bear those ills we have
Than fly to others that we know not of?

Spiritual insight reveals that Hamlet is right. We cannot escape life's experiences, be they ever so rough, by fleeing to another environment. All the conditions in this world have been constructed by the people who inhabit the world, and each individual is a builder of it and personally responsible for his immediate environment.

It is the mind that makes the man, and the mind and the thoughts of the mind endure even though the body be dissolved. So let no man think that he can escape the creations of his mind by breaking the physical chains that bind him to the earth. Nor does death in any of its phases relieve him of the states of mind that dominated him at the time of passing. The law of God is not mocked at any time or under any circumstances. "Whatsoever a man soweth, that shall he also reap." What we have sown in the flesh we shall reap in the flesh unless we repent, change our minds. When we do repent, we shall break mortal thoughts and ascend into a spiritual thought realm, the kingdom of God. This ascension we do not attain by dying physically but by dying to ill thoughts and living in true, good thoughts while still in the flesh. "Yet in my flesh shall I see God."

"The Word became flesh, and dwelt among us," says John in the very first chapter of his gospel.

Of all the great spiritual teachers of the ages Jesus has given us the most vivid and vital evidence of God as Father and guide. We say as Philip did, "Show us the Father, and it sufficeth us." The disciples were looking for a flesh-and-blood God. Do not the majority of Christians today look forward to seeing sometime, somewhere, a flesh-and-blood God sitting on a throne? Jesus replied, "He that hath seen me hath seen the Father."

He then explained that He was in the Father and the Father in Him. Yet His listeners did not understand, because they had not been trained to think metaphysically. God is Spirit, omnipresent Spirit-mind; and in Him "we live, and move, and have our being."

"God lives in me; no more I pine;
For love, and health, and joy are mine."

That God is the animating principle of all creation is not a new or startling teaching. It has been the conclusion of thinking minds ever since the birth of logic, and it will never be discarded so long as the faculty of logic continues to be exercised. Where there is an effect there must be a cause, and no amount of sophistry will erase the straight line from premise to conclusion. Timid men will cry pantheism and scare both themselves and others with a bugaboo they do not understand. Nevertheless the fact remains that intelligence and design and all the other evidences of an omnipresent planning Mind are so palpable in us and the world about us that we cannot boast of our sanity and at the same time deny them.

When logic presents these mighty truths to us and we begin to turn our attention to the omnipresent principle eternally active and flashing its presence into us and the whole universe, we awaken within ourselves a consciousness of it, and it begins to think and plan through us.

This is the first movement of Omnipresence, creating man as a self-conscious replica of itself, that is, of God. This replica is the Son of God or Christ, the exact reproduction in miniature of the mighty cosmic Mind. When this man of cosmic Mind arrives at full manifestation of Himself in habitation and place, we have Jesus Christ, the Son of God or God glorified in man. Jesus in ecstasy beholding this climax exclaimed "Glorify thou me with thine own self with the glory which I had with thee before the world was."

So if we have not begun our glorification by realizing this quickening life within, let us commence right now to recognize it in thought and word. James Russell Lowell wrote, "It may be that the longing to be so helps make the soul immortal." A great truth, spoken by a great man. Desire from within shoots a ray of energy from the imprisoned I AM to the all-infolding Spirit, and a thread of golden light unites parent and child. Darwin taught that desire for light in the protoplasmic cell shot a ray from its center to its surface and formed the primary eye. If this be true, and it seems logical, it is possible for us to animate the thirty-nine trillion cells estimated by Doctor Crile to be present in the body and eventually make them all luminous, as did Jesus. Thus science is revealing to us the movements of mind in forming the primary or physical body, which by the quickening of the Spirit is raised to the glorified immortal body.

We should not lose sight of the fact that the completion of this glorified body that God has planned for us devolves on us. We must become conscious of God-Mind and co-operate with it in making His plan manifest in us. As Jesus said, "My Father worketh even until now, and I work."

The childlike simplicity of this primary work seems so insignificant that great men who have delved into philosophy and worked with weighty intellectual problems deem it beneath them to become as a little child and concentrate their thoughts on nursery rhymes. They do not realize that instead of molding and animating the cells of their bodies they have projected their thoughts outwardly in speculating about the universe and its laws. So the cells left to themselves gradually starve for want of mind stimulation and finally die.

If you, dear reader, have attained eminence in some earthly field of action and yet have not demonstrated health, it may be that you need to take sound words in some simple form and go unto your Lord.

The Spirit of Him that raised up Jesus dwells in me, and I am made whole. Paul wrote, "But if the Spirit of him that raised up Jesus from the dead dwelleth in you, he that raised up Christ Jesus from the dead shall give life also to your mortal bodies through his Spirit that dwelleth in you." Few Christians realize the vital truth in this statement by Paul, although it is but one of many of like character to be found in his writings. Paul taught that what Spirit did for Jesus it would do for all who follow Him and adopt His methods of spiritual self-development.

Jesus claimed like results for His followers. In Matthew 19:28 it is written, "Verily I say unto you, that ye who have followed me, in the regeneration when the Son of man shall sit on the throne of his glory, ye also shall sit upon twelve thrones, judging the twelve tribes of Israel."

The promises of the power of Spirit to transform man from a mortal to an immortal state are producing a great company of spiritual-minded persons in the world today who work in the silence and speak but little about their heavenly experiences. In this way Spirit is forming a mighty Christian army that, when the need arises, will come out of its obscurity and save our civilization from extinction.

Although these spiritually quickened souls, often widely separated, may be working alone, they are bound together by the Holy Spirit, and the bond of brotherhood that unifies them is far more enduring than any human relationship. They are developing latent faculties of the soul that will make them superpowered men and women.

In order to establish and perpetuate the new order of life that is being poured into earth's mental atmosphere from on high it is absolutely essential that a people be prepared who can make use of the finer forces of the mind. The great initial outpouring of Spirit took place at the Pentecostal baptism more than nineteen centuries ago. The few who received this primal baptism are the seed from which has sprung a multitude. The trillions of cells forming the body of Jesus swim in omnipresence awaiting our appropriation. They are the living, quickening seeds of new life.

I am strengthened and healed by the power of the Spirit in the inner man.

We all need a better acquaintance with that phase of creative Mind that reveals and forms a connecting link between the Most High and the mind of the natural man. Most of us have not made conscious contact with the Spirit within but are thinking and acting in the outer crust of our being. Consequently we cannot hold communion with God in His omnipotence but must have a mediator or equalizer of the light and power that proceeds from the originating source of existence.

This is illustrated in high-powered electric systems: a transformer is necessary to lower the voltage and adapt it to the capacity of small industrial motors. If the full current from one of the big electric cables were turned directly into our small motors it would burn them up.

If the full current of God life were turned directly into the ordinary man's nervous system, it would destroy it. An equalizer has been provided--the Holy Spirit or Spirit of truth--through Jesus Christ.

Our human family has lost contact with the Spirit of truth, and our only salvation is through a soul strong enough to re-establish the connection. Jesus Christ released the electric atoms in His body and formed a conduit in the ether through which divine life is again flowing to the inhabitants of this planet. Without this purified life substance we should be unable to receive life or any message direct from God.

In John 14:16 Jesus said, "And I will pray the Father, and he shall give you another Comforter, that he may be with you for ever, even the Spirit of truth: whom the world cannot receive." Again in John 16:14 He makes His identity with the Spirit of truth stronger: "He shall glorify me: for he shall take of mine, and shall declare it unto you."

All who have faith enough to believe these things are comforted and guided by the Spirit of truth. Read John 17:20: "Neither for these only do I pray, but for them also that believe on me through their word."

It is the Spirit of truth that talks to us in dreams, visions, and inner urges. The more we acknowledge the Spirit as our indwelling inspiration and life the stronger its consciousness will be to us.

Through the Spirit of truth God moves the whole creation; hence any man may constantly increase his understanding of the source and relation of all things by claiming his unity with the Spirit of truth.

Question Helps

Chapter I - Be Thou Made Whole

1. In what respect do the words Christ and Jesus differ in meaning?
2. What is the supreme attainment of every man?
3. Is it possible for the Christ to experience death, burial, and resurrection?
4. When and where does resurrection take place? How did Jesus resurrect His body?
5. Do the words we use have any bearing on the results we get?
6. Why is it that man has not brought forth a greater degree of the Christ perfection?
7. Are infirmities permanent? How overcome?
8. Why did Jesus never give His personality any credit for the wonderful works He did?
9. Do all men have access to the Christ within?
10. Should man give more attention to the healing power of nature?
11. Should the student give his undivided attention to one system of development or should he study many? Explain fully.
12. Are there any short cuts into the kingdom of heaven?
13. Explain what is meant by the "end of the world," as brought out in the lesson?
14. Describe the means by which Jesus undertook to establish the kingdom of heaven on earth.

God Presence

Chapter II - God Presence

1. How may we know more of God and of ourselves?
2. Explain the meaning of "God is the health of His people."
3. Does God ever will man to be sick? Does He ever use His power to punish His creations?
4. How may we say that the attributes of God are expressed?
5. Should man ever think of God as being separate from him or outside him?
6. Explain how mind is the connecting link between God and man.
7. What is the proper procedure in realizing God as health? Is it looked on as practical by the world at large?
8. Explain the "still small voice."
9. Explain God as principle. Should the truth that God is principle lead us to infer that He is cold and unfeeling?
10. What part does man play in the forming of things?
11. Is God ever absent from His creations?
12. Since intelligence is the light of the world, how may we increase our intelligence?

Realization Precedes Manifestation

Chapter III - Realization Precedes Manifestation

1. How are we able to know that mind is the source of all things?
2. How should we regard miracles?
3. Is it possible for us to do the works that Jesus did?
4. Is it possible to explain the laws governing religion from a scientific viewpoint?
5. What part does concentration play in our demonstrations?
6. Give the metaphysical meaning of the word realization.
7. What does faith have to do with the realization of one's ideals?
8. Are all prayers answered?
9. The text mentions a realm where no effort is required to gain the answer to questions. Explain.
10. What is the supreme realization of man?

Producing Results

Chapter IV - Producing Results

1. What states of mind are necessary if we are to realize perfect health?
2. To what phase of being should a person give his
attention in order to understand the Scriptures?
3. How can healing be instantaneous?
4. Explain the meaning of the word sin.
5. What is it to forgive sin?
6. Should one ever think of oneself as being born in sin? What should be one's viewpoint?
7. What is the foundation of the Jesus Christ kingdom?
8. What part does love play in our unfoldment?
9. Explain fully the meaning of the Trinity.
10. What mental attitude should man have toward his body?

The Omnipotence Of Prayer

Chapter V - The Omnipotence of Prayer

1. Why is it necessary to affirm a thing one already knows to be true?
2. Should everyone pray? Why?
3. Explain why Jesus advised us to ask for what we want.
4. Is asking always a part of prayer? What other forms of prayer are there?
5. Is it ever good for one to be self-righteous? 6. What is the key to all mysteries?
7. What part do faith and understanding play in a perfect demonstration?
8. What is the real foundation of effective prayer?
9. Is it essential to have great faith in order to demonstrate?
10. Is silent prayer more effective than audible prayer? Why?
11. What state of mind is necessary if we are to receive clear revelations?
12. Why are some healings slow even though prayers are said?

God Said, And It Was So

Chapter VI - God Said, and It Was So

1. Explain fully in your own words the power of healing words.
2. Did Jesus ever write? Through what channel have we received His words?
3. From what standpoint did Jesus say that His words are spirit and are life?
4. Does the word of itself have power? What must we do to give full force to our words?
5. Is Truth ever the formulated doctrine of any church, creed, or sect? Where may we find Truth?
6. What must we do to keep successfully in mind the words of Jesus?
7. Is moral goodness always an indication of spirituality?
8. What determines the character and the results of our words?
9. Is it necessary for us to feel our oneness with God in order to believe in His omnipotence?
10. What does the healing of the man at the Pool of Bethesda represent?
11. Is it ever possible for anyone to do our spiritual work for us?
12. Explain how Jesus made His teachings available to all.

Indispensable Assurance

Chapter VII - Indispensable Assurance

1. Is man's desire for a fuller and more excellent life a natural and orderly one? Explain fully.
2. Give in your own words a definition of faith. Is it

natural for man to have faith?

3. Is it a falsehood to deny sickness in the face of its appearance?

4. How are we to get more life?

5. Is it a fact that faith is blind?

6. How are we to emulate Jesus? Is it necessary to do so in order to do the works of God?

7. Give three steps that are necessary in demonstration.

8. Would you call Jesus a master scientist? What did He mean when He said, "In my Father's house are many mansions"?

9. Is it better to seek understanding through intellectual reasoning or through divine inspiration?

10. Just what do our thoughts and words have to do with our demonstrations?

11. Is it always necessary for us to be receptive in order to be healed? Does God ever do things for us against our will?

12. Give the difference between a genius and an ordinary man from the metaphysical viewpoint.

13. Is it sufficient to be inspired by an ideal, or is something else needed?

14. Should one ever take the attitude that things as they are cannot be changed?

15. Explain what is meant by giving up the personal and taking up the universal.

The Fullness Of Time

Chapter VIII - The Fullness of Time

1. What part does order play in life?
2. Explain fully the power of words.
3. Is there any limit to the power of thought?
4. What should be our attitude toward hurry?
5. How may we become conscious of our I AM?
6. How is soul growth related to bodily health?
7. Explain the relation between law and order. What part does law and order play in the divine scheme of things?
8. What is the difference between natural law and divine law?
9. Were the works that Jesus performed really miracles? Why?
10. Is it good to deny the existence of the things of the world?
11. Is it necessary to enter fully into the kingdom in order to realize results?
12. Give some of the signs that follow the giving of attention to Spirit.

Healing Through Praise And Thanksgiving

Chapter IX - Healing through Praise and Thanksgiving

1. Has praise any commercial value? Any spiritual value? Explain.
2. How is the body restored to perfection?
3. How should the various writers of the Bible be judged?
4. Is it possible for us to be of service in establishing peace on earth?
5. In your own words tell how the new Christianity and physical science are working together.
6. Where is heaven, and how is it formed?
7. Explain what Jesus meant when He said that the bread and wine was His body and His blood.
8. Does man have the power to form and reform the universal energy?
9. Is there more than one God?
10. Explain in your own words the meaning of the four horses mentioned in the 6th chapter of Revelation.

"I Am The Way, And The Truth, And The Life"

Chapter X - I Am the Way, and the Truth, and the Life

1. Explain why the word of Spirit is next to Spirit in power.
2. Compare Jehovah and Christ. How should one go about choosing healing words?
3. Why do we find it advantageous to use the name Jesus Christ?
4. Did Jesus discover the principles He taught and demonstrated?
5. Give the difference between the real spiritual I AM and the personality. How did Jesus handle this proposition? Is it possible for us to do likewise?
6. What is the difference between Jehovah God and Elohim God?
7. Does the individual I AM contain infinite creative capacity?
8. Can the unseen forces be mechanically demonstrated? How?
9. What did Jesus mean when He said that we should be judged by our words? What is meant by the "day of judgment"?
10. Explain fully the change from the natural life to the spiritual life. What did Paul mean when he said, "I die daily?"
11. What must be our viewpoint if we are to be saved?
12. Should we expect healing today the same as in the time of Jesus' ministry on earth?

Healing Power Of Joy

Chapter XI - Healing Power of Joy

1. Explain how joy acts on fear.
2. Explain the relation between happiness and health.
3. Do you think that singing can be of benefit toward the realization of perfect health?
4. Explain how the whole universe is in vibration.
5. What part does zeal play in our unfoldment? Explain fully.
6. What is the cause of man's seeming lack of vital energy?
7. Explain the importance of faith. How is faith quickened?
8. Does man's thinking have much to do with his spiritual progress?
9. Why is it necessary first to study mind in order to understand the real character of God?
10. What should we do to bring the Spirit into our consciousness?

Holy Spirit Fulfills The Law

Chapter XII - Holy Spirit Fulfills the Law

1. Explain the Holy Spirit from the viewpoint of the Christian metaphysician and the physical scientist.
2. How should a good Christian healer regard the Holy Spirit?
3. Should we ever hesitate to call on the Holy Spirit?
4. Did God create man with a perfect body or perfect-body idea?
5. Did Jesus die on the cross? Explain how He was able to resurrect His body.
6. Is it to our benefit to know that mind rules matter? Explain.
7. Is it possible to escape life's experiences by a change of environment or by death?
8. Can "ascension" be gained through physical death?
9. What did Jesus mean when He said, "He that hath seen me hath seen the Father"?
10. Is it necessary for man to become as a little child? Explain fully.
11. Why is it that man must have a mediator in order to contact God? Who is this mediator?
12. Since man has seemingly lost contact with Spirit, what is his only salvation?

Mysteries of John

Foreword

METAPHYSICAL BIBLE students recognize in the Gospel of John a certain spiritual quality that is not found in the other Gospels. Although this is not true of all Bible readers, it may be said that those who look for the mystical find it in the language of this book. The book is distinctive in this respect and is so successful in setting forth metaphysical truths that little interpretation is necessary. Only in a few instances does the original writing conceal the deep truths that the student seeks to discern. Written language is at best a reflection of inner ideas, and even though a teacher couples ideas and words as adroitly as Jesus does, elucidation is sometimes difficult.

Nevertheless ideas are catching, and this may be the best reason for publishing another book about this spirit-arousing Fourth Gospel. We are all heavily charged with ideas, and when these ideas are released they spring forth and pass from mind to mind, being "recorded" as they fly, and when they are expressed the whole race is lifted up--if the idea is charged with the uplifting Spirit. Jesus was God's idea of man made manifest in the flesh; so He was warranted in making that dynamic assertion, "I, if I be lifted up from the earth, will draw all men unto myself." Nowhere in all literature has this truth of the unity of God, man, and creation been so fearlessly expressed and affirmed by man as in the Book of John.

Here the question arises as to God's responsibility for all that appears in the flesh, both good and evil, which seems to confound our logic and understanding. We are in human consciousness the fruit of a tree that stemmed from the soil of Being. The laws instituted in the aeons and ages of the past still prevail in the present. Interpreting Being from a personal standpoint, we have ignored the principles and laws at the very foundation of all creation and substituted a personal God, and many contradictions have followed. Now through the unfoldment of the spiritual man implanted in us in the beginning we are discerning the unchangeable laws of the good and the absolute necessity of conforming to them.

So we see that Jesus taught plainly that God functions in and through man and nature instead of being a person somewhere in the skies; also that we demonstrate God by making His Spirit manifest in our life. "He that hath seen me hath seen the Father." Socrates was asked, "What is a good man?" He replied, "A man who does good." Again he was asked, "What is good?" " What the good man does," he replied.

No extended definition of good is necessary to those who follow Jesus; even converted savages understand good and do it. The universal desire among awakened Christians to love God and man is part of the law constantly operating through man when he finds his right relation to God.

The status of evil is that of a parasite. It has no permanent life of itself; its whole existence depends on the life it borrows from its parent, and when its connection with the parent is severed nothing remains.

Apparent evil is the result of ignorance, and when the truth is presented the error disappears. Jesus called it a liar and the father of lies.

Men personalize good and evil in a multiplicity of gods and devils, but Truth students follow Jesus in recognizing the supreme Spirit in man as the "one God and Father of all."

Chapter I

> "In the beginning was the Word, and the Word was with God, and the Word was
> God. 2 The same was in the beginning with God. 3 All things were made through
> him; and without him was not anything made that hath been made. 4 In him was
> life; and the life was the light of men. 5 And the light shineth in the darkness,
> and the darkness apprehended it not."

IN PURE METAPHYSICS there is but one word, the Word of God. This is the original creative Word or thought of Being. It is the "God said" of Genesis. The Greek original refers to it in the 1st chapter of John as the logos. The Greek word cannot be adequately translated into English. In the original it denotes wisdom, judgment, power, and in fact all the inherent potentialities of Being. This divine logos was and always is in God; in fact it is God as creative power. Divine Mind creates under law; that is, spiritual law. Man may get a comprehension of the creative process of Being by analyzing the action of his own mind. First is mind, then the idea in mind of what the act is to be, then the act itself. Thus the Word and the divine process of creating are identical.

Apart from mind nothing can be made. Even man, in his forming and bringing anything into manifestation, uses the same creative process that God used; to the degree that the qualities of the one Mind enter into man's thought in the process his work will be enduring.

The divine idea--the Christ or Word of God--is always everywhere present.

Among the four Gospels that of John is readily discerned by metaphysicians as a symbolical life of Jesus and should appear first in the New Testament, corresponding to the first chapters of Genesis. Quite a few Bible critics so consider it, among them Ferrar Fenton, who gives it first place in his "Complete Bible in Modern English."

John explains that all existence is spiritual, that it comes to man as a gift, and that Christ is its fulfillment. "In the beginning was the Word, and the Word was with God, and the Word was God."

"The Word" is the English translation of the Greek logos, which means a thought or concept and also the word that is an expression or utterance of the same. It also involves the logical relation between idea and expression; hence our word logic, which also derives from logos.

Our attention is called to the 1st chapter of Genesis: "And the Spirit of God moved upon the face of the waters. And God said, Let there be light: and there was light."

Here in detail, day by day, or period by period, creation is ideated.

The parallel between Genesis and John is shown by the manifestation of the ideal man. In Genesis Adam appears first. In John it is John the Baptist, who is said to "bear witness" to the coming man, Jesus. In Genesis man was given dominion over all things; in John "all things were made through him."

John the Baptist represents the natural man, the physical man, who is the nucleus around which the spiritual man builds. Man may be compared to a house, the foundation being rock, the superstructure lighter material. The rock upon which Jesus built was not material: it was mental; its symbol, Peter, was a mind receptive to spiritual Truth and spiritual substance.

The first Adam was formed of the "dust of the ground," representing radiant substance instead of gross earth.

So John the Baptist was more than the perfect physical man. He was the illumined natural man. He preached and baptized his disciples and with spiritual vision saw the unfoldment of the natural man into the Christ man.

Spiritual man is the true light "which lighteth every man, coming into the world." The world was made by him and yet "knew him not."

There is a creative force constantly at work in man and all creation, but it is not recognized. It is Spirit-mind shining consciously in the minds and hearts of those who recognize it. Those who ignore this light do not "apprehend" it, and to them it is nonexistent.

"But as many as received him, to them gave he the right to become children of God, even to them that believe on his name."

> [6] There came a man, sent from God, whose name was John. [7] The same came
> for witness, that he might bear witness of the light, that all might believe through
> him. [8] He was not the light, but came that he might bear witness of the light.

Man in his darkened, ignorant state dwells in a realm of material thoughts and perceives nothing higher until he arrives at the point in his unfoldment where he is ready to receive understanding of the Christ Truth. Then he enters into the John the Baptist or intellectual perception of Truth. The intellectual perception of Truth by the natural man (John the Baptist) is not the true light (the Christ) but bears witness to the light and prepares the way for its dawning in consciousness.

> [9] There was the true light, even the light which lighteth every man, coming into
> the world. [10] He was in the world, and the world was made through him, and
> the world knew him not. [11] He came unto his own, and they that were his own
> received him not.

The true light (the Christ or Word) that lights every man coming into the world is and ever has been in man. Even the outer man was formed and came into existence through it. Up to a certain stage in his unfolding man does not recognize this truth; now however this mystery, which is "Christ in you, the hope of glory," is being revealed to the race with more and more clarity and with greatly increased power.

> [12] But as many as received him, to them gave he the right to become children of
> God, even to them that believe on his name: [13] who were born, not of blood, nor
> of the will of the flesh, nor of the will of man, but of God.

According to the 12th and 13th verses, the same truth that held good for Jesus will hold good for as many as receive Him (the Christ) and believe in His resurrecting power as Jesus believed in it.

> [14] And the Word became flesh, and dwelt among us (and we beheld his glory, glory
> as of the only begotten from the Father), full of grace and truth.

Jesus recognized this truth that the Christ, the divine-idea man or Word of God, was His true self and that He was consequently the Son of God. Because Jesus held to this perfect image of the divine man, the Christ or Word entered consciously into every atom of His being, even to the very cells of His outer organism, and transformed all His body into pure, immortal, spiritual substance and life. Thus "the Word became flesh." The resurrecting of His whole being included His body. Jesus entered alive and entire into the spiritual realm.

> [15] John beareth witness of him, and crieth, saying, This was he of whom I said,
> He that cometh after me is become before me: for he was before me. [16] For of
> his fulness we all received, and grace for grace. [17] For the law was given through
> Moses; grace and truth came through Jesus Christ. 18 No man hath seen God
> at any time; the only begotten Son, who is in the bosom of the Father, he hath
> declared him.

"The law was given through Moses." Moses represents a phase of the evolutionary process in man. "The law"–the outer commandments--cannot redeem. "Grace and truth came through Jesus Christ"; that is, the real saving, redeeming, transforming power came to man through the work that Jesus did in establishing for the race a new and higher consciousness in the earth.

We can enter into that consciousness by faith in Him and by means of the inner spirit of the law that He taught and practiced.

The 18th verse teaches that through the Christ in us we come into an understanding of the Father, since the Son (the Word) ever exists in God, and Father and Son are one and are omnipresent in man and in the universe. Spirit Truth is discerned through Spirit only; not in outer ways or through intellectual perception do we come to know God.

> *19* And this is the witness of John, when the Jews sent unto him from Jerusalem
> priests and Levites to ask him, Who art thou? 20 And he confessed, and denied
> not; and he confessed, I am not the Christ. 21 And they asked him, What then?
> Art thou Elijah? And he saith, I am not. Art thou the prophet? And he answered,
> No. 22 They said therefore unto him, Who art thou? that we may give an answer
> to them that sent us. What sayest thou of thyself? 23 He said, I am the voice of
> one crying in the wilderness, Make straight the way of the Lord, as said Isaiah the
> prophet. 24 And they had been sent from the Pharisees. 25 And they asked him,
> and said unto him, Why then baptizest thou, if thou art not the Christ, neither
> Elijah, neither the prophet? 26 John answered them, saying, I baptize in water: in
> the midst of you standeth one whom we know not, 27 even he that cometh after
> me, the latchet of whose shoe I am not worthy to unloose. 28 These things were
> done in Bethany beyond the Jordan, where John was baptizing.

In the regeneration two states of mind are constantly at work. First comes the cleansing or denial state, in which all the error thoughts are eliminated. This includes forgiveness for sins committed and a general clearing up of the whole consciousness. The idea is to get back into the pure, natural consciousness of Spirit. This state of mind is typified by John the Baptist, who came out of the wilderness a child of nature whose mission it was to make straight the way for One who was to follow.

This putting away of sin from the consciousness (baptism through denial, plus forgiveness) is very closely allied to the deeper work that is to follow; so much so that to the observer it seems the same. Hence the followers of John, when they saw the works he did, asked if he was the Messiah. His answer was that the One who followed him was to baptize with Holy Spirit.

From this we discern that mental cleansing and the reforms that put the conscious mind in order are designed to prepare the way for that larger and more permanent consciousness which is to follow. This is the denial of "self" or personality. Jesus said, "If any man would come after me, let him deny himself." We are all guilty in a way of undue devotion to personal aims, which are always narrow and selfish. So long as these exist and take the place of the rightful One there is no room for the higher self, the Christ of God.

The recorded "This is the Son of God" is a reference to a matter of first importance in the regeneration. The recognition of man as the Son of God and the establishment in the mind of the new relations between the divine Father and the Son are essential to the process. If we do not affirm our sonship, with all its privileges and powers, we are sure to belittle ourselves and make limitations that prevent us from entering into the fullness of the Godhead. "Be perfect, as your heavenly Father is perfect."

> 29 On the morrow he seeth Jesus coming unto him, and saith, Behold, the Lamb of
> God, that taketh away the sin of the world! 30 This is he of whom I said, After me
> cometh a man who is become before me: for he was before me. 31 And I knew him
> not; but that he should be made manifest to Israel, for this cause came I baptizing
> in water. 32 And John bare witness, saying, I have beheld the Spirit descending
> as a dove out of heaven; and it abode upon him. 33 And I knew him not; but he
> that sent me to baptize in water, he said unto me, Upon whomsoever thou shalt
> see the Spirit descending, and abiding upon him, the same is he that baptizeth in

> the Holy Spirit. 34 And I have seen, and have borne witness that this is the Son
> of God.

Metaphysically interpreted, John the Baptist symbolizes in each individual the natural man, but with an illumined intellect. His face is turned toward the light in the measure that he recognizes and pays homage to the higher self within the individual. John baptized with water all those who believed that Jesus was soon to make His appearance. This is a cleansing, purifying process, preparing the individual to see spiritually and to discern spiritually.

The Father-Mind is the living principle, the absolute, the unlimited. The Son is the living Word. "Word" is used to designate man's I AM identity. The Holy Spirit is the action or outpouring or activity of the living Word. This activity produces what may be termed the light of Spirit, the breath of God, the "personality" of Being. The outpouring of the Holy Spirit is the sign by which the natural man recognizes the divine. Jesus, who became the "Lamb of God" or perfect expression of God, baptized in the Holy Spirit.

> 35 Again on the morrow John was standing, and two of his disciples; 36 and he
> looked upon Jesus as he walked, and saith, Behold, the Lamb of God!

By cultivation the spiritual mind becomes an active factor in consciousness. It has to be desired and sought before it becomes a part of one's conscious life. John the Baptist (the natural conscious mind) is expecting, looking for, and earnestly desiring a greater realization of Spirit. He knows that he is not fulfilling the Christ ideal of manhood; hence his prophecy of One who is to come, "the latchet of whose shoe" he is not worthy to loose.

This willingness to give up the natural man to the divine is a most propitious sign in one who is in the regenerative process. Many persons are ambitious to put on Christ, but are not willing to give up the present man in order to do so. John the Baptist had a following, yet he was willing that his disciples should go to Jesus. He openly acknowledged Him as the "Lamb of God." This was his acknowledgment of the Christ Mind. That mind has no personal ambition; it is innocent, loving, and obedient to the call of God.

> 37 And the two disciples heard him speak, and they followed Jesus. 38 And Jesus
> turned, and beheld them following, and saith unto them, What seek ye? And they
> said unto him, Rabbi (which is to say, being interpreted, Teacher), where abidest
> thou? 39 He saith unto them, Come, and ye shall see. They came therefore and saw
> where he abode; and they abode with him that day: it was about the tenth hour.
> 40 One of the two that heard John speak, and followed him, was Andrew, Simon
> Peter's brother. 41 He findeth first his own brother Simon, and saith unto him, We
> have found the Messiah (which is, being interpreted, Christ). 42 He brought him
> unto Jesus. Jesus looked upon him, and said, Thou art Simon the son of John:
> thou shalt be called Cephas (which is by interpretation, Peter).

When the conscious mind recognizes the Christ Mind, the various faculties gradually awaken and attach themselves to it. Andrew is the first apostle mentioned, and with him was one whose name is not given here but who is supposed to have been John (love). Love is modest and retiring, "seeketh not its own." Andrew represents the strength of the mind, which, greatly rejoiced when it finds the inexhaustible source of all strength, exclaims, "We have found the Messiah."

Strength is clearly related to substance (Simon), which in spirit we call faith. "Faith is the substance of things hoped for" (A.V.). What we hope for and mentally see as a possibility in our life comes into visibility, and we call it substantial.

> 43 On the morrow he was minded to go forth into Galilee, and he findeth Philip:
> and Jesus saith unto him, Follow me. 44 Now Philip was from Bethsaida, of the city
> of Andrew and Peter. 45 Philip findeth Nathanael, and saith unto him, We have

found him, of whom Moses in the law, and the prophets, wrote, Jesus of Nazareth,
the son of Joseph. 46 And Nathanael said unto him, Can any good thing come out
of Nazareth? Philip saith unto him, Come and see. 47 Jesus saw Nathanael coming
to him, and saith of him, Behold, an Israelite indeed, in whom is no guile! 48
Nathanael saith unto him, Whence knowest thou me? Jesus answered and said
unto him, Before Philip called thee, when thou wast under the fig tree, I saw thee.
49 Nathanael answered him, Rabbi, thou art the Son of God; thou art King of
Israel. 50 Jesus answered and said unto him, Because I said unto thee, I saw thee
underneath the fig tree, believest thou? thou shalt see greater things than these. 51
And he saith unto him, Verily, verly, I say unto you, Ye shall see the heaven opened,
and the angels of God ascending and descending upon the Son of man.

The name Philip means "lover of horses," and Philip is symbolic of the vigor, power, vitality, and energy of the mind. Philip, Andrew, and Peter are of the same "city," Bethsaida. The name Bethsaida means "house of fishing," and Bethsaida signifies a group of thoughts in consciousness that have as their central idea a belief in the increase of ideas and their expression and manifestation in outer form.

Nathanael (representing the imagination) is also called Bartholomew. In the realm of the real (Israel) the imaging power of the mind is guileless, innocent of error images. It is open and receptive to the beauty and perfection of Being. It is the faculty of imagination that makes the great artist and the great poet. It is the guileless innocence of the Nathanael state of mind that causes the religious enthusiast to believe all things about Spirit and the world invisible. Exercised without Christ understanding, the imagination becomes delusory. It is the image maker in the psychic; the clairvoyant may be deceived by its conjuring power. In itself it is not error, but it may, like all the other faculties, be used in erroneous ways. When the Mind of Spirit uses it, as in the case of Jesus' discerning Nathanael when he was under the fig tree, it is without guile; and in God's communication with man this faculty plays an important part.

Among the apostles, Bartholomew represents the imagination. He is called Nathanael in the 1st chapter of John, where it is recorded that Jesus saw him under the fig tree, the inference being that He discerned Nathanael's presence before the latter came into visibility. This would indicate that images of people and things are projected into the imaging chamber of the mind and that by giving them attention one can understand their relation to outer things. Mind readers, clairvoyants, and dreamers have developed this capacity to varying degree. Consciousness is what is concerned with soul unfoldment both primarily, and secondarily and all the way! Forms are always manifestations of ideas. Whoever understands this can interpret the symbols shown him in dreams and visions, but lack of understanding of this law makes one a psychic without discernment.

With this spiritual faculty it is possible for man to penetrate into the "fourth dimension" or what is usually called the "kingdom of the heavens" and to discern the trend of the spiritual forces. The angels of God are spiritual forces active in the Sons of God, the spiritually quickened.

The open and receptive and believing mind can see the things that take place in the Christ Mind, thus transcending the capacity of the unillumined natural man.

Chapter II

SPIRITUALLY A marriage represents the union of two dominant states of consciousness. Mary, the mother of Jesus, represents intuition, the spiritual soul, Eve, "the mother of all living." Jesus is the personal I AM and His apostles are the twelve faculties.

Cana is a "place of reeds"; so is the larynx found in the body. The name Galilee means "to whirl"; air is rapidly forced through the larynx in speaking or singing. The apostles represent the dominant nerve centers, the spiritual symbolism of each being concealed in the name. Philip means "one who is fond of horses." The horse symbolizes vigor, vitality, power. Vigor or its opposite, weakness, is betrayed by the voice, so we designate Philip as the power faculty, and his place in body expression is in the larynx (at Cana).

Water may be compared to natural or human life, and wine to spiritual life. In the regeneration spirit and body are united, but before this union can be accomplished the exhausted natural life must be quickened with spirit (symbolized by the turning of water into wine). This lack of vitalizing life is first realized by Mary, the source of all life, but Jesus, the directive I AM in all bodily activities, does not feel that He is yet ready to perform this seeming miracle and pleads delay: "Mine hour has not yet come."

But the urge of the inner forces is strong and the confident mother is sure that her son can do all things: "Whatsoever he saith unto you, do it."

The water pots filled to the brim with water by the servants represent the extent to which nature is prepared to fulfill the transformation from negative life to spiritual life through the power of the word of the Master, Jesus: "Draw out now, and bear to the ruler of the feast." The ruler of the feast, the supreme I AM, pronounced the transformed water to be superior to the best wine.

This transformation of the negative, watery fluid of the organism into vitalizing Spirit is accomplished by adding to every word a spiritual idea. The idea of omnipresent life will then quicken the natural life in man, and it will make conscious contact with the one life and draw it out for the benefit of the many.

When the I is "lifted up" there is a higher vital action imparted to the whole consciousness. Jesus said, "I, if I be lifted up from the earth, will draw all men unto myself." The lifting up of the I is the result of spiritual perception of Truth. When we discern the real truth of being and our relation to it, there is a new and higher consciousness established. This greater energy is first imparted to the soul or thought realm and through it to the body. This whole process is under law. There is a definite consecutive connection of thought and thing, through laws that may be discerned by man and used universally. At the close of chapter 1, Jesus had caught sight of the spiritual realm and said: "Ye shall see the heaven opened, and the angels of God ascending and descending upon the Son of man."

This high perception of man's union, through the I AM, with the divine harmony sets up a sympathetic vibration that is imparted to every part of consciousness. The marriage that took place in Cana of Galilee symbolizes this union in which the negative watery elements of the body were "lifted up" to wine or Spirit. A Bible authority says that His remark is more correctly stated in the words: "Woman, what is there between me and thee?" This interrogation depicts the questioning attitude of the personal I AM, Jesus. It is not clear in its understanding of what is to be done. It is looking forward to a time when it will act, but its "hour is not yet come." We find ourselves wanting to see all the steps of our actions before we begin, but in spiritual processes we have to proceed without foreknowing the various steps. If we go ahead and speak the word, the law will see us through. The elemental forces of Being (servants) are at hand to carry out our orders, and the intuitive perfection of Truth (woman) within us commands that those forces do our bidding.

The symbolism of this miracle has to do with the abundance of vital energy that may be generated from a union of man with the "water of life" or nerve substance in the various centers of his organism. With every thought we are putting the nerve substance into a state of action, and it rushes to any part of the body that is the center of attention. When we have been much excited or interested there is a concentration of vitality in the head, and if we do not know how to restore and equalize this vitality again in the body, we have a headache or the stuffy condition called a cold. To equalize: Center the attention in the larynx and declare, "All equalizing, harmonizing power is given unto me in mind and body."

In regeneration there is a permanent transmutation of physical vitality into higher consciousness, and a new element is introduced into the organism. "The ruler of the feast" (the Lord) praises the transmuted substance as the best offered at the wedding feast.

> 12 After this he went down to Capernaum, he, and his mother, and his brethren, and his disciples; and there they abode not many days.

Capernaum designates or represents an inner conviction of the abiding compassion and restoring power of Being. When one enters this state of consciousness a healing virtue pours out of the soul and transforms all discord into harmony.

Jesus and His mother and His brethren and His disciples went into this state of consciousness.

> 13 And the passover of the Jews was at hand, and Jesus went up to Jerusalem.

It is the nature of thought to repeat itself. At each repetition it will grow stronger or weaker as it is consciously recognized or ignored by man. Thus we can cultivate a good movement of the mind by giving it a special affirmation (feast). The Feast of the Passover that Jesus went up to Jerusalem to attend symbolizes an escape from bondage. When we begin to discipline our mind we always go up in consciousness, because it is from our spiritual height that we see things clearly and in their right relation.

> 14 And he found in the temple those that sold oxen and sheep and doves, and the changers of money sitting.

When we throw the light of Spirit into the subconscious courts of the body temple, we find queer and often startling conditions there. One would hardly expect to see butcher stalls and money-changers in a temple built for the worship of God, yet similar conditions exist in all of us.

> 15 And he made a scourge of cords, and cast all out of the temple, both the sheep and the oxen; and he poured out the changers' money, and overthrew their tables;
> 16 and to them that solddoves he said, Take these things hence; make not my Father's house a house of merchandise.

So the body temple must be cleansed; it is the house of God ("for we are a temple of the living God"), and it should be put in order. The first step in this cleansing process is to recognize its need. The next step is the "scourge of small cords" (A.V.): to formulate the word or statement of denial. When we deny in general terms we cleanse the consciousness, but secret sins may yet lurk in the inner parts. The words that most easily reach these hidden errors are not great ones, such as "I am one with Almightiness; my environment is God" but small, definite statements that cut like whipcords into the sensuous, fleshly mentality.

To get perfect results it is necessary to deal with our mind in both the absolute and the relative. In the early morning we may affirm, "All the affairs of my life are under the law of justice, and my own comes to me in ways divine," and before noon find ourselves searching the papers for advertisements of bargains in the stores. Such an experience shows that we have not gone into the temple and tipped over the tables and scattered the coins.

> 17 His disciples remembered that it was written, Zeal for thy house shall eat me up.

Excessive zeal in observing the forms of religious worship eats up the truly spiritual. "The zeal of thine house hath eaten me up." When we become very zealous in observing the rites of the church, we are prone to forget the church itself, which is Christ.

The light of Jesus Christ is, symbolically, the life of everyone who enters the same state of mind that He did. You always reap the consequences of your thought, and to enter the Christ Mind you have but to think along Jesus Christ lines.

Every man produces a thought atmosphere that has character and power in proportion to his ability as a thinker. Power increases with expansion; in thought, power is great or small as the ideals are high or low. When you follow narrow ideals your thought atmosphere is correspondingly contracted; but mental breadth enlarges and strengthens it in all directions.

"How can a man conceal himself?" said Confucius. In the light of the ever-present thought atmosphere with which we surround ourselves, he cannot. Nearly all people have the ability of sensing the thought atmosphere of those they meet; and a man may cultivate this ability to project himself until he becomes an open book and the air about him is filled with his silent yet potent words, ever telling what he has thought.

The thought atmosphere is a real, substantial thing, and has in it all that makes the body. We have a way of considering the things we cannot see as unsubstantial, and although we are told that we cannot conceal ourselves we go right on believing that we can. Hence it is good for us to know that of a truth we do carry about with us this open book of our life, out of which all persons read whether we realize it or not. Some people are good thought readers while others are dull, but all can read a little, and you cannot conceal yourself. Also your thought atmosphere is constantly printing its slowly cooling words on your body, where they are seen of men. But with a little practice we can feel the thought force of this atmosphere that surrounds us and gradually gain a realization of its existence that is as real as that of the outer world.

"Think on these things," said Paul. Think about Christ as a life force penetrating your whole being. Try to feel this force as an energy pulsating through every nerve and fiber of your body. Then imagine you can see this life force as a light lighting up every cell. Light represents intelligence, and when the light in you breaks forth into understanding you will know that there is a spiritual mind that is as much greater than the ordinary mind as the sun is greater than the moon. In Him is life, and this life is the light of men.

> 18 The Jews therefore answered and said unto him, What sign showest thou to us,
> seeing that thou doest these things? 19 Jesus answered and said unto them, Destroy
> this temple, and in three days I will raise it up. 20 The Jews therefore said, Forty
> and six years was this temple in building, and wilt thou raise it up in three days? 21
> But he spake of the temple of his body. 22 When therefore he was raised from the
> dead, his disciples remembered that he spake this; and they believed the scripture,
> and the word which Jesus had said.

That the temple referred to means the body is clearly stated in verse 21: "But he spake of the temple of his body." Man's ability to preserve his body from destruction is the proof that he has mastered his mind. So long as our body shows signs of decay it is evident that we have not cast out of the inner realms the "thought butchers" that for a sacrifice kill doves, sheep, oxen, and goats. The allusion here is to the destructive thoughts lying deep in the consciousness at the very issues of life.

The "three days" are spirit, soul, and body, the three "degrees" or parts of man's consciousness. When the I AM of man has purified and mastered these three, man is in the dominion proclaimed for him in the 1st chapter of Genesis; the Scripture or Word of God is fulfilled in him, and his faculties (disciples) recognize and respond to it every time that the uplifting word (the resurrecting word) is proclaimed.

> 23 Now when he was in Jerusalem at the passover, during the feast, many believed
> on his name, beholding his signs which he did. 24 But Jesus did not trust himself

> unto them, for that he knew all men, [25] and because he needed not that any one should bear witness concerning man; for he himself knew what was in man.

Truth is of the absolute order and does not have to be proved. Jesus recognized this fact and therefore did not feel it necessary to place any great value on the opinion of those who had not yet fully attained spiritual consciousness.

Chapter III

NOW there was a man of the Pharisees, named Nicodemus, a ruler of the Jews: 2 the same
came unto him by night, and said to him, Rabbi, we know that thou art a teacher come from
God; for no one can do these signs that thou doest, except God be with him.

THIS 3d chapter of John opens with a narrative of Nicodemus, "a ruler of the Jews," his visit to Jesus "by night" (meaning the darkness of intellectual understanding), and his confession: "Thou art a teacher from God; for no one can do these signs that thou doest, except God be with him."

Jesus told him that he must be "born anew," "of water and the Spirit." Here is a recognition by the Master of the operation of the divine law of evolution.

All "inheritance" of ideas and beliefs has a mental basis. We "inherit" some states of mind from our ancestors. An "inherited" or transmitted religion is a dark state, if there is no real understanding in it. This is the Nicodemus mentality. Nicodemus was a Pharisee and a ruler of the Jews. He represents the Pharisaical side of our mentality that observes the external forms of religion without understanding their real meaning. We accept our parents' religious affiliations without giving any thought to their origin. There was a time when it was considered unfilial and an evidence of disobedience for the children to join any other church than that to which their parents belonged. The Jews were especially rigid in their adherence to their traditional religion, and they proudly referred to their fathers Abraham, Isaac, and Jacob, who were taught of God.

This conservative religious thought preserves the church as an institution and restrains the individual from becoming religiously erratic. Nicodemus was a friend of Jesus', but his defense of the Master was put in the form of a question, reminding the Sanhedrin of the Jewish law that every man must be heard or given a chance to defend himself before being condemned. The "ruler of the Jews" did not press his championship of his friend before the Sanhedrin, and the assistance that he gave at the tomb of Jesus was safe enough, once the prosecutors and executioners had finished their work and turned their attention elsewhere.

Nicodemus was not acquainted with the power of Spirit and really had no understanding of regeneration, although he was a "teacher of Israel" (Israel representing thoughts that pertain to the religious department of the mind).

> 3 Jesus answered and said unto him, Verily, verily, I say unto thee, Except one be
> born anew, he cannot see the kingdom of God. 4 Nicodemus saith unto him, How
> can a man be born when he is old? can he enter a second time into his mother's
> womb, and be born? 5 Jesus answered, Verily, verily, I say unto thee, Except one
> be born of water and the Spirit, he cannot enter into the kingdom of God. 6 That
> which is born of the flesh is flesh; and that which is born of the Spirit is spirit. 7
> Marvel not that I said unto thee, Ye must be born anew. 8 The wind bloweth where
> it will, and thou, hearest the voice thereof, but knowest not whence it cometh, and
> whither it goeth: so is every one that is born of the Spirit.

The Pharisees refused to be baptized by John. They did not consider that they needed the repentance that he demanded. They thought they were good enough to take the high places in the kingdom of God because of their popularly accepted religious supremacy. Many people refuse to deny their shortcomings. They hold that they are perfect in Divine Mind and that it is superfluous to deny that which has no existence. But they are still subject to the appetites and passions of mortality, and will continue to be until they are "born anew."

The new birth is an uncertainty to the intellectual Christian, hence there has gradually evolved a popular belief that after death the souls of those who have accepted the church creed and have been counted Christians will undergo a change. But in His instructions to Nicodemus Jesus makes no mention of a resurrection after death as having any part in the new birth. He cites the ever present though unseen wind as an illustration of those who are born of Spirit. The new birth is a change that comes here and now. It has to do with the present man, that he may be conscious of the "Son of man," who is the real I AM in each individual. "And no one hath ascended into heaven, but that descended out of heaven, even the Son of man, who is in heaven."

This chapter of John contains some of the vital truths taught in Christianity: the evolution of man from natural to spiritual consciousness, and the incarnation of Jesus Christ as the divine pattern for all men who are seeking the way of life.

Christianity teaches the complete law of evolution as compared with the partial exposition of the law made by Darwin and associates. Christianity describes God as Spirit creating by a process comparable to the mental processes with which we are all familiar. "God said," and thus God created that which was to appear, God planned man and the universe, and through His word projected them into creation as ideal principles and immanent energies acting behind and within all visibility. But we should remember that Spirit could not emerge from the formless into the formed without creating relations, which necessitated laws operating through man and all things as essential factors in an orderly universe. Thus even God becomes subject to His laws or commandments. God the universal Spirit first appears as spiritual man. The next step in evolution is the appearance of the idea of spiritual man in the natural or Adam man. This man was primitively identified with an infinite capacity for expansion. When he recognizes his identity as being that of his source, Spirit, he expands in divine order and brings forth only good. When he deserts his spiritual anchorage and gives attention to external experiences and sensations, he falls into a world in which a diversity of results obtain that he calls good and evil. Thus man eats "of the fruit of the tree of the knowledge of good and evil." In these few words is summed up the fall of man from an Edenic state, where he had the constant inspiration of creative Mind, to a consciousness of matter and the desperate struggle of personality for existence.

The natural man must evolve into the spiritual. "And as Moses lifted up the serpent in the wilderness, even so must the Son of man be lifted up."

We are told here that "the light is come into the world, and men loved the darkness rather than the light." World chaos results from the lack of spiritual light. We may plan peace and achieve it, but if this peace is not based on divine law, evolving love, and that law incorporated into the pact of peace as well as into the minds of those who sign that pact, we shall have no permanent peace.

> 9 Nicodemus answered and said unto him, How can these things be?

There is but one real man, the ideal or spiritual man that God created. Jesus was explaining to Nicodemus the evolution of this spiritual man from his ideal to his manifest state. Man is fundamentally spiritual and so remains throughout his various manifestations. He comes out of heaven, manifests himself as a personality in the earth, and returns to heaven. The first Adam was in Paradise, and after his fall enough of his spiritual nature remained to keep him alive. Without this animating Spirit the whole human family would have perished with the fall of Adam. Faith in Spirit and the ultimate dominance of the good in man will finally restore him to the heaven from which he descended.

The new birth is simply the realization by man of his spiritual identity, with the fullness of power and glory that follows.

> 10 Jesus answered and said unto him, Art thou the teacher of Israel, and under-
> standest not these things? 11 Verily, verily, I say unto thee, We speak that which
> we know, and bear witness of that which we have seen; and ye receive not our
> witness. 12 If I told you earthly things and ye believe not, how shall ye believe if
> I tell you heavenly things? 13 And no one hath ascended into heaven, but he that
> descended out of heaven, even the Son of man, who is in heaven. 14 And as Moses
> lifted up the serpent in the wilderness, even so must the Son of man be lifted up;
> 15 that whosoever believeth may in him have eternal life.

16 For God so loved the world, that he gave his only begotten Son, that whosoever
believeth on him should not perish, but have eternal life. *17* For God sent not the
Son into the world to judge the world; but that the world should be saved through
him.

"For God so loved the world, that he gave his only begotten Son, that whosoever believeth on him [His own divine self] should not perish, but have eternal life." Not only are we to believe in our own divinity, but we are to accept the example of that divinity expressed through Jesus Christ.

To believe in Jesus is to believe that in the regenerate state we are to be, like Him, "joint-heirs with Christ." This belief must then lead us to a desire and an effort to attain our inheritance, because then we know that there is no other thing in the universe worth striving for. Every person in his real, true self desires to be just as great and just as good as it is possible for him to be. The open door to the attainment of this objective is to believe in one's own divinity and then to raise oneself to its level by following the example of Jesus.

This text reveals the heart of the glad tidings of Jesus Christ to mankind. In love God gave His only-begotten Son, the fullness of the perfect-man idea in Divine Mind, the Christ, to be the true, spiritual self of every individual. By following Jesus' example of recognizing and acknowledging the Christ in our every thought, word, and deed, thus unifying ourselves with His completeness, the outer will become as the inner; we shall be like Christ; we shall know Him as He is. He who truly believes "cometh not into judgment, but hath passed out of death into life."

18 He that believeth on him is not judged: he that believeth not hath been judged
already, because he hath not believed on the name of the only begotten Son of God.
19 And this is the judgment, that the light is come into the world, and men loved
the darkness rather than the light; for their works were evil. 20 For every one that
doeth evil hateth the light, and cometh not to the light, lest his works should be
reproved. 21 But he that doeth the truth cometh to the light, that his works may
be made manifest, that they have been wrought in God.

Salvation from the results of error thought begins at once when we have faith in the power of the Lord Jesus Christ to save us from the judgment. He comes to us in Spirit to do away with the effects of transgression of the law. When we perceive the way of righteousness and Truth and follow it, there comes to us a new light, an understanding of the law, and we enter the kingdom of God here and now. "Even the Son of man, who is in heaven."

22 After these things came Jesus and his disciples into the land of Judaea; and there
he tarried with them, and baptized. 23 And John also was baptizing in AEnon near
to Salim, because there was much water there: and they came, and were baptized.
24 For John was not yet cast into prison. 25 There arose therefore a questioning
on the part of John's disciples with a Jew about purifying. 26 And they came unto
John, and said to him, Rabbi, he that was with thee beyond the Jordan, to whom
thou hast borne witness, behold, the same baptizeth, and all men come to him. 27
John answered and said, A man can receive nothing, except it have been given him
from heaven. 28 Ye yourselves bear me witness, that I said, I am not the Christ, but,
that I am sent before him. 29 He that hath the bride is the bridegroom: but the
friend of the bridegroom, that standeth and heareth him, rejoiceth greatly because
of the bridegroom's voice: this my joy therefore is made full. 30 He must increase,
but I must decrease.

31 He that cometh from above is above all: he that is of the earth is of the earth,
and of the earth he speaketh: he that cometh from heaven is above all. 32 What he
hath seen and heard, of that he beareth witness; and no man receiveth his witness.

> 33 He that hath received his witness hath set his seal to this, that God is true. 34
> For he whom God hath sent speaketh the words of God: for he giveth not the
> Spirit by measure. 35 The Father loveth the Son, and hath given all things into his
> hand. 36 He that believeth on the Son hath eternal life; but he that obeyeth not
> the Son shall not see life, but the wrath of God abideth on him.

Jesus represents the Christ. Judea represents praise. John the Baptist and Jesus represent co-operation between the intellect and the Spirit.

Metaphysically interpreted, John the Baptist represents the intellectual concept of Truth and his baptizing means a mental cleansing. The name Salim means "peace." "Near Salim" signifies the illumined consciousness of spiritual life and peace in the individual. The water refers to a natural rising in consciousness of the cleansing power of the thought and word of purification and life. The Jew symbolizes an inquiring thought. John candidly explained that he had said before that Jesus was the Christ, the Saviour, and that he, John, must decrease while the Christ must increase. However John declared that he truly believed Jesus to be the Saviour and that all who believed should receive eternal life. But John must decrease, and yet by his own admission those who believe are to have everlasting life.

Metaphysically interpreted, John the Baptist (representing the illumined intellect) decreases on the sense plane in proportion as the intellect is lifted up in Spirit and is in truth swallowed up in spiritual consciousness. The faculty decreases on one plane only to be reborn on a higher one. The illumined intellect wholly co-operates with Spirit, so there is a merging and blending of these powers until the mere intellect ceases to be mere intellect and is swallowed up in Spirit. This is the ideal unfoldment. There are those who are so bound in their own beliefs, who are so set on the letter of the law, that they think intellectuality is the highest unfoldment. They have not yet attained the ability to perceive or receive the things of Spirit. Those in the John the Baptist process of unfoldment willingly cooperate with the Christ every step of the way. The truth is that we are all under the law of infinite expansion, and the development of the race must go forward. Therefore, it is said that "the Son of man must be lifted up."

An example of how the intellect serves may be readily illustrated by the use of the x in algebra. The x stands for the unknown quantity. When the problem is worked out the x is erased. Thus the intellect is the tool of Spirit just as the x is a tool used in the mathematical operation. In the John the Baptist consciousness we obey and conform our thinking to the requirements of the spiritual instead of the natural. Spirit life is something that has enduring qualities. It is superior to the life that goes and comes through death and rebirth.

When the redeemed intellect is fully merged with the Christ light, then the indwelling Spirit of truth is free to perform many so-called miracles. It bridges over difficulties and cements the forces of the soul into one perfect instrument of God for achieving the glory of God. When one reaches this plane spiritual unfoldment goes forward by leaps and bounds.

In order to fulfill the divine law of his being man must realize that he is the Son of God in manifestation, that he came from above and is above all; also that in his evolution he leaves the earthly consciousness and ascends into the spiritual under a law of mind. "He that cometh from above is above all: he that is of the earth is of the earth, and of the earth he speaketh." For he whom God hath sent speaketh the words of God. "The Father loveth the Son, and hath given all things into his hand."

Chapter IV

THE NAME Samaria means "watchtower"; and Samaria represents that department of the objective consciousness which functions through the head. The name Sychar means "drunken," and the place symbolizes a confused state of mind. Sychar was located near the parcel of ground that Jacob gave to his son Joseph; physiologically it corresponds to the forehead, seat of intellectual perception. Here also is Jacob's well--inspiration through the intellect alone.

Jesus--I AM--has been compassing the whole man, from within to without, and the I AM "rests" at the point where the intellectual and the spiritual meet.

> 7 There cometh a woman of Samaria to draw water: Jesus saith unto her, Give me to
> drink. 8 For his disciples were gone away into the city to buy food. 9 The Samaritan
> woman therefore saith unto him, How is that thou, being a Jew, asketh drink of
> me, who am a Samaritan woman? (For Jews have no dealings with Samaritans.)
> 10 Jesus answered and said unto her, If thou knewest the gift of God, and who it
> is that saith to thee, Give me to drink; thou wouldest have asked of him, and he
> would have given thee living water. 11 The woman saith unto him, Sir, thou hast
> nothing to draw with, and the well is deep: whence then hast thou that living
> water? 12 Art thou greater than our Father Jacob, who gave us the well, and drank
> thereof himself, and his sons, and his cattle? 13 Jesus answered and said unto her,
> Every one that drinketh of this water shall thirst again: 14 but whosoever drinketh
> of the water that I shall give him shall never thirst; but the water that I shall give
> him shall become in him a well of water springing up unto eternal life. 15 The
> woman saith unto him, Sir, give me this water, that I thirst not, neither come all
> the way hither to draw.
>
> 16 Jesus saith unto her, Go, call thy husband, and come hither. 17 The woman
> answered and said unto him, I have no husband. Jesus saith unto her, Thou saidst
> well, I have no husband: 18 for thou hast had five husbands; and he whom thou
> now hast is not thy husband: this hast thou said truly. 19 The woman saith unto
> him, Sir, I perceive that thou art a prophet. 20 Our fathers worshipped in this
> mountain; and ye say, that in Jerusalem is the place where men ought to worship.
> 21 Jesus saith unto her, Woman, believe me, the hour cometh, when neither in this
> mountain, nor in Jerusalem, shall ye worship the Father. 22 Ye worship that which
> ye know not: we worship that which we know; for salvation is from the Jews. 23
> But the hour cometh, and now is, when the true worshippers shall worship the
> Father in spirit and truth: for such doth the Father seek to be his worshippers.
> 24 God is Spirit: and they that worship him must worship in spirit and truth. 25
> The woman saith unto him, I know that Messiah cometh (he that is called Christ):
> when he is come, he will declare unto us all things. 26 Jesus saith unto her, I that
> speak unto thee am he.
>
> 27 And upon this came his disciples; and they marvelled that he was speaking with
> a woman; yet no man said, What seekest thou? or, Why speakest thou with her?
> 28 So the woman left her waterpot, and went away into the city, and saith to the
> people, 29 Come, see a man, who told me all things that ever I did: can this be
> the Christ? 30 They went out of the city, and were coming to him.

Jesus preached one of His greatest sermons to the woman at the well; she was a Samaritan, a heathen. ("Jews have no dealings with Samaritans.") Her highest concept of God was that of a being who had to be worshiped in some temple in Jerusalem or in a certain mountain. Jesus told her, "God is Spirit: and they that worship him must worship in spirit and truth."

To worship God truly we must know where He is and how to approach Him. If, as many teach, God lives in heaven, and heaven is located somewhere in the skies, we have a consciousness of separation from Him, and our approach to Him is uncertain.

But when we know the truth about God, that He is an omnipresent Spirit manifesting Himself to our mind when we think of Him as one with us in Spirit and responding to our every thought, then we know Him as He is.

This lesson on omnipresence needs constant repeating because we function mentally and physically, the material or manifest predominating. Here we are told that Jesus went from Judea to Galilee. Judea connotes Spirit and Galilee connotes manifestation. Jesus told the woman that salvation came from the Judeans or spiritual-minded. It is easy to understand God as Spirit and man as His spiritual offspring.

The "well of water springing up into eternal life" is the fount of Christ inspiration within man's consciousness. When the seal of material thought is broken this inner spiritual life flows forth peacefully, majestically, vitalizing and renewing mind and body. In the clear light of Truth we are conscious of life as unchanging, eternal.

The Samaritan woman represents the duality of the soul or subconsciousness. It is not the true source of wisdom, although many searchers after Truth fail to distinguish between its revelations and those of Spirit. In Hindu metaphysics it is known as the human and animal soul.

The Samaritans claimed to be descendants of Jacob, and they used portions of the Hebrew Scriptures, but in the eyes of the Israelites the Samaritans were pretenders, not true followers of Jehovah. Thus spiritually enlightened people see in psychic and spiritistic phenomena and the revelations of that branch of occultism an imitation of Truth, without a true understanding of its relation to Spirit.

But the soul must have Truth, and Christ recognizes the soul as worthy; hence this wonderful lesson of John 4:9-26 given to one auditor. The soul draws its life from both the earthly side of existence (Jacob's well) and the spiritual (the Jew), but is destined to draw from a higher fount, omnipotent Spirit. Jesus asked the woman for a drink, which indicates the universality of the spiritual life, present in the Samaritan woman as well as in Jesus.

"The gift of God" to man is eternal life. The soul informed of this truth asks the Father for the manifestation of this life, and there gushes forth a never-failing stream. But where sense consciousness is dominant the soul is slow to see the realities of ideas, thoughts, and words; the sight is fixed on material ways and means: "Thou hast nothing to draw with ... whence then hast thou that living water?" This is a fair setting forth of the status of the questioning ones of this day who ask the explanation of spiritual things on a material basis.

The Christ is a discerner of thoughts and reads the history of the soul as an open book. When Jesus displayed this ability to the woman, she at once had faith in Him and accepted Him as a prophet, not because she understood His doctrine, but because He had told her of her past: "Come, see a man, who told me all things that ever I did."

In its natural state the soul is attached to localities, forms, and conditions in the world. It believes in the importance of places of worship and in the observance of outward forms. The Mind of Spirit puts all such formalities aside and proclaims the universality of spiritual forces. "God is Spirit." "Neither in this mountain, nor in Jerusalem, shall ye worship the Father." The soul, by falling into forms of worship, fails to get the true understanding, but the Christ-minded know Spirit. They enter into the consciousness of the formless life and substance and they are satisfied.

The Jews represent spiritual understanding, inspiration; the Gentiles represent material understanding. Salvation comes only through spiritual inspiration. This is the inner interpretation of Jesus' words "Salvation is from the Jews."

The "woman of Samaria" is a combination of the intellectual and emotional side of the soul. Jesus met her beside Jacob's well (inspiration through the intellect alone) in the city of Sychar (a confused state of mind). The I AM (Jesus) has power to harmonize the intellect by the power of Spirit. But before the I AM can do this, it must get the intelligent attention of the mixed state of consciousness symbolized by Sychar and the Samaritans. Being a combination of both Hebrew and heathen blood, the Samaritans were a mixed race; the woman at the well recognized the separation that exists between absolute Truth and the mixed thoughts of intellect. Jesus is not afraid of being contaminated by such communion. He is willing to imbibe the inspiration of this realm of mind, and in so doing He comes in touch with its interests.

The Jesus consciousness is appealing to intellectual people to recognize the gift of God, the Spirit of universal love and brotherhood. It invites their thoughts to receive the living inspiration, which may be had for the asking. But man must ask. "Ask, and ye shall receive."

The questioning, analytical attitude taken by the woman at the well represents the tendency of intellect to argue: "I see no visible means whereby you can get the everlasting water of life. Are you greater than all the precedents and antecedents of intellectual inheritance and experience?" These assumptions of the spiritual-minded that they have a truth higher than human reason seem to be farfetched and ephemeral. These are but a few of the many questions and objections of the intellectually wise.

Nevertheless spiritual perception continues to affirm that it has the inspiration that will never slacken or prove wanting. The mortal understands so little that it is constantly asking for more. It is never satisfied with itself or with the knowledge that it finds; but whoever drinks of the true spiritual inspiration will never thirst. It will prove a "well of water springing up unto eternal life."

The outer symbol of worship is adoration, homage; but worship in Spirit and Truth involves absolute union with the character of the object of worship. Therefore in order to fulfill the requirements of spiritual worship, a right understanding of God and a development in oneself of His Spirit are necessary.

> [31] In the mean while the disciples prayed him, saying, Rabbi, eat. [32] But he said
> unto them, I have meat to eat that ye know not. [33] The disciples therefore said
> one to another, Hath any man brought him aught to eat? [34] Jesus saith unto them,
> My meat is to do the will of him that sent me, and to accomplish this work. [34]
> Say not ye, There are yet four months, and then cometh the harvest? behold, I say
> unto you, Lift up your eyes, and look on the fields, that they are white already unto
> harvest, [36] He that reapeth receiveth wages, and gathereth fruit unto life eternal;
> that he that soweth and he that reapeth may rejoice together. [37] For herein is the
> saying true, One soweth, and another reapeth. [38] I sent you to reap that whereon
> ye have not labored: others have labored, and ye are entered into their labor.

On the divine side of his being man makes contact with spiritual ideas, which are the source of external substance or food. The natural man (represented by the disciples) thinks that the substance necessary for food must be put through the material process of planting and harvesting, but in Spirit the pure substance is always at hand ready to be appropriated by the inner consciousness. In states of high spiritual realization the desire for material food vanishes. Jesus fasted for forty days and "afterward hungered."

> [39] *And from that city many of the Samaritans believed on him because of the word of the*
> *woman, who testified, He told me all things that ever I did.* [40] *So when the Samaritans*
> *came unto him, they besought him to abide with them: and he abode there two days.* [41]
> *And many more believed because of his word;* [42] *and they said to the woman, Now we be-*
> *lieve, not because of thy speaking: for we have heard for ourselves, and know that this is*
> *indeed the Saviour of the world.*

There are always those at hand who need help, and that is our chance to administer aid. The woman who received help from Jesus at the well fled to the city to tell the people of Him. The result was that many came to Him, and He ministered to them all, proving that salvation is for all alike. "God is no respecter of persons." Salvation comes to everyone who assimilates and appropriates these truths and lets them find expression in and through him. Jesus healed and freed those to whom He ministered, and they believed, not because of what the woman said but because they themselves witnessed what Jesus Himself did.

> 43 And after the two days he went forth from thence into Galilee. 44 For Jesus
> himself testified, that a prophet hath no honor in his own country. 45 So when he
> came into Galilee, the Galilaeans received him, having seen all things that he did
> in Jerusalem at the feast: for they also went unto the feast.

Jesus came into Galilee, and the Galileans received Him. Spiritually interpreted, this means that the indwelling Christ reaches spiritual consummation, spiritual unity with the original Spirit, in the measure that it manifests life and functions in Spirit consciousness. Life activity (Galilee) is omnipresent, and man needs to apprehend the laws of Spirit, the laws governing all manifest things and his relation to all things.

The natural man looks up to what he considers mysterious and wonderful. He is not impressed by anything he thinks he knows and understands. Miracles to him are expected to come forth from some miraculous background. Therefore, Jesus, the carpenter's son, was of too common origin for His native companions to have any great faith in His claims of spiritual inspiration. "No man is a hero to his tailor." Therefore the Master "did not many mighty works there [in Nazareth] because of their unbelief."

> 46 He came therefore again unto Cana of Galilee, where he made the water wine.
> And there was a certain nobleman, whose son was sick at Capernaum. 47 When
> he heard that Jesus was come out of Judaea into Galilee, he went unto him, and
> besought him that he would come down, and heal his son; for he was at the point
> of death. 48 Jesus therefore said unto him, Except ye see signs and wonders, ye will
> in no wise believe. 49 The nobleman saith unto him, Sir, come down ere my child
> die. 50 So Jesus saith unto him, Go thy way; thy son liveth. The man believed the
> word that Jesus spake unto him, and he went his way. 51 And as he was now going
> down, his servants met him, saying, that his son lived. 52 So he inquired of them
> the hour when he began to amend. They said therefore unto him, Yesterday at the
> seventh hour the fever left him. 53 So the father knew that it was at that hour in
> which Jesus said unto him, Thy son liveth: and himself believed, and his whole
> house. 54 This is again the second sign that Jesus did, having come out of Judaea
> into Galilee.

It is believed by many professing Christians that the healing of the nobleman's son was a miracle performed only to furnish proof that Jesus came from God. A Bible commentator who is counted very wise in Bible interpretation has said: "Miracles have been wrought only to authenticate the bearers of supernatural revelation, so when a revelation is really being given, the dull minds of men should be compelled to discern, and attend to it by works so evidently due to divine power as to demonstrate that the speaker must bring a message directly from God." Yet Jesus Himself taught that those who believed on Him should do the works that He did and greater works.

The fact is that the healing of the nobleman's son is being duplicated every day of the year by modern followers of Jesus' methods, followers who have numberless absent patients, whom they never see yet whom they heal as effectually as Jesus healed the nobleman's son. Unity has similar cases every day, and the testimonials that we receive bear witness to the efficacy of our healing ministry. The light of Truth is shining more brightly today than ever before. The same faith that healed the nobleman's son will heal all persons who open their minds to it and let go of prejudice and unbelief. This fact is being demonstrated to all who are willing to believe.

Faith on the part of the patient or of someone connected with him is found to be an important factor in absent healing. This nobleman had faith that Jesus could heal his son, and when Jesus uttered the positive truth "Go thy way; thy son liveth," he "believed the word."

Spiritual healing is so marvelous and so far beyond the range of human explanation that it may appear to be supernatural. We cannot explain it clearly, but this we know: When we attain oneness with the invisible force that moves the mind, a new and higher energy sweeps through us; the thought is ablaze, and even our spoken words seem alive. When the word or spiritualized thought is sent to a receptive mind, it is conducted like the oscillations of the wireless telegraph; there is a universal thought ether that carries the message.

When the word goes forth from a spiritual center (represented by Jesus and His apostles) it becomes a continuous life-giver to all who believe in the spiritual as the source of life. Through faith they "tune in" and catch the message from the living word. "The words that I have spoken unto you are spirit, and are life." "Heaven and earth shall pass away: but my words shall not pass away."

Chapter V

JERUSALEM IS the spiritual center in consciousness. A feast in Jerusalem is a receptive state of mind toward all spiritual good, and the appropriation of that good for future use. Jerusalem means "city of peace." When we get deep down into the silent recesses of our soul we realize a stillness and sweetness beyond expression. There is a great peace there, the "peace of God, which passeth all understanding," and a welling up of an indescribable substance that fills the whole consciousness at the point where the inflow of original substance takes place.

> 2 Now there is in Jerusalem by the sheep gate a pool, which is called in Hebrew
> Bethesda, having five porches. 3 In these lay a multitude of them that were sick,
> blind, halt, withered, (waiting for the moving of the water. 4 for an angel of the
> Lord went down at certain seasons into the pool, and troubled the water whoso-
> ever then first after the troubling of the water stepped in was made whole, with
> whatsoever disease he was holden--margin.) 5 And a certain man was there, who
> had been thirty and eight years in his infirmity. 6 When Jesus saw him lying, and
> knew that he had been now a long time in that case, he saith unto him, Wouldest
> thou be made whole? 7 The sick man answered him, Sir, I have no man, when
> the water is troubled, to put me into the pool: but while I am coming, another
> steppeth down before me. 8 Jesus saith unto him, Arise, take up thy bed, and walk.
> 9 And straightway the man was made whole, and took up his bed and walked.

Sheep are the most harmless and innocent of all animals, and they represent the natural life that flows into man's consciousness from Spirit. It is pure, innocent, guileless; and when we open our mind to this realization of Spirit life we open the gate by the sheep market.

Here is a pool called Bethesda (meaning "house of mercy" or "place of receiving and caring for the sick"). There are also five porches or covered colonnades. This "pool" represents the realization in consciousness that our life is being constantly purified, healed, and made new by the activity of mind. Physically this is expressed in the purification and upbuilding of the blood by coming in contact with the oxygen of the air in the lungs. The ebb and flow of the waters of the pool is constant, and when our mind is active all the depleted blood corpuscles are purified and renewed.

This great multitude of "sick folk" (depleted life corpuscles) lies near this pool, under the "five porches" (five senses). The "five-sense" consciousness does not realize the power of the I AM to quicken these inner functions of man's organism; it lets weak, depleted life cells accumulate and burden its system, when a thought of the activity of life would, through the divine law, set them free from their helplessness.

It is not necessary that all the purification and renewing of the depleted corpuscles take place through the lungs when man understands the power of the I AM to declare the word of activity. Jesus, the I AM of Spirit, did not tell the man to go down into the pool and be healed, but said, "Arise, take up thy bed, and walk." Thus we see that the work of the Spirit is not confined to physical activities, although it does not ignore them. If your lung capacity is not equal to the purification of your blood, increase it by declaring the law of active life. Anemic blood may be made vigorous and virile by daily centering the attention in the lungs and affirming them to be spiritual, and under the perpetual inflow of new life and the outflow of old life the lungs will do your will.

Do not be limited by so-called established laws of nature, or by man's mortal thought that if you have reached the age of "thirty-eight" the life current is beginning to wane, that your "sabbath" or day of rest is setting in. It is "lawful" in Spirit to declare the perpetual activity of life anywhere, at any time, and under all circumstances. Divine life takes no cognizance of the laws that the intellect has set up for governing it. Life is ever active. It is constantly present in all its fullness and power, and it has no day of rest or "sabbath."

> Now it was the sabbath on that day. 10 So the Jews said unto him that was cured, It
> is the sabbath, and it is not lawful for thee to take up thy bed. 11 But he answered
> them, He that made me whole, the same said unto me, Take up thy bed, and walk.
> 12 They asked him, Who is the man that said unto thee, Take up thy bed, and walk?
> 13 But he that was healed knew not who it was; for Jesus had conveyed himself away,
> a multitude being in the place. 14 Afterward Jesus findeth him in the temple, and
> said unto him, Behold, thou art made whole: sin no more, lest a worse thing befall
> thee. 15 The man went away, and told the Jews that it was Jesus who had made
> him whole. 16 And for this cause the Jews persecuted Jesus, because he did these
> things on the sabbath. 17 But Jesus answered them, My Father worketh even until
> now, and I work. 18 For this cause therefore the Jews sought the more to kill him,
> because he not only brake the sabbath, but also called God his own Father, making
> himself equal with God.

These particular Jews had no understanding of the real "sabbath," which is a state of consciousness attained through meditation and the realization that the law is fulfilled in both thought and act.

The "sabbath of the Lord" has nothing to do with any day of the week. God did not name days and weeks, nor has He darkened His clear concepts of Truth by the time element.

Therefore, it is during the period of rest known as the "sabbath" that the demonstrations come forth, the state of consciousness in which the man that was sick let go of all false appearances and took up his bed and walked.

Many times much outer discord is avoided by the Christ's seemingly withdrawing from the outer until the quibbling intellect has somewhat spent its fury. ("Jesus had conveyed himself away.") Then the Christ reappears and reveals to the demonstrating thought added light: "Sin no more, lest a worse thing befall thee."

God-Mind is the living power back of all nature, causing the flowers to bud and to bloom and the grass to spring up. Jesus explained the outer working of this law in a very few words when He said, "My Father worketh even until now, and I work."

This divine creative power works continually one day just the same as any other day. Metaphysically we realize that this great creative force is God-Mind in action, and that it can not only create but also re-create. Therefore when Jesus spoke the word for him the sick man through this redeeming agency was instantly made whole. As all sickness is the result of sin, he who was healed was admonished to refrain from again breaking the law lest a worse sickness befall him.

Jesus was introducing into the consciousness of man the new truth that God is indeed the loving Father of all. But the intellectualists (represented by the Pharisees) could not receive it.

"He not only brake the sabbath [from the viewpoint of the Pharisees], but also called God his own Father, making himself equal with God."

Here again the Jews thought it blasphemy even to consider spiritualizing their nature until they knew in deed and in truth that God was their Father and that all that the Father had was theirs.

> 19 Jesus therefore answered and said unto them, Verily, verily, I say unto you, The
> Son can do nothing of himself, but what he seeth the Father doing: for what
> things soever he doeth, these the Son also doeth in like manner. 20 For the Father
> loveth the Son, and showeth him all things that himself doeth: and greater works
> than these will he show him, that ye may marvel. 21 For as the Father raiseth the
> dead and giveth them life, even so the Son also giveth life to whom he will. 22
> For neither doth the Father judge any man, but he hath given all judgment unto
> the Son; 23 that all may honor the Son, even as they honor the Father. He that
> honoreth not the Son honoreth not the Father that sent him. 24 Verily, verily, I say
> unto you, He that heareth my word, and believeth him that sent me, hath eternal
> life, and cometh not into judgment, but hath passed out of death into life. 25 Verily,

> verily, I say unto you, The hour cometh, and now is, when the dead shall hear the
> voice of the Son of God; and they that hear shall live. 26 For as the Father hath life
> in himself, even so gave he to the Son also to have life in himself: 27 and he gave
> him authority to execute judgment, because he is a son of man. 28 Marvel not at
> this: for the hour cometh, in which all that are in the tombs shall hear his voice,
> 29 and shall come forth; they that have done good, unto the resurrection of life;
> and they that have done evil, unto the resurrection of judgment.

The Father is the great source of all light and all understanding, and the Son is the idea that expresses the light and the wisdom of God.

The Son is the idea of God-Mind, of man in his perfection. Under divine law man makes manifest what God has in His mind.

The divine idea, the Christ, has been given eternal life and has the power to impart it to the Adam man. In addition to this He has been given judgment: He determines how the life shall be made manifest. The Father of life is a great river in the Garden of Eden, which represents man's innate capacity ready to obtain expression in all wisdom and understanding.

We honor the Christ when we recognize it as having the authority of God. In its life-giving capacity it is equal to God and has the power of God. When that is enthroned in us which possesses spiritual identity we have the realization that we are speaking the word right from the Father. Jesus in this state of unfoldment proclaimed: "The words that I say unto you I speak not from myself: but the Father abiding in me doeth his works."

In this way God is most fully manifest in His "divine idea" or Son, the Christ in man.

What men need above all else in this day is more wisdom, more discretion, in the use of the life they have. More life accompanied by the same old destructive ignorance in using it would but add to their misery. Thus God does not dictate what shall be man's choice with respect to this or any other act. If man discovers the law through which life is made manifest in his consciousness, he may use it blindly and ignorantly if he so elects. But he must also abide by the results of his choosing, and this is where man sets up his wail of sorrow: he does not like to reap his sowing.

Death came into our world through the ignorant use of life, and death can be put out only by a wise use of life. Death is the result of a wrong conception of life and its use. In the beginning of man's experiments with the powers of Being, he had no conception of death. His consciousness was intact and his unfoldment in wisdom was gradual and orderly. But his desire to experiment predominated. Sensation was sweet and enticing; it absorbed so much of his attention that he forgot wisdom--he "hid" from his Lord, and the result was separation from his Eden, the divine harmony of the law of spiritual unfoldment.

In raising the dead there are then two factors to deal with. The thought of the reality of death and the fear of death have both played destructive roles in the race consciousness, and they must be taken up and dissolved. The total unreality of death must be portrayed to the deluded consciousness. The omnipresence and the omnipotence of life are beyond dispute, and there can be no question that death is a condition set up in human consciousness. God is not dead; He does not recognize or countenance death. Neither does man when freed from its delusion. Jesus said: "Follow me . . . Leave the dead to bury their own dead."

The first step in demonstrating over death is to get the belief entirely out of the mind that it is God-ordained or is of force or effect anywhere in the realm of pure Being.

The next step is to live so harmoniously that the whole consciousness will be not only resurrected from its belief in death but so vivified and energized with the idea of undying life that it cannot be dissolved or separated from its vehicle, the body.

If our thoughts are good they work for good in our life, and if they are bad they are objects of redemption.

> 30 I can of myself do nothing; as I hear, I judge: and my judgment is righteous;
> because I seek not mine own will, but the will of him that sent me. 31 If I bear

witness of myself, my witness is not true. 32 It is another that beareth witness of
me; and I know that the witness which he witnesseth of me is true. 33 Ye have sent
unto John, and he hath borne witness unto the truth. 34 But the witness which
I receive is not from man: howbeit I say these things, that ye may be saved. 35
He was the lamp that burneth and shineth; and ye were willing to rejoice for a
season in his light. 36 But the witness which I have is greater than that of John;
for the works which the Father hath given me to accomplish, the very works that
I do, bear witness of me, that the Father hath sent me. 37 And the Father that
sent me, he hath borne witness of me. Ye have neither heard his voice at any time,
nor seen his form. 38 And ye have not his word abiding in you: for whom he sent,
him ye believe not. 39 Ye search the scriptures, because ye think that in them ye
have eternal life; and these are they which bear witness of me; 40 and ye will not
come to me, that ye may have life. 41 I receive not glory from men. 42 But I know
you, that ye have not the love of God in yourselves. 43 I am come in my Father's
name, and ye receive me not: if another shall come in his own name, him ye will
receive. 44 How can ye believe, who receive glory one of another, and the glory
that cometh from the only God ye seek not? 45 Think not that I will accuse you
to the Father: there is one that accuseth you, even Moses, on whom ye have set
your hope. 46 For if ye believed Moses, ye would believe me; for he wrote of me.
47 But if ye believe not his writings, how shall ye believe my words?

The Christ is the perfect God idea, which is ever in touch with its source. The Christ therefore realizes always that it can of itself do nothing, and places all judgment in the law. The laws of God are unchangeable. Man neither makes nor creates anything of permanence; he discerns what God has created and conforms to it in thought and act.

Judgment, when expressed on the mortal plane of consciousness, often is the expression of a critical and backbiting disposition. Man's safety lies in recognizing his need and balancing his judgment faculty with love. Then there will spring forth a new conquering power, which will express itself in righteousness and justice without condemnation.

The substitution of the Scriptures for the living Word of God is undoubtedly one of the reasons why the promise of Jesus to His followers of the ability to do mighty works has not been fulfilled. The Jews of Jesus' time had done this very thing: they had substituted the Book of Moses for the living Word and had so materialized their minds and their religion that they did not know the Messiah when He came. Jesus accused them of this, saying: "Ye search the scriptures, because ye think that in them ye have eternal life; and these are they which bear witness of me; and ye will not come to me, that ye may have life."

The Scriptures alone are not sufficient to impart spiritual understanding. The Pharisees were inveterate students of the Hebrew Scriptures, but Jesus accused them repeatedly of lack of understanding. The Bible is a sealed book to one whose own spiritual understanding has not been quickened by the living Word. "The word is very nigh unto thee, in thy mouth, and in thy heart, that thou mayest do it." Jesus so identified Himself with the living Word that His words became, like it, creative. He submerged His personality in God-Mind until He became the expression of that Mind, the idea clothed in flesh. "And the Word became flesh, and dwelt among us." Then instead of memorizing whole chapters of the Bible let us quicken our mind and our body with the creative word and thereby escape death. "Verily, verily, I say unto you, If a man keep my word, he shall never see death."

The Pharisaical mind thinks that salvation lies in the Scripture itself, when in fact the Scripture simply bears witness of the Saviour. The need is not to concentrate on the letter of the law but to live the Truth and let the divine principles find expression through the soul. Thus man learns to travel the path that leads to light and peace and satisfaction.

There is no necessity of accusing our brother. The law itself works everything out in perfect justice. In fact Moses symbolizes this progressive or "drawing-out" process, which in the individual works from within upward, and in the universe appears as the upward trend of all things.

The idea that the Bible is the living Word of God has diverted the attention of Christians from the one creative Word ever since the original translators dropped the little word "ye" from the sentence (in John 5:39) in which Jesus criticized the Jews for their much study of the Scriptures and thereby made their study a command. Modern translators have corrected this attempt to make Jesus an indorser of the printed word, and it is now made clear that overstudy of the letter may prevent one from making unity with the Word of God manifest, Jesus the Christ.

Chapter VI

WE INCREASE our vitality by blessing and giving thanks in spirit. To bring about this increase efficiently we must understand the anatomy of the soul and mind centers in the body.

It has been found by experience that a person increases his blessings by being grateful for what he has. Gratitude even on the mental plane is a great magnet, and when gratitude is expressed from the spiritual standpoint it is powerfully augmented. The custom of saying grace at the table has its origin in man's attempt to use this power of increase.

A woman who had been left with a large family and no visible means of support related in an experience meeting how wonderfully this law had worked in providing food for her children. In her extremity she had asked the advice of one who understood the law, and she had been told to thank God silently for abundant supply on her table, regardless of appearances. She and her children began doing this, and in a short time the increase of food was so great at times that it astonished them. Her grocer's bill was met promptly, and in most marvelous ways the family was supplied with food. Never after that time did they lack.

In all its work the I AM (Christ) uses the faculties of the mind. The I AM is Spirit, and it cannot move directly on substance or formed states of consciousness. It uses the spiritual faculties as its agents. The name Philip means "power," and Jesus appealed to Philip to know how these hungry "thoughts" or people were to be fed. Jesus did this to "prove him." This means that power is still under the limitations of sense. It looks on the visible supply and judges its capacity from that viewpoint. Andrew (strength), brother of Peter (faith), has a slight perception of true supply on the seven-sense plane of consciousness (represented as the lad with five loaves and two fishes). This is a good beginning for the I AM. If you have a consciousness of the capacity that is involved in the natural man's sevenfold nature, you have a good foundation on which to build the twelvefold or spiritual man.

Having quickened your idea of power and strength in universal Spirit, you "sit down" or center your forces within you and begin to bless and give thanks. In divine order you make connection with the universal, vital energy of Being and fill your whole consciousness with vitality. The surplus energy settles back into the various centers as reserve force (the twelve baskets that remained over). Thus you learn to live by "the living bread which came down out of heaven," the very flesh or substance of eternal life.

Jesus and His disciples were on a mountain when this great increase of substance took place, which indicates a high state of consciousness. An eminent British scientist, Sir James Jeans, says that it may be that the gods that determine our fates are our own minds acting on our brain cells and through them on the world about us. Here is stated a profound truth that, accepted and tested, will demonstrate supply to meet every need. Science says that we live in an invisible ether pregnant with the essence of all visible things, that this essence is wrapped up in the atom, and that it awaits an as yet undiscovered law to set it free. Jesus knew the law and through Him we may know it. In World War II science used this power in the destructive atom bomb. Jesus used it constructively in feeding the five thousand.

> 15 Jesus therefore perceiving that they were about to come and take him by force,
> to make him king, withdrew again into the mountain himself alone.

Spirit always has the power and the ability to handle any situation. Jesus knew His time had not yet come. He had not yet developed the spiritual power necessary to meet the many demands made on Him. The way out was to withdraw from public work for a season. Those who are evolving spiritually know whether or not they are equal to certain demands made on them, and they withdraw to the within for further spiritual realization and power.

> 16 And when evening came, his disciples went down unto the sea; 17 and they en-
> tered into a boat, and were going over the sea unto Capernaum. And it was now
> dark, and Jesus had not yet come to them. 18 And the sea was rising by reason of

a great wind that blew. 19 When therefore they had rowed about five and twenty
or thirty furlongs, they behold Jesus walking on the sea, and drawing nigh unto
the boat: and they were afraid. 20 But he saith unto them, It is I; be not afraid. 21
They were willing therefore to receive him into the boat: and straightway the boat
was at the land whither they were going.

To walk on the sea as Jesus did, without sinking down into the waves, required established faith in the power of Spirit.

We cannot walk on the waves of life in our own personal strength. If we remember to call on the strength of Christ we are sustained by unlimited power, by the real self.

22 On the morrow the multitude that stood on the other side of the sea saw that
there was no other boat there, save one, and that Jesus entered not with his disciples
into the boat, but that his disciples went away alone 23 (howbeit there came boats
from Tiberias nigh unto the place where they ate the bread after the Lord had given
thanks): 24 when the multitude therefore saw that Jesus was not there, neither his
disciples, they themselves got into the boats, and came to Capernaum, seeking
Jesus. 25 And when they found him on the other side of the sea, they said unto
him, Rabbi, when camest thou hither? 26 Jesus answered them and said, Verily,
verily, I say unto you, Ye seek me, not because ye saw signs, but because ye ate of
the loaves, and were filled. 27 Work not for the food which perisheth, but for the
food which abideth unto eternal life, which the Son of man shall give unto you:
for him the Father, even God, hath sealed. 28 They said therefore unto him, What
must we do, that we may work the works of God? 29 Jesus answered and said unto
them, This is the work of God, that ye believe on him whom he hath sent. 30 They
said therefore unto him, What then doest thou for a sign, that we may see, and
believe thee? what workest thou? 31 Our fathers ate the manna in the wilderness;
as it is written, He gave them bread out of heaven to eat. 32 Jesus therefore said
unto them, Verily, verily, I say unto you, It was not Moses that gave you the bread
out of heaven; but my Father giveth you the true bread out of heaven. 33 For the
bread of God is that which cometh down out of heaven, and giveth life unto the
world. 34 They said therefore unto him, Lord, evermore give us this bread. 35 Jesus
said unto them, I am the bread of life: he that cometh to me shall not hunger, and
he that believeth on me shall never thirst. 36 But I said unto you, that have seen
me, and yet believe not. 37 All that which the Father giveth me shall come unto
me; and him that cometh to me I will in no wise cast out. 38 For I am come down
from heaven, not to do mine own will, but the will of him that sent me. 39 And
this is the will of him that sent me, that of all that which he hath given me I
should lose nothing, but should raise it up at the last day. 40 For this is the will of
my Father, that every one that beholdeth the Son, and believeth on him, should
have eternal life; and I will raise him up at the last day.

41 The Jews therefore murmured concerning him, because he said, I am the bread
which came down out of heaven. 42 And they said, Is not this Jesus, the son of
Joseph, whose father and mother we know? how doth he now say, I am come
down out of heaven? 43 Jesus answered and said unto them, Murmur not among
yourselves. 44 No man can come to me, except the Father that sent me draw him:
and I will raise him up in the last day. 45 It is written in the prophets, And they
shall all be taught of God. Every one that hath heard from the Father, and hath
learned, cometh unto me. 46 Not that any man hath seen the Father, save he that
is from God, he hath seen the Father. 47 Verily, verily, I say unto you, He that
believeth hath eternal life. 48 I am the bread of life. 49 Your fathers ate the manna
in the wilderness, and they died. 50 This is the bread which cometh down out of

heaven, that a man may eat thereof, and not die. [51] I am the living bread which came down out of heaven: if any man eat of this bread, he shall live for ever: yea and the bread which I will give is my flesh, for the life of the world.

[52] The Jews therefore strove one with another, saying, How can this man give us his flesh to eat? Jesus therefore said unto them, Verily, verily, I say unto you, Except ye eat the flesh of the Son of man and drink his blood, ye have not life in yourselves. He that eateth my flesh and drinketh my blood hath eternal life: and I will raise him up at the last day. For my flesh is meat indeed, and my blood is drink indeed. He that eateth my flesh and drinketh my blood abideth in me, and I in him. As the living Father sent me, and I live because of the Father; so he that eateth me, he also shall live because of me. This is the bread which came down out of heaven: not as the fathers ate, and died; he that eateth this bread shall live for ever. These things said he in the synagogue, as he taught in Capernaum.

Here the multitudes (meaning a multitude of thoughts) are really seeking comfort and consolation ("they themselves got into the boats and came to Capernaum, seeking Jesus"). They had entered into that inner conviction of the abiding compassion and restoring power of God.

In the universal Mind principle, which Jesus called "the Father," there is a substance that also includes the mother or seed of all visible substance. It is the only real substance because it is unchangeable, while the visible substance is in constant transition.

The origin or source of all substance is the idea of substance. It is purely spiritual and can be apprehended only by the mind. It is never visible to the eye, nor can it be sensed by man through any of the bodily faculties. Bible authorities say that the Almighty God in Genesis should have been translated El Shaddai, "the breasted one." Thus God is found to include both the male and the female principle.

When the mind has centered its attention on this idea of substance long enough and strongly enough, it generates the consciousness of substance, and through the powers of the various faculties of the mind in right relation it can form visible substance. Jesus in this way brought into visibility the loaves and fishes to feed the five thousand.

But this faculty of dealing with ideas is open to all men and women. It is not given to privileged persons and withheld from all others.

Jesus knew this, and He also knew that every man must center his attention on this spiritual substance and bring forth its fruits, just as He did. But those whose attention has long been centered in things visible are slow to appreciate this fact.

Jesus fed the multitude in an easy way, and they followed Him over the sea in boats apparently in order to get more food; at least that is the motive Jesus attributed to them.

Then He tells them plainly that they must not labor for the food that perishes but for the food that "abideth unto eternal life."

When they asked how they should do these "works of God" or so-called miracles, He said, "Believe on him whom he hath sent." One translation says, "Believe in him." Man is to believe in the spiritual presence of the living God even as one "sent"; that is, entered into the consciousness.

All shall attain who believe or have faith in the spiritual source of life. Whoever comes to this Christ realm in the heavens all about us will be moved by its will, which is the will of the Father. There will be no loss, no failure in this realm, and whoever enters into the Mind of Spirit will have poured out to him its life essence and be wholly raised up from material conditions when arriving at the "last day" (the last degree of understanding).

Moses caused manna to fall from heaven to feed the Children of Israel. The body of Christ is a spiritual substance that we incorporate into consciousness through faith out of the heavens of mind. That the food we eat has a spiritual source is proved by those who fast in spiritual faith much longer and easier than those who are forced to starve.

> [60] Many therefore of his disciples, when they heard this, said, This is a hard saying;
> who can hear it? [61] But Jesus knowing in himself that his disciples murmured at
> this, said unto them, Doth this cause you to stumble? [62] What then if ye should
> behold the Son of man ascending where he was before? [63] It is the spirit that giveth
> life; the flesh profiteth nothing: the words that I have spoken unto you are spirit,
> and are life. [64] But there are some of you that believe not. For Jesus knew from
> the beginning who they were that believed not, and who it was that should betray
> him. [65] And he said, For this cause have I said unto you, that no man can come
> unto me, except it be given unto him of the Father.

> [66] Upon this many of his disciples went back, and walked no more with him. [67] Je-
> sus said therefore unto the twelve, Would ye also go away? [68] Simon Peter answered
> him, Lord, to whom shall we go? thou hast the words of eternal life. [69] And we
> have believed and know that thou art the Holy One of God. [70] Jesus answered
> them, Did not I choose you the twelve, and one of you is a devil? [71] Now he spake
> of Judas, the son of Simon Iscariot, for he it was that should betray him, being
> one of the twelve.

Jesus said, "It is the spirit that giveth life; the flesh profiteth nothing: the words that I have spoken unto you are spirit, and are life." Being, the original fount, is an impersonal principle; but in its work of creation it puts forth an idea that contains all ideas: the Logos, Word, Christ, the Son of God, or spiritual man. This spiritual man or Christ or Word of God is the true inner self of every individual. Man therefore contains within himself the capacities of Being, and through his words uses the creative principle in forming his environment, good or bad. So we make our own heaven or hell.

The ideas that make words constructive are those of life, love, wisdom, substance, power, strength, and all other ideas that express divine attributes. Words carrying the life idea produce a vitalizing and life-giving effect. Words that express divine love are harmonizing and unifying in their effect.

Words are made active in the body through their receptivity by the mind and are carried into the body through the subconsciousness by one's thought. Constructive words that renew the body are made a part of the body consciousness by prayer and meditation. These are the words that are Spirit and give life.

Many people start out to walk in the light of Spirit, to unfold Truth, but they become entangled in their own misgivings and disbelief and therefore return to their old limited way of life.

After these events Jesus went to Galilee (the "whirl of life"), for He did not walk in Judea (praise) because the Jews sought to kill him. The Jews (the Pharisaical Jews in this instance) believed in the letter of the law rather than the spirit.

Chapter VII

JESUS WAS DEVELOPING His spiritual nature, which is under spiritual law. The Pharisaical Jews followed the letter of the law, which resists and seeks the destruction of the Christ. The Christ usually moves in secret. It does its spiritual work quietly instead of showing off. Some of the multitude thought Jesus was a good man; others thought He had led the people astray. This represents the quibbling of the lesser mind.

> 14 But when it was now the midst of the feast Jesus went up into the temple, and
> taught. 15 The Jews therefore marvelled, saying, How knowest this man letters,
> having never learned? 16 Jesus therefore answered them, and said, My teaching
> is not mine, but his that sent me. 17 If any man willeth to do his will, he shall
> know of the teaching, whether it is of God, or whether I speak from myself. 18 He
> that speaketh from himself seeketh his own glory: but he that seeketh the glory
> of him that sent him, the same is true, and no unrighteousness is in him. 19 Did
> not Moses give you the law, and yet none of you doeth the law? Why seek ye to
> kill me? 20 The multitude answered, Thou hast a demon: who seeketh to kill thee?
> 21 Jesus answered and said unto them, I did one work, and ye all marvel because
> thereof. 22 Moses hath given you circumcision (not that it is of Moses, but of the
> fathers); and on the sabbath ye circumcise a man. 23 If a man receiveth circumcision
> on the sabbath, that the law of Moses may not be broken; are ye wroth with me,
> because I made a man every whit whole on the sabbath? 24 Judge not according to
> appearance, but judge righteous judgment.
>
> 25 Some therefore of them of Jerusalem said, Is not this he whom they seek to
> kill? 26 And lo, he speaketh openly, and they say nothing unto him. Can it be
> that the rulers indeed know that this is the Christ? 27 Howbeit we know this man
> whence he is: but when the Christ cometh, no one knoweth whence he is. 28 Jesus
> therefore cried in the temple, teaching and saying, Ye both know me, and know
> whence I am; and I am not come to myself, but he that sent me is true, whom ye
> know not. 29 I know him; because I am from him, and he sent me. 30 They sought
> therefore to take him: and no man laid his hand on him, because his hour was not
> yet come. 31 But of the multitude many believed on him; and they said, When the
> Christ shall come, will he do more signs than those which this man hath done? 32
> The Pharisees heard the multitude murmuring these things concerning him; and
> the chief priests and the Pharisees sent officers to take him. 33 Jesus therefore said,
> Yet a little while am I with you, and I go unto him that sent me. 34 Ye shall seek
> me, and shall not find me: and where I am, ye cannot come. 35 The Jews therefore
> said among themselves, Whither will this man go that we shall not find him? will
> he go unto the Dispersion among the Greeks, and teach the Greeks? 36 What is
> this word that he said, Ye shall seek me, and shall not find me; and where I am,
> ye cannot come?

Jesus' disciples wanted Him to go up to Jerusalem for one reason: to prove that He was the Christ, but He realized that He had not yet attained the necessary power. After they had departed He got more spiritual consciousness and was moved to go under the protection of Spirit, and in this state of mind the Jews could not lay their hands on Him or injure Him in any way. Jesus, like all persons who are growing spiritually, felt the power within Him to be much stronger than He could manifest without. He wanted to prove to His friends that He was the Christ but doubted His ability.

He was not speaking from Himself for His own glory, but He was seeking the glory of Him that sent Him.

The all-knowing Christ Mind can easily handle the Pharisaical mind that is following the letter of the law. The intellectual mind cannot understand the claim of the spiritual that it can go where it cannot be found by those present. The mind that functions in matter cannot comprehend a state in which matter can pass through matter.

> 37 Now on the last day, the great day of the feast, Jesus stood and cried, saying, If
> any man thirst, let him come unto me and drink. 38 He that believeth on me, as
> the scripture hath said, from within him shall flow rivers of living water. 39 But
> this spake he of the Spirit, which they that believed on him were to receive: for
> the Spirit was not yet given; because Jesus was not yet glorified.

Jesus realized that man's real thirst is for Spirit and that this thirst can only be quenched through an outpouring of the Holy Spirit within the soul, which thrills one with new life and energy and vitality.

If we have understanding faith we know that there is no cessation of life and that we have only to open our consciousness more and more to the Spirit of life in order to realize that from within flow rivers of living water.

The Holy Spirit was in evidence before the time of Jesus, but He gave a new impetus to this indwelling helper and promised that the holy Comforter would be with us throughout all time.

> 40 Some of the multitude therefore, when they heard these words, said, This is
> of a truth the prophet. 41 Others said, This is the Christ. But some said, What,
> doth the Christ come out of Galilee? 42 Hath not the scripture said that the Christ
> cometh of the seed of David, and from Bethlehem, the village where David was?
> 43 So there arose a division in the multitude because of him. 44 And some of them
> would have taken him; but no man laid hands on him.

When one is in a mixed state of consciousness there is always dissension and questioning. However when one is born anew into the Christ consciousness all things are made clear.

"For all shall know me, From the least to the greatest of them."

> 45 The officers therefore came to the chief priests and Pharisees; and they said unto
> them, Why did ye not bring him? 46 The officers answered, Never man so spake. 47
> The Pharisees therefore answered them, Are ye also led astray? 48 Hath any of the
> rulers believed on him, or of the Pharisees? 49 But this multitude that knoweth not
> the law are accursed. 50 Nicodemus saith unto them (he that came to him before,
> being one of them), 51 Doth our law judge a man, except it first hear from himself
> and know what he doeth. 52 They answered and said unto him, Art thou also of
> Galilee? Search, and see that out of Galilee ariseth no prophet.

The "chief priests" of the Pharisaical consciousness are the highest thoughts in authority in the Pharisaical hierarchy. The "officers" are thoughts that execute the law. However, when it reaches a certain state of unfoldment even the Pharisaical mind, which believes in the strict letter of the law, is open to conviction if it can entertain a higher truth safely. This is proved by Nicodemus' spiritual conversion. The Pharisaical side of man's mind in its faithful adherence to religious forms eventually becomes aware of the presence of divine power. This truth was in evidence when the officers replied, "Never man so spake," revealing that the higher light of the Christ had found entrance into their consciousness.

Chapter VIII

JESUS' GOING UP into the Mount of Olives means the soul's ascending to the state of consciousness where absolute Truth is manifest and from this high vantage point teaching a lesson in brotherly love to the intellectual faculties. Sometimes the intellectual faculties imagine they are in supreme authority, as in this case, where the woman caught in adultery is presented as an example. "Now, spiritual man, what are you going to do about that?

Under the law, we are told, we must stone her." Jesus, here symbolizing the indwelling Christ, writes on the ground and says, "He that is without sin among you, let him first cast a stone at her." The intellectual faculties, thus trapped in their own conceit, slink away.

The Christ questions this adulterous state of consciousness: "Woman, where are they? did no man condemn thee?" The reply is "No man, Lord." The final injunction is "Neither do I condemn thee: go thy way; from henceforward sin no more." Thus the overcoming power of the Christ Mind is doing its perfect work.

> 12 Again therefore Jesus spake unto them, saying, I am the light of the world: he
> that followeth me shall not walk in the darkness, but shall have the light of life. 13
> The Pharisees therefore said unto him, Thou bearest witness of thyself; thy witness
> is not true. 14 Jesus answered and said unto them, Even if I bear witness of myself,
> my witness is true; for I know whence I came, and whither I go; but ye know not
> whence I come, or whither I go. 15 Ye judge after the flesh; I judge no man. 16 Yet
> and if I judge, my judgment is true; for I am not alone, but I and the Father that
> sent me. 17 Yea and in your law it is written, that the witness of two men is true. 18
> I am he that beareth witness of myself, and the Father that sent me beareth witness
> of me. 19 They said therefore unto him, Where is thy Father? Jesus answered, Ye
> know neither me, nor my Father: if ye knew me, ye would know my Father also.
> 20 These words spake he in the treasury, as he taught in the temple: and no man
> took him; because his hour was not yet come.

The Christ within is always declaring, "I am the light of the world: he that followeth me shall not walk in the darkness, but shall have the light of life." The first lesson in spiritual development to be learned is that everyone has within him the light of divine understanding. Those who do not recognize that they have this inner light are thinking intellectually instead of spiritually. The Christ light comes forth from God and under all circumstances is aware of its source. It places all judgment in the Father, knowing that its light is from that source alone. The intellectual man has no conception of this truth but depends more on man-made judgment.

Jesus (symbolizing the Christ) was working in the substance consciousness and under the light of Spirit and was master of the situation. Therefore no man took Him, because His hour was not yet come. He put all protection under God, who was ever-present as His witness and defense.

> 21 He said therefore again unto them, I go away, and ye shall seek me, and shall
> die in your sin: whither I go, ye cannot come. 22 The Jews therefore said, Will
> he kill himself, that he saith, Whither I go, ye cannot come? 23 And he said unto
> them, Ye are from beneath; I am from above: ye are of this world; I am not of
> this world. 24 I said therefore unto you, that ye shall die in your sins: for except
> ye believe that I am he, ye shall die in your sins. 25 They said therefore unto him,
> Who art thou? Jesus said unto them, Even that which I have also spoken unto you
> from the beginning. 26 I have many things to speak and to judge concerning you:
> howbeit he that sent me is true; and the things which I heard from him, these
> speak I unto the world. 27 They perceived not that he spake to them of the Father.
> 28 Jesus therefore said, When ye have lifted up the Son of man, then shall ye know
> that I am he, and that I do nothing of myself, but as the Father taught me, I speak

these things. 29 And he that sent me is with me; he hath not left me alone; for I
do always the things that are pleasing to him. 30 As he spake these things, many
believed on him.

Jesus, symbolizing the I AM, the Christ, again is proclaiming Truth from the absolute standpoint. As He persists the light of Christ eventually does filter into consciousness. Through self-righteous adherence to outer forms man resists his true unfoldment or evolution. The egotistical personality assumes that its world of phenomena is real and that all talk about disappearing into spirit is illusion. Sanctimoniousness develops from the belief that intellect can be spiritually sanctified. The spiritual mind (the I AM) is the Saviour and is working to come into evidence. It is working to redeem the self-righteous, Pharisaical, intellectual man. When this man has been lifted up, "then shall ye know that I am he, and that I do nothing of myself, but as the Father taught me. I speak these things."

31 Jesus therefore said to those Jews that had believed him, If ye abide in my word,
then are ye truly my disciples; 32 and ye shall know the truth, and the truth shall
make you free. 33 They answered unto him, We are Abraham's seed, and have never
yet been in bondage to any man: how sayest thou, Ye shall be made free? 34 Jesus
answered them, Verily, verily, I say unto you, Every one that committeth sin is the
bondservant of sin. 35 And the bondservant abideth not in the house for ever: the
son abideth for ever. 36 If therefore the Son shall make you free, ye shall be free
indeed.

An understanding of Truth comes only to those who abide faithfully in the teachings of Jesus. They alone are free who persist in holding to the true view of life, regardless of preaccepted theories, and who obey only the voice of the higher self, which holds them to an unswerving performance of the right, both mental and outer, instead of following the voice of their own desires.

The subject of freedom is inexhaustible. The quest of freedom is endless and is unfulfilled save in the Christ consciousness. The Jews did not understand the teachings of Jesus on this subject. As the chosen people, they were in bondage to racial pride, and their intemperance in this regard was difficult to uproot.

The "house" is man's body. No one who allows intemperate desires to rule his life and to gain expression through his thought and conduct can hope to remain long in the body or to experience in it any measure of true satisfaction. Only the "Son," the self-forgetting, loving, helpful concentration of all the powers on the gaining of a higher understanding of the forces that control mankind, can bring full and complete freedom. Once this power of concentration is gained and practiced, perfect freedom is indeed assured. But concentration does not spring, perfect and full-fledged, from beneath the fleeting wing of the random resolve; it requires the faithful giving of oneself to the practice of the presence of God. "Abideth" entails a continuing in the Christ state of mind and heart.

Jesus in effect said, "If you live in the spirit of My teachings, you will become truly My disciples, and you will be freed from all your limitations through the understanding of Truth that comes to you as the result of your steadfastness."

37 I know that ye are Abraham's seed: yet ye seek to kill me, because my word hath not free
course in you. 38 I speak the things which I have seen with my Father: and ye also do the
things which ye heard from your father. 39 They answered and said unto him, Our father
is Abraham. Jesus saith unto them, If ye were Abraham's children, ye would do the works
of Abraham. 40 But now ye seek to kill me, a man that hath told you the truth, which I
heard from God: this did not Abraham. 41 Ye do the works of your father. They said unto
him, We were not born of fornication; we have one Father, even God.

Those who think of themselves as descended from human ancestors are in bondage to all the limitations of those ancestors, regardless of their claims to the contrary. It is a falling short of the full stature of man to regard himself as descended from the human family. This is a sin that keeps the majority of men in bondage to sense consciousness. The Jews were proud of their ancestors, Abraham, Isaac, and Jacob, who did things that in our day would make them candidates for the penitentiary. Polygamy might be mentioned as an example.

The worship of ancestors is observed in our own day by those who eagerly search the records of royalty for a family coat of arms or trace their ancestry back to William the Conqueror. The one and only way to get free of this burden of race heredity is to proclaim your divine sonship. If you believe that God is your Father, acknowledge Him, and He will acknowledge you.

A short definition of sin is ignorance. If you knew your spiritual origin and all the purity and power that it includes, you would not be subject to the race tendencies that sway the mind of the flesh. This is the freedom of the Son of God; the shackles of false thoughts are loosed, and there is the open light of heaven instead of the darkness of sense consciousness.

It seems incredible that men should seek to destroy and kill out of their thoughts this superconscious mind, but such is the self-sufficiency of ignorance identified with human lineage. Mortality has failed generation after generation, yet men cling to it as the summum bonum of existence, and antagonize the Spirit.

> 42 Jesus said unto them, If God were your Father, ye would love me: for I came
> forth and am come from God; for neither have I come of myself, but he sent me.
> 43 Why do ye not understand my speech? Even because ye cannot hear my word.
> 44 Ye are of your father the devil, and the lusts of your father it is your will to do.
> He was a murderer from the beginning, and standeth not in the truth, because
> there is no truth in him. When he speaketh a lie, he speaketh of his own: for he
> is a liar, and the father thereof. 45 But because I say the truth, ye believe me not.
> 46 Which of you convicteth me of sin? If I say truth, why do ye not believe me?
> 47 He that is of God heareth the words of God: for this cause ye hear them not,
> because ye are not of God. 48 The Jews answered and said unto him, Say we not
> well that thou art a Samaritan, and hast a demon? 49 Jesus answered, I have not a
> demon; but I honor my Father, and ye dishonor me. 50 But I seek not mine own
> glory: there is one that seeketh and judgeth.

It is hard for the intellect to realize the spiritual "I AM THAT I AM." It always argues back and forth, endeavoring to prove that the intellect itself is the highest authority.

Jesus condemned the sins of the intellect, of which self-righteousness is the greatest, as worse than moral sins. Compare this scathing arraignment of the arrogant Jews with the ready forgiveness for the adulteress. The pompous ecclesiastical dignitary is much harder to reach with Truth than the repentant moral sinner.

Any thought that does not have its origin in the one divine source is a liar and the father of all lies.

> 51 Verily, verily, I say unto you. If a man keep my word, he shall never see death.
> 52 The Jews said unto him, Now we know that thou hast a demon. Abraham died,
> and the prophets; and thou sayest, If a man keep my word, he shall never taste of
> death. 53 Art thou greater than our father Abraham, who died? and the prophets
> died: whom makest thou thyself? 54 Jesus answered, If I glorify myself, my glory
> is nothing: it is my Father that glorifieth me; of whom ye say, that he is your
> God; 55 and ye have not known him: but I know him; and if I should say, I know
> him not, I shall be like unto you, a liar: but I know him, and keep his word. 56
> Your father Abraham rejoiced to see my day; and he saw it, and was glad. 57 The
> Jews therefore said unto him, Thou art not yet fifty years old, and hast thou seen
> Abraham? 58 Jesus said unto them, Verily, verily, I say unto you, Before Abraham

was born, I am. [59] They took up stones therefore to cast at him: but Jesus hid himself, and went out of the temple.

"Verily, verily, I say unto you, If a man keep my word, he shall never see death. The Jews said unto him, Now we know that thou hast a demon. Abraham died, and the prophets; and thou sayest, If a man keep my word, he shall never taste of death."

If the would-be overcomer will diligently meditate on these words, the light of Truth will gradually break in. Then he will know that the Christ, the I AM THAT I AM, was before Abraham and also that the old "church father" Abraham was spiritually quickened to the degree that he was constantly seeking the light. "Your father Abraham rejoiced to see my day; and he saw it, and was glad."

It was the Christ in Jesus who exclaimed, "Before Abraham was born, I am." Christ, the spiritual man, spoke often through Jesus, the natural man. We know that Christ, the spiritual man, could not have experienced death, burial, and resurrection. The experiences were possible only to the mortal man, who was passing from the natural to the spiritual plane of consciousness.

The word of God is the word that conveys to the world the ideas of the Most High. It is not the Most High in His wholeness, but it carries with it the power behind the throne, because "the three agree in one," the Father (principle), the Son (the ideal), and the Holy Ghost, (the formative word).

Jesus said, "If a man keep my word, he shall never see death." The "word" here referred to is not comprehended by the spoken or written word of Jesus but rather the original creative Word of God, the Logos. This is the Logos or God Word that the Gospel of John states "became flesh, and dwelt among us (and we beheld his glory, glory as of the only begotten from the Father)." According to the Bible, the words of Jesus were more powerful than those of any other man who ever lived. He infused the divine-life idea into His words until they made direct union with the creative Word of the Father.

When man in faith makes this intimate connection between his mind and the Father's, he enters into what may be termed the "river of life," and he has ability to take others with him into the waters that cleanse, purify, and vitalize so perfectly that death is swallowed up in life and man lives right on without the tragedy of death. Such a man was, and is, Jesus the Christ, and the promise is that all who incorporate in mind and body the living creative Word, as He did, will with Him escape death. This promise of the overcoming power of the Word has been interpreted to mean death of the soul after physical death, but there is no foundation for this assumption. Jesus overcame death of the body. His followers are expected to do the same.

Chapter IX

THERE ARE SINS of omission and sins of commission. This text illustrates a sin of omission. The man born blind had not sinned, neither had his parents sinned.

In this whole chapter the Christ is declaring, "I am the light of the world." When our blind, stumbling thoughts awaken to the reality of the Christ, darkness falls away and we see clearly.

The inquiry "Who sinned, this man, or his parents, that he should be born blind?" indicates a previous incarnation of the man in the fleshly body, in which he might have sinned. Belief in successive incarnations of man was accepted by all the scriptural writers who were spiritually wise. The tents and tabernacles in which the Children of Israel lived in the wilderness are symbols of the fleshly body that men put on and off, again and again. Solomon's Temple is a symbol of the regenerated body of man; when man attains this body he will cease to die and reincarnate. In order to build this indestructible body we must make manifest in ourselves the works of God. The Pharisees were very strict in their observance of the external ritual but had no knowledge of the inner spiritual law that expressed its perfection in health of body.

The sin of omission is even greater than the sin of commission. There is some hope for the one who is an active sinner; but what can we expect of one who makes no effort to do anything for himself, who simply drifts with the tide, or looks to others to do all things? Before he was healed, the blind man was a sinner of omission. He was a blind beggar, a person who had no perception of his own capacity, or no confidence in his power to rise superior to conditions in the material realm. When man fails to apprehend his mission and to do the work of bringing forth the good that is allotted to him, he remains in darkness. His blindness is that sin of omission which is present in every man who does not realize his place in the Godhead. If a man fails to do that which he is told from within is the right thing to do, he is sinning, and he will remain in darkness to just the degree that he sins.

The works of God that we are to make manifest are the perfect ideas of a perfect-man idea in Divine Mind. "Ye therefore shall be perfect, as your heavenly Father is perfect." We are to bring forth in ourselves the perfection of Being. If through neglect, laziness, or belief in inability we fail to do this, we fall under the judgment of the constantly operating law of life, which is inwardly urging us and in all the visible and invisible forms of nature is commanding: "Go forward."

The world is full of people who are in this beggarly blind state. They sit by the wayside and wait for the workers to give them pennies and crusts, when they themselves might be the producers of their own good. The remedy for their situation is for them to deny material darkness, ignorance, and inability in themselves. By putting the clay upon the blind man's eyes Jesus illustrated how man makes opaque his understanding by affirming the power of material conditions to hamper and impede his spiritual and material growth. The washing away of this clay by the man himself shows that by our own volition and our own efforts we must deny away these seeming mountains of environing conditions.

The starting point of man's reformation is in the mind. He must begin to handle situations mentally at first; as he proceeds to do away with thought limitations, surrounding conditions will gradually change, and he will find himself "seeing" as a result of his efforts to do the will of the one supreme Mind.

When we begin to deny away the limitations of old material race thoughts and to affirm illumination from the Christ within us, we are sure to arouse the "Jews" and the "Pharisees" in our mental realm. They are our tendencies to cling to the letter of the word, to the forms of religion, and to deny the power of Spirit actually to illumine our mind and transform our entire being. If after we are awakened we are bold in the declaration of Truth, as this man was when he was healed, we may experience much opposition from our old formal religious ideas. If we listen to them all, we may feel as though we were no longer in spiritual favor. But we need not fear; we shall become conscious of the Christ again, and He will reveal Himself to us. Then we shall worship Him truly.

Chapter X

THE DOOR OF YOUR mind is your open-mindedness. "I am the door of the sheep." "Sheep" are your thoughts. "A thief and a robber" is mortal thought. The "porter" is the will. The "good shepherd" is the spiritual I AM.

All forces that come into your consciousness in any other way than through your own I AM are thieves and robbers. No man can be saved from the limitations and mistakes of ignorance except through his own volition.

There is a widespread belief that we can turn over to those who have better understanding the straightening out of our tangled thoughts. Such help may be extended temporarily, but it always proves "a thief and a robber" in the end. The true healer is always the teacher and instructs his patients how to open the door to the "good shepherd," the divine I AM.

> 7 Jesus therefore said unto them again, Verily, verily, I say unto you, I am the door
> of the sheep. 8 All that came before me are thieves and robbers: but the sheep did
> not hear them. 9 I am the door; by me if any man enter in, he shall be saved, and
> shall go in and go out, and shall find pasture. 10 The thief cometh not, but that
> he may steal, and kill, and destroy: I came that they may have life, and may have it
> abundantly. 11 I am the good shepherd: the good shepherd layeth down his life for
> the sheep. 12 He that is a hireling, and not a shepherd, whose own the sheep are
> not, beholdeth the wolf coming, and leaveth the sheep, and fleeth, and the wolf
> snatcheth them, and scattereth them: 13 he fleeth because he is a hireling; and
> careth not for the sheep. 14 I am the good shepherd; and I know mine own, and
> mine own know me, 15 even as the Father knoweth me, and I know the Father;
> and I lay down my life for the sheep. 16 And other sheep I have, which are not
> of this fold: them also I must bring, and they shall hear my voice; and they shall
> become one flock, one shepherd. 17 Therefore doth the Father love me, because I
> lay down my life, that I may take it again. 18 No one taketh it away from me, but
> I lay it down of myself. I have power to lay it down, and I have power to take it
> again. This commandment received I from my Father.

"The good shepherd layeth down his life for the sheep." This means that the high spiritual I AM lets itself become identified with the limitations of self-consciousness that it may lift all up to the spiritual plane. "I lay down my life, that I may take it again."

When we open the door of the mind by consciously affirming the presence and power of the divine I AM in our midst, there is a marriage or union of the higher forces in being with the lower, and we find that we are quickened in every part; the life of the I AM has been poured out for us. Thus Christ becomes the Saviour of the whole world, by pouring this higher spiritual energy (His blood) into human consciousness, which each must take for himself and identify himself with. The individual I AM is the only door through which it can get into our thoughts in a legitimate way. If it comes through mediumship or hypnotism or mental suggestion, without our willing co-operation, it is "a thief and a robber."

There is but one life-giver, one Saviour, the Christ; and the only door through which the divine essence can come to us is through our own I AM. Jesus of Nazareth points the way, but everyone must take up his cross and follow Him, must "overcome" as He overcame.

> 19 There arose a division again among the Jews because of these words. 20 And
> many of them said, He hath a demon, and is mad; why hear ye him? 21 Others
> said, These are not the sayings of one possessed with a demon. Can a demon open
> the eyes of the blind?

The word Jews in this instance refers to the Pharisaical Jews who are following the letter of the law. There is always a division among the intellectually wise and an arguing back and forth. It is the Christ consciousness alone that seeks the unity of all things.

[22] And it was the feast of the dedication at Jerusalem: [23] it was winter; and Jesus was walking in the temple in Solomon's porch.

Partaking of a feast in Solomon's Porch in the Temple symbolizes our peaceful thought people appropriating spiritual substance in an outer state of consciousness (porch).

[24] The Jews therefore came round about him, and said unto him, How long dost thou hold us in suspense? If thou art the Christ, tell us plainly. [25] Jesus answered them, I told you, and ye believe not: the works that I do in my Father's name, these bear witness of me. [26] But ye believe not, because ye are not of my sheep.

In this Scripture Jesus symbolizes the I AM or Christ, and the Jews symbolize our high-brow intellectual thoughts, which hold to the letter of the law to such an extent that they cannot let the spiritual word expand in and through the consciousness.

[27] My sheep hear my voice, and I know them, and they follow me: [28] and I give unto them eternal life; and they shall never perish, and no one shall snatch them out of my hand. [29] My Father, who hath given them unto me, is greater than all; and no one is able to snatch them out of the Father's hand. [30] I and the Father are one.

"My sheep hear my voice." The sheep are our gentle, obedient thoughts that are always open to the inspiration of the Christ. Man's soul is encased in the body, with its great organ or instrument from which issues forth the human voice. When man is established in his I AM power and dominion, His voice is strong and vibrant and commanding. God revealed Himself to the prophets of old through the "still small voice." While it is not audible it is distinct and clear. Many ask how to distinguish the real voice. They hear voices and voices but do not understand how to distinguish the real one. If man follows the Holy Spirit, the one teacher, if he concentrates on the power of the word and holds continuously for the leading of the Spirit of truth, he will enter into a state of spiritual discernment in which he can readily distinguish the still small voice.

[31] The Jews took up stones again to stone him. [32]Jesus answered them, Many good works have I showed you from the Father; for which of those works do ye stone me? [33] The Jews answered him, For a good work we stone thee not, but for blasphemy; and because that thou, being a man, makest thyself God. [34] Jesus answered them, Is it not written in your law, I said, Ye are gods? [35] If he called them gods, unto whom the word of God came (and the scripture cannot be broken), [36] say ye of him, whom the Father sanctified and sent into the world, Thou blasphemest; because I said, I am the Son of God? [37] If I do not the works of my Father, believe me not. [38] But if I do them, though ye believe not me, believe the works: that ye may know and understand that the Father is in me, and I in the Father. [39] They sought again to take him: and he went forth out of their hand.

40 And he went away again beyond the Jordan into the place where John was at the first baptizing; and there he abode. 41 And many came unto him; and they said, John indeed did no sign: but all things whatsoever John spake of this man were true. 42 And many believed on him there.

After the Christ has done a positive work it always withdraws to an inner state of consciousness in order to replenish its power before it goes forth to achieve again. Into this state of consciousness opposing intellect cannot find entrance. But after a season the Christ again penetrates into the Jordan or subconsciousness made up of thoughts good, bad, and indifferent. Here man is in an ignorant and unredeemed state. His concepts are turbulent with materiality.

However here again the light of the Christ penetrates, and many believe and receive the Truth. Jesus has made conscious unity with His supermind or I AM mind and through it with the Father. This is the only way in which any man can attain perfection.

Here again Jesus emphasizes the importance of works to prove one's claims of spiritual authority and power. "If I do not the works of my Father, believe me not." The world is full of religious leaders who cannot do the works promised by Jesus, and yet they are accepted as His representative. He said, "These signs shall accompany them that believe."

Chapter XI

THE NAME Lazarus means "whom God helps." Metaphysically interpreted, Lazarus represents the spiritual strength that comes to man through his recognition of God as his supporting, sustaining power. When man fails to recognize God as the origin and support of his life, spiritual understanding becomes weak in him and he sinks into materiality. To all intents he is dead to the Truth of his own being. The devotional soul, Mary, and the practical soul, Martha, are sisters in this intellect, and although like all women they have faith in the Spirit, they allow themselves to fall under the thought of mortal law and believe in the reality of death. The whole world is under the hypnotism of this material belief, and it is making tombs for thousands every day.

Out of a torpid condition of soul like that of Lazarus the I AM (Jesus) calls forth the living Spirit of the Christ, and reawakens by one word the consciousness of true understanding in man and the quickened perception of his faculties.

The name Thomas means "twin." Spiritually considered, Thomas is understanding, whose twin is Matthew, the will. Matthew, metaphysical twin of Thomas, is not so described in the Scriptures; spiritually he is identified as the co-ordinating faculty. In a well-balanced mind understanding is followed by action.

Intellectual understanding assures us of the truth of our sense impressions. It says, "Seeing is believing." According to this dictum, if we should see written on a blackboard, "Two plus two equals six," we should be called on to accept as true a contradiction of the principles of mathematics.

> *17 So when Jesus came, he found that he [Lazarus] had been in the tomb four days already. 18 Now Bethany was nigh unto Jerusalem, about fifteen furlongs off; 19 and many of the Jews had come to Martha and Mary, to console them concerning their brother. 20 Martha therefore, when she heard that Jesus was coming, went and met him: but Mary still sat in the house. 21 Martha therefore said unto Jesus, Lord, if thou hadst been here, my brother had not died. 22 And even now I know that, whatsoever thou shalt ask of God, God will give thee. 23 Jesus saith unto her, Thy brother shall rise again. 24 Martha saith unto him, I know that he shall rise again in the resurrection at the last day. 25 Jesus said unto her, I am the resurrection, and the life: he that believeth on me, though he die, yet shall he live; 26 and whosoever liveth and believeth on me shall never die. Believest thou this? 27 She saith unto him, Yea, Lord; I have believed that thou art the Christ, the Son of God, even he that cometh into the world. 28 And when she had said this, she went away, and called Mary her sister secretly, saying, The Teacher is here, and calleth thee. 29 And she, when she heard it, arose quickly, and went unto him. 30 (Now Jesus was not yet come into the village, but was still in the place where Martha met him.) 31 The Jews then who were with her in the house, and were consoling her, when they saw Mary, that she rose up quickly and went out, followed her, supposing that she was going unto the tomb to weep there. 32 Mary therefore, when she came where Jesus was, and saw him, fell down at his feet, saying unto him, Lord, if thou hadst been here, my brother had not died. 33 When Jesus therefore saw her weeping, and the Jews also weeping who came with her, he groaned in the spirit, and was troubled, 34 and said, Where have ye laid him? They say unto him, Lord, come and see. 35 Jesus wept. 36 The Jews therefore said, Behold how he loved him! 37 But some of them said, Could not this man, who opened the eyes of him that was blind, have caused that this man also should not die? 38 Jesus therefore again groaning in himself cometh to the tomb. Now it was a cave, and a stone lay against it. 39 Jesus saith, Take ye away the stone. Martha, the sister of him that was dead, saith unto him, Lord, by this time the body decayeth; for he hath been dead four days. 40 Jesus saith unto her, Said I not unto thee, that, if thou believedst, thou shouldest see the glory of God? 41 So they took away the stone. And Jesus lifted up his eyes, and said, Father, I thank thee that thou heardest me. 42 And I knew that thou hearest me always: but because of the multitude that standeth*

around I said it, that they may believe that thou didst send me. [43] *And when he had thus spoken, he cried with a loud voice, Lazarus, come forth.* [44] *He that was dead came forth, bound hand and foot with grave-clothes; and his face was bound about with a napkin. Jesus saith unto them, Loose him, and let him go.*

Jesus represents man in the regeneration; that is, man in the process of restoring his body to its natural condition, where it will live right on perpetually without old age, disease, or death. A necessary step in this process of body restoration is the quickening of the sleeping Lazarus, who represents the vitalizing energies in the subconsciousness that feed the body and give it the life force that renews its youth.

Jesus was at Bethany near Jerusalem. Metaphysically Jerusalem represents a point in consciousness where the spiritual energy of life is strong enough to vitalize adjacent body substance (Bethany, "house of figs"). Jesus vitalized and baptized His soul and body with spirit life when He denied the power of death over Lazarus and affirmed the resurrecting life. We can do the same thing when we do it in His name. Jesus' groaning and weeping represent the seemingly insurmountable conditions that are just before us.

We should ever remember that the youth we love so well never dies; it is merely asleep in the subconscious--Jesus said that Lazarus was not dead. People grow old because they let the youth idea fall asleep. This idea is not dead but is sleeping, and the understanding I AM (Jesus) goes to awaken it. This awakening of youthful energies is necessary to one in the regeneration. The body cannot be refined and made, like its Creator, eternal before all the thoughts necessary to its perpetuation are revived in it. Eternal youth is one of these God-given ideas that man loves. Jesus loved Lazarus.

The outer senses say that this vitalizing force of youth is dead in man, that it has been dead for so long that it has gone into dissolution, decay; but the keener knowledge of the spiritual man proclaims, "Our friend Lazarus is fallen asleep; but I . . . awake him out of sleep."

Bringing this sleeping life to outer consciousness is no easy task. Jesus groaned in spirit and was troubled at the prospect. The higher must enter into sympathy and love with the lower to bring about the awakening--"Jesus wept." But there must be more than sympathy and love--"Take ye away the stone." The "stone" that holds the sleeping life in the tomb of matter in subconsciousness is the belief in the permanency of present material laws. This "stone" must be rolled away through faith. The man who wants the inner life to spring forth must believe in the reality of omnipresent spiritual life and must exercise his faith by invoking in prayer the presence of the invisible but omnipresent God. This reveals to consciousness the glory of Spirit, and the soul has witness in itself of a power that it knew not.

In Spirit all things are fulfilled now. The moment a concept enters the mind, the thing conceived is consummated through the law that governs the action of ideas. The inventor mentally sees his machine doing the work designed, though he may be years short of making it do that work. The spiritual-minded take advantage of this law and affirm the completeness of this ideal, regardless of outer appearances. This stimulates the energy in the thought process and gives it power beyond estimate. This is the step that Jesus took when He lifted up His eyes and said: "Father, I thank thee that thou heardest me. And I knew that thou hearest me always." The sleeping youth (Lazarus) does not at once respond, but the prayer of thanksgiving that is now in action gives the assurance that calls it at the next step to the surface--"Lazarus, come forth."

Jesus "cried with a loud voice." This emphasizes the necessity of working strenuously to project the inner life to the surface. Beginners find it easy, under proper instruction, to quicken the various life centers in the body and co-ordinate them as a body battery that, under the direction of the will, throws a current of energy to any desired place. A time comes when the outer flesh must be vitalized with this inner life; then arises the necessity of using the "loud voice" as the propelling force. This is removing from the face the "napkin," which represents conscious intelligence made manifest.

Freedom from all trammels is necessary before the imprisoned life can find its natural channel in the constitution. "Loose him, and let him go" means unfettered life expressing itself in joyous freedom of Spirit. The flesh would take this vital flood and use it in the old way, put new wine into old bottles, but Spirit guides those who trust it, and leads them in righteous ways when they listen patiently to the inner guide.

This raising of Lazarus is performed every day by those who are putting on the new Christ body through the resurrected Christ life.

> 45 Many therefore of the Jews, who came to Mary and beheld that which he did,
> believed on him. 46 But some of them went away to the Pharisees, and told them
> the things which Jesus had done.

Interpreted within ourselves, there are always the thought forces that believe the Truth and accept the so-called miracles of the Christ, but there are also those that question and resort to the Pharisees (the strict intellectual phase of mind) for their stamp of approval.

> *47 The chief priests therefore and the Pharisees gathered a council, and said, What do we?*
> *for this man doeth many signs. 48 If we let him thus alone, all men will believe on him:*
> *and the Romans will come and take away both our place and our nation. 49 But a certain*
> *one of them, Caiaphas, being high priest that year, said unto them, Ye know nothing at*
> *all, 50 nor do ye take account that it is expedient for you that one man should die for the*
> *people, and that the whole nation perish not. 51 Now this he said not of himself: but being*
> *high priest that year, he prophesied that Jesus should die for the nation; 52 and not for the*
> *nation only, but that he might also gather together into one the children of God that are*
> *scattered abroad. 53 So from that day forth they took counsel that they might put him to*
> *death.*

In this instance the Pharisees represent a congregation of intellectual thought people called together to counsel with one another. The Romans symbolize the rule of the natural man. The intellectual Pharisee is always jealous of his religious rights and fearful of being robbed of his own. He observes the forms of religion but neglects the spirit. He does not understand the activities of the Christ Mind and therefore fears it.

Another tendency of the intellect is to question and argue back and forth. The high priest symbolizes the highest spiritual thought force in authority that has an inkling of Truth, and he perceives that the Christ will eventually give His life for the redemption of all. The narrow intellect, however, does not have the spiritual viewpoint and seeks to destroy the saving spiritual power.

> *54 Jesus therefore walked no more openly among the Jews, but departed thence into the*
> *country near to the wilderness, into a city called Ephraim; and there he tarried with the*
> *disciples. 55 Now the passover of the Jews was at hand: and many went up to Jerusalem*
> *out of the country before the passover, to purify themselves. 56 They sought therefore*
> *for Jesus, and spake one with another, as they stood in the temple, What think ye?*
> *That he will not come to the feast? 57 Now the chief priests and the Pharisees had given*
> *commandment, that, if any man knew where he was, he should show it, that they might*
> *take him.*

When a state of consciousness is not open to Truth, the Christ (in this Scripture symbolized by Jesus) withdraws to an inner sanctum (here symbolized by Ephraim, a name that means "doubly fruitful"), where closer union with the great divine source is found. Jesus therefore walked no more openly among the Jews.

The Feast of the Passover represents a passing from a lower state of consciousness to a higher. For the spiritual passover the devout always seek the city of peace (Jerusalem). No matter in what state of consciousness one may be functioning there is always that within which craves something better. The intellect, continuing to believe it is to be the highest authority, would kill out the Christ.

Chapter XII

BETHANY MEANS "a place of fruits," dates, bread, that is, substance. Whenever we make a mental demonstration we get a certain result in our body. This is called the "fruit" of our thought.

When Jesus went to Bethany He realized the fruit or effect of raising Lazarus; that is, the quickening of certain sleeping energies in His body consciousness.

This realization is a feast to the soul and body, a filling of the whole man with a sense of satisfaction. Martha, the practical soul, and Mary, the devotional, serve the Master. Martha provides the material necessities and Mary the spiritual, while Lazarus sits at meat (abides as the living substance of the subconsciousness).

Mary, the devotional side of the soul, is grateful for the awakening of her brother Lazarus, because she depends for her manifestation on the subconscious life that he represents. When the soul is lifted up in prayer and thanksgiving, there follows an outflow of love that fills the whole "house" or body with its odor. The anointing of Jesus' feet represents the willingness of love to serve. When Jesus washed the feet of His apostles He said, "He that is . . . greater among you, let him become as the younger; and he that is chief, as he that doth serve."

> [4] *But Judas Iscariot, one of his disciples, that should betray him, saith,* [5] *Why was not this ointment sold for three hundred shillings, and given to the poor?* [6] *Now this he said, not because he cared for the poor; but because he was a thief, and having the bag took away what was put therein.* [7] *Jesus therefore said, suffer her to keep it against the day of my burying.*
> [8] *For the poor ye have always with you; but me ye have not always.*

> [9] The common people therefore of the Jews learned that he was there: and they came, not for Jesus' sake only, but that they might see Lazarus also, whom he had raised from the dead. [10] But the chief priests took counsel that they might put Lazarus also to death; [11] because that by reason of him many of the Jews went away, and believed on Jesus.

Judas Iscariot (sense consciousness) is incarnated selfishness, and his every thought is to build up personality. When Mary anoints the feet of Jesus (when love pours out her precious substance, diffusing its essence throughout the whole man), Judas inquires why the ointment was not sold and the proceeds given to the poor. The Judas consciousness believes in poverty and has no understanding of the true law of supply. All that comes into consciousness is selfishly appropriated and dissipated by this thief, yet he produces nothing. Sense consciousness is the enigma of existence, and in it is wrapped up the mystery of individuality. Jesus knew that through this department of His being He would be betrayed, but He made no effort to defeat the act of Judas. Sense consciousness betrays man every day, yet it would be unwise wholly to destroy it before its time, because at its foundation it is good; it has simply gone wrong; it "hath a devil."

Love is the "greatest thing in the world," according to Henry Drummond, who analyzed it in a masterly manner. Jesus acknowledged the power of love when He said, "Suffer her to keep it against the day of my burying." When personality is hurt to the death and surrenders all, love pours her balm over every wound and the substance of her sympathy infuses hope and faith into the discouraged soul. A noted mental healer relates that her husband was dying of consumption. She had treated him in every way known to her science without results, when one day in her agony she exclaimed, "I will give my whole life to save you." Immediately, she says, a great flood of substance seemed to roll forth from her heart toward her husband, and from that day he began to improve, and he finally got well. This was the precious ointment of love, poured out for him when he was buried in the consciousness of death, and it resurrected him. Divine Love hath a balm for every ill.

> [12] On the morrow a great multitude that had come to the feast, when they heard that Jesus was coming to Jerusalem, [13] took the branches of the palm trees, and went forth to meet him, and cried out, Hosanna: Blessed is he that cometh in the name of the Lord, even the King of Israel. [14] And Jesus, having found a young ass, sat thereon; as it is written, [15] Fear not, daughter of Zion: behold, thy King cometh, sitting on an ass's colt. [16] These things understood not his disciples at the first: but when Jesus was glorified, then remembered they that these things were written of him, and that they had done these things unto him. [17] The multitude therefore that was with him when he called Lazarus out of the tomb, and raised him from the dead, bare witness. [18] For this cause also the multitude went and met him, for that they heard that he had done this sign. [19] The Pharisees therefore said among themselves, Behold how ye prevail nothing; lo, the world is gone after him.

The triumphal entry of Jesus into Jerusalem and His reception by the multitude represents a transient and external enthusiasm, the result of demonstrations in the outer. This multitude that went forth to meet Him, crying, "Hosanna: Blessed is he that cometh in the name of the Lord," did so because they had witnessed the raising of Lazarus. Their homage to Jesus was based on the "signs" that they had witnessed, and not on that deep inner conviction of Truth that attests the sincere followers.

A large proportion of those who espouse the cause in this day do so from the "signs" standpoint. They have observed some demonstration, and accept the philosophy as they would a new patent medicine, and they change their doctrine as readily as the doser does his drug.

> [20] Now there were certain Greeks among those that went up to worship at the feast: [21] these therefore came to Philip, who was of Bethsaida of Galilee, and asked him, saying, Sir, we would see Jesus. [22] Philip cometh and telleth Andrew: Andrew cometh, and Philip, and they tell Jesus. [23] And Jesus answereth them, saying, The hour is come, that the Son of man should be glorified. [24] Verily, verily, I say unto you, Except a grain of wheat fall into the earth and die, it abideth by itself alone; but if it die, it beareth much fruit. [25] He that loveth his life loseth it; and he that hateth his life in this world shall keep it unto life eternal. [26] If any man serve me, let him follow me; and where I am, there shall also my servant be: if any man serve me, him will the Father honor.

Common sense often saves a man from the fanaticism of religious enthusiasm. The Greeks represent the practical side of man's nature. They ask Philip for an interview with Jesus, and Philip tells Andrew. All this means that it is through the power (Philip) and strength (Andrew) in man that the sense reason acts, and when the I AM is called down from its lofty spiritual enthronement to the contemplation of practical life, there is a restoration of equilibrium. Then it recognizes the law of giving its exalted ideality to the earthly consciousness, that it may also be lifted up. To the higher consciousness this seems like the death of an ideal, but it is only a temporary submergence, which has its resurrection in a great increase of life and power. Thus we lose our life in the service of the good, and count it of no value in order to find it again in Spirit.

> [27] Now is my soul troubled; and what shall I say? Father, save me from this hour. But for this cause came I unto this hour. [28] Father, glorify thy name. There came therefore a voice out of heaven, saying, I have both glorified it, and will glorify it again. [29] The multitude therefore, that stood by, and heard it, said that it had thundered: others said, An angel hath spoken to him. [30] Jesus answered and said, This voice hath not come for my sake, but for your sakes.

Jesus' mission on earth was to save the race from bondage, from sin, sickness, and death. This Scripture reveals that Jesus had been able to realize the Truth in this regard and that the time was now approaching for the demonstration. In the face of it all, He realized He was on new ground and there was that within Him which was troubled. "Father, save me from this hour. But for this cause came I unto this hour. Father, glorify thy name." From within Him came the reassuring voice of God: "I have both glorified it [the name] and will glorify it again." This means that Jesus' heavenly credentials were sufficient and that there was nothing to fear. The demonstration must eventually be forthcoming.

> 31 Now is the judgment of this world: now shall the prince of this world be cast
> out. 32 And I, if I be lifted up from the earth, will draw all men unto myself. 33 But
> this he said, signifying by what manner of death he should die. 34 The multitude
> therefore answered him, We have heard out of the law that the Christ abideth for
> ever: and how sayest thou, The Son of man must be lifted up? who is this Son of
> man? 35 Jesus therefore said unto them, Yet a little while is the light among you.
> Walk while ye have the light, that darkness overtake you not: and he that walketh
> in the darkness knoweth not whither he goes. 36 While ye have the light, believe
> on the light, that ye may become sons of light.

The multitude here referred to is the multitude of thoughts within the soul that is endeavoring to lay hold of the laws of spirituality. Jesus' admonition was "Yet a little while is the light among you. Walk while ye have the light, that darkness overtake you not."

> 36 These things spake Jesus, and he departed and hid himself from them. 37 But
> though he had done so many signs before them, yet they believed not on him: 38
> that the word of Isaiah the prophet might be fulfilled, which he spake,

Lord, who hath believed our report?
And to whom hath the arm of the Lord been revealed?
39 For this cause they could not believe, for that Isaiah said again,
40 He hath blinded their eyes, and he hardened their heart;
Lest they should see with their eyes, and perceive with their heart,
And should turn,
And I should heal them.

> 41 These things said Isaiah, because he saw his glory; and he spake of him. 42
> Nevertheless even of the rulers many believed on him; but because of the Pharisees
> they did not confess it, lest they should be put out of the synagogue: 43 for they
> loved the glory that is of men more than the glory that is of God.

By a "prophet" within the soul is understood the capacity to read out of the law and to perceive to what degree the soul can really demonstrate spirituality. It is revealed that in this Scripture the Pharisaical intellect was in authority, compelling the soul forces that were beginning to understand Truth but that still loved the glory that is of men more than the glory that is of God to do obeisance to it.

> *44 And Jesus cried and said, He that believeth on me, believeth not on me, but on him that*
> *sent me. 45 And he that beholdeth me beholdeth him that sent me. 46 I am come a light*
> *into the world, that whosoever believeth on me may not abide in the darkness. 47 And if*
> *any man hear my sayings, and keep them not, I judge him not: for I came not to judge the*
> *world, but to save the world. 48 He that rejecteth me, and receiveth not my sayings, hath*
> *one that judgeth him: the word that I spake, the same shall judge him in the last day. 49*
> *For I spake not from myself; but the Father that sent me, he hath given me a command-*
> *ment, what I should say, and what I should speak. 50 And I know that his commandment*

is life eternal; the things therefore which I speak, even as the Father hath said unto me, so I speak.

In this Scripture Jesus (symbolizing the indwelling Christ) is declaring to the whole soul consciousness that the preponderance of power is spiritual. Spiritual character is the rock foundation of Being; therefore He is urging the multitude of thoughts to realize that their redemption comes through decreeing their oneness with Spirit and that the will of God is active in consciousness.

The realization of divine unity is the highest that we may attain. This is true glory, the blending and merging of the whole being in Divine Mind. "Build yourself into God and you will find yourself in heaven right here and now."

Chapter XIII

WE HAVE PROOF on every side that through our mind we are unified into the one Mind. Through the interflowing of mind and Mind we act and react on each other, and "no man liveth unto himself alone." By this mind contact we all become responsible for the good or bad conditions in our neighbors and remotely for that of the whole race. Christianity teaches that sin came into the world through the sin of one man, Adam, and that it is cast out by the righteousness of one man, Jesus. This was demonstrated by the projection into the race consciousness of the blood or spiritually quickened life energy of Jesus as a solvent for sin.

Satan represents the adverse ego in the race that opposes and resists the divine law, and Judas is its personal representative. Jesus purified all the elements composing His blood, smashed the atoms and released the electrons into the race consciousness, subjecting them to the will and appropriation of anyone who exercises sufficient faith and the desire to attain that end. Giving up this life essence was a great sacrifice on the part of Jesus; it was trusting to others His very life essence to be appropriated by them and restored to Him when all have attained the purity of the principles that it represents.

In this episode Jesus is about to make the great sacrifice; the passing over from one state of consciousness to another is about to take place. Then He ceases to be the great leader of men and through surrender of the most precious possession of man, his life, Jesus becomes the lowly servant of us all.

By His acts Jesus taught as many lessons in soul unfoldment as by His words. Soul unfoldment means the bringing forth of divine ideas in the soul or consciousness of man and the bringing of these ideas into expression in the body. Jesus told His disciples that those who would become truly great must serve. Those who have become great have first learned, as a matter of course, to serve and in so doing have found their own good.

The undisciplined disciples had disputed about who should have the higher places in the kingdom, who should be the greatest, who should sit at the right hand of the Master and who at the left. Jesus cited to them the little child's guilelessness and trustfulness and willingness to learn. He also showed them the difference between divine greatness and the human idea of greatness. Finally He told them that whoever would be great among them should be their minister or servant, even as the Son of man came to minister and to "give his life a ransom for many." To have everything done for one is to remain a child, but to do for others is to reach man's estate. Jesus gave His very life in service to the world, and He left us an example that we should follow. We should be eager to become as unselfishly humble and willing to minister to others for their eternal good as He was.

> 6 So he cometh to Simon Peter. He saith unto him, Lord, dost thou wash my feet?
> 7 Jesus answered and said unto him, What I do thou knowest not now; but thou
> shalt understand hereafter. 8 Peter saith unto him, Thou shalt never wash my feet.
> Jesus answered him, If I wash thee not, thou hast no part with me. 9 Simon Peter
> saith unto him, Lord, not my feet only, but also my hands and my head. 10 Jesus
> saith to him, He that is bathed needeth not save to wash his feet, but is clean every
> whit: and ye are clean, but not all. 11 For he knew him that should betray him;
> therefore said he, Ye are not all clean.

> 12 So when he had washed their feet, and taken his garments, and sat down again,
> he said unto them, Know ye what I have done to you? 13 Ye call me, Teacher, and,
> Lord: and ye say well; for so I am. 14 If I then, the Lord and the Teacher, have
> washed your feet, ye also ought to wash one another's feet. 15 For I have given you
> an example, that ye also should do as I have done to you. 16 Verily, verily, I say
> unto you, A servant is not greater than his lord; neither one that is sent greater
> than he that sent him. 17 If ye know these things, blessed are ye if ye do them.

Spiritual consciousness puts all men and all things on a common level. In the sight of God there is no great, no small. The principle of life (that is, God immanent in the universe as the great underlying cause of all manifestation) supplies the humble, unlearned laborer as fully and as freely as it supplies the most cultured person. Those who "put . . . on . . . Christ" (develop a consciousness according to the Christ standard) disregard rank and title.

Some years ago two humble missionary workers who had been in China were received into the home of a wealthy woman in America who was interested in foreign missions. When the hour of departure came, they walked two blocks to the elevated train to save taxi fare. Their hostess, who lived simply and did not even keep an automobile, insisted on accompanying them to the station and helped them carry their hand baggage. She had given millions to the cause of health and education in India and China, yet she was completely democratic and simple.

The feet are the willing and patient servants of the body. They go all day at the bidding of the mind, and upon them rest many of the burdens that result from material thoughts. The more we believe in the false importance of matter the greater is the burden laid upon our feet and the more tired they become.

By washing the feet of His apostles Jesus denied the race idea of matter as all-important and taught the value of service. Even Peter (spiritual faith) had to be cleansed of his belief in the seeming reality of material conditions. It seems a menial thing to wash another's feet, but Jesus taught and exemplified the willingness of divine love to serve in humble ways and thus redeem man from the pride of the flesh.

As through His great love Jesus cleansed our understanding, so should we cleanse the understanding of our fellows. He delegates to His disciples and students of every age and land the power to cleanse man's mind of false standards of life. This Christ cleansing through love is not only a teaching; it is also a life to be lived. The true teacher of practical Christianity must be a Christian, a follower of Jesus in all His ways. Those who, like Judas, are possessed of the adverse mind should receive the same humble service, the same lesson that is given to persons who are true and faithful.

> 18 I speak not of you all: I know whom I have chosen: but that the scripture may be
> fulfilled, He that eateth my bread lifted up his heel against me. 19 From henceforth
> I tell you before it come to pass, that, when it is come to pass, ye may believe that
> I am he. 20 Verily, verily, I say unto you, He that receiveth whomsoever I send
> receiveth me; and he that receiveth me receiveth him that sent me.

> 21 When Jesus had thus said, he was troubled in the spirit, and testified, and said,
> Verily, verily, I say unto you, that one of you shall betray me. 22 The disciples looked
> one on another, doubting of whom he spake. 23 There was at the table reclining
> in Jesus' bosom one of his disciples, whom Jesus loved. 24 Simon Peter therefore
> beckoneth to him, and saith unto him, Tell us who it is of whom he speaketh. 25
> He leaning back, as he was, on Jesus' breast saith unto him, Lord, who is it? 26
> Jesus therefore answereth, He it is, for whom I shall dip the sop, and give it him.
> So when he had dipped the sop, he taketh and giveth it to Judas, the son of Simon
> Iscariot. 27 And after the sop, then entered Satan into him. Jesus therefore saith
> unto him, What thou doest, do quickly. 28 Now no man at the table knew for
> what intent he spake this unto him. 29 For some thought, because Judas had the
> bag, that Jesus said unto him, Buy what things we have need of for the feast; or,
> that he should give something to the poor. 30 He then having received the sop
> went out straightway: and it was night.

The Christ symbolized by Jesus is eternally the I AM, though the disciples may not fully understand. The Judas faculty, the sum of the unredeemed life forces, is bound to betray until it is spiritualized. Jesus (the Christ) knew that this unredeemed condition was bound to bring about tragedy. The physical life represented by Judas may be ambitious, selfish, proud, tyrannical, but we cannot do without it. The false must be overcome. When faith and love ask questions the way for illumination and revelation is opened.

> 31 When therefore he was gone out, Jesus saith, Now is the Son of man glorified,
> and God is glorified in him, 32 and God shall glorify him in himself, and straightway
> shall he glorify him. 33 Little children, yet a little while I am with you. Ye shall
> seek me: and as I said unto the Jews, Whither I go, ye cannot come; so now I say
> unto you. 34 A new commandment I give unto you, that ye love one another; even
> as I have loved you, that ye also love one another. 35 By this shall all men know
> that ye are my disciples, if ye have love one to another.

When a soul makes complete union with God-Mind there is always an outpouring of the Holy Spirit upon it. This is true glorification, the acknowledgment by the Father that the Son is indeed lifted up (glorified).

Jesus at this point was in a high spiritual state of consciousness; in fact, He had made a perfect at-one-ment with the Father. He was aware that even His apostles had not attained His glory. In the meantime love is the great harmonizer, and finally love is the fulfillment of the law.

> 36 Simon Peter saith unto him, Lord, whither goest thou? Jesus answered, Whither
> I go, thou canst not follow me now; but thou shalt follow afterwards. 37 Peter saith
> unto him, Lord, why cannot I follow thee even now? I will lay down my life for
> thee. 38 Jesus answereth, Wilt thou lay down thy life for me? Verily, verily, I say
> unto thee, The cock shall not crow, till thou hast denied me thrice.

When Jesus said that He was going away, Peter said he wanted to go with Him. He said he would lay down his life for Jesus. But the Master's insight into the state of consciousness represented by Peter gave Him foreknowledge of what would happen. He warned Peter of his coming failure, and He was prepared for the confusion and scattering of the disciples. He knew that eventually Peter would regain and express the Christ faith and that His band of followers would preserve Christianity for posterity but first they must be spiritually unfolded as He was.

Chapter XIV

WE BELIEVE IN God. It follows logically that we believe also in the manifestation of God, the ideal man. This proposition once accepted, there dawns on the understanding the truth of an intimate relation existing between Father and Son. The Father, God, "Spirit," is within the Son as the animating principle. The full recognition by man of this indwelling Spirit, as it was in Jesus, makes man the central figure and ruling power in the manifest universe. "The kingdom of God is within you."

"Many mansions" means many abiding places. "Mansion" comes from the Latin manere, to remain. The meaning of Jesus was that He was making a permanent abiding place for those who believed in His teaching and accepted Him for what He really was--God manifest. The idea usually held out is that Jesus was preceding His disciples to heaven, where He would await and welcome them. But there is no such meaning in the text. The permanent abiding place to which Jesus invites His friends is "prepared" by Him: He makes the place Himself, in fact He is the place. "Where I am, there ye may be also:

> [4] And whither I go, ye know the way. [5] Thomas saith unto him, Lord, we know not whither thou goest; how know we the way? [6] Jesus saith unto him, I am the way, and the truth, and the life: no one cometh unto the Father, but by me. [7] If ye had known me, ye would have known my Father also: from henceforth ye know him, and have seen him. [8] Philip saith unto him, Lord, show us the Father, and it sufficeth us. [9] Jesus saith unto him, Have I been so long time with you, and dost thou not know me, Philip? he that hath seen me hath seen the Father; how sayest thou, Show us the Father? [10] Believest thou not that I am in the Father, and the Father in me? the words that I say unto you I speak not from myself: but the Father abiding in me doeth his works. [11] Believe me that I am in the Father, and the Father in me: or else believe me for the very works' sake.

"Whither I go, ye know the way." The intellectual man, Thomas, claims ignorance and says he does not know the place or the way. Then Jesus reveals the spiritual Truth to which He has gradually been leading their minds, saying, "I am the way, and the truth, and the life: no one cometh unto the Father, but by me." An understanding of man's spiritual nature reveals his unity with the omnipresent principle of life, the Father. Jesus the Christ is in the Father, and the Father is in man. Whoever sees the spirituality of man in himself or others sees the Father. The Father principle may be so developed in man that it will move him unerringly in all his ways, and the Father may even speak words through his mouth. When this point is reached the question of man's unity with the Father principle is wholly removed, the manifestation of wisdom and power in him proving that a higher principle is at work through him. "Believe me for the very works' sake."

But Philip (the power of the word) says, "Show us the Father." This faculty must be raised to the realization of the omnipresence of Spirit by an acknowledgment that the word of the I AM spoken through it is not of the mortal but of God. "The words that I say unto you I speak not of myself: but the Father abiding in me, doeth his works."

> [12] Verily, verily, I say unto you, He that believeth on me, the works that I do shall he do also; and greater works than these shall he do; because I go unto the Father. [13] And whatsoever ye shall ask in my name, that will I do, that the Father may be glorified in the Son. [14] If ye shall ask anything in my name, that will I do.

"Whatsoever ye shall ask in my name, that will I do." There is no limit here. "Whatsoever" covers everything. Then why do we not receive at all times when we ask in His name? Because we have not demonstrated the power of His name. The name stands for the spiritual man, and it is this name or sign of God with us that rewards our faith. Had we a check signed by a well-known financier we should not hesitate to present it at the bank and get the money. The same confidence in the life-giving and success-producing power of the risen Christ must be established in us. When we reach out into the great invisible spiritual substance all about us and think of ourselves as its expression, confidently expecting it to manifest itself through us, it will do so. If at the first trial we do not succeed, let us keep trying until we do succeed; for the promise can be proved true, "If ye shall ask anything in my name, that will I do."

> 15 If ye love me, ye will keep my commandments. 16 And I will pray the Father, and
> he shall give you another Comforter, that he may be with you for ever, 17 even the
> Spirit of truth: whom the world cannot receive; for it beholdeth him not, neither
> knoweth him: ye know him; for he abideth with you, and shall be in you. 18 I
> will not leave you desolate: I come unto you. 19 Yet a little while, and the world
> beholdeth me no more; but ye behold me: because I live, ye shall live also. 20 In
> that day ye shall know that I am in my Father, and ye in me, and I in you. 21 He
> that hath my commandments, and keepeth them, he it is that loveth me: and he
> that loveth me shall be loved of my Father, and I will love him, and will manifest
> myself unto him. 22 Judas (not Iscariot) saith unto him, Lord, what is come to pass
> that thou wilt manifest thyself unto us, and not unto the world? 23 Jesus answered
> and said unto him, If a man love me, he will keep my word: and my Father will
> love him, and we will come unto him, and make our abode with him. 24 He that
> loveth me not keepeth not my words: and the word which ye hear is not mine, but
> the Father's who sent me.

In this Scripture Jesus, representing the I AM, gives assurance of divine co-operation to those who are loyal in thought and word to the Truth. You now know the relation in which you stand to the Father. Spiritually you are one, but to sustain this spiritual relation until it is fully manifested in your body and environment requires attention. The concrete aspect of Truth, represented by the personality of Jesus, must be taken away before you can understand Truth in its abstract or universal sense. Then withdrawing your attention from the letter or personality and centering it on Truth in its spiritual essence, you find that there is an intelligible side to that which seems vague and indefinite. The Comforter, the Advocate, the Spirit of truth is omnipresent as divine wisdom and power, which are brought into active touch with our consciousness through our believing in Him. In "the world"–on the phenomenal side--we cannot know this guide and helper, but having learned the truth about the omnipresence of Spirit, with all the abundance of life, love, Truth, and intelligence through which it is made manifest, we at once begin to realize that the Mighty One dwells with us, and "shall be in you."

The going away of the I AM was apparent to sense consciousness only--the "world beholdeth me no more"–but the larger range of consciousness beholds an expansion of the sense of divine identity and life, "Ye behold me: because I live, ye shall live also." With this expansion of the sense of our divine identity comes a perception of our unity with the Father, and the absolute identity of our sense-limited I with the universal I AM, the Christ. "In that day ye shall know that I am in my Father, and ye in me, and I in you."

The question is frequently asked, Is it not presumptuous for us, who have at first no realization of their truth, to make the statements that Jesus made? No, it is not; because in Spirit we are all that He claimed for Himself, and in no other way except affirming this truth can we make it manifest. All who experiment with words find that they generate force in the mind and eventually affect the body. Jesus urged His disciples to believe on Him, to keep His commandments, His sayings, His words, and they went forth and did wonderful works in "the name of . . . Jesus Christ."

In this Scripture Jesus says that those who keep His commandments thus show their love for Him and that He will love them and manifest Himself to them. Understanding as we do the affinity that similar thoughts have for one another, we perceive why keeping "my word" and believing "in me" were so powerfully urged by Jesus. He transcended men in His high statements, and His work corresponded to them, and knowing this law that like thoughts and words swiftly seek unity, He took advantage of it to lift us all up to His high standard.

But we must get out of the "world" or letter before we can touch this spiritual potency. Judas asked why it was that Jesus would manifest Himself to them and not to the world. Jesus' answer is right in line with this mental law of words by which the speaker is put in contact with those who have uttered similar words: "If a man love me, he will keep my word: and my Father will love him, and we will come unto him, and make our abode with him. He that loveth me not keepeth not my words: and the word which ye hear is not mine, but the Father's who sent me."

> 25 These things have I spoken unto you, while yet abiding with you. 26 But the
> Comforter, even the Holy Spirit, whom the Father will send in my name, he shall
> teach you all things, and bring to your remembrance all that I said unto you. 27
> Peace I leave with you; my peace I give unto you: not as the world giveth, give
> I unto you. Let not your heart be troubled, neither let it be fearful. 28 Ye heard
> how I said to you, I go away, and I come unto you. If ye loved me, ye would have
> rejoiced, because I go unto the Father: for the Father is greater than I. 29 And now
> I have told you before it come to pass, that, when it is come to pass, ye may believe.
> 30 I will no more speak much with you, for the prince of the world cometh: and
> he hath nothing in me; 31 but that the world may know that I love the Father, and
> as the Father gave me commandment, even so I do. Arise, let us go hence.

The Father is principle. The Son is this Father principle revealed in a creative plan. The Holy Spirit is the executive power of both Father and Son.

The Holy Spirit is not all of Being, nor the fullness of Christ, but an emanation or "breath" sent forth to do a divine work. Thus circumscribed, the Holy Spirit may in a sense be said to take on the characteristics of personality, but personality that for capacity transcends all man's conceptions.

The Holy Spirit was before the time of Jesus. However Jesus' life and demonstration gave a new impetus to it. The Holy Spirit or Spirit of truth is man's one sure guide in his spiritual ongoing. An outpouring of the Holy Spirit always brings peace and infinite faith in the Father through the Son.

(See John 15:17-27 for further interpretation.)

Chapter XV

METAPHYSICALLY stated, the Father is the God-Mind; Jesus is the individual incarnation of that Mind, here called the true vine. "Every branch in me" means the faculties of mind, and the "fruit" is the thought.

The law is that an unused faculty atrophies and withers away. This is true of everything in existence. Inertia and nonuse soon bring stagnation, corruption, death, and disintegration. We have accepted this so universally as a fact of nature that its original character as an intelligent force has been overlooked. All the teaching of the Scriptures is that a failure to use a talent or faculty meets with a reprimand from the Father-Mind. The over-careful servant who buried his talent had it taken away from him and given to the one who had increased his the most. This also has been observed in its negative aspect--a faculty overused draws its vitality from the others and eventually depletes them seriously, unless they are developed by balanced exercise. This is a law of our being, and we should regard it as an intelligent principle instead of a blind force, as we usually do.

> 3 Already ye are clean because of the word which I have spoken unto you. 4 Abide
> in me, and I in you. As the branch cannot bear fruit of itself, except it abide in the
> vine; so neither can ye, except ye abide in me. 5 I am the vine, ye are the branches:
> He that abideth in me, and I in him, the same beareth much fruit: for apart from
> me ye can do nothing. 6 If a man abide not in me, he is cast forth as a branch,
> and it is withered; and they gather them, and cast them into the fire, and they are
> burned. 7 If ye abide in me, and my words abide in you, ask whatsoever ye will, and
> it shall be done unto you. 8 Herein is my Father glorified, that ye bear much fruit;
> and so shall ye be my disciples. 9 Even as the Father hath loved me, I also have
> loved you: abide ye in my love. 10 If ye keep my commandments, ye shall abide in
> my love; even as I have kept my Father's commandments, and abide in his love. 11
> These things have I spoken unto you, that my joy may be in you, and that your joy
> may be made full. 12 This is my commandment, that ye love one another, even as
> I have loved you.

The soul in conscious touch with the Father-Mind and striving to fulfill the divine law brings the power of true words to bear in the purifying and cleansing of its faculties. "Ye are clean because of the word which I have spoken unto you." The necessity of abiding in the I AM in order to bear much fruit is affirmed. When our faith attaches itself to outer things, instead of the spiritual I AM, it ceases to draw vitality from the one and only source of all life, divine Principle. The only door to this life is the I AM. This abiding is a conscious centering of the mind in the depths within us by means of repeated affirmations of our faith and trust in it. This day-by-day repeating of affirmations finally opens a channel of intelligent communication with the silent forces at the depths of Being, thoughts and words flow forth from there, and an entirely new source of power is developed in the man.

When the thought or "word" of Truth from the supreme I AM of consciousness, becomes an abiding fact in our mind, we need no longer strive in external ways; we have but to express a deep desire in the soul and it is fulfilled. "Ask whatsoever ye will, and it shall be done unto you."

This constant affirming, with faith in the I AM within us, more and more establishes us in command of the real forces of Being. The abiding in the Spirit opens up the various spiritual powers one after the other. Love is a great force that dissolves all the opposers of true thought and thus smooths all the obstacles of life. This leads to joy, another positive force that has not been bearing fruit because of the obstructions heaped upon it by our failure to fulfill the law of All-Good. This wonderful kingdom within the soul is developed through the keeping of the "commandments"; that is, the commanding, controlling, and directing of every thought according to the harmonious law of love toward others. There is no occult mystery connected with this development of the soul forces; it is simply thinking and acting in terms of the law of love in our intercourse with our fellow men.

> 13 Greater love hath no man than this, that a man lay down his life for his friends. 14 Ye are my friends, if ye do the things which I command you. 15 No longer do I call you servants; for the servant knoweth not what his lord doeth: but I have called you friends; for all things that I heard from my Father I have made known unto you. 16 Ye did not choose me, but I chose you, and appointed you, that ye should go and bear fruit, and that your fruit should abide: that whatsoever ye shall ask of the Father in my name, he may give it you.

In this Scripture we see Jesus realizing that His apostles had made wonderful progress and were functioning on the spiritual plane. Therefore, He no longer considered them of the world but knew definitely that henceforth they were to do the works of Him that sent them. As co-workers with Him, He called them "friends." In all His ministry Jesus taught freedom of the individual. We are not "servants" but agents free to do as we will.

> 17 These things I command you, that ye may love one another. 18 If the world hateth you, ye know that it hath hated me before it hated you. 19 If ye were of the world, the world would love its own: but because ye are not of the world, but I chose you out of the world, therefore the world hateth you. 20 Remember the word that I said unto you, A servant is not greater than his lord. If they persecuted me, they will also persecute you; if they kept my word, they will keep yours also. 21 But all these things will they do unto you for my name's sake, because they know not him that sent me. 22 If I had not come and spoken unto them, they had not had sin: but now they have no excuse for their sin. 23 He that hateth me hateth my Father also. 24 If I had not done among them the works which none other did, they had not had sin: but now have they both seen and hated both me and my Father. 25 But this cometh to pass, that the word may be fulfilled that is written in their law, They hated me without a cause. 26 But when the Comforter is come, whom I will send unto you from the Father, even the Spirit of truth, which proceedeth from the Father, he shall bear witness of me: 27 and ye also bear witness, because ye have been with me from the beginning.

The Comforter or Holy Spirit is the law of God in action, and when thought of in this way it appears to have personality. From this truth the Hebrews got their conception of the personal, tribal God.

The functions ascribed to the Holy Comforter or Holy Spirit or Spirit of truth imply distinct personal subsistence: He is said to speak, search, select, reveal, reprove, testify, lead, comfort, distribute to every man, know the deep things of God, and He can be known by man only through his spiritual nature.

(See John 14:25-31 for further interpretation.)

Chapter XVI

JUST AS JESUS knew He was persecuted and would be persecuted so He knew that His followers would be persecuted. The ignorant persecute those whom they do not understand or revere.

The Pharisaical or worldly state of mind has no conception of the higher realm within but thinks it governs the whole man and is jealous of any attempt to usurp its power. Hence persecution follows.

While Jesus knew that His apostles did not fully comprehend all that He said, He was encouraging them to go forth in their spiritual strength and to travel the road that was ahead of them.

> 7 Nevertheless I tell you the truth: It is expedient for you that I go away; for if I
> go not away, the Comforter will not come unto you; but if I go, I will send him
> unto you. 8 And he, when he is come, will convict the world in respect of sin,
> and of righteousness, and of judgment: 9 of sin, because they believe not on me;
> 10 of righteousness, because I go to the Father, and ye behold me no more; 11 of
> judgment, because the prince of this world hath been judged. 12 I have yet many
> things to say unto you, but ye cannot bear them now. 13 Howbeit when he, the
> Spirit of truth, is come, he shall guide you into all the truth: for he shall not speak
> from himself; but what things soever he shall hear, these shall he speak: and he
> shall declare unto you the things that are to come.

Jesus understood that the apostles must make their own demonstration and could not lean on Him. Therefore He directed them to the Holy Comforter or Holy Spirit, which is the law of God in action and the one supreme teacher. Eventually this Spirit leads us into all Truth. "One jot or one tittle shall in no wise pass away from the law." Justice and righteousness must be meted out. The Holy Spirit is the Comforter or God's love in action, which like a mother guides and helps and forgives all who seek her.

> 14 He shall glorify me: for he shall take of mine, and shall declare it unto you. 15
> All things whatsoever the Father hath are mine: therefore said I, that he taketh
> of mine, and shall declare it unto you.

The Holy Spirit is the dispenser of divine substance, and all prosperity demonstrations are made through Him. The widow's mite was more than the gift of the rich because the widow had blessed it and it was her all. It is not the size of the object but the blessing behind it that counts. Like the little children blessed by Jesus, the mite, being blessed, increases mightily.

> 16 A little while, and ye behold me no more; and again a little while, and ye shall
> see me. 17 some of his disciples therefore said one to another, What is this that he
> saith unto us, A little while, and ye behold me not; and again a little while, and
> ye shall see me: and, Because I go to the Father? 18 They said therefore, What is
> this that he saith, A little while? We know not what he saith. 19 Jesus perceived
> that they were desirous to ask him, and he said unto them, Do ye inquire among
> yourselves concerning this, that I said, A little while, and ye behold me not, and
> again a little while, and ye shall see me? 20 Verily, verily, I say unto you, that ye shall
> weep and lament, but the world shall rejoice: ye shall be sorrowful, but your sorrow
> shall be turned into joy. 21 A woman when she is in travail hath sorrow, because
> her hour is come: but when she is delivered of the child, she remembereth no more
> the anguish, for the joy that a man is born into the world. 22 And ye therefore
> now have sorrow: but I will see you again, and your heart shall rejoice, and your
> joy no one taketh away from you.

The Christ always goes into the secret place by Himself in order to hold for greater strength and illumination, and when He attains this strength and illumination He comes out and demonstrates what He has received from the Father. Our thoughts get panicky and don't understand,

and each time the Christ withdraws in order to receive new inspiration from God they are sorrowful; but when He comes forth and demonstrates, their sorrow is turned into joy. Ultimately they will come into the light of Truth and understand what the indwelling Christ demonstrates when He goes into the silence to renew His strength. This is also true of the individual who is trying to "put on Christ."

Spiritual perception reveals to us that we are not persons but ideas in the cosmic Mind.

Jesus knew that the hour for His crucifixion was approaching. Crucifixion means the giving up of the whole personality. This was the demonstration that the Master was facing. However, He knew His spiritual power, and He was well aware that He would rise from the dead, would again be with His disciples, and would be more able than ever to instruct them in the mysteries of Being. "I will see you again."

> 23 And in that day ye shall ask no question. Verily, verily, I say unto you, If ye shall
> ask anything of the Father, he will give it you in my name. 24 Hitherto have ye
> asked nothing in my name: ask, and ye shall receive, that your joy may be made
> full. 25 These things have I spoken unto you in dark sayings: the hour cometh,
> when I shall no more speak unto you in dark sayings, but shall tell you plainly of
> the Father. 26 In that day ye shall ask in my name: and I say not unto you, that I
> will pray the Father for you; 27 for the Father himself loveth you, because ye have
> loved me, and have believed that I came forth from the Father. 28 I came out from
> the Father, and am come into the world: again, I leave the world, and go unto the
> Father. 29 His disciples say, Lo, now speakest thou plainly, and speakest no dark
> sayings. 30 Now know we that thou knowest all things, and needest not that any
> man should ask thee: by this we believe that thou camest forth from God. 31 Jesus
> answered them, Do ye now believe? 32 Behold, the hour cometh, yea, is come, that
> ye shall be scattered, every man to his own, and shall leave me alone: and yet I am
> not alone, because the Father is with me. 33 These things have I spoken unto you,
> that in me ye may have peace. In the world ye have tribulation: but be of good
> cheer; I have overcome the world.

"In that day ye shall ask me no question" means that the apostles would have unfolded to the point where they would understand the laws of Spirit and would be able to read out of the law for themselves.

The "dark sayings" refers to the darkened consciousness that cannot see the true light. But this Scripture indicates that "the night is far spent, and the day is at hand." The apostles are coming into a great illumination and will be able to go direct to the Father for light and guidance and power. Hitherto the apostles have been students. Now they are to come into a consciousness in which they can tap the great universal reservoir and receive therefrom. They are to realize that Omniscience knows all things, and they have only to unify their consciousness with that of Omnipresence in order to enter into the state where the true light leads into perfect understanding.

(See John 14:12-14 for further interpretation.)

Chapter XVII

IN THIS SCRIPTURE Jesus was asking of the Father as never before. To glorify means to magnify with praise, to enhance with spiritual splendor. to adorn. Jesus was asking for a full and complete unification of His consciousness with that of the Father. Jesus realized that He had been given all authority over the flesh. He was holding the realization not only for His own glorification but also for that of His disciples. Jesus realized that in this union a full understanding of God and His laws would be revealed, which would naturally make clear to Him the way of eternal life.

> 4 I glorified thee on the earth, having accomplished the work which thou hast given me to do. 5 And now, Father, glorify thou me with thine own self with the glory which I had with thee before the world was. 6 I manifested thy name unto the men whom thou gavest me out of the world: thine they were, and thou gavest them to me; and they have kept thy word. 7 Now they know that all things whatsoever thou hast given me are from thee: 8 for the words which thou gavest me I have given unto them; and they received them, and knew of a truth that I came forth from thee, and they believed that thou didst send me. 9 I pray for them: I pray not for the world, but for those whom thou hast given me; for they are thine: 10 and all things that are mine are thine, and thine are mine: and I am glorified in them. 11 And I am no more in the world, and these are in the world, and I come to thee. Holy Father, keep them in thy name which thou hast given me, that they may be one, even as we are. 12 While I was with them, I kept them in thy name which thou hast given me: and I guarded them, and not one of them perished, but the son of perdition; that the scripture might be fulfilled. 13 But now I come to thee; and these things I speak in the world, that they may have my joy made full in themselves. 14 I have given them thy word; and the world hateth them, because they are not of the world, even as I am not of the world. 15 I pray not that thou shouldest take them from the world, but that thou shouldest keep them from the evil one. 16 They are not of the world, even as I am not of the world. 17 Sanctify them in the truth: thy word is truth. 18 As thou didst send me into the world, even so sent I them into the world. 19 And for their sakes I sanctify myself, that they themselves also may be sanctified in truth. 20 Neither for these only do I pray, but for them also that believe on me through their word; 21 that they may all be one; even as thou, Father, art in me, and I in thee, that they also may be in us: that the world may believe that thou didst send me. 22 And the glory which thou hast given me I have given unto them; that they may be one, even as we are one; 23 I in them, and thou in me, that they may be perfected into one; that the world may know that thou didst send me, and lovedst them, even as thou lovedst me. 24 Father, I desire that they also whom thou hast given me be with me where I am, that they may behold my glory, which thou hast given me: for thou lovedst me before the foundation of the world. 25 O righteous Father, the world knew thee not, but I knew thee; and these knew that thou didst send me; 26 and I made known unto them thy name, and will make it known; that the love wherewith thou lovedst me may be in them, and I in them.

Jesus must have been the product of a former cycle of time, and He had previously made the perfect union in the invisible with the Father.

In proportion as people understand and have faith in Jesus as their actual Saviour from sin, and in proportion as they are set free from appetite, passion, jealousy, prejudice, and all selfishness, they experience wholeness of mind and body as the result. The ultimate result of this knowledge and of daily practice in overcoming (even as Jesus Himself overcame) will be a new race that will demonstrate eternal life--the lifting up of the whole man--spirit, soul, and body--into the Christ consciousness of oneness with the Father. This is indeed true glorification. By means of the reconciliation, glorification, and at-one-ment that Jesus re-established between God and man we can regain our original estate as sons of God here upon earth.

To comprehend this glorification requires a deeper insight into creative processes than the average man and woman have attained, not because they lack the ability to understand but because they have submerged their thinking powers in a grosser thought stratum. So only those who study Being from the standpoint of pure mind can come into an understanding of the transfiguration and of the part that Jesus played in opening the way for humanity to enter into the glory that was theirs before the world was formed.

In its highest form, prayer is an exalted state of consciousness in which self-interest is lost in the desire to do good to everybody. Jesus always prayed the unselfish prayer. There are as many kinds of prayer as there are people in the universe. Those who pray for some personal good have no conception of the ecstasy of those who utterly forget self in their supplications for the good to be given to others. Yet all kinds of prayers are fulfilled. "Ask whatsoever ye will, and it shall be done unto you."

Those who spend much time in the Spirit come to be so much in love with it that they find it hard to endure the selfishness of the world, which they are tempted to leave entirely. Mystics and spiritual adepts withdraw to caves and the wilderness, as far from the haunts of men as they can get, because of the evil they see and feel so vividly. Then it becomes a real struggle to keep the self in the world. It is not right for one who has found this divine Truth within himself to withdraw from those who are ignorant of it and enjoy his riches alone. We should not think of being taken out of the world, but rather should we strive to keep our faculties from evil.

When we have found our being in God, we are no longer identified with the world; our interest is in spiritual things, and all our prayers are lifted up. "They are not of the world, even as I am not of the world." Through our intense realization of the eternal good and our unity with it we become so saturated with the thought of good that we are impregnable to evil. Thus we find that the doctrine of sanctification is based on Truth, and that it is possible for us to become so good in purpose that everything we do will turn to good. But we must certainly sanctify ourselves in Christ and persistently send forth the word of purity and unselfishness to every faculty in order to demonstrate it. We must not confine our prayer for perfection to ourselves alone but make it for them also that believe on Christ "through their word."

The realization of divine unity is the highest that we can attain. This is true glory, the blending and merging of the whole being into Divine Mind. "I in them, and thou in me, that they may be perfected into one."

This merging of God and man does not mean the total obliteration of man's consciousness but its glorification or expansion into that of the divine. This is taught in Hindu philosophy as the absorption of the soul into Nirvana, which has been erroneously interpreted as the total loss of individual consciousness instead of its majestic expansion.

Chapter XVIII

THE NAME KIDRON means "turbid stream." Kidron represents the current of confused thoughts that sometimes pour in upon us when we try to go into the silence. The "garden" locates the current in the world of universal thought. But this is a small matter compared with the activity of the great personal self in the subjective consciousness, Judas, who "knew the place," and took advantage of its darkness to capture the I AM. He came with a "band" (combative thoughts) and "officers from the chief priests and the Pharisees" (the idea of priestly authority and religious guidance from the standpoint of the letter), bearing "lanterns and torches and weapons" (light of the intellect, the torch of reason, and the force of circumstances).

Judas, representing the life principle, at this phase of overcoming is not fully redeemed from carnal thoughts and desires.

When Jesus went "over the brook Kidron" and entered the garden of Gethsemane, He passed in His own consciousness from the without to the within.

> 4 Jesus therefore, knowing all the things that were coming upon him, went forth,
> and saith unto them, Whom seek ye? 5 They answered him, Jesus of Nazareth.
> Jesus saith unto them, I am he. And Judas also, who betrayed him, was standing
> with them. 6 When therefore he said unto them, I am he, they went backward,
> and fell to the ground. 7 Again therefore he asked them, Whom seek ye? And
> they said, Jesus of Nazareth. 8 Jesus answered, I told you that I am he; if therefore
> ye seek me, let these go their way: 9 that the word might be fulfilled which he
> spake, Of those whom thou hast given me I lost not one. 10 Simon Peter therefore
> having a sword drew it, and struck the high priest's servant, and cut off his right
> ear. Now the servant's name was Malchus. 11 Jesus therefore said unto Peter, put
> up the sword into the sheath: the cup which the Father hath given me, shall I not
> drink it?

For the moment the personal will (the officers and soldiers, the executors of man-made laws) is here overcome. The second question is of the personality and milder. Jesus realizes that the time has come for Him to prove that the principles of almighty God are invulnerable and must stand. The I AM faced the condition unafraid (Jesus representing the I AM, answered, "I am he").

Your faith in the righteousness of your cause (Peter) may lead you to combat the ruling religious thoughts, and in your impetuosity you resent their counsel (Malchus, counselor) and deny their capacity to receive Truth (cut off the right ear); but good judgment and a broad comprehension of the divine overcoming through which you are passing will cause you to adopt pacific means. "Put up the sword into the sheath."

"The cup which the Father hath given me" is the consciousness of eternal life. This must be attained by a crucifixion, an utter "crossing out," of the personal self, both on its objective and subjective planes of volition; hence "they led him to Annas" that other processes of the divine law might be carried out.

> 12 So the band and the chief captain, and the officers of the Jews, seized Jesus and
> bound him, 13 and led him to Annas first; for he was father in law to Caiaphas,
> who was high priest that year. 14 Now Caiaphas was he that gave counsel to the
> Jews, that it was expedient that one man should die for the people.

"The band and the chief captain, and the officers of the Jews" are found in the intellectual realm, and it is before this tribunal that the Christ appears, to be tested and tried. Annas was a leading factor in the persecutions at the time of the ministry and crucifixion of Jesus. He represents intellectual opposition to spiritual Truth. His son-in-law Caiaphas, the high priest, represents a ruling religious thought force that is also entirely intellectual. He belongs to the religious world of forms and ceremonies, the "letter" of the word. The ruthlessness of these men shows how a merely formal religion will persecute and attempt to kill the inner Christ Spirit and all that pertains to it.

> [15] And Simon Peter followed Jesus, and so did another disciple. Now that disciple
> was known unto the high priest, and entered in with Jesus into the court of the
> high priest; [16] but Peter was standing at the door without. So the other disciple,
> who was known unto the high priest, went out and spake unto her that kept the
> door, and brought in Peter. [17] The maid therefore that kept the door saith unto
> Peter, Art thou also one of this man's disciples? He saith, I am not. [18] Now the
> servants and the officers were standing there, having made a fire of coals; for it was
> cold; and they were warming themselves: and Peter also was with them, standing
> and warming himself.

Simon Peter followed Jesus, and so did another apostle. Simon Peter (symbolizing the faculty of faith) and the "other disciple" (John, symbolizing love) always sustain and support the I AM man in every trial.

> [19] The high priest therefore asked Jesus of his disciples, and of his teaching. [20]
> Jesus answered him, I have spoken openly to the world; I ever taught in synagogues,
> and in the temple, where all the Jews come together; and in secret spake I nothing.
> [21] Why askest thou me? ask them that have heard me, what I spake unto them:
> behold, these know the things which I said. [22] And when he had said this, one
> of the officers standing by struck Jesus with his hand, saying, Answerest thou the
> high priest so? [23] Jesus answered him, If I have spoken evil, bear witness of the
> evil: but if well, why smitest thou me? [24] Annas therefore sent him bound unto
> Caiaphas the high priest.

> [25] Now Simon Peter was standing and warming himself. They said therefore unto
> him, Art thou also one of his disciples? He denied, and said, I am not. [26] One of
> the servants of the high priest, being a kinsman of him whose ear Peter cut off,
> saith, Did not I see thee in the garden with him? [27] Peter therefore denied again:
> and straightway the cock crew.

The high priest who questioned Jesus symbolizes a form of religious thoughts in man that follows the set rule of the letter of the law with little or no thought of its inner spiritual importance. Jesus (here representing the Christ) sets forth the Truth in plain, concise language, which however has no significance for the person functioning on the natural-religious plane of existence.

> [28] They lead Jesus therefore from Caiaphas into the Praetorium: and it was early;
> and they themselves entered not into the Praetorium, that they might not be defiled,
> but might eat the passover. [29] Pilate therefore went out unto them, and saith, What
> accusation bring ye against this man? [30] They answered and said unto him, If this
> man were not an evil-doer, we should not have delivered him up unto thee. [31]
> Pilate therefore said unto them, Take him yourselves, and judge him according to
> your law. The Jews said unto him, It is not lawful for us to put any man to death:
> [32] that the word of Jesus might be fulfilled, which he spake, signifying by what
> manner of death he should die.

The Praetorium symbolizes a state of despotism, where force and cruelty and tyranny exist. The Jews, symbolizing intellectual spirituality, would because of their religious traditions turn the Jesus over to barbarians to be crucified.

The Jewish priesthood taught persecution as the unavoidable heritage of their race; even Jesus told His followers that they would suffer persecution when they taught His doctrine. At the age of thirteen a Jewish boy is considered a man ready to meet "persecution" and receives the blessing of the rabbi. Although it is true that the spiritual mind and the mortal are at war, metaphysicians see that the persecution of the Jews in every land is the result of the affirmation of the law of persecution by those with the power of the word. "Every idle word that men shall speak, they shall give account thereof."

> 33 Pilate therefore entered again into the Praetorium, and called Jesus, and said
> unto him, Art thou the King of the Jews? 34 Jesus answered, Sayest thou this of
> thyself, or did others tell it thee concerning me? 35 Pilate answered, Am I a Jew?
> Thine own nation and the chief priests delivered thee unto me: what hast thou
> done? 36 Jesus answered, My kingdom is not of this world: if my kingdom were
> of this world, then would my servants fight, that I should not be delivered to the
> Jews: but now is my kingdom not from hence. 37 Pilate therefore said unto him,
> Art thou a king then? Jesus answered, Thou sayest that I am a king. To this end
> have I been born, and to this end am I come into the world, that I should bear
> witness unto the truth. Every one that is of the truth heareth my voice. 38 Pilate
> saith unto him, What is truth?
>
> And when he had said this, he went out again unto the Jews, and saith unto them,
> I find no crime in him. 39 But ye have a custom, that I should release unto you one
> at the passover: will ye therefore that I release unto you the King of the Jews? 40
> They cried out therefore again, saying, Not this man, but Barabbas. Now Barabbas
> was a robber.

The Jews and the high priests and the officers who represent intellectual religious thought forces continued to work for Jesus' execution because they realized within their hearts that He was indeed a King, and they feared His spiritual power. The point to be considered by every follower of Jesus is His continued assertion that He is a King, right in the face of the desertion of His subjects and His imminent death; "a king! aye, a king! and every inch a king."

Barabbas was a prisoner charged with insurrection and murder. He was held at Jerusalem, and the Jews demanded that he be released instead of Jesus.

Metaphysically Barabbas represents the adverse consciousness (rebellion and hatred) to which man gives himself when he allows himself to oppose the Christ. Man gives free rein to this adverse consciousness when he would destroy the Christ or true spiritual I AM in himself, since it is through the Christ alone that an overcoming can be gained over the Adversary. This adverse state of thought (Barabbas) is of its father the Devil.

Chapter XIX

THE CONTEST FOR supremacy between the intellectual forces, represented by Pilate, and the pseudospiritual, represented by the Jews, is portrayed in John 19. Both contenders realize that it is a momentous occasion, and they seek to shift the responsibility for the destruction of the coming King Jesus and His rule. The rabble (sense consciousness) arrays Him in mock royal robes and a crown and cries, "Hail, King of the Jews!" Thus the sense man jeers at religion. To the ruling intellect Jesus has committed no wrong, and it beholds Him as a morally good man, saying, "Behold, the man!" When the Jews renew their cry of "Crucify him" because He claims to be the Son of God and a temporal ruler who is against Caesar, Pilate is troubled and appeals to Jesus, who replies that His rule is from above. When the Jews urge that Jesus is scheming to undermine and destroy Caesar's temporal rule Pilate becomes alarmed and calls a rehearing at Gabbatha (in Hebrew, a knoll or hill). We see at once that this signifies a high plane of human understanding.

Here Pilate (the intellect) again shifts the burden of rule to the Jews (the claimed spiritual authority) and says, "Shall I crucify your King?" The Jews betray their allegiance to temporal things by replying, "We have no king but Caesar." The decision to crucify Jesus was a combination of intellect and pseudo Spirit and was carried out, as indicated, by the co-operation of those taking part. "Then therefore he [Pilate] delivered him unto them [the Jews] to be crucified," and "the soldiers therefore ... crucified Jesus."

The Crucifixion took place at Golgotha, "The place of a skull" (the front brain, the seat of the will and conscious understanding, the throne of the mind, where all ideas are tested and either enthroned or cast out). In the crucifixion of Jesus both Pilate and the Jews (both the intellect and the ruling spiritual ideas) unite in casting out the claim that man is the Son of God. Although Jesus (representing the spiritual man) was not allowed to establish His conscious rule in the front brain, He left a great unified doctrine of truth (represented by the seamless garment that the soldiers found they could not separate). So for two thousand years this Truth has endured and is now being made king in the conscious minds of those who believe. Before the Son of God is enthroned the tables must be turned, the intellect and the pseudospiritual must be crucified, and the great I AM elevated to the high place.

Jesus paid the supreme tribute to woman when on the cross He recognized her and designated her as the mother and preserver of love, to abide in the home of His beloved disciple John.

Jesus became one of our human family for a purpose, to make it possible for us to attain spiritual consciousness, which we could not do without the example of someone who had attained the goal. That we are sons of God is merely an idea until it has been demonstrated and enthroned in consciousness. Man is a child of evolution, the evolution of the perfect man implanted in us as by the Father-Mind. We were on the way to final demonstration of the Son of God when we lost our way in the delusions of sense. A guide and helper became absolutely necessary. Jesus assumed this dangerous and humiliating role. He had to become one of us in flesh and intellect, and it is this flesh-and-intellect man whose career is represented as being consummated in the offer of vinegar made to Him at His last human breath on the cross. So it was not Jesus the man of great ideas that was crucified; it was the flesh-and-intellect man, who cried out, "My God, my God, why hast thou forsaken me?"

> 31 The Jews therefore, because it was the Preparation, that the bodies should not
> remain on the cross upon the sabbath (for the day of that sabbath was a high day),
> asked of Pilate that their legs might be broken, and that they might be taken away.
> 32 The soldiers therefore came, and brake the legs of the first, and of the other that
> was crucified with him: 33 but when they came to Jesus, and saw that he was dead
> already, they brake not his legs: 34 howbeit one of the soldiers with a spear pierced
> his side, and straightway there came out blood and water. 35 And he that hath seen
> hath borne witness, and his witness is true: and he knoweth that he saith true, that
> ye also may believe. 36 For these things came to pass, that the scripture might be

fulfilled, A bone of him shall not be broken. [37] And again another scripture saith,
They shall look on him whom they pierced.

The "Preparation" refers to the observances preliminary to the celebration of the Jewish Sabbath, or to the festival the day before the Sabbath. Among the Jews there was a law to the effect that a lifeless body should not remain upon the cross on the Sabbath, as this was a day set aside for rest and freedom from all troubled or contentious thoughts. Hence Jesus' body was ordered removed.

The Jews asked that the legs of Jesus might be broken and also those of the malefactors that were crucified with Him. Crushing the bones destroyed the last vestige of life in the body. Jesus appeared to be dead, but the inference is that He still retained contact with the bone marrow from which the blood or life is produced.

The fact that the demand of the Jews was not executed shows the higher law was at work and not a bone of Jesus' body was broken. The Scripture prophecy was carried out even to the piercing of His side, the place nearest the heart, the abode of love.

This whole Scripture reveals how those established in the intellect will seek to kill out the Christ, and also how they are ultimately defeated in His victory over death.

[38] And after these things Joseph of Arimathea, being a disciple of Jesus, but secretly
for fear of the Jews, asked of Pilate that he might take away the body of Jesus: and
Pilate gave him leave. He came therefore, and took away his body. [39] And there
came also Nicodemus, he who at first came to him by night, bringing a mixture of
myrrh and aloes, about a hundred pounds. [40] So they took the body of Jesus, and
bound it in linen cloths with the spices, as the custom of the Jews is to bury.

[41] Now in the place where he was crucified there was a garden; and in the garden a new
tomb wherein was never man yet laid. [42] There then because of the Jews' Preparation (for
the tomb was nigh at hand) they laid Jesus.

Jesus rested in the tomb of Joseph of Arimathea. Arimathea represents an aggregation of thoughts of lofty character, a high state of consciousness in man. Joseph represents a state of consciousness in which we increase in character along all lines. We not only grow into a broader understanding but we also increase in vitality and substance. Jesus' resting in Joseph's tomb symbolizes the truth that Jesus was resting in the consciousness of vitality and substance, was growing into a broader understanding, and was in truth gathering strength for the great demonstration over death to follow.

Chapter XX

ON THE RESURRECTION morning the friends and followers of Jesus seemed to have forgotten His promise that He would rise from the dead, and they looked for His body in the tomb. This incident shows that when the belief in death has overshadowed us, it darkens our understanding; we must pass from under this cloud before we can be conscious of the presence of awakened life. Mary was searching for her Lord and Master in the tomb even while He was at her side. John and Peter, failing to find Him where they expected Him to be, "went away again unto their own home."

Don't look in the tomb for the one you loved. Spirit is not confined in the chambers of the dead. When we fail to realize the new life in Christ we are sorrowful indeed. It is then that we should turn back to Christ Jesus (the I AM) who stands nearby and who says to the soul, "Why weepest thou? whom seekest thou?" Grief and the search for the lost one in some external place are then done away with quickly. The ascending thought of the I AM is the saving idea. "I ascend unto my Father and your Father, and my God and your God."

A resurrection takes place in us every time we thus rise to a realization of the perpetual indwelling life that connects us with the Father. We leave in the tomb of matter the graveclothes of mortal sense (the sense of being mortal), which are thoughts of man's limitation and inevitable subjection to material laws. Material laws are the laws that man has made for himself and his world.

The I AM is Spirit, but in order to rise into the realm of pure ideas it must not be attached to the clinging affections of the soul. (Jesus said to Mary, "Touch me not.") The two angels, "one at the head, and one at the feet, where the body of Jesus had lain," represent the positive words of life that bring spiritual powers to bear that lift the body out of matter into Spirit. These two bright and shining powers are possessed of animated intelligence as they say to the weeping Mary: "Why seek ye the living among the dead? He is not here, but is risen."

The most effective consolation that we can give to those who are immersed in the grief of separation and loss is to deny for them the human belief in death and affirm in thought, word and citations of Scripture the omnipresence of life. This dissipates the flood of sorrow thoughts that submerges the souls of those who mourn. Jesus did not want the sorrowing Mary thought to touch Him. The spiritual mind does not grieve; it does not look to matter and the limitations of the flesh for life eternal, and it dissipates the thoughts of sorrow by a denial of their reality or power to affect the mind of the Son of God.

Always keep to your highest thoughts and deny every suggestion of sorrow or loss. The children of darkness wear sackcloth and sit in ashes, but the children of light rejoice, look up ("ascend" in every thought to the Father of life and light), and are set free thereby from the burden of grief and from belief in death and separation.

> [19] When therefore it was evening, on that day, the first day of the week, and when
> the doors were shut where the disciples were, for fear of the Jews, Jesus came and
> stood in the midst, and saith unto them, Peace be unto you. [20] And when he had
> said this, he showed unto them his hands and his side. The disciples therefore
> were glad, when they saw the Lord. [21] Jesus therefore said to them again, Peace
> be unto you: as the Father hath sent me, even so send I you. [22] And when he had
> said this, he breathed on them, and saith unto them, Receive ye the Holy Spirit:
> [23] whose soever sins ye forgive, they are forgiven unto them; whose soever sins ye
> retain, they are retained.

Christianity began with Jesus Christ, was carried on by the apostles and the Seventy whom Jesus sent out two by two; then by other persons as they came into an understanding of Truth. This process of Christianizing will continue until the entire race is redeemed from error. Even so, as our faculties, our senses, and our thoughts learn the truth, they in turn give light and life to the thoughts that are still in darkness. In this way the entire man becomes established in immortality, eternal life.

Jesus Christ commissioned His followers to make disciples of all nations. This commission was given to them on a mountain in Galilee. A mountain always symbolizes spiritual elevation or a high place in consciousness. When the spiritually awakened and spiritually taught faculties and thoughts assemble with the I AM in spiritual consciousness, they are sent throughout the entire man, to the very outermost parts of the body consciousness.

In order to make the world Christian individuals must become Christian. The Christ Spirit must enter everyone. The Christ is knocking at the door of every heart, and He will enter when He is invited to come in. The mind that is open to Truth invites Christ to enter. When all men are filled with the Christ consciousness, international law will embody the Christ standard and the Christ kingdom will be established in the earth.

> 24 But Thomas, one of the twelve, called Didymus, was not with them when Jesus
> came. 25 The other disciples therefore said unto him, We have seen the Lord. But
> he said unto them, Except I shall see in his hands the print of the nails, and put my
> finger into the print of the nails, and put my hand into his side, I will not believe.
>
> 26 And after eight days again his disciples were within, and Thomas with them.
> Jesus cometh, the doors being shut, and stood in the midst, and said, Peace be unto
> you. 27 Then saith he to Thomas, Reach hither thy finger, and see my hands; and
> reach hither thy hand, and put it into my side: and be not faithless, but believing.
> 28 Thomas answered and said unto him, My Lord and my God. 29 Jesus saith unto
> him, Because thou hast seen me, thou hast believed: blessed are they that have not
> seen, and yet have believed.
>
> 30 Many other signs therefore did Jesus in the presence of the disciples, which are
> not written in this book: 31 but these are written, that ye may believe that Jesus is
> the Christ, the Son of God; and that believing ye may have life in his name.

Thomas is the apostle of Jesus who represents the understanding faculty of the natural man. Understanding and will function or should function in unison; each has its center of activity in the front brain, the forehead.

Among the apostles of Jesus Thomas stood for the head, representing the reason and intellectual perception. Jesus did not ignore Thomas's demand for physical evidence of His identity but respected it. He convinced Thomas by corporeal evidence that there had been a body resurrection and that it was not a ghost body that he saw but the same body that had been crucified, as was evidenced by the wounds that Thomas saw and felt.

The peace of Jesus came through the knowledge that there is no reality in death but that life is from everlasting to everlasting. He had proved His power to overcome the last enemy, death, and therefore He was established in "the peace of God, which passeth all understanding."

Jesus manifested Himself to the Eleven, and He upbraided them for disbelieving the accounts of His resurrection. Apparently the resurrection of Jesus is a great mystery, and to those who read the Bible in the letter and have no discernment of the power of Spirit to transform the body it must remain a mystery. The question often is asked whether or not we believe that Jesus rose from the dead with the same flesh body in which He walked the earth and, if so, what became of that body.

In former times believers accepted it as a miracle and made no attempt to explain the law by which it was accomplished, but blind faith is not so popular in the church as it once was, and skeptics are more bold. The school of "high criticism" is openly attacking Bible occurrences that it cannot account for under natural law. Thinking people are seeking a comprehensive explanation of the so-called miracles of the Bible. They wish to know how Jesus did His mighty works, including the resurrection of His body. The historical account makes clear that the flesh body that had been crucified was the body that Jesus had after His resurrection.

That Jesus knew how to restore life to dead organs is evidenced by His healing of paralytics, blind people, and in three cases by raising those who had died. He knew a way of restoring life that others living in His age did not know. He tried to explain it to His disciples and companions, but they did not understand. He told them that He would come to life again, but they seemed to have no comprehension of what He was saying. They thought He was talking to them about the Temple at Jerusalem, but He was talking of His body temple, which He could lay down and take up at will.

It is not at all surprising that the very near friends of Jesus were filled with astonishment and fear when they found that He was not in the tomb where they had laid Him. They could not understand that for years He had been training His soul to accomplish this very thing. He had spent whole nights in prayer, and through the intensity of His devotions had made union with Divine Mind. This union was so full and so complete that His whole being was flooded with spiritual life, power, and substance and the wisdom to use them in divine order. In this manner He projected the divine-body idea, and through it His mortal body was transformed into an immortal body. This was accomplished before the Crucifixion, and Jesus knew that He had so strengthened His soul that it would restore His body, no matter how harshly the body might be used by destructive man.

Jesus had obtained power on the three planes of consciousness: the spiritual, the psychical, and the material. After His resurrection He held His body on the psychical and the astral planes for forty days, and then translated it to the spiritual, where it exists to this day as a body of ethereal substance directed and controlled by His thought and mind force. Having a body of spiritually electrified atoms, Jesus is able to quicken the bodies of people who attract His presence by believing in Him; He radiates a glorious life that energizes those who believe in His power.

By positive affirmations we must all appropriate this same Christ life, substance, and Truth as ours individually and as the very foundation and substance of our body.

Thousands in this day have found the law that Jesus demonstrated and the inner meaning of the Truth that He taught. They are working, praying, denying, affirming, concentrating, willing. They are in all ways building up the perfect-idea body, transforming flesh corruptible into substance incorruptible. Thus they are following Jesus in the regeneration. When they have renewed every organ and every part both within and without, and have put away all evidences of old age, the world at large will begin to accept their claims as true: that the destiny of all men is to transform the body of flesh into a body of Spirit and thus immortalize it. In this manner death is to be overcome and the earth made the dwelling place of immortal men.

This process of revealing and making use of the hidden forces of nature has already begun in the use of electricity, the radio, X rays, radar, and other invisible energies. The discovery that the atom has an electrical center was the first scientific break into omnipresent spiritual life. This life will be exploited by men until they exhaust the capacity of the machines they build to utilize it; then they will look for more efficient agents, which they will find in the development of the human body. Man's body directed by his mind is the only dynamo that can generate life and control it. Men can now build machines that smash the atom and liberate its latent forces, but the released energy can destroy the machinery and even the bodies of those who set it free.

Nature has within her all the elements necessary to the construction of heaven here on the earth and in the ether surrounding the earth. It won't be long before we shall be constructing houses in the air, but we must first learn how to levitate our body, as did Jesus; then resurrection will be part of our spiritual evolution and we shall know experimentally what Jesus meant by His death and resurrection, also just where He lives at the present time and what is required of us before we can meet Him in the heavens.

Chapter XXI

WHEN THE DISCIPLES had toiled all night in their fishing boats without results, Jesus suddenly appeared on the shore and called to them, "Cast the net on the right side of the boat, and ye shall find." The result was 153 large fishes, so heavy that the net could not be lifted into the boat, yet it did not break. Man's mind is the net that catches thoughts, which are the basis of external conditions. The sea is the mental realm in which man exists. Toil of all kinds is a combination of mental and physical exertion. When the mind is exalted toil is easy. By using his mind man invents machinery that relieves him from wearying muscular labor. In a larger way the spiritual man uses his mind and takes advantage of divine guidance to lighten his toil.

The net of man's thought works hard and long in the darkness of human understanding and gains but little, but once the Christ Mind is perceived and obeyed the net is cast on the "right side," and success follows. The "right side" is the side on which man realizes the truth that inexhaustible resources are always present and can be made manifest by those who exercise their faith in that direction.

Whoever seeks supply through Spirit and submits his cause to the law of justice and righteousness always succeeds. The reason why men fail to demonstrate the many promises of divine support is that they cling to some selfish or unjust thought. "Seek ye first his kingdom, and his righteousness; and all these things shall be added unto you."

The bread and fish that Jesus provided on the shore represents the supply of Spirit for the needs of the body. Not only does the Father provide for man in the natural world, as by the draught of fishes, but in the invisible world of substance are elements that correspond to the material things. Bread symbolizes the substance of the omnipresent Christ body and fish the capacity of increase that goes with it. Fish are the most prolific of all living things and aptly exemplify the ability of increase inherent in the Christ substance.

> [15] *So when they had broken their fast, Jesus saith to Simon Peter, Simon, son of John, lovest thou me more than these? He saith unto him, Yea, Lord; thou knowest that I love thee. He saith unto him, Feed my lambs.* [16] *He saith to him again a second time, Simon, son of John, lovest thou me? He saith unto him, Yea, Lord; thou knowest that I love thee. He saith unto him, Tend my sheep.* [17] *He saith unto him the third time, Simon, son of John, lovest thou me? Peter was grieved because he said unto him the third time, Lovest thou me? And he said unto him, Lord, thou knowest all things; thou knowest that I love thee. Jesus saith unto him, Feed my sheep.* [18] *Verily, verily, I say unto thee, When thou wast young, thou girdest thyself, and walkedst whither thou wouldest: but when thou shalt be old, thou shalt stretch forth thy hands, and another shall gird thee, and carry thee whither thou wouldest not.* [19] *Now this he spake, signifying by what manner of death he should glorify God. And when he had spoken this, he saith unto him, Follow me.* [20] *Peter, turning about, seeth the disciple whom Jesus loved following; who also leaned back on his breast at the supper, and said, Lord, who is he that betrayeth thee?* [21] *Peter therefore seeing him saith to Jesus, Lord, and what shall this man do?* [22] *Jesus saith unto him, If I will that he tarry till I come, what is that to thee? follow thou me.* [23] *This saying therefore went forth among the brethren, that that disciple should not die: yet Jesus said not unto him, that he should not die; but, If I will that he tarry till I come, what is that to thee?*

> [24] *This is the disciple that beareth witness of these things, and wrote these things: and we know that his witness is true.*

> [25] *And there are also many other things which Jesus did, the which if they should be written every one, I suppose that even the world itself would not contain the books that should be written.*

Three times Jesus asked Simon Peter, "Lovest thou me?" Peter's spiritual advancement hinged on his possession of love, and the test of love is its willingness to serve. It is quite evident that Jesus was trying to teach Peter that if he loved truly he would serve.

Faith must be established in love and must work by love; and every faculty of man must be established in love and work by love if perfect harmony and good are to be realized. Faith established in love and working by love will remain steadfast at all times, under all circumstances; it will be our sustaining power during our every hour of need.

In verse 18 of this chapter Jesus explains further what He meant by His questioning. Faith (Peter), when it first begins to awaken to the Christ ideal, sees the unlimited possibilities that are presented in this new life; it realizes that it can bring into manifestation anything that may be desired. In its more mature state it realizes the necessity for service in a universal sense. The giving up of the personal self (with the consequent working from a universal standpoint) is the death whereby we are to glorify God. However, laying hold of Spirit and its power should accompany the denial of self.

Faith (symbolized by Peter) is the faculty on which depends continuous supply; hence Peter is challenged with the thought of love toward Christ three times. Faith must be in loving communion with the Christ Mind in order to draw down to the thoughts (sheep) the necessary supply. Man does not live by bread alone but by words and thoughts from God. These come into consciousness through mental and spiritual laws. Peter's three successive affirmations of love represent fulfillment of the close Christ union in spirit, soul, and body. Faith at the beginning is wistful, vigorous, vacillating, but in its maturity it gives itself wholly to Spirit and is willing to die to self. This is the "manner of death" by which faith glorifies God: being absorbed into the Divine Mind.

Through repeated affirmations of love toward Christ, man develops a consciousness of divine love that abides at the heart center and fills the whole body with ecstasy. This consciousness is "the disciple whom Jesus loved."

Jesus revealed the mind of the Father. This mind is the life and intelligence of man as well as the substance that provides for all his needs. This providing power of the Father, Jesus brought out prominently, and He showed in various ways how easy it is to obtain supply by trusting God. This teaching is not an encouragement to man to be idle, but rather to be active and trustful, constantly looking to Spirit instead of matter as the source of his good.

The actual resurrection of Jesus in a body that corresponds to the physical is not a subject open to debate by the followers of Jesus Christ. The historical evidence is ample to convince any unprejudiced mind. However, the study of the constituent parts of man, his spirit, soul, and body, reveals man's innate capacity to overcome the disintegrating effects of error thinking and living, and his ability, by conforming to the standards laid down by Jesus, to destroy the seeds of death and implant health and eternal life in his body.

To the oft-repeated question "If Jesus resurrected His physical body why is He not visible here among us?" we would say that Jesus overcame the sins that caused our original fall from the perfect body of the Adamic man to the diseased and dying body in which the race is now existing. When we have purified our mind and body and cast out every evil thought, our body will become transparent to human sight, as is Jesus' body. The idea that a transparent body is thin air, a ghost, is wholly wrong. Science says that the invisible electrical units composing the atom are millions of times more powerful than any visible thing. When the atomic energy in the atomic bomb was released great cities were destroyed. Jesus told His followers that when they were gathered in that upper room in Jerusalem the Holy Spirit would descend upon them with power; and they were transformed from ignorant men into linguists of unbelievable ability.

Paul says, "Be ye transformed by the renewing of your mind." When we accomplish this transformation we shall see Jesus as He is and as we must all be in the resurrection from the dead and dying body in which we are now functioning. This is not to be accomplished by a great miracle at some appointed time in the future, but day by day we shall be resurrected out of the darkness of sense into the glorious light of Spirit.

Atom-Smashing Power of Mind

Forward

A great many passages in this book testify to Charles Fillmore's persistent interest in what is popularly called atomic energy and the promise held out by its development of a better world for mankind. As he rejoiced in the scientific achievement of its discovery so he tirelessly devoted his thought to its guidance into the channels of peaceful use. On every occasion he urged those having to do with its development to make sure that this unique form of energy, this great gift of the Father, would not be used to worsen life and destroy mankind.

From another standpoint Charles Fillmore's mind was simply fascinated by the idea of the atom, this infinitesimal particle of substance, and the enormous energy locked up in it. At times he thought of it as the most perfect representation in the manifest world of that divine mental or spiritual energy which pervades all things and which, when properly expressed through the minds of His children, serves so greatly to glorify God. At other times he thought of it as the very essence of this mental or spiritual energy, Spirit-mind itself! The reader will find each one of these standpoints set forth over and over--perhaps vaguely and mystically at times--but ever testifying to the alertness and vitality of Charles Fillmore's mind and his unflagging interest in everything in his world.

As will be readily recognized by Unity readers, the articles appearing as chapters in this book, were originally published in Unity magazine over a period of half a century, one of them going back as far as the year 1898.

In the last paragraph of Chapter VIII the author gives his readers a clear formula for dealing with the problem of the atom:

"The great and most important issue before the people today is the development of man's spiritual mind and through it unity with God. . . . The taproot of all our confusion is our failure to use our mind intelligently. We can only think as God would have us think by adjusting our thoughts to divine ideas. Religion and all that it implies in prayer and recognition of God in idea and manifestation is the one and only way out of the chaos in which we find ourselves. We must therefore begin at once to develop this unity with the Father-Mind by incorporating divine ideas into all that we think and speak."

Chapter I - The Atomic Age

THE MAJORITY of people have crude or distorted ideas about the character and the location of Spirit. They think that Spirit plays no part in mundane affairs and can be known by a person only after his death.

"But Jesus said, 'God is Spirit'; He also said, 'The kingdom of God is within you.' Science tells us that there is a universal life that animates and sustains all the forms and shapes of the universe. Science has broken into the atom and revealed it to be charged with tremendous energy that may be released and be made to give the inhabitants of the earth powers beyond expression, when its law of expression is discovered.

"Jesus evidently knew about this hidden energy in matter and used His knowledge to perform so-called miracles.

"Our modern scientists say that a single drop of water contains enough latent energy to blow up a ten-story building. This energy, existence of which has been discovered by modern scientists, is the same kind of spiritual energy that was known to Elijah, Elisha, and Jesus, and used by them to perform miracles.

"By the power of his thought Elijah penetrated the atoms and precipitated an abundance of rain. By the same law he increased the widow's oil and meal. This was not a miracle--that is, it was not a divine intervention supplanting natural law--but the exploitation of a law not ordinarily understood. Jesus used the same dynamic power of thought to break the bonds of the atoms composing the few loaves and fishes of a little lad's lunch--and five thousand people were fed.

"Science is discovering the miracle-working dynamics of religion, but science has not yet comprehended the dynamic directive power of man's thought. All so-called miracle workers claim that they do not of themselves produce the marvelous results; that they are only the instruments of a superior entity. It is written in I Kings, 'The jar of meal wasted not, neither did the cruse of oil fail, according to the word of Jehovah, which he spake by Elijah.' Jesus called Jehovah Father. He said, 'The works that I do in myFather's name, these bear witness of me.'"

Jesus did not claim to have the exclusive supernatural power that is usually credited to Him. He had explored the ether energy, which He called the 'kingdom of the heavens'; His understanding was beyond that of the average man, but He knew that other men could do what He did if they would only try. He encouraged His followers to take Him as a center of faith and use the power of thought and word. 'He that believeth on me, the works that I do shall he do also; and greater works than these shall he do.'

"The great modern revival of divine healing is due to the application of the same law that Jesus used. He demanded faith on the part of those whom He healed, and with that faith as the point of mental and spiritual contact He released the latent energy in the atomic structure of His patients and they were restored to life and health.

"Have faith in the power of your mind to penetrate and release the energy that is pent up in the atoms of your body, and you will be astounded at the response. Paralyzed functions anywhere in the body can be restored to action by one's speaking to the spiritual intelligence and life within them. Jesus raised His dead bodies in this way, and Paul says that we can raise our body in the same manner if we have the same spiritual contact.

"What have thought concentration and discovery of the dynamic character of the atom to do with prayer? They have everything to do with prayer, because prayer is the opening of communication between the mind of man and the mind of God. Prayer is the exercise of faith in the presence and power of the unseen God. Supplication, faith, meditation, silence, concentration, are mental attitudes that enter into and form part of prayer. When one understands the spiritual character of God and adjusts himself mentally to the omnipresent God-Mind, he has begun to pray aright.

"Audible prayers are often answered but the most potent are silently uttered in the secret recesses of the soul. Jesus warned against wordy prayers--prayer uttered to be heard of men.

He told His disciples not to be like those who pray on the housetop. 'When thou prayest, enter into thine inner chamber, and having shut thy door, pray to thy Father who is in secret, and thy Father who seeth in secret shall recompense thee.'

"The times are ripe for great changes in our estimate of the abiding place and the character of God. The six-day creation of the universe (including man) is described in Genesis is a symbolic story of the work of the higher realms of mind under divine law. It is the privilege of everyone to use his mind abilities in the superrealms, and thereby carry out the prayer formula of Jesus: 'Seek ye first his kingdom, and his righteousness; and all these things shall be added unto you.'"

The foregoing extract is from the "Health and Prosperity" column in Unity for May, 1927. These comments are peculiarly applicable to the present and also to a subject that has been agitating the public mind for some time, the atomic bomb.

Of all the comments on or discussions of the indescribable power of the invisible force released by the atomic bomb none that we have seen mentions its spiritual or mental character. All commentators have written about it as a force external to man to be controlled by mechanical means, with no hint that it is the primal life that animates and interrelates man's mind and body.

The next great achievement of science will be the understanding of the mental and spiritual abilities latent in man through which to develop and release these tremendous electrons, protons, and neutrons secreted in the trillions of cells in the physical organism. Here is involved the secret, as Paul says, "hid for ages and generations . . . which is Christ [superman] in you, the hope of glory." It is through release of these hidden life forces in his organism that man is to achieve immortal life, and in no other way. When we finally understand thefacts of life and rid our minds of the delusion that we shall find immortal life after we die, then we shall seek more diligently to awaken the spiritual man within us and strengthen and build up the spiritual domain of our being until, like Jesus, we shall be able to control the atomic energy in our bodies and perform so-called miracles.

The fact is that all life is based upon the interaction between the various electrical units of the universe. Science tells us about these activities in terms of matter and no one understands them, because they are spiritual entities and their realities can only be understood and used wisely by the spiritually developed man. Electricians do not know what electricity is, although they use it constantly. The Christian uses faith and gets marvelous results, the electrician uses electricity and also gets marvelous results, and neither ofthem knows the real nature of the agent he uses so freely.

The man who called electricity faith doubtless thought that he was making a striking comparison when in fact he was telling a truth, that faith is of the mind and it is the match that starts the fire in the electrons and protons of innate Spirit forces. Faith has its degrees of voltage; the faith of the child and the faith of the most powerful spiritual adept are far apart in their intensity and results. When the trillions of cells in one's body are roused to expectancy by spiritual faith, a positive spiritual contact results and marvelous transformations take place. When Jesus asked His patients, "Believe ye that I am able to do this?" He was making such a contact. Also when He told those to whom He ministered, "Thy faith hath made thee whole," He used the same law. When He turned water into wine and fed five thousand by multiplying a few loaves and fishes, He performed in a masterly and beneficial way what our scientists made possible in a destructive way by releasing through the atomic bomb thepent-up forces of Spirit.

Scientists have invented a machine that records the forces of thought. Every thought expressed by the mind radiates an energy as it passes through the brain cells, and this machine measures the force of these radiations. Sir James Jeans, the eminent British scientist, gives a prophecy of this in one of his books. He says in substance that it may be that the gods determining our fate are our own minds working on our brain cells and through them on the world about us. This will eventually be found to be true, and the discovery of the law of release of the electronic vitality wrapped up in matter will be the greatest revelation of all time.

When we awake to the fact that every breath we draw is releasing this all-potent electronic energy and it is shaping our lives for good or ill, according to our faith, then we shall begin to search for the law that will guide us aright in the use of power.

People the world over were amazed and terrified when they read of the destruction wrought on the cities and people of Japan by two atomic bombs. But do we realize that millions of people are killed every year by atomic force? Doctors tell us that it is the toxin generated in our own bodies that kills us. What produces this destructive force? It must be our own minds, and the remedy must also be in a change in mind. Paul expressed this when he said, "Be ye transformed by the renewing of your mind."

All persons who have dismissed the idea of miracle in the marvelous works of Jesus and His followers, have looked forward to a time when the law they used would be explained, but nearly all expected it to come through spiritual means. But now science has opened up a kingdom having all the possibilities of the kingdom of heaven taught by Jesus. However Jesus said this kingdom is within us and would be exercised constructively through our minds under divine law. The latest discovery of science shows that through the development of the atom a power will be cast right into our midst that will in its physical aspect make the earth equal to our wildest dreams of heaven. Broadcasting stations sending out on the ether light, heat, power, will be established the world over, and every householder will have receiving sets which he can turn on or off at will. The cost will be negligible. Lighter-than-air forms of building material will be discovered and our dwellings will float in the air and be transported from place to place like airplanes. Even the climate of the whole planet may be transformed, destructive forces no longer possible, and peace reign forever. Labor as we now have it will disappear, production will become so easy that a man will in a week raise enough food to last him a year. Everybody will produce abundantly. Everybody will have everything he wants, and no one will slave for wages. Art, science, religion, music, and the finer things of life will be for all the people and those who do not expand their minds to enjoy the finer things of life will be out of step with the times.

Our men of science have found the key that unlocks the door to the physical realm in the kingdom of the heavens, but the spiritual domains are yet to be found and their doors unlocked by the multitude. There must be a change of mind by the people of the earth before the tremendous uplift to be wrought by atomic energy can become beneficial and permanent. Greed and selfishness will find a way to exploit it to boost their ambition unless they are taught the truth. We should therefore redouble our efforts to show man that the power that rules the world is within him. "Greater is he that is in you than he that is in the world."

Chapter II - The Restorative Power of Spirit

NOT ONLY our Bible but the scriptures of all the nations of the world testify to the existence of an invisible force moving men and nature in their various activities. Not all agree as to the character of this omnipresent force, universal Spirit, but it serves the purpose of being their god under whatever name it may appear. Different nations ostensibly believe in the same scriptures, but they have various concepts of the universal Spirit; some conceive it to be nature and others God. Robert Browning says, "What I call God . . . fools call Nature."

Our Bible plainly teaches that God implanted in man His perfect image and likeness, with executive ability to carry out all the creative plans of the Great Architect. When man arrives at a certain point in spiritual understanding it is his office to co-operate with the God principle in creation. Jesus had reached this point, and He said, "My Father worketh even until now, and I work."

It is possible for man to form states of consciousness that are out of harmony with the God principle, but these do not endure, and through experience man learns to adjust his thought to that of God. "I will be what I will to be" is basic in all creation and it proves itself in the face of human reason and logic. God is free to do as He wills, and He has implanted that same freedom in man. When we understand this ego-forming capacity of man and even of nature, we have the key that unlocks the many mysteries and contradictions that appear in every walk of life.

As the animating life of all things God is a unit, but as the mind that drives this life He is diverse. Every man is king in his own mental domain, and his subjects are his thoughts. When the king of Babylon called Daniel to interpret his dream of the image with the head of gold and feet of clay, the prophet prefaced his interpretation with these words, which contain in essence the kingly authority of every man:

"Thou, O king, art king of kings, unto whom the God of heaven hath given the kingdom, the power, and the strength, and the glory; and wheresoever the children of men dwell, the beasts of the field and the birds of the heavens hath he given into thy hand, and hath made thee to rule over them all: thou art the head of gold."

"Thou art the head of gold" is true of every man, but in his ignorance man thinks he is the feet of clay. This thought of his own inefficiency darkens his mentality, and when the Lord attempts to communicate with him in symbols he has to call upon external sources to explain them.

People in this atomic age civilization ask why God does not reveal Himself now as He did in Bible days. The fact is that God is talking to people everywhere, but they do not understand the message and brush it aside as an idle dream. We need to divest ourselves of the thought that Daniel and Joseph, in fact all the unusually wise men of the Bible, were especially inspired by God, that they were divinely appointed by the Lord to do His work. Everything points to their spiritual insight as the result of work on their part to that end. Daniel as a youth had been taught to worship Jehovah, the one and only God. He restrained the gross appetites of the flesh and thereby made himself receptive to Spirit. "But Daniel purposed in his heart that he would not defile himself with the king's dainties, nor with the wine which he drank." He begged that he and his companion be allowed to eat herbs and drink water, which was granted; and the record says that at the end of even a ten-day test they were in better condition physically than all the youths that ate of the king's dainties, that God gave them knowledge and skill, and that Daniel had "understanding in all visions and dreams."

The body is the instrument of the mind, and the mind looks to the Spirit for its inspiration. A very little observation shows that the purer the mind the greater its capacity to receive and interpret the ideas imparted to it by the Spirit. It does not require a doctor's diagnosis to prove that alcohol confuses the mind and injures the body. The daily toll of automobile accidents proves that drivers with alcohol in their stomachs are trifling with death. Although Paul advises that we eat what is set before us, asking no questions, experience proves that the advice of Daniel leads to better health and clearer thinking. Paul is credited with a giant intellect, but when he advised Timothy to take a little wine for his stomach's sake, we know that he was not inspired by the Spirit of wisdom.

Not only the Scriptures that we look to for authority in our daily living but also the experience of ourselves and our neighbors proves that those who cultivate communion with the Father within become conscious of a guiding light, call it what you will.

Those who scoff at this and say that it is all the work of the imagination are deluding themselves and ignoring a source of instruction and progress that they need above all things. If this sense world were the only world we shall ever know, the attainment of its ambitions might be sufficient for a man of meager outlook and small capacity, but the majority of us see ourselves and the world about us in a process of transformation that will ultimate in conditions here on the earth far superior to those we have imagined for heaven."Great is the mystery of godliness," and still greater is the capacity for godliness. When Spirit responds to the seeking mind and begins to reveal the magnitude of that undiscovered country within us, we long for a new language with words describing glories beyond all human comparison. Even our so-called physical body reveals a radiant body (which Jesus referred to as sitting on the throne of His glory) that interlaces the trillions of cells of the organism and burns as brightly as an electric light. Jesus gave His apostles a glimpse of this radiant body when He was transformed before them. "And as he was praying, the fashion of his countenance was altered, and his raiment became white and dazzling."

Jesus was very advanced, and His radiant body was developed in larger degree than that of anyone in our race, but we all have this body, and its development is in proportion to our spiritual culture. In Jesus this body of light glowed "as he was praying." Jesus' body did not go down to corruption, but He, by the intensity of His spiritual devotion, restored every cell to its innate state of atomic light and power. When John was in the state of spiritual devotion Jesus appeared to him, "and his eyes were as a flame of fire; and his feet like unto burnished brass."Jesus lives today in that body of glorified electricity in a kingdom that interpenetrates the earth and its environment. He called it the kingdom of the heavens.

We do not have to look to the many experiences recorded in the Bible of the spiritually illumined to prove the existence of the spiritual supersubstance. Peopleeverywhere are discovering it, as they always have in every age and clime. Unless it is put under control of the Christ Mind it takes on psychic and "spooky" expressions, which distort the soul instead of unfolding it under divine law, and drive its victims into our psychopathic sanatoria. However, men will continue to pray, and prayer releases the innate glory of God-Mind, so we must be taught how to establish our identity with the Christ and through it to gain the mastery of the stored-up riches of the man invisible.

The metaphysical literature of our day is very rich with the experiences of those who have found through various channels the existence of the radiant body. One example is Angela Morgan's book "Behold the Angel!" Miss Morgan's writing in this book is a radical departure from her well-known poetical vein. She is specific and to the point in announcing her revelations. She says in the foreword:

"This is a book about the radiant body, the living self of every human being; the immortal structure which is the real self even now in this moment of time". The author, through intense conviction and the validity of recent experience, writes in concrete terms of what to her is as real as flesh, bones, blood, and muscle. There is, behind this "veil of flesh," an actual flamelike structure invisible to our everyday, limited perception. When I say it is "radiant," I mean it literally. . . . It is vividly alive, glorious as the sunrise.

She tells of numerous instances in which she saw hands and feet and other parts of her body lighted or really transformed by the flame invisible.

This convincing confession of Miss Morgan prompts me to tell of my development of the radiant body, during half a century's experience. It began when I was mentally affirming statements of Truth. Just between my eyes, but above, I felt a "thrill" that lasted a few moments, then passed away. I found I could repeat this experience with affirmations. As time went on I could set up this "thrill" at other points in my body and finally it became a continuous current throughout my nervous system. I called it "the Spirit" and found that it was connected with a universal life force whose source was the Christ. As taught in the Bible, we have through wrong thinking and living lost contact with the parent life. Jesus Christ incarnated in the flesh and thereby introduced us by His Word into the original Father life. He said, "If a man keep my word, he shall never taste of death." I have believed that and affirmed His words until they have become organized in my body. Sometimes when I make this claim of Christ life in the body I am asked if I expect to live always in this flesh. My answer is that I realize that the flesh is being broken down every day and its cells transformed into energy and life, and a new body is being formed of a very superior quality. That new body in Christ will be my future habitation.

I have found that the kingdom of God is within man and that we are wasting our time and defeating the work of the Spirit if we look for it anywhere else.

Chapter III - Spiritual Obedience

> I fairly sizzle with zeal and enthusiasm and spring forth with a mighty faith to do the things that ought to be done by me. —CHARLES FILLMORE

ZEAL is the great universal force that impels man to spring forward in a field of endeavor and accomplish the seemingly miraculous. It is the inward fire that urges man onward, regardless of the intellectual mind of caution and conversation.

Paul, the zealot whose name was first Saul, metaphysically is a symbol of varied significance. He was born of Jewish parents in Tarsus, Asia Minor, a city of considerable culture and refinement. He was reared as a Pharisee and educated as a rabbi in schools in Jerusalem. His one conception of salvation did not go beyond that of obtaining it through a perfect performance of the works of the law. But in truth he was a man of deep religious character and worshiped the living God.

He was on his way to Damascus to persecute the disciples of Jesus, no doubt in one instant "breathing threatening and slaughter against the disciples of the Lord" and in the next swearing allegiance to the living God whom he worshiped. "As he journeyed ... suddenly there shone round about him a light out of heaven: and he fell upon the earth." Because of the great blaze of illumination he was struck temporarily blind.

Thus through the spiritual power of his own mind, apparently by accident, he broke into the ethers where his consciousness was flooded with spiritual light, and he heard the voice of Jesus saying: "Saul, Saul, why persecutest thou me? . . . and when his eyes were opened, he saw nothing; and they led him by the hand, and brought him into Damascus." This experience illumined, expanded, and enriched his whole being, and eventually led him into his life's work: preaching the gospel of Jesus Christ to the whole Gentile world.

Paul presents a tremendous outpouring of zeal; first on the intellectual plane as champion of the law and the prophets, afterward as a disseminator of the freeing doctrine of the Christ. He was a "chosen vessel" of the Lord, and "not disobedient unto the heavenly vision." Yet on several occasions he allowed his zeal to run away with his better judgment and as a result suffered many things.

Zeal should be tempered with wisdom. It is possible to be so zealously active on the intellectual plane that one's vitality is consumed and there is nothing left for spiritual growth. "Take time to be holy." Never neglect your soul. To grow spiritually you should exercise your zeal in spiritual ways.

As children of God our place is at the right hand of the Father. When man really realizes this, he calls down upon himself the baptism of the Holy Spirit. He soon learns that obedience to Spirit increases his power to control his thoughts and thus make his world conform to the divine standard.

When man is obedient to Spirit he will not suffer burdens. To trust Spirit he must know of its guidance by experience. By those who have not learned the guidance of Spirit, that experience must be acquired. Man is spirit and must find himself before he can communicate with universal Spirit.

Paul had his weak points, but he was a great apostle and made Jesus' doctrine live. No doubt the light of spiritual understanding with which his consciousness was flooded at the time of his conversion carried him a long way in his ministry. His fearlessness was the strong point of his character. To him the gospel came first and the things of the world second. This is what made him a great apostle of the Lord. When will and understanding are joined in consciousness man is equal to any emergency.

Without doubt the secret of Paul's great illumination at the time of his conversion is that in previous lives he had built up a spiritual consciousness, and on his way to Damascus he "stirred up" the gift that was within him. The new race that is now being born on this planet will develop these unused resources of the mind by realization, audible prayer, and thanksgiving and bring to the surface the riches of both the subconscious and the superconscious mind.

Above all other Bible writers Paul emphasizes the importance of the mind in the transformation of character and body. In this respect he struck a note in religion that had been mute up to this time; that is, that spirit and mind are akin and that man is related to God through his thought. Paul sounds again and again in various forms this silent but very essential chord in the unity of God and man and man and his body. All Christian metaphysicians are indebted to him for many quotable Scriptures that fortify their position that the mind is the center of man's world around which, to him, all things revolve.

Spiritual realization changes things. In scientific prayer realization is the high point of attainment. With concentrated spiritual attention man can affirm in faith that God Spirit is present and that he, man, is one with the God presence.

That there is a certain unity also between the mind and the elements, mystics contend, and this is borne out by the power exercised by Jesus when He stilled the wind and stopped the storm.

The question is often asked, Does the race mind affect nature and to what extent? Some geologists surmised that exploding bombs might have been the cause of the Japanese earthquake following World War II. Science cannot verify this surmise, although it does teach the unity of all things.

When the scientific world investigates the so-calledmiracles of religion and discovers that they are being duplicated continually, the power of mind over matter will be heralded as of great importance to both religion and science.

Prayer gives spiritual poise to the ego, and it brings forth eternal life when spiritually linked with the Christ. "If a man keep my word, he shall never see death."

Jesus understood the realm of divine substance, and it was obedient to His word. He will continue to draw upon this omnipresent source of power and also include us in its life-giving energy if we will abide with Him in the Spirit. When we understand the innate capacity of the mind raised to spiritual dominion we cannot but have an increase of faith equal to doing the works of Jesus, and even greater works, as He promised.

Machines that measure the energy used by the mind acting on the brain cells have already been invented, but there is no account of the brain voltage of a person in prayer. When such measurements have been made we shall know something of the capacity of the mind in its highest range of expression. Jesus also called attention to the power of a group praying with Him. "For where two or three are gathered together in my name, there am I in the midst of them."

The first mention of this dynamic power of the Spirit is found in Acts 1 and 2, when the early followers of Jesus were gathered in the "upper chamber." They all became spiritual dynamos, as revealed in the Greek word translated "power." These disciples had been with Jesus for over three years, but did not have the inspiration or power that was poured out upon them at this historical gathering, which has ever since been an outstanding example of the marvelous spiritual experiences of those who are of one mind and heart in their group worship of Jesus the Christ. It is recorded that the Spirit came upon them like a wind and sat upon each of them in"tongues . . . of fire."

To one who gains even a meager quickening of the Spirit, Christianity ceases to be a theory; it becomes a demonstrable science of the mind.

We must not anticipate better social and economic conditions until we have better men and women to institute and sustain those conditions.

Jesus said that He was the bread and substance that came down from heaven. When will our civilization begin to realize and appropriate this mighty ocean of substance and life? A finer civilization than now exists has been conceived by many from Plato in his "Republic" to Edward Bellamy in "Looking Backward." But a new and higher civilization will be developed only through the efforts of higher and finer types of men and women. Philosophers and seers have looked forward to a time when this earth would produce superior men and women, but save Jesus none has had the spiritual insight to declare, "Verily I say unto you, This generation shall not pass away, until all these things be accomplished." The Greek word genea, here translated "generation," does not mean a little span of thirty-three years of life, but covers the whole race history in its multitudinous births and deaths, incarnations and reincarnations throughout the millions of years since we began to function in creative Mind. It is out of this race that the new race is to come forth. "Ye are the people." The time is at hand for those who are spiritually ripe to stand forth and realize their spiritual identity. Jesus pointed to this when He said, "Say not ye, There are yet four months, and then cometh the harvest? behold, I say unto you, lift up your eyes, and look on the fields, that they are white already unto harvest."

Prayer, communion with God within, realization, awakens spiritual consciousness and develops true spiritual character. It is the only way to cleanse and perfect the mind and thus permanently heal the body. It is good to get still and think about the inexhaustible resources of infinite Mind; about its presence in all its fullness and its readiness to manifest itself when the law is complied with. Pray with persistence and pray with understanding. Be instant in prayer; and never allow anything to keep you from having your daily quiet hour of communion with God, your own indwelling Father.

One day little Billy and Johnny were climbing around in an old apple tree. Finally they walked out on a limb, and were holding to the boughs above them. But the limb on which they were standing proved to be rotten and gave way, and the boys came tumbling down to the ground. Johnny was hurt and began to cry. But Billy got up with a smile on his face and began brushing the dirt off his clothes.

"Why ain't you hurt?" moaned Johnny. "You was out further on the limb than me." "I prayed," was the happy reply. "You didn't have no time to pray," retorted Johnny. "But it didn't catch me, because I was already prayed up ahead," explained Billy. "So I wasn't scared. I know'd I'd be all right."

"Behold, the man!" Jesus Christ is the type of a new race now forming in the earth. Those who incorporate into consciousness the Christ principles are its members. Sir Francis Galton, the father of eugenics, says: "There is nothing either in the history of domestic animals or in that of evolution to make us doubt that a race of sane men may be formed, who shall be as much superior mentally and morally, as the modern European is to the lowest of the primitive races." It is now being revealed in the renaissance of Christianity, which is pouring its light out upon the world, that this new race is forming in the souls of the spiritual-minded in every nation of the earth. These are "the called" of Scripture, who are being gathered together in spiritual consciousness, and will eventually come forth to rule the world with Jesus Christ. Emerson says: "Great hearts send forth steadily the secret forces that incessantly draw great events, and wherever the mind of man goes, nature will accompany him, no matter what the path."

Let us remember that God is Spirit and all that emanates from God is spiritual, including man. The dominion that God gave to man in the beginning, as recorded in Genesis, is a dominion over spiritual ideas, which are represented in the allegory by material symbols. Hence to exercise his dominion man must understand the metaphysical side of everything in existence. Mind is at the bottom of all life and substance. The mind was not "invented" by the brain, but it has evolved the brain as its most efficient instrument.

Divine Mind is the one and only reality. When we incorporate the ideas that form Divine Mind into our mind and persevere in those ideas, a mighty strength wells up within us. Then we have a foundation for the spiritual body, the body not made with hands, eternal in the heavens. When the spiritual body is established in consciousness, its strength and power is transmitted to the visible body and to all the things that we touch in the world about us.

In the economy of the future man will not be a slave to money. Humanity's daily needs will be met in ways not now thought practical.

In the new economy we shall serve for the joy of serving, and prosperity will flow to us and through us in ripplingstreams of plenty. The supply and support that love and zeal set in motion are not yet largely used by man, but those who have tested this method are loud in their praise of its efficiency.

Chapter IV - I AM - or Superconsciousness

SUPERCONSCIOUSNESS is the goal toward which humanity is working. Regardless of appearances there is an upward trend continually active throughout all creation. The superconsciousness is the realm of divine ideas. Its character is impersonal. It therefore has no personal ambitions; knows no condemnation; but is always pure, innocent, loving, and obedient to the call of God.

The superconsciousness has been perceived by the spiritually wise in every age, but they have not known how to externalize it and make it an abiding state of consciousness. Jesus accomplished this, and His method is worthy of our adoption, because as far as we know, it is the only method that has been successful. It is set forth in the New Testament, and whoever adopts the life of purity and love and power there exemplified in the experiences of Jesus of Nazareth will in due course attain the place that He attained. Jesus acknowledged Himself to be the Son of God. Living in the superconsciousness calls for nothing less on our part than a definite recognition of ourselves as sons of God right here and now, regardless of appearances to the contrary. We know that we are sons of God; then why not acknowledge it and proceed to take possession of our God heirdom?

That is what Jesus did in the face of the most adverse conditions. Conditions today are not so inertly material as they were in Jesus' time. People now know more about themselves and their relation to God. They are familiar with thought processes and how an idea held in mind will manifest itself in the body and in affairs; hence they take up this problem of spiritual realization under vastly more favorable conditions. An idea must work out just as surely as a mathematical problem, because it is under immutable law. The factors are all in our possession, and the method was demonstrated in one striking instance and is before us. By following the method of Jesus and doing day by day work that comes to us, we shall surely put on Christ as fully and completely as did Jesus of Nazareth.

The method by which Jesus evolved from sense consciousness to God consciousness was, first, the recognition of the spiritual selfhood and a constant affirmation of its supremacy and power. Jesus loved to make the highest statements: "I and the Father are one." "All authority hath been given unto me in heaven and on earth." He made these statements, so we know that at the time He was fully aware of their reality. Secondly, by the power of His word He penetrated deeper into omnipresence and tapped the deepest resources of His mind, whereby He released the light, life, and substance of Spirit, which enabled Him to get the realization that wholly united His consciousness with the Father Mind.

In making His great overcoming Jesus applied the principles of Being scientifically, and He instructed His followers to do as He did. No one can get a copyright on the principles of Truth any more than he can get a corner on the air. Truth is free; it is Spirit, and cannot be kept from the spiritually minded, nor can it be confined within the bounds of any religious organization. In the light of modern science the miracles of the Bible can be rationally explained as Mind acting in an omnipresent spiritual field, which is open to all men who develop spiritually. "Ye who have followed me, in the regeneration when the Son of man shall sit on the throne of his glory, ye also shall sit upon twelve thrones, judging the twelve tribes of Israel."

"He that overcometh, I will give to him to sit down with me in my throne."

Overcoming is a change of mind from error to Truth. The way of overcoming is first to place one's self by faith in the realization of Sonship, and second, to demonstrate it in every thought and act.

The Word is man's I AM. The Holy Spirit is the "outpouring" or activity of the living Word. The work of the Holy Spirit is the executive power of Father (mind) and Son (idea), carrying out the creative plan. It is through the help of the Holy Spirit that man overcomes. The Holy Spirit reveals, helps, and directs in this overcoming. "The Spirit searcheth all things, yea, the deep things of God." It finally leads man into the light.

The work that the overcomer does for the world is to help establish a new race consciousness, "new heavens and a new earth, wherein dwelleth righteousness." By being true to his highest understanding of Truth the overcomer never swerves to the right nor left for any reason.

The work that the overcomer does for the world is to help establish a new race consciousness, "new heavens and a new earth, wherein dwelleth righteousness." By being true to his highest understanding of Truth the overcomer never swerves to the right nor left for any reason.

This has been going on for a number of years. Whenever they undertake to joke him about his seemingly tame choice he is overjoyed. He feels he is testifying for the Lord and is thankful just for the opportunity. However he says that first one and then another of his friends has come to him privately and asked him how he has the nerve always to turn down the drinks. He tells them he stands in the strength of the Lord and that it is no problem at all for him. They usually admit they wish they had as much backbone as he. This gives him the opportunity to present a word for the practical use of Truth.

The mind of man is built on Truth, and the clearer man's understanding of Truth is the more substantial his mind becomes. It is through progressive, step-by-step spiritual unfoldment that Truth is demonstrated. The truths of Being are scientific, and undoubtedly Jesus understood and taught the properties of the cosmic ether under the name of "the kingdom of the heavens."

Science rightly understood is of inestimable value to religion, and Christianity in order to become the world power that its founder envisioned, must stress the unfoldment of the spiritual mind in man in order that he may do the mighty works promised by Jesus.

When Jesus went up into the mount to pray He was transfigured before His apostles Peter, James, and John. True prayer brings about an exalted radiation of energy, and when it is accompanied by faith, judgment, and love, the word of Truth bursts forth in a stream of light that, when held in mind, illumines, uplifts, and glorifies.

Jesus recognized Mind in everything and called it "Father." He knew that there is a faith center in each atom of so-called matter and that faith in man can move upon the faith center in so-called matter and can remove mountains.

He developed spiritual faith in His own mind, which moved upon the cells of His body and released the power He used in His resurrection and ascension.

We cannot separate Jesus Christ from God or tell where man leaves off and God begins in Him. To say that we are men as Jesus Christ was a man is not exactly true, because He had dropped that personal consciousness by which we separate ourselves from our true God self. He became consciously one with the absolute principle of Being. He proved in His resurrection and ascension that He had no consciousness separate from that of Being, therefore He really was this Being to all intents and purposes.

Yet He attained no more than what is expected of every one of us. "That they may be one, even as we are" was His prayer.This is all accomplished through the externalization of the superconsciousness, which is omnipresent and ever ready to manifest itself through us as it did through Jesus. Let "Christ be formed in you."

In Acts 1:8 Jesus said: "But ye shall receive power, when the Holy Spirit is come upon you."

Through the Holy Spirit, man not only has power to keep the words of Jesus but also to do the works that He did, even "greater works."

Modern science tells us that in the trillions of cells in our body there are imprisoned electronic energies beyond all possibility of estimate; that a single teardrop has within its atoms dynamic force enough to blow up a six-story building. Man is coming into an understanding of how to release these mighty powers and use them in regenerating soul and body.

Jesus taught that the realities of God are capable of expression here in this world and that man within himself has God capacity and power. Jesus was crucified because He claimed to be the Son of God. Yet the Scriptures, which the Pharisees worshiped, had this bold proclamation, which Jesus quoted to them from Psalms 82:

"I said, Ye are gods, And all of you sons of the Most High."

Jesus differed from other men in that He proved by His works that He was the Son of God, while the average man is still striving to attain that excellency. The reports by His followers of what He taught clearly point to two subjects that He loved to discourse upon. The first was the Son of God: He was the Son of God. Secondly: We might all become as He was and demonstrate our dominion by following Him in the regeneration. In order to follow Jesus in the regeneration we must become better acquainted with the various phases of mind and how they function in and through the body.

He who has caught the significance of man, and who and what man is, never allows himself to accept any erroneous conclusions as to his final destiny. He does however know there is a way provided by which he can not only free himself from the claims of materiality but also by his efforts open the way for many others to do likewise. No person ever demonstrated his God-given powers in even a small way but what he helped others to do the same. Preaching is good, but precept is better. "I, if I be lifted up from the earth, will draw all men unto myself."

In Isaiah 65:17 we read: "Behold, I create new heavens [ideals] and a new earth [manifestation]; and the former things shall not be remembered, nor come into mind."

The body that is formed in regeneration absorbs the substance of the body of flesh, and makes out of it a new body in divine order, under the law of the Christ Mind. In this process the physical body dies so that the Christ body may live; but the spiritual ego, the I AM, remains consciously active throughout the process of development that Paul referred to when he said: "I die daily."

In spiritual understanding we know that all the forces in the body are directed by thought and that they work in a constructive or a destructive way, according to the character of the thought. Medicine, massage, and all the material means accomplish but incomplete, unsatisfactory, temporary results, because they work only from the outside and do not touch the inner springs that control the forces. The springs can only be touched by thought. There must be a unity between the mind of man and Divine Mind so that ideas and thoughts that work constructively unto eternal life may be quickened in the mind and organism of man.

Jesus unfolded the consciousness of the Absolute. Through the quickening of the Spirit we are loosed from all limiting ideas and are set free in the Christ consciousness or realization of the Absolute. The consciousness of the Lord Jesus Christ is of limitless life, strength, power, wisdom, love, and substance that are everywhere present, always present.

We are told in John that the world could not contain the books that would be written if all the things that Jesus did were put into writing. But enough is given in the story of His life and in the writings of the apostles concerning Him to bear witness to that which is daily being revealed in this day of fulfillment. Those who are consecrated to Truth and fully resolved to follow Jesus all the way are spiritualizing the whole man, including the body, which is being redeemed from corruption. Those who are living as Jesus lived are becoming like Him. "God is not the God of the dead, but of the living."

Resurrection takes place in people who are alive. One does not go into the grave to be resurrected and to enter the heavenly state of those raised in Christ.

Chapter V - The Day of Judgment

AS WE COME to a realization of an entirely different consciousness new relations are set up that it is sometimes difficult to explain to one who believes in time and space.

In the Bible description of the "day of judgment" the Son of man has always been represented as Jesus Christ, who is to be surrounded by angels and sit on a throne passing judgment after death upon the just and the unjust. But we understand the Son of man to be the spiritual man, that which is ideal, unlimited, and divine. We come into entirely different relations when we affirm, "I am a divine being." When we affirm this we begin to pass judgment. We are the same man, but divine ideas (angels) must come into our consciousness. Then we begin to judge and know that our everyday thoughts are different from our divine, ideal thoughts. We judge between our good thoughts and our evil thoughts, our unlimited and our limited thoughts.

It is said we are to be judged after death according to deeds done in the body, which are kept on record like books that are balanced; and if the balance is found to be in our favor we go up, and if against us we go down. But if we are spiritual now--divine--this spiritual part has dominion, and we begin to exercise this dominion. The moment we catch sight of this we begin to judge. We begin to put the thoughts that are good on the right and the others on the left. All our ideas of the attributes of our divine self we put on the right hand of power, while the thoughts of disease, death, limitation and lack we put on the left--denied, cut off.

This is not to occur after death. It is to begin right now! We don't say that all is evil; that would be mental suicide. We just say it is a "goat thought." We do not kill it but transform it. After separating our innocent sheep thoughts, we begin to have fine, high, discriminating judgment.

Then the Son of man has come in His glory, surrounded by His angels (ideas). We know that He is limitless. "I am now a son of God," we say. "I am divine." These angels (ideas) take their places on the throne with the Son of man and judgment begins immediately.

Then today is the day of judgment!

We may have the perception and may see the angels (ideas) but we have not passed judgment. We do not judge until we begin to deny and affirm. Judgment commences the moment you accept the truth of your divine sonship.

"Then shall the King say to them on his right hand, Come, ye blessed of my Father, inherit the kingdom prepared for you from the foundation of the world."

Who is the king? The center of consciousness, the I AM, and the I AM has power to just the extent you have the courage to assert your power. We must all step forth and assert, "All authority hath been given unto me in heaven and on earth." If the central spark is like the divine, then we have all power.

We are here as the king, and we say to our true thoughts (angels), "Come . . . inherit the kingdom prepared for you from the foundation of the world." Then all is ours. There is no limit. We ask what we will and it is done unto us. All good that we can conceive of is now ours. Is there evidence of the oak in the acorn? No! But there is a pattern of an oak there, and this pattern or image is what makes the tree. The image in mind makes the condition.

Now is the time to plant the seed thought of the conditions we desire by saying, "Come my good thoughts, let us inherit our kingdom."

We do not fear anything, for we have separated our sheep from the goats; we have set our true thoughts on the right and have denied our error thoughts any power whatever. "I was hungry, and ye gave me to eat; I was thirsty, and ye gave me drink; I was a stranger, and ye took me in; naked, and ye clothed me; I was sick, and ye visited me; I was in prison, and ye came unto me."

We understand that our good thoughts always minister to us in days of despondency and discouragement. We rest in the thought that we have done a good deed in such and such an instance or that we have been good at such and such a time. These are the thoughts that minister to us. These thoughts are not conscious; but they are laying the foundation for the coming of the Lord, so they say: "When saw we thee hungry, and fed thee? or thirsty, and gave thee drink? When saw we thee a stranger, and took thee in? or naked, and clothed thee? Or when saw we thee sick, or in prison, and came unto thee?"

Every thought of goodness makes a place, a form, and sets up a friendly habit in the mind that is permanent and that in your time of need ministers to you. You are glad to accept this ministry, for you have done good because the Spirit of good is working through you. Thus you reap the benefit of all the good you have ever done or thought. Your thoughts give back results of the same nature as themselves. If in the silence you have earnestly held to the pure and good you have built in you a place for the pure and good. Every true thought has made a place in your mind and when you are about to judge you will recognize it, although you did not realize it at the time you sent it forth.

We are carried along by these thoughts until we reach the consciousness of our I AM power. We do not know we are building ourselves, our environment, our world, until we reach this consciousness. Then judgment of our world begins and is passed on our thought creations. Suppose we have tried to cast the beam out of our eye so that we might help our brother. This act will answer in our judgment day, "I was that 'least' one."

Come into the kingdom of mind. Here everything that is in Principle is yours. These error thoughts and misconceptions of Truth are only age-lasting, not everlasting.

Everything, all good, is to be gathered up, and everything is good at its center. The essence of your body is good and of true substance. When you sift your consciousness of all but the real and true, the body becomes full of light. The diamond owes its brilliance to the perfect arrangement of the innumerable little prisms within it, each of which refracts the light of the other. Man's body is made up of centers of consciousness--of light--and if arranged so they radiate the light within you, you will shine like the diamond. All things are in the consciousness and you have to learn to separate the erroneous from the true, darkness from light. The I AM must separate the sheep from the goats. This sifting begins right now and goes on until the perfect child of God is manifest and you are fully rounded out in all your Godlike attributes.

Chapter VI - Thou Shalt Decree A Thing

As imagination bodies forth
The forms of things unknown, the poet's pen
Turns them to shapes, and gives to airy nothing.A local habitation and a name.
-SHAKESPEARE-

TO DECREE with assurance is to establish and fix an ideal in substance. The force behind the decree is invisible, like a promise to be fulfilled at a future time; but it binds with its invisible chains the one who makes it. We have only a slight conception of the strength of the intangible. We compare and measure strength by some strong element in nature. We say "strong as steel." But a very little thought will convince us that mental affirmations are far stronger than the strongest visible thing in the world. The reason for this is that visible things lack livingness. They are not linked with energy and intelligence as are words. Words charged with power and intelligence increase with use, while material things decrease.

It is not necessary to call the attention of metaphysicians to the fact that all visible things had their origin in the invisible. The visible is what remains of an idea that has gradually lost its energy. Scientists say that this so-called solid earth under our feet was once radiant substance. Nothing is really "solid" but the atomic energy latent in everything. They tell us that it takes some six billion years for uranium to disintegrate and become lead, and this rate of disintegration has helped scientists determine the age of the earth as about two billion years.

Since nothing is lost in the many transformations that occur in nature, what becomes of the energy that is being released in the disintegration that is going on in our earth? The answer is that a new earth is being formed in which matter will be replaced by atomic energy. This process of refining matter into radiant substance is taking place not only in the natural world but in our bodies also. In fact the speed with which the transformation takes place depends on the character of the thoughts that we project into our brains and through them into our bodies and the world about us. This is why we should spiritualize our thoughts and refine the food we eat to correspond. The press announces a great shortage of meat all over the world, with alarming predictions of malnutrition and race deterioration. Instead of a calamity this meat shortage will prove a blessing. New and better foods will be found to replace the corrupt flesh with which people have been stuffing their stomachs. The call for stimulants that the fermenting mess produces in digestion will diminish, and a purer, sweeter body and saner mind will follow. The peoples of Europe, forced by the economic conditions brought about by wars, are adopting a simpler diet, with better health; so says the public press. Thus what seems calamity turns out to be a source of joy.

At the present writing there is a housing shortage everywhere and the lack of materials and competent labor indicate that several years will elapse before the need is met. This is counted a calamity; but is it? The inventive genius of man is planning houses of glass and other materials that will be much less expensive--more durable and in every respect superior to the present homes. When man gets his ingenious mind into action he always meets every emergency with something better. These many examples of the power of man's mind should make us pause when we are tempted to consider any situation disastrous or nearly so. Every adverse situation can be used as a spur to urge one to greater exertion and the ultimate attainment of some ideal that has lain dormant in the subconsciousness. The pessimist moans, "I could make a better world than this." The optimist sings, "Go to it; that's what God put you here for."

People everywhere on earth are now realizing as never before that the well-being of this world rests with its inhabitants. It is no longer a religious dogma or a philosophical theory that the destiny of the race is in the hands of man. God has given all things to us to use as we shall determine. We can use the atomic energy to destroy or construct as we decree. "Behold, I set before you the way of life and the way of death." The dominion and authority God gave to His image-and-likeness man has assumed such reality that even the most trivial person can understand it and tremble at the prospect of what might come to pass if that dominion were used by vicious men. Those who have recklessly gone on living without seeking the wisdom of the source of life are now asking what shall be done to save us from the insanity that would destroy our world. The one and only answer, of course, is that the moral and spiritual standard of the race must be raised the world over as the one and only ultimate source of safety. This means that every person must begin on himself and, as it dawns, let the light shine by imparting it to others. If this method were followed universally the millennium would be upon us in a marvelously short time. This is not a religious question but a matter of life or death; not a question of hell after death but of survival here and now of everybody and everything one holds dear. There are Hitlers still alive and others reincarnating. They must all be educated morally and taught the nearness of the spiritual man and the necessity of his incorporation into the consciousness of the natural man before permanent life can be established in the individual. This work is to be done for our race right here on this planet, and for this reason we who love the Lord and greatly desire that His law be fulfilled are calling on all people to make haste and accept the abundant life and light that He so freely offers.

The Bible records many instances where marvelous results followed the observance of religious rites in which trumpets took a leading part. The priests under Moses were ordered to blow trumpets before the Ark; Gideon and his three hundred overcame a large army of Midianites by flashing lights, shouting, and blowing trumpets; the walls of Jericho fell as the result of trumpet and voice vibrations. Isaiah says: "And it shall come to pass in that day, that a great trumpet shall be blown; and they shall come that were ready to perish in the land of Assyria [the psychic realm], and they that were outcasts in the land of Egypt [materialism]; aud they shall worship Jehovah in the holy mountain in Jerusalem [spirituality]."

The trumpet sets up sharp vibrations in the ether, which cause disintegration when they impinge upon an object in the mental or material realms. These realms Isaiah symbolically refers to as Assyria and Egypt. Trained metaphysicians produce like results through the spiritual word, uttered audibly or silently or both. It is in this field of Spirit that Unity people are destined to do a great work in helping to educate people everywhere. By declaring and decreeing spiritually the words of Jesus and Jehovah we send into the ether a spiritual force that shatters the fixed states of consciousness holding millions in evil ways. In this way the doors of mental prisons will be opened to multitudes of sin-bound souls. Anyone who has faith in Spirit and the power of the word spoken in faith can send it forth, and like the radio oscillation, it will be picked up by receptive minds everywhere.

"Let your light shine before men; that they may see your good works, and glorify your Father who is in heaven."

Chapter VII - Thinking in the Fourth Dimension

SCIENTISTS TELL us that the discoveries that their efforts are revealing convince them that they are just on the verge of stupendous truths. Christianity spiritually interpreted shows that Jesus understood the deeper things of God's universe. He understood exactly what the conditions were on the invisible side of life, which is termed in His teaching the "kingdom of God" or the "kingdom of the heavens." We are trying to connect His teaching with modern science in order to show the parallel; but as He said in Mark 4:23, "if any man hath ears to hear, let him hear." This means that we must develop a capacity for understanding in terms of the atomic structure of the universe.

Unless we have this spiritual capacity we do not understand. We think we have ears, but they are attuned to materiality. They do not get the radiations from the supermind, the Christ Mind. Physiology working with psychology is demonstrating that hearing and seeing can be developed in every cell in the body, independent of ears and eyes. We hear and see with our minds working through our bodies. This being true, the capacity to hear may extend beyond the physical ear into the spiritual ethers, and we should be able to hear the voice of God. This extension of hearing is what Jesus taught. "If any man hath ears to hear, let him hear."

Then we are told that we must "take heed" what we hear. Many of us have found that as we develop this inner, spiritual hearing, we hear voices sometimes that do not tell the truth. These deceptive voices can be hushed by affirming the presence and power of the Lord Jesus Christ. As you unfold your spiritual nature, you will find that it has the same capacity for receiving vibrations of sound as your outer, physical ear has. You do not give attention to all that you hear in the external; you discriminate as you listen. So in the development of this inner, spiritual ear take heed what you hear: discriminate.

Jesus said, "For he that hath, to him shall be given: and he that hath not, from him shall be taken away even thatwhich he hath." How can what a man has not be taken away? We believe in our mortal consciousness that we have attained a great deal, but if we have not this inner, spiritual consciousness of reality our possessions are impermanent. Then we must be careful what we accumulate in our consciousness, because "he that hath, to him shall be given." The more spiritual Truth you pile up in your mind, the more you have of reality, and the larger is your capacity for the unlimited; but if you have nothing of a spiritual character, what little you have of intellectual attainment will eventually be taken away from you.

The kingdom of the heavens, the new dimension of mind and energy that is being unfolded today in the spiritual ethers by the discoveries of the scientists, should not be divorced from the kingdom of heaven taught by Jesus. Jesus taught in parables because His listeners were not trained in science.

We know that the kingdom of the heavens or kingdom of God is not a place in the skies but an ideal state in creative mind, ready to be ushered into the minds of men.

We have thought that this kingdom of God was to be introduced into the world in a miraculous way. At the very beginning of His ministry Jesus announced, "The time is fulfilled, and the kingdom of God is at hand"; but it did not then appear. He said, "The kingdom of God cometh not with observation." Its source is not in outer things; it comes from sources within man. So we know that we must develop spiritual understanding and spiritual power in some respects exceeding that of Jesus. "He that believeth on me, the works that I do shall he do also; and greater." Man is the outpicturing of the infinite and creative Mind, and all the capacity of this great Mind is his by inheritance.

Jesus taught that man is the light of God. Without man God should be deaf and dumb and blind. Did you ever think that you are God's ears and God's mouth and God's eyes? You have doubtless heard these statements before, but you have taken them metaphorically; but it is true that man is God, formulated.

God is Spirit, it is plainly taught, and the omnipotent, omnipresent essence from which all things proceed. Both science and religion agree on the fundamental fact that God is the source of all creation. Just how God puts Himself into His creation is not so universally understood or accepted. But Paul says that God is in us all and through us all and above us all; that is, God saturates us. God as Spirit is the ether or soil in which we grow as human plants.

Jesus compared this soil of God to the soil necessary to the vegetable kingdom, in which seed is cast and springs up and grows and unfolds by a series of orderly stages: "first the blade, then the ear, then the full grain in the ear." This seed is the God word, and it is tremendously prolific, much more so than any material seed.

When man points his mind toward God and allows his zeal to run in a single channel, he may become God-intoxicated. Peter the Hermit became intoxicated with the idea that God wanted Jerusalem rescued from Moslem rule, and he rode up and down Europe on his little mule shouting, "God wills it." His fanatical zeal started the Crusades that rolled from Europe to Palestine for nearly two hundred years.

When we recognize that great teachers and leaders of the race have really developed and expressed a superconsciousness that is potential in all persons, we have raised the hopes and the capacities of men from the human to the divine. These scientific discoveries are proving that God is impartial and absolutely just in all His relations with humanity. When the natural world is scientifically and universally revealed, a great school of instruction in soul unfoldment will be established right here in our midst, and its results will be beyond all our present imaginings.

The mysteries of the supermind have always been considered the property of certain schools of occultists and mystics who were cautious about giving their truths to the masses for fear that in their ignorance these might misuse them. But now the doors are thrown wide open, and whosoever will may enter in.

Our attention in this day is being largely called to the revolution that is taking place in the economic world, but a revolution of even greater worth is taking place in the mental and spiritual worlds. A large and growing school of metaphysicians has made its advent in this generation, and it is radically changing the public mind toward religion. In other words, we are developing spiritual understanding, and this means that religion and its sources in tradition and in man are being inquired into and its principles applied in the development of a new cosmic mind for the whole human family. So we need a larger realization of the importance of man and the importance of every one of us in manifesting the God who is Spirit.

We have thought that the burden rested on God alone and that we were merely puppets in His hands; but Jesus taught otherwise, and our science proves that man dominates nature when he affirms his mental supremacy. We are told that today we have invented machines that can produce faster than we yet know how to use, that our markets may be glutted with the products of these mechanical inventions, and that the products may become so cheap that those who produce them will come to want. We have wished that everything we touched might turn to gold; it has come to pass and we are paralyzed by the pressure of the stuff we have piled up in our ingenuity and selfishness. We cannot eat it ourselves, and our greed makes us fearful that we shall lose all of it if we pass it out freely to others.

So the great need of the whole human family is to know this one supreme law of God as Spirit manifesting itself in the mind of man. It is then necessary that we understand our own importance as God manifestations. We should understand that we are not separate nor insignificant but the vital, important, integral parts of a mighty whole. Jesus realized the importance of the superman as a thinking power expressing God-Mind when He said, "No one cometh unto the Father, but by me."

We have thought that we were to accept Jesus as our Saviour, that He made propitiation for our sins, and that that was what He meant when He said we could not reach the Father except through Him. We have thought that He meant His personality and His great sacrifice; and we now have to admit that in its deeper, spiritual significance this is in a measure true. But in a more personal and intimate way we are vitally and spiritually intersphered with the Christ Mind in God, and we cannot measure up to and express our divinity unless we accept Jesus' standard of the importance of man and the necessity of man in the great creative scheme of life.

All persons in rare moments catch glimpses of this creative plan as a whole, and of man's importance in its beauty and perfection. But this subject is so deep and so far-reaching that it can be realized in small degree only by those who have developed spiritual sight and feeling, and practice thinking in the fourth dimension, or kingdom of God.

Chapter VIII - Is This God's World

WHY DOESN'T God do something about it?" This oft-repeated query, uttered by the skeptical and unbelieving, is heard day in and day out. Imitating the skeptics, Christian believers everywhere are looking to God for all kinds of reforms in every department of manifest life and also are charging Him with death and destruction the world over.

One who thinks logically and according to sound reason wonders at the contradictions set up by these various queries and desires.

Is God responsible for all that occurs on this earth, and if not all, how much of it?

The Bible states that God created the earth and all its creatures, and last of all man, to whom He gave dominion over everything. Observation and experience prove that man is gaining dominion over nature wherever he applies himself to that end. But so much remains to be gained, and he is so small physically that man counts himself a pygmy instead of the mental giant that he is.

All the real mastery that man attains in the world has its roots in his mind, and when he opens up the mental realm in his being there are no unattainables. If the conquests of the air achieved in the last quarter of a century had been prophesied the prophets would have been pronounced crazy. The fact is that no one thinking in the old mind realm can have any conception of the transformation of sound waves into electromagnetic waves and back again into words and messages of intelligence. Edison admitted that his discovery of the phonograph was an accident and that he never fully understood how mechanical vibrations could be recorded and be reproduced in all forms of intelligent communication.

Reasoning in terms of matter, no one can understand how words and music and pictures can be carried over long distances through space without conflict and then be reproduced by a mechanical device with perfection and accuracy.

Now that man has broken away from his limited visualizations and mentally grasped the unhampered ideas of the supermind, he is growing grandly bold and his technical pioneers are telling him that the achievements of yesterday are as nothing compared to those of tomorrow. For example, an article by Harland Manchester condensed in the Reader's Digest from Scientific American tells of the "micro-waves" that are slated for a more spectacular career in the realm of the unbelievable than anything that has preceded them. This article describes in detail some of the marvels that will evolve out of the utilization of microwaves, among which may be mentioned "private phone calls by the hundreds of thousands sent simultaneously over the same wave band without wires, poles or cables. Towns where each citizen has his own radio frequency, over which he can get voice, music, and television, and call any phone in the country by dialing. Complete abolition of static and interference from electrical devices and from other stations. A hundred times as much 'space on the air' as we now have in the commercial radio band. A high-definition and color television network to cover the country. And, perhaps most important of all, a nation-wide radar network, geared to television, to regulate all air traffic and furnish instantaneous visual weather reports to airfields throughout the land."

Add to this the marvels promised by the appliers of atomic energy and you have an array of miracles unequaled in all the bibles of all the nations of the world.

It is admitted by those who are most familiar with the dynamic power of these newly discovered forces that we do not yet know how to protect our body cells from the destructiveness of their vibrations. Very thick concrete walls are required to protect those who experiment with atomic forces. One scientist says that the forces released from the bombs that were used on the Japanese cities in 1945 may affect those who were subjected to them and their descendants for a thousand years. Experimentation proves that we have tapped a kingdom that we do not know how to handle safely.

It is quite obvious that these forces, if they could be utilized, would vastly improve our standard of living and that they were planned for us by creative Mind. If we cannot control them, why did God allow us to discover them? And now that we are turning them loose in space all about us, what are we going to do about it? Also how do we reconcile this situation with the observation of the Psalmist:

"Thou makest him to have dominion over the works of thy hands; Thou hast put all things under his feet."

The fact is that we have reached a point in race evolution where we are forced to give attention to the refinement of the body. Our religion has too long taught that the body is dust and ashes and that it is its destiny to die and be left to the worms. The deterioration of the body cells must be arrested and a new and more powerful life force injected into the physical organism. This is plainly part of the teaching of Jesus. He said, "I came that they may have life, and may have it abundantly." He told his followers that when they went to that upper room in Jerusalem they would receive the baptism of the Holy Spirit with power. The original Greek says that they would receive dynamic energy. All baptisms with Spirit impart vitalizing life to the recipient, and the joy of quickened vitality should be felt and retained as part of the physical regeneration.

The divine unction imparted by spiritual baptism also contains all the healing forces of X rays, ultraviolet rays, sunshine, and in fact all the radiant restorative forces now so widely used as healing agents. But the energy imparted by Spirit is so tempered that it never injures but always heals. That this is not true of the shocks given by mechanical generators is evidenced by the scars they often leave. A prayer treatment by an experienced spiritual healer is a baptism, with power proportioned to the spiritual understanding of the healer. The lowest method of imparting spiritual baptism is by the laying on of hands and prayer. The highest is realizing the Holy Spirit presence and its expression through the power of the word. Jesus began His ministry by doing the former, but at the end He sent His word and healed by means of it.

God created the fundamental ideas culminating in the idea of ideal man. This ideal man has power to mold God's creation into any manifestation he may choose. If he consults the Father and projects his thoughts in accordance with the law, perfect manifestation follows. As Jesus said, "My Father worketh even until now, and I work."

One who understands this relation of man to his creator can assert with confidence that this is man's world and always will be. By right thinking man can have the co-operation of God in producing manifestations and thereby can set up the kingdom of God in the earth; or he can ignore God and attempt to form a world and govern it without divine aid. We are now living in a civilization dominated by human thought, and confusion is the result.

How many ages and aeons have passed since man lost contact with God no one can tell. We have about six thousand years of history and no heavenly conditions are recorded. Caves and sand drifts reveal the remains of man in combat with the gorilla for half a million years, with man himself sunk almost to the level of the monkey. When man dropped out of the ethers and became one of the primates mortal understanding has not yet discerned, but the distortions in the earth and all nature bear evidence of a terrible shock.

We know that our home is not altogether on the earth but also in the air, over which we must gain dominion before we can have a fit dwelling place. We are now gaining this dominion by mechanical means. This will be followed by the development of a human organism that, unified with Spirit, will transport us everywhere in air and on earth.

The great and most important issue before the people today is the development of man's spiritual mind and through it unity with God. There seem to be things in more immediate need of being done to alleviate present conditions, but the taproot of all this confusion is our failure to use our minds intelligently. We can only think as God would have us think by adjusting our thoughts to divine ideas. Religion and all that it implies in prayer and recognition of God in idea and manifestation is the one and only way out of the chaos in which we find ourselves. We must therefore begin at once to develop this unity with the Father mind by incorporating divine ideas into all that we think and speak.

Chapter IX - Demonstrating Christ Thought by Thought

> Behold, what God hath wrought! An ideal man, a mighty man--A man supreme, who thought by thought Must demonstrate what God hath wrought.–CHARLES FILLMORE

|MANIFEST MAN, personal man, began evolving the ideal man, that is, "putting on Christ," ages and aeons ago. We are now nearly midway in this evolution. The age of this evolution might be determined if we could count the trillions of cells in our body where are inscribed the experiences we had in the ages we have lived. However we know by inspiration and analogy that our conscious creation began with this earth. If science says the earth has been two billion years in evolving, that is our age. When the morning stars were forming we were here.

He who reads the "signs of the times" discerns spiritually that we are now in the midst of a race transition in which we are taking a very pronounced upward swing in the development of the ideal man implanted in us in the beginning. A new concept of God, man, and the universe is upon us. We must realize all this and go upward with the mighty urge for higher things. Will God take us up to an imaginary heaven in a chariot of fire, or do we use our mind to lift ourselves heave nward? "God helps those who help themselves" holds good in the heavens as in the earth. We begin right where we are to bring forth the kingdom of God within us. Every problem of life can be successfully solved if we begin with the use of the I AM on the various planes of mind. It is not we alone; it is when we realize that we can connect ourselves with the Father-Mind and prove what Jesus said--"I speak not from myself: but the Father abiding in me doeth his works"–that our potential almightiness begins to appear.

If you are given to worry and anxiety, think about the fearless confidence and trust of the Spirit. This will at once relieve your mind of the thoughts that have stirred you, and the power of the Spirit will begin its work of straightening out your affairs. If you are overwhelmed with material work and the call of the outer world, stop and concentrate in the I AM and say: "I am Spirit. I do not believe in matter or material conditions. I have power, because I know that all power is in Divine Mind. Divine Mind now sets my thoughts and all my affairs in divine order, and I rest in the confidence and peace of thekingdom within."

You can have a well body, but you must begin to build it with your word. Instead of laying up weak and sick words in your body, begin now to speak words of strength and health--and keep at it. Do not look at what has been. Lot's wife tried that, and she never got beyond the past. Clear out of your mind all rubbish about disease, and you will find that none has any lodgment in your body. The thought makes the body and determines the condition it lives in. Thoughts of health are living, eternal things, and they work with the irresistible power of almightiness to tone up the organism to their own high state of harmony and capability.

There is but one way to establish harmony in the home, and that is to establish it first in the individual. It is the law of Spirit that we must be that which we would draw to us. If we would draw to us love, we must be love, be loving and kind; if we would have peace and harmony in our environment, we must establish it within ourselves. We must faithfully and persistently deny the appearance of that which seems to be inharmonious and silently and faithfully affirm the omnipresent peace, love, and harmony that we want to see manifested. That which we hold in consciousness will be made manifest for us, therefore we should not hold the thought of anything that we do not want to see appear.

There is a relation between thinking and eating, and as you grow spiritually the character of your food and all that pertains to eating may have to be changed in conformity with the new order of things. If you will leave meat and all animal products out of your food you will see a change for the better. But above all, keep your thought mastery and do not be controlled by appetite. Do not fear to eat. Eat with thanksgiving and bless your food.

If you are looking to mental science alone for help you are certain to be disappointed; "for neither is there any other name under heaven, that is given among men, wherein we must be saved" than the name of Jesus Christ. Jesus' teaching is something deeper and farther reaching than mere mental science. It is not something that works things out for us in the personal but is a power that transforms the whole man.

Here is what Judge Troward said on this subject:

> *"I have studied the subject (mental science) now for several years, and have a general acquaintance with the leading features of most of the systems which unfortunately occupy attention in many circles at the present time, and I have no hesitation in saying that to the best of my judgment all sorts and descriptions of so-called occult study are in direct opposition to the real life-giving Truth.*
>
> *We hear a great deal in these days about "initiation," but believe me, the more you try to become a so-called "initiate," the further you will put yourself from living life. I speak after many years of careful study and consideration when I say that the Bible and its revelation of Christ is the one thing really worth studying, and it is a subject large enough in all conscience, embracing as it does our outward life of everyday concerns, and also the inner springs of our life and all that we can in general terms conceive of as life".*

Just in proportion as a person yields willingly and obediently to the transforming process does he demonstrate the Truth. All that pertains to self must be put away as fast as it is revealed, and that which is of the universal, the Christ, must take its place.

Be still and witness the salvation of the Lord. You doubtless fully know that this stillness in the secret place of the Most High is not mental torpor, but a quiet tranquillity that holds itself in an equipoise of spiritual security. You have done your part when your true word has gone forth. Now rest at the center and say: "It is well; Thy work is sure; I am satisfied." Do not argue with anyone, nor discuss the matters that you have submitted to Spirit; simply say, "All is well; it is finished."

Every man who accomplishes things sees first in his mind what he wishes to do. He puts away all doubt. It makes no difference how small or how large the thing you want to do may be; if you have an unlimited confidence in your ability to do it, you will do it. Nothing can in any way impede or defeat you. Faith is the highest expression of belief or confidence. It is that something in man which says: "I believe in the possibilities of things that I cannot see. I believe in the possibility of Divine Mind doing in this age, right now, everything that was ever done in any age." When we believe this and hold to it, putting aside all doubt and whatever suggests failure, the thoughts of faith begin to accumulate substance, and fulfillment follows.

In order to realize Truth and to demonstrate it you must live it. If anyone appears careless, simply deny it and affirm order and harmony. Allow nothing in the external to disturb your poise and dominion. That is the way of love. When you refuse to see negative things they will disappear, and you will be surprised to see how you will change. Your mind, body, and affairs are the expression of your thoughts, so if you are not happy, change your mental habits. This may not seem practical to you at first, but if you will faithfully practice the Golden Rule and send only thoughts of love to everyone, you will witness practical results. You can cultivate the habit of seeing the good, the true, the bright side of every subject, and then with your friends you can bring this side out in conversation, thus keeping yourself positive and poised, and at the same time sowing the seed of Truth in the minds of others.

The "leading of the Spirit" is not something mysterious. When you open your mind to the wisdom of God in the silence, you should claim in faith that you have received, and trust that the Spirit does guide you. "Christ Jesus . . . was made unto us wisdom"; and the more you affirm that Christ is your wisdom the more you will realize the order and harmony that result from the directing power of divine wisdom. But do not be surprised and disappointed if everything does not work out according to your old ideas.The all-seeing Mind should not be judged by the dim and short vision of the mortal. What may at first seem to you failure may prove to be a clearing away of rubbish that will open the way in mind to a larger life.

Jesus showed by His life and teachings that it is the will of God for men to be well. A clear understanding of this is necessary if one wants to demonstrate health. Where there is a belief that God wills sickness and suffering, His love and power are shut out of consciousness. Spiritual healing depends on faith, and there cannot be faith while the mind is holding thoughts directly opposed to the possibility of healing. It is therefore very necessary to dwell much on the love and power of God so that a steady, unwavering faith may be established.

The subconscious realm of mind is the realm that contains all past thoughts. First, we think consciously and this thought becomes subconscious, carrying on its work of building up or tearing down, according to its character.The subconscious mind cannot take the initiative, but depends on the conscious mind for direction. When one is quickened of Spirit, one's true thoughts are set to work and the subconscious states of error are broken up and dissolved. In one's daily silence and communion with God, thoughts from the subconsciousness come into the conscious realm of mind to be forgiven and redeemed. Flesh heredity is denied and inheritance from God affirmed, which enables man consciously to draw divine ideas from the one Mind. These ideas are established in consciousness and the whole mentality is at one with Christ, the divine-man idea.

All wisdom is implanted in us by divine intelligence, which is another name for God. In the degree that we awaken to the consciousness of our inherent wisdom, in that degree we are responsible to the Father and are required to render unto Him the fruitage of our wisdom. All of us unfold according to our understanding and realization. Whether our understanding is small or large, we must measure up to or demonstrate that which has been given us. "To whomsoever much is given, of him shall much be required."

The phrase "body of Christ" has a threefold significance. First, as regards its application to the body of Jesus, in Matthew 26:26, 27 Jesus called the bread He had blessed His body and the wine His blood. Out of this came the symbolic rite of the Lord's Supper. All symbols are useful to the extent that they point man to the realities for which they stand. When this reality is discerned the symbols are understood. Jesus dwelt continually in the consciousness of being the very substance and life of God. "He that hath seen me hath seen the Father." Through the conscious realization of His oneness with God His body became a "body of life," spiritual substance, His blood the life of God. This is the body and blood He gave as a "ransom for many"; the understanding that the Christ body comes not by the grave but through our daily realization of the omnipresence of substance and life and our union with it.

Secondly, the words "body of Christ" refer to man's spiritual body. "Until Christ be formed in you." When we appropriate words of Truth, "eat them," so to speak, we partake of the substance and life of Spirit and build the Christ body. This is partaking of the body and blood of Jesus Christ, the true sacrament that vitalizes the body by renewing the mind. Every student of Truth builds the Christ body as he constantly abides in the Christ Mind through daily meditation upon words of Truth.

Thirdly, the phrase "body of Christ" applies to the group of people who find perfect unity in Spirit, free from all the limitations and authority of creed. Such a group is free from bondage to the letter and subject only to the Spirit of truth. Jesus Christ is the head of this body, and its members are joined through a recognition of universal Spirit. This "body of Christ" is sometimes referred to as the "church of Christ." This latter term is commonly misunderstood in that many sects call themselves the "church of Christ," each believing they are the chosen of God. God is not partial and does not choose. Man exercises that privilege, and if he chooses to conform to the "law of the Spirit of life in Christ Jesus" he becomes a member of the church of Christ and is recognized by the Father. There is unity only in Spirit, and "God is Spirit." All personal opinions upon which creeds are based disappear before the spiritual understanding that the only real unity is the body of Christ, His church. All who measure up to the Christ standard, forsaking everything pertaining to the personal, limited self, bringing forth the unlimited fruits of the Spirit, are members of this body, the "body of Christ." Through this body is to come the "restoration of all things, whereof God spake by the mouth of his holy prophets that have been from of old."

Chapter X -Truth Radiats Light

ALTHOUGH Paul did not demonstrate complete overcoming, as Jesus did, he saw in man as a mystery the truth that had been lost sight of for "ages and generations . . . which is Christ in you, the hope of glory." We are urged by both Jesus and Paul to glorify God in our bodies. The body is the fruit of the mind, therefore we must become better acquainted with the mind and with the supermind in order to glorify the body.

The fact is that the entire theme of the Bible is man and his various states of mind, represented as persons, tents, tabernacles, temples. In Exodus we read, "Let them make me a sanctuary, that I may dwell among them." It is explained that this sanctuary was to be the meeting place of the people and their God and eventually the dwelling place of Jehovah. Jehovah means the I AM, which is also the meaning of the Christ or the supermind. Where in all the universe can man meet the supermind save in his own mind and body?

We are then compelled to conclude that the Tabernacle of the Israelites and the Temple of Solomon are symbols of man's body, the real meeting place of Jehovah.

Paul says, *"We are a temple of the living God; even as God said, I will dwell in them, and walk in them."*

When Solomon was preparing to build the Temple he soliloquized: "But who is able to build him a house, seeing heaven and the heaven of heavens cannot contain him? who am I then, that I should build him a house, save only to burn incense before him?" The burning of incense in the house of Jehovah represents the spiritualization of the fine essences of the body through adoration and exalted thoughts. When the mind is lifted up in meditation and prayer the whole body glows with spiritual light.

This spiritual light transcends in glory all the laws of matter and intellect. Even Moses could not enter the Tabernacle when it was aglow with this transcendent light. It is written that the Israelites did not go forward on days when the cloud remained over the Tabernacle, but when the cloud was taken up they went forward. This means that there is no soul progress for man when his body is under the shadow of a "clouded" mind, but when the cloud is removed there is an upward and forward movement of the whole consciousness (all the people).

We are warned of the effect of thoughts that are against or opposed to the commandments of Jehovah. When we murmur and complain we cloud our minds, and Divine Mind cannot reach us or help us. Then we usually loaf until something turns up that causes us to think on happier things, when we go forward again.

Instead of giving up to circumstances and outer events we should remember that we are all very close to a kingdom of mind that would make us always happy and successful if we would cultivate it and make it and its laws a vital part of our life. "The joy of Jehovah is your strength."

You ask, "How can I feel the joy of Jehovah when I am poor, or sick, or unhappy?" Jesus said, "Come unto me, all ye that labor and are heavy laden, and I will give you rest."

Here is the first step in getting out of the mental cloud that obscures the light of Spirit. Take the promises of Jesus as literally and spiritually true. Right in the midst of the most desperate situation one can proclaim the presence and power of Christ, and that is the first mental move in dissolving the darkness. You cannot think of Jesus without a feeling of freedom and light. Jesus taught freedom from mortality and proclaimed His glory so persistently that He energized our thought atmosphere into light. This light is Spirit power, and it can be seen and felt by anyone who will call on the name Christ and expect it to raise him quickly out of depression and negative states of mind into the power and zeal of an overcomer through Christ.

The Scriptures state that when Moses came down from Mount Sinai with the Ten Commandments his face shone so brilliantly that the Children of Israel and even Aaron, his own brother, were afraid to come near him until he put a veil over his face. The original Hebrew says his face sent forth beams or horns of light.

The Vulgate says that Moses had "a horned face"; which Michelangelo took literally, in his statue of Moses representing him with a pair of horns projecting from the head. Thus we see the ludicrous effect of reading the Bible according to the letter.

Our men of science have experimented with the brain in action, and they tell us that it is true that we radiate beams when we think. The force of these beams has been measured.Here we have further confirmation of the many statements in the Bible that have been taken as ridiculous and unbelievable or as miracles. Persons who spend much time in prayer and meditate a great deal on spiritual things develop the same type of face that Moses is said to have had. We say of them that their face fairly shine when they talk about God and His love. John saw Jesus on the island of Patmos, and he says, "His countenance was as the sun shineth in his strength."

I have witnessed this radiance in the faces of Truth teachers hundreds of times. I well remember one class lesson during which the teacher became so eloquent that beams of light shot forth from the head and tongues of fire flashed through the room, very like those which were witnessed when the followers of Jesus were gathered in Jerusalem.

We now know that fervent words expressed in prayer and song and eloquent proclamations of spiritual Truth release the millions of electrons in our brain cells and through them blend like chords of mental music with the Mind universal. This tendency on our part to analyze and scientifically dissect the many supposed miracles recorded in the Bible is often regarded as sacrilegious, or at least as making commonplaces of some of the very spectacular incidents recorded in Scripture.

In every age preceding this the priesthood has labored under the delusion that the common people could not understand the real meaning of life and that they should therefore be kept in ignorance of its inner sources; also that the masses could not be trusted with sacred truths, that imparting such truths to them was like casting pearls before swine.

But now science is delving into hidden things, and it is found that they all arise in and are sustained by universal principles that are open to all men who seek to know and apply them.

So the time has arrived when all shall know the Truth, "from the least to the greatest of them." Of course there are many sides to Truth. What we mean by Truth is concerned with the great fundamental questions that have always perplexed and at the same time engaged the profoundest attention of men: What is the character of God? How does God create? What is the real character of man, and what relation does he bear to his source? What is the ultimate destiny of man and the universe?

These are some of the fundamental questions that meet us at every turn. They have been answered by both philosophers and priests in every age, yet they still remain largely unanswered in the popular estimation. Of course the priests think they have the answer, but they offer no proof save that of inspiration. The philosophers and scientists are not satisfied with the answers of the spiritually inspired. They want facts, and they are testing the seen and the unseen for forces that respond to certain laws without variation or deviation. They claim that the theological explanation of creation by Moses and the location and description of the kingdom of heaven by Jesus are not specific enough and cannot be definitely and scientifically proved; all of which is approximately true. Popular religion does not attempt to harmonize its fundamental facts with the findings of science, and in its ignorance it fights science and thinks that science is destroying the faith of the people in things spiritual.

Anyone who will search for the science in religion and the religion in science will find that they harmonize and prove each other. The point of unity is the Spirit-mind common to both. So long as religion assumes that the Spirit that creates and sustains man and the universe can be cajoled and by prayer or some other appeal can be induced to change its laws, it cannot hope to be recognized by those who know that unchangeable law rules everywhere and in everything.

Again, so long as science ignores the principle of intelligence in the evolutionary and directive forces of man and the universe, just so long will it fail to understand religion and the power of thought in the changes that are constantly taking place in the world, visible and invisible.

Chapter XI - The Only Mind

I SAY, *"An idea comes to me."* Where did it come from? It must have had a source of like character with its own. Ideas are not visible to the eye, they are not heard by the ear, nor felt, nor tasted, yet we talk about them as having existence. We recognize that they live, move, and have being in the realm that we term mind.

This realm of mind is accepted by everybody as in some way connected with the things that appear, but because it is not describable in terms of length, breadth, and thickness, it is usually passed over as something too vague for consideration.

But those who take up the study of this thing called mind find that it can be analyzed and its laws and modes of operation understood.

To be ignorant of mind and its laws is to be a child playing with fire, or a man manipulating powerful chemicals without knowing their relation to one another. This is universally true; and all who are not learning about mind are in like danger, because all are dealing with the great cause from which spring forth all the conditions that appear in the lives of all men and women. Mind is the one reservoir from which we draw all that we make up into our world, and it is through the laws of mind that we form our lives. Hence nothing is as important as a knowledge of mind, its inherencies, and the mode of their expression.

The belief that mind cannot be understood is fallacious. Man is the expression of mind, dwells in mind, and can know more clearly and definitely about mind than about the things that appear in the phenomenal world.

It is only from the plane of mind that one can know Truth in an absolute sense. That which we pronounce truth from the plane of appearances is relative only. The relative truth is constantly changing, but the absolute Truth endures; and what is true today always was and always will be true.

It does not require scholastic culture to understand mind. Persons who do not even know how to read or write may be very adept in the realm of pure mind. It does not follow that he who talks most fluently about mind knows the most. He may theoretically perceive the underlying principles without realizing their working factors in his own being.

Mind is not language; mind is not formulation. These are outgrowths of mind; they are man's way of communicating to his fellow man the concepts of his mind. Thus very simple persons, from the world's standpoint, frequently know a great deal about mind and its operation that they are unable to express in language.

Women as a rule know more about pure mind on its own plane than men, because they trust that inner faculty of pure knowing called intuition more fully than men. The medically wise of the world today cannot comprehend how a quiet little person who knows nothing about physiology or medication can sit down beside their dying patients and bring them back to health without apparently doing anything. And they never will know until they delve behind a knowledge of externality and learn mind to mind the workings of Spirit.

Some persons confound the realm of knowledge about things formulated through the intellect with pure knowledge. Intellect and its plane of activity are not pure mind as the realm of matter is not Spirit.

The same essences of being enter into both, but wisdom is sadly lacking in the intellectual realm. Intellect has formulated its conclusions from the sense side of existence instead of from the spiritual side, and these two sides are divergent.

No one can know about the potentialities of mind and how they are manifested except through a study of mind itself without any reference whatever to things or their relations. One may logically deduce a system of being from abstract intellectual reasoning, but it will lack the living fire that accompanies pure mind.

Those who study mind know the same things; and though they be dumb, they enjoy the communion that ever goes on in thought. No one should for a moment imagine that because he lacks the technical education of the world that he is therefore not fitted to study the science of mind. No matter how ignorant you may be of the world's ways or God's ways, if you will give your mind to the attention of the one Mind, you will in due season become wise. This great law of mind and Mind recognizing each other and flowing together in unbroken wisdom has been known in all ages and among all peoples. The scribes and Pharisees who knew the life and lack of scholastic advantages of Jesus, the carpenter's son, exclaimed in amazement, "How knoweth this man letters, having never learned?"

Mind is the great storehouse of good from which man draws all his supplies. If you manifest life, you are confident that it had a source. If you show forth intelligence you know that somewhere in the economy of Being there is a fount of intelligence. So you may go over the elements that go to make up your being and you will find that they draw their sustenance from an invisible and, to your limited understanding, incomprehensible source.

This source we term Mind, because it is as such that our comprehension is best related to it. Names are arbitrary, and we should not stop to note differences that are merely technical. We want to get at the substance which they represent.

So if we call this invisible source Mind it is because it is of like character with the thing within our consciousness that we call our mind. Mind is manyfold in its manifestations. It produces all that appears. Not that the character of all that appears is to be laid to the volition of Mind; no, but some of its factors enter into everything that appears. This is why it is so important to know about Mind, and how its potentialities are made manifest.

So we know that that which we term Mind is the reservoir of the universe and man and that in it is stored up all that we may desire. So it behooves us to study this great reservoir and learn its laws. We call it Mind because through our study it has disclosed to us a quality that is not apprehended by those who study it in its phenomenal aspect. The physical scientist tells us that there is a universal energy in which all motion, light, heat, color, and the like, have their origin.

We claim that what they have discovered is the power side of God and that there is another factor that they have not discovered but that is associated with the universal energy. That factor is divine wisdom. They admit that there is evidence of design in the varied and beautiful manifestation of this universal energy, but they are at a loss for a way to make the acquaintance of the designer. To know this designer and manipulator of the substance and energy of the universe is what our system of mind development teaches. It instructs you how to acquaint yourself with the qualities of Mind and through them to seize upon the substance and life of the universe and bring them into harmonious relations in your body and affairs. This is something that few learned physical scientists have attempted, and here is a field of discovery upon which few have yet launched forth. In fact but few of the materialistic school have ever caught the first ray of this light. They have, it is true, longed to know more about the wisdom of the Creator, but it does not seem to have dawned upon them that the wisdom of God is just as much present everywhere as energy and substance. By all the methods known to their science they have tested the many elements of the formed and formless earth and air and noted the methodical and orderly workings of each under certain conditions. They speak of molecular attraction, repulsion, polarity, and the like. Some have said that every atom of matter is apparently intelligent; but as these atoms do not speak their particular language, they have taken for granted that they could not hold converse with them on the plane of mind.

This is where we have set up a study that makes of every atom in the universe a living center of wisdom as well as life and substance.

We claim that on its plane of comprehension man may ask the atom or the mountain the secret that it holds and it will be revealed to him. This is the communication of mind with Mind; hence we call Mind the universal underlying cause of existence and study it from that basis.

God is Mind, and man made in the image and likeness of God is Mind, because there is but one Mind, and that the Mind of God. The person in sense consciousness thinks he has a mind of his own and that he creates thought from its own inherent substance. This is a suppositional mind that passes away when the one and only real Mind is revealed. This one and only Mind of God that we study is the only creator. It is that which originates all that is permanent; hence it is the source of all reality. Its creations are of a character hard for the sense man to comprehend, because his consciousness is cast in a mold of space and time. These are changeable and transient, while the creations of the one Mind are substantial and lasting. But it is man's privilege to understand the creations of the one Mind, for it is through them that he makes his world. The creations of the one Mind are ideas. The ideas of God are potential forces waiting to be set in motion through proper formative vehicles. The thinking faculty in man is such a vehicle, and it is through this that the visible universe has existence. Man does not "create" anything if by this term is meant the producing of something from nothing; but he does make the formless up into form; or rather it is through his conscious co-operation that the one Mind forms its universe. Hence the importance of man's willing co-operation with God in every thought, because unless he is very wise in his thinking, he may be sending forth malformations that will cause both himself and the universe trouble.

Thinking is a process in mind by and through which the abstract is made concrete. It is the process of working up into things those ideas in the one Mind which are not things. God does not see things nor conditions as man sees them, except through the thinking faculty in man (represented by man in the Godhead).

The ideas of Divine Mind are whole and complete in their capacity to unfold perpetually greater and more beautiful forms according to the thinking capacity in man. Man catches mental sight of an idea in Divine Mind and proceeds to put it in terms comprehensible to him on his plane of consciousness. All ideas have their origin in Divine Mind, but their character as unfolded by man depends entirely upon his acquaintance with God. The idea of a house as formulated by man varies all the way from a wigwam to the most magnificent castle. The original idea of a house, as it exists in God's mind, cannot be anything less than the perfected consciousness of man, of which his body is a symbol. This is the temple "not made with hands," and it is the only temple acceptable to God.

No man can acceptably serve God or do His will until he understands the fundamental principles of thinking and how thoughts are made manifest as forms or states of consciousness. This is revealed by the Father to everyone who seeks to know His law and to follow it. When man has thus sought the Father with an eye single to His guidance, he begins to know that certain relations exist between him and the Father and that only through a maintenance of those relations can he come into harmony with God and do His will.

The idea of the man separated in consciousness from Divine Mind is that he was arbitrarily created by God, who could have chosen or not chosen to create him, and that not being responsible for his existence, man has a perfect right to be rebellious and petulant if hardships come into his life. This is a childish view of the great plan of creation, in which man is such an important factor. It is only when man becomes meek and lowly, an obedient receptacle for the Spirit of God, that he sees the divine plan of creation and his place in it. Then he becomes a willing co-operator, because his understanding accepts the law as it is and knows that it cannot be changed by either God or man. They are so intimately linked together that the harmony of existence depends upon their mutual understanding. When this is established by man's willing obedience and acceptance of his part of the work, a new order of things is set up and a new creation inaugurated. The first step in this new order is the realization by man that he is in the world to do a specific work. As Jesus said at the age of twelve, "Knew ye not that I must be in my Father's house?" and in His last prayer are these words, "I glorified thee on the earth, having accomplished the work which thou hast given me to do."

The Father has sent each one of us out to do a certain work. Are we doing that work? Have we asked what it is? Or are we aimlessly wandering about the earth trying to find satisfaction in the fleeting things of sense?

"Ye shall know the truth, and the truth shall make you free."

This truth is that of the relation of man to God and of how creation is carried forward. The God-man relation is in one sense like that of father and child; in another sense it is like that of creator-creative instrument and creation manifest. Man constitutes the instrument of God through which He brings his potentialities into visibility. As such an instrument man is in a measure a dictator as to how it shall be done. That is, man has discretionary power or free will. Freedom of will is illusionary however because if man wills to carry on creation in defiance of the divine plan and order, his creations in due time fall into chaos through lack of coherency. God fixes the plan of the structure and gives into the hands of man all the materials for building. Man may also know the plan and build according to it, or he may go ahead without consulting the plan. Humanity has built age after age only to find that its structures do not endure. They are faulty because the divine plan has not been consulted by the builder.

Mind is the storehouse of ideas. Man draws all his ideas from this omnipresent storehouse. The ideas of God, heaven, hell, devils, angels, and all things have their clue in Mind. But their form in the consciousness depends entirely upon the plane from which man draws his mental images. If he gets a "clue" to the character of God and then proceeds to clothe this clue idea with images from without, he makes God a mortal. If he looks within for the clothing of his clue idea he knows God to be the omnipresent Spirit of existence.

If man gets the clue idea from heaven and hell and devils and angels and looks without for clothing for his idea, he makes a locality in the skies and calls it heaven, and another under the earth and calls it hell. But if he goes to the Father for information he finds both heaven and hell within his own consciousness, both the result of his own thought.

So it is of the utmost importance that we know how we have produced this state of existence which we call life; and we should be swift to conform to the only method calculated to bring harmony and success into our life, namely to think in harmony with the understanding derived from communion with the God-Mind.

Chapter XII - Contact with the Christ Mind

WE MAY TAKE it for granted on the basis of many Scripture passages that all of us who accept God as an associate in life are consciously in intimate contact with the Holy Spirit. However it will strengthen our faith and greatly add to the effectiveness of the Holy Spirit in its work with us if we understand its character and the law under which it co-operates with us in the development of mind, body, and affairs.

Theologians differ in their conceptions of the Holy Spirit. Some define it as a principle, but the majority refer to itas "He"; that is, as the third person of the Trinity. In the Scriptures it is named variously. In Genesis 1:2 it is spoken of as "the Spirit of God" moving upon the face of the waters. We read in Job 33:4:

"The Spirit of God hath made me, And the breath of the Almighty giveth me life."

Bible authorities (Scofield, for example) say that wherever the name El Shaddai occurs in the Hebrew Scriptures it should have been translated "Nourisher" or "Strength-giver," which in Hebrew is the feminine name for God. This verse may be read:

"The Spirit of God hath made me,And the breath of the mother giveth me life."

In Psalms 104:30 it is written, "Thou sendest forth thy Spirit." The Spirit is omnipresent, as revealed in the 139th Psalm:

"Whither shall I go from thy Spirit?
Or whither shall I flee from thy presence?"

Read all this psalm for a comprehension of the universality of the Holy Spirit's work in the creation of man and his evolution. The Holy Spirit in Divine Mind corresponds to our thought in our minds. God is Mind; God's idea of His creation is His Son, and this Son (idea), executing the plans of God (the original Mind) corresponds to our thinking in its work of devising plans. We may ideate without restriction, but when we come to the execution of our ideas we have to respect certain laws, which we sometimes consider restrictions. So we can ideate the unlimited Divine Mind, but when this Mind is brought into our world or consciousness it is limited to our conception of it.

With a clear understanding of the relation that ideas bear to their manifestation, we can approach God with confidence; then we have access to the real, unlimited creative ideas, and we co-operate with the Holy Spirit and get greater results. We can thus lay hold of a healing or a prosperity thought and confidently affirm that in mind we are quickened and made whole; that we are prospered, and that we are successful in all our ways, because we are working with and through the whole Spirit of God the Holy Spirit of wisdom and love.

In Matthew Jesus asked the Pharisees, "What think ye of the Christ? whose son is he? They say unto him, The son of David. He saith unto them, How then doth David in the Spirit call him Lord, saying,

"The Lord said unto my Lord,
Sit thou on my right hand,
Till I put thine enemies underneath thy feet?"

"If David then calleth him Lord, how is he his son?"

This lesson, which Jesus gave to His disciples, brings out clearly the relation that the universal or Jehovah-Mind bears to the personal or Christ Mind. This also suggests that David was not the forebear of Christ, but that the Lord or Christ of David existed before the human person was born. It follows that the Christ in Jesus existed before the personality. This is true of all of us. Christ is the spiritual mind in every individual, and the spiritual mind is the offspring of the universal or Jehovah-Mind.

When Paul said, "Until Christ be formed in you," he referred to the development in man of the super-mind.

All the divine perfection that exists in the universal Jehovah-Mind can be brought into direct contact with its image and likeness, the Christ, imprinted in the beginning in each individual.

As he develops spiritually man releases, rounds out, and fully expresses that divine perfection which is potentially in his soul.

The affirmation of any good statement of health puts us in conscious contact with the Christ Mind universal and quickens and releases the energy stored up in the subconscious mind, and the process of rejuvenation begins its work. This renewal of man's youth through the recognition of Jehovah confirms Psalm 103:

> Bless Jehovah, Oh my soul;
> And all that is with me, bless his holy name
> Bless Jehovah, Oh my soul,
> And forget not all his benefits:
> Who forgiveth all thine iniquities;
> Who healeth all thy diseases;
> Who redeemeth thy life from destruction;
> Who crowneth thee with lovingkindness
> and tender mercies;
> Who satisfieth thy desire with good things,
> So that thy youth is renewed like the eagle.

All those who in faith have persistently applied this law of spiritual acknowledgment of the Christ have received benefits that bear witness to the fact that man can overcome sin, sickness, and old age and rise out of the race belief in human limitation, and finally attain eternal life as Jesus attained it.

Jesus warned us not to lay up treasure in a material way but to be "rich toward God," as taught in the 12th chapter of Luke. Jesus was rich toward God in that He knew how to release the creative substance implanted in Him from the beginning. This same substance is within every one of us; when released, it makes contact with the universal substance, and invisible currents of supply begin to carry their riches to us. It is not necessary that we understand scientifically all the activities of the pent-up substance in our minds, although we shall eventually understand every step of the way.

A simple word of blessing poured out upon that which we have or that which we can conceive as possible for us as sons of the all-providing God will at least begin to release the superabundance of Spirit substance, and we shall have an inner confidence and faith in the providence of our Father.

Jesus warned us not to be anxious about temporal needs but to pray, believing, and to bless and give thanks; then right in the face of seeming insufficiency we should be enabled to demonstrate plenty. Jesus illustrated this when He showed how giving thanks in a devout consciousness for this inner substance would multiply the apparently insignificant resources (the five loaves and two fishes) until they became sufficient to meet the hunger of more than five thousand persons.

A textbook on the redemption or reconstruction of man should cover every phase of human character. Human egotism should be repressed; man's spiritual identity exalted. Remedies for the greatest evils of humanity should be given plentifully, and the lesser evils minimized.

Our Scriptures, plus the guidance of "the Spirit of truth" recommended by Jesus, form such a textbook for Christians. In this combination is found instruction fitted to the needs of the multitude. The timid and fearful read, "Have not I commanded thee? Be strong and of good courage; be not affrighted, neither be thou dismayed: for Jehovah thy God is with thee whithersoever thou goest."

How an inflated personal ego usurps and finally destroys the spirituality of one who once was anointed king of Israel is illustrated in the life of Saul. The stimulation of the spiritual ego is forcefully taught and demonstrated by prophets and great religious leaders. It is written in the Psalms:

> "I said, Ye are gods,
> And all of you are sons of the Most High."
> Jesus reiterated this and was denounced by the Pharisees because He declared, "I and the Father are one."

Christian metaphysicians have discovered that man can greatly accelerate the growth in himself of the Christ Mind by using affirmations that identify him with the Christ. These affirmations often are so far beyond the present attainment of the novice as to seem ridiculous, but when it is understood that the statements are grouped about an ideal to be attained, they seem fair and reasonable.

The spiritual man is clothed by the aspirations, the thoughts, and the acts of the natural or physical man. It is here, in this realm of so-called matter, that character is formed. By faith, prayer, meditation, and inward resolutions man identifies himself with the spiritual man and forms in both mind and body the things affirmed. There was no visible evidence of Jesus' unity with the Father when He affirmed, "I and the Father are one." His disciples said, "Lord, show us the Father, and it sufficeth us." So we find that we must be true to our ideas, and clothe them with an assumption of their tangibility even before they have appeared. We must pray, believing that we have received and we shall receive.

States of mind established in the consciousness gather to themselves vitamins, cells, nerves, muscles, the flesh itself. To see oneself in mind spiritually courageous, strong, and healthy will instill health in the primal elements of the organism, which in due season will work to the surface in a perfect body.

We must all learn to look to the mental man for causes. For example, no one but a metaphysician knows the origin of disease germs. The physician takes it for granted that disease germs exist as an integral part of the natural world; the metaphysician sees disease germs as the manifested results of anger, revenge, jealousy, fear, impurity, and many other mind activities. A change of mind will change the character of a germ. Love, courage, peace, strength, and good will form good character and build bodily structures of a nature like these qualities of mind.

The same general law is carried out in everything with which man has to do. Financial success or failure depends on the attitude of mind active in both those who achieve success and those who fall under the negations of failure. To attain prosperity, think about prosperity, industry, and efficiency. Fill your mind to overflowing with thoughts of success; realize that the fullness of all good belongs to you by divine right. To this add a feeling of happiness and joy and you have the recipe for abundant and lasting prosperity.

Chapter XIII - Metaphysics of Shakespeare

IN DISCUSSIONS of Shakespeare and his plays we hear little about what may be termed the by-products of the great dramatist's mind; for usually the dramatic incidents of the plays occupy the attention of the reader to the exclusion of the more subtle threads of philosophy and soul culture. Shakespeare was a great teacher, and his mind grasped the salient issues in the practical world in which he lived and often forged away ahead into realms that modern research and discovery pronounce miraculous.

Psychological insight is essential in discerning the spiritual wisdom of Shakespeare. The intellectual reader will miss entirely the references to a supermind that crop out in all his dramas. Bible readers know that spiritual things are spiritually discerned. This is also strikingly true of Shakespeare's works.

In the fantasy "Midsummer Night's Dream" Shakespeare tells how the imagination gives to airy nothings a local habitation and a name:

I never may believe
These antique fables, nor these fairy toys.
Lovers and madmen have such seething brains,
Such shaping fantasies, that apprehend
More than cool reason ever comprehends.
The lunatic, the lover, and the poet
Sees Helen's beauty in a brow of Egypt:
The poet's eye, in fine frenzy rolling,
Doth glance from heaven to earth,
from earth to heaven;
And as imagination bodies forth
The forms of things unknown, the poet's pen
Turns them to shapes, and gives to airy nothing
A local habitation and a name.
Such tricks hath strong imagination,
That, if it would but apprehend some joy,
It comprehends some bringer of that joy;
Or in the night, imagining some fear,
How easy is a bush supposed a bear!

In his infancy Shakespeare was baptized in the church, but his little-known history does not testify to his devotion. However his writings betray a very deep spiritual understanding. Neither was he a mystic. The fine understanding of psychology displayed by many of the Shakespearean characters must have been gained by soul development attained by the author in previous incarnations.

We should look for the antecedents of Shakespeare among the early church fathers, where the spiritual man was quickened and the culture of the soul given supreme attention. There is no record that he was taught in any schools except those of the village of Stratford, where he was born. Because of this many have asked, "Where has this man gained wisdom?"

The intellectuals have carried this lack of academic background and evidence of great supermind ability so far that they have assumed that some other person, notably Lord Bacon, is the author of Shakespeare's plays. The claim rests on very flimsy proofs and is not at all accepted by those who discern the capacity of the soul to attain understanding and carry it forward from one incarnation to another.

The claim that Shakespeare was not a scholar must be admitted. He made numerous errors of which a scholar would not be guilty. But Shakespeare was a genius of the people, not a pedant. He forged his way beyond the boundaries of the cultured intellect into the realms of fantasy and mysticism, and gave "local habitation and a name" to "airy nothing." Let us be thankful that Shakespeare was not a scholar.

Shakespeare portrayed every form of human character hundreds of years before there was such a thing as psychoanalysis, and psychologists today find in him and the puppets of his brain their most prolific examples of the subtleties of the mind.

Shakespeare did not write about himself, and we have no worldly knowledge of how such an apparently unlettered man could gain such command of language and such familiarity with men and nature. Like Jesus, he knew what was in man. Such discernment comes only with ages of experience, and we are safe in asserting that Shakespeare was a very old soul and that he inherited from previous lives a culture that made him a mastermind. We all have an untapped mind of knowledge in our subconscious mind, and it requires a mastermind to uncover it. Inspiration and rediscovery are the positive and negative poles of the mind. Shakespeare's writings indicate that he drew upon both these sources and concentrated the product in thought of the highest nobility coupled in the same scenes with shocking vulgarity. Shakespeare wrote down both what he got from the memories below and from the heavens above. Many persons whose normal thoughts are pure as snow are often shocked and puzzled at their incongruous and sometimes lascivious dreams. A maturer development will reveal that the I AM has taken advantage of the sleeping conscious mind and renewed associations with things sealed up in the depths of the subconscious mind.

That Shakespeare was familiar with a world beyond the grasp of the sense is quite evident from the words he puts into the mouths of his players. His statements about dreams, visions, witches, and prophecies, and various other references to the unseen world show that he had faith and sight above the ordinary dweller in sense.

In the play "Julius Caesar" Calpurnia, wife of Caesar, has a dream warning her of the impending danger to her husband, and she begs him not to go to the senate on the fateful day. His friends urge him to go, and he explains his reason for wanting to stay at home.

Calpurnia here, my wife, stays me at home:
She dreampt to-night she saw my statue,
Which like a foundation with an hundred spouts,
Did run pure blood, and many lusty Romans
Came smiling and did bathe their hands in it:
And these does she
apply for warningsand portents
And evils imminent, and on her knee
Hath begged that I will stay at home to-day.

Decius argues that the dream has been misinterpreted. He says:

It was a vision fair and fortunate:
Your statue spouting blood in many pipes,
In which so many smiling Romans bathed,
Signifies that from you great Rome shall suck
Reviving blood, and that great men shall press
For tinctures, stains, relics, and cognizance.

Here Shakespeare reveals an acquaintance with both the literal and the allegorical meaning of dreams. Modern metaphysicians have discovered by experience that the interpretation of dreams requires the finest kind of discrimination. Some dreams are cast in the phenomenal and are given for enlightenment of the dreamer about outer events, while others are parables. Calpurnia has the discerning mind, and in the same context remarks,

There is one within
Besides the things that we have heard and seen.

The developing soul meets many situations in mind that require superior wisdom to handle. Helps of a limited character may be had from without, but the final and only safe guide is the Spirit within. The breadth and depth of Shakespeare's mind proves that he had in many lives cultivated the habit of drawing upon the fount of all wisdom within his own soul.

Spiritualists claim that spirit guidance was discovered by the Fox sisters in Hydesville, New York, less than a century ago, yet we find it portrayed in a dozen of Shakespeare's plays. Hamlet is infuriated by the graphic description by his father's ghost of his murder by the king, Hamlet's uncle. He prefaces the gruesome details with the often quoted prelude:

> I could a tale unfold whose lightest word
> Would harrow up thy soul, freeze thy young blood,
> Make thy two eyes, like stars,
> start from their spheres,
> Thy knotted and combined locks to part
> And each particular hair to stand on end,
> Like quills upon the fretful porpentine.

That Shakespeare has a certain knowledge of the status of those who have left the body is evidenced by the regrets of the ghost of Hamlet's father at his untimely violent demise.

Of life, of crown, of queen, at once dispatched:

> Cut off even in the blossoms of my sin,
> Unhousel'd, disappointed, unaneled;
> No reckoning made, but sent to my account
> With all my imperfections on my head.

That departed ones continue to live in a realm very near to that in which we live Shakespeare accepted as a matter of course. He makes them a vital part of so many scenes that we cannot help concluding that their existence to him was not open to question. The only place where there is any doubt suggested is in Act III, Scene 3, of "The Winter's Tale," in which Antigonus says:

> I have heard, but not believed, the spirits
> o' the dead
> May walk again: if such thing be, thy mother
> Appeared to me last night, for ne'er was dream
> So like a waking.

Then follows a vivid description of the mother, who "in pure white robes . . . thrice bowed before me."

Although spiritualism is not accepted by metaphysical Christians in the terms in which it is presented by its exclusive followers, it is a question of psychology and must be explained by those who teach Truth. Shakespeare did not teach religion but the facts of life as he saw them. The continuous existence of man after death of the body is one of the facts of man's spiritual life and should be so recognized and its place defined in psychology. Religion is concerned primarily with spiritual things, the psychical world is secondary.

Although he may not have applied the law of spiritual healing to himself he saw the possibility, and in many forceful phrases and subtle inferences he exalted the inherent power of man. Although Macbeth was cast in the role of a man of desperate and unsatisfied ambition, Shakespeare put into his mouth a proclamation any man can make and be strengthened by:

> The mind I sway by and the heart I bear
> Shall never sag with doubt nor shake with fear.

Shakespeare saw what was coming in true healing; that is, the restoration of the mind through right thinking. On this point he says:

Canst thou not minister to a mind diseased,
Pluck from the memory a rooted sorrow,
Raze out the written troubles of the brain,
And with some sweet oblivious antidote
Cleanse the stuff'd bosom of that perilous stuff
Which weighs upon the heart?

Shakespeare was familiar with all the superstitions of his age. His characters are witches, seers, soothsayers, astrologers; he shows familiarity with forces that in our day are considered occult and spooky. They believed in signs and omens, the control of men by the sun, moon, and stars--astrology. Yet the fallacy of such concepts of mortality was usually pointed out. In "King Lear" Edmund is made to say:

This is the excellent foppery of the world, that when we are sick in fortune--often the surfeit of our own behavior--we make guilty of our disasters the sun, the moonand the stars: as if we were villains by necessity, fools by heavenly compulsion; knaves, thieves, and treachers, by spherical predominance; drunkards, liars and adulterers, by an enforc'd obedience of planetary influence; and allthat we are evil in, by a divine thrusting on: an admirableevasion of whoremaster man, to lay his goatish dispositionto the change of a star.

In "Julius Caesar," where Brutus and Cassius are discussing the dominance of Caesar, Cassius says:

Ye gods! it doth amaze me
A man of such feeble temper should
So get the start of the majestic world
And bear the palm alone. . . .
Why, man, he doth bestride the narrow world
Like a Colossus, and we petty men
Walk under his huge legs and peep about
To find ourselves dishonorable graves.
Men at some time are masters of their fates:
The fault, dear Brutus, is not in our stars,
But in ourselves, that we are underlings.

The oft-discussed metaphysical question of the origin of evil and the source of good is settled in a concise statement by Hamlet:

"There is nothing either good or bad, but thinking makes it so."

Many years ago the London Times announced a contest to test the value that the English people placed on Shakespeare. The subject voted on was, in substance, What do you consider of the greatest value to Great Britain, Shakespeare or the Empire of India? Shakespeare won!

People the world over will readily concur in this estimateof the mind supreme in Shakespeare. He was "not for a season, but for all time." He excelled as a dramatist, but as we have shown by these few extracts, he was also a metaphysician, a prophet, and a poet. The plots of his many plays are largely adaptations from other authors, but their glorification by Shakespeare's genius transformed them and may be likened to the glorification of the natural man by the genius of Jesus. For example, Pythagoras taught that the universe was harmonized in a masterful symphony, with suns, stars, and planets as notes on the staff supreme. Shakespeare evidently got from this his cue for the exquisite lines uttered by Lorenzo:

How sweet the moonlight sleeps upon this bank!
Here we will sit, and let the sounds of music
Creep in our ears: soft stillness and the night
Become the touches of sweet harmony.
Sit, Jessica. Look how the floor of heaven
Is thick inlaid with patines of bright gold:

There's not the smallest orb which thou behold'st
But in his motion like an angel sings,
Still quiring to the young-eyed cherubins;
Such harmony is in immortal souls;
But whilst this muddy vesture of decay
Doth grossly close it in, we cannot hear it.

Chapter XIV - The Body

A GREAT DEAL is said in the Bible about man's body. In fact, the Bible is a mystical record of the various bodies in which the souls of men have lived. Bodies show the different states of mind of those who inhabit them, ranging all the way from the Adam embodiment and environment up to the Christ body and its freedom from environment. It is fair to say that the Bible is the allegorical record of man under many aliases, in many bodies.

In all the history of man he has appeared under all sorts of masks, which he has called his bodies, ranging from a corrupt and distorted body up to the "glorious body" of Christ.

The resurrection of the body is the paramount theme of the New Testament and in fact the all-embracing yet veiled subject of the entire Bible. Immortality has been the engrossing subject of man's thought since the record of the race began. Passage after passage might be cited from the Bible illustrating what man's body potentially is and how it should be controlled and governed so as to gain for its possessor the greatest amount of harmony in life.

Now, mark you, man is not solely his body, for man is more than body, but without a body there could be no visible man. Yet the body is not man, but man will forever possess a body. If the body is not man and man could not be without a body, and since the body is constantly changing, what is man?

You see at once that man is not body, but that the body is the declaration of man, the substantial expression of his mind. We see so many different types of men that we are bound to admit that the body is merely the individual's specific interpretation of himself, whatever it may be. Man is an unknown quantity; we see merely the various ideas of man expressed in terms of body, but not man himself. The identification of man is determined by the individual himself, and he expresses his conception of man in his body.

Some persons have tall bodies; some have short ones. Some have fat bodies; some have slim ones. Some have distorted bodies, some have symmetrical ones. Now, if the body is the man, as claimed by sense consciousness, which of these many bodies is man?

The Bible declares that man is made in the "image" and after the "likeness" of God. Which of the various bodies just enumerated is the image and likeness of God?

The New Testament maintains that man's body is the dwelling place of the Spirit of God: "Know ye not that your body is a temple of the Holy Spirit which is in you? . . . glorify God therefore in your body." Yet it is written that the Man of Galilee casts devils out of this temple of God. How could devils infest the temple of God?

Some persons contend that man's body is corrupt from birth, and others affirm that it is the glorious masterpiece of God.

We find however that those who say that they despise the body are loath to part with it, for the reason that they cannot adequately conceive of man without a body, and it is better to have some kind of a body than to run the risk of not having any. The body that these persons possess is their only means of identifying themselves. They do not fancy the idea of risking another, and possibly a worse body, so they hold onto the one they have as long as they are able, regardless of its frailties. The chances of getting a new body seem so uncertain that we all strive to keep the one we have.

Let us repeat that the body of man is the visible record of his thoughts. It is the individual's interpretation of his identity, and each individual shows in his body just what his views of man are. The body is the corporeal record of the mind of its owner, and there is no limit to its infinite differentiation. The individual may become any type of being that he elects to be. Man selects the mental model and the body images it. So the body is the image and likeness of the individual's idea of man. We may embody any conception of life or being that we can conceive. The body is the exact reproduction of the thoughts of its occupant. As a man thinks in his mind so is his body.

You can be an Adam if you choose, or you can be a Christ or any other type of being that you see fit to ideate. The choice lies with you. The body merely executes the mandates of the mind.

The mind dictates the model according to which the body shall be manifested. Therefore as man "thinketh within himself [in his vital nature], so is he." Each individual is just what he believes he is.

It is safe to say that nine hundred and ninety-nine persons out of every thousand believe that the resurrection of the body has something specifically to do with the getting of a new body after death; so we find more than ninety-nine per cent of the world's population waiting for death to get something new in the way of a body. This belief is not based on the principles of Truth, for there is no ready-made-body factory in the universe, and thus none will get the body that he expects. Waiting for death in order to get a new body is the folly of ignorance. The thing to do is to improve the bodies that we now have; it can be done, and those who would follow Jesus in the regeneration must do it.

The "resurrection" of the body has nothing whatever to do with death, except that we may resurrect ourselves from every dead condition into which sense ignorance has plunged us. To be resurrected means to get out of the place that you are in and to get into another place. Resurrection is a rising into new vigor, new prosperity; a restoration to some higher state. It is absurd to suppose that it applies only to the resuscitation of a dead body.

Paul hints at a time when the body will be changed, and he says it is when "death is swallowed up in victory." Here are Paul's words: "When this corruptible shall have put on incorruption, and this mortal shall have put on immortality . . . Death is swallowed up in victory."

This transformation is worked out by the individual himself, and is not the result of physical death but rather of the death or annihilation of the erroneous beliefs that ignorance has stored in the cells of the body. It is first a mental resurrection, followed by a body demonstration.

It is the privilege of the individual to express any type of body that he sees fit to ideate. Man may become a Christ in mind and in body by incorporating into his every thought the ideas given to the world by Jesus.

"But we all, with unveiled face beholding as in a mirror the glory of the Lord, are transformed into the same image from glory to glory, even as from the Lord the Spirit."

Divine mind has placed in the mind of everyone an image of the perfect-man body. The imaging process in the mind may well be illustrated by the picture that is made by light on the photographic plate, which must be "developed" before it becomes visible. Or man's invisible body may be compared to the blueprint of a building that the architect delivers to the builder. Man is a builder of flesh and blood. Jesus was a carpenter. Also He was indeed the master mason. He restored the Lord's body ("the temple of Jehovah") in His mind and heart (in Jerusalem).

When we call ourselves fleshly, mortal, finite, we manifest it bodily upon a fleshly, mortal, and finite plane. We sow to the flesh and of the flesh reap corruption. The time has arrived for the whole human family to repudiate the estimate of man as corrupt and instead to think of him as he was designed by creative Mind. "This corruptible must put on incorruption, and this mortal must put on immortality," said Paul.

We must stop calling the body flesh and blood, and see it as it is in Spirit-mind, pure and incorruptible. This realization of man's perfect body will arrest decay, disintegration, and death.

We must rise above material thoughts into spiritual realization, and live, move, and have our being in a divine reality. When our views of man are elevated to spiritual understanding, we shall begin to express bodily perfection. Our thoughts must be perfect before we can expect to manifest perfection in body. The issues of life are within man; the body is merely the record of the mind of the individual.

Jesus demonstrated for us the highest type of embodiment. He brought His body under the mastery of His mind. He said, "I have power to lay it down, and I have power to take it again." What Jesus did we all can do, and it is fair to say that His is the normal standard for every individual and that every other expression of life is abnormal, the result of insufficient Christ elements. Paul says, as quoted, "Ye are the body of Christ," and he says this to emphasize the fact that Christ is the one true pattern for man and that each of us should achieve the fulfillment of the divine design. "Let us make man in our image, after our likeness."

Jesus was the only man who ever proclaimed with authority, "He that hath seen me hath seen the Father." Jesus was the divine oracle; His mind was unified with the universal Mind principle; this same principle obtains in a degree today in those who identify themselves with Spirit instead of with the flesh. We need not "look . . . for another" in whom to witness the Christ, as did John the Baptist, but we must look for Christ in ourselves, precisely as the man Jesus found the Christ in Himself.

The statement "Ye are the body of Christ" promises the possibility of a universal incarnation of the Christ and does not in any sense narrow it down to one single individual.

Again Paul's words "Glorify God . . . in your body" proclaim the fact that the God nature may become manifest in every individual. What is the chief object of man? To glorify God in his body; this is the true answer. Have the courage to make the heroic attempt to give personal expression to God. And how shall we do this? By mentally agreeing that we are potentially the Christ and capable of making a divine presentation of ourselves to the Father. We must rise to the conscious realization that every thought of mind, every atom of body, every molecule of being, every function of nature, and every force is divine, and that all of these do and shall vibrate to the harmonies of Spirit. This is the resurrection of man; there is none other.

By so doing we establish our ego, our I AM identity with Divine Mind, and enter with Jesus into joint heirship to the heavenly inheritance of power, peace, prosperity, and perfection.

All the so-called human or earthly spheres of operation are reflections of the divine, and by considering them we may gain an intellectual concept of spiritual realities, but we should ever remember that spiritual things are "spiritually judged." By this higher renewal of the mind we shall be bodily transformed, and prove those things that are good, perfect, and true.

The resurrection of the body is not dependent for its demonstration on time, evolution, or any of the man-made means of growth. It is the result of the elevation of the spiritually emancipated mind of the individual.

Step by step, thought added to thought, spiritual emotion added to spiritual emotion--eventually the transformation is complete. It does not come in a day, but every high impulse, every pure thought, every upward desire adds to the exaltation and gradual personification of the divine in man and to the transformation of the human. The "old man" is constantly brought into subjection, and his deeds forever put off, as the "new man" appears arrayed in the vestments of divine consciousness.

All have hope and find deep consolation, aye, assurance in the belief of the final redemption of the body; and this universal feeling is born of the legitimacy of the faith that this redemption must eventuate, that perfection is the ultimate goal of man's being, and that death and separation must disappear from human experience.

How to accomplish the resurrection of the body has been the great stumbling block of man. The resurrection has been a mere hope, and we have endeavored to reconcile a dying body with a living God, but have not succeeded. No amount of Christian submission or stoical philosophy will take away the sting of death. But over him who is risen in Christ "death no more hath dominion."

Chapter XV - Faith Precipatations

WHEN ASKED what electricity is, a scientist replied that he had often thought of it as an adjunct to faith, judging from the way it acts.

This linking of faith and electricity seems at first glance fantastic, but when we observe what takes place when certain substances in solution and an electric current are brought in conjunction, there seems to be a confirmation of the Scripture passage: "Now faith is assurance of things hoped for."

Just as the electric current precipitates certain metals in solution in acid, so faith stirs into action the electrons of man's brain; and acting concurrently with the spiritual ethers, these electrons hasten nature and produce quickly what ordinarily requires months of seedtime and harvest.

The widow, in the time of Elisha, was so distressed with debt that she had even mortgaged to slavery her two children. She appealed to the prophet, who said, "What hast thou in the house?" She replied, "Thy handmaid hath not anything in the house, save a pot of oil." He told her to borrow all the empty vessels her neighbors had and then to go into the house and shut the door, and to pour the oil in the pot into all those vessels; which she did until they were all full. She then paid her debts and had plenty left.

Jesus fed four thousand persons at one time and five thousand at another by the same means. He also "precipitated" the elements of wholeness many times and healed the multitude. He required co-operation in faith on the part of those He healed in order thus to complete the healing circuit.

Speedy answers to prayer have always been experienced and always will be when the right relations are established between the mind of the one who prays and the spiritual realm, which is like an electrical field. The power to perform what seems to be miracles has been relegated to some God-selected one; but now we are inquiring into the law, since God is no respecter of persons, and we find that the fulfillment of the law rests with man or a group of men, when they quicken by faith the spiritual forces latent within them.

The reason why some prayers are not answered is lack of proper adjustment of the mind of the one who prays to the omnipresent creative spiritual life.

Jesus was the most successful demonstrator of prayer of whom we have any record, and He urged persistence in prayer. If at first you don't succeed, try, try again. Like Lincoln, Jesus loved to tell stories to illustrate His point, and He emphasized the value of persistence in prayer. He told of a woman who demanded justice of a certain judge and importuned him until in sheer desperation he granted her request.

Every Christian healer has had experiences where persistent prayer saved his patient. If he had merely said one prayer, as if giving a prescription for the Lord to fill, he would have fallen far short of demonstrating the law. Elijah prayed persistently until the little cloud appeared or, as we should say, he had a "realization"; then the manifestation followed.

The Bible is treasured as the word of God because it records so many of these apparent miracles; but the fact is that all over this land enough demonstrations of the supermind are taking place every day to fill many books of the size of the Bible. Some of them are recorded, and people read about them, but these are few compared with the many that are taking place. All of which goes to prove that there is a restorative law that, if taken advantage of, will heal the world of all its ills.

Many of the old-school faith healers object to the scientific explanation of the healing process. They have believed in a personal God and that all superworld forces are set in motion by His personal intervention. However it is much more satisfying to logical minds to know that God is the law and that the Spirit that we have thought of as a projection of Him is in fact He Himself in His own spiritual identity. This is the teaching of Jesus, and our men of science are proving it to be true. An understanding of this all-accessible Truth is making seers, prophets, and mighty men of God out of pygmies. On every hand men of mediocre ability are becoming world leaders through exploiting the supermind qualities that they have merely glimpsed as existing within them.

These ephemeral Caesars have gained in inkling of the disciplined mind's dominion and are using it to control the negative mass thought, and through the hypnotic force of words they evolve chaos and dark night the world over.

When men accept and understand Jesus' teaching about the mastery of the spiritual man, all the evils that arise from these upstart saviors will disappear. But now in the night of mind's eclipse

"We petty men
Walk under his huge legs, and peep about
To find ourselves dishonorable graves."

Then the question arises, If this supermind ability is in every man, why is it not more widely understood and used?

There are several answers to this pertinent question, the most plausible being the lack of human initiative. Men prefer to let others do their thinking for them. This is especially true in religious matters. The race thought has been so saturated with the belief that spiritual revelation must come through some authorized channel that the man without an ecclesiastical degree is timid about expressing an opinion about God or man's spiritual nature.

Jesus broke this hypnotic spell when without ecclesiastical authority He claimed to be the Son of God.

We should remember that Jesus included as sons of God all those who, as He said, are "my sheep," that is, follow Him. He quoted Psalm 82, in which it is written,

"I said, Ye are gods
And all of you sons of the Most High."

The church elders and the people cried, "Crucify him!" Jesus taught great truths, which were grasped by but a few open-minded followers, and they formed a new church. After doing mighty works for hundreds of years they in turn, built an ecclesiastical hierarchy from which the common people were excluded. The Church Fathers gathered and selected certain religious manuscripts and compiled the Bible, which they proclaimed to be the very word of God, to be read and interpreted by those only having the authority of the church.

Here again we see positive thought submitting to negative thought, thereby keeping the world in darkness for ages.

As Luther started the Protestant Reformation so we are now at the beginning of another reformation, in which the freedom and power of man spiritually will not only be taught but demonstrated.

The supermind demonstrations that mark this modern religious reformation seem so at variance with nature that they are still looked upon as miracles, notwithstanding the fact that logic and science shout from the housetops the universality of law.

Those who study the spiritual import of Jesus' teaching have revealed to them a mental technique for which no adequate language has yet been invented.

The Jews demanded of Jesus that He tell them plainly, and His reply was that His works would testify that He was the Son of God and that He and the Father were one. We who have experienced Spirit baptism freely testify to the dynamic thrill that ripples through the nerves for days and months and is often repeated in silent meditation for years after the first outpour. Thus revelation, observation, and actual experience prove that man develops spirituality according to the divine pattern called in Genesis the image and likeness of God.

The natural man in the physical world is merely the beginning formation of the man planned by creative Mind. When the natural man finishes his unfoldment he enters the next stage, that of the Christ man illustrated by Jesus. Jesus was the first man or "fruit" of the earth's first age, that of the natural man. He opened the way for all those who aspire to the attainment of immortality.

To the present time the followers of Jesus have been told by spiritual leaders that He taught the immortality of the soul only. But now it is revealed that He immortalized His body and said, "Follow me." It was man's sins that brought death to his body, and his redemption must include the healing of the body. When the mind is healed of its sins the body will respond. "Your body is a temple of the Holy Spirit, which is in you, which ye have from God."

So we find as we study and apply the doctrine of Jesus that the body must be included. Faith in the omnipresent pure substance precipitates the substance in the body and we are transformed.

Proofs may be found in profusion that the divine law of body restoration is in action in a large way right here in our midst. The literature of Unity teems with testimonials of persons who have been healed and are grateful to God for renewed health, strength, prosperity, and happiness. Thus it is not necessary to strengthen your faith by reading about the work of God in ages past; you can personally consult your neighbor, who can doubtless tell you of marvels fully as great as any recorded in the Bible.

The majority of cases that come to us belong to the class of the discouraged woman told of in Luke 8:43, "who spent all her living upon physicians, and could not be healed." Doctors have pronounced them incurable, and as a last resort they turn to God. The hardest part of the work in their healing is to get out of their minds the verdict of the doctor that their cases are incurable. We have discovered that there are no incurables. "With God all things are possible." Any experienced metaphysical healer will tell you that he has been the instrument through which all the popular diseases have been healed.

Some of the stories told by patients are beyond human credence; for example, the restoration of the eyes of a man from which they had been removed, and the growth of the nose of a woman who had lost it by disease. These are very rare but well authenticated in metaphysical circles. I am not prepared to give the names of these cases, but I can testify to my own healing of tuberculosis of the hip. When a boy of ten I was taken with what was at first diagnosed as rheumatism but developed into a very serious case of hip disease. I was in bed over a year, and from that time an invalid in constant pain for twenty-five years, or until I began the application of the divine law. Two very large tubercular abscesses developed at the head of the hip bone, which the doctors said would finally drain away my life. But I managed to get about on crutches, with a four-inch cork-and-steel extension on the right leg. The hip bone was out of the socket and stiff. The leg shriveled and ceased to grow. The whole right side became involved; my right ear was deaf and my right eye weak. From hip to knee the flesh was a glassy adhesion with but little sensation.

When I began applying the spiritual treatment there was for a long time slight response in the leg, but I felt better, and I found that I began to hear with the right ear. Then gradually I noticed that I had more feeling in the leg. Then as the years went by the ossified joint began to get limber, and the shrunken flesh filled out until the right leg was almost equal to the other. Then I discarded the cork-and-steel extension and wore an ordinary shoe with a double heel about an inch in height. Now the leg is almost as large as the other, the muscles are restored, and although the hip bone is not yet in the socket, I am certain that it soon will be and that I shall be made perfectly whole.

I am giving minute details of my healing because it would be considered a medical impossibility and a miracle from a religious standpoint. However I have watched the restoration year after year as I applied the power of thought, and I know it is under divine law. So I am satisfied that here is proof of a law that the mind builds the body and can restore it.

Chapter XVI - The Seed is the Word

BEING HAS two aspects: the invisible and the visible, the abstract and the concrete. The visible comes forth from the invisible, and this coming forth is always according to a universal method of growth from minute generative centers. All forms are built according to this law. From center to circumference is the method of growth throughout the universe. The one who studies form alone and expects to learn from it and its transformations the secret of existence never goes back to the "seed"; never catches sight of the Spirit moving upon every generating center.

Causes are always invisible: spiritual. "God is spirit," and "the seed is the word of God." Thus that which produces the seed is the Spirit. It is popularly presumed that the seed produces after its kind that which appears. This is a superficial conclusion, and a moment's logical consideration will convince anyone that a thing so small, a cause so insignificant as compared with the effect, could not produce without being possessed of an anterior principle results so large and varied. The oft-repeated illustration of the acorn's having folded within its heart the oak is not correct. The acorn of itself is powerless to produce anything, but as an avenue through which interior forces become exterior it is important.

We should never lose sight of the fact that things are but the evidence of intelligence and power. In and of themselves they are without causative power in any way. The seed is the symbol of the Word of God, and in its generative qualities it represents the apparent insignificance of the Word as it goes forth from its invisibility and silence. But this Word is a generative center with all the possibilities of God at its call. It is the idea of God, the image and likeness. It is just like God in its essentials, and needs only to be planted in fertile ground to produce the living picture of which it is the image. In its highest degree of expression this is man. Christ is the Word of God. It was in the beginning with God, and is now with God. It came forth from God. It became flesh and dwelt among men. It always dwells among men; it is the real originating center through which man draws all his intelligence, life, love, substance. It is the one point at which we tap the divine storehouse; it is the inlet and outlet of God.

So the "seed," that is, "the word of God," is man; not the external thinking personality that has a consciousness of separation, but the internal spiritual germ. The central seed is the generative center from which the personal man forms himself. He draws upon the universal forces within and without, just as the tree draws upon the invisible Spirit, manifesting itself in earth, air, and water. He may be totally unconscious of this situation in certain stages of his building, but this does not nullify the fact. The fact that the babe is not conscious of the method of its sustenance during the first months of its prenatal life has no weight with those who have observed the law.

Man is the idea of God, and the idea of God is the word of God. Man is not a thing of small beginnings but of infinite beginnings. His resource is the Infinite, and he draws his substance from an inexhaustible store. He is never at a loss for supply, be it ever so scarce in the markets of the world.

At the heart center of everyone is the "seed . . . the word of God." It is there as a door opening into the infinite. Man opens this door or closes it at his will. Some open it just a little crack and others not at all. Some open the door wide, and they manifest such rare powers that they are exalted, even deified, by those who have closed their own doors. This little inner door is a door of great promise; he who opens it wide finds on its inner side the kingdom of God. It is the way into the kingdom. It is the Christ Spirit speaking through those who have opened: "I am the door."

It is strange but true that the inner "seed" of God may have been so neglected as to have been entirely forgotten by some people. They may have a slight recollection of having at some remote period been in a state in which they did not have to endure the burdens of self-sustenance, but this is so faint that it is like a dim, faraway dream. When a man has thus forgotten the seed and has sought other means of growth, he loses his symmetry. He becomes gnarled and crooked.

His body is filled with knots, and his limbs die before their time. This is the paralysis of nonrecognition of the generative seed. No true growth results from earth and air alone. Man does not live by bread alone, but by every word proceeding out of the mouth of God. This "word of God" is the "seed"; that is, man's real self, because it is the umbilical cord that forever connects him with the infinite fountain of supply. No growth takes place except through this "seed," this high idea of what man is. Any other idea is a reflection, and there are reflections in descending degree, until man finds himself comparing himself with his own creations--worm of the dust.

As Emerson says:

"Whilst a necessity so great caused the man to exist, his health and erectness consists in the fidelity with which he transmits influences from the vast and universal to thepoint on which his genius can act.The ends are momentary; they are vents for the currents of inward life which increases as it is spent. A man's wisdom is to know that all ends are momentary, that the best end must be superseded by a better. But there is a mischievous tendency in him to transfer his thoughts from the life to the ends, to quit his agency and rest in his acts: the tools run away with the workman, the human with the divine. I conceive a man as always spoken to from behind, and unable to turn his head and see the speaker. In all the millions who have heard the voice, none ever saw the face. As children in their play run behind each other, and seize one by the ears and make him walk before them, so is the spirit our unseen pilot. That well-known voice speaks in all languages, governs all men, but none ever catches a glimpse of its form. If the man will exactly obey it, it will adopt him, so that he shall not any longer separate it from himself in his thought; he shall seem to be it, he shall be it. If he listen with insatiable ears, richer and greater wisdom is taught him; the sound swells to ravishing music, he is borne away as with a flood, he becomes careless of his food and of his house, he is the tool of ideas, and leads a heavenly life. But if his eye is set on the things to be done, and not on the truth that is still taught, and for the sake of which the things are to be done, then the voice grows faint, and at last is but a humming in his ears. His health and greatness consist in his being the channel through which heaven flows to earth, in short, in the fullness in which an ecstatical state takes place in him. It is pitiful to be an artist, when by forbearing to be artists we might be vessels filled with the divine overflowings, enriched by the circulations of omniscience and omnipresence."

Let not this seed of God within you lie fallow for want of conscious recognition on your part. You want to express all the possibilities of Being, which you can do if you will acknowledge the source through which they methodically come forth.

Many people think man grows a little differently from other things. They are sure he is a special creation, formed by the Lord God in a miraculous way, from the "dust of the ground" and "set up against de palin's to dry"! This style of creation will do for the backwoods preacher but not for thinking people. Man is the creation of God. God creates in a definite manner. Man is created in a definite manner. He comes forth into the visible world in a regular, everyday sort of a way, through the simple process wrapped up in the mystery of this inner "seed."

To think that man is created in any but a methodical way is to think without reasonable consideration. There is no evidence anywhere of a miraculous creation of anything, and it is folly to assume that the Almighty stepped out of His course to make man. Man in his divine selfhood makes himself. His process is precisely that of God's, through the power of his word. Without the Christ word man has no life in him. Man does not make anything that lasts unless it has its point of departure in this inner seed idea of the Father. Men think they are building, but they are deceived. They may spend thousands of years rearing states of consciousness that in the day of judgment between the real and the evanescent must be dissolved into the vapor of nothingness.

Every idea is a seed, and will bring forth according to its character, modified somewhat by the kind of mind soil in which it is planted. There is a law of growth in mind parallel with that of earth. A thistle seed will always produce thistles, regardless of the character of the soil; a low ideal will likewise work out low conditions in a high type of mind. You that find lodgment and produce crops in other receptive minds.

But each man is a gardener who has absolute charge of his mind and can determine just what kind of seeds shall be planted in his domain. What he says is law in the garden ofwhich he has control. If he is lax, shiftless, and ignorant of his privileges, he may let the thistle seeds from foolish minds blow over his fence and take root in his garden. But it is not at all necessary. By his simple word of command he can protect his domain from all intruders. Not all men know this, nevertheless it is true.

Chapter XVII - The Resurrecting Power of the Word

IT IS PLAINLY taught in the Bible that God created a spiritual, undying man; that death came into the world through transgression of the law, called sin; that sin was the work of one man, and that sin would be overcome by one man. "As in Adam all die, so in Christ shall all be made alive." Jesus Christ is the fulfillment of that promise.

The race has so long existed in the negative mental conditions that bring sickness and finally death that it is very difficult to convince men that they can live forever in their bodies. They have been taught that death is natural, that death is part of the scheme of life, that through death we progress to better conditions. This negative teaching has been a part of the race thought so long that death has been accepted as the necessary end of existence. But such is not the teaching of Christianity.

Every organ of the body is capable of being constantly renewed through the inflow of an unseen force called mind or life or Spirit. Therefore we should be continually renewing and spiritualizing the body. But we are not doing so because of our lack of faith in our possibilities as offspring of universal life. We find it hard to believe that the renewing and spiritualizing of the body can be accomplished, yet the history of the Hebrew race (considered as an allegory) shows that this is possible.

We look on the wanderings of the Children of Israel in the wilderness as typical of our wanderings through the wilderness of materiality and ignorance on our way to the Promised Land; but we have always put the Promised Land away off somewhere in heaven! The teaching of Jesus is that we can demonstrate over all the ills of the body, all the discords and inharmonies of the flesh, and finally overcome death as He did, here and now.

The lesson of Easter, when learned, convinces us that one man demonstrated what has been taught throughout the centuries in the religion of Christianity. Jesus evidently did not know in the beginning of His life that He was to make this great demonstration. He was a carpenter and worked with Joseph, but for thirty years He must have been growing in spiritual power. In meditation He doubtless caught glimpses of the great Truth, and it dawned on Him that He was the man who had been selected, or that through His own demonstration He had attained the ability, to overcome the negative thoughts, the sins that were tearing down the bodies of the race, and that He had the power to gain complete mastery of the human weakness called death.

When Jesus received the illumination and stepped forth as a teacher, He found it very difficult to impress on others that He was anything more than one of the common people. He claimed immortality, He claimed that He was the Messiah they had been looking for, and they said in effect: "This is ridiculous. We know this man. He is Jesus, the son of Mary and Joseph. We know Him and His brothers and His sisters. We have been brought up with Him. It is absurd to think that a man can step right out of the common herd and become the Messiah."

It is an adage that a great man is not without honor except in his own country. From the physical viewpoint we are part of the common people and we will not concede that one of our number can by any possibility become divine. The Scriptures plainly teach that Jesus' own followers did not believe His claim that He was divine. They admitted that He was a great teacher. He taught truths that they accepted in the abstract, but they were not ready to concede that one of their number had attained the demonstration of Truth. In a sort of wonderment Jesus' disciples followed Him, but they had not grasped the underlying truths that He was teaching: that the body is the temple of the living God, and that the man Jesus could lay it down or take it up; that He was going to make a demonstration over death that would satisfy not only them but the whole world; that when He was ready He was going up to Jerusalem to be crucified there. Christian metaphysicians see symbology in all this, but it actually took place.

Jesus knew that He must demonstrate over death and that He must prepare for that test. He told all His friends that He was going to accomplish this thing, but they were incredulous. Peter attempted to dissuade Jesus from His announced purpose of going to Jerusalem to be crucified, but Jesus would not be swerved from His course. We often think that if Jesus would only come now and make a demonstration over death, we should all believe. Probably only a handful of us would accept Him if He came among us today and made such a demonstration. The newspapers would say it was a fake, a trick. The scribes and the Pharisees and the doubters reported that the soldiers were paid to open the tomb and let Jesus escape. Incredulity exists today. That is the reason why the demonstration of eternal life is so difficult. That is the reason why after two thousand years the world at large is not convinced that it is possible for man to be raised out of the thought that death is inescapable. Even after Jesus demonstrated resurrection the disciples found it hard to believe Him.

A woman was the first person to come to Jesus' tomb after His resurrection. Women are more receptive to Truth than men. Women have more spirituality and faith than men, but if today a man died who had claimed that he would resurrect his body on a certain day, it is doubtful whether even the women would go to the tomb to see that resurrection. Mary and the other women did not go to the tomb of Jesus expecting Him to be there alive. They did not expect to see Him come out of the tomb; on the contrary they had spices and herbs for the embalming of His body. The body was not there and they began to inquire about it. The angel told them, "He is risen"; but they could not believe it, and they looked into the tomb. There were the grave clothes, but the body of Jesus was gone. The disciples, when told that Jesus had risen, were skeptical. We are told that Jesus walked with two of them on the way to Emmaus and explained the Scriptures to them. After a time they recognized Him; then He disappeared from their midst.

Shortly after the incident at Emmaus Jesus appeared again to the Eleven, and to prove to them that He had the same body that He had had before His resurrection, He "showed them his hands and his feet," and He ate a piece of broiled fish. After that He disappeared again. All this would be thought "spooky" in our day, and we cannot blame the apostles for being "amazed."

Followers of Jesus do not understand the difference between the astral or ghostly body of the dead and the resurrected body of Jesus. There is a difference made by the mental power of the individual and the way he thinks about life, soul, spirit, and matter. If we believe that the body is the temple of the living God, we shall follow Jesus in the resurrection.

Why are we not resurrecting the body? Why are we giving it up to disintegration? Sin is the cause of death; then it must be that through the elimination of sin we shall come into eternal life and save the body from the disintegrating effects of death. In fact we are all striving for the resurrection of the body when we try to overcome its oncreeping feebleness. But our efforts are material instead of spiritual. We should remember that "it is the spirit that giveth life; the flesh profiteth nothing." We try in many ways to renew the life supply within us.

Some very absurd methods have been advocated by so-called scientists to perpetuate man's life, to make him healthier, wealthier, happier. We all want more life, more happiness, more good; and we can have everything we want if we comply with the divine law as Jesus did. The body is composed of elements that are essentially perfect. We have not understood the law of harmony and have therefore thrown these primal perfect elements out of adjustment. By our thoughts we are continually moving the cells of the body. The original impetus is given by the conscious mind, hence we must regulate our thinking to the end that harmony be set up in the cellular life throughout the organism.

It is very evident that Jesus understood the science of right thinking. We hate our enemies and have bodily disorders as a result. Jesus said, "Love your enemies." This is but one of many laws of mind activity that Jesus carried out in His life. We must first follow Jesus in controlling our thoughts; then we shall be able to follow Him in the resurrection.

Jesus controlled His thoughts by harmonizing them, by continually thinking constructively, by continually bringing into action in His conscious mind all the mental factors that lead to the new life, to the understanding of what life is. We know that the body is destroyed by discord, by fever, and by other inharmonies. Fever is but a clashing of the cells of the organism, a tearing down process; but back of fever are harsh thoughts. We can trace every ill to some thought. We must eliminate these sinning thoughts. The sinning thought is the thought that fails to measure up to the high calling; it is not a true thought. We have limited our ideas to a small realm. We have thought that sin covered only the transgressions of the moral man. But I assure you that sin becomes visible in the physical; hence we should look for a physical resurrection after we have crucified the carnal mind.

Jesus laid great stress on the power of the word. The word has two activities: One is that of the still small voice in the silence, and the other is that of the "loud voice" that was used by Jesus when He raised Lazarus from the dead. In the beginning "God said, Let there be"–and there was. We are the offspring of God, and our words have power proportionate to our realization of our in-dwelling spiritual kingdom. In the world today there is ample evidence of the power of words to move multitudes. That same power can heal and make people happy. If you will recognize this power and increase it and apply it in all your thoughts and acts, the impetus given to your spoken thought will produce a body so constructed, so harmonized that it will renew itself and never allow you to go to the grave. Jesus did a work of this kind. He said that a man would be held accountable for his slightest word. Jesus sent His word to heal people. He said, "If a man keep my word, he shall never taste of death." What were His words? They were words of life, of peace, or harmony. "Ye have heard that it was said, An eye for an eye, and a tooth for a tooth," but "This is my commandment, that ye love one another." So long as we have destructive thoughts, so long as we war in thought with our neighbor next door or on the other side of the earth, just so long shall we have inharmony, just so long shall we fall short of being true followers of Jesus. We must love, we must forgive, we must harmonize our thoughts under the divine law; then we shall heal and resurrect the body.

Chapter XVIII - Transfiguration

Be ye transformed by the renewing of your mind.

TRANSFIGURATION is always preceded by a change of mind. Our ideas must be lifted from the material, the physical, to the spiritual. But first we need to realize that it is possible for us to be transfigured as well as to understand the law by which transfiguration is brought about.

The meaning of the Transfiguration has never been understood by those who read the Scriptures as history. The transfiguration of Jesus has always been considered a historical event, and its allegorical meaning overlooked. To get the real meaning of the Transfiguration, we must regard the experience of Jesus on the mount as typical of what often takes place in those who are growing in spiritual consciousness.

We have evidences every day of the power of thought to transfigure the countenance. We know that it is possible for a person to be transformed in a degree by the thoughts that flit through his mind from moment to moment, but we do not know his capacity for transfiguration, which is unlimited, nor the part it plays in his attainment of the Christ consciousness and the Christ body.

The real object of existence is to bring forth the perfect man and attain eternal life. Eternal life must be earned. It is usually assumed that man does not die, and this is true of the I AM; but how about the consciousness, the soul? "The soul that sinneth, it shall die" is the testimony of the Scriptures. That only lives which conforms to the principle of eternal life.

Spirit exists eternally in God-Mind, of which we must become conscious. This consciousness is soul and is the tangible part of soul. God-Mind gives us the opportunity to incorporate into our consciousness His attributes. These attributes are spiritual life, love, wisdom, strength, power, in fact the essence of all good, which we realize first in mind, then in body and affairs. Thus God gives us the spiritual perfection that we are to manifest and retain eternally in consciousness. This is His Son or Christ.

Jesus taught that we must attain the consciousness of eternal life, that we have no life in us until we have attained this consciousness. Until we demonstrate over death, the death of the body, we are in a transitory state of existence.

Then the real object of existence is to attain the consciousness of eternal life and to manifest all that is potentially involved in us by our Creator. The Spirit--I AM or ego in man is eternal, but there must be a consciousness of this quality of eternity; there must be a consciousness of the image-and-likeness man. There must be in every one of us a realization of that Spirit which has in it--involved in its being--all that exists in the universal. If we do not realize this, if we do not make it ours, we must eventually go back to the universal. Jesus was the great way-shower to the attainment of this realization of Spirit, and we shall miss "the prize of the high calling" if we do not enter the path that He trod and that He pointed out in many parables, illustrations, and experiences.

Then this overcoming or lifting up of man is a process through which we are all passing if we have been converted to the Christ way of life. Transfiguration plays a part and an important part in this evolution of the soul. When we see the parallel between our experiences and the transfiguration of Jesus we gain confidence to go forward.

In our study and application of the Christian life we all have times when we are spiritually uplifted. Such a time is marked by a form of spiritual enthusiasm, which is brought about by statements of Truth made by ourselves or others--prayers, words of praise, songs, meditations--any statement of Truth that exalts the spiritual realms of the mind. Jesus was lifted up by Peter, James, and John (faith, judgment, and love). Whenever we dwell on these virtues and try to live up to them, they are exalted in consciousness, and they go up with us to the mount of Transfiguration. You may not always realize this. You may think that the uplifting was just a passing exaltation, but it stamps itself on your soul and body and marks the planting of a new idea in the upward trend of the whole man.

What is your attitude toward these times when you feel the mighty uplift of Spirit? Do you give them their due importance; or when you again come down into the valley, do you groan and question and wonder why you do not abide in your exaltation, why there seems a falling away of the mind from it?

Right here we must be wise and understand the relation of the higher principles of man and their action in the redemption of soul and body. Do not lose sight of the fact that the whole man must be spiritualized. Some people get into the habit of going up in spirit to the mount of Transfiguration, and they find it so enticing that they refuse to descend to the valley again. Then soul and body are left to go their own way, and a separation ensues. Such persons dwell continually on the heights and ignore the essential unity of Spirit, soul, and body. Many delusions arise among Christians because they lack understanding of the law of the idea and its manifestations. All things, all actions, all principles, are working toward the unity of God, man, and the universe. But there must be a readjustment and a cleansing of the whole mass. If there are things, whether mental or physical, that are not up to the high standard of Spirit, they must die. Jesus on the mount spoke of His death that was to follow. This death is of the material perception of substance and life, which is reflected in man's body of flesh. This must perish. The limited concept of matter and of a material body must be transformed so that the true spiritual body may appear.

We find that at every upward step we take in our evolution there is a sloughing off of, a doing away with, some parts of consciousness that do not accord with the higher principles. Jesus referred to it as the planting of a seed in the ground and its dying before it can bring forth the new life. The real life chit in the seed does not die. It lives and multiplies when rid of its husk of bondage. In the refinement of metals the fire, which is life, fuses the whole mass. Then the molten elements form a new base; the precious metals go by themselves and the dross goes by itself. The dross is poured off and thrown away, the precious metals are saved.

Much the same thing takes place in the action of Spirit, soul, and body when a person goes into the high consciousness and is transfigured. Some persons call it conversion, some illumination, some the lifting-up power of Spirit. Whatever you call it, it is the same thing. When the white heat of God life comes upon man, there is exaltation and transfusion of elements. The result of soul exaltation is a finer soul essence forming the base of a new body substance. The passing away of the dross of materiality is a form of death.

You have doubtless wondered: "Why is it that, after I have had an uplift, after I have had a high realization, or a strong treatment, I have to meet so many errors? It seems to me that the negative side piles in on me the next day or the next few weeks stronger than ever."

The cause of this is a gathering together of the evil and the good; the day of judgment has arrived, and you are the judge. You may even be buried for "three days" in that material consciousness which has not yet come to the full light. But when you know the law that Spirit is always with you you have nothing to fear, if you hold steadily to the Christ presence that you realized in the mount of Transfiguration.

Having once seen Truth, having once had the illumination, you find that the next step is to demonstrate it and not to be cast down or discouraged by the opposite. When the crucifixion comes and you are suffering the pangs of dying error, you may cry out, "My God, my God, why hast thou forsaken me?" forgetting for the time the promises in the mount of Transfiguration. This is when you need to realize that you are passing through a transforming process that will be followed by a resurrection of all that is worth saving.

Transfiguration is an essential step in every forward movement of men and nations. All philosophers have observed it in its various phases. Carlyle says: "Once risen into this divine white heat of temper, were it only for a season and not again, it is henceforth considerable through all its remaining history. And no nation that has not had such divine paroxysms at any time is apt to come to much."

Paul saw it in its work in man, when he wrote, "For our citizenship is in heaven; whence also we wait for a Saviour, the Lord Jesus Christ: who shall fashion anew the body of our humiliation, that it may be conformed to the body of his glory." "Then shall the righteous shine forth as the sun in the kingdom of their Father." "We know that, if he shall be manifested, we shall be like him; for we shall see him even as he is." "As we have borne the image of the earthy, we shall also bear the image of theheavenly."

It is quite essential that those who are striving for "the prize of the high calling of God in Christ Jesus" cling to their ideal as real. It should not be regarded in the light of a past event or of a future achievement, but as fulfillment here and now. This is illustrated in the communion of Moses and Elijah with Jesus on the mount, Moses representing the law, Elijah its fulfillment. Jesus is the I AM, in which both the past and the future are joined. But Peter, not understanding the lesson, wanted to make three tabernacles, representing the tendency of man to separate and localize that which is spiritual and universal.

When the voice of Principle proclaimed the spiritual man's presence--"This is my beloved Son, in whom I am well pleased; hear ye him"–there were no promises of the past or the future. Time has no power over one who dwells in the mind of God. There is no time to the mind of one who realizes omnipresence. Nothing will transfigure the race and renew the body so rapidly as the denial of both past and future. Persons get childish because they let their thoughts dwell upon the past. Fear of the future weakens the virile life, and the feet stumble. The Son of God is vigorous with the increasing life that is perpetually flowing forth from the Father. When man realizes the omnipresent life his whole organism is vitalized, and the soul is glorified. When man is in spiritual consciousness his soul shines with an energy that electrifies the outer clothing. Those little points of magnetic light, which we have all observed upon removing our clothing at night, are weak manifestations of the aura of the soul, which can be magnified until the whole body is ablaze with it.

Some Christians teach the saving of the soul and the perishing of the body. Jesus taught the saving of both soul and body. It is true that this mortal body must be transfigured; it is but a picture or symbol of the real, the spiritual body, which is the "Lord's body." The "Lord's body" is the body of Spirit, the divine idea of a perfect human body. When one realizes this new body, the cells of the present body will form on new planes of consciousness, they will aggregate around new centers, and the "Lord's body" will appear.

"But we all, with unveiled face beholding as in a mirror the glory of our Lord, are transformed into the same image from glory to glory, even as from the Lord the Spirit."

When the body is devitalized by excessive labor, dissipation, or any loss of vital force, its aura shrinks away and a consciousness akin to that of being unclothed is evident. To dream of being naked or partly clothed is a warning by Spirit that the reserve vital force has been dissipated and the natural clothing of the body removed. Continuous disregard of the law of conservation of vital force is followed by various diseases and finally death. During sleep the system, under natural law, seeks to equalize the vital forces, and it does so if the intellectual concentration has not been too great. A dream of falling means that this force, which has been piled up in the head, is falling down into the lower channels of the body, and is restoring equilibrium at the expense of harmonious reaction. When the mind is adjusted to the divine law, all the vital forces flow harmoniously and the aura glows about the body as a beautiful white light, protecting it from all discord from without and purifying it continually from within. This is the state of the perfected man described in Revelation 1:14-16.

"And his head and his hair were white as white wool, white as snow; and his eyes were as a flame of fire; and his feet like unto burnished brass . . . and his voice as the voice of many waters. . . . and his countenance was as the sun shineth in his strength."

Chapter XIX - The End of The Age

IN ALL AGES and among all people, there have been legends of prophets and saviors and predictions of their coming. Anticipation of a messiah has not been confined to the Occident, for several of the prominent religions of the Orient have prophesied a messiah. The fact that all who believe in the principle of divine incarnation have long strained their eyes across the shining sands in an effort to catch sight of the coming of one clothed with the power of heaven, should make us pause and consider the cause of such universality of opinion among peoples widely separated. To dismiss the subject as a religious superstition is not in harmony with unprejudiced reason. To regard these prophecies merely as religious superstitions rules out traditions that are as tenable and as reliable as the facts of history. There is a cause for every effect, and the cause underlying this almost unanimous expectation of a messiah must have some of the omnipresence of a universal law.

In considering a subject like this, which demonstrates itself largely on metaphysical lines, it is necessary to look beyond the material plane to the realm of causes.

The material universe is but the shadow of the spiritual universe. The pulsations of the spiritual forces impinge upon and sway men, nations, and planets, according to laws whose sweep in space and time is so stupendous as to be beyond the ken or comprehension of astronomy. But the fact should not be overlooked that higher astronomy had its votaries in the past. The Magi and the illumined sages of Chaldea and Egypt had astronomical knowledge of universal scope. It was so broad, so gigantic, so far removed from the comprehension of the common mind of their day that it always remained the property of the few. It was communicated in symbols, because of the poverty of language to express its supermundane truths. In the sacred literature of the Hindus are evidences of astronomical erudition covering such vast periods of time that modern philosophers cannot or do not give them credence, and they are relegated to the domain of speculation rather than of science. However the astronomers of the present age have forged along on material lines until now they are beginning to impinge upon the hidden wisdom of the mighty savants of the past.

There is evidence that proves that the ages of the distant past knew a higher astronomy than do we of this age, and that they predicted the future of this planet through cycles and aeons--its nights of mental darkness and the dawn of its spiritual day--with the same accuracy that our astronomers do its present-day planetary revolutions.

Jesus evidently understood this higher astronomy, and He knew that His work as a teacher and demonstrator of spiritual law was related to it, yet not controlled by it. He co-operated with the "law . . . and the prophets," as far as they went, but He knew the higher law of the Christ man and affirmed His supremacy in the words: "All authority hath been given unto me in heaven and on earth."

Jesus evidently understood the aeons or ages through which the earth passes. For example, in Matthew 13:39, our English Bible reads: "The enemy that sowed them is the devil: and the harvest is the end of the world; and the reapers are angels." In the Diaglott version, which gives the original Greek and a word-for-word translation, this reads: "THAT ENEMY who SOWED them is the ADVERSARY; the HARVEST is the End of the Age; and the REAPERS are Messengers." In this as in many other passages where Jesus used the word "age," it has been translated "world," leading the reader to believe that Jesus taught that this planet was to be destroyed.

So we see that the almost universally accepted teaching of the end of the world is not properly founded on the Bible. The translators wanted to give the wicked a great scare, so they put "the end of the world" into Jesus' mouth in several instances where He plainly said "the end of the age."

The Bible is a textbook of absolute Truth; but its teachings are veiled in symbol and understood only by the illumined. The old prophets knew that the earth would become spiritualized in time, and they looked forward and saw it as a self-luminous planet. This is plainly stated in numerous places in the Scriptures. Isaiah says: "Arise, shine; for thy light is come, and the glory of Jehovah is risen upon thee. . . . Violence shall no more be heard in thy land, desolation nor destruction within thy borders . . . The sun shall be no more thy light by day; neither for brightness shall the moon give light unto thee: but Jehovah will be unto thee an everlasting light, and thy God thy glory." John in Revelation also saw a like condition when he prophesied: "And there shall be night no more; and they need no light of lamp, neither light of sun; for the Lord God shall give them light."

Job wrote:

"Canst thou lead forth the Mazzaroth
['the signs of theZodiac' (margin)]
in their season? . .
Knowest thou the ordinances of the heavens?
Canst thou establish the dominion thereof in the earth?"

In accordance with the prophecies of the ancients, our planetary system has just completed a journey of 2,169 years, in which there has been wonderful material progress without its spiritual counterpart. But old conditions have passed away and a new era has dawned. A great change is taking place in the mentality of the race, and this change is evidenced in literature, science, and religion. There is a breaking away from old creeds and old doctrines, and there is a tendency to form centers along lines of scientific spiritual thought. The literature of the first half of the twentieth century is so saturated with occultism as to be an object of censure by conservatives, who denounce it as a "lapse into the superstition of the past." Notwithstanding the protests of the conservatives, on every hand are evidences of spiritual freedom; it crops out in so many ways that an enumeration would cover the whole field of life.

This is surely the coming of the spirit of Christ or Truth, just as was prophesied: "For yourselves know perfectly that the day of the Lord so cometh as a thief in the night." "And it shall come to pass afterward, that I will pour out my Spirit upon all flesh; and your sons and your daughters shall prophesy, your old men shall dream dreams, your young men shall see visions."

It is evident that Jesus and His predecessors had knowledge of coming events on lines of such absolute accuracy as to place it in the realm of truth ascertained, that is, exact science.

That knowledge of our planet is daily becoming more refined, is admitted by material scientists, but that it will ever become spiritualized, as was declared by the ancients, they do not yet admit.

The evidences of a radiant condition of matter on our planet, are so plain that even the most skeptical are loath to deny them, and they must eventually be accepted by all scientists. The physicists are rapidly altering their viewpoint. They are working out their researches in the mental realm. Recently one of the greatest of them, Professor Robert Andrews Millikan, wrote that "matter is no longer a mere game of marbles played by blind men. An atom is now an amazingly complicated organism, possessing many interrelated parts and exhibiting many functions and properties--energy properties, radiation properties, wave properties, and other properties, quite as mysterious as any that used to masquerade under the name of 'mind.' Hence the phrase 'All is matter' and 'All is mind' have now become mere shibboleths completely devoid of meaning."

But these material evidences of a new era are not necessary to the sensitive ones who feel it in the very atmosphere and who are thrilled by the light of the Christ principle. To those who hunger after righteousness, this Christ principle is the elixir of eternal life; but those who are wedded to things material would better beware! The race is changing its vibrations to a higher rate, and the higher types of the race must keep the equipoise by unfolding spiritually or they will lose their hold. Cases of loss of mental poise are now getting so numerous as to attract the attention of the medical world, and these cases will increase in frequency in the future, unless there is a stronger development of the spiritual nature of men. Old things are passing away!

Do you belong to the old, or are you building anew from within and keeping time with the progress of the age? The "harvest" or "consummation of the age" pointed out by Jesus is not far off. This is no theological scare; it is a statement based on a law that is now being tested and proved.

Listen to your inner voice; cultivate the good, the pure, the God within you. Do not let your false beliefs keep you in the darkness of error until you go out like a dying ember. The divine spark is within you. Fan it into flame by right thinking, right living, and right doing, and you will find the "new Jerusalem."

That Jesus was the fulfillment in the flesh of the long-looked-for Messiah is accepted by those who have had spiritual illumination, and is believed by millions who have not had this illumination. Many have not lifted up the Son of man in themselves, but they have faith that Jesus did. Those who study the life of Jesus in its personal aspect, to the exclusion of the spiritual, sense the wonderful possibilities within man and the universe. One who does not develop his own spiritual nature cannot see the spiritual nature in Jesus or in other men who are following Jesus in the regeneration.

Man employs a divine-natural law of growth or evolution before he reaches the divine spiritual. Those under the divine-natural law are referred to in the Bible as the "children of God." However it is possible for the "children of God" to forge ahead of the average in spiritual understanding and power, and to become those who are called "sons of God." All great spiritualleaders have been of the latter class. They see that

"The fault . . . is not in our stars, But in ourselves, that we are underlings."

What we all need is a fuller understanding of the spiritual laws lying back of the phenomena of existence. "It is the spirit that giveth life; the flesh profiteth nothing." Christians should seek the undying life and law of Jesus and the creative substance of His body instead of the historical man of Nazareth. Abstract Truth is good as a beginning for the aspiring man, but Truth incarnated through a great One is a dynamic booster, and we all intuitively unite with such a one as Jesus, and are set free from our human limitations by the vision and quickening that contact with the Christ gives us.

It is a strange fact that in attempts to get the world's estimate of great men the name of Jesus has seldom been suggested. One would think that the army of men and women teaching the doctrines of this greatest of men, would put His name at the head of the list. Our attention is always called to the classifications "secular" and "religious" to explain why Jesus is not included among the world's great men. In fact, Jesus is not considered a man but a god, and in this fact we find another of the many separations that systematized religion has made between the spiritual and the material.

The secular world has been taught that Jesus was so superior to mortal man that He can be thought of only as a god. This removes Him from us all as a man whose character we may emulate and as an example of what we may become and places His attainments far beyond human possibilities.

But Jesus laid no claim to that superiority over other men with which the church so persistently invests Him. His teaching is that all who keep the divine law as He kept it will become like Him and His disciples. "Neither for these only do I pray, but for them also that believe on me through their word." "I in them, and thou in me, that they may be perfected into one; that the world may know that thou didst send me, and lovedst them, even as thou lovedst me."

By separating Jesus from the rest of the race we close the door against the real man, the man that every personal man must progress into. "My little children, of whom I am again in travail until Christ be formed in you," said Paul. There is a great awakening, in all parts of the world, to the absolute necessity and immediate possibility of a race of men patterned after Jesus of Nazareth. Thus is germinating the seed of the new race that Jesus sowed. "Except a grain of wheat fall into the earth and die, it abideth by itself alone; but if it die, it beareth much fruit." Jesus taught the highest Truth ever given to the world, but in addition to His doctrines He gave the race His purified, glorified body. He purified and spiritualized the natural blood until it became a spiritual life stream, into which all may enter and be cleansed. He spiritualized the cells of His corruptible body and set them free in "the heavens," where we may all appropriate or "eat" them. The heavenly kingdom to which Jesus so often referred is the unlimited spiritual consciousness where mind and body are equal in all activities. When we come into the full consciousness of "the heavens," the body will respond instantly to every thought; then time, space, and all the limitations of matter will disappear. It is in this consciousness that Jesus now lives; His "second coming" will be the revealing to men and women everywhere that He has not been absent at any time. "Lo, I am with you always."

The heavenly signs of the second coming of the Son of man are in the cosmic ether, which is now known to science as interpenetrating all things. In the invisible ether, we shall eventually find a complete record of the history of the race, which spiritually developed man will be able to read as easily as he now reads the daily paper. Sir James Jeans in his book "The Mysterious Universe" says: "We must think of space as being drenched with almost all the cosmic radiation which has ever been generated since the world began. Its rays come to us as messengers not only from the farthest depths of space, but also from the farthest reaches of time. And, if we read it aright, their message seems to be that somewhere, sometime, in the history of the universe, matter has been annihilated, and this not in tiny, but in stupendous amounts."

Jesus named God-Mind the "KINGDOM of the HEAVENS." According to the original Greek, as given in the Emphatic Diaglott, He said: "Reform! because the ROYAL MAJESTY of the HEAVENS has approached." Bible translators have not understood the spiritual meaning of the Scriptures, and they have nearly always translated the word "heavens" in the singular, making it read "heaven." This error has misled many into thinking that Jesus, in His many parables and comparisons, referred to a place called heaven. But it is apparent that in these parables and comparisons He was trying to explain to His hearers the character of the omnipresent substance and life that has all potentiality and is the source of everything that appears on the earth.

The coming in the clouds of the heavens of the "Son of man sitting at the right hand of Power," as Jesus told the high priest, is the "second coming," and we should look nowhere else for the advent of the risen Christ. Christ is today "sitting at the right hand of Power," which represents spiritual power expressed; the clouds of heaven being the obscurity in which sense consciousness holds the light of Truth.

Let us cease expecting Christ to come in bodily form; let us turn our attention to His risen body already with us. In this way we shall co-operate with Him in setting up the kingdom of the heavens on the earth. In Matthew 24-23-27 Jesus gave the strongest kind of warning against the idea of the personal appearance of the Christ. This passage concludes with these words: "For as the lightning cometh forth from the east, and is seen even unto the west; so shall be the coming of the Son of man." These are Jesus' own words, and they should have greater weight than Paul's theory that Jesus will appear with a great shout in the clouds of heaven, which has been interpreted literally as the personal appearance of Jesus in the sky.

The world needs the Christ consciousness. The need implies that the attainment is near at hand. There are men and women who gaze up into the heavens for Christ, as did the early disciples, instead of looking within their own heart and mind. "Ye men of Galilee, why stand ye looking into heaven?" Only believe in the omnipresent Christ and you will behold Him sitting on the right hand of Power within your own being!

All who believe that Christ is here now should teach it and preach it with all possible zeal.

The people are longing and reaching out for the healing hand of the Lord Jesus Christ.

There is great need of leadership under the Christ whose banner is love.

The Prince of Peace should be invited to the peace conferences that are held by war-taxed and war-weary peoples.

Christ righteousness should be dominant in settling the differences between capital and labor.

Our schools in every grade need to teach the moral standard of Christ as fundamental to all true character.

When our children have the Christ Spirit pointed out to them as being within and as a living fount of health, wealth, and happiness, they will quickly accept it.

Then the ambition of men will be to compete in bringing forth Truth, goodness, and righteousness; and evil and sin, with its sickness and poverty, will disappear from the earth.

Question Helps

Chapter I

The Atomic Age

1. What great truth have our scientists revealed to man by breaking into the atom? Tell in your own words how both Elijah and Jesus used the same energy that was discovered by them.

2. Did Jesus claim to have the exclusive supernatural power that is usually credited to Him? Explain.

3. To what is the revival of the divine law of healing due? How may the sick be restored to life and health?

4. What have thought concentration and discovery of the dynamic character of the atom to do with prayer? Explain.

5. Of what is the six-day creation of the universe (described in Genesis) a story? Explain how the privileges of the superrealm are open to all.

6. What will be the next great achievement of science?

7. How is man to achieve immortal life?

8. What part does faith play in the transformation of man?

9. What does the latest discovery of science reveal? Explain fully.

10. What must come about before mankind can truly receive the beneficial and permanent uplift to be wrought by atomic energy?

Chapter II

The Restorative Power of Spirit

1. Explain the spiritual import of Jesus' words "My Father worketh even until now, and I work."
2. What is the meaning of "I will be what I will be"?
3. In what sense is every man a king?
4. How does man's belief in his own inefficiency hinder his spiritual progress?
5. Why is a vegetarian diet inducive to a high state of spiritual unfoldment?
6. How does man become conscious of the guidance of Spirit?
7. It is possible for us to develop a radiant body temple?
8. In what state of existence is Jesus manifesting Himself today?
9. How does man save himself form unpleasant psychic or "spooky" experiences in the process of transmuting his body from the physical to the supersubstance state?
10. Give in your own words Charles Fillmore's account of the development of the radiant body within himself.

Chapter III

Spiritual Obedience

1. What is spiritual zeal?

2. While on his way to Damascus to persecute the Christians the zealous Saul's concept of religion went through a complete change. Explain fully.

3. Why should zeal be tempered with wisdom?

4. Why should man be obedient to Spirit? Explain.

5. Above all other Bible writers what important point did Paul emphasize?

6. What does prayer do for man?

7. Explain the outpouring of the dynamic power of Spirit as recorded in Acts 1 and 2.

8. Jesus said that he was the bread and substance that came down from heaven. When will our civilization begin to realize and appropriate this boundless substance and life?

9. What is the dominion that God gave man in the beginning? Explain.

10. In the economy of the future what will take place?

Chapter IV

I Am or Superconsciousness

1. Define superconsciousness.
2. Explain how Jesus externalized the superconsciousness, thus making it an abiding place for the race.
3. Explain the method by which Jesus evolved from sense to God consciousness.
4. How does man overcome all error beliefs?
5. Explain how the mind of man is built on Truth.
6. What great truth did Jesus prove by His resurrection and ascension?
7. What accomplishments are possible to man through the Holy Spirit?
8. Modern science reveals that imprisoned within the cells of man's body are electronic energies beyond possibility of estimate. Of what practical use is this knowledge to man today?
9. Can man free himself and others from the claim of materiality? Explain.
10. How is man loosed from all limiting thoughts and set free in the Christ consciousness

Chapter V

The Day of Judgment

1. Define the term "Son of man."
2. When do we begin to pass judgment? Explain.
3. How do we separate our good thoughts from thoughts of disease, death, lack, and the like?
4. How do we handle our "goat" thoughts?
5. At what stage of unfoldment do we begin to have fine, discriminating judgment?
6. "Then shall the King say unto them on the right hand, Come, ye blessed of my Father, inherit the kingdom prepared for you from the foundation of the world." Who is the King? Explain.
7. How do we reap the benefit of all the good we have ever done or thought?
8. When is everything in Principle ours?
9. Explain how the body becomes full of light.
10. In this connection what is the work of the I AM?

Chapter VI

Thou Shalt Decree a Thing

1. How does man fix an ideal in substance?
2. Define "the visible."
3. Since nothing is really lost, what becomes of the energy that is being released in the disintegration that is going on in the earth?
4. How may man develop a purer, sweeter body and a saner mind?
5. Explain how the destiny of the race is in the hands of man.
6. What will save the race from being destroyed?
7. Name at least three instances in the Bible where marvelous results followed the blowing of trumpets used in the observance of religious rites.
8. Explain how these results were accomplished.
9. How does the trained metaphysician produce like results?
10. Explain how faith plays an important part in broadcasting messages of light to receptive minds.

Chapter VII

Thinking In The Fourth Dimension

1. Do the stupendous truths science is discovering today parallel the truths of the invisible side of life that Jesus taught? Explain.

2. It is necessary for man in the present day to develop a capacity for understanding in terms of the atomic structure of the universe? Give reasons for your answer.

3. Define Jesus' words "If any man hath ears to hear, let him hear."

4. In developing the inner ear we sometimes hear deceptive voices. How may this situation be handled scientifically?

5. Give your interpretation of these words of Jesus: "For unto every one that hath shall be given, and he shall have abundance: but from him that hath not, even that which he hath shall be taken away."

6. Should the discoveries of science be divorced from the kingdom of the heavens taught by Jesus? Explain.

7. Are the mysteries of the supermind open to all alike? What is the result?

8. Does man have power to dominate nature? Explain.

9. What is the great need of the whole human family?

10. Explain the need for a larger realization of the importance of man in manifesting God.

Chapter VIII

Is This God's World?

1. Is God responsible for all that occurs on this earth, and if not, how much?

2. "Thou makest him [man] to have dominion over the works of thy hands: Thou hast put all things under his feet." Explain the significance of these words of the Psalmist in relation to the atomic bomb.

3. Eventually how may our standard of living be vastly improved by the utilization of atomic forces?

4. Is it necessary today to give more attention to the refinement of the body temple?

5. Explain the difference between a prayer treatment given by an experienced spiritual healer and the shocks given by mechanical generators.

6. Is this God's world? Give reasons for your answer.

7. Is it possible to determine how many ages have passed since man lost contact with God? Explain.

8. Where is man's home?

9. What is the great and important issue before the people today?

10. What is the one and only way out of the chaos?

Chapter IX

Demonstrating Christ Thought By Thought

1. What great truth do the "signs of the times" reveal?
2. How can fear and worry and other limitations be overcome?
3. How can we demonstrate a well body?
4. What is the one way to establish harmony in the home?
5. Explain why we should yield obediently to the transforming process of Spirit.
6. What parts do imagination and faith play in demonstration?
7. Is it necessary to live the Truth in order to demonstrate it? Explain.
8. Is there anything mysterious in being led by Spirit? Explain.
9. How are errors in the subconscious mind eliminated?
10. Define the phrase "body of Christ" in its threefold significance.

Chapter X

Truth Radiates Light

1. Define body temple and explain what is necessary in order to glorify the body.

2. In Exodus we read, "Let them make me a sanctuary, that I may dwell among them." Give the metaphysical meaning of
this Scripture.

3. What does it mean to burn incense in the house of Jehovah?

4. What is the result when our mind is lifted up in prayer

5. The Israelites did not go forward in the wilderness on days when the cloud remained over the Tabernacle but only when the cloud was lifted. Give the metaphysical meaning of this.

6. What is the first step in getting out of a mental cloud?

7. When Moses came down from Mount Sinai with the Ten Commandments his countenance shone so brilliantly they had to put a veil over his face. Explain from a scientific viewpoint.

8. What effect do fervent words expressed in eloquent proclamations of spiritual Truth have upon man?

9. Do you consider the tendency on the part of metaphysicians to analyze scientifically these experiences sacrilegious? Give reason for your answer.

10. When the student searches for the science in religion and the religion in science what does he discover? Please amplify.

Chapter XI

The Only Mind

1. Explain in your own language where ideas come from and in what realm they operate.
2. Can man analyze mind and understand its laws and modes of operation? Give reason for your answer.
3. On what plane alone can we know Truth in an absolute sense? Explain.
4. What relation do language and formulation bear to mind?
5. Explain the difference between intellectual knowledge and pure spiritual knowing.
6. Regardless of lack of technical education, what results when man gives his mind to the attention of the one Mind?
7. What is the great difference between what the physical scientist calls "universal energy" and the metaphysician calls God-Mind?
8. Explain how man is a co-creator with God.
9. When man seeks the Father with an eye single to His guidance what is the result?
10. What is man's first step after he has learned spiritual obedience?

Chapter XII

Contact With The Christ Mind

1. Is man consciously in intimate contact with the Holy Spirit? How may an understanding of Holy Spirit activity strengthen man's faith?

2. What is the meaning of the name El Shaddai?

3. Explain how the Holy Spirit in Divine Mind corresponds to man's thought in his mind.

4. How may we approach God with confidence; and what is the result?

5. Explain in your own words the relation of the universal or Jehovah-Mind to the personal or Christ Mind.

6. How may we get into conscious contact with the Christ Mind and demonstrate over sin, sickness, and death? Explain fully.

7. Jesus taught that the true way to demonstrate abundance is to be "rich toward God." Explain in your own words how this sure law of demonstration operates.

8. Why should human egotism be repressed? Explain fully.

9. How can man greatly accelerate the formation in him of the Christ Mind?

10. Give fully the origin of anger, revenge, fear, poverty, failure, and the like, and explain how these error conditions can be changed into love, courage, peace, prosperity, and success.

Chapter XIII

Metaphysics Of Shakespeare

1. Give in your own words an estimate of the true character of Shakespeare.

2. What do Shakespeare's writings reveal as regards his spiritual understanding?

3. Where would you look for the antecedents of Shakespeare? Give reasons for your answer.

4. Every soul has an untapped mine of knowledge in the subconscious mind, inspiration and rediscovery being the positive and negative poles of the mind. What was the relation of Shakespeare's thought to these sources of knowledge? Explain.

5. In Shakespeare's play "Julius Caesar" what is revealed by the two different interpretations of Calpurnia's dream?

6. In "Hamlet" Hamlet's father's ghost appears and gives a Graphic description of how he had been murdered by the king. What does this reveal as to Shakespeare's thought?

7. Shakespeare did not teach religion but the facts of life as he saw them. Explain.

8. Although Shakespeare may not have applied the law of spiritual healing to himself, is there evidence that he perceived the possibility of such healing? Give reasons for your answer.

9. While Shakespeare was familiar with the superstitions of his age, did he usually point out the fallacies in them? Explain.

10. Does the genius displayed in Shakespeare's writings belong wholly to the men and women of his time or to all generations? Give reasons for your answer.

Chapter XIV

The Body

1. Define the Bible in terms of the subject presented in this chapter.

2. What is the paramount theme of the New Testament and in fact the veiled theme of the entire Bible?

3. According to the explanation given in this chapter, what is man? Does man really despise his body? Explain.

4. What is the body?

5. Is the belief that the resurrection of the body has to do with the getting of a new body after death founded on the principles of Truth? Give reasons for your answer.

6. Give explanation of Paul's words "When this corruptible shall have put on incorruption, and this mortal shall have put on immortality . . . Death is swallowed up in victory."

7. How may men become a Christ in mind and in body?

8. Explain in your own words how a pattern of the perfect body is stamped in every soul and how this pattern may be brought into manifestation.

9. Explain how Jesus, who overcame death even in the body, is our normal standard.

10. How do we establish our ego, our I AM identity with Divine Mind, and step by step eliminate the old and put on the new?

Chapter XV

Faith Precipitations

1. Compare the way electricity operates on the physical plane with the way faith operates in the realm of mind

2. Did Jesus require co-operation in faith on the part of those He healed in order to complete the healing circuit? Why is this necessary?

3. (a) When are speedy answers to prayer experienced?

(b) With whom does the fulfillment of the law rest?

4. (a) Did Jesus teach persistence in prayer? Explain.

(b) What is the teaching of Jesus about God's being the law as well as the Spirit?

5. Explain how ephemeral Caesars become world leaders Today. Explain fully.

6. If the supermind ability is in every man, why is it not more widely understood and used?

7. When and how was the hypnotic spell of ecclesiastical authority broken, and how long was it in abeyance? Explain.

8. Explain in your own words the reformation of which we have today seen only the beginning.

9. Did Jesus teach the immortality of the body as well as of the soul? Explain.

10. Are there any incurable diseases? Explain fully.

Chapter XVI

The Seed Is The Word

1. In your own words explain Being in its twofold aspect.

2. What is the word of God?

3. Do “things” have causative power? Explain.

4. Define man and explain how he draws his substance from the infinite storehouse.

5. Give the metaphysical meaning of the statement "I am the door.”

6. When man ceases to remember the source of his being what Is the result?

7. Interpret Jesus’ words “Man shall not live by bread alone, but by every word that proceedeth out of the mouth of God.”

8. Is there any evidence that man is a miraculous creation? Explain.

9. Explain in your own words the statement that every idea is a seed and brings forth according to its character.

10. Man’s mind is a garden, where he is in control and himself determines just what kind of seed words are to grow there. Elaborate.

Chapter XVII

The Resurrecting Power Of The Word

1. Jesus Christ is the fulfillment of the promise. "As in Adam all die, so also in Christ shall all be made alive." Explain.

2. Why is it difficult for man to realize that he can overcome the negative conditions called sickness and death?

3. What unalterable truth does the Easter lesson reveal to us?

4. When Jesus received His illumination and stepped forth as a teacher did He meet with any opposition? Explain.

5. If a demonstration of resurrection were to take place today, what would be the attitude of men in general?

6. Explain the difference between the astral or ghostly body of the dead and the resurrected body of Jesus.

7. How may we come into eternal life and save the body from the disintegrating effects of death?

8. What has right thinking to do with making the demonstration of eternal life? Explain.

9. (a) What are the two activities of the word mentioned in this chapter?

(b) What determines the measure of power possessed by our words?

10. Explain in your own language the meaning of the Scripture "If a man keep my word, he shall never taste of death."

Chapter XIX

The End Of The Age

1. Throughout the ages all nations and all peoples have been looking for the coming of One clothed with the power of heaven. Explain this idea from a metaphysical standpoint.

2. Did Jesus understand the higher astronomy of past ages? What was his attitude toward it?

3. Is the accepted teaching of "the end of the world" founded on the Bible? Explain.

4. As the mentality of the race changes as evidenced in literature, science, and religion is there a corresponding growth in spiritual freedom? Give full explanation.

5. Explain how to hold fast to the Christ principles in order to retain mental balance during the present time, in which the race is changing its vibrations to a higher rate.

6. Who are the "children of God"? Who are the "sons of God"?

7. How do we enter into a fuller understanding of the spiritual laws lying back of the phenomena of existence?

8. Explain fully why we should not separate Jesus from the rest of the race but should look upon Him as our way-shower.

9. Give a scientific explanation of the second coming of the Son of man. Give reasons for your answer.

10. What does the great need in the world today of the Christ consciousness imply? Give reasons for your answer.

The Revealing Word

Foreword

The Revealing Word offers Truth students the metaphysical meanings and uses of words and phrases that frequently appear in Unity publications, and many that appear in the Bible. Whereas Unity's Metaphysical Bible Dictionary explains the esoteric meanings of scriptural proper names, The Revealing Word is devoted mostly to common names. In addition to words that have religious significance, hundreds of words that are in everyday use appear in this book. Thus the reader is given inner meanings that he or she can apply to daily living. All things in life are expressed in words. Equipped with the inner meanings of words, a person can control all the issues of his or her life, from the insignificant to the great.

abate--To lessen; to moderate. In making a demonstration, when we reach the point where the mind changes from the negative to the positive state the troubled thoughts begin to abate. A certain set of negative ideas has run its course, and the restorative thought forces are in evidence.

Abba--A word of endearment signifying father. It is only as we come to know our sonship, our true relation to God, that we enter into the consciousness of love and tender affiliation with Spirit, signified by the word Abba. (see Mark 14:36)

abdicate--To let go; to relinquish; to renounce. The ability to abdicate is twofold in action: it eliminates the error, and it expands the good. When the ego consciously lets go and willingly gives up its personal ideas and loves, it has fulfilled the law of denial and is restored to the Father's house.

abide--To continue in a fixed thought of God, the All-Good; to dwell in the Christ consciousness. "If ye abide in me, and my words abide in you, ask whatsoever ye will, and it shall be done unto you" (John 15:7).

Abiding--A conscious centering of the mind in divine Principle within us by means of repeated affirmations of our faith and trust in Principle.

abiding Presence--Christ, the presence of light, peace, joy, love, life, and substance that is ever within, about, before, and beside man. (see presence of God)

absolute, the--Divine Mind; unlimited Principle; the almighty One; the all-pervading Spirit; the Infinite; the Eternal; the Supreme Being. The one ultimate creative Mind; the Source of all things. That which is unconditioned, unlimited, unrestricted, and free from all limitations. The self-existent God.

Absolute, to place judgment in the--The metaphysician finds it necessary to place his judgment in the Absolute in order to demonstrate His supreme power. This is accomplished by first declaring that one's judgment is spiritual and not material, that its origin is in God, that all its conclusions are based on Truth, and that they are absolutely free from prejudice, false sympathy, or personal ignorance.

Absolute, treating in the--Treating in the consciousness of the Spirit of God; affirming the absolute Truth of Being for man.

Absolute, unification of man with the--Man unifies himself with the Absolute through recognition that he is the son and heir of the Father, in whose image and likeness he was created. By realizing the Mind of Christ, he becomes one with the Absolute.

abstract, the--The realm of pure ideas such as goodness, purity, wisdom, and love.

abundance, spiritual--Ideas in consciousness of the omnipresent supply and support of the one Mind; invisible substance, with infinite capacity of expansion when held in mind, affirmed, and praised. "All things whatsoever the Father hath are mine" (John 16:15).

abundance, steps in demonstrating--First, we must recognize abundance as an idea that is real and has the power to expand. Then, we must talk abundance--choose words representing abundance--and thus build up an invisible world of substance. In this way, we build or form in our mind that which draws to us an abundance of every good thing. "For whosoever hath, to him shall be given" (Luke 8:18).

accident--An unfortunate event that takes place without our conscious foreknowledge.

accidents, cause and cure of--The cause of all accidents lies in sense consciousness. To be free from all accidents, we must raise our consciousness, so that it is spiritually positive and Christlike. Then we shall attract only good.

accuser--Opposer; hater; an enemy. (see Devil and Satan) The accuser is overcome by casting him down in the name of Jesus Christ.

achievement, universal desire for--The craving for accomplishment, innate in every man. The universal desire for worth-while achievement, giving a mighty impulse to all things, is divinely good.

acquisitiveness--The desire to acquire. It is a legitimate faculty of mind, but covetousness is the Judas trait. When a man seeks to acquire from God only, acquisitiveness builds up his consciousness, but when he oversteps the law and seeks that which belongs to another his acquisitiveness becomes a destroyer. (see covetousness)

activity, spiritual--Thoughts in relation to spiritual Principle. Mind movement in accordance with the activity of Divine Mind.

Adam--Red; reddish. The first movement of mind in its contact with life and substance. Adam was created from the "dust of the ground" (Gen. 2:7). Dust represents the radiant earth or substance. When spiritual man (I AM) enters into this substance and makes use of the God ideas inherent in him, he brings forth the ideal body in its elemental perfection. Adam was first perfect as an idea in elemental divinity.

Adam man--Unregenerate sense man; antichrist: the man who has fallen away from spirituality. Originally Adam was the spiritually illumined man of God. The Adam man was primitively identified with an infinite capacity for expansion. When he recognizes his identity as spiritual he expands in divine order and brings forth only good.

Adam man, ills of--The many ills of the Adam man grew out of his belief that he could satisfy and nourish himself with material food and drink alone. To feed the body is not enough. The spiritual man hungers for the bread of life and thirsts for living water, even the Word of God.

Adam man, transformation of--We are not to erase Adam, but we are to transform him by the renewing of our mind. "And be not fashioned according to this world: but be ye transformed by the renewing of your mind, that ye may prove what is the good and acceptable and perfect will of God" (Rom. 12:2).

adjustment--The rearrangement of thoughts according to the divine order of the Christ Mind; a bringing of man's consciousness into exact correspondence with God's perfect harmony, or heaven. "And the crooked shall become straight, and the rough ways smooth" (Luke 3:5).

adultery--Mixed thoughts, errors that have their existence in the unregenerated feelings; thoughts that have not come under the dominion of the I AM.

Adversary, the--The vain imagination that there could, in reality, be anything opposed to Divine Mind, or could be any separation of man from it, led to the forming of a state of mind that is described in the Bible as the "adversary." We find that the various names--Satan; Devil; Adversary; accuser; carnal mind; old man; man of sin; and personality--all refer to the consciousness that man has built up in his ignorance of his true estate.

affirm--To hold steadfast in mind or to speak aloud a statement of Truth.

affirm the salvation of the Lord--To realize silently and to declare audibly that the Christ within us is taking charge of all our affairs.

affirmation--A positive statement of Truth. By the use of affirmations we claim and appropriate that which is ours in Truth. (see denial)

affirmation, act of--The "yes" action of the mind; the act of affirming; the declaring of Truth; the mental movement that asserts confidently and persistently the Truth of Being in the face of all appearances to the contrary.

affirmation and denial--Two movements of the mind that express power to accept or to reject, to lay hold of or to let go. (see denial)

affirmation, how made--Affirmations do not have to be made only in set terms such as, "I affirm my body to be spiritual." The sum total of thought in all its positive aspects composes the affirmations that bring ideas into form.

affirmation, purpose of--To establish in consciousness a broad understanding of the divine principles on which all life and existence depend. By affirming Truth we are lifted out of false thinking into the consciousness of Spirit.

affirmation, remedial effects of--All unrighteous conditions may be adjusted through affirming the power of the great universal Spirit of justice. Affirm: "The infinite Spirit of love and justice is now operating in all my affairs, and all is well."

age--A cycle or a dispensation. Jesus was acquainted with cycles or ages of spiritual development of which the natural man knew nothing. Jesus came at the end of an age. Age to mortal man is the measurement of the life or existence of a person or thing. It is based on the false concept of time as reality. "What is the signal of Your presence, and the completion of this age?" (Matt. 24:3, Fenton.)

air--The deific breath of God. It symbolizes a purifying, vitalizing power that revives and makes alive.

alchemy, divine--Transmutation; changing in action and in character from the mortal into the spiritual. It has been said that the mind is the crucible in which the ideal is transmuted into the real.

alcoholism--A diseased condition brought about by one who, thirsting for the true stimulation of Spirit, resorts to the excessive use of false stimulants, such as alcoholic beverages. The way to demonstrate over this condition is to turn wholeheartedly to Spirit and to realize and to affirm that the desire for false stimulants is dissolved and dissipated and that the pure spiritual life of Christ satisfies and uplifts.

allegiance to the Father--The consciousness that divine wisdom is guiding the universe and man, which gives man a feeling of security. Allegiance to the Father signifies a constant devotion to and trust in the Father.

allegory--A symbolical representation of Truth. "Which things contain an allegory" (Gal. 4:24).

All-Good--Divine Mind; God; the principle of divine benevolence that permeates the universe.

almighty--All-powerful; having all power or force to accomplish anything. All things are possible with God, because He is infinitely all-mighty. All the power, all the force, all the might of the universe are God's; He is, in truth, almighty God. "Jehovah appeared to Abram, and said unto him, I am God Almighty" (Gen. 17:1).

Alpha and Omega--The beginning and the end; the Son of God; all in all. "I am the Alpha and the Omega" (Rev. 22:13).

altar--Stabilized place of worship. A fixed, definite center in consciousness; the place in consciousness where we meet the Lord and are willing to give up our sins, to give up the lower for the higher, the personal for the impersonal.

The altar mentioned in Rev. 11:1 symbolizes the consciousness of full consecration that takes place first in the temple of worship within: "Present your bodies a living sacrifice, holy, acceptable to God, which is your spiritual service" (Rom. 12:1).

altar, brazen, of temple worship--Represents the generative life.

altar, golden, of incense--Symbolizes the establishing of permanent resolutions of purity and covenants with the higher law of obedience, although it may entail daily sacrifice. (This applies to the altar of the burnt offerings also.)

altar, to an unknown God--A yearning to know the unrevealed Spirit and a reaching out for a fuller realization of its source.

alternate between good and evil--To swing the mind from good to evil and vice versa, with consequent variation in the application of Truth principles. Alternation is fatal to realization. "For let not that man think that he shall receive anything of the Lord; a double-minded man, unstable in all his ways" (James 1:7,8).

ambition--A subtle mental force that drives men toward their goals. If it is dedicated wholly to Spirit and acts from Principle, it will work for good. If its motto is, "The end justifies the means," it is a menace.

ancestors--Forefathers. Those who think of themselves as descended from human ancestors are in bondage to all the limitations of those ancestors, regardless of their claims to the contrary. It is a falling short of the full stature of man to regard himself as descending from the human family. This is the sin that keeps the majority of men in bondage to sense consciousness.

angel--A messenger of God; the projection into consciousness of a spiritual idea direct from the Fountainhead, Jehovah. "And there appeared unto him an angel of the Lord standing on the right side of the altar" (Luke 1:11). The word of Truth, in which is centered the power of God to overcome all limited beliefs and conditions.

angel, of Jehovah--The quickening thought of God appearing in the form of light or divine intelligence, intuition, and understanding.

angels, ascending and descending--The imaging power of the mind receiving divine ideas and reflecting them into the consciousness.

angels, office of--To guard, to direct, and to redeem the natural forces of the body and mind, which have in them the future of the whole man.

anointed of God, the--One who is conscious of the real spiritual outpouring from the source of his being; a consecrated person, "The Spirit of the Lord is upon me, because he anointed me" (Luke 4:18).

anointing--A symbolical expression of the pouring out of the spirit of love on one who has faith in God. Rubbing with oil; consecrating the body with the living Spirit of Christ. "But thou, when thou fastest, anoint thy head, and wash thy face" (Matt. 6:17).

antichrist--That which denies or opposes the idea that the Christ dwells in and is the true self of each individual. The active effort in the world to exalt death and to delude men into believing that death is the way to eternal life is an instance of work that is antichrist. Such a thought is opposed to Christ. Jesus came to deliver the human race from death and to fulfill in man God's perfect will, abundant life. The antichrist thoughts must be persistently denied. The perfect will of God for all men is abundant life, not death.

anxiety--A form of fear; a negative mental attitude that keeps God's good from man.

apostles--Those sent forth; messengers; ambassadors; active spiritual thoughts. Jesus conferred this title on the Twelve whom He sent forth to teach and to heal.

In order to command our powers and to bring them into unity of action, we must know what they are and their respective places on the staff of Being. The Grand Man, Christ, has twelve powers of fundamental ideas, represented in the history of Jesus by the Twelve Apostles. So each of us has twelve faculties or fundamental ideas to make manifest, to bring out, and to use in the attainment of his ideals. There are innumerable other ideas, but each one stems from some one of these fundamental ideas.

Jesus' twelve apostles were: Peter (faith); Andrew (strength); James, son of Zebedee (wisdom or judgment); John (love); Philip (power); Bartholomew (imagination); Thomas (understanding); Matthew (will); James (order); Simon the Cananaean (zeal); Thaddaeus (renunciation or elimination); and Judas (life conserver). (see disciple, calling of)

appetite--Either the craving of the sense man for fulfillment of his fleshly desires or the hunger and thirst of the spirit for its divine inheritance. "But he awaketh . . . and, behold, he is faint, and his soul hath appetite" (Isa. 29:8).

appetite, carnal or sensual--A hunger and thirst for sensual pleasures; misdirected effort to obtain satisfaction through feeding the insatiable sense man. All indulgence of such appetite must be denied out of man's consciousness before Christ can be manifested.

appreciation--The act of appreciating; esteeming. Spiritually, man's mind esteems to a great measure the loveliness and power of omnipresent God, All-Good. "I will give thee thanks with my whole heart" (Psalms 138:1).

appropriation--The act of taking possession of something. To appropriate the word of Truth is to take the substance of the word into one's mind and heart.

ark--A holy place; a sanctuary; a tabernacle; the Christ center within wherein man is one with pure Being.

ark, Noah's--Symbolizes the spiritual part of oneself, built in the midst of the flood of error. One builds one's ark on the scientific understanding of the wisdom, presence, and power of God and on the affirmations of what one is in Spirit.

The only refuge from the Flood (see Gen. 6:18) was the ark of Jehovah. The ark represents a positive, saving state of consciousness, which agrees with or forms a covenant with the principle of Being, with subconscious inspiration, with Christ. This ark is the product of "rest" (Noah) in the spiritual part of us, right in the midst of the flood of error.

Ark of the Covenant--Represents the original spark of divinity in man's being, which is a sacred and holy thing. On its development depends man's immortality. The original spark (Ark of the Covenant) occupies the most holy place in the body temple and must be cared for with great devotion; otherwise, the spiritual forces are scattered.

No human hand is allowed to touch this ark of the covenant. No human thought can enter the sacred precincts, which are kept veiled from all eyes.

armor of God--The robe of righteousness. Error cannot enter the consciousness that is strongly fortified with the light, life, power, and substance of Spirit.

ascension--The ascending or progressive unfoldment of man from the animal to the spiritual. It is measured by three degrees or states of consciousness: first, the animal; second, the mental or psychical; and third, the spiritual. Jesus first manifested Himself as the man on the physical plane, from which He was resurrected to the mental or psychical; from thence He ascended to the spiritual.

asceticism--The practice of severe self-denial; the attempt to deny the body itself as an evil thing instead of beholding it as the sacred temple of the living God to be revered, respected, and loved.

aspirations--The deep longing of man for union with his source, with his Father-Mother, God.

"As the hart panteth after the water brooks,
So panteth my soul after thee, O God.
My soul thirsteth for God, for the living God"
(Psalms 42:1, 2).

ass--In Oriental countries in Bible times kings and rulers rode the ass, and it was the accepted bearer of royalty. The animal part of the human consciousness is typified by the ass, and the purpose of Jesus' riding an ass into Jerusalem was to portray the mastery by the I AM of the animal nature and its manifestation (colt). Jerusalem is the city of peace or spiritual consciousness. The characteristics of the ass are stubbornness, persistency, and endurance. To ride these is to make them obedient to one's will.

association, spiritual--Living in an uninterrupted relationship with ideas that come into consciousness from God.

astrology--"The pseudo science which treats of the influence of the stars upon human affairs, and of foretelling terrestrial events by their position and aspects" (Webster). Astrology represents the belief in man that his good depends wholly on something outside himself--his ruling star, fate, providence--instead of depending on the power of his own thoughts to establish within himself and his world what he wills.

It is true that we are in sympathy with all nature, which includes the earth, the sun, the moon, and the stars. These are all ensouled, and their actions can affect us when we do not believe in a higher power. But there is a higher power in everyone: Spirit. In Genesis it is stated that spiritual man, the image-and-likeness man, was given dominion over all creation.

astronomy--"The science which treats of the celestial bodies, their magnitudes, motions, constitution, etcetera" (Webster).

The material universe is only the outpicturing of the spiritual universe. The pulsations of the spiritual forces impinge on and sway men, nations, and planets according to laws whose sweep in space and time is so stupendous as to be beyond the ken or comprehension of astronomy. But the fact should not be overlooked that higher astronomy had its votaries in the past. The Magi and the illumined sages of Chaldea and Egypt had astronomical knowledge of universal scope.

There is evidence that proves that the sages of the distant past knew a higher astronomy than do we of this age and that they predicted the future of this planet through cycles and aeons--its nights of mental darkness and the dawn of its spiritual day--with the same accuracy that our astronomers do its present-day planetary revolutions.

Jesus evidently understood this higher astronomy, and He knew that His work as a teacher and demonstrator of spiritual law was related to it, yet not controlled by it. He co-operated with the "law . . . and the prophets," as far as they went, but He knew the higher law of the Christ man and affirmed His supremacy in the words, "All authority hath been given unto me in heaven and on earth" (Matt. 28:18).

atmosphere--Individually, an extension of consciousness; collectively, the pervading influence of the predominating thoughts.

atom--"One of the small parts out of which any physical quantity is built up" (Webster). A particle charged with tremendous energy that may be released and made to give to man powers beyond expression. Jesus used the dynamic power of thought to break the bonds of the atoms composing the few loaves and fishes of the boy's lunch--and five thousand persons were fed. Material science says that each atom of matter has force and intelligence and a certain individuality; hence, it is a form of mind.

atonement--Reconciliation between God and man through Christ; the uniting of our consciousness with the higher consciousness. Jesus became the way by which all who accept Him may "pass over" to the higher consciousness. We have atonement through Him.

attainment, intellectual –Intellectual attainments are not in themselves of use in matters spiritual. They have their end in teaching the student how to command his faculties and to bring them into subjection. We must drop them out of our mind as quickly as we can and be willing to commence anew in the school of the higher life. Let us affirm often: "I am meek and lowly of heart. I am led of the Spirit."

attainment, spiritual--A laying hold of the high and lofty ideas of the Christ Mind; the bringing of spiritual ideas into manifestation in one's mind, body, and affairs.

attention--(see concentration)

attitude--The state of mind in relation to some matter or situation; a mental position. Attitude of mind toward environment determines the nature of man's environment. A positive attitude draws the good; a negative attitude brings its train of sin, sickness, poverty, and death. "For as he thinketh within himself, so is he" (Prov. 23:7).

attributes of Being--That which is inherent in the twelve powers of faculties.

augury--The blind following of the commands of some omen or voice, not of Spirit.

aura--The thought emanation that surrounds every person. As to whether it is an illumined aura, or medium, or dark and cloudy depends on the dominant thought force of each person. The aura around the bodies of sincere, honest persons is usually bright blue or some modification of blue. The aura is not visible to all persons, but only to those who have their psychical nature quickened on the spiritual plane.

There are in the world today men and women who have followed the teaching of Jesus and developed in their bodies a superenergy or life that not only permeates the physical structure but envelops it in a luminous aura that can be and is felt by both themselves and others. Spirit reveals that spiritual thinking breaks open the physical cells and atoms and releases their imprisoned life, which originally came from Divine Mind. Jesus carried this process so far that His whole body was transformed and became a conscious part of the Father's life and intelligence. (see halo and radiation)

aura, how created--Prayer liberates the energies pent up in the mind and body. Those who pray much create a spiritual aura that eventually envelops the whole body. The bands of light painted by artists around the heads of saints are not imaginary; they actually exist and are visible to the sharp eye of the painter. Luke testifies (9:29) that when Jesus was praying "his countenance was altered, and his raiment became white and dazzling." After Moses had been praying on the mountain his face shone so brightly that the people could not look at it, and he had to wear a veil.

authority--Rightful power; mastery; or dominion. "For he taught them as having authority" (Mark 1:22).

authority, having--Inspired by Spirit within. The Spirit of truth is the one and only authority in the study of Truth. (see John 16:13)

authority, parental--Human parental authority is a thought of bondage or slavery in mortal consciousness based on desire of parents to domineer and to wield power. Divine parental authority is child guidance based on love and understanding. It includes willingness to grant freedom to the child by helping him to know and to live Truth.

autosuggestion--The conscious impression of selected thoughts on the subconscious mind by oneself.

avarice--Inordinate greed for material riches. (Symbolized by "the money-changers.") The avaricious suffer most in body and are the most difficult to heal, because of the mental bias that prompts them to get all things as cheaply as possible, including the kingdom of heaven.

avarice, how to be free from--Establish in consciousness the idea of giving generously and freely, not from compulsion or for the sake of reward but from the pure love of giving.

awakening, spiritual--Becoming conscious of the things of Spirit, or God.

B

Baal worship--Putting nature before God in earth, air, and water; giving the substance of mind and body to the things of sense. It is a form of idolatry. "Thou shalt have no other gods before me" (Exod. 20:3).

babe--Metaphysically, a new state of consciousness; innocent and childlike.

babe in Christ--One whose face is turned toward the light, but who has not yet come into a deep understanding of Truth.

baptism--The spiritual cleansing of the mind. Typifies the cleansing power and work of Spirit that redeems men from sin. It is the first step in the realization of Truth. When the baptizing power of the word is poured on a center in consciousness, it dissolves all material thought, and through this cleansing, purifying process, the individual is prepared to see and to discern spiritually.

The two baptisms, those of John and Jesus, represent the two common steps in spiritual development, denial and affirmation, or the dropping of the old and laying hold of the new. In the first baptism, that of John, through the power of the word, the sense man is erased from consciousness, and the mind is purged and made ready for the second baptism, that of Jesus. In the second baptism, the creative law of divine affirmation, set into action by supreme Mind, lights its fires at the center of man's being, and when thus kindled raises soul and body to a high degree of purity. This process is known as regeneration.

baptism, Pentecostal--The great initial outpouring of Spirit that took place more than nineteen centuries ago. The primal baptism of the Holy Spirit. (see Acts 2:1-4)

baptism, the Holy Spirit--A quickening of the spiritual nature that is reflected in mind and body. Spiritual baptism has power; it is affirmative; it is positive. This outpouring of the Holy Spirit is the second baptism. Christ represents this phase of baptism. It is the most precious gift of God and comes to those who steadfastly seek first the kingdom of God and His righteousness. "He shall baptize you in the Holy Spirit" (Matt. 3:11).

beatitudes, Jesus'–Jesus in exaltation is blessing spiritual man with the attributes of God and also blessing the natural man with the attributes of the spiritual man. (see Matt. 5:3-11)

beauty, spiritual--The loveliness of God beheld in His creations by the eye of man. Spiritual man beholds this divine loveliness everywhere. "He hath made everything beautiful in its time" (Eccles. 3:11).

beholding--We are transformed by beholding. Whatever we persistently behold we manifest. Our looking into the perfect pattern, the indwelling Christ, and beholding His perfection transforms us into His likeness.

Being--God; the Mind of the universe composed of archetype ideas: life, love, wisdom, substance, Truth, power, peace, and so forth. Being is omnipresent, omnipotent, omniscient; it is the fullness of God, the All-Good.

Being, personal and impersonal nature of--Being is not only impersonal Principle as far as its inherent and undeviating laws are concerned, but also personal as far as its relation to each of us is concerned. We as individuals do actually become a focus of universal Spirit.

Being, the law of growth and--Being exists under two phases: invisible and visible, abstract and concrete. The visible comes forth from the invisible, and this coming forth is always according to a universal method of growth from minute generative centers. From center to circumference is the plan of procedure throughout the universe. To study form alone and to expect to learn from it and its evolutions the secret of existence does not enable one to catch sight of Spirit moving upon every generating center.

belief--An inner acceptance of an idea as true. Belief is closely related to faith. Belief functions both consciously and subconsciously. Many false individual and race beliefs are very active below the conscious level. To erase these hidden error beliefs, a comprehensive program of denial is necessary.

belief in separateness, results of--The belief in separateness from God Mind leads to ignorance and death. All intelligence and life are derived from the one Mind. When man thinks of himself as being alone, he cuts himself off in consciousness from the fount of inspiration. "For apart from me ye can do nothing" (John 15:5).

believe on the Son--We must come to His terms of expression. We do not believe that there are other sons wiser than He and that from them we can get wisdom, guidance, and understanding. We believe that He is, as far as we are concerned, the only begotten Son of the Father.

Bethesda, Pool of--"House of mercy; house of healing." Represents the realization in consciousness that our life is being constantly purified, healed, and made new by the activity of mind. Physically, this is expressed in the purification and upbuilding of the blood by its coming in contact with the oxygen of the air in the lungs.

Bible--The sacred and inspired Scriptures of the Christian religion. It is a divine "book of life" rather than merely a history of people, and it bears "witness unto the word" of God (Acts 14:3).

Bible characters--The characters of the Bible represent ideas in one's own mind. When this symbolism is understood one can follow the characters in their various movements and thus find the way to solve all one's life's problems.

Bible, place in Truth study--The Bible is a recital of what has taken place in the consciousness of man, of the results of his working, either intelligently with the law or unintelligently against it, in seeking his own salvation. It gives an explanation of spiritual law as applied to man and tells him how to find the kingdom of heaven within.

Bible, spiritual interpretation of the--A spiritual interpretation of the Bible demands that the meaning of every figure, type, parable, and symbol must be in harmony with the fundamental principles of Being.

birth, new--The awakening of man to a consciousness of his unity with the one universal Spirit; the change from mortal to spiritual consciousness through the begetting and quickening power of the word of Truth. It is the change that comes here and now. Jesus made no mention of resurrection after death as having any part in the new birth. "Except one be born anew, he cannot see the kingdom of God" (John 3:3).

birth, new, change following--When man is begotten and born of the Word he is no longer "flesh . . . as grass" (I Pet. 1:24) but is eternal and abiding, not subject to death and corruption.

birth, new, effect of--Begetting and quickening take place in man's inner consciousness, but the process of being "born anew" (John 3:3) includes the whole man, spirit, soul, and body. To be born again is to be made "a new creature" (II Cor. 5:17) having "this mind in you, which was also in Christ Jesus" (Phil. 2:5) and a body like unto His glorious body.

black magic--Jesus said that the kingdom of heaven had been taken by violence and force. "And from the days of John the Baptist until now the kingdom of heaven suffereth violence, and men of violence take it by force" (Matt. 11:12). It is possible to use the life, substance, and power that form the basis of the kingdom of heaven in selfish ways. This is black magic and is the work of the selfish personality that Jesus refers to in Matt. 10:28, "Fear him who is able to destroy both soul and body in hell."

blasphemy--Impious or irreverent thoughts toward God, such as sickness, poverty, death. "But the blasphemy against the Spirit shall not be forgiven" (Matt. 12:31).

bless--To invoke good upon; to call forth the action of God; to confer God's good on something or someone.

blessedness of God--The joy that comes from God to those whose thoughts are stayed on Him. "Everlasting joy shall be unto them" (Isa. 61:7).

blessing, power of--Blessing imparts the quickening spiritual power that produces growth and increase. It is the power of multiplication.

blood--Expresses a spiritual principle that has been introduced into the race mind through the purified Jesus. It is a spiritual principle in that it rests on pure ideals; yet it is manifested in mind and body in concrete form when rightly appropriated. That it can be appropriated and used to the purification of the mind and the healing of the body, thousands are proving in this day.

Through His experience on the Cross, where His precious blood was spilled, through His suffering there, Jesus lowered His consciousness to the consciousness of the race, thereby administering to the whole race a blood transfusion, imparting to man the properties of Being that will restore him to his divine estate. Such a transfusion not only revives us in temporal ills, but begins in the body a purifying and energizing process that will finally save us from death.

blood of Christ--The life contained in God's Word. Therefore, it is spiritual energy that purifies and redeems man by pouring into his life currents a new and purer stream. This divine energy cleanses the consciousness of dead works to enable man to serve the living God.

blood of Jesus--That which represents the principle of eternal life. Jesus raised the life activity of His blood and revealed its spiritual potency. In this respect it became part of the spiritual life of the race and is thus accessible to all persons. It is after this manner that we drink His blood. "Except ye eat the flesh of the Son of man and drink his blood, ye have not life in yourselves" (John 6:53).

blood of the Lamb--The innocent, undefiled life, or the primal life of Being, which Jesus made accessible to all those who believe in Him as the revealer of the pure life of God the Father. "These are they that come out of the great tribulation, and they washed their robes and made them white in the blood of the Lamb" (Rev. 7:14).

blood, spilling of--(see meat eating)

boat--Symbolizes a positive, sustaining state of consciousness that prevents one from sinking into a negative condition (water) and bears up the faculties of the mind.

body--The outer expression of consciousness; the precipitation of the thinking part of man. God created the idea of the body of man as a self-perpetuating, self-renewing organism, which man reconstructs into his personal body. God creates the body idea, or divine idea, and man, by his thinking, makes it manifest. As God created man in His image and likeness by the power of His word, so man, as God's image and likeness, projects his body by the same power.

All thoughts and ideas embody themselves according to their character. Material thoughts make a material body. Spiritual thoughts make a spiritual body.

body, disintegration of the, cause and remedy--The body disintegrates because generation after generation men have tried to bring forth after the wisdom of Satan instead of the wisdom of God. Jesus made the unity between the superconsciousness in the top brain and the life center, and by following His methods and identifying ourselves with His spiritual consciousness we may get back into our former spiritual estate in the Garden of Eden. "As in Adam all die, so also in Christ shall all be made alive" (I Cor. 15:22).

body, effects of sin and righteousness on the--The body is destroyed, made sick unto death by sin and ignorance; the body is made alive in Christ through understanding and righteousness. "The wages of sin is death; but the free gift of God is eternal life in Christ Jesus" (Rom. 6:23).

body, given benefit of salvation--The body receives the benefit of salvation through prayer and spiritual meditation. In this way the substance of Spirit is carried by living words of Truth into every part of the body, and its quickening power makes alive the whole organism.

body, how to make perfect--Man may have a perfect body and a perfect world when he understands and uses the perfect word, the complete word, the word that contains all the attributes of God. When the words of man are charged with a full understanding of Divine Mind and its inhering ideas and he consciously applies this knowledge in all his feeling, thinking, speaking, and living, he will be able to show forth a perfect body and a perfect world.

body, how transformed--The body is transformed by the renewing of the mind. By affirmation the mind lays hold of living words of Truth and builds them into mind and body. When we enter into and abide in the Son of God consciousness we have eternal life, and the body is transformed into pure flesh manifesting the perfection of Spirit.

body, natural forces of the--The natural forces of the body are eager to co-operate with man in manifesting a perfect body. Man must co-operate with them by obeying divine law.

body, redemption of the--The body is made and sustained by thought. Its character is like the thought that made it. Every thought has in it an idea of substance and life. When the mind of man is in conscious union with Divine Mind his body manifests perfection.

The body can be redeemed only by man's taking it beyond the three dimensions of the earthly realm and raising it to the fourth dimension. The earthly body is substance in its gross form and as such is still subject to the physical laws that operate in gross substance. But when perfect ideas of life and substance are attained in consciousness, the three dimensions of mind, idea, and expression will be embraced in the fourth dimension of realization or Divine Mind. Then the same spiritual conditions will be found in manifestation as are in Spirit or God-Mind.

body, spiritual--The perfect manifestation of a divine idea. It is composed of spiritual substance so pure that no disintegrating force can be found in it. This body of pure Spirit is the very temple of the living God; a radiant, beautiful body illumined with the eternal light of Spirit. "That they may behold my glory, which thou hast given me" (John 17:24).

body of Christ--The body that is the result of spiritual thought. It maintains its unity with Spirit, even in manifestation. This is first individual, and then universal, including all men.

body of Christ, members of the--All those who forsake everything pertaining to the personal, limited self and measure up to the Christ standard in thoughts and acts, thus bringing forth the unlimited fruits of Spirit, are members of the one body: the body of Christ.

body of light--Jesus, dwelling continually in the consciousness of Being, the very substance and life of God, had conscious realization of His actual oneness with Spirit. His body became a "body . . . of light" (Luke 11:34) spiritual substance, the very essence of Being. "He that hath seen me hath seen the Father" (John 14:9).

bondage--Undue attachment to thoughts in personal consciousness, such as race, class, sex, age, or personality. "Whatsoever thou shalt bind on earth shall be bound in heaven and whatsoever thou shalt loose on earth shall be loosed in heaven" (Matt. 16:19).

bosom, Abraham's--The peace and contentment that come to those who trust God.

bounty, the Lord's--The generosity of God.

bread--Representative of universal substance. The substance of the omnipresent Christ body. Our daily bread is the sustenance for spirit, mind, and body. Some of this daily bread is appropriated in the form of food. There is substance in words of Truth, and this substance is appropriated by prayer and meditation on Truth.

bread, breaking of--Stirring into action, in consciousness, of the inner substance of Spirit (bread) and the concentrating of mind on it as the real possession. "And they continued stedfastly in the apostles' teaching and fellowship, in the breaking of bread and the prayers" (Acts 2:42).

bread from heaven--Descent into man's consciousness of ideas that are manifested as manna, which feeds and refreshes. "I have meat to eat that ye know not" (John 4:32).

bread of life--The word of Truth that imparts new vitality to mind and body. "Thou shalt eat bread at my table continually" (II Sam. 9:7).

breastplate--The breastplate of the high priest of Israel had on it twelve precious stones, representing the twelve tribes of Israel. This means that the twelve faculties of the mind must be massed at the great brain center called the solar plexus breath--The inner life flow that pulsates through the whole being. The breathing of the manifest man corresponds to the inspiration of the spiritual man. When any man is inspired with high ideas he breathes "into his nostrils the breath of life" (Gen. 2:7).

breath of the Almighty--The inspiration of Spirit; the silent movement of God within our being.

"There is a spirit in man,

And the breath of the Almighty giveth them understanding"(Job 32:8).

The breath of God, which became the soul of the man manifestation, includes all emotions and energies that move in and through the organism, and it is always designated as feminine. Psyche is the name of that subtle essence that flows in and out of the great heart center called in physiology the cardiac plexus. The name Psyche, which figures in Greek mythology, means breath, life. Psyche is represented as one of the three daughters of a king. These three "daughters" are spirit, soul, and body. Psyche is the soul in its many earthly experiences, in its failures and its successes.

breathing--The symbol of inspiration. Jesus breathed on His apostles and said to them, "Receive ye the Holy Spirit" (John 20:22).

brotherhood--An established thought in high spiritual consciousness. This thought springs from the understanding that God is the one Father and that all men are brothers.

burdens--Beliefs in ill-health, lack, personal responsibility, prejudice, fear, condemnation, and all other negative things. Truth will make us free from each one of these burdens.

burning bush--When we arrive at a four-sided or balanced state of mind, the light of intuition or flame of fire burns in our heart, yet it is not consumed; there is no

loss of substance. In thinking there is a vibratory process in the brain that uses up nerve tissue, but in the wisdom that comes from the heart the "bush" or tissue is not consumed. This thinking in wisdom is "holy ground," or substance in its spiritual wholeness; that is, the idea of substance in Divine Mind.

by night--In the darkness of intellectual consciousness. Nicodemus visited with Jesus "by night" (John 3:2).

calf of gold--Represents the tendency of man to form images after the pattern that he sees with the eye rather than from the ideals that rise in the silent meditations of the mind.

Calvary--(see Golgotha)

camel--In individual consciousness the camel is a symbol of power, endurance, strength, and patient perseverance.

candlestick--The candlestick of the Temple represents the intelligence in man. The "seven golden candlesticks" of Rev. 1:12 are receptacles of spiritual light.

capacity, spiritual--Transcending intellectual knowledge. Nearly everyone has at some time touched this hidden wisdom and been more or less astonished at its revelations.

cause and effect--The law of sequence; the balance wheel of the universe. This law, like all other divine laws, inheres in Being and is good. "Whatsoever a man soweth, that shall he also reap" (Gal. 6:7). Man lives in two worlds, the world of cause (the within) and the world of effect (the without).

causes, primal--Primal causes are complete, finished, absolute. All that man manifests has its origin in a cause that we name Divine Mind. The one Mind is absolute, and all its manifestations or effects are in essence like itself. This being true in logic, it is not a difficult matter to arrive at the conclusion that the effect proves the character of the cause.

cells of the body--Structural and functional units of organism made up of atoms composed of electrons and protons, which, in reality, have their origin in the supermind.

These cells are adjusted one to the other through associated ideas. When divine love enters into man's thought process every cell is poised and balanced in right order. Law and order rule in the cells of the body with the exactness that characterizes their action in the worlds of a planetary system.

center in consciousness--A faculty through which a mind quality is expressed. When a center loses its power it should be baptized by the word of Spirit. This cleanses all material thought; impotence is vitalized with new life, and the whole subconsciousness is awakened and quickened.

chaos--Disorder; confusion; discord. Chaos in body and affairs results from chaos in mind, a product of the sense man.

character, spiritual--The true estimate of man's qualities. Character building is ever from within outward. Spiritual discernment of the reality of man's origin and being in God is the only enduring foundation of character.

cheerfulness--A steady, quiet, beautiful expression of the joy of God. It is conducive to good health because it frees one from tension.

chemicalization--A condition in the mind that is brought about by the conflict that takes place when a high spiritual realization contacts an old error state of consciousness.

The mind of man is constantly at work, and this work results in the production of thought forms. These thought forms assume individual definiteness; they take on personality, which works out into the body. Whenever a new spiritual idea is introduced into the mind, some negative belief is disturbed. It resists. With this resistance comes more or less commotion in the consciousness. This is called chemicalization. This can be greatly modified or eliminated by putting the mind in divine order through denial.

If the cleansing baptism of denial does not precede the Holy Spirit's descent, there is conflict in the consciousness--the old error thoughts contend for their place, refuse to go out, and a veritable war is the result. When the conscious mind has been put in order, the Holy Spirit descends with peace like a dove.

cherubim--Protection; sacred life. The inner, spiritual life is protected from the outer, coarser consciousness. The cherubim spread their wings over the place of the Ark and covered it. Also in the Scriptures cherubim are symbolic figures representing the attributes and majesty of God.

childlike--(see meek)

Children of Israel--The thoughts of reality or the true ideas about Being that have to be brought out in every part of man's consciousness. These thoughts are brought down from the land of Canaan into Egypt (the flesh consciousness) and, for a season, are submerged in the fleshly realm, or thoughts in form.

Heaven, according to Jesus, is within man; and with this understanding we see that the escape of the Israelites from Egypt is paralleled by the escape of man from ignorance and materiality.

chosen of God--God has chosen each of us as a medium for the expression of Himself as love, life, wisdom, abundance, health, and so forth. "Ye did not choose me, but I chose you, and appointed you, that ye should go and bear fruit" (John 15:16).

chosen people--The "royal priesthood" making up the Christ body; by overcoming, they have incorporated into their consciousness the attributes of God. They are the living expression of His righteousness and glory.

Christ--The incarnating principle of the God-man; the perfect Word or idea of God, which unfolds into the true man and is blessed with eternal life by measuring up to the divine standard, thus fulfilling the law of righteousness. "Thou art my beloved Son, in thee I am well pleased" (Mark 1:11).

Christ is the divine man. Jesus is the name that represents an individual expression of the Christ idea. Christ existed long before Jesus. It was the Christ Mind in Jesus that exclaimed, "And now, Father, glorify thou me with thine own self with the glory which I had with thee before the world was" (John 17:5).

Christ abides in each person as his potential perfection. Jesus Christ, the embodiment of all divine ideas, exists eternally in the Mind of Being as the only begotten Son of God, the "Messiah" or "anointed one," and is the living Principle working in man. (See the way and Jesus)

Christ and Jehovah--Jehovah of the Old Testament is the I AM, or Christ of God invisible; the Messiah is the promise of the visible manifestation of that I AM, or Christ, and Jesus Christ is the fulfillment in man of that original spiritual I AM, or Jehovah.

Christ, abide in--To dwell continually in the consciousness of Christ to the point of realization of unity with the Father and Son. To abide in Christ is to live in the perfection of God-Mind, the thought of God, the living Christ.

Christ, birth of--Man is the bringing forth (the birth) of God's idea of man, the Christ of God. This is done through the quickening power of the word of Truth. The birth of Christ is the beginning in the inner realms of consciousness of a higher set of faculties, which, when grown to full stature, will save the whole man from ignorance, sickness, and death.

Christ, first coming of--The dawning in mind that spiritual man is the real Son of God.

Christ, formation of--When man appropriates words of Truth he partakes of that which forms the spiritual soul, substance, and life of Spirit and which manifests as Christ in the perfect body. Every student of Truth is letting "Christ be formed" (Gal. 4:19) in him when he constantly abides in the Christ Mind through daily meditating on words of Truth.

Christ, indwelling--The Son of God or spiritual nucleus within each person. All our thoughts must harmonize with this spiritual center before we can bring into expression the divine consciousness. Each man has within himself the Christ idea, just as Jesus had. Man must look to the indwelling Christ in order to recognize his sonship, his divine origin and birth, even as did the Saviour. This real self is "closer . . . than breathing, and nearer than hands and feet." It is the kingdom of God in each person. "Neither shall they say, Lo, here! or, There! for lo, the kingdom of God is within you" (Luke 17:21).

Christ in you--The true light, which guides every man coming into the world, is, and ever has been, in man. Even the outer man was formed and came into existence through it. This is "Christ in you, the hope of glory" (Col. 1:27).

Christ, joint heirs with--We are joint heirs with Christ to all that the Father has. This truth alone--the belief that in the regenerate state we are to be like Jesus, who became Christ manifested--leads us to a desire and an effort to attain our inheritance of eternal life here and now, because we know that there is no other thing in the universe worth striving for.

Christ, second coming of--The awakening and the regeneration of the subconscious mind through the superconscious or Christ Mind.

Christ body, work of the--The work of the Christ body is the "restoration of all things, whereof God spake by the mouth of his holy prophets that have been from of old" (Acts 3:21). (see body of Christ)

Christian conversion--A letting go of sin; a moral cleansing. This type of conversion is good as far as it goes, but it is far from complete. (see conversion)

Christianity--The science of eternal life. It is governed by scientific principles of mind action, which are really the foundation of all the various sciences.

Christianity began with Jesus and was carried on by His apostles. He commanded them to cast out demons, to heal the sick, to make the blind to see, even to raise the dead. Whenever Truth is declared in the name of Jesus Christ, the demons of fear and disease are cast out.

Christianity, esoteric--Christianity that deals with the deep metaphysical truths that Jesus taught. "The letter killeth, but the spirit giveth life" (II Cor. 3:6).

Christianity, exoteric--Christianity that deals with the letter or surface meaning of the teachings of Jesus.

Christianity, practical--The teachings of Jesus practically applied to the everyday life of man. Practical Christianity is not a term applied to an arbitrary theory of human origin; neither is it a revelation to humanity from some prophet whose word alone must be taken unquestionably as authority. It is, in this respect, different from most religious systems of the world. Its students are not asked to believe anything that they cannot logically demonstrate to be true. Thus, it is the only system of religion before the people today that, because of its universal appeal to the pure reason in man, can be accepted and applied by every nation under the sun.

Christian, or Gentile--In the New Testament symbology Christian typifies the spiritual and Gentile the material.

church--The word church is derived from a Greek word meaning "the Lord's house." The individual's consciousness is his "Lord's house," and assembled within it are groups or aggregations of ideas (thought centers). The spiritualized will carries to the different "churches" (thought centers) the word of Truth and builds them up into a knowledge of their perfection and divinity by training them in spiritual thinking.

church of Christ--Spiritual consciousness, first individual, then collective. In the general usage the word church applies to persons who have been "born anew" (John 3:3) through the quickening power of the word, gathered together in one body, their union being typified by the human body.

Jesus never organized a church on earth; neither did He authorize anyone else to do so. He said to Peter, "Upon this rock I will build my church" (Matt. 16:18). He did not tell Peter that he was to be the head of the church, with a line of popes to follow. He said, "I will build my church" (ecclesia, assembly, or called-out ones). Jesus is still the head of His "assembly," and its only organization is in Spirit. He gave but one guide, one source from which His followers should receive their inspiration: "The Holy Spirit, whom the Father will send in my name, he shall teach you all things, and bring to your remembrance all that I said unto you" (John 14:26).

circulation, spiritual--The inner stream of life, substance, and intelligence flowing freely through the entire being.

circumcision--Symbolical of the cutting off of mortal tendencies; indicative of purification and cleanliness under divine law. Circumcision is fulfilled in its spiritual meaning by the freeing of the individual from the law of sin and death. "Circumcision is that of the heart, in the spirit not in the letter" (Rom. 2:29).

clairvoyance--"The power of discerning objects not present to the senses but regarded as having objective reality" (Webster). Intuitive perception; clear vision. Everything that takes place in the world of manifestation first takes place in the realm of thought. If one is spiritually quickened to the measure that he can discern the thought movements, he can gain a foreknowledge of what is about to occur.

coats of skins--The body of flesh. Man was connected originally with the spiritual-body idea, but when he took on personal consciousness he was given "coats of skins," which, under divine law, corresponded with the quality of his thought world. When spiritual thought becomes supreme in consciousness, the coats of skins will give way to the manifestation of the spiritual body, which is the immortal body that was spoken of by Paul.

coat without seam--The "coat . . . without seam," which the soldiers did not separate, represents the great unified doctrine of Truth that Jesus left (John 19:23). (see vesture of Jesus)

cocreator, man with God--"My Father worketh even until now, and I work" (John 5:17). God creates in the ideal, and man carries out in the manifest world what God has idealized. Jesus treats this relation between the Father and the Son in the 5th chapter of The Gospel According to John: "The Son can do nothing of himself, but what he seeth the Father doing: for what things soever he doeth, the Son also doeth in like manner" (John 5:19).

Comforter, the--The Holy Spirit, the only authorized interpreter of the gospel of Jesus; He who gives comfort and cheer and reveals the Truth of God to us.

commandments--Having to do with the law or the orderly working out of divine principles. Moses represents the "Thou shalt not" phase of law; Jesus represents the "Thou shalt" phase of law.

commandments, to keep His--This is to command, to control, and to direct every thought according to the harmonious law of love one to another.

communion--Sharing the deep aspirations of our heart with the indwelling Father and hearing His "still small voice" (I Kings 19:12).

communion, kept secret--There are times when it is to our own spiritual benefit and to God's glory to keep things concealed and, like Mary, to ponder them in our heart until due time for expression. There are joys of the Spirit that are secret between a man and his Lord. One feels a sense of condemnation and depletion if he talks too freely about his communion with the Lord.

companionship--Association of those who are in divine harmony. This perfect fellowship is best found by those who practice quiet communion with God.

compass, points of the--In scriptural symbology east means the within, which is spiritual; west, the without, which is expression; north, the above, or intellect; south, the below, or physical.

compassion, divine--In the heart of God exists an eternal tenderness and mercy for His children. "Jehovah is gracious, and merciful" (Psalms 145:8).

compassion, human--A characteristic of love and mercy prompted by an understanding heart. A compassionate mind sees the error, but does not condemn. "Neither do I condemn thee: go thy way; from henceforth sin no more" (John 8:11).

compensation, law of--The order under which one receives just remuneration. The law of compensation is universal and not subject to personal demands. If the mind is turned toward man as one's recompense, it is turned away from divine law.

concentration--A thought center; a nucleus of faith or spiritual confidence. The centering of the attention on a particular idea. Concentration forms a mental loadstone in the mind to which thought substance rushes like iron filings to a magnet, bringing the forces, whether mental or physical, to a common purpose.

conception--Power of forming ideas in substance; the embodiment of an idea.

condemnation, dangerous--According to Webster, condemn means "to pronounce to be wrong." There is always a cause for every mental tangent, and that which would kill the sense man, root and branch, has its point of departure from the line of harmony in the thought of condemnation. In John the Baptist it seemed a virtue, in that he condemned his own errors, but this led to his condemnation of Herod, through which action he lost his life. We are to learn from this that condemnation is a dangerous practice.

conditions, evil--In Divine Mind there is no recognition of evil conditions. Such conditions have no basis of reality. To rid ourselves of any appearance of evil, let us change our thought at once and begin to build a consciousness that knows nothing but good. Let us affirm: "I am a child of the Absolute. God is good, and I am His perfect child. Everything that comes into my life is good."

conqueror--Metaphysically, one who attains mastery over sense consciousness. "We are more than conquerors through him that loved us" (Rom. 8:37).

conscience--There is a divine goodness at the root of all existence. It is not necessary to give in detail the place of abode of each sentient part of this central goodness, for it is there, wherever you look, and whenever you look. No man is so lowly but that at the touch of its secret spring this divine goodness may be brought to light in him. This goodness sleeps in the recesses of every mind and comes forth when least expected. Many stifle it for years, maybe for ages, but eventually its day comes, and there is a day of reckoning. This is the law of universal balance--the equilibrium of Being. It cannot be put aside with transcendental philosophies or metaphysical denials any more than it can be smothered in the forces of the blind passions.

Whoever has felt the prick of conscience has been spoken to by the Holy Spirit. Whoever has sat at the feet of his own inner convictions has been aware of God's presence.

conscience, accusing--A state of mind that refuses to remit past sins and keeps one in a state of self-condemnation and remorse.

conscious mind--The mind that makes one know of one's mental operations and states of consciousness; that phase of mind in which one is actively aware of one's thoughts. The mind through which man establishes his identity.

consciousness--The sense of awareness, of knowing. The knowledge or realization of any idea, object, or condition. The sum total of all ideas accumulated in and affecting man's present being. The composite of ideas, thoughts, emotions, sensation, and knowledge that makes up the conscious, subconscious, and superconscious phases of mind. It includes all that man is aware of--spirit, soul, and body.

It is very important to understand the importance of our consciousness in spiritual growth. Divine ideas must be incorporated into our consciousness before they can mean anything to us. An intellectual concept does not suffice. To be satisfied with an intellectual understanding leaves us subject to sin, sickness, poverty, and death. To assure continuity of spirit, soul, and body as a whole, we must ever seek to incorporate divine ideas into our mind. A consciousness of eternal life places one in the stream of life that never fails.

consciousness, ascend in--Rise to the spiritual realms of mind.

consciousness, body--The subconscious mind in its work in the body--repairing, renewing, and conducting the functions of the body in harmony and health if right ideas are given to it, or disintegrating the organism and producing inharmonious action of the functions if untrue thoughts are sown in the mind.

consciousness, centers of--The subconscious realm in man has twelve great centers of action. Each of these twelve centers has control of a certain function in mind and body. The twelve centers are: faith, strength, judgment, love, power, imagination, understanding, will, order, zeal, renunciation (or elimination), and life.

consciousness, Christ--Consciousness built in accordance with the Christ ideal, or in absolute relationship to the Father. The perfect mind that was in Christ Jesus.

consciousness, illumined--A mind purified by the light of Truth.

consciousness, inner--The realm of the supermind as contrasted with the outer or conscious mind.

consciousness, material--A state of mind based on belief in the reality of materiality, or things as they appear. It is carnal mind expressing its unbelief in the omnipresence of God.

consciousness, negative--A mind filled with un-God-like thoughts, such as fear, hate, greed, lust, resentments, discouragement, sickness, and poverty.

consciousness, positive--A mind filled with God's thoughts, such as power, strength, generosity, purity, and optimism.

consciousness, sense--A mental state that believes in and acts through the senses. To rise out of sense consciousness, we determine to return to conscious oneness with God. "I will arise and go to my Father" (Luke 15:18).

consciousness, Son of God--A state of mind that is conscious of God's ideal man.

consciousness, spiritual-- (see Christ consciousness)

consciousness, total--Conscious, subconscious, and superconscious phases of mind working as a whole, as a unit.

consecration--The dedication of one's everyday thought to God; a complete surrender of oneself to God. The entire mind is brought under the control of the Christ consciousness with whole-souled devotion to spiritual ideas. It is the one way to perfect peace of mind. Consecration also means the application of all one's tact, skill, and inspiration to bringing other men into the Christ light. Thus, the whole world is to be brought into the Christ fold and transformed by Truth. "Who then offereth willingly to consecrate himself this day unto Jehovah" (I Chron. 29:5).

contemplation--A form of meditation; a thought of becoming a child of God.

convalescence--That period during which pure life from on high is cleansing the consciousness, and the waters of negation are receding. The body does not always at a single bound regain its natural condition, but there is a gradual recovery.

conversion--"The experience associated with and involving a definite and decisive adoption of religion, especially a Christian religion" (Webster). Conversion is a change of heart and is a real experience, but it is merely introductory to the new life in Christ. When a person arrives at a certain exalted consciousness through the exercise of his mind in thinking about God and His laws, he is lifted above the thoughts of the world into a heavenly realm. This is the beginning of his entry into the kingdom of heaven. When man attains this high place in consciousness he is baptized by the Spirit; that is, his mind and even his body are suffused with spiritual essences, and he begins the process of becoming a new creature in Christ Jesus.

conviction--The state of being convinced. Metaphysically, it is the divine assurance that comes to one when he is fully satisfied of the worth of Truth. Conviction refuses to be influenced by the senses because it is founded in spiritual thought.

cords, scourge of--The specific statement of denial. General denial cleanses the consciousness, but secret sins may yet lurk in the inner parts. Small definite statements that cut into them like whipcords will erase these specific transgressions. "And he made a scourge of cords, and cast all out of the temple, both the sheep and the oxen" (John 2:15).

corruptible--The corruptible body is that which is subject to decay. When it is transformed into the spiritual body, it becomes incorruptible and is forever enduring. "This corruptible must put on incorruption" (I Cor. 15: 53).

cosmos--Order; system; harmony; the opposite of chaos. The universe is a cosmos because it expresses Divine Mind, the essence of all harmony and order.

country, far--A state of consciousness in which man has separated himself from an intimate spiritual association with the Father and thereby does not have the benefit of divine wisdom in his affairs.

courage--A spiritual quality that enables one to remain poised and centered in God amidst great difficulties and danger. The realization that the almighty God of the universe is a spiritual presence which is constantly striving to express in and through us fills us with new courage and a fearlessness that is beyond description. "Be strong, and let your heart take courage" (Psalms 31:24).

covenant--A solemn agreement or compact between two or more parties. "My covenant shall stand fast with him" (Psalms 89:28).

covenant, new--Jesus established a new and higher consciousness for man and taught and practiced the truth of the inner kingdom. This teaching is known as the "new covenant" (Heb. 12:24). The new covenant is to be written in the heart of each person.

Covenant, Ark of the--(see Ark of the Covenant)

covetousness--Insatiable desire to possess that which belongs to another. Covetousness has no wisdom. When a man gives up to its demands he does foolish things to gain possession of the coveted object. "Thou shalt not covet" (Exod. 20:17). (see acquisitiveness)

creation--The original plan of an idea in Spirit. Back of the visible universe are both the original creative ideas and those that are brought forth as earthly things. In the creative process Divine Mind first ideates itself. In the Scriptures this idea is named Jehovah, meaning I AM the ever living--He who is eternal. The creation is carried forward through the activity of the Holy Spirit.

The order of creation is from the formless to the formed, from the invisible to the visible. This goes on perpetually, and there is never a beginning or an ending to the process. The ideal is continually pouring itself into its creation and lifting it higher and yet higher. Apart from mind nothing can be done. Man, in his forming and bringing things into manifestation, uses the same creative process in mind that God uses. First is mind; then the idea in mind; then the materialization of the idea.

creation, described in Genesis--The 1st chapter of Genesis describes the creative action of universal Mind in the realm of ideas and does not pertain to the manifest world. This truth is substantiated in the 2d chapter, where it is stated that there was not a man to till the soil. This proves conclusively that the first creation described is in the realm of ideas.

(The account of creation rendered by Ferrar Fenton gives an enlightening translation from the Hebrew: "By periods God created that which produced the Suns; then that which produced the Earth" [Gen. 1:1]. This is in line with Truth.)

creative force in man--Spirit-mind is the creative force constantly working in man and all other creation. Those who fail to recognize Spirit-mind shining within them dwell in a continuous state of darkness and ignorance. To them the almighty Christ is nonexistent. "And the light shineth in the darkness; and the darkness apprehended it not" (John 1:5).

creative intelligence--Mind of God forever upbuilding His universe.

creative Principle--God as the cause and moving force in and through all creation.

Cross--The Cross represents that state of consciousness termed "mortal mind." This is the "carnal mind" of Paul also, and it burdens the body with its various erroneous beliefs. "He went out, bearing the cross for himself" (John 19:17). The center of action of this "carnal mind" is in the brain, and it is here that it has to be met in the final overcoming that the I AM undertakes. "The place called The place of a skull" (John 19:17).

The Cross is not a burden as commonly understood, but a symbol of the forces in man adjusted in their right relation.

crown--That which imparts honor or splendor. Highest state or quality. The crown of eternal life is the prize to all who overcome carnal mind.

crucifixion--The crossing out in consciousness of errors that have become fixed states of mind; the surrender or death of the whole personality in order that the Christ Mind may be expressed in all its fullness.

The crucifixion of Jesus represents the wiping of personality out of consciousness. We deny the human self so that we may unite with the selfless. We give up the mortal so that we may attain the immortal. We dissolve the thought of the physical body so that we may realize the spiritual body.

cup--The consciousness of eternal life. This must be attained by an utter crossing out of the personal self. This is "the cup which the Father hath given me" (John 18:11).

curse--To affirm evil for or on something or someone. Cursing has a variety of meanings as used in the Scriptures. The whole human family is pictured as under the curse of God for not bringing forth spiritual good, because of disobedience and failure to observe divine law. "If ye will not hear, and if ye will not lay it to heart, to give glory unto my name, saith Jehovah of hosts, then will I send the curse upon you, and I will curse your blessings; yea, I have cursed them already, because ye do not lay it to heart" (Mal. 2:2).

God is love, and God's law of love cannot be broken. Man brings evil on himself by not obeying the law. Jesus redeemed mankind from the ancient curse of Jehovah, but men are themselves responsible for avoiding transgression of the law. "Christ redeemed us from the curse of the law" (Gal. 3:13).

D

dainties, king's--That which pertains to sensual gratification.

dark sayings--Refers to the darkened consciousness that cannot yet see the true light. Jesus knew that the apostles would soon reach the point where they would be able to go direct to the Father for light and guidance. Then He would not have to speak to them in "dark sayings" that they could not understand, but could speak to them "plainly of the Father" (John 16:25).

darkness--The ignorance of the sense man; the absence of Truth (light) in consciousness. Darkness represents undeveloped capacity. It is caused by lack of love. "He that saith he is in the light and hateth his brother, is in the darkness" (I John 2:9).

dawn--Spiritual perception as a dawning light in consciousness, increasing as one turns steadily toward Truth.

day--Represents the state of mind in which intelligence dominates. The idea back of day is light, or the dispensation of intelligence. In the Scriptures day and night are symbols for degrees of unfoldment, day being understanding; night, ignorance. (see night)

day, last--All shall attain who believe or have faith in the spiritual source of life. Whoever enters into the Mind of Spirit will have poured out to him its life essence and be wholly raised up from material conditions when arriving at the "last day"–the last degree of understanding.

day of judgment--Any day in which we get the result in body and affairs of some thought or word that we have expressed.

day of rest--The true day of rest is the consciousness of universal peace that constitutes the kingdom of heaven. This peace is eternal, and when man becomes conscious of it his "day of rest" has begun to dawn. This rest comes from the understanding that now in Christ all things are complete.

days, three--The three days that Jesus was in the tomb represent the three steps in overcoming error. First, nonresistance and humility; second, the taking on of divine activity, or accepting the will of God; third, the assimilation and fulfillment of divine will.

daydreamer--One having ideas brilliant beyond description, but which are not clothed in the habiliments of action. He perceives an idea, but does not give it form by infusing into it the substance of living faith. He falls short by failing to realize that there are two sides to every proposition, the image and the expression.

death--Physical dissolution of the body; the outer symbol of mental negation or spiritual inertia. As commonly interpreted, death is the absence of life in the body. Death is caused by man's failure to comply fully with God's law. It is the result of sin and has no uplifting power. A falling short of the law of life is sin. Sin causes discord in mind, which produces a separation between spirit and body. Through believing in error and dissipating the life substance, the mind loses hold of its consciousness of life and enters into negation, and dissolution takes place. The result is death of the body temple. "The wages of sin is death; but the free gift of God is eternal life" (Rom. 6:23).

If, through the power of our thought and word, we affirm the opposite of life and talk about the absence of life, we rob the body cells of their natural element. This treatment will eventually bring death to the organism. Let us not say, "I am tired"; "I am weak"; "I am sick." Rather, let us say, "I am strong"; "I am well"; "I am alive with the life of God now and forevermore."

death, an enemy of man--Death is not a friend but an enemy and must be overcome. Death does not change man and bring him into the resurrection and eternal life. Death has no place in the Absolute.

In the world today there is an active effort to exalt death and to delude men into believing that death is the way to eternal life in heaven. Such a thought is opposed to the teachings of Jesus, because Jesus came to deliver the human race from death and to fulfill in man God's perfect will: abundant life. Jesus made no mention of resurrection after death as having any part in the new birth. The new birth is a change that comes here and now. It has to do with the present man, that he may become conscious of Christ within himself. Those who are guided by the Spirit of truth understand the life teaching and are not led astray by any philosophy that makes death and the grave necessary factors in spiritual growth.

death, a sleep--Death is but a prolonged sleep, the result of thought inharmony so great that the body cannot stand the strain and collapses. Then, instead of being in a body when he awakes, man finds that he is in the realm of thought without a vehicle adequate to his full expression, and he is forced by divine law again to build an organism.

death, first and second--The first death is the death of the light and life of Spirit in man's consciousness. The second death is a cessation of vital force and action in the body. It occurs when the mind completely loses control of the body. The functional activities cease, and the physical organism dissolves.

death, how to overcome--The Christ man goes through the various centers of the body and rebuilds them with his word. The abiding consciousness of life fills every cell of the body with its quickening energy, and the body becomes immortal.

debt--A contradiction of the universal equilibrium. There is no such thing as lack of equilibrium in all the universe; therefore, in Spirit and in Truth there is no debt.

Debts are produced by thoughts of lack, impatient desire, and covetousness. A thought of debt will produce debt. As long as we believe in debt, we shall go into debt and accumulate the burdens that follow this thought. When such thoughts are erased from consciousness, our debts are overcome and paid in full.

debt, how to overcome--Thoughts of abundance will more quickly and surely bring what is ours to us than any thoughts we can hold about debtors discharging their obligations to us. We are to see abundance everywhere and to affirm it, not only for ourselves but for everyone else. We shall fill our mind with thoughts of divine love, justice, peace, and forgiveness. This will pay our debts of love, which will bring to us abundance to meet every obligation.

decree--To command; to ordain. To decree with assurance is to establish and to fix an ideal in substance. The force behind the decree is invisible, like a promise to be fulfilled at a future time; but it binds with its invisible chains the one who makes it. We have only a slight conception of the strength of the intangible. We compare and measure strength by some strong element in nature. We say that something is as "strong as steel." But a little thought will convince us that mental affirmations are far stronger than the strongest visible thing in the world. The reason for this is that visible things lack livingness. They are not linked with energy and intelligence as are words. Words charged with power and intelligence increase with use, while material things decrease.

Deity, the--The Supreme Being; God.

delusion--False perception. Delusion occurs only in that realm which is not established by the divine Logos, God's creative Word.

demon--This word is used in Matt. 8:28-34, when the demons ask to be sent into the swine. The demons of the parable represent error states of mind that have been quickened by Truth and are repentant. When one knows the work of Jesus in regenerating or reconstructing the mind and body and that this work is typical of what all have to do, one sees that negative thoughts have to be dealt with. One also understands that the demons or devils are error states of mind that have to be lifted up by the quickening power of Spirit. (see Christianity and Devil)

demonstrate--"To prove by reasoning, as by deduction; to establish as true" (Webster). To demonstrate Truth is to effect a change of consciousness. This includes the elimination of error and the establishment of Truth.

demonstration--The proving of a Truth principle in one's body or affairs. The manifestation of an ideal when its accomplishment has been brought about by one's conformity in thought, word, and act to the creative Principle of God.

It is a metaphysical law that there are three steps in every demonstration: the recognition of Truth as it is in Principle; holding an idea; and acknowledging fulfillment. "Whatsoever ye shall ask in prayer, believing, ye shall receive" (Matt. 21:22).

demonstration, complete--God expressed in all fullness; the putting on of Christhood, which Jesus accomplished.

demonstration, spiritual--A spiritual realization followed by the manifestation in the outer of the Truth that has been realized within.

demonstration, the great--That which crowns all others and includes all others--the demonstration of eternal life; the truth that life is omnipresent and eternal and that it is ours just to the measure that we appropriate it.

demonstrator--One who understands and conforms to any point of divine law. He may demonstrate much or little; he may deal with his whole consciousness or merely with his outer mentality. (see overcomer) denial--The mental process of erasing from consciousness the false beliefs of the sense mind. Denial clears away belief in evil as reality and thus makes room for the establishing of Truth.

Carnal consciousness is made up of a multitude of false individual and race beliefs. Through denial we get rid of these shadows of reality. We cleanse the temple of the mind of these thieves and robbers of our good. In so doing, we make way for the planting of the seeds of Truth that will bring to us an ever-increasing supply of good. (see affirmation)

denials, as related to affirmations--A denial is a relinquishment, and it should not be made with too much vehemence. Let us make our denials as though we were gently sweeping away cobwebs, and our affirmations in a strong, bold, positive attitude of mind. When we poise ourselves in Divine Mind our affirmations and denials will be made in right relation. We will know just when to let go of a thought and when to lay hold of another.

deny himself--When a man denies himself he denies personality; he denies that the world of appearance is real. "If any man would come after me, let him deny himself . . . and follow me" (Mark 8:34).

desert place--A desert place in the consciousness of man is a seeming lack of substance and life. In Truth desert places do not really exist. From the viewpoint of Spirit there is no lack. Where God is, there are His inexhaustible resources; God is everywhere present.

desire--An expression of the inmost being of man; the onward impulse of an ever-evolving man. It springs from deep within Being and it has enduring power. Deep desire is essential to spiritual growth. It is desire--earnest, intense desire--that draws the whole being up out of mortality and its transient joys into the power to appreciate and to receive real spiritual blessings.

desire, repressed--Desire that is forced out of consciousness into the subconscious mind without transmutation according to spiritual law.

desire to excel--The inspiration of the Holy Spirit, which ever urges us to forsake earthly things and to desire that which is of heaven. Desire to excel should be encouraged and cultivated in the right direction. It is in all men.

destiny--The goal toward which man's own thoughts are leading him. In the beginning he was destined to bring forth God's perfect pattern and he must eventually reach this supreme goal. Man's destiny is to go from glory to glory.

development--Increase in conception and expression of the qualities that belong to Divine Mind. The development or correction of all present ideas underlying one's manifestation, and the training of them to conform to the divine idea of man.

Devil--The mass of thoughts that has been built up in race consciousness through many generations of earthly experiences and crystallized into what may be termed human personality, or carnal mind, which opposes and rejects God.

The "devil" is a state of consciousness adverse to the divine good. Other names for this state of consciousness are the Adversary, carnal mind, the accuser, and the old man. There is no personal devil. God is the one omnipresent Principle of the universe, and there is no room for any principle of evil, personified or otherwise.

Devil, how to overcome the--The Devil is overcome by denying his existence and by affirming universal Christ love for God and all men. The devils that we encounter are fear, anger, jealousy, and other similar negative traits, and they are in ourselves. Christ gives us the power to cast out these devils, thereby cleansing our consciousness.

digestion, spiritual--Absorbing Truth into the consciousness through meditation.

discern--"To lay hold of with the understanding, especially that which is hidden or obscure; to divine" (Webster). To apprehend the Truth of Being; to look through appearances and to behold the reality of omnipresence.

discerning the Lord's body--(see I Cor. 11:29) To discern the Lord's body is to recognize that it is substance and life, and it is formed within man, and that it is, in the larger sense, made up of members in whom the Christ body has been individually formed.

discernment, spiritual--That inner spiritual faculty by which man may receive the revelations of God-Mind. The faculty by which we inwardly know that which is spiritual. It indicates the ready insight into divine law that was the glory of the Master.

disciple--"One who receives instruction from another" (Webster). (see apostles)

disciple, calling of--To call a disciple (or apostle) is mentally to recognize that disciple; it is to identify oneself with the intelligence working at a center: for example, judgment at the solar plexus. To make this identification, one must realize one's unity with God through Christ, Christ being the Son-of-God idea always existing in man's consciousness.

disciples in the upper room--The gathering of the disciples (or apostles) in the upper room symbolizes the concentration of the faculties at the center of spirituality in communion with the Father.

discrimination--The ability to distinguish qualities or values, enabling one intelligently to choose the desirable.

disease--An inharmonious condition in mind and body brought about by error thinking. Ignorance causes all disease "My people are destroyed for lack of knowledge" (Hosea 4:6). Organic disease has its origin in mind as truly as any other manifestation. It has become subconscious and needs the power of the Christ Mind to reach and to dissolve the error thoughts that are causing the disease.

dispensation, new--The great outpouring of power, love, and spiritual life that is now taking place in all who acknowledge the I AM presence.

dispensation, old--The Mosaic dispensation.

divine--Godlike; godly; of the nature of God.

divine ideal--The Christ man; the divine idea of man.

divine law--The logical process by which Principle or God manifests.

Divine Mind--God-Mind; ever-present, all knowing Mind; the Absolute, the unlimited. Omnipresent, all-wise, all-loving, all-powerful Spirit.

There is but one Mind, and that Mind cannot be separated or divided, because, like the principle of mathematics, it is indivisible. All that we can say of the one Mind is that it is absolute and that all its manifestations are in essence like itself.

Divine Mind, creative power of--The functioning of the principles of Being; Spirit in action. Mind is not a thing; Mind is. It is that which, through orderly processes, produces things. Divine Mind first conceives the idea, then images its fulfillment. Man, acting in co-operation with Divine Mind, places himself under this same creative law and thus brings his ideas into manifestation.

divine motherhood--The brooding, nourishing element of Divine Mind, in which spiritual ideas are brought to fruition.

divine order--Order is the first law of the universe. Indeed, there could be no universe unless its various parts were kept in perfect order. The facts of Spirit are of spiritual character and, when understood in their right relation, they are orderly. Orderliness is law and is the test of true science.

divinity within us--The true spiritual man, the Christ that is the real of every man.

doctrine of church--A teaching peculiar to a church or to churches in general.

doctrine of Unity, value of the--Unity doctrine is of practical, everyday value to everyone who follows its instructions because it shows man that he is his own minister, lawyer, and doctor and that he has within himself the storehouse from which he can supply every need. It is the doctrine that Jesus proclaimed with original simplicity. It asks man to return again to the estate of simplicity in which he was as a little child, believing implicitly what the Father tells him from the inner recesses of his own being. It has been found to be a good doctrine because it has opened to man a new world, and he sees how, through it, shall be brought about the fulfillment of the promise: "And he [God] shall wipe away every tear from their eyes; and death shall be no more; neither shall there be mourning, nor crying, nor pain, anymore: the first things are passed away" (Rev. 21:4).

domination--"Exercise of power in ruling; often, arbitrary or insolent sway" (Webster). One person should never dominate another because it weakens the will of the one dominated and makes the will of the one who dominates hard and unyielding.

dominion--"Supreme authority, sovereignty" (Webster). As a perfect child of God, man is born to complete dominion over all creation. Dominion is an inner consciousness obtained only through mind discipline. This supreme authority comes as man realizes his oneness with the Father.

dominion, urge to exercise--The power and right of dominion and authority are innate within man, having been implanted there by Divine Mind at man's creation.

door--The door of our mind is the I AM. "I am the door of the sheep" (John 10:7). The "sheep" are our thoughts. There is but one life-giver, one Saviour, the Christ; and the only door through which the divine essence can come to us is through our own I AM.

door of the temple--The "door of the temple which is called Beautiful" (Acts 3:2) is the way that opens to spiritual illumination, to an understanding of how to lay hold of and to apply spiritual law.

double-mindedness--Contemplation of a world both good and evil; mental acceptance of a principle of evil as well as of good. This constitutes a denial of God as omnipresent good.

doubt--"Unsettled state of opinion concerning the reality of the truth of something" (Webster). Doubt is the Satan of every man. Doubt is the root of weakness, mental and physical. If men had faith in themselves, in the ability of Spirit within them, they would become giants, where they are but pygmies.

dove--Symbolizes peace of mind and confidence in divine law. The dove is nonresistant. In this state of consciousness we rest in Spirit.

drink of the cup--To drink of the cup from which Jesus drank is to rise above all sensuality, to gain mastery over every impulse of mind and body, and to devote one's whole life to Spirit.

drunkard--"One who habitually drinks strong liquors immoderately" (Webster). The first step in healing the drunkard in ourselves or another is to withdraw all condemnation and censure and to affirm the law of love. There is a very close connection in Being between love and life.

A man once testified that he healed himself of drunkenness by saying, whenever the desire for liquor came to him, "I do not love whisky; I love God."

duality--(see double-mindedness).

dust, shake off the--To deny all seeming materiality. "And whosoever shall not receive you, nor hear your words, as ye go forth out of that house or that city, shake off the dust of your feet" (Matt. 10:14).

dying--The state of negation in man's consciousness wherein he is failing to retain possession of his body.

dying to self--Signifies man's willingness to die to the little personal self, so that he may be absorbed into Divine Mind. To lay down the mortal thought of life and to take up the spiritual idea of life opens the door to the realization that the I AM has creative power and can express the life manifestation in divine order.

ears--Represent the obedience and receptivity of the mind.

earth--Metaphysically speaking, the earth represents the consciousness of the physical body.

east--The within. As used in Matt. 2:1, the word in the original is plural; thus, from the regions of interior wisdom come thoughts of reverence and rich gifts of substance, understanding, and every spiritual help for the Christ child, whose growth in consciousness has begun.

Easter--The awakening and raising to spiritual consciousness of the I AM in man, which has been dead in trespasses and sins and buried in the tomb of materiality.

eat and drink--To appropriate; to become conscious of the food that "abideth unto eternal life," and to use it.

eat of the tree of life--The eternal life of God is within every man. When we consciously realize the presence of this life in every part of our organism we are eating of the tree of life.

eating--Eating is symbolical of mental appropriation of thoughts of substance. "Thy words were found, and I did eat them; and thy words were unto me a joy and the rejoicing of my heart" (Jer. 15:16).

Supplying the physical needs does not solve the whole problem of hunger for man, for his hungers are as varied as his interests and desires. They include his thoughts and feelings as well as his physical needs. When Jesus said, "He that eateth me, he also shall live because of me" (John 6:57), He referred to the appropriation of spiritual substance by man, and not to his eating of material food. We "eat" spiritual things when we affirm that we are strengthened and sustained by spiritual substance.

When in the holy silence you nourish your consciousness on God's word, you are eating of the "hidden manna" (Rev. 2:17), the bread that gives everlasting life. The Lord's Supper (Matt. 26:26-31) is a mental feast.

eating of the tree of good and evil---Appropriating the consciousness of both good and evil.

To "eat" is to appropriate the substance of ideas through thinking about them. "Evil" represents error-thought combinations; that part of consciousness which has lost sight of true principles and through sensation becomes enamored of the thing formed. Form has its place in creation, but it is subject to the creative idea that begets it. The activity of an idea in man's mind produces sensation. To become involved in the sensation of an idea to the exclusion of control is to eat of the "tree of the knowledge of good and evil" and to die to all consciousness of the original idea.

ecclesia--The church of Jesus Christ: the called-out ones.

Eden, Garden of--Represents a region of Being in which are provided all primal ideas for the production of the beautiful. As described in Genesis, it represents, allegorically, the elemental life and intelligence placed at the disposal of man and through which he is to evolve both mind and body.

The human body with its psychical and spiritual attributes comprises a miniature Garden of Eden. When man develops spiritual insight and in thought, word, and act voluntarily operates in accord with divine law, then rulership, authority, and dominion become his in both mind and body. "The kingdom of God is within you" (Luke 17:21). (see Garden of Eden)

education, spiritual--To draw forth from within, through meditation and prayer, the deep truths of God.

ego--The I. The ego is man, and by reason of his divinity he makes and remakes as he wills. In this lie his greatest strength and his greatest weakness. The ego of itself is possessed of nothing. It is a mere ignorant child of innocence floating in the Mind of Being, but through the door of its consciousness must pass all the treasures of God.

ego, adverse--When the ego attaches itself to sense consciousness, it builds the antichrist man, who has no basis in reality. This is known as the adverse ego. It is the adverse ego that causes all the trouble in the world. Its selfishness and greed make men grovel in the mire of materiality, when they might soar in the heavens of spirituality.

ego, spiritual--The true self; an individualized center of God consciousness; I AM; conscious identity.

egotism--A state of consciousness built up by the will functioning in the sense world. In this false expression it looks upon itself as great, honorable, mighty. Supreme egotism stops the flow of spiritual life in the organism, and body atrophy sets in.

Egypt--Mental bondage to sense thoughts; material consciousness. It pertains to the physical sense of life, the corporeal organism.

elimination--(see renunciation)

Elohim God--The original Mind in creative action. El means "the strong and ever-sustaining one," and Alah, "to swear or formulate by the power of the Word." Elohim thus represents the universal Principle of Being that designed all creation.

El Shaddai--(see almighty)

emanate--"To issue forth from a source" (Webster). In metaphysics, emanation usually refers to the silent influence of Mind of Spirit.

emotion--Undisciplined or uncontrolled forces. Subnormal or supernormal activity of mental or physical forces. Excitement of the feelings.

It is found that for each bad emotion there is a corresponding chemical change in the tissues of the body that is life-depressing and poisonous. Contrariwise, every good emotion makes a life-promoting change. Thus, it follows that it pays to think good thoughts and to do good acts for one's own sake.

"end of the world"–Literally, "the completion of this eon." This does not refer to the physical world, but to the present era or age; or individually, to the end of a certain state of consciousness.

The "end of the world" is the separation of the true from the false in consciousness, when the wisdom and understanding of Spirit are so developed in us that we, of our own accord, choose whom we will serve and select that which is right in the sight of God. "The world passeth away, and the lust thereof" (I John 2:17).

"The end of the world" is sometimes translated "the End of the Age" ("Emphatic Diaglott"), thus giving a clearer meaning to the text. The world, the age, the old order of things shall come to an end and pass away; and the new world, the new age, "wherein dwelleth righteousness," will be established.

energy--The power of God within us to accomplish. Strength or vigor of expression. Internal or inherent power, as of the mind; capacity of acting, or producing an effect. Power forcibly exerted; force or action. Zeal in motion, the forerunner of every effect.

enthusiasm--"Ardent zeal or interest; fervor. Divine inspiration or possession" (Webster). It is a powerful expression of a living interest; it is active and vital. Enthusiasm is another word for zeal, and zeal is a great stimulator of man. You cannot think of or repeat the word zeal without evoking a certain mental thrill that spurs you to action in some direction.

entity--"A thing which has reality and distinctness of being either in fact or for thought" (Webster).

entities, protective--The shepherds who were watching their flocks by night at the time of Jesus' birth symbolize protective entities of God that have kept watch over the soul in its sleep between incarnations.

environment--Surroundings. Our consciousness is our real environment. The outer environment is always in correspondence to the thoughts making up our consciousness.

"Thou hast made the Most High thy habitation; There shall no evil befall thee" (Psalms 91:9, 10).

equivalent--"Equal in force or authority" (Webster). Our demonstrations are equivalent to the power and illumination contained in our realizations. We receive according to our capacity to receive.

error--That which is untrue. Error thoughts represent belief in thoughts and beliefs not of God. Error thoughts have no foundation in Truth. They originate in the intellect. They are eliminated by one's denying their reality and power, and affirming the Truth of Being.

essence, spiritual--The substance in which all things exist and out of which all things are made.

eternal--Without beginning or end; timeless; everlasting in duration. "The eternal God is thy dwelling-place" (Deut. 33:27).

ether--The spiritual substance in which we live, move, and have our being and out of which can be made whatever we desire. Some scientists teach that space is heavily charged with energies that would transform the earth if they could be controlled. Arthur Eddington says that about half the leading physicists assert that the ether exists and the other half deny its existence; but, in his words, "Both parties mean exactly the same thing, and are divided only by words."

One with spiritual understanding knows that the ether exists as an emanation of Mind and should not be confused in its limitations with matter. Its being is governed and sustained by ideas, and ideas have no physical dimensions.

evil--That which is not of God; unreality; error thought; a product of the fallen human consciousness; negation.

Evil is a parasite. It has no permanent life of itself; its whole existence depends on the life it borrows from its parent, and when its connection with the parent is severed nothing remains. In Divine Mind there is no recognition of evil conditions. Such conditions have no basis of reality. They are conjurations of a false consciousness. Apparent evil is the result of ignorance, and when Truth is presented the error disappears.

There is but one presence and one power, God omnipotent. But man has the privilege and freedom of using this power as he will. When he misuses it he brings about inharmonious conditions. These are called evil. Evil appears in the world because man is not in spiritual understanding. He has not learned that all is Mind; neither has he conformed to the law of Mind, with the result that inharmony appears in his body and affairs. He can do away with evil by learning rightly to use the one Power. If there were a power of evil, it could not be changed.

evil, overcoming--Evil must be overcome with good. We must dwell in the good so wholly that all the substance of our thoughts and our being is given over to the promotion of the good. This is a mental process in which all negation (evil) is denied, and creative, fearless affirmation of God's perfect good is steadfastly adhered to.

evolution--The development achieved by man working under spiritual law. It is the result of the development of ideas in mind. What we are is the result of the evolution of our consciousness, and this consciousness is the result of seed ideas sown in the mind. In the beginning, God implanted His perfect word--involved this seed word into each man. Evolution is the unfolding in consciousness of that which God involved in man in the beginning. (see involution)

evolution, spiritual--The unfolding of the Spirit of God into expression. The Christ or Son of God evolution in man is plainly taught in the New Testament as the supreme attainment of every man. "For the earnest expectation of the creation waiteth for the revealing of the sons of God" (Rom. 8:19).

exaltation--A lifting up; a raising up of the consciousness in man from a physical and mental basis to the spiritual. Affirm: "I hear the voice of God within me and I am exalted."

exercise--The act of training the mind to think of God's attributes as forces that are being incorporated into the mind as one incorporates strength into the body. "Exercise thyself unto godliness" (I Tim. 4:7).

exercises, spiritual--Prayer, meditation, worship, and fasting from erroneous ideas.

existence--"State or fact of having being" (Webster); manifestation. The object of man's existence is to bring forth in the race that which exists in God.

exorcist--One who uses a holy name to cast out evil spirits; an imitator of Truth who is not in the understanding of the change of heart and thought that must accompany all true healing. (see Acts 19:13-16)

expectation--Anticipation of divine good. Looking about for the wondrous benefits God has prepared for us.

In every person is that which causes him always to hope for and to expect that which is good and true. This very expectation helps the good to become active.

experimentation--Man is a free agent. He can open his mind to divine wisdom and know creative law, or he can work out his unfoldment through experimentation. Our race is in the experimental stage. In our ignorance we transgress the law to the very limit, and then a great reaction sets in, a general condition that is negative to the point of dissolution. Then, that in us which always looks obediently to God in an extremity is awakened, and we seek divine guidance.

external forms of religion, worship of--Undue attention to ritual and ceremony. Concern with the letter and not the spirit of religion.

eye, inner--Spiritual vision; intuitive seeing with the eye of Truth.

eye, single--Searching quality of mind with keen observation that selects only that which is good. The single eye is open and receptive only to the guiding light of Spirit.

eyes, blind--A darkened consciousness. When we are exalted and illumined through Truth darkness disappears. "And in that day shall the deaf hear the words of the book, and the eyes of the blind shall see out of obscurity and out of darkness" (Isa. 29:18).

faculty, spiritual--An individualized center of God consciousness. The twelve faculties or ideas in Divine Mind are: faith, strength, wisdom or judgment, love, power, imagination, understanding, will, order or law, zeal, renunciation, and life. Man takes control of his faculties through exercising the will.

There are two ways to develop the spiritual faculties: through the evolutionary law of experience and trial (the school of the twelve sons of Jacob); or by the direct power of the Word, or the I AM (the purifying of the twelve apostles of Jesus). The law of Moses and the experiences of the Children of Israel under the old dispensation represent the first; and the transforming power of the true Word, or gospel of Jesus Christ, as set forth in the New Testament, is the second. When Divine Mind is looked to as the one and only guide, the faculties of man are developed in an orderly manner through the power of the Word. "For sin shall not have dominion over you: for ye are not under law, but under grace" (Rom. 6:14).

faculties, awakened--Faculties of mind that have been expanded until they function in harmony with Divine Mind.

failure--Inability, through a lack of power, to make a demonstration. Seeming failure is often a steppingstone to something higher.

faintheartedness--Uncourageous thoughts, lacking ability and efficiency.

faith--The perceiving power of the mind linked with the power to shape substance. Spiritual assurance; the power to do the seemingly impossible. It is a magnetic power that draws unto us our heart's desire from the invisible spiritual substance. Faith is a deep inner knowing that that which is sought is already ours for the taking "Now faith is assurance of things hoped for" (Heb. 11:1).

A close analysis shows that faith is the foundation of all that man does. Jesus spoke of a new condition for the upliftment of the race. He called it the "kingdom of the heavens." He said it must be built upon the foundation typified by Peter (rock), who represents faith. This is proof that faith is closely related to the enduring, firm. unyielding forms of substance. The development of the faith faculty is a key to spiritual realization. "According to your faith be it done unto you" (Matt. 9:29).

Faith in God is the substance of existence. To have faith in God is to have the faith of God. We must have faith in God as our Father and source of all the good we desire.

Faith is more than mere belief. It is the very substance of that which is believed. It works by love. Thoughts of condemnation, enmity, and resistance must be released and divine love declared; then faith will work unhindered.

Faith working in spiritual substance accomplishes all things. This is the faith that cooperates with creative law. When faith is exercised deep in spiritual consciousness, it finds its abode; and under divine law, without variation or disappointment, it brings results that are seemingly miraculous.

faith, blind--An instinctive trust in a power higher than ourselves. Because blind faith does not understand the principles of Being, it is liable to discouragement and disappointment.

faith, center of--The pineal gland, located in the middle of the brain, is the center of faith in the body of man. Concentration of thought on this center opens the mind of man to spiritual faith.

faith compared with trust--Trust is a weaker brand of faith, but better than mistrust. As a rule, persons who merely trust the Lord do not understand divine law. If they had understanding, they would affirm the presence and power of God until the very substance of Spirit would appear in manifestation.

faith cure--Another name for spiritual healing.

faith, how cultivated--By studying the experiences of Peter (the apostle representing faith), we obtain suggestions on the development of this faculty. The vacillating allegiance of Peter to Jesus illustrates the growth of faith in one who has not developed this faculty. Faith is built up through denial of all doubt and fear and continuous affirmations of loyalty to the divine idea, the higher self. One must have faith in one's spiritual capacity and depend on it in the face of adverse appearances.

faith in oneself--The ground for man's faith in himself is the truth that he is a son of God and, as such, he inherits the divine nature. Man should have faith in himself because he cannot be successful in any line without such faith.

faith, intellectual--The faith that has its seat of action in the intellect only. Intellectual man has faith in his art, in his science, or in his philosophy, which answers his purpose for the time being.

faith of Jesus--Jesus did not claim an exclusive supernatural power, which we usually accredit to Him. He had explored the ether energy, which He called the "kingdom of the heavens"; His understanding was beyond that of the average man. However, He knew and said that other men could do what He did if they would only have faith. He encouraged His followers to take Him as a pattern for faith and to use the power of thought and word. Divine healing is due to the application of the same law that Jesus used. In most instances, He demanded faith on the part of those He healed; and with this faith as a point of mental and spiritual contact, He released the latent energy in the atomic structure of the ones in need of healing, and they were restored to life and health. "He that believeth on me, the works that I do shall he do also; and greater works than these shall he do" (John 14:12).

faith, prayer of--The act of mentally taking that which is desired. Jesus said, "All things whatsoever ye pray and ask for, believe that ye receive them, and ye shall have them" (Mark 11:24).

faith thinking--The most important power of man is the original faith-thinking faculty. All of us have the thinking faculty located in the head, from which we send forth good, bad, and indifferent thoughts. If we are educated and molded after the average pattern of the human family, we may live a lifetime and never have an original thought. The thinking faculty is supplied with the second-hand ideas of our ancestors, the dominant beliefs of the race, or the threadbare stock of the ordinary social swim. This is not faith thinking. Faith thinking is done only by one who has caught sight of the Truth of Being and who feeds his thinking faculty on images generated in the faith center. Faith thinking is not merely an intellectual process based on reasoning. The faith thinker does not compare, analyze, or draw conclusions from known premises. He does not take appearances into consideration; he is not biased by precedent. His thinking gives form, without cavil or question, to ideas that come straight from the eternal fount of wisdom. His perception impinges on the spiritual, and he knows.

faith, understanding--Faith that functions from Principle. It is based on knowledge of Truth. It understands the law of mind action; therefore, it has great strength. To know that certain causes produce certain results gives a bedrock foundation for faith.

faithless generation--A generation that lacks the spiritual faith and power to do the works Jesus would have it do, such as healing the sick and making the blind to see.

fall--A retrogression in consciousness from the pristine Christ Mind to the personal and sense mind of the Adam man.

false claims--Those who make the indwelling Spirit of truth their guide and authority will not be deceived by false claims made either by other persons or by institutions. The safe way is to trust the Spirit of truth continually for protection from false beliefs.

family, the Christ--Jesus said: "Who is my mother and my brethren? And looking round on them that sat round about him, he saith, Behold my mother and my brethren! For whosoever shall do the will of God, the same is my brother, and sister, and mother" (Mark 3:33-35).

family, the universal--If God is the Father of all, then all men and women are brothers and sisters in a universal family. In the Christ consciousness we are all one.

famine--Lack of faith in God's power to prosper.

fasting--Denial; abstinence from error thoughts, to the end that we may meditate on Truth and incorporate it into our consciousness of oneness with the Father.

fate--"That which is destined or decreed; appointed lot. Fate suggests inevitability and immutability in strict use, but usually carries no clear implication of whether it is good or evil" (Webster). Man, through his thought, is working out his own salvation; he is created in the image and likeness of God and is finally to reach "the goal unto the prize of the high calling of God in Christ Jesus" (Phil. 3:14).

Father--God through His Holy Spirit is the Father.

Father and Son--The Father-Mind is the living Principle, the Absolute, the Great Unlimited. The Son is the living Word.

Father and Son, result of knowing both--When we are quickened in spiritual understanding, we experience a renewal of mind and a transformation of body. The mortal becomes immortal, the corruptible becomes incorruptible. It is the resurrection into eternal life.

Father of lights--Source of profound understanding, illumination, wisdom. Through our realization of and meditation on spiritual illumination, we open the way for these spiritual gifts to be showered upon us.

Father-Principle--The exact and immutable Principle of Being, lying back of all existence as cause, and approachable only along lines of perfect law. It is omnipresent and is not subject to change or open to argument.

Father's house, the--The Christ consciousness. It is the center of man's consciousness and is made manifest to him by mind processes alone.

favor of God--Good realized through faithful obedience; the orderly unfoldment in mind and body that results from meditation and prayer; a blessing that comes to us through obedience to Spirit. The bringing about of an inner spiritual strength, resulting in the development of all parts of mind and body.

fear--"Painful emotion marked by alarm; dread; disquiet" (Webster). Fear is one of the most subtle and destructive errors that the carnal mind in man experiences. Fear is a paralyzer of mental action; it weakens both mind and body. Fear throws dust in our eyes and hides the mighty spiritual forces that are always with us. Blessed are those who deny ignorance and fear and affirm the presence and power of Spirit.

fear, how to overcome--Fear is cast out by perfect love. To know divine love is to be selfless, and to be selfless is to be without fear. The God-conscious person is filled with quietness and confidence.

fear of God--"Only fear Jehovah, and serve him in truth with all your heart" (I Sam. 12:24). In this scriptural passage the word fear is used with Webster's meaning: "Awe; profound reverence, especially for the Supreme Being."

fearfulness--State of mind that is full of fear. Fearfulness is a parasite; it drives away divine guidance and produces weakness of the heart.

feast--Appropriation in a large measure; that is, laying hold of divine potentialities.

feast in Jerusalem--A receptive state of mind toward all spiritual good. It is the realization of the unfailing substance of Divine Mind. A great peace is there--"the peace of God, which passeth all understanding" (Phil. 4:7)–and a welling up of an indescribable substance that fills the whole being with satisfaction.

feast, marriage--Conscious union between spirit or mind and body in the silent influx of substance; the union of man with Spirit. A thirsting for things of Spirit is necessary before one can come to the spiritual marriage feast. Great desire for the light and purity of Spirit is the power that prepares man for this greatest of feasts. (see Matt. 22:1-15) feast, Sabbath--The inflow of spiritual substance that we realize when we enter the silence.

feeding the five thousand--In the universal Mind is a substance that Jesus called the "Father," which is also the seed of all visible substance. It is the only real substance because it is unchangeable, while visible substance is in constant transition.

An idea is purely spiritual and can be apprehended only by the mind. It is never visible to the eye but can be sensed by man through any of his spiritual functions. When the attention has been centered on the idea of substance long enough and strongly enough, a consciousness of substance is generated; and, by the powers of the various faculties of the mind in right relation, visible substance is formed. In this way, Jesus brought into visibility the loaves and fishes to feed the five thousand.

feeling--Feeling is external to thought; behind every feeling or emotion there lies thought, which is its direct cause. To erase a feeling, a change of thought is required.

feet--Represent the phase of the understanding that connects us with the outer or manifest world and reveals the right relationship toward worldly conditions in general. We can take possession of all substance that we comprehend and understand, in the name of I AM. This is the meaning of Josh. 1:3: "Every place that the sole of your foot shall tread upon, to you have I given it, as I spake unto Moses."

feet, washing of--The denial of materiality is illustrated in Jesus' washing of the apostles' feet (John 13:5-10). Even Peter (who represents faith) must be cleansed from belief in the reality of material conditions. To wash another's feet seems a menial thing, but in this humble way Jesus taught and exemplified the willingness of divine love to serve, so that man may be redeemed from the pride of the flesh.

feminine--The divine feminine in man is the mother phase of Being. God, through His Holy Spirit, is the Father.

field--Outside the house of God. "He that soweth the good seed is the Son of man; and the field is the world" (Matt. 13:37-38).

fiery furnace--A state of mind in which one goes through a purifying process, and evil and error are destroyed.

fire--Symbolizes cleansing and purification, but it is more than a symbol. Material fire is the symbol, and the fire of Spirit is the reality. The whole universe is alive with a divine, living, spiritual energy that consumes all the dross of sense and materiality. It is a fire that burns eternally. Because this is true, some have assumed that disobedient, sinful persons are to live forever in everlasting torment. But if the fire is eternal, the dross is not, and when the error is consumed the burning stops. The fire consumes only when it meets anything unlike itself. In purified man it is manifested as his eternal life.

fire of God--The Word of God in action. It burns out the dross of negative consciousness and reveals the Christ.

fire, tongues of--Illumination of thought, in demonstration of Spirit's presence and power.

firmament--Faith in mind power, a firm, unwavering place in consciousness. The firmament in the midst of the waters is an idea of confidence or faith in the invisible.

first-born--The "first-born" of every state of consciousness is the personal I. When the flood of light from the universal is let in through our declaration of the one wisdom and one love, this I of every mortal state of consciousness is slain, and there is a "great cry in Egypt; for there was not a house where there was not one dead" (Exod. 12:30).

fish--Represent ideas of multiplication and fecundity. Accounts in which Jesus figures as a party to fish eating are symbolical of the mental side of eating, which is the appropriation of ideas.

The reason Jesus so often used fish to illustrate His teaching is that He was a living demonstration of ideas, and all that He did was in the realm of ideas rather than in the realm of effects. Fish represent ideas in which there is great possibility of increase; Jesus used these ideas to represent the inexhaustible, everywhere present abundance.

fishers of men--Spiritually quickened men who are strongly fortified in Truth and able to help others to find the light.

flame of fire--Light of understanding that flames up in the heart, yet does not consume substance. (see burning bush)

flash of intelligence--The musical genius says he hears the music in a flash and is often at his wit's end to transcribe it fast enough. Many an immortal poem or prose work has been flashed from the mind of the author without any apparent effort on his part. But if all the prayers and mind efforts of literary geniuses were inquired into, it would be found that there had been heroic mental effort somewhere at some time. The realization of perfection takes root in the mind and may come forth in a flash.

flesh--Mortal consciousness expressing itself through appetite. It is overcome by denying that appetite is physical and by affirming it to be spiritual.

flesh, carnal or sensual--A malformation of the substance idea of Being. It must be transformed by right conception of divine perfection before the mortal can put on the immortal.

fleshpots of Egypt--The pleasures of sense.

flocks--Symbolical of thoughts. "Tend the flock of God which is among you" (I Pet. 5:2).

food--A symbol of appropriation. Bread represents the flesh; it is an outer form of the inner substance. (see drink of the cup)

All food is primarily mental, and in the process of digestion and assimilation it becomes part of the body structure, making cells like itself in character. If we wish to bring into manifestation the perfect spiritual body, we should feed on words of Truth--foods that are spiritual in character--avoiding all that carry with them into the system a mental atmosphere of sensuality, fear, or any other discord.

foods, solid--The deeper truths that require much study, meditation, prayer, and concentration in order that they may be appropriated and assimilated by the mind.

food, spiritual--Thoughts and words of Truth; the word of God.

"food which perisheth"–The race consciousness strives for the things of sense, but one who has found the real substance and source of supply proclaims, "Work not for the food which perisheth, but for the food which abideth unto eternal life" (John 6:27).

forces, creative--Active physical or mental forces, having the capacity to produce or to create.

forehead--The seat of perception. The forehead is the center of consciousness, which the understanding of Truth seals; that is, it secretly unites the consciousness with Christ.

forerunner of Spirit--As symbolized by John the Baptist, the perception of Truth that prepares the way for Spirit through a letting go of old concepts and beliefs.

forgiveness--A process of giving up the false for the true; erasing sin and error from the mind and body. It is closely related to repentance, which is a turning from belief in sin to belief in God and righteousness. A sin is forgiven when one ceases to sin, and true forgiveness is only established through renewing the mind and body with thoughts and words of Truth.

Forgiveness really means the giving up of something. When you forgive yourself, you cease doing the things that you should not do. Jesus said that man has power to forgive sin. Sin is the falling short of divine law, and repentance and forgiveness are the only means that man has of getting out of sin and its effect and coming into harmony with the law.

It is through forgiveness that true spiritual healing is accomplished. Forgiveness removes the errors of the mind, and bodily harmony results in consonance with divine law.

The law is Truth, and Truth is all that is good. There is no power or no reality in sin. If sin were real and enduring, like goodness and Truth, it could not be forgiven but would hold its victim forever. When we enter into the understanding of the real and the unreal, a great light dawns on us, and we see what Jesus meant when He said, "The Son of man hath authority on earth to forgive sins."

forgiveness, necessity of--Our first work in any demonstration is to contact God; therefore, we must forgive all men their transgressions. Through the divine law of forgiveness we cleanse our mind so that the Father can forgive us.

form--"The shape and structure of anything" (Webster). All forms are manifestations of ideas. Back of the universe are both the original creative idea and the cosmic rays that form into earthly things.

fornication--Debasement of the spiritual nature, caused by functioning in carnal consciousness.

fornication, abstaining from--Refusing to entertain mortal tendencies and dwelling in spiritual consciousness.

forsaking all for Christ--Giving up everything pertaining to the personal man, so that the Mind of Christ may be perfectly incorporated into consciousness.

fourth dimension--A transcendent realm that Jesus called the "kingdom of the heavens." Here one can discern the trend of spiritual forces and see with the spiritual vision of the Christ Mind.

The fourth dimension (which embraces and encompasses the other three dimensions) is also realization, the doing away with time and space and all conditions. The human mind, with its limited reasoning faculties, is bound by time, space, and conditions and can get no farther into the spiritual than reason will take it, but when we go beyond reason into the realm of realization, then we have attained the consciousness of pure being, the fourth-dimension mind.

frankincense--"A fragrant gum resin" (Webster). Metaphysically, it represents in man the transmutation of the material consciousness into the spiritual.

freedom--The quality or state of being without thought or restraint, bondage, limitation, or repression; having a sense of complete well-being. It is a result of regulating one's life according to Principle, not according to what anyone else may think or say.

We can never know the full meaning of freedom until we abide in the Christ consciousness. Without prayer and spiritual meditation there can be no concept of spiritual freedom and, therefore, no demonstration of it. It is gained only through spiritual development gained in long hours of communion with God in the silence. Liberation from bondage comes as we seek first the perfect Mind of Christ. "If therefore the Son shall make you free, ye shall be free indeed" (John 8:36).

free will--Man's inherent freedom to act as he determines. There can be no perfect expression without perfect freedom of will. If man determines to act in accord with divine law, he builds harmony, health, happiness, and eternal life, which is heaven.

fruitfulness--The rich consciousness man develops as the result of high realizations of Truth.

fruit of the vine--The "fruit of the vine," which man drinks anew in the Father's kingdom, is the consciousness of spiritual life direct from the Fountainhead. (see Matt. 26:29)

fulfill--"To carry into effect; to realize or manifest completely" (Webster). To fulfill the law of his being, man must proclaim the true word and thought of unity with God.

fulfillment of righteousness--Attained through affirmation of Truth and denial of error. As man dwells "in the secret place of the Most High," "under the shadow of the Almighty" (Psalms 91:1, 2), he will fulfill all righteousness.

garden--The spiritual body in which man dwells when he brings forth thoughts after the pattern of original divine ideas. This "garden" is the substance of God.

Garden of Eden--Represents a region of Being in which are provided all primal ideas for the production of the beautiful; the elemental life and intelligence placed at the disposal of man, through which he is to evolve.

Man's body temple is the outer expression of the Garden of Eden. God gave it to man "to dress it and to keep it." (see Gen. 2:15) Man's primary work in the earthly consciousness is to use his creative power to preserve harmony and order in his world and to conserve his powers for divine direction. (see Eden, Garden of)

garment--The radiation or aura that surrounds the body.

garment, Jesus' seamless--The indivisible garment that Jesus wore next to His body. It was a thought garment woven without a break of His high realizations of Truth. These realizations of Truth not only infolded Him but firmly interlaced the substance of both His spiritual and body consciousness.

gate, narrow--The spiritual mind, which requires absolute conformity to Truth and measures all things by the gauge of Truth. The way is "straitened" because it requires only Truth to be recognized, and it rules out untruth or evil.

gate, wide--The easy, negative way by which men conform to sense consciousness and the pleasures of the world, with the result that their mind-muscle becomes soft and flabby. When trials come men find that they are not able to cope with them.

gates, twelve--The twelve faculties of mind. Before these faculties become avenues through which we enter into the city of God, they must be purified according to the standards of Spirit.

Gehenna--Represents the cleansing fire of Spirit, which consumes all the dross of sense and materiality. (see hell)

generation--Procreation. The law of generation is undoubtedly the mystery of mysteries in human consciousness. Men have probed, with more or less success, all the secrets of nature, but of the origin of life they know comparatively nothing. It is only when the inquiring mind transcends the human and rises into the spiritual realm that light comes.

generic--"Pertaining to, or having the rank of, a genus" (Webster). Family; kind. Adam was generic man, the whole human race epitomized in an individual man idea. "Let the earth put forth grass, herbs yielding seed, and fruit-trees bearing fruit after their kind" (Gen. 1:11).

Genesis--Source or origin. The first of the "five books of Moses," giving an account of creation from a metaphysical viewpoint.

genius--One who lets Spirit within him speak out, regardless of how different the utterances may be from those of persons who pose as authorities. He has absolute faith in his spiritual revelations and fearlessly proclaims them. He is a pioneer and a leader. He listens to his own inner voice and has faith in his God-given ability.

ghosts--Thoughts objectified. They are nothing except mind projections.

giants--The Philistines and all the other giants of the Promised Land represent the untrained or undeveloped states of mind in the subconsciousness that Truth is to subdue and to discipline. When they become obedient to the law of Being they will be man's servants, gladly doing his bidding.

gift--"Every good gift and every perfect gift is from above, coming down from the Father of lights" (James 1:17). God's greatest gift to man is the power of thought, through which he can incorporate into his consciousness the Mind of God.

gift, spiritual--The manifestation of Spirit in each of the members of the Christ body according to each man's receptivity; giving to each member a particular work in the redemption of the individual.

gifts, of the Magi--Offerings of love to the Christ; inner resources open to the Christ Mind.

giving, and receiving--It is necessary to give freely if we are to receive freely. The law of receiving includes giving. The knowledge that substance is omnipresent and that man cannot, therefore, impoverish himself by giving (but rather will increase his supply) will enable man to give freely and cheerfully. "Freely ye received, freely give" (Matt. 10:8). (see receiving)

glorify--To magnify with praise; to enhance with spiritual splendor; to adorn. Glorification is the highest spiritual state of consciousness attainable by man.

glory--Realization of divine unity; the blending and merging of man's mind with God-Mind.

goat--Metaphysically, the goat symbolizes resistance and opposition. It is a phase of personality. We resist Spirit on one hand and we resist fellow men on the other. Resistance to the Lord is to be killed out entirely, and resistance to our fellowmen is to be sent into the wilderness (denied a place in consciousness).

God--The almighty One; the Creator; the ruler of the universe; the Infinite; the Eternal. God is not person but Principle. He is the underlying, unchangeable Truth "with whom can be no variation, neither shadow that is cast by turning" (James 1:17). God as principle is absolute good expressed in all creation. When men know God and worship Him "in spirit and truth" (John 4:24), they recognize Him as this great goodness, omnipresent, omniscient, and omnipotent. "Blessed be . . . God . . . the Father of mercies and God of all comfort" (II Cor. 1:3)

God is personal to us when we recognize Him within us as our indwelling life, intelligence, love, and power. There is a difference between a personal God and God personal to us. Since the word personal sometimes leads to misunderstanding, it would probably be better to speak of God individualized in man rather than of God personal to man.

When we identify ourselves with Him as our indwelling Father, He seems to us to be personal; however, it is not in a personal sense, but in the universal identification of ourselves with Him that we come into the God consciousness. The personal is limited. The universal, or God consciousness, is unlimited.

God is that from which all love springs. His character is taught in the name Father, representing the love, protection, and providing care of God for man, His offspring. He is life and love and wisdom and power and strength and substance.

We do not see God with our physical eyes except as He manifests Himself through His works. His attributes are, therefore, brought into expression by man, who is His son and who is like Him in essence. If we would make of ourselves channels through which He can come forth into expression and manifestation, we must endeavor to raise our thought and feeling to God's level.

God, accessibility of--God is approachable, available, and usable to all who draw nigh unto Him. God is Spirit, the principle of intelligence and life, everywhere present at all times. He is, forever, as accessible as a principle of mathematics or music. "The Father abiding in me" (John 14:10).

God as health--God is absolute wholeness and perfection. Man's recognition of his oneness with this perfect wholeness through Christ brings him into the consciousness of his indwelling life and health. "I in them, and thou in me, that they may be perfected into one" (John 17:23).

God as law--Principle in action.

God as lawgiver--The law of God in action is the Holy Spirit; in that action He appears as having individuality. When prophets and mystics come into conscious mental touch with this executive lawgiver, He uses them as mouthpieces by which He guides and directs His people.

God as life--God as life is made manifest in the living. Life cannot be analyzed by the senses. It is beyond their grasp; hence, it must be cognized by the higher consciousness.

God as mind--The connecting link between God and man. God-Mind embraces all knowledge, wisdom, and understanding and is the source of every manifestation of true knowledge and intelligence. God as principle cannot be comprehended by any of the senses. But the mind of man is limitless, and through it he may come into touch with Divine Mind. The one Mind is a unit and cannot be divided. The individual mind is a state of consciousness in the one Mind.

God as principle--The unchangeable life, love, substance, and intelligence of Being. Principle does not occupy space; neither has it any limitations of time or matter, but it eternally exists as the one underlying cause out of which come forth all true ideas.

God as Spirit--God is Spirit, and Spirit is located and appears wherever it is recognized by an intelligent entity. It thus follows that whoever gives his attention to Spirit and seals his identification with it by His word, starts a flow of Spirit life and all the attributes of Spirit in and through his consciousness. To the extent that man practices identifying himself with the one and only source of existence, he becomes

Spirit, until finally the union attains a perfection in which he can say with Jesus, "I and the Father are one" (John 10:30).

God as substance--This does not mean matter, because matter is formed while God is the formless. The substance that God is lies back of all matter and all forms. It is that which is the basis of all form yet enters not into any form as finality. It cannot be seen, tasted, or touched. Yet it is the only enduring substance in the universe.

God as Truth--The eternal verity of the universe and man.

God, centered in--To have the attention focused on spiritual ideas and ideals.

God, creative process of--Christianity describes God as Spirit, creating by a process comparable to the mental processes, with which we are all familiar. First, mind, then the idea (word) in mind of what the act shall be, then the act itself. God planned man and the universe, and through the expression of His word projected them into creation, as ideal principles and imminent energies acting behind and within all visibility. The creative processes of Divine Mind are continuously operative; creation is going on all the time, but the over-all plan, the design in Divine Mind, is finished.

God's creations are always spiritual. This includes spiritual man (God-man) through whom all things, including personal man (Adam man) are brought into manifestation. Spiritual man is the acme or pinnacle of God's creation--the image and likeness of God. "Thou art my beloved Son, in thee I am well pleased" (Mark 1:11).

God, demonstrating--To demonstrate God means to make His Spirit manifest in one's life.

God immanent--This refers to the all-pervading and indwelling presence of God, the life and intelligence permeating the universe. Jesus lovingly revealed that the Father is within man, forever resident in the invisible side of man's nature. Paul also set forth this truth when he wrote of "one God and Father of all, who is over all, and through all, and in all" (Eph. 4:6).

God, jealous--God is not jealous as men count jealousy, but He is jealous of principle, from which no lapses are tolerated. Man's failure to observe divine law causes it to react on him.

God-man--The man that God created in His image and likeness, and present within all men.

God manifest--God manifest is really greater than God principle; the man who has demonstrated the God character is greater than the untried man. Jesus proclaimed, "I and the Father are one" (John 10:30). He had all the possibilities of Principle and, in addition, He demonstrated a large degree of its possibilities. In this respect, Jesus is the great Way-Shower and helper for all men.

God presence, unity with--To make oneself conscious of the presence of God, one must consistently affirm oneness with this presence. Say: "I have faith in God; I have faith in Spirit; I have faith in things invisible. I am one with God."

God, reconciliation with--To be reconciled with God means to be willing that His will be done; that is, that limitations, personality, ignorance shall give way so that the perfection and righteousness of Divine Mind may be expressed. Reconciliation takes place by man's surrender of an adverse will and an acceptance of that "mind . . . which was also in Christ Jesus" (Phil. 2:5).

God, responsibility to--Truth is implanted in us by divine intelligence. To the degree that we awaken to the consciousness of the inherent wisdom, to this degree are we responsible to the Father and required to render unto Him the fruitage of our wisdom. Each of us unfolds according to understanding and realization. Whether our understanding is little or great, we must demonstrate the Truth we know. If our understanding is much, much is required of us.

"God said"–The same as "Mind thought," by which all things were brought forth. (see 1st chapter of Genesis)

God transcendent--This suggests God as above and beyond His creation. That God is remote from the practical affairs of man or from man's own experience is a false belief. God (perfection) is not out of reach of His offspring; neither is He something beyond and above man. Tennyson tells us that "closer is He than breathing, and nearer than hands and feet."

God, will of--God's will is always perfection and all good for all His children; perfect health in mind and body; abundance of every good thing including joy, peace, wisdom, and eternal life. He does not will suffering or imperfection in any form.

The belief that God wills both good and evil is false; the truth is that God is all good and only good can come to man from Him. If man experiences error and inharmony, he brings them upon himself by his failure to harmonize his thoughts, words, and acts with the Lord, or divine law. (see will, divine)

God's name--God's name represents wholeness. It is holy, perfect. God is everywhere present. When we think of God as being anything less than that which is perfect and whole, we are taking His name in vain. "Thou shalt not take the name of Jehovah thy God in vain" (Exod. 20:7).

gold--Metaphysically, gold represents spiritual gifts; the riches of Spirit. The gold that the Wise Men brought to the Christ child was a consciousness of the omnipresent richness of substance. To follow Jesus in the demonstration of prosperity, we must charge our mind with wise and rich ideas.

golden candlesticks--Receptacles of spiritual light.

golden scepter--A rod; symbol of wisdom held out when the king (the will) is willing to listen to reason.

Golgotha--"The place of a skull" (Matt. 27:33). The skull is the place where the intellect is crossed out, so that Spirit may win eternal ascendancy. Jesus (the intellectual) was crucified at "The place of a skull," so that Christ (Truth) might become all in all.

good, the--The Absolute; the incomparable; that which is godly in its character. God is omnipresent All-Good. "Why callest thou me good? none is good save one, even God" (Mark 10:18).

good and evil states of consciousness--Good and evil states of consciousness form the heavens and the hells of the race. We go in mind to heaven or hell every time we mentally project thoughts that "chord" with that particular state. When we establish an enduring consciousness of good, evil disappears as darkness before light.

goodness, reward of--There is always a saving grace in divine goodness; and if we have ever done a kind act, it has been preserved in the careful records of memory and will come forth when we most need it.

gospel--An Anglo-Saxon word derived from God (good) and spell (story, tidings). It is now universally identified with Jesus' mission and the doctrine that has grown out of it--that system of religious beliefs centered about the teachings of Jesus.

The gospel of Jesus is that every man can become God incarnate. It is not alone a gospel of right living, but also shows the way into dominion and power equal to and surpassing that of Jesus of Nazareth. "He that believeth on me, the works that I do shall he do also; and greater works than these shall he do; because I go unto the Father" (John 14:12).

grace--Good will; favor; disposition to show mercy; aid from God in the process of regeneration. "By grace have ye been saved" (Eph. 2:5).

"Grace and truth came through Jesus Christ" (John 1:17); that is, the real saving, redeeming, transforming power came to man through the work that Jesus did in establishing for the race a new and higher consciousness in the earth. We can enter into this consciousness by faith in Him and by means of the inner spirit of the law that He taught and practiced.

gratitude--Gratitude and thanksgiving are both necessary in demonstrating prosperity through divine law. Be grateful to God and thankful to the friends whom He uses to supply you.

All metaphysicians have found by experience that being thankful for what they have increases the inflow. Gratitude is a great mind magnet, and when it is expressed from the spiritual standpoint it is powerfully augmented. The saying of grace at the table has its origin in this idea of the power of increase through giving thanks.

graven image--Idol. We set up a graven image when we image God as a material form or location in substance. (see image)

gravitation--The love force in nature; the power of attraction among physical bodies.

greatest in God's kingdom--When Jesus washed the feet of His apostles He brought home to His followers that he who willingly performs lowly, humble service for others, with no thought of personal distinction, is greatest in God's kingdom.

greed, freedom from--A result of the habit of tithing, which establishes a consciousness of giving and keeps one's mental channel free from material selfishness.

Greek--Metaphysically, a term for intellectual reasoning. In Acts 11:20-24, the truth regarding the new teaching of Jesus is beginning to reach the old reasoning of the intellect, and the wall of old ideas is being broken down.

ground, holy--Substance in its spiritual wholeness, or the idea of substance in Divine Mind. When we realize his idea we let go of all limitation and are conscious only of the Absolute.

growth--Increase by assimilation of new substance; multiplication. We grow by incorporating spiritual substance into our consciousness. The law of growth is in beholding. When we behold the body as anything other than its divine idea, we hold it there (in error, sin, discord). To behold ourselves free from these keeps us manifesting freedom.

growth, spiritual--The increase of God in man. All growth is first in mind and depends on the standards we are holding in mind. A high spiritual standard has lifting power. All growth and unfoldment are based on the law. What we earnestly desire and persistently affirm will be ours if we "faint not" (Gal. 6:9).

guidance, spiritual--The impressions that come from the Spirit of truth within man.hades--A Greek word, often translated hell. It is supposed to refer to the unseen world, or the abode of the dead. In reality, however, the word has reference to the grave or the "pit." Hades refers to the outer darkness, the realm of sense, in contrast to the inner or luminously spiritual hallow the name of God--To realize that His name means wholeness and perfection for us.

halo--The artists of old always painted saints with an emanation or circle of light around the head, which custom contained a grain of truth. It is from the I AM center in the crown of the head that we draw all new inspiration, all new ideas. When they contact man's consciousness these new inspirations, new ideas, break forth as a soft golden light (pure wisdom) that surrounds the head. This is known to spiritually quickened men as the halo. (see aura)

hand--Represents executive ability; the doing of things; outer or manual power.

hardening--Refusing to accept guidance of Spirit. Willful ignorance of the God principle in man's own being, or disobedience to the indwelling Christ.

harmony, divine--Perfect accord with the goodness, the beauty, and the righteousness of omnipresent Spirit. Everything is governed by fixed law, and harmony is its expression. This is illustrated by the living body, which is a sensitive instrument, responsive to the touch of the Master, I AM.

harmony, divine, how lost--When the will is centered in the external and loses sight of the ideal, it breaks the connection between Spirit and manifestation, and thus man loses the harmony that is his under divine law.

harmony, divine, how restored--Through a knowledge of the Truth of Being man is restored to divine harmony. He must know the Truth about himself and conform to it in all his thinking, and not be misled by appearances.

hate--Extreme antipathy, intense aversion, lingering antagonism. Dislike is a mild form of hate. Both hatred and dislike are antichrist, and have no place in the superconsciousness.

hate, bodily effects of--Hate burns out the vital spark in the glands, much as an excessively high current burns out a fuse in your house lighting system. Then the light goes out and death of the body sets in.

hate, remedy for--Love, peace, and harmony are the only remedies that count. "God is love" (I John 4:8), and to live in God-Mind,

man must cultivate love until it becomes the keynote of his life.

head--The center from which the mind expresses various thoughts and ideas.

heal--"To make hale, sound, or whole" (Webster). To bring forth the perfect Christ man that exists within each of us.

healer--One who heals the sins of man, and restores him to his original, sinless state. The healer is the focal center of faith; through him faith reaches the patient, directly or by means of someone very much interested in him.

healer, natural--One who has a great compassion and yearning to help humanity out of its errors and suffering. When one enters this state of consciousness a healing virtue pours out that changes all discord to harmony.

healing--"Restoring to original purity or integrity" (Webster). The first step in all spiritual healing is to believe, and the next step is openness and receptivity to the stream of healing life. Through the exercise of faith and our words, our spiritual quality is fused into unity with the power of Christ and the work is marvelously accomplished.

All healing is based on mental cleansing. When the mind is free from error thoughts, harmony in the body ensues. Permanent healing is never accomplished until the mental cause of the disease, the error thought, is removed. Jesus was a true healer, and when He cast out the error that caused the condition, He said, "Sin no more, lest a worse thing befall thee" (John 5:14). The "thing" was caused by sin. Thus the true way to heal is to find the mental cause and destroy it forever.

healing, absent--Healing of an individual by a person who is not in the physical presence of the one being healed.

healing and will power--Through the use of the will, it is possible to bring about an appearance of health. This is not spiritual healing; it is a species of mind dominance.

healing, medical and spiritual--Permanent healing is never gained through medication or drug curing. Spiritual healing restores to perpetual health because it erases the error thought and cleanses the mind. "Though your sins be as scarlet, they shall be as white as snow" (Isa. 1:18).

healing name--Any declaration man may make, in which the name Jesus Christ is used reverently, will contact the spiritual ether where the Christ I AM lives and will open the mind and body to the inflow of spiritual healing power. Affirm: Through Jesus Christ, vitalizing energy floods my whole being, and I am healed.

healing, psychical--Healing on the mental plane.

healing virtue--The restoring power of Being. "For power came forth from him, and healed them all" (Luke 6:19).

healing word--The healing word is not a special creation to meet an emergency. The word goes forth and establishes that which is. It does not heal anything--in its perfection there is nothing to heal. Its office is to behold the perfection of Being.

health--A state of being sound or whole in mind and body. Oneness with the Christ Mind assures perfect health. Health is the normal condition of man, a condition true to the Truth of his being. Health is from within and does not have to be manufactured in the without. It is the very essence of Being, universal and enduring.

That which seems to be sickness does not exist in Truth. When man becomes so much at one with God-Mind that he abides in the consciousness of health, he enters the eternal peace in which he knows that "it is finished" (John 19:30). To know God as health one must take up the study of the healthy mind and make it and not physical appearance the basis of every calculation.

health and the word--Experiences, innumerable times repeated, prove the power of words to bring health. Health is potential in the real of your being. Health can always be demonstrated through the power of the spoken word.

hearing--Ability to look deeper than words and catch the inner meaning. "He that hath ears, let him hear" (Matt. 13:9). In many places the Bible indicates that the ear referred to is not the physical organ but the listening mind.

The "ear" that conceives and really hears is the auditory center in the brain. It is here that the mind grasps and analyzes the sound vibrations.

heart--The heart is love, the affectional consciousness in man. It is the faculty through which man receives love from Being. The heart, however, is but the visible expression of an invisible center of consciousness. It is the center from which the divine substance is poured forth. Everyone uses his heart center when he sends forth a loving thought.

As used in Scripture, the word heart represents the subconscious mind. "Out of the abundance of the heart his mouth speaketh" (Luke 6:45).

heart, good and evil--The heart of the unregenerate man is both good and evil, but the evil is without foundation in Being, and has no sustaining power outside man's belief in its reality. When the heart is purged of all thoughts adverse to good, man consciously contacts the underlying God substance.

heaven--The Christ consciousness; the realm of Divine Mind; a state of consciousness in harmony with the thoughts of God. Heaven is everywhere present. It is the orderly, lawful adjustment of God's kingdom in man's mind, body, and affairs.

Jesus, of all those claiming intimate acquaintance with spiritual things, gave heaven definite location. "The kingdom of God is within you" (Luke 17:21). Heaven is within every one of us; a place, a conscious sphere of mind, having all the attraction described or imagined as belonging to heaven. But this kingdom within is not material, it is spiritual.

heaven and earth--Two states of mind, the ideal and the manifestation. According to Revelation 21:1 we are to have new ideals with manifestations in the earth to correspond.

God visioned two planes of consciousness, the heaven and the earth, or more properly, "the heavens and the earth." One is the realm of pure ideas; the other, of thought forms. Heaven is the orderly realization of divine ideas. Earth is the manifestation of these ideas.

heaven, firmament of--The consciousness of Truth that has been formulated and established.

heaven, restoration to--Faith in Spirit and the ultimate dominance of the good in all men will finally restore man to the heavenly consciousness from which he descended.

heifer--The heifer, she-goat, ram, turtledove, and young pigeon that Abram was instructed to take (Gen. 15:9) represent beliefs on the sense plane that must be sacrificed. The thought of physical strength must be given up, and its spiritual source must be realized. The human must be given up in order that the divine will may prevail. All subconscious resistance to the working of the divine law must be denied away.

hell--Symbolized in the Bible as Gehenna, Ge Hinnom, the Valley of Hinnom--a place outside Jerusalem where the city's refuse was burned. It symbolizes that purifying fire which consumes the dross of man's character.

Metaphysically, hell represents a corrective state of mind. When error has reached its limit, the retroactive law asserts itself, and judgment, being part of that law, brings the penalty, called hell, upon the transgressor. This penalty is not punishment, but discipline. If the transgressor is repentant and obedient, he is forgiven. (see fire, hades)

hell of fire--The "hell of fire" spoken of in Scripture is the purifying fire or power of the Spirit. Its purpose is the cleansing and purification of man.

heredity, flesh--The belief that man has his being from man. The law is that like begets like, and this law is set into operation in a way adverse to Truth when man holds himself as the offspring of mortal man. It is overcome by the Truth that God is Father, that man's real source is God, and that his inheritance is the perfection and wholeness of God. When this Truth is perceived we begin to understand and take on the characteristics of our divine Father. If we believe that God is our Father, and acknowledge Him, He will acknowledge us.

"hid with Christ in God"–The lifting up of the Christ in man in order that his physical and mental nature may be drawn into the universal perfection. Man dies to the old life of sense and lives under a new commandment. "For ye died, and your life is hid with Christ in God" (Col. 3:3).

hireling--The hireling state of mind is that in which one is constantly looking for rewards. This cultivates selfishness, which is the foundation of fear.

hoarding--Gathering things together in the external. This is a vain effort to avert an imagined shortage in the future. "Lay not up for yourselves treasures upon the earth, where moth and rust consume . . . but lay up for yourselves treasures in heaven, where neither moth nor rust doth consume" (Matt. 6:19,20).

hold all persons in Truth--Never to think evil of anyone, no matter how much error he may seem to express, but to see all as they really are in Spirit: perfect, harmonious, joyous, and prosperous.

hold a thought--To search out and absorb to one's consciousness, through the process of meditation and prayer, the Truth contained in spiritual words. To repeat some statement of Truth in the silence and meditate on it until it becomes a living word in the consciousness, illuminating and upbuilding mind and body.

holding a mental picture--This is a work that lies deeper than the outer man discerns. The subconscious mind must enter into the process and desire intensely the good that is to be demonstrated. This deep desire keeps in mind an image of that which is to be brought into manifestation.

holding to Principle--Standing steadfast by a statement of Truth in the face of seeming error; insisting on the divine accuracy of one's faith. Demonstration will follow.

holy--"Spiritually whole; of unimpaired innocence" (Webster). Holiness is wholeness in Spirit, mind, and body. In this state of consciousness man is aware of the all-pervading glory of God.

Holy Communion--To establish our acceptance of the Christ we celebrate Holy Communion within our mind and heart. "And as they were eating, Jesus took bread, and blessed, and brake it; and he gave to the disciples, and said, Take, eat; this is my body. And he took a cup, and gave thanks, and gave to them, saying, Drink ye all of it; for this is my blood of the covenant . . . I shall not drink henceforth of this fruit of the vine, until that day when I drink it new with you in my Father's kingdom" (Matt. 26:26-29).

The bread used in the churches typifies substance, which we consider the Lord's body, a body of spiritual ideas. The wine used symbolizes His blood, life, or the circulation of divine ideas in our consciousness that will purify our mind and heart and renew our strength, freeing us from all corruption, sin, and evil, and bringing forth in us the abundant unlimited life of God. Through the appropriation and assimilation of substance and life in consciousness, we blend our mind with the Father-Mind, or universal Mind of God, and there is a harmonizing of every fiber of the body with Christ. As our mind and heart are cleansed of untrue thoughts and beliefs, our body will take on the life and light of divinity. Eventually, the body will become living light, as was shown in the transfiguration of Jesus.

Holy Ghost--(see Holy Spirit)

holy ground--(see ground, holy)

holy, holy, holy--The word of Truth; the statement of wholeness of the whole body; a spiritual perception of the all-pervading glory of divine perfection.

holy of holies--The most sacred inner realm of consciousness wherein man comes into awareness of the presence of Spirit.

Holy Spirit--The activity of God in a universal sense. The moving force in the universe taken as a whole. The Spirit is the infinite "breath" of God, the life essence of Being. "And when he had said this, he breathed on them, and saith unto them, Receive ye the Holy Spirit" (John 20:22).

Holy Spirit is the love of Jehovah taking care of the human family. The Holy Spirit is in the world today with great power and wisdom, ready to be poured upon all who look to it for guidance. Its mission is to bring all men into communion with God; to guide men in order that they will not mistake the way into the light.

The Holy Spirit is third in the Trinity, which in theology is designated: Father, Son, and Holy Spirit. In metaphysics we approach the Trinity and more readily realize its meaning through the terms mind, idea, and expression. To be "filled with the Holy Spirit" is to realize the activities of Spirit in individual consciousness. The quickening of a man by the Holy Spirit is peculiar to each individual and must be experienced to be understood.

The Holy Spirit is authority on the gospel of Jesus. It is the only authority that Jesus ever recognized, and whoever attempts to set forth His gospel from any other standpoint is in the letter and not the spirit. No man can know what Jesus' doctrine is except he gets it direct from the one and only custodian. It is not to come secondhand, but each for himself must receive it from the Holy Spirit, which is sent by the Father in the name of the Son.

Holy Spirit, sin against--Resistance to Spirit. So long as it continues, it shuts out the forgiving love of God.

Holy Spirit and the Word--The Word is man's I AM identity. The Holy Spirit is the outpouring or activity of the living Word. The activity produces the light of Spirit, the Truth of God, the personality of Being.

holy temple--The redeemed spiritual body.

honesty--The divine law in action, which reveals that man must give an equivalent (equal value) for everything that he gets. "That we may lead a quiet and peaceable life in all godliness and honesty" (I Tim. 2:2, Scofield).

hope (and faith)–Hope is the expectation of good in the future. It is a quality (good as far as it goes) of sense mind because it is subject to time. Faith is the certain knowledge that our good is ours right now. It is of God; it goes beyond time and space.

horns, ram's--Adverse conditions. The blowing of the ram's horn represents the denial of adverse conditions and the affirmation of the power of Spirit.

horses, four--(see 6th chapter of Revelation.) The four horses and their riders are, first, "a white horse," representing the power of the Christ; second, "a red horse [war]: and to him that sat thereon it was given to take peace from the earth"; third, "a black horse" [commercialism]: "A measure of wheat for a shilling, and three measures of barley for a shilling"; and fourth, "a pale horse: and he that sat upon him, his name was Death."

Prodigious preparation for war by nations, incited by the greed for gain, will lead them to "let slip the dogs of war" unless the rider of the white horse comes forth "conquering, and to conquer."

hosannas--Represent the joyful obedience and homage that all the thoughts in one's consciousness give when an error state of mind is overcome.

house--The house that God builds and dwells in is man's body. "Know ye not that your body is a temple [house] of the Holy Spirit?" (I Cor. 6:19). The body temple. "For we are a temple of the living God" (II Cor. 6:16).

humanity--The garden of God, of which the soil is the omnipresent thought substance.

humility--"Freedom from pride and arrogance" (Webster). Recognition that the personal man by himself is ineffectual. "I can of myself do nothing" (John 5:30). "The Father abiding in me doeth his works" (John 14:10).

True humility is needed very much in the Christ-centered individual. The true Christian is humble. He knows the nothingness of the lesser self in man and the allness of Christ.

hypocrite--In classic Greek, the word meant an actor in a theater; so the word came to mean anyone who pretends to be one thing while really he is something far different.

Appearing to be lovingly thoughtful for others, while thinking only of self and reputation, is to deserve only the reward of a hypocrite. No wise man would seek the reward of empty applause, which might satisfy the boastful giver. A modest man asks the approval of Spirit only. (see Matt. 6: 1-18)

I AM--Spiritual identity; the real or Christ Mind, of each individual. The I AM Being. God is I AM, and man, His offspring, is also I AM. I AM is the indwelling Lord of life, love, wisdom, and all the ideas eternally in Divine Mind.

The I AM is the metaphysical name of the spiritual self, as distinguished from the human self. One is governed by Spirit, the other by personal will. Christ and Jehovah are the scriptural names for spiritual I AM. Jesus called it the Father. I AM is eternal, without beginning or ending: the true spiritual man whom God made in His image and likeness.

The I AM has its being in heaven; its home is in the realm of God ideals. It is the center around which all the thoughts of man revolve. The narrow concept of the personal I AM should be led out into the consciousness of the great and only I AM. Man identifies himself with that to which he attaches his I AM, and whatever he identifies himself with, that he manifests. Hitch your I AM to the star of Christ, and infinite joy will follow as night the day.

I AM identity--As the will of God, man represents I AM identity. Individual consciousness is like an eddy in the ocean--all the elements that are found in the ocean are also found in the eddy, and every eddy may, in due course, receive and give forth all that is in the ocean. This is individual consciousness, freedom to act without dictation of any kind, selfhood without consciousness of cause, the power to make or break without limitation.

I AM, used adversely--Man seeking happiness through sense pleasure. This is sin (missing the mark), and the wages are pain, sickness, poverty, and death. Think I AM in harmony with God-Mind, and health, wealth, and harmony will be yours.

"I am the light of the world"–(John 8:12). Refers to Christ as the expresser of Truth in all its aspects.

idea--Original, primary, or unlimited thought of Being; in God-Mind the eternal Word or Logos.

The first-born of everything in the universe is an idea in Divine Mind. The divine idea of the universal creation is called in Scripture Christ, "who is the image of the invisible God, the first born of all creation" (Col. 1:15). Everything is first an idea in mind, and this law holds good, not only in the creations of God, but in the forms made by man as well. The table upon which you write was first an idea in the mind of the maker. All creation is summed up or concentrated in man. Everything found in the universe is found in his constitution. "In him dwelleth all the fulness of the Godhead bodily" (Col. 2:9).

idea, Christ--The one complete idea of perfect man in Divine Mind. Jesus is the name that represents an individual expression of the Christ idea. Jesus Christ is the name often applied to the man of Galilee who demonstrated perfection. Christ Jesus is the idea that is being expressed by men as a result of their faith in and understanding of Truth. In this idea are involved all the potentialities of that which is to be evolved through man. The idea itself becomes the evolving power through which it makes its inherencies manifest.

Christ ideas are the most heavily charged with Spirit. Every expressed idea of the Christ Mind is powerful in raising consciousness. Jesus could well say, "I, if I be lifted up from the earth, will draw all men unto myself" (John 12:32).

ideas are catching--We are all heavily charged with ideas, and when these ideas are released they spring forth and pass from mind to mind, being "recorded" as they fly; when they are expressed the whole race is lifted up--if the idea is charged with the uplifting Spirit.

ideas, relation of, to the mind--As the son is to the father, so is the idea to the mind. Mind is one with its ideas, so the Father (God-Mind) is one with its offspring, the idea, the Son. Mind is coexistent with its ideas, and there is continual interaction and communion.

ideal--A mental pattern of perfection.

ideal, divine--The Christ man; the divine idea of man.

ideal of Spirit--The ideals in the Mind of Being that produce the perfect creation.

ideal unfoldment--When the illumined intellect wholly co-operates with Spirit there is a merging and blending of these powers until the intellect ceases to be mere intellect and is lost in Spirit.

idealism, divine--God's standard of perfection.

idol--In scriptural language, a false god. Even as Jesus was tempted by Satan, we are often tempted to worship the false gods of greed, covetousness, jealousy, retaliation, and other forms of negation.

ignorance, how dissolved--Ignorance (lack of knowledge) that results from association with ignorant minds can be dissolved by using the Word.

ills, cause of--Anger, jealousy, fear, hate, lust often cause ills of the body. These result from our failure to adjust our mind to Divine Mind. When the sinning state of mind is forgiven and the heavenly state of mind established, man is restored to his primal and natural wholeness. "The Son of man hath authority on earth to forgive sins" (Luke 5:24). This is wholly a mind process. All wrong and right conditions of man result from his thinking. "As he thinketh within himself, so is he" (Prov. 23:7).

illumination--The light of Christ; spiritual understanding; intuitive knowing. Spiritual illumination is a state of consciousness resulting from Holy Spirit baptism. It is good to affirm: "Christ radiance lights my mind, and my whole being is illumined with Truth."

illumined consciousness--A mind purified by the light of Truth.

illumined thoughts--Thoughts quickened through their conscious relationship to Spirit.

illusion--(see ghosts)

image--"A mental representation of anything not actually present to the senses" (Webster). Everything that is manifested was first a mental picture and was brought into expression by the forming power of the imagination. Man accumulates a mass of ideas about substance and life, and with his imagination he molds them into shape. Each one of us must not only see the image of our desires as a theory, but we must also form it into a living, breathing thing through every motive and act.

Man gets the ideal images necessary to express his perfect organism from the one perfect Mind. The perfect body will be demonstrated through his beholding the perfect, eternal, living, glorified Christ body.

image, graven--(Exod. 20:4). Graven images of God are made by mental pictures. The thought of God as a great king in a place called heaven makes just such a material image in our thought realm, and we grow to believe in and worship such an imaginary being, instead of the true God, who is Spirit.

imagination--The faculty of mind that images and forms; the power to shape and form thought. The imaging faculty presides at the nerve center between the eyes. Through this faculty the formless takes form.

With our imagination we lay hold of ideas and clothe them with substance. The body is the product of the mind. What man pictures or imagines in his mind will eventually appear in his body. In the communication of God with man, the imaging power of the mind plays an important part. It receives divine ideas and reflects their character to the consciousness. According to Scripture this is the opening of the heavens and the seeing the "angels of God ascending and descending upon the Son of man" (John 1:51).

immaculate conception--(Luke 1:26-35). The coming into activity of the Christ in us is the result of an exalted idea sown in the mind. Therefore Mary, the soul, becomes devout and expectant and believes in the so-called miraculous as a possibility. Mary expected the birth of the Messiah as the Holy Spirit had promised. She was overshadowed by that high idea, and it formed in her mind the seed that quickened into the cell. In due season there were aggregations of cells strong enough in their activity, and what is called the birth of Jesus took place.

Metaphysically interpreted, Mary, the virgin mother, represents a pure state of mind that ponders spiritual things and believes in revelations from angels and messengers from God.

Mary was "found with child of the Holy Spirit," which refers to the miraculous conception by which the Virgin Mary is held to have conceived without original sin. Joseph, not fully understanding the prophecy, "was minded to put her away privily," which refers to the fact that in the first stages of the birth of Christ in us we do not understand the process, and sometimes are moved to put it away from us.

immanent--Indwelling, abiding in, remaining or operating within. God is immanent in all creation including man. "One God and father of all, who is over all, and through all, and in all" (Eph. 4:6).

Immanuel (or Emmanuel)–A Hebrew word meaning "God with us." The consciousness that God is with us and we are one with Him. The understanding of how "the Word became flesh" (John 1:14).

immortal--Not subject to death; that which has everlasting existence; incorruptible.

impulse--Metaphysically, a movement of mind that urges man on to spiritual achievement. That which urges man to go forward. Thought activity that arises in the inner, or spiritual mind.

impurity, how eliminated--The consciousness of personal impurity is taken away through the realization of divine purity in thoughts and words.

incarnate Word of God--The word of God made flesh. Spiritual man, Christ, is the incarnate Word of God.

incense--A symbol of prayer. There must be a constant going forth of the word of the Spirit, proclaiming Truth. This spiritual essence should radiate from center to circumference, and permeate the whole consciousness.

The symbology of the burning of incense (Luke 1:9) is transmutation. The finer essences of the body are transmuted to what may be termed the fourth or radiant dimension, and a firm foundation laid for an organism of permanent character. Paul calls it the "celestial" body (I Cor. 15:40). This process of transmutation takes place whenever the I AM makes union in the body with the Lord, or higher self.

incorporate--To unite with or introduce into a body. We incorporate spiritual substance into our body through prayer.

individuality--The true self; that which is undivided from God; our spiritual identity; the God part of us. That which characterizes one as a distinct entity or particular manifestation of divine Principle. Individuality is eternal; it can never be destroyed. (see personality)

infinite--That which embraces all. The totality of Being including all knowledge, all space, all life; the complete all. That which was from the beginning, is now, and ever shall be. Without end or limitation. It is that which is boundless, immeasurable, inexhaustible. God is infinite and eternal.

influence--"Emanation or effusion, especially of a spiritual or moral force" (Webster). One's mental attitude, thoughts, and words are the creative or destructive influences in one's world. Do not say: "I am sick," "I am poor," "I am unhappy." Say: "I am well," "I am at peace," "I am wealthy."

inheritance--"A possession or blessing" (Webster). Man's inheritance from God is divine ideas. These ideas find expression, and the expression forms what man calls his good. Back of the expression is the idea.

iniquities--The mental habits that shut God out of the consciousness.

injustice--"Violation of another's rights; wrong" (Webster). The belief in injustice may be overcome by understanding the divine law of justice and fixing faith firmly in it. The remedy for all that appears unjust is denial of condemnation of others or self. Thus the healing and forgiving law of Christ is allowed to function. Say: "I deny all condemnation, judgment, and criticism of myself and all others."

inn--(Luke 10:34). One's pure thought; the price of the care received there is paid through overcoming.

inner chamber--(Matt. 6:6). The place within where we consciously meet God. It is also called the "secret place of the Most High" (Psalms 91:1), and the "Holy of holies" (Heb. 9:3). Jesus names it "the Father in me" (John 14:11), and "the kingdom of God . . . within you" (Luke 17:21).

insanity--An unbalanced condition of the faculties of mind. The remedy is to know and realize that the unclouded Christ Mind dominates all one's thinking, and that there is perfect balance and control in both mind and body.

inspiration--Inbreathing of Spirit. The breath of God infused into man, endowing him with super light and life. "He breathed on them, and saith unto them, Receive ye the Holy Spirit" (John 20:22).

inspiration, original--The writings of the Hebrew prophets are good examples of original inspiration, which is divine wisdom.

inspiration, spiritual--An inflow of divine ideas; activity of a spiritual character; understanding that comes from God.

instinct--"The native or hereditary factor in behavior" (Webster). It is akin to intuition. Man instinctively trusts in a higher power.

integration--When all the desire of the mind and heart is to express God, man is made whole, unified, integrated. "Blessed are your eyes, for they see; and your ears, for they hear" (Matt. 13:16). Man is spiritually integrated when he experiences unity of mind and body through the Christ consciousness.

integrity, spiritual--That quality of the consciousness which makes one unswerving in his conformity to the divine standard.

intellect--"The power or faculty of knowing" (Webster). Intellect is not wise. Wisdom is not its office. Intellect is the executive officer of wisdom, and can do right only when faithfully carrying out the instruction of its principal. Intellect follows the letter of the law.

It is hard for the intellect to realize the spiritual "I AM THAT I AM" (Exod. 3:14). The intellect always argues back and forth, endeavoring to prove that it is the highest authority. Jesus condemned the sins of the intellect, of which self-righteousness is the greatest, as worse than moral sins. People who live wholly in the intellect deny that man can know anything about God, because they do not have quickened faith.

intellectualism--Knowledge as independent of feeling. Literal knowledge without consideration of the Spirit. The devotee of intellectualism is often impractical and unsuccessful; he has accumulated more knowledge than he has wisdom and power to apply.

intelligence--The expression of man's powers and capacities through the avenue of the limited mental attitude termed the intellect. When the same avenue loses its boundaries and catches sight of the great sea of infinite understanding, which is always open to it, it takes on that phase of knowing more properly termed wisdom.

intelligence, divine--Intelligence that accords with or comes from Divine Mind. The next great proclamation of scientific minds will be that one directive intelligence is an essential cause of the harmonious universe.

intemperance--"Immoderate indulgence of appetites or passions" (Webster). Men need and desire the stimulant of Spirit, but not being in spiritual understanding they do not know what it is they crave and they seek satisfaction in material things.

intuition--The natural knowing capacity. Inner knowing; the immediate apprehension of spiritual Truth without resort to intellectual means. The wisdom of the heart. It is very much surer in guidance than the head. When one trusts Spirit and looks to it for understanding, a certain confidence in the invisible good develops. This faith awakens the so-called sixth sense, intuition, or divine knowing. Through the power of intuition, man has direct access to all knowledge and the wisdom of God.

invisible, the--Reality that cannot be seen, touched, or comprehended by any of the outer senses. In this realm a great and mighty work is being accomplished.

invocation--The calling forth of the presence of Spirit through the power of the Word.

involution (and evolution) – Involution (infolding) always precedes evolution (unfolding). That which is involved in mind evolves through matter. (see evolution) jealousy--A form of mental bias that blinds the judgment and causes one to act without weighing the consequences. The remedy is a dismissal of the negative thoughts that cause one to be jealous, followed by a fuller trust in the great all-adjusting power of God.

Jehovah--The I AM, the spiritual man, the image and likeness of Elohim God. In the King James Version of the Bible the Hebrew "Jehovah" has been translated "Lord." Lord means an external ruler. Bible students say that Jehovah means the self-existent One, the I AM. Then instead of reading "Lord" we should read I AM. It makes a great difference whether we think of I AM, self-existence within, or "Lord," master without. All Scripture shows that Jehovah means just what God told Moses it meant: I AM. "This is my name for ever, and this is my memorial unto all generations" (Exod. 3:15).

Jehovah, anger of--The anger and wrath of Jehovah are symbolical of the divine law in man in its often strenuous work of revealing and erasing error from the consciousness.

Jehovah God--The most inclusive name for Being. Jehovah represents the individual I AM and God (Elohim) the Universal Principle.

Jerusalem--"Habitation of peace." The spiritual center in consciousness. In man it is the abiding consciousness of spiritual peace. When we go deep into the silent recesses of our beings, we realize a stillness and sweetness beyond expression. A great peace is there--the "peace of God, which passeth all understanding" (Phil. 4:7). This is the point in consciousness where the Spiritual energy of life is strong enough to vitalize adjacent body substance. The substance is physically a nerve center just back of the stomach; spiritually it is the realization of the unfailing substance of Divine Mind.

Jerusalem, feast in--Metaphysically, a receptive state of mind toward all spiritual good.

Jerusalem, new--Spiritual consciousness. It is founded on the twelve fundamental ideas in Divine Mind, each represented by one of the precious stones. (Revelation 21: 19, 20) It is also represented by an association of all people in peace, based on spiritual understanding, purity, and a willingness to be united with Christ.

Jesus--The Man of Nazareth, son of Mary; the Saviour of mankind according to present-day Christian belief. Metaphysically He is the I AM in man, the self, the directive power, raised to divine understanding and power--the I AM identity.

As the result of lack of conscious connection between the thinking faculty and the fountainhead of existence, humanity had reached a very low state. Then came Jesus of Nazareth, whose mission was to connect the thinker with the true source of thought. Thinking at random had brought man into a deplorable condition, and his salvation depended on his again joining his consciousness to the Christ. Only through that connection could he be brought back into his Edenic state--the church of God.

It is plain to any reasonable, unprejudiced mind that Jesus of Nazareth was a religious reformer with a mission from on high, that He had an insight into those things which are ever mysteries to men immersed in the sense consciousness, and that through His knowledge, and in harmony with His mission, He set into motion spiritual ideas that ever since His ministry have been operative in the world. It is evident to even a cursory reader of His life and teachings that He was the representative of a thoroughly organized plan to help men into a higher realization of God and their relation to Him.

Jesus was keenly conscious of the character of God and His own relationship to Him. He knew God as unlimited love and as ever-present, abundant life; He knew Him as wisdom and supply. He knew God as Father, who is ever ready and willing to supply every need of the human heart. He knew that as Son of God He had access to every blessing, to all the wisdom, love, and help of the Father-Mind. Jesus did not simply believe that the words He spoke were true, He knew that they were true. His words were pregnant with meaning; they were vital, living words, which carried conviction and which produced immediate results.

Jesus is the Way-Shower. He came that we might have life more abundantly; that is, He came to awaken man to the possibilities of his own nature. "As he is . . . so are we in this world" (I John 4:17). He came to bear witness to Truth. He used the one true way to the realization of eternal life and the universal consciousness, therefore His influence on the race cannot be measured. It is infinite and eternal. (See Christ and the way)

Jesus, crucifixion of--The Jews were under the dominion of an earth-minded priesthood. They were in a state of ignorance as regards spiritual things and did no thinking for themselves. Hence, they could not recognize or comprehend the things of which Jesus spoke to them. They were looking for a temporal king who would restore to them, by war and conquest, the earthly glory of Solomon. When Jesus tried to teach them of Spirit, of a spiritual idea, the Christ within themselves, "the hope of glory," (Col. 1:27) that would free them from every bondage of mind, body, and environment, they crucified Him.

Jesus Christ--Christ is the perfect idea of God for man. Jesus is the perfect expression of the divine idea Man. Jesus Christ is a union of the two, the idea and the expression, or in other words, He is the perfect man demonstrated.

Jesus' prayers were answered because He always dwelt in the consciousness of perfect harmony with the Father. When we ask in His name, it is with an earnest desire for that consciousness which Jesus possessed. The Christ within each of us is ever seeking perfect expression, and it should be our earnest effort to have our mind and heart clear and open channels in order that He may more perfectly work through us. When we ask in the name of Christ Jesus we ask in the consciousness that in reality we are perfect children of the Father. This harmonious relationship between God and man is attained by prayer and meditation and by constantly affirming God's presence and power. If we would have God manifest through us, we must endeavor to raise our thoughts and feelings to the standard of God.

Jew--Broadly speaking, a Hebrew. Metaphysically, a thought springing from and belonging to the praise and inner-life consciousness of the individual.

Jewess--The soul or feminine aspect of that in consciousness for which a Jew stands.

jewels--"Jewels of silver, and jewels of gold" (Exod. 12:35) represent wisdom and love in the external sense, which are to be asked for or demanded by the Children of Israel. This means that we are to affirm that all wisdom and all love, even in their most external manifestations, are spiritual. This puts Spirit in control both within and without.

John the Baptist--Represents the natural man, the physical man. His face is turned toward the light in the measure that he recognizes and pays homage to the higher self within the individual. The intellectual perception of Truth by the natural man (John the Baptist) is not the true light (the Christ) but bears witness to the light and prepares the way for its dawning in consciousness.

joy--The happiness of God expressed through His perfect idea--man. Joy and gladness are strength-giving, especially if the mind is fixed on the things of Spirit. Affirm: "The joy of the Lord is my strength."

Judas--Represents the ego that has possession of the sex, or life, center in the organism and is using it for its own selfish ends. Judas was a "thief." The selfish use of the life and vitality of the organism for the gratification of sense pleasure robs the higher nature, and the spiritual man is not built up. This is the betrayal of Christ.

judgment--Mental act of evaluation through comparison or contrast. Spiritual discernment; the inner voice through whose expression we come into a larger realization of ourselves.

Judgment is a faculty of the mind that can be exercised in two ways--from sense perception or spiritual understanding. If its action be based on sense perception its conclusions are fallible and often condemnatory; if based on spiritual understanding, they are safe.

judgment, day of--That period in man's development when the law of justice and righteousness begins to be felt in his consciousness, and he finds himself in the midst of experiences where he must learn the law and conform to it.

The great judgment day of Scripture indicates a time of separation between the true and the false. There is no warrant for the belief that God sends man to everlasting punishment. Modern interpreters of the Bible say that the "hell of fire" (Matt. 5:22) referred to by Jesus means simply a time in which purification is taking place.

judgment seat--The "judgment-seat" (Rom. 14:10) is within man. A judging, or discerning between the true and the false, is going on daily in us as overcomers; we are daily reaping the results of our thoughts and our deeds.

justice--When judgment is divorced from love, and works from the head alone, there goes forth the human cry for justice. In his mere human judgment man is hard and heartless; he deals out punishment without consideration of motive or cause, and justice goes awry. When justice and love meet at the heart center, there are balance, poise, and righteousness.

There is an infinite law of justice that may be called into activity. When we call our inner forces into action, the universal law begins its great work in us, and all the laws both great and small fall into line and work for us. The true way to establish justice is by appealing directly to the divine law

K

karma--"The whole ethical consequence of one's acts considered as fixing one's lot in the future existence" (Webster). The accumulated effects of the sins of past lives; the burden that those who believe in karma expect to carry for ages, or until they work out of it. They are weary treadmill travelers from birth to death, and from death to birth. There is no such hopeless note in the teachings of Jesus. He came to bring a full consciousness of abundant life, complete forgiveness, redemption from all sin, and victory over death and the grave, thus delivering man from any occasion for re-embodiment and from all bondage to karma.

"keep my word"–(John 8:51). Treasure the words of Jesus as a saving balm in time of need.

"keys of the kingdom of heaven"–(Matt. 16:19). Affirmation and denial. (see affirmation; denial)

king (righteous)–The executive faculty in every man whose life is guided, governed, and directed by Spirit.

"king of the Jews, this is the"–(Luke 23:38). This means that the word of the I AM goes forth as a ruling suggestion in the spiritual and intellectual. In the physical is goes forth in the individual consciousness, but the doing away with the limitations of mortal mind pulls down all walls of partition, and the whole man accepts the word of Truth.

kingdom of God--The Christ consciousness, kingdom of heaven.

kingdom of heaven--The kingdom of heaven is the realm of divine ideas, producing their expression, perfect harmony. It is within man.

kingdom within--That realm in man's consciousness where he knows and understands God.

knowing--There is in man a knowing capacity transcending intellectual knowledge. Nearly everyone has at some time touched this hidden wisdom and has been more or less astonished at its revelations. The knowing that man receives from the direct fusion of the Mind of God with his mind is real spiritual knowing.

knowledge--"Acquaintance with fact; hence, scope of information" (Webster). Intellectual knowledge is independent of feeling; it is literal knowledge without consideration of the Spirit. Man can store up a great fund of knowledge gleaned from books and teachers, but the most unlettered man who sits at the feet of his Lord in the silence comes forth radiant with the true knowledge, that of Spirit.

lack--"Fact or state of being deficient or wanting" (Webster). In the great Mind of Spirit there is no thought of lack. Such a thought has no rightful place in man's mind. Deny all thoughts of lack; affirm God's ever-present abundance in all your affairs.

ladder, Jacob's--Represents the step-by-step realization by means of which man assimilates the divine ideas of Truth that come to him from Jehovah.

lamb--Represents innocent, guileless forms of life on the animal plane of consciousness.

lamb, killed and eaten in the night--Represents the giving up of the animal life propensity in the mortal body. The command is that the lamb shall be without spot or blemish, and be wholly eaten after being roasted with fire. This refers to the complete transmutation and surrender of the human life to Spirit after it has been purified by the fires of regeneration.

Lamb of God--The pure life and substance of Being. By His overcoming Jesus restored to mankind the consciousness of this pure life and substance, which flows into man's consciousness through the spiritual body. Its nature is to vivify with perpetual life all things that it touches. Jesus is called "the Lamb of God" (John 1:29).

language--An arbitrary arrangement of sounds used to express thoughts. Thus the same thought in the minds of two men may be beyond their power to communicate to each other because they are not familiar with the intellect's provincial dialect. If these men were conscious of the mental plane where images are the basis of language, they would have no trouble in communicating though they were born of diverse races. The image of a horse in one mind would be seen by the other mind instantly, and communication be easy. The common language of mankind is based on thought images. We shall never realize the universal language that is the dream of the philologist until we have dropped the arbitrary word plane and ascended into the realm of thought images.

laver--Basin or bowl. The laver with water therein is the word of denial ever at hand ready to cleanse every impure thought that comes into consciousness.

law--The faculty of the mind that holds every thought and act strictly to the Truth of Being, regardless of circumstances or environment. Law is a mathematical faculty. It places first things first.

Laws of mind are just as exact and undeviating as the laws of mathematics. To recognize this is the starting point in finding God.

Man does not make the law; the law is, and it was established for our benefit before the world was formed. Back of the judge is the law out of which he reads. Laws, whether natural or artificial, are but the evidence of an unseen power.

The development of man is under law. Creative mind is not only law, but is governed by the action of the law that it sets up. We have thought that man was brought forth under the fiat or edict of the great creative Mind that can make or unmake at will, or change its mind and declare a new law at any time. But a clear understanding of ourselves and of the unchangeableness of Divine Mind makes us realize that everything has its foundation in a rule of action, a law, that must be observed by both creator and created.

law, all-providing--God is the all-providing law. He is the spiritual substance out of which is made everything the race needs; the Father who supplies all His children bountifully out of His own abundance.

God is Mind; man, the offspring of God, is mind. To know the law of God, man must adjust his mind to God-Mind. The first step in applying this law is recognition of it as Truth. Unless God is known as the source of all supply, men look to the material world for support. This violates the law and breaks the connection with the one Source of all good.

law, divine--Divine law is the orderly working out of the principles of Being, or the divine ideals, into expression and manifestation throughout creation. Man, by keeping the law of right thought, works in perfect harmony with divine law, and thus paves his way into spiritual consciousness.

Divine law cannot be broken. It holds man responsible for the result of his labors. It is revealed to the mind of man through his consciously thinking on spiritual ideas.

The law that Moses laid down for the Children of Israel was one of denial and affirmation, principally denial. The law that Jesus gave was one of affirmation and love. So in taking control of the forces within, keep on the affirmative side. Let the preponderance of your thought be positive, and do not spend much time saying, "I am not." You may find it helpful sometimes to say, "I am not afraid," but more often you should say, "I am bold, fearless, courageous."

law, evolutionary--Upward trend of all things; in the individual the rising of man from sense consciousness to spiritual consciousness. This law is set into action by our thinking and is continually supported by our thoughts.

law, generic--The law that operates in each group; that from which anything springs; the germ seed that brings forth after its kind.

law, mortal--The law of limitation that man has made for himself.

law, natural--The law of seed, cultivation, and harvest that natural man is subject to for the provision of his wants.

law of attraction--The law that all conditions and circumstances in affairs and body are attracted to us to accord with the thoughts we hold steadily in consciousness.

law of conservation--Building up a large reserve consciousness of substance, life, strength, and power, instead of laying up material treasures. This is done through prayer.

"Lay not up for yourselves treasures upon the earth, where moth and rust consume, and where thieves break through and steal: but lay up for yourselves treasures in heaven, where neither moth nor rust doth consume, and where thieves do not break through nor steal" (Matt. 6:19, 20).

law of giving and receiving--The law of substance that equalizes all things. To realize and maintain divine order, substance must have both an inlet and an outlet in consciousness, and must be kept moving.

To demonstrate substance as supply, the law governing it must be recognized and kept. Those who, from pride or ignorance, do not open themselves to the inflow of substance do not demonstrate supply, and all who by selfishness refuse it an outlet, also fail. Everyone must receive freely and give as freely as he receives. Disregard of the basic principle of supply frequently hinders man's realization of the divine good. Readiness to give and readiness to receive are equally essential.

law of infinite expansion--The principle of never-ceasing growth and development toward the fulfillment of God's perfect idea that is firmly fixed in all creation.

law of justice--Many persons doubt that there is an infinite law of justice working in all things. Let them now take heart and know that this law has not worked in their affairs previously because they have not "called" it into activity at the creative center of consciousness. (see justice)

law of righteousness--The law of spiritual and mental growth that is raising man from sense consciousness to spiritual consciousness. The nature of the universe is purity and goodness. By abiding in the Christ consciousness, man aligns himself with this divine law. He becomes the "light of the world" (Matt. 5: 14).

law of sin and death--A misnomer. Sin and death are contrary to the law of love and life. They are false beliefs endowed with power through man's erroneous thinking. This seeming law can be transcended by application of the higher and true law of immutable good. Law is Truth, and in Truth all is good. There is no Truth and no reality in sin.

law of thought purification--A rule of mind action whereby man overcomes "the world, the flesh, and the devil" by building the pure Christ consciousness.

law, transgression of--Thinking thoughts that violate the principle of harmony inherent in Being. Such transgression is followed by evil conditions. Through the strength, power, purity, and love that Jesus imparted to the race mind, we can rise superior to the penalty of transgressed law and live forever in our present body forms made glorious.

law written in our "inward parts"–A law either in or around the cells, that controls their formation and duplicates the pattern laid down ages ago in mother Eve and father Adam. "I will put my law in their inward parts, and in their heart will I write it; and I will be their God, and they shall be my people" (Jer. 31:33).

"Lazarus, come forth"–(John 11:43). This refers to the power of the Word to arouse mind energy to such an extent that the physical becomes immersed in the healing life, enabling the spiritually perfect man to come into manifestation.

leaven--The leaven is the Truth. "The kingdom of heaven is like unto leaven, which a woman took, and hid in three measures of meal, till it was all leavened" (Matt. 13:33). When a word of Truth seems to be hidden in the mind, it is not idle but is quietly spreading from point to point. This process continues until the whole consciousness is vitalized by Spirit.

"Take heed, beware of the leaven of the Pharisees and the leaven of Herod" (Mark 8:15). In this case, the leaven represents limited thoughts. When we attempt to confine the divine law to the customary avenues of expression and scoff at anything beyond, we are letting the leaven of the Pharisees work in us. When we allow the finer forces of the body to fulfill lust and appetite, we are letting the leaven of Herod work to our undoing.

"Wherefore let us keep the feast, not with old leaven, neither with the leaven of malice and wickedness, but with the unleavened bread of sincerity and truth" (I Cor. 5:8).

letting go of the old--Erasing from consciousness thoughts contrary to Truth. This is done by denial.

liberation--We are not to be liberated through suppression of sense or by violent overcoming; but through a steady, step-by-step demonstration over every error.

life--That expression of Being which manifests as animation, activity, vigor. Life and substance are ideas in Divine Mind. Life is the acting principle; substance is the thing acted upon. In the phenomenal world, life is the energy that propels all forms to action. Life is not in itself intelligent; it requires the directive power of an entity that knows where and how to apply its force in order to get the best results.

In order to give man a body having life in itself, God had to endow him with a focal life center, located in the generative organs. This center of activity in the organism is also the seat of sensation, which is the most subtle and enticing of all factors that enter into being. But these qualities (sensation and generation) are necessary to man's character, and without them he would not be the complete representative, or image and likeness, of God.

Life does not emanate from the mind; it is not a psychic or purely mental quality, nor does it spring from the physical. Life is divine, spiritual, and its source is God, Spirit. The river of life is within man in his spiritual consciousness. He comes into consciousness of the river of life through the quickening of Spirit. He can be truly quickened with new life and vitalized in mind and body only by consciously contacting Spirit. This contact is made through prayer, meditation, and good works.

life, crown of--Living eternally in the presence of God. Its attainment depends on the understanding of the science of right thinking.

life, higher--The higher life is a higher state of mind. We know it when we realize I AM the Son of God.

lifted up in consciousness--Resurrected. One who has discovered the Truth of Being is raised, lifted up in consciousness, resurrected daily out of his old, subconscious, negative thought condition into the one positive Reality.

light--The understanding principle in mind. In divine order it always comes first into consciousness. Light is a symbol of wisdom. When Jesus said, "I am the light of the world" (John 8:12), He meant that He was the expresser of Truth in all its aspects.

light, inner--The illumination of Spirit resident in the center of every man's being.

lightning--Represents force, light, power. Jesus said, "Think not that I came to destroy the law or the prophets: I came not to destroy, but to fulfill" (Matt. 5:17); that is, He came to demonstrate that natural and spiritual law are one. He foresaw this very period when "the powers of the heavens shall be shaken" (Matt. 24:29)–that is, the mental realms were to be broken up--and He attributed this phenomenon to the coming of the Christ as "lightning."

limitation--Thoughts in consciousness that are narrow or restricted and which keep one in bondage to error. Belief in lack, illness, sin, or death are limitations in consciousness.

lion--"And one of the elders saith unto me, Weep not; behold, the Lion that is of the tribe of Judah, the Root of David, hath overcome to open the book and the seven seals thereof" (Rev. 5:5). The lion symbolizes courage, fearlessness, initiative, life. We must have the courage to enter fearlessly into the overcoming life and into the understanding of things. But courage alone will not do. We must have reverence of spiritual things--a devotional attitude--in order to receive spiritual inspiration. The phrase, "of the tribe of Judah," bespeaks this reverential nature and attitude.

lips, sinful--Lips that utter faultfinding words, condemnatory words. The law is, "The lips of the wise shall preserve them" (Prov. 14:3).

logic--(derived from the word Logos, which see). A rational relation or connection between idea and expression. Logic in its strictest sense is the only accurate method of arriving at Truth. Any system of philosophy or religious doctrine that does not admit of the rules of perfect logic in reaching its conclusion from a stated premise, must be outside the pale of pure reason and in the realm of man-made dogma. Logic and Logos are almost synonymous terms, and the highest scriptural authority tells us that all things were made by the Word. Hence, the word of reason or the reasonable word is the very foundation of the universe. Therefore, to know accurately about the reality of things we must disregard all appearances as indicated by the five senses, and go into pure reason--the Spirit from which was created everything that has permanent existence.

Logos--The Word of God; the divine archetype idea that contains all ideas: the Christ, the Son of God, spiritual man in manifestation. Divine Mind in action. This supreme idea is the creative power, the Christ consciousness formulated by universal Principle.

Logos, law of the--The law of divine creation produces the order and harmony of perfect thought. Law puts first things first. It is a rule of action.

An understanding of the Logos reveals to us the law under which all things are brought forth, the law of mind action. Divine Mind creates by thought, through ideas.

Lord--The activity of the spiritual I AM as the ruling consciousness. The Lord God of the Scriptures is Christ, the Spiritual Man; our divine consciousness; the creative power within us.

Lord, absence from--A state in which both mind and body are functioning in carnality.

Lord is One, the--Oneness of thought and purpose in the individual, as well as the one Presence and one Power--the omnipotent good, which man must know and consider in his contact with the world without. The principle of oneness controls life.

Lord, wrath of the--(see wrath of God)

Lord's Prayer--A series of ideas illustrative of man's relationship to his Creator.

Lord's Supper--(Matt. 26:26-30). Metaphysically, God's covenant with mankind, through His perfect idea, Christ Jesus. This compact was completed through Jesus' breaking the bread and blessing the cup. The bread symbolizes spiritual substance, or the body. The wine symbolizes the blood of Jesus, or spiritual life.

We eat the body of Jesus by affirming the one spiritual substance to be the substance of our body and we drink His blood by affirming and realizing our oneness with the one divine, omnipresent life of Spirit.

love--The pure essence of Being that binds together the whole human family. Of all the attributes of God, love is undoubtedly the most beautiful. In Divine Mind, love is the power that joins and binds in divine harmony the universe and everything in it; the great harmonizing principle known to man.

Divine love is impersonal; it loves for the sake of loving. It is not concerned with what or who it loves, nor with a return of love. Like the sun, its joy is in the shining forth of its nature. "Love suffereth long, and is kind; love envieth not; love vaunteth not itself, is not puffed up" (I Cor. 13:4).

Love is an inner quality that sees good everywhere and in everybody. It insists that all is good, and by refusing to see anything but good it causes that quality finally to appear uppermost in itself, and in all things.

Love is the great harmonizer and healer. Whoever calls on God as Holy Spirit for healing is calling on divine love. Divine love will bring your own to you, adjust all misunderstandings, and make your life and affairs healthy, happy, harmonious, and free, "Love therefore is the fulfilment of the law" (Rom. 13:10).

luck--All things come about through law. Men sometimes blindly keep the law or part of it for a time, and it works for them. Not understanding the cause that produced their success, they call it "luck" and build up a belief in "chance."

lust of the flesh--Sense consciousness, which causes man to be tempted. So long as he is ruled by the serpent of sense, man is not fulfilling divine law. The activity of the cleansing, refining process of Spirit is hindered in man when he lets lustful desire enter the love consciousness.

magnify the Lord--The mind possesses magnifying power, which it exercises habitually, either consciously or unconsciously. This power makes the mind the fertile side of man's nature, out of which spring "the issues of life." We magnify the Lord by anticipation, by expecting, by declaring that only the good is true, by steadfastly declaring that every blessing is ours now.

malefactors, crucified with Jesus--Represent duality--belief in good and evil, past and future--comprising all the thought consciousness of opposites that has been built up since man began to eat, or enter into the conscious knowledge of "good and evil" (Gen. 2:17).

mammon--Treasure; wealth; the material or worldly thought and belief regarding riches, possessions, and wealth, compared with the true inner riches of the mind, which are the understanding and the realization of the spiritual substance, life, and intelligence that lie back of every outer manifestation.

man--An idea in Divine Mind; the epitome of being. The apex of God's creation, created in His image and likeness.

Man appears unlike God because he, through disobedience, fell into sin. Through accepting race thoughts, man has adopted wrong ideas about himself and his relation to his Source. He has believed that he is unlike God and separate from Him, and these concepts have, by the law of thought, become manifest.

Ideal man is the perfect man, the Christ, the offspring of Divine Mind. Manifest man should be as perfect as the ideal, and he will be when the individual identifies himself with the Christ. When he is identified with anything less than perfection he manifests some degree of imperfection.

Man makes his world through the activity of ideas in his consciousness--ideas of wisdom, power, intelligence. The real man is the embodiment of God, and all the God-substance and the power to make it active is inherent within him.

When we are quickened to spiritual understanding and fully realize the true character of God and our own nature as the image, or idea, of God we will begin to live as Jesus lived in order that we may bring forth the likeness. To perceive the true character of God and His attributes and then to grasp our relationship to Him is to realize that His attributes are our attributes, His power is our power; His character is our character.

man, age of--Man is not limited in life. He has existed with the Father always. At the very beginning of creation he was born into being through the Son, the Christ, the perfect, ideal man whom God made in His image and likeness.

"Jesus said . . . Before Abraham was born, I am" (John 8:58).

man, duality of--Man is a duality in seeming only. He is a unit when he knows himself. His ignorance of himself and his relation to God is the cause of the seeming duality. When wisdom comes to him and he makes wisdom his own, there is no longer war between the ideal man in God and the becoming man in the Lord God.

man, fall of--The result that follows man's failure to recognize his divinity. By his error he falls into a state of consciousness where he is bound in limitation and error. He falls short of his divine possibilities.

man idea--Before there could be a man there must have been an idea of man. God, the Father, Divine Mind, had an idea of man, and this idea is his Son, the perfect man idea, the offspring of God-Mind. This Son is the Christ, the only begotten of the Father. The Son, being the express image and likeness of the Father, is perfect, even as the Father which is in heaven is perfect. All that we find in Divine Mind we find in its offspring, "who is the image of the invisible God, the firstborn of all creation" (Col. 1:15). "In him dwelleth all the fulness of the Godhead bodily" (Col. 2:9).

man, illumined intellectual--John the Baptist represents the illumined intellectual man who perceives with spiritual vision the unfoldment of this natural, intellectual man into the Christ man.

man, mortal--An error concept or expression of man, a misunderstanding of his true nature that results in an untrue expression of God-given powers and ends in death.

man, new--(Eph. 4:24; Col. 3:10). The "new man" is born of a divine idea through the overshadowing of the Holy Spirit. This idea is that man is a spiritual being; he is a "holy thing."

man of sin--The "man of sin" is the carnal mind in each individual, and it always opposes and misrepresents the Truth; sometimes it poses as an angel of light and Truth. Everyone who overcomes this inner adversary will be saved from all deception that may be practiced by anybody or anything that claims the place of the Lord Jesus Christ.

man, sense--The earth man, who lives through his senses. He gathers his information and makes his judgments from evidence gathered by the senses. He seeks his pleasure through the satisfaction of his sense appetites. He is the false man, the antichrist man.

man, Son of--Unregenerate man; personality, the name of the personal consciousness. The spiritual man is God's Son; the personal man is man's son.

man, spiritual--The sum total of the attributes or perfect idea of Being, identified and individualized. This man is the "only begotten Son" (John 3:16) of God.

Jehovah, or "I AM THAT I AM" (Exod. 3:14), is the name of this divine man. He was manifested as the higher self of Jesus. In the New Testament He is called the Christ. Jesus named Him the "Father in me" (John 14: 10). He called Him Father more than forty times.

man, ungodly--The ungodly man is unlike God; he seeks to accumulate material riches, to gain worldly knowledge or fame. He does not know God as the prosperity of himself and all others. "But the way of the wicked [ungodly] shall perish" (Psalms 1:6).

manna--The bread of life; the Word of God. Represents the realization that the divine substance is everywhere present, in every part of the consciousness.

manger--Represents the animal life of the body in which the new life is first manifested.

manifestation--The materialization of a Truth idea; the coming forth into visibility of that which has been affirmed; the appearance of an idea.

mansions, many--(John 14:2). Degrees of realization of the Truth of Being. The "place" that Jesus prepared is a definite state of realization of Truth into which may come all who take up the same denials and affirmations that He took up.

mantle of Elijah--Represents the reflected power that falls on us and becomes the abiding part of our consciousness, after we have declared the Truth in the highest until it makes visible the mental currents ("chariots") and vital powers ("horsemen") of Being (II Kings 2:12).

mark on Cain--The mark set on Cain to keep him from being slain was the consciousness of his divine origin. No matter how deep in transgressions the body may be, it still bears the stamp of God.

marriage, spiritual--Spiritually, marriage represents the union of two dominant states of consciousness. When we open the door of the mind by consciously affirming the presence and power of the divine I AM in our midst, there is a marriage or union of the higher forces in being with the lower and we find that we are quickened in every part; the life of the I AM has been poured out for us.

masters--Certain persons who call themselves "masters" claim that they have forged ahead of the race in their understanding and use of some of the powers of mind and have in personal egotism set up kingdoms and put themselves on thrones. These so-called "masters" and members of occult brotherhoods are attracting susceptible minds away from the straight and narrow path and leading them to believe that there is a short cut into the kingdom. Jesus described the situation forcibly and clearly in Matthew 24:24: "For there shall arise false Christs, and false prophets, and shall show great signs and wonders; so as to lead astray, if possible, even the elect."

mastery and dominion--We demonstrate mastery and dominion by persistently thinking thoughts of power and strength in the absolute principle of Truth, and through the I AM establishing them in our own consciousness.

materiality--The concept that the material universe is real, that the three-dimension world really exists. The truth is that the material world is a limitation of the four-dimension world; it has no permanent existence and will come to an end. This is attested to by both religion and science.

matter--Man's limited concept of divine substance that he has "formed" in consciousness; a thought of substance as dense, solid, weighty, and separate from the spiritual life that underlies it. When man is quickened of the Spirit he knows Spirit to be all, in all, and he gives all thought to this reality.

matter, rule of--That state of man where material ideas and standards are the established rule of his life and actions.

meat eating--Meat eating stimulates the sense man and interferes with the development of spiritual power. For many reasons it is better to abstain from a meat diet. First, because of the command, "Thou shalt not kill" (Exod. 20:13). Injustice and cruelty react on the one who practices them, whether he himself kills or partakes of that which has been killed for him by others. Meat eating requires the spilling of blood, which destroys Truth in consciousness. Destructive ideas are introduced into the stomach, producing doubts and fears and physical inharmonies. The love of God should be expressed toward all animals.

meditation--Continuous and contemplative thought; to dwell mentally on anything; realizing the reality of the Absolute; a steady effort of the mind to know God; man's spiritual approach to God.

The purpose of meditation is to expand the consciousness Christward; to bring into realization divine Truth; to be transformed in spirit, soul, and body by the renewing of the mind.

meek, the--Anyone highly trained to react to all negative stimuli with love instead of with "an eye for an eye." "Blessed are the meek: for they shall inherit the earth" (Matt. 5:5).

men of Israel--The religious thoughts and aspirations of man, which give him access to resurrection life through faith in the Christ.

men of valor, mighty--Strong, courageous, conquering thoughts expressed by man, inspired by the establishment of praise (Judah) and faith (Benjamin) in consciousness.

mental assimilation--The mind assimilates what it affirms.

mental atmosphere--Surrounding or prevailing mental influence. Your mental attitude, thoughts, and words are creative or destructive influences in your world.

mental discipline--The practice of the daily training of the mind through denials of error and affirmations of Truth.

mental premise--A basic mental premise is an original proposition of Truth that serves as the ground for affirmation, such as, "All is good."

mentality, adverse--The mortal mind with its beliefs and thoughts opposed to the perfect Mind of Christ is the adverse mentality. All sin, suffering, disease, and death are the work of the adverse mentality.

merchant--One who is seeking the "jewel" of spiritual good, through exchange of thought, discussion, and argument. In order to attain the inner pearl, the unadulterated Truth, man must give up the so-called values and realize his oneness with the Christ within.

mercy--Christlike treatment toward the suffering. The important point in desiring to be merciful is righteous adjustment, as this results in true overcoming.

messenger--An intellectual perception of Truth that cleanses the mind and heart and leads to the coming or conscious presence of the indwelling Spirit of truth, the Christ.

messengers of God--Spiritual thoughts that always bring messages of light and point the way to a harmonious co-operation between the indwelling love of the heart and the understanding of the head.

Messiah--The promise of the visible manifestation of the Christ. Christ is the fulfillment in man of this promise.

metaphysician--One skilled in the science of Being; a student and teacher of the laws of Spirit.

metaphysics--The systematic study of the science of Being; that which transcends the physical. By pure metaphysics is meant a clear understanding of the realm of ideas and their legitimate expression.

microbes, how formed--Microbes or germs are formed by the power of thought. Thoughts become entities and have identity according to the character of the thought in the mind of the thinker. Error thoughts make disease microbes. Positive thoughts form intelligent body-builders.

middle wall of partition--The division between the conscious mind and the subconscious mind, caused by man's lack of understanding of his true I AM nature. This partition is broken down by the realization and manifestation of the one Divine Mind.

midnight--The darkened negative state of consciousness.

millennium--Man has for untold ages looked forward to a millennium day. That day will always be in the future until we let go of our thought of a future. The millennium day is now. It is established today--this very hour.

millstone--A seeming hindrance of an earthly nature; a heavy burden.

Mind--By the term Mind, we mean God--the universal Principle, which includes all principles.

As an aid in understanding how the universal Mind creates, we can observe the action of our own mind because we are the offspring of the one Mind and we bring forth in like manner. "The Son can do nothing of himself, but what he seeth the Father doing: for what things so-ever he doeth, these the Son also doeth in like manner" (John 5:19).

Man in the consciousness of the one Mind has no sense of apartness. Through affirmation he can attune himself to Being, transmute his thoughts into ideas, and accomplish the seemingly impossible.

mind--The starting point of every act and thought and feeling; the common meeting ground of God and man. God is mind, and we cannot describe God with human language, so we cannot describe mind. We can only say: I am mind; I know. God is mind; He knows.

The mind is the seat of perception of the things we see, hear, and feel. It is through the mind that we see the beauties of the earth and sky, of music, of art, in fact, of everything. That silent shuttle of thought working in and out through cell and nerve weaves into one harmonious whole the myriad moods of mind, and we call it life.

mind, affirmative state of--A binding, holding process. If man affirms his unity with the life, substance, and intelligence of God, he lays hold of these spiritual qualities.

mind, carnal--Misuse of mind powers, arising from ignorance of the relationship between God and man. A state of consciousness formed about a false ego or false concept of man. All the "works of the flesh" (Gal. 5:19) are the product of carnal mind.

mind, change of--A change of mind is the very first requisite of the new life in Christ. We go into this new and higher state of consciousness as we would go into another country. The kingdom of heaven is right here in our midst and will become tangible reality to us when we have developed the faculties necessary to comprehend it.

mind, fixed state of--A combination of thoughts in consciousness that is hard to change; ideas that have crystallized.

mind, mortal--Error consciousness in unregenerate man, or man composed of ungodlike thoughts. It is the opposite of the Christ Mind, which is the perfect Mind of God in man. Mortal mind gathers its information through the senses. It judges by appearances, which are often false judgments. Man must renounce this false state of mind if he is to be one with God. Mortal mind breeds sin, poverty, sickness, and death.

mind of the flesh--(Rom. 8:7) Mixed thoughts, selfishness, fear, and the like. These thoughts are what we find in persons of Gentile consciousness, and in the regeneration they must be eliminated.

mind, subconscious--The sum of all man's past thinking; also his memory. The subconscious mind sometimes acts as though separate from the conscious mind: for instance, in dreams. The subconscious mind has no power to do original thinking. It can act only upon what is given to it through the conscious or the superconscious mind.

mind, three phases of--Conscious mind, subconscious mind, and superconscious mind, called the Lord. The superconscious mind transcends both the conscious and subconscious phases of mind. The harmonious working together of these three seemingly separate minds is necessary to the bringing forth of the latent possibilities of man.

miracle--"An event or effect in the physical world beyond or out of the ordinary course of things, deviating from the known laws of nature, or transcending our knowledge of these laws" (Webster). In reality miracles are events that take place as a result of the operation of a higher, unknown law. All true action is governed by law. Nothing just happens. All happenings are the result of cause and can be explained under the law of cause and effect.

Mighty things have been wrought in the past by those who had mere blind faith to guide them. To faith we now add understanding of the law, and our achievements will be a fulfillment of the promise of Jesus, "He that believeth on me, the works that I do shall he do also; and greater works than these shall he do" (John 14:12).

mist--Lack of clear understanding between the earth consciousness and the spiritual Mind.

money--A medium of exchange and a measurement of value. The materialization of spiritual substance. The symbol of the idea of prosperity.

Money is a symbol that represents values in goods, land, or service. Substance in the form of money is given to us for constructive uses. The money idea is good and draws to us good when we are functioning in divine order.

Love of money is the root of much evil. Man should love the source of all money, God.

money changers--Dishonest thoughts of materialism and greed. The consciousness must be cleansed of these if the body temple is to be kept pure and holy.

moon--Represents personal intelligence; the intellect.

Its light is supplied by the sun, symbol of spiritual light.

mortal beliefs--Beliefs in sickness, sin, poverty, trouble, accident, and death, which are prevalent in the race mind.

mortal consciousness--Consciousness of self as separate from God. This is a false consciousness. Consciousness must harmonize with God-Mind to be free from thoughts of poverty, sin, sickness, and death.

mortal ego--Identification of the I AM with the whole array of false race and individual mental patterns.

mortal plane--That realm of ideas conceived in mortal, or material consciousness.

mortal words--Words spoken by the intellectual man. They are empty because they lack the life and substance necessary to impart spiritual life and nourishment to the mind.

motherhood, divine--The brooding, nourishing element of Divine Mind, or God, in which spiritual ideals are brought to fruition.

mountain--A mountain represents an exalted state of mind where the divine plan may be perceived and unfolded; a state of spiritual realization.

The "high mountain" to which personality carries us in our spiritual uplift is the consciousness of power over mortal thought in all its earthly avenues of expression. Going up into the mountain to pray means elevating our thoughts and our aspirations to the spiritual viewpoint.

mule--Represents human will. When it is ridden and is obedient, it infers subjection of that faculty to the established order.

multitude--The "great multitude" of John 6:5 is composed of our own hungry thoughts. They want an influx of the Truth of Spirit into consciousness. "Man doth not live by bread only, but by everything that proceedeth out of the mouth of Jehovah doth man live" (Deut. 8:3).

mustard seed--The mustard seed comparison shows the capacity of the apparently small thought of Truth to develop in consciousness until it becomes the abiding place of a higher range of thoughts (birds of the air).

myrrh--An aromatic gum resin; a slightly pungent perfume, used for incense. Metaphysically myrrh represents the eternity of Spirit, an emblem of the Resurrection, an ointment of love.

mystic--One who has intimate, firsthand acquaintance with God; a man of prayer. Jesus was the greatest mystic of all ages.

mysticism--The practice of the presence of God; the life of prayer that results in intuitive knowledge and experience of God.

The Bible contains more high mysticism than all other books. Spiritual things are spiritually discerned. It is necessary to call on one's own spiritual light to enter into the deep mysticism of the Bible.

name--An arbitrary appellation received in the language of the intellect describing a mental image or thought picture.

In the English language we have a very careless way of expressing the recondite meaning of words, but in the Hebrew the name of every person or thing represents its character. Every name in the Scriptures has an inner meaning. For instance, Bethlehem means "house of bread," and indicates the nerve center at the pit of the stomach through which the universal substance joins with the refined or spiritualized chemical products of the body substance.

The Scriptures give much importance to the naming and numbering of the prophets and peoples. The Lord always gave the wise men and leaders new names when they achieved some signal victory. The record abounds with such examples. When the great Jehovah sent Moses to bring the Children of Israel out of Egypt He gave the name by which He was to be known: "I AM THAT I AM."

name, God's--To describe God is to give Him limitation, hence He could not be given a fairer designation than "I AM THAT I AM." This is without confines or bounds and it allows unlimited expansion in every direction.

Metaphysicians have found that this name held in mind persistently gives the mind freedom from narrow beliefs. It lets the imagination soar away from its dimensional concepts of God, and there flows into the mind in consequence a whole flood of expanded ideas.

name of Jesus--Spiritual understanding proves that the name of a great character carries his name potency and that wherever his name is repeated silently or audibly his attributes become manifest. Jesus knew this, and He commanded His disciples to go forth in His name. The marvelous healing works that they did in His name prove the great spiritual power resident in His name.

napkin--Represents that in which something is hid. Too often we keep concealed a bit of Truth or a talent that should be taken out and put to some good use. (see Luke 19:20)

narrow door--The open mind that measures all things by the gauge of Truth. This way is "straitened" because it requires that only Truth be recognized, and it rules out untruth or evil.

nations--Aggregations of thoughts in the mind that are to be instructed through the faculties.

nature--The intellect's name for God. Men fall short when they seek to find God by studying nature. Instead of molding and animating the cells of their bodies, they project thought outward in speculating about the universe and its law.

Nature is the servant of mind, and when lawful thoughts are enthroned in consciousness nature restores the natural harmony existing between Spirit, soul, and body. When man asserts his divine supremacy he dominates nature.

nature, animal--The undisciplined nature in man or that phase of his being which has been allowed to express according to the desires of sense.

nature, restorative power of--This is the name given by doctors to the Spirit of health, which is always right at hand awaiting an opportunity to enter in to make whole and to harmonize all discords in the body.

neck--The seat of the power faculty in man.

necromancy--An activity of man's mind used adversely in which he is in league with hidden forces such as mesmerism and black magic and uses them in selfish ways.

negation--The unreal; that which has no basis in reality.

negative--The state of consciousness that repels good and attracts its own likeness, lack. Poverty is the negative side of plenty; sickness is the negative side of health; death is the negative side of life. These states result from the mind's being allowed to image anything contrary or adverse to the one almighty resource, God.

negative, dealing with--Denial of error thoughts and beliefs.

nerve fluid--A spiritual fluid that God is propelling throughout man's whole being continually, as the electromagnetic center of every physically expressed atom. This wonderful stream of nerve fluid finds its way over all the nerves in man's body temple, giving him the invigorating, steadying power of the Holy Spirit.

nerves--"Cordlike or filamentous bands of nervous tissue that connect parts of the nervous system with the other organs of the body, and conduct nervous impulses to or away from these organs" (Webster). The nerves have been described as wires over which messages are sent to and from the brain. Every emotion and every feeling that is transmitted over the nerves to the brain is registered and translated into thought, which may be expressed through the spoken word.

net--Man's mind is the net that catches thoughts, which are the basis of external conditions. This net works hard and long in the darkness of human understanding and gains but little, but once the Christ Mind is perceived and obeyed the net is cast on "the right side," and success follows.

new birth--The realization by man of his spiritual identity, with the fullness of power and glory that follows.

A birth is a coming into a state of being. Man first is born, or comes into a state of physical being; he thinks of himself as flesh, material. The "new birth" is the coming into a higher state of being that is alive to the fact that man is like God, one with God.

newness of life--Understanding of the spiritual facts of being.

new race--The race of men expressing the perfection of God as typified in Jesus. All men are potential members of this new race; they can become a part of it by following and demonstrating the Christ principle.

New Thought--A mental system that holds man as being one with God (good) through the power of constructive thinking.

night--Represents human understanding in which man's thought net works long and hard with little gain.

nonresistance--A passive state of mind. The law of nonresistance as taught by Jesus is demonstrated only by erasing from the individual consciousness every thought of personal rights.

nostrils--Represent openness to the inspirations of Divine Mind.

numbered--To be numbered is to be especially designated as having place, relation, importance, and necessity. If you are numbered you are one of the factors that enter into the great problem of life. To number and to name mean one and the same thing. If you are numbered you are therefore recorded in the annals of heaven and the omnipresent Father knows you by a name peculiar to Spirit.

O

obedience, spiritual--Obedience comes through understanding man's relation to God. When we show forth wisdom and purity and the perfect Principle that is God, we are obedient to Him.

object of man's existence--The mortal concept of the object of man's existence is personal pleasure and profit. The spiritual concept is to express God.

obsession--All conscious thought may become subconscious. An error may be held in mind until it is firmly fixed or crystallized and so strong that it takes control of a man. Such controlling mental states are false states of consciousness. Anger, jealousy, greed, appetite, passion are traits that, when allowed to become dominant, are obsessions, and are the "demons" that are to be cast out.

occultism--The belief that secret and mysterious powers can control the visible world. This procedure is not the way of the Christ Mind. "For there is nothing hid, save that it should be manifested; neither was anything made secret, but that it should come to light" (Mark 4:22).

offerings, freewill--"Freely ye received, freely give" (Matt. 10:8) is a law of life, and all must conform to it in order to realize their highest good and to receive abundantly. Giving measures the receiving.

oil, anointing--The thought of love, which is poured over anything, making it holy or a perfect whole. "Love . . . is the fulfillment of the law" (Rom. 13:10).

ointment--Symbolizes affirmation of peace, poise, and gladness.

ointment in alabaster cruse--The conserved nerve fluid that is stored up in the secret recesses of the body.

ointment, precious--Fragrance of love with which understanding (feet) is often bathed.

old age--A false belief deeply imbedded in the race mind. It accepts biological law as the ultimate for man instead of the law of God--which is eternal life in the body.

Omega--(see Alpha and Omega)

omnipotence--Infinite power. God is infinite power. All the power there is. All-powerful.

omnipresence--God is Mind. The one Mind contains all, and all ideas exist in the one Mind. God is everywhere present. There is no place where God is not. He is in all, through all, and around all. Omnipresence is a spiritual realm that can be penetrated only through the most highly accelerated mind action, as in prayer.

omniscience--God as omniscience is all-knowing, all-knowledge.

omniscient--All-knowing; infinite knowledge and wisdom. Divine Mind is omniscient. It knows all.

one life and one intelligence--There is one Spirit; one principle of life, love, intelligence, and goodness in, through, and over all, even God, the good omnipotent.

one Mind--There is but one Mind. Every individual and the various phases of character that make that individual are but states of consciousness in the one Mind.

one presence and one power--God, Spirit, is the only presence in the universe, and is the only power. He is in, through, and around all creation as its life and sustaining power.

one Spirit-Mind--God is the one Spirit-Mind in which all ideas of life, love, substance, intelligence, and power originate.

opposition in consciousness--The effort of old states of mind to continue exercising dominion in the face of new ideas becoming active in mind.

optimism--The inclination to expect good; the practice of seeing God (All-Good) everywhere. A sturdy belief in the goodness of reality.

order--The divine idea of order is the idea of adjustment, and as this is established in man's thought, his mind and affairs will be at one with the universal harmony.

ordinances of Jehovah--"The ordinances of Jehovah are true, and righteous altogether" (Psalms 19:9). Ordinances are established rules, and here we have the divine law under a slightly different aspect. When a man keeps the law of his being, he is guided into greater sureness and definiteness of understanding.

organic regeneration--To become conscious of divine substance, affirm your unity with it until you feel it as an exquisite vibration in every part of your body. This is the baptism of the Holy Spirit so often referred to by the apostles, and when you feel it you may know that you are tasting the "hidden manna" (Rev. 2:17), that you have begun organic regeneration that will be completed in immortality in the body, "the body of Christ" (I Cor. 12:27).

organs of the body--All outward conditions are the result of ideas that have first appeared in mind. The organs of the body are bundles of ideas that have organized themselves about a working center. They have their positive pole in mind, and it is there that we should look for the means to regulate them.

"our daily bread"–(Matt. 6:11). Our daily bread is the sustenance for spirit, soul, and body. Some of this "daily bread" is appropriated in the form of food. But man does "not live by bread alone, but by every word that proceedeth out of the mouth of God" (Matt. 4:4). There is substance in words of Truth, and this substance is appropriated by prayer and meditation on Truth.

outer understanding – Man's intellectual consciousness that gathers knowledge and substance for personal advancement and gain. This is not true spiritual understanding, but is a hireling, a stranger, so far as concerns the getting of good by waiting on the inner teacher, the Spirit of truth.

overcome the world--To correct thoughts that fall short of the divine ideal.

overcomer--One who recognizes the Truth of his being and is renewing his mind and body and affairs by changing his thoughts from the old mortal beliefs to the new as he sees them in Divine Mind. He demonstrates the divine law, not only in surface life but in innermost consciousness. Spiritual power, mastery, and dominion are attained by the overcomer. "He that overcometh, I will give to him to sit down with me in my throne" (Rev. 3:21).

overcoming--"Gaining superiority; winning" (Webster). Through thought mastery, sense man is overcome. The victorious thought of love defeats the thoughts of hate and fear. "Be of good cheer; I have overcome the world" (John 16:33).

overcoming, spiritual--Dealing with the problems of life in spiritual understanding and demonstrating over error through the keeping of spiritual laws.

oversoul--The universal Principle, the absolute One, God, Being. The absolute reality. The oversoul is the divine thought man. Jesus is the expressed oversoul of this planet.

pagan--One in any age who believes in the power of material things.

paganism--The religion of pagans, pertaining to idolatrous worship. The worship of money as God is a form of paganism.

pain--An indication that the vital forces of the body are at work to bring about health.

palm trees--Metaphysically, realizations in the physical of unlimited resource of strength.

pantheism--"The doctrine that the universe, taken or conceived of as a whole, is God; the doctrine that there is no God but the combined forces and laws which are manifested in the existing universe" (Webster).

In its last analysis what we call nature, pantheists would name God. Metaphysically, pantheism refers to God as omnipresence, the one living, all-powerful, intelligent Mind, pervading and sustaining all things and directing them in love, wisdom, and order.

Pantheism and the teachings of Unity differ widely: pantheism diminishes the importance of the individual, while Unity teaches that man always retains his individual identity in God-Mind.

parable--A brief symbolical story told to illustrate Truth. "He taught them many things in parables" (Mark 4:2).

paradise--A state of high spiritual consciousness.

parsimony--In mortal consciousness, the idea of closeness in expenditures; undue thrift. Indicates lack of understanding of accessibility of supply through omnipresent substance.

Passover--Outwardly a Jewish feast; symbolically, a mental attitude in which we are bridging over from an old state of consciousness and entering a new. In taking on the Christ consciousness men pass over from the mortal to the spiritual consciousness.

pasture--Metaphysically, a pasture represents substance in a form in which it can be utilized by the individual. "He maketh me to lie down in green pastures" (Psalms 23).

patience--An attitude of mind characterized by poise, inner calmness, and quiet endurance, especially in the face of trying conditions. Patience has its foundation in faith, and it is perfected only in those who have unwavering faith in God. "The proving of your faith worketh patience" (James 1:3).

pattern--The divine incarnation of Jesus is the divine pattern for all men who are seeking the Christ way of life.

peace--Harmony and tranquillity derived from awareness of the Christ consciousness. "Peace I leave with you; my peace I give unto you" (John 14:27). Steadfast affirmations of peace will harmonize the whole body structure and open the way to attainment of health conditions in mind and body.

Until world peace is based on the divine law of love and this law incorporated into the pact of peace as well as into the minds of those who sign the pact, there will be no permanent peace.

peacemaker--One who has the ability to say "peace" to the turbulent waves of thought and have them obey. A peacemaker is one who reduces to peace and harmony all the thoughts of strife, anger, and retaliation in his own mind. The ability to say "peace" to thoughts, and have them obey, entitles man to sonship of the Most High. "Blessed are the peacemakers: for they shall be called sons of God" (Matt. 5:9).

pearl of great price--The Truth that no man can afford to barter away, although all the kingdoms of the earth and the glory of them be weighed in the balance against this one treasure.

Pentateuch--The first five books of the Bible, called the books of law, or the books of Moses.

Pentecost--The "day of Pentecost" was with the Israelites the great "feast of harvest," or "day of the first-fruits" (Exod. 23:16; Num. 28:26).

"That day of Pentecost" signifies a gathering of spiritual powers for the purpose of harvesting the first fruits of Spirit; otherwise, a dedicating of these new forces of Spirit to unselfish service in the vineyard of the Lord.

The first Pentecost after Jesus' ascension was the time of the first recorded coming of the Holy Spirit baptism upon His apostles and immediate followers. The descent into consciousness of the Jesus Christ life may have taken place on the day of Pentecost in the company of the apostles as described. They were in the upper room of the mind, which is a spiritual state of mind, and had been praying for ten days with one accord for the fulfillment of the promise of the Holy Spirit as given by Jesus. This attitude of many minds forms a mental magnet and brings about results in flashes of light and spiritual illumination. Religious revivals have demonstrated this to greater or lesser degree.

people, holy--The members of the body of Christ are called a holy people because they are different from the world about them in that they refer all things to the in-dwelling Presence. In their method of praying and of attaining health and plently, in their manner of conversation, and in all vital points their lives are set to a higher standard than that of the people of the world.

perception, spiritual--Apprehension of Truth through intuition; the ability to perceive spiritually; the faculty of seeing spiritual reality in spite of appearances that may suggest the contrary.

perfection--A state of consciousness completely free from any shadow of negation.

perfection, attainment of--Jesus said, "Ye therefore shall be perfect, as your heavenly Father is perfect" (Matt. 5:48). We attain divine perfection through spiritual aspiration, by never ceasing to erase false thoughts and by affirming Truth as the law of our being.

perseverance--Metaphysically, to persist in pursuit of Truth. Through perseverance we make connection with the higher realms of consciousness.

persistency--The inner spiritual quality of an abiding conviction that urges one on to accomplishment. Persistency in prayer awakens the spiritual consciousness. When this awakening has been accomplished, one is in a constant state of thanksgiving and praising, and the joy of a conscious union with creative Mind is realized.

personal aims--Personal aims are concerned exclusively with one's own welfare. They are always narrow and selfish. So long as these exist and take the place of the rightful one, there is no room for the higher self, the Christ of God. "Let him deny himself . . . and follow me" (Matt. 16:24).

personal man--Adam.

personality--The sum total of characteristics that man has personalized as distinct of himself, independent of others or of divine principle. The word personality as used by metaphysicians is contrasted with the word individuality. Individuality is the real; personality is the unreal, the mortal, the part of us that is governed by the selfish motives of the natural man. (see individuality)

Personality is a veil or mask worn by man that conceals the real, the spiritual I AM. Jesus shattered this mask and revealed Christ, the true man of God.

Individuality is Jehovah, ideal man; image and likeness of Elohim, universal creative Mind.

Personality is Adam, man formed by Jehovah and commanded to develop his individuality in Eden, an environment of all potential possibilities.

Personality is what man seems to be when he thinks in his three-dimensional consciousness; individuality is what he really is when he thinks in his unlimited spiritual consciousness.

As the true Christ self emerges, personality decreases. The real self, the individuality, begins to express. "He must increase, but I must decrease" (John 3:30).

pessimism--An unhappy mental state resulting from beholding the shadow of reality, termed evil.

pests--All vermin and pests of every kind come from wrong thoughts and expressions of life in man and by man. God is life, and all life springs from the one perfect life-idea. Man brings the life of God into manifestation through his thoughts, words, and acts. Through ignorance and wrong thinking man has worked out of divine order with the great principle of life and has brought about the different manifestations of life that prey on and torment him today.

Pharisee--One who observes the letter of the religious law but not its spirit; lacking in understanding of the Truth.

The Pharisees were hypocrites. Jesus denounced them with greater severity than any other class of sinners. They pretended to practice the divine law, but failed to do so. They represent the son who said, "I go, sir; and went not" (Matt. 21:30).

Physician, the Great--The omnipresent, healing, in-dwelling Spirit of Jesus Christ.

pillar of cloud--Light of spiritual understanding to guide us.

pillar of fire--Witness of the Spirit on the altar of love as a glow of light that opens the understanding.

"place" that Jesus prepared--(John 14:2) Jesus said He had prepared a "place" for us. This "place" is a spiritual current in the cosmic ether in which we live, and we can feel it when we direct our attention to Jesus Christ in prayer and meditation. "The kingdom of God is nigh" (Luke 21:31).

planes--The different realms of ideas in which men function. There are many planes of life, one above or below another, yet not conflicting. All creation is based on life activity, or as it is called in physical science, rates of vibration. A certain activity in the life current forms worlds on a plane, which we may call the physical; a little increase in the vibratory rate makes another system, which we may designate as the psychical; a still higher rate makes a universe where spiritual ideas prevail.

These are all interlaced and interblended in the presence around and within us, hence the "kingdom of God is within you" (Luke 17:21), or "among you," as one translator gives it.

plumb line--The divine law that measures uprighteousness or integrity.

poise--A state of consciousness that beholds the world from the harmony of the Christ Mind; a freedom from personal thinking.

pool--Metaphysically, the realization in consciousness that our life is being constantly purified, healed, and made new by the activity of mind.

poor in spirit--Those who have denied personal consciousness. They are poor in the spirit of selfishness, but rich in the Spirit of Christ. "Blessed are the poor in spirit: for theirs is the kingdom of heaven" (Matt. 5:3).

poverty, cure for--When love has begun its silent pulsations at one's center of consciousness, one cannot remain in want or poverty. From the invisible currents of the inner ether, love will draw to any man all that belongs to him, and all belongs to him that is required to make him happy and contented.

power--Man's innate control over his thoughts and feelings. A quickening from on high must precede his realization of dominion. "Ye shall receive power, when the Holy Spirit is come upon you" (Acts 1:8). God is All-Power, thus all things are possible with Him.

The mind and the body of man have power to transform energy from one plane of consciousness to another. This is the power and dominion implanted in man from the beginning. The climax of man's power and dominion is set forth in the resurrection and ascension of the type man, Jesus.

In mind, power is increased through exalted ideas. These show us the relation between the world without and the mind within, and we find that they are parallel. Whatever you see in the external, you may be assured has its parallel in mind.

The same law is operating in the spiritual realm and the material realm under different masks of manifestation. The one thing to understand is that whatever we see without is controlled by something within. This law, once revealed to the mind, clears up the whole creation, and shows how God works.

Man is the power of God in action. To man is given the highest power in the universe, the conscious power of thought. There is a universal, creative force that urges man forward to the recognition of the creative power of his individual thought. This thought is elemental, and all its attributes come under the dominion of man. When he co-operates with Principle, man sits on the throne of his authority and the elemental force is subject to him.

Spiritual power is omnipresent. It is released in our body by spiritualizing our consciousness. This divine energy will surge through us as we erase negative thoughts from consciousness and become one with God-Mind.

powers, man's twelve--Faith, wisdom, love, life, power, strength, imagination, understanding, will, law of order, zeal, renunciation.

practical Christianity--The teachings of Jesus practically applied in one's daily life.

praise--The quality of mind that eulogizes the good; one of the avenues through which spirituality expresses.

The purpose of praise is to awaken in ourselves a higher realization of the omnipresence and power of God. Prayer and praise change man, not God. The mental attitude that praise sets up stimulates, quickens, whirls into action, and finally establishes in character the ideals of which they are the vehicle.

Through an inherent law of mind action we increase whatever we praise. The whole creation responds to praise, and is glad. Animals and children quickly respond to praise. One can praise a weak body into strength, a fearful heart into peace and trust, shattered nerves into poise and power, a failing business into prosperity and success, want and insufficiency into supply and support.

We make practical application of the law of praise by giving thanks always for all things, recognizing that "to them that love God all things work together for good" (Rom. 8:28).

prayer--Communion between God and man. This communion takes place in the innermost part of man's being. It is the only way to cleanse and perfect the consciousness and thus permanently heal the body.

Prayer is the most highly accelerated mind action known. It steps up mental action until man's consciousness synchronizes with the Christ Mind. It is the language of spirituality; when developed it makes man master in the realm of creative ideas.

Prayer is more than supplication. It is an affirmation of Truth that eternally exists, but which has not yet come into consciousness. It comes into consciousness not by supplication but by affirmation.

Do not supplicate or beg God to give you what you need, but get still and think about the inexhaustible resources of infinite Mind, its presence in all its fullness, and its constant readiness to manifest itself for you when its laws are complied with. This is what Jesus meant when He said, "Seek ye first his kingdom, and his righteousness; and all these things shall be added unto you" (Matt. 6:33).

It is necessary to pray believing that we have received because God is all that we desire. The good always exists in Divine Mind as ideas, and we bring it into manifestation through the prayer of faith, affirmation, praise, and acknowledgment.

All through the Scriptures, the different attitudes of mind necessary in prayer are pointed out. We are told to be instant in prayer, to pray with the Spirit, to pray in understanding. We have thought that prayer was something we could go to, in any way, at any time. But we have learned that to get results, we must pray with persistence and understanding, and with faith. This practice establishes a consciousness where doubt cannot enter. Jesus was in this consciousness. Is it possible for the ordinary man? Yes. But he must watch and pray. He must not only pray; he must watch also.

These are the seven necessary conditions for true prayer:

1. God should be recognized as Father.

2. Oneness with God should be acknowledged.

3. Prayer must be made within, in "the secret place" (Psalms 91).

4. The door must be closed on all thoughts and interests of the outer world.

5. The one who prays must believe that he has received.

6. The kingdom of God must be desired above all things, and sought first.

7. The mind must let go of every unforgiving thought.

prayer, chamber of--"Enter into thine inner chamber and . . . shut thy door" (Matt. 6:6). The inner chamber is the "secret place of the Most High" (Psalms 91:1). It is the very depths of a man's consciousness. To enter it is to turn the attention from the without to the within. To "shut thy door" is to still the senses and close the mind against every disturbing exterior thought.

prayer, intercessory--The 17th chapter of John is known as the intercessory prayer. In this chapter Jesus first prayed for Himself, then for His apostles, and then for all who would accept salvation through Him, which prayer is extended to all generations.

"And now, Father, glorify thou me with thine own self with the glory which I had with thee before the world was. I manifested thy name unto the men whom thou gavest me out of the world" (John 17:5, 6). "I pray for them: I pray not for the world, but for those whom thou hast given me" (John 17:9). "Neither for these only do I pray, but for them also that believe on me" (John 17:20).

prayer for health--This prayer is the one most quickly answered, because natural laws that create and sustain the body are really divine laws. When man silently asks for the intervention of Spirit in restoring health, he is calling into increased activity the natural forces of the body. Through prayer the mind is renewed and the body transformed.

predestination--"The preordination of men to everlasting happiness or misery" (Webster). Since man is created in the image and after the likeness of God, he is predestined to bring the perfect pattern into expression. "I am God Almighty; walk before me, and be thou perfect" (Gen. 17:1).

The belief that God makes men do certain things cannot be true in a single instance, because, if it were, man would not be a free agent. If God interfered with man's will in some things, it would follow that He could interfere in any and all things. Logic and observation clearly reveal the freedom of man in everything. He was given freedom of thought, and must work out his own salvation.

It is well to use daily an affirmation such as this in the name of Jesus Christ: I am the son of God, and the Spirit of the Most High dwells in me. I am the lord of my mind, and express only that which is constructive and upbuilding. I am predestined to be the perfect expression of my Father, and the fullness of all good is mine.

predictions--The law of mind action will bring to pass what man believes in and expects. If he has faith in what he has been told by mediums and fortunetellers, he brings it to pass himself by his faith.

preparation, the--(John 19:31). Refers to the observances preliminary to the celebration of the Jewish Sabbath, or to the festival the day before the Sabbath. Among the Jews there was a law to the effect that a lifeless body should not remain on the cross on the Sabbath, as this was a day set aside for rest and freedom from all troubled or contentious thoughts.

presence of God--The awareness of Spirit within one's own being. It manifests as increased life, peace, love, and a deep sense of spiritual joy. (see abiding Presence)

presents--The presents that the Wise Men brought are symbolical of the inner resources open to the Christ child. They may be from the stored-up good deeds and thoughts of previous incarnations that the wisdom within carefully guards and gives to a man as an inheritance.

pride, spiritual--A form of personal vanity over spiritual achievement; a proud personal spirit; a "holier than thou" attitude.

"Blessed are the poor in [personal] spirit: for theirs is the kingdom of heaven" (Matt. 5:3).

priests--Metaphysically, ideas of priestly authority and the religious guidance of the intellect. The "priests and Levites" represent our so-called natural religious tendencies. These officiate in the rites and ceremonies of the tent, or tabernacle, and when the more permanent structure (temple) is built, they bring up all the "holy vessels" from the tent or tabernacle.

primary law and secondary law--Primary law is the one law of God. Secondary law is the law of diet, of economics, of medicine, and many other secondary things. A true metaphysician always looks to the law of God.

prince of Peace--Jesus is the Prince of Peace. When asking the Father for that which belongs to the Son under the divine law, man should assume the power and dignity of the Prince of Peace. He should not crawl and cringe before an imaginary king on a throne but rather feel that he is the image of an invisible Being who created him to represent His mightiness as well as His loving-kindness. We should affirm with conviction those mighty words of Jesus: "All authority hath been given unto me in heaven and on earth" (Matt. 28:18).

Principle--Fundamental Truth. Divine Principle is fundamental Truth in a universal sense, or as pertaining to God, the Divine. It is the underlying plan by which Spirit (God) moves in expressing itself; the oversoul of this planet which works its way into expression through Jesus.

God immanent in the universe is the great underlying cause of all manifestation; the source from which form proceeds. Although Principle is formless, it is that by which all form is produced.

Principle is the I AM of every man. As the principle of music moves through tones, so does the principle of mind move through ideas. A word is a spoken thought, or idea. Therefore, God as creative Mind, moves through the expressed thought of Divine Mind, referred to in Scripture as the Word of God.

progress, spiritual--Growth in the conception and expression of spiritual ideas.

Promised Land--Metaphysically, a realization of divine substance. It is the foundation of the substratum of the new body in Christ. It is not a dream that man is to possess a body of immortality.

When there wells up in a man a great desire to be free from the bondage of ignorance and the animal propensities, his journey to the Promised Land begins.

promises, God's--Free will gives to man the privilege to accept or reject the promises of God. If he rejects them there is no way for them to be fulfilled in him.

No one who holds back part of the price can find the way into the kingdom. The works of the flesh must be entirely overcome. Every flesh desire must be put away so that the pure and holy desires of the Christ man may be given expression. All the life substance must be conserved, spiritualized, and used in making the body whole and perfect like the body of the Lord Jesus Christ.

prophet--One who receives the inspiration of Spirit, understands spiritual law, and imparts it to others. The prophets of old seemed to stand between God and the people; it was through them that the people received divine guidance.

Metaphysically, the prophet is that in us which discerns the working of the law. Transgressed law brings its own punishment, and it is the prophet of the Lord that sees its outworking in our life. It is the prophet in us that often warns and keeps us from transgressing the law, because we discern what the result will be.

prophets, false--Deceptive thoughts that have been built up by error; selfish desires. False prophets are the representations of deceptive religious thoughts. They seem innocent and harmless like sheep, but are in reality selfish and dangerous. "Beware of false prophets, who come to you in sheep's clothing, but inwardly are ravening wolves" (Matt: 7:15).

proselyte--Metaphysically, one who has turned away from the old, set, religious forms and ceremonies, and realizes Truth for himself.

proselyting--The act of one endeavoring to convert another to his way of thinking. This is not in accord with divine law. The Spirit of truth within is man's one and only guide.

No one has the right to dictate what another shall do. However, we do teach principles boldly without regard to whether mortal man accepts or rejects. It is ours to give forth the Truth; the responsibility of acceptance rests with those who hear. If the higher self hears the Word and the lower self resists and rebels, that is a matter for the individual to work out according to his own choice and faith.

prosperity--The consciousness of God as the abundant, everywhere present resource, unfailing, ready for all who open themselves to it through faith. "They that seek Jehovah shall not want any good thing" (Psalms 34:10).

Prosperity is based on the conscious possession of the idea of God's abundance back of all things. Things come and go, but the idea of abundance endures. Things appear at its command. Jesus had no visible possessions, but He could supply thousands of persons with food through praising and giving thanks to the invisible Spirit of plenty.

The difference between spiritual prosperity and material prosperity is that spiritual prosperity is founded on understanding of the inexhaustible, omnipresent substance of Spirit as the source of supply; the material belief is that the possession of things constitutes prosperity.

"Lay not up for yourselves treasures upon the earth . . . but lay up for yourselves treasures in heaven" (Matt. 6:19-20).

In demonstrating prosperity, you should praise and give thanks for every little evidence of financial improvement. Be confident of the immediate co-operation of God's Spirit with you in bringing to pass that for which you have given thanks. The divine resource never fails. God is the omnipresent, unfailing resource for all who trust Him and who make all their thoughts chord with Divine Mind. God is your prosperity. Stamp this thought daily on your mind and you will reap financial success.

Giving in the right mental attitude creates prosperity. Giving with the fear of lack leads to poverty. Giving with the thought of a large resource opens the way for a large income. "Give, and it shall be given unto you; good measure, pressed down, shaken together, running over" (Luke 6:38).

psalm--The Truth of God spoken in poetry or music; a hymn of praise or joy; spiritual aspiration of the soul. "Is any cheerful? let him sing praise" (James 5:13).

psyche--A word prominent in Greek mythology, meaning "the soul." Psyche may be thought of as man in his many earthly experiences, in his failures and his successes.

psychic--Pertaining to mental powers not common to ordinary man; mental powers outreaching the scope of the physical man, but not yet quickened to the standard of Spirit.

Man has a body in the ether that is the counterpart of the physical. It is through this psychic body that he has sensations in the physical. It is possible to think of the psychic body and cultivate its sensations until it appears as real as the physical. Many persons have done this until they have formed a psychic world consciousness and are often unable to separate it from the physical. To them the realm of thought forms is the finality of creation instead of the mental pictures of that which is about to appear.

The first step of a Truth student in handling the psychic forces of consciousness is the same as that in handling any other, and that is to realize that God is the one and only power; to declare with Byron: "There is no god but God!–to prayer--lo! God is great!

Next make conscious contact with this all-powerful God-Mind and realize that every phase of the mind, every thought is brought into the captivity of the Christ, and that through your I AM power and dominion you are master over every situation.

psychoanalysis--Analysis of the subconscious mind. The followers of Jesus go one step farther in mind therapy than the psychoanalyst; they incorporate Spirit with soul and make Spirit the primal source and sustainer of both soul and body. "It is the spirit that giveth life" (John 6:63).

psychology and religion--Thought control is imperative, and there is urgent need of teachers on both the mental and spiritual plane of consciousness if the race is to go forward in development. To this end there needs to be more co-operation between these two schools, because they complement each other. Religion becomes practical and effective in everyday life when it incorporates psychology as part of its litany. Without religion psychology is weak in its fundamentals, and without psychology religion fails to give proper attention to the outlet of its ideals. The fact is that religion, comprehended in its fullness, includes psychology. Jesus was a profound psychologist.

The carping critic cries, "Your religion is psychology instead of Christianity." Our answer is that the new Christianity includes an understanding of psychology and does not stop with an analysis of the mind but goes on to the highest phase of mind's possibilities, unity with Spirit.

punishment--Man does not receive punishment from an outside force. Man punishes himself by holding false thoughts. He escapes from punishment as soon as he aligns his thought with that of God.

pure in heart--The "pure in heart" are those who are completely free from all anxiety, resentment, selfishness, lust, and every other form of antichrist thought and feeling. "Blessed are the pure in heart: for they shall see God" (Matt. 5:8).

purity of the Christ Mind--The deep purity and mighty strength of the Christ Mind are made manifest in men as they develop spiritually. Instead of consciously and unconsciously tempting one another in sense ways, these qualities in each will incite in the other holy aspirations to fulfill the law of righteousness. "And every one that hath this hope set on him purifieth himself, even as he [the Father] is pure" (I John 3:3).

purification of blood--If your lung capacity is not equal to the purification of your blood, increase it by declaring the law of active life. Anemic blood may be made vigorous and virile by daily centering the attention in the lungs and affirming them to be spiritual, and under the perpetual inflow of new life and the outflow of old life the lungs will do your will.quality, spiritual--That which is characteristic of one's spiritual nature. High spiritual qualities are established in man's body consciousness through prayer and profound spiritual aspiration.

Q

quickening, spiritual--An inflow of divine vitality into the body, which follows the affirmation of Truth. To quicken is to make alive. The quickening of the Spirit in the mortal body makes it eternal and incorruptible, not subject to death and corruption.

Spiritual quickening is a waking up of the whole man to the full consciousness of what he is in the sight of God. The sense man is only half-awake, going about in a dream and thinking it is real life. The word of God is quick, and when it enters into a man he stands upright on his feet, his divine understanding, and he knows and sees himself as he is. He is wide awake, alert, quick, and powerful.

"But if the Spirit of him that raised up Jesus from the dead dwelleth in you, he that raised up Christ Jesus from the dead shall give life also to your mortal bodies through his Spirit that dwelleth in you" (Rom. 8:11).

quietness--When the mind is stilled, when all the clamor of the external world is silenced, one experiences the quietness of God. "In returning and rest shall ye be saved; in quietness and in confidence shall be your strength" (Isa. 30:15).

race consciousness--The human race has formed laws of physical birth and death, laws of sickness and physical inability, laws making food the source of bodily existence, laws of mind that recognize no other source of existence except the physical. The sum total of these laws forms a race consciousness separate from and independent of creative Mind. When creative Mind sought to help men spiritually, the mind of the flesh opposed it and made every effort to solve its problems in its own way. The great need of the human family is mind control. Jesus showed us that mastery is attained through realization of the power of Spirit.

race errors--Erroneous race thoughts that bind mankind to sin, disease, poverty, war, calamity, and death.

race mind--Totality of beliefs, thoughts, memories, feelings, and experiences of the race. Man has built into the race mind a consciousness of corruptible flesh instead of the inherent incorruptible substance of God-Mind.

radiation--An extension of consciousness. Jesus' soul radiation or aura was so powerful that it perpetually stimulates to greater achievement, and thrills with new life all who enter its sphere of influence. (see aura)

rain--Metaphysically, an outpouring of Spirit that constantly refreshes and enriches man's developing thoughts. The descent of potential ideas into substance. The rain that "watereth the earth" represents the love of God, which comes into mind when summoned and needed.

raising of Lazarus--The restoration in consciousness of the idea of youth, which is asleep in the subconsciousness.

rats--Represent destructive, undermining, gnawing thoughts.

raven, going forth of a--The raven's going forth represents the reaching out of the thought from within to connect with the outer world. There is an individual consciousness, which is the ark, and a universal consciousness, which is the heavens and the earth.

rays--All mental action radiates rays of light. Clairvoyants and psychics have long claimed that they can see these rays surrounding not only human beings, but animals, plants, and even stones. Their claims have been considered chimerical until in the last few years, when science found that it can measure the force of these invisible rays. The character of the thoughts colors the emanations of these rays. If the thoughts pertain to the things of sense, the rays are dark and weak; if the affectional and intellectual nature is active, they become highly colored and forceful. When the mind is exalted in prayer, a dazzling light radiates from all parts of the body, but especially from the head.

rays, healing--Spiritual rays superior to the ultraviolet rays that come from the sun. They heal both mind and body.

reality--That which is abiding, eternal, and unchangeable, the same "yesterday and to-day, yea and for ever" (Heb. 13:8). The basic principles of mathematics and music are real, because they are not subject to change. A wrong application of their principles may produce discord, but the principles are not disturbed. God is the one harmonious Principle underlying all being and the reality out of which all that is eternal comes.

All causes are in mind. Error thoughts produce the mental and physical inharmonies called disease. These effects are not enduring and eternal. Error can be erased from the mind and be made to disappear from the body.

realization--The deep inner conviction and assurance of the fulfillment of an ideal. It means at-one-ment, completion, perfection, wholeness, repose, resting in God. It is the dawning of Truth in the consciousness. When realization takes place, one abides in the light of God-Mind. It is the inner conviction that prayer has been answered, although there is as yet no outer manifestation.

The supreme realization is unity with God-Mind, complete oneness with the Christ consciousness. This highest realization is taking place more widely today among men than at any time in all history. Jesus fully attained this supreme realization.

realm, spiritual--The higher realm of consciousness built in accordance with the Christ ideal. The realm of Spirit is wherever God is working to express Himself. When man as principle becomes the perfect image and likeness of God, no other realm will appear to have being.

rebellion--Open defiance and resistance to an authority to which one owes allegiance. One rebels because he believes he is not being rightly governed, his conditions are not satisfactory. Man has been taught that God brought on him sickness, poverty, inharmony, and that these conditions are the will of God. While he recognizes that God is supreme ruler and governor of all things, man rebells at such conditions being imposed on him. As soon as a man comes into the understanding that his own thoughts and words are the cause of the conditions in his life, he no longer rebels and blames God. He uses his creative thought power, he sets the Word into right activity, and good comes into his life.

receiving--(see giving)

receptivity, spiritual--The attitude of mind that awaits the higher way as a little child awaits the helping hand of a parent. It is not the arbitrary disciplinarian, but the loving, tender, understanding heart that in visible life lightens the intricate problems that perplex the mind. When one who is receptive and obedient gives himself unreservedly to Spirit and receives without antagonism its guidance, he is delighted with the possibilities that are disclosed to him in caring for his physical and spiritual needs. He then begins to realize what Jesus meant when He said, "If any man would come after me, let him deny himself, and take up his cross, and follow me" (Matt. 16:24).

recompense--The satisfaction and uplift that one feels after a realization of Truth.

re-creation--The process of redemption; a gradual transformation that takes place as man pays the price, gives up self, and allows Spirit to work in mind and body.

redemption--The process by which the life and substance of man's lesser self are brought to conform to the standards of his spiritual self. The body is redeemed from destruction by attaining spiritual consciousness on earth. "For this corruptible must put on incorruption" (I Cor. 15:53).

regeneration--A change in which abundant spiritual life, even eternal life, is incorporated into the body. The transformation that takes place through bringing all the forces of mind and body to the support of the Christ ideal. The unification of Spirit, soul, and body in spiritual oneness.

Regeneration begins its work in the conscious mind and completes it in the subconsciousness. The first step is cleansing or denial in which all error thoughts are renounced. This includes forgiveness for sins committed and a general clearing of the whole consciousness. After the way has been prepared, the second step takes place. This is the outpouring of the Holy Spirit.

reincarnation--When a soul leaves the body, it rests for a season. Then innate desire for material expression asserts itself, and the ego seeks the primal cell and builds another body. This is reincarnation. Reincarnation will continue until the ego awakens to the Christ Mind and through it builds an imperishable body.

The law of Being is broken by sin and death. Resurrection or regeneration in this body here and now--not reincarnation--is the aim of overcomers. Reincarnation is the result of man's use of the great forces of Mind, enabling an ego or soul that has been separated from the vehicle of expression (the body) again to attract to it the necessary substance to reconstruct the body-consciousness and to have another opportunity for the demonstration of the Truth of Being, but reincarnation is not a part of the divine plan and does not lift man out of mortal limitations. It is not an aid to spiritual growth, but merely a makeshift until full Truth is discerned.

relaxation--A letting go of tenseness in mind and body. Abatement of strain. Loosening the tight mental grip we have on ourselves in order that the healing Christ life may flow freely through our being. "Come unto me . . . and I will give you rest" (Matt. 11:28).

religion--A systematic exposition on the awareness of a deity who is the supreme ruler of heaven and earth; that which arouses reverence and love for a supreme being. There is a wide range of religious experience between the blindly groping faith that caused men to pass their children through the fire as sacrifice to their deities, and the divine consciousness of Jesus, who submitted His body to the purifying fire of the Spirit and came forth alive with a life that never dies.

In the study of things pertaining to religion we should keep in mind the three activities of consciousness: spiritual, psychical, and physical. The spiritual is the realm of absolute principles; the psychical is the realm of thought images; the physical is the realm of manifestation. The well-balanced, thoroughly developed man, of which Jesus is the type, comprehends and consciously adjusts his spirit, soul, and body as a whole, and thereby fulfills the law of his being. Those who are on the way to this attainment have various experiences, which are symbolically set forth in the Scriptures.

renunciation--A letting go of old thoughts in order that new thoughts may find place in consciousness. A healthy state of mind is attained when the thinker willingly lets go the old thoughts and takes on the new. This is illustrated by the inlet and outlet of a pool of water. The center of renunciation, sometimes called elimination, in the lower part of the abdomen, carries forward the work of elimination of error thoughts from the mind and waste from the body.

repentance--A turning from a belief in sin and error to a belief in God and righteousness; a reversal of mind and heart in the direction of the All-Good. When we repent, we break with mortal thought and ascend into a spiritual thought realm, the kingdom of God.

The Greek word metanoia is translated "repentance," which has been interpreted to mean an admission to God of sorrow for past sin and a resolve to be good in the future. The field of action for that which has been assumed to be goodness in the sight of God has nearly always been in conduct.

There is always hope for the repentant sinner. A repentant state of mind is an exceedingly good state for one who has been on the error side. If you find yourself suffering the result of transgressed law, begin at once a righteous repentance. As soon as you repent and recognize that the way of Spirit is the way of pleasantness, your sins are forgiven you, and you are made whole and well.

repetitions, vain--When we rehearse affirmations just because they are given to us to hold, with no thought of their inner reality, or if we are in a doubtful state of mind, they become "vain repetitions." It is true that a declaration of Truth may not at first repeating find lodgment in consciousness and that we may repeat it over and over before it becomes a living word, but the attitude of mind as we go through this process is the seed that bears fruit, the assurance of the harvest. Nothing outside of man can affect him when he is in contact with his inner spiritual source.

resistance--The greatest disintegrating element in the human consciousness is resistance. Beware of every form of fighting, and of all thoughts of a destructive character. Thoughts build or destroy, and they will work in your mind and body in an adverse way and tear down the good you desire to build up if you do not form them with care.

A mental state of resistance indicates an unyielding personal will. Evil has no power except that which man gives it by his thought. Resisting evil is a way of affirming its power. A positive, fearless attitude in facing the appearance of evil overcomes it, and this attitude comes from the understanding that evil has no power.

restitution--The resurrection of man to the divine image and likeness in mind and body and to the dominion that has been his from the beginning. The restitution work also includes the earth, which is to be redeemed from the curse that fell on it through sin. It is to blossom and bring forth and be a paradise, a fitting home for redeemed man.

restlessness--The unsatisfied longing of a man for God. Restlessness cannot be satisfied by change of climate or environment or by travel or by any other outward change. Only by a man's finding his center in God can restlessness and discontent be satisfied.

"For he satisfieth the longing soul,

And the hungry soul he filleth with good"

(Psalms 107:9).

restorative power of nature--The term given by doctors to the Spirit of health, which is always right at hand awaiting opportunity to enter in to make whole and to harmonize all discord in the body.

resurrection--The restoring of mind and body to their original, undying state. This is accomplished by the realization that God is Spirit and that God created man with power like that which He Himself possesses. When man realizes this, his mind and body automatically become immortal. "If the Spirit of him that raised up Jesus from the dead dwelleth in you, he that raised up Christ Jesus from the dead shall give life also to your mortal bodies through his Spirit that dwelleth in you" (Rom. 8:11). The word resurrection also suggests that there has been a falling short of the divine standard; therefore, the necessity of being restored and revived. Through resurrection man becomes an inhabitant here and now of "a new heaven and a new earth" (Rev. 21:1).

Jesus was raised from the dead. He overcame death in the body. "For since by man came death, by man came also the resurrection of the dead." Physical death is not necessary. "We all shall not sleep, but we shall all be changed" (I Cor. 15:21, 51).

The power of the resurrection is the Christ. "I am the resurrection, and the life" (John 11:25). This resurrection is not of the future, "but hath now been manifested by . . . our Saviour Christ Jesus, who abolished death, and brought life and immortality to light" (II Tim. 1:10).

Christ, absolute Principle, the God-idea man, is the true resurrecting power and life in each of us here and now. Jesus resurrected His body through the spiritual I AM dwelling in Him.

The resurrection takes place in us every time we rise to Jesus' realization of the perpetual indwelling life that is connecting us with the Father. A new flood of life comes to all who open their minds and their bodies to the living word of God.

revelation--An unveiling, a disclosure of Truth, making known that which is hidden. The revelation of Christ to all men is the ultimate revelation.

Divine revelation is much more common than is understood. The Spirit of truth is revealing the hidden wisdom to thousands on every hand. Poets and writers of Truth are being inspired of the Most High. Quiet citizens in every walk of life are the recipients of the divine word. Every man who has earnestly asked for divine guidance, or who has earnestly desired to do right in the sight of God and man, is being taught by the Holy Spirit.

reverence--The attitude of reverence is an important feature in developing the Christ consciousness. Without it the mind loses a certain necessary connection with Spirit and lacks that central poise of faith that gives a religious tenor to the process.

rich young man--(Mark 10:17-27). Personality; the state of consciousness in man that lays hold of the world of form, seeking satisfaction in personal possessions and in fulfilling the letter of the law.

righteousness--A state of harmony established in consciousness through the right use of God-given attributes. It leads directly to eternal life. Truth working in consciousness brings forth the perfect salvation of the whole man--Spirit, soul, and body--and righteousness (right relation) is expressed in all his affairs.

right side--The "right side" (John 21:6) is always on the side of Truth, the side of power. Whenever you, the master, are there, the nets are filled with ideas, because you are in touch with the infinite storehouse of wisdom.

rites--The rites and ceremonies of the priests in the tabernacle or temple represent the action of spiritual forces in developing the body. The great object of man's existence in planetary consciousness is to build a body after the ideals given by the Lord. The physical body is the tabernacle or temporary structure in and through which the enduring body is formed, and regeneration is a combination of chemical, mental, and spiritual processes.

river of life--The source of the natural healing impulse that constantly reconstructs the organism. When a man in faith makes intimate connection between his mind and the Father's, he enters into the river of life. And he has the ability to take others with him into the waters that cleanse, purify, and vitalize.

rod--Metaphysically, the power of the I AM in spiritual consciousness; I AM mastery and dominion.

roll, burning of--The burning of the roll (Jer. 36th chapter) represents a denial by the spiritual thought working in consciousness. To go forward to more advanced demonstrations, we must give up the present ruling ideas.

When we reach a point in our ongoing where there is necessity of greater spirituality, our own meditations reveal to us that the way is through reforming our methods of thought and life. This is the intuitive perception of the progressive trend of all things, which is symbolized in the burning of the "roll" by the king. The lesson is that we shall read out of the "roll" of the higher wisdom the new revelations of Truth that are being constantly presented to us and be open and receptive to divine evolution.

room, upper--The storehouse of ideas. The I AM center is in the crown of the head and dispenses the substance and life and intelligence of Spirit.

rulership--In personal rulership the great ones exercise authority; he who rules lords it over his subjects. In spiritual rulership he who serves best is greatest and is ruler through true merit. (see Matt. 20:25-28)

Jesus is the greatest ruler the world has ever known because He served humanity best, even to overcoming death itself; through His demonstration the way to eternal life was opened to humanity.

sabachthani--In sabachthani we find the root idea of loosening, setting free; letting alone and forsaking are secondary developments. The real root idea of the word expressed the cutting loose of bondage, or freeing from slavery.

On the cross Jesus cried, "Eli, Eli lama sabachthani?" that is, "My God, my God, why hast thou forsaken me?" (Matt. 27:46).

Metaphysically, sabachthani is the cry of the soul at the darkest hour of crucifixion. When the sensual is passing away it seems as though man were giving up his life, including every good. The sensual looms so large at this hour that, for the time being, it shuts God from the consciousness of the individual who is going through the experience. But God never forsakes His children; there can be no real separation from the divine, and a glorious resurrection into a greater degree of spiritual life than was ever realized before always follows each letting go of the old.

Sabbath--The true Sabbath is that state of spiritual attainment where man ceases from all personal effort and all belief in his own works, and rests in the consciousness that "the Father abiding in me doeth his works" (John 14:10). When we understand the true spirit of the Sabbath, we cease following prescribed rules laid down by a church and open our mind to God's rest and peace. We rest from outer work, cease daily occupation, and give ourselves up to meditation or the study of things spiritual.

The Sabbath is kept any time we enter into spiritual consciousness and rest from thoughts of temporal things. We let go of the external observance of days, because every day is a Sabbath on which we retire into Spirit and worship God.

sacrifice--A refining process that is constantly going on in consciousness; the renunciation of old beliefs that seem good for new ideas that are more of the nature of Christ.

salt of the earth--The thoughts in man that understand, love, and obey Truth as Jesus taught and demonstrated it.

salvation--The restitution of man to his spiritual birthright; regaining conscious possession of his God-given attributes. It comes as the result of redemption; the change from sin to righteousness. Salvation comes to man as a free gift from God. It embodies a knowledge of God that frees one from all limitations and points the way by which mind and body may be lifted up to the spiritual place of consciousness.

The belief that Jesus in an outer way atoned for our sins is not salvation. Salvation is based solely on an inner overcoming, a change in consciousness. It is a cleansing of the mind, through Christ, from thoughts of evil.

sanctification--The putting on of the nature of God and rising to the plane of dominion that gives man peace and satisfaction; the purity and holiness of the Christ consciousness. "This is the will of God, even your sanctification" (I Thess. 4:3).

sanctuary of the soul--The secret place within man's being where he has a rendezvous with God.

Satan--The Adversary, the great universal negative whose power is derived from the unlawful expression of man's own being. The serpent as "Satan" is sensation suggesting indulgence in pleasures beyond the law fixed by creative Mind.

Saviour--The Christ Mind is our Saviour. Through the Christ Mind we find salvation from poverty, sickness, sin, and death.

sayings of Jesus--To keep the sayings of Jesus is to take the spiritual principles that He enunciated and square our own life by them, that is, use them as a working basis in all the life processes.

science, spiritual--Science is the systematic and orderly arrangement of knowledge. Spiritual science, which is the orderly arrangement of the truths of Being, does not always conform to intellectual standards, but it is still scientific. Spiritual science treats of absolute ideas, while mental science treats of limited thoughts.

scribes--Scribes represent the thoughts that come to us from the outer world; Spirit inspires us from within. When Spirit speaks, no person can be quoted as authority--the Truth itself is authority, and it bows to no human exponent.

"For he taught them as having authority, and not as the scribes" (Mark 1:22).

Scriptures--Although the Holy Scriptures are almost universally considered to be the printed Bible only, the real Scriptures are the book of life within our own consciousness. The written word, however, is meant as a clue to a more vital part of the Scriptures than appears, since there is both a literal and a spiritual significance to them.

The Scriptures are not like other books. They have an enduring life, because of the spiritual quality given them by the writers. They are a profitable source of instruction in righteousness, as they set forth the principle, or law, of eternal life.

The Scriptures contain in symbol a most wonderful description of the creative action of Divine Mind, and one who studies the Bible merely as a historical record or as a guide to morals fails to sound the depths of these ancient writings.

Truth students recognize that Bible history is something more than history. For example, they see in the journey of the Israelites to the Promised Land, a picture of man's progress from sense consciousness to spiritual consciousness.

season of fruits--Bringing forth of the various powers of consciousness.

second coming--The second coming is the result of building the principles of Being into the soul of man, where they begin to express through him.

The events in the life of Jesus of Nazareth represent certain stages of spiritual growth in natural man. Jesus was the incarnation of the Son of God, and was the great Example, the Way-Shower, and manifested the Mind of God. If we are to attain full sonship we must follow His example. The second coming is right upon us. The Spirit of the Lord Jesus is here right now, and has been ever since He gave His spiritual body and blood to the race consciousness.

"secret place of the Most High"–(see inner chamber)

sects--In the spiritual interpretation of fundamental principles that underly the Scriptures, there are no sects, no differences among Truth students. But when the Bible is read according to the letter instead of the spirit, each reader views it from his own personal standpoint. This gives rise to a variety of opinions. Many a person who has what he considers the right viewpoint, tries to gain a following and convert others to his ideas, and in this way sects have been formed.

seed--The creative idea inherent in the Word. Its nature is inherited from its parent source, God. The "seed," that is, "the word of God," is the real man--not the external thinking personality that has consciousness of separation, but the internal Spirit center. The seed is a generative center through which intelligence manipulates substance and produces form. In itself it is powerless to produce anything, but it is the avenue through which interior forces manifest in the outer. Man draws on the universal forces within and without, just as the tree draws on the invisible Spirit and earth, air, and water.

The illustration of the mustard seed is used to show the capacity of the apparently small thought of Truth to develop in consciousness until it becomes the abiding place of a higher range of thoughts (birds of the air).

"seek the things that are above"–(Col: 3:1). Seek spirituality, instead of materiality. Seek to unfold the Christ Mind and to abide in spiritual consciousness. This leads into the path of peace, joy, and abundance of all good.

selah--Tranquil, secure, at rest, silence, pause, quiet. Selah is that state of mind in which we relax from affirming Truth and wait on God in the stillness. Then the Holy Spirit may reveal more of its inspirations to us and may establish us more firmly in divine harmony and good.

self-control--The capacity to direct one's behavior in right ways.

One who tries to establish self-control through will power and suppression never accomplishes permanent results. Self-control is accomplished when all the forces of man come in touch with the divine will and understanding.

self--Christ, the divine idea, is the true self of every man. Adam, the natural man, is the incomplete self. The fulfillment of self is accomplished as man puts on the Christ.

selfishness--Overconcern for one's own interests or comfort and disregard for the welfare of others. Selfishness leads to strife, followed by anger and hate. These emotions generate thought currents that burn up the body cells in somewhat the way a live wire sears flesh. Selfishness is often the cause of unhappiness.

self-love--Care for one's own happiness and well-being. This care is entirely compatible with justice, generosity, and love for others.

"Thou shalt love the Lord thy God with all thy heart, and with all thy soul, and with all thy strength, and with all thy mind; and thy neighbor as thyself" (Luke 10:27).

selling one's birthright--When one denies his true inheritance as a son of God, in thought, word, or deed, he is to that extent selling his birthright.

sensation--A state of excited interest or feeling derived from stimulation of the sense organs. Spirituality, lifts up this divine creation and restores it to its pristine beauty. Through cultivation of the spiritual nature, sensation is crowned with purity, and the son of man becomes aware of God's presence in his body as life, power, love, and joy.

sense consciousness--A mental state formed from believing in and acting through the senses. It is the serpent consciousness, deluded with sensation.

Judgments based on outer appearances--the senses--produce discordant thoughts, jealousies, and a host of limiting beliefs.

senses, how to develop the--By declaring our senses to be spiritual and by speaking the increasing word of the I AM to every one of them, we multiply their capacities and give them a sustaining vigor and vitality. This is done through the simple word of the I AM, backed up by the realization of its spiritual power.

separation from God--Man, being the offspring of God, has the power to create. He has used his privilege and created a realm of error thought, which separates him in consciousness from the Father.

separation of religion and state--Some statesmen and politicians urge the separation of religion and state because they do not understand the true character or mission of religion. The clergy are responsible for this misconception; they emphasize the saving of the soul, that it may be prepared to dwell happily in heaven after death. This teaching removes religion from its true field of work, which is making people better and happier here and now. As a result of this teaching that the greater rewards of religion will come after death, Christianity has been robbed of the major part of its power as a harmonizer of worldly affairs. Jesus did not promise rewards after death, but on the contrary, emphasized service in this world as the supreme thing. Mortal man thinks leadership is evidence of greatness, but Jesus taught that greatness is attained through service.

seraphim--Ideas of purity; the cleansing power of exalted ideas.

serpent--Sense consciousness or the desire of unspiritualized man for sensation. He seeks satisfaction through the appetite. By listening to the serpent of sense, man falls to his lowest estate.

sheep--Harmless and innocent animals; they represent the natural life that flows into man's consciousness from Spirit. It is pure, innocent, guileless.

The separation of goats from sheep is a mental process wherein the good, obedient, and profitable thoughts (sheep) are retained (placed on the right hand). The stubborn, selfish, useless thoughts (goats) are put away (placed on the left hand).

Sheba--The Queen of Sheba indicates the ruling intelligence of the whole consciousness pertaining to the part of being that has to do with nature.

shepherds--The shepherds watching by night are the protecting entities of God that watch over us. They are the conservers and protectors. To affirm "Jehovah is my shepherd" is to acknowledge that God (Spirit) is the source of understanding and of all help.

seven--the number seven represents fullness in the world of phenomena; seven refers to the divine law of perfection for the divine-natural man.

seven golden candlesticks--Refers to the seven nerve centers in the organism that have been quickened, purified, and transmuted into spiritual intelligence.

seven stars--The sevenfold powers of man in intelligent action are represented by the seven stars.

shoes--Represent the words with which understanding (Truth) is clothed. When holy ground, or substance in its spiritual wholeness, is approached by man he must put off from his understanding all limited thoughts about the Absolute--he must put his shoes off his feet.

shortcomings--Mental transgressions, which must be mentally denied. Many persons refuse to deny their shortcomings. They hold that they are perfect in Divine Mind and that it is superfluous to deny that which has no existence. But they are still subject to the appetites and passions of mortality, and will continue to be until they are "born anew." The Pharisees refused to be baptized by John. They did not consider that they needed the repentance that He demanded. They thought they were good enough to take the high places in the kingdom of God because of their popularly accepted religious supremacy.

silence, the--A state of consciousness entered into for the purpose of putting man in touch with Divine Mind so that the soul may listen to the "still small voice" (I Kings 19:12).

When one goes into the silence he enters the "secret place of the Most High," the closet of prayer within. He closes the door and in the stillness of that meeting place he prays to God, he communes with God, and he meditates on Truth. Then he listens to what God has to say to him.

silver and gold--Symbolize love and wisdom.

sin--Missing the mark; that is, falling short of divine perfection. Sin is man's failure to express the attributes of Being--life, love, intelligence, wisdom, and the other God qualities.

Sin (error) is first in mind and is redeemed by a mental process, or by going into the silence. Error is brought into the light of Spirit and then transformed into a constructive force. "Be ye transformed by the renewing of your mind" (Rom. 12:2).

Through the Christ Mind, our sins (wrong thinking) are forgiven or pardoned (erased from consciousness). When we have cast all sin (error thought) out of our mind, our body will be so pure that it cannot come under any supposed law of death or corruption.

singing--Singing, praising, and thanksgiving are the great building impulses of man. Never repress the desire to give thanks through happy songs and words of praise. (see song)

Singing restores harmony to tense nerves because its vibrations stir them to action, thus making it possible for the ever-waiting, healing Spirit to get in. The organ of the human voice is located right between the thyroid glands, the accelerators of certain important body functions. To a greater or lesser degree every word one speaks vibrates the cells up and down the body, from front brain to abdomen.

single eye--The single eye sees only God (good) everywhere. This perfect vision heals all disease in mind, body, and affairs. "The lamp of the body is the eye: if therefore thine eye be single, thy whole body shall be full of light" (Matt. 6:22).

six days of creation--The six great ideal projections from Divine Mind, each more comprehensive than its predecessor. The climax is reached when that phase of Being called man appears, having dominion over the ideas that have gone before.

sleep--Sleep is a great harmonizer of discordant thoughts. It "knits up the ravell'd sleave of care." We do not know the deep mysteries of sleep or what goes on in the soul when the sense man is in repose. Those who go into the "deep silence" produce a state of consciousness analogous to sleep. All the outer thoughts are stilled, and the soul listens to the "still small voice." It may also see symbols, feel the inner forces, or catch divine ideas fresh from the Fountainhead. Those who are expert in concentrating the attention on inner planes of Being find that a great rest and peace comes to them. Upon emerging from one of these sweet periods of communion with the Lord, they feel as if they have had a night of refreshing sleep.

solar plexus--The vital center of the organism, through which the subconscious mind connects with the physical body. The solar plexus is a large nerve center lying back of the pit of the stomach, and it controls the activity of the stomach.

Solomon's Temple--With its inner and outer courts, it is a symbolical representation of man's body.

Son of God--The fullness of the perfect-man idea in Divine Mind, the Christ. The true spiritual self of every individual. The living Word; the Christ idea in the Mind of God.

The Son ever exists in God. Father and Son are one and are omnipresent in man and the universe. Jesus represents God's idea of man in expression (Son of man); Christ is that idea in the Absolute (Son of God). The Christ is the man that God created in His image and likeness, the perfect-idea man. He is the real self of all men.

Son of man--That in us which discerns the difference between Truth and error. When we get this understanding we are in a position to free our soul from sin and our body from disease, which is the effect of sin. The Son of man must be lifted up, and there is no way to do this except through prayer.

son, prodigal--The "two sons" of Luke 15:11 are the two departments of the soul, or consciousness. The son who stayed at home is the religious or moral nature; the son who went into the far country is the human phase of the soul, in which are the appetites and passions. Going into a "far country" is separating the consciousness from the parent Source.

The first step in complying with the law of return to the Father's house is repentance and confession. Confession should be made to God. If we are truly repentant, the Father will forgive; He will have compassion, and the bounty of Divine Mind will be poured out on us.

When we make unity between the outer sense and the inner Spirit (the return of the prodigal son to the Father's house), there is great rejoicing; the outer is flooded with the vitality (robe), unending power is put into his hand (ring), and his understanding (feet) is strengthened. The "fatted calf" is the richness of strength always awaiting the needy soul. When all these relations have been established between the within and the without, there is rejoicing. The dead man of sense is made alive in the consciousness of Spirit--the lost is found.

song--(see singing)

sonship--Man, through Christ within, is God's son. Man reveals his sonship to himself and to others by claiming it; by declaring that he is not a son of mortality but a son of God; that the Spirit of God dwells within him and shines through him; that this Spirit is Christ, Son of God.

soul--Man's consciousness; the underlying idea back of any expression. In man, the soul is the many accumulated ideas back of his present expression. In its original and true sense, the soul of man is the expressed idea of man in Divine Mind.

Man is Spirit, soul, and body. Spirit is the I AM, the individuality. The body is soul expressing, and soul includes the conscious and subconscious minds. Soul makes the body, the body is the outer expression of the soul, and bodily health is in exact correspondence to the health of the soul.

soul development--The unfoldment of divine ideals in the soul, or consciousness of man, and the bringing of these ideals into expression in the body.

soul, duality of the--That phase of the soul named subconsciousness, which draws its life from both the earthly side of existence and the spiritual; it answers to both good and evil, light and darkness.

soul, food for the--The soul is fed by thought; the true soul food is the Word of God. The Word of God when properly appropriated makes the soul immortal.

source of all good--God is the source of all good. All good things flow to us from Him through love and grace. "All that is mine is thine" (Luke 15:31).

sowing--Every thought is a seed and brings forth after its kind. Every carnal thought, or thought of selfishness in any form, is seed sown to the flesh. It brings forth error and builds up flesh consciousness. The fruit of this sowing is death and corruption.

Every spiritual thought is a seed sown to the Spirit. Spiritual thoughts feed and nourish and build up the spiritual man. The result is life and immortality to the whole man: Spirit, soul, and body.

Spirit--God as the moving force in the universe; Principle as the breath of life in all creation; the principle of life; creative intelligence and life.

We sometimes discover within ourselves a flow of thought that has been evolved independently of the reasoning process and we are puzzled about its origin and its safety as a guide. In its beginnings this seemingly strange source of knowledge is turned aside as a day-dream; again it seems a distant voice, an echo of something that we have heard and forgotten. One should give attention to this unusual and usually faint whispering of Spirit in man. It is the development in man of a greater capacity to know himself and to understand the purpose of creation.

When one concentrates all the faculties on Truth ideas, the conscious mind and superconscious mind blend, and there is a descent of spiritual energies into soul and body. Then the faculties receive new power to express Truth and the body is renewed.

Spirit of truth--The Mind of God in its executive capacity; it carries out the divine plan of the originating Spirit. It proceeds from the Father and bears witness of the Son.

The Spirit of truth is God's thought projecting into our mind ideas that will build a spiritual consciousness like that of Jesus. The Spirit of truth watches every detail of our life, and when we by affirmation proclaim its presence, it brings new life into our body and prosperity into our affairs.

Spirit of wholeness--The Holy Spirit of the New Testament. In Greek mythology the Holy Spirit is symbolized by the goddess Hygeia. Modern medical men call it the restorative power of nature. (see Holy Spirit)

spiritual cosmogony--Spiritual interpretation of the creation of the universe. When science admits that the ether is moved by omnipotent Mind, the Bible will show forth a complete spiritual cosmogony.

spiritual discernment--Intuitive knowing of that which is true of God, or Spirit.

spiritual healer--One who helps man reform so that bodily healing follows as a natural consequence. In order to have bodily perfection it is necessary to bring the mind to a state of righteousness. This is the work of the spiritual healer.

spiritual quickening--Making active according to spiritual standards, by being linked to the activity of God-Mind.

spirituality--The consciousness that relates man directly to his Father-God. It is quickened and grows through prayer and other forms of religious thought and worship.

"spears into pruning-hooks"–(Isa. 2:4). Sharp, penetrating thoughts of cruelty turned into helpful ways.

stand--To hold fearlessly to the truth that Spirit is doing its perfect work and that there is no cause for alarm. Endurance is necessary to a soldier, and everyone who aspires to win the good fight of self must be able to stand against whatever comes. But before we can stand we must be prepared to meet adverse thoughts and overcome unworthy desires.

standards--Man's intellectual standards are determined according to the judgments of the senses. The one true standard of thinking is absolute Truth.

star--Represents man's first awakening before he realizes his Christ wisdom and power. The morning star heralds the coming of light and the glory of the sun. In like progressive unfoldment, the mind has its star of promise, which leads on to wisdom, then to final glory in the sun of righteousness, which is the Son of God.

star of Bethlehem--Symbolizes our inner conviction of our divine sonship. This inner conviction of our ability to accomplish whatever we undertake calls forth the very best in us and helps us to succeed where others of equal ability fail. The accumulated wisdom and experience of a man (the Wise Men from the East) rejoice when faith in one's destiny to do the will of God begins to rise within, and all the riches of wise experience, such as gifts of gold, frankincense, and myrrh, are bestowed on the young child. These gifts represent the subconscious reserve forces of the organism that enter into and form the new man in Christ.

stiff-necked--Self-sufficient, obstinate; descriptive of one who has attained a degree of spiritual dominion but is not obedient to the Spirit of truth.

stillness--A mental state of infinite peace, rest, and tranquillity where man's senses are hushed and he abides in God. "Be still, and know that I am God" (Psalms 46:10).

"still small voice"–The voice of Spirit speaking within the depths one's being. The "still small voice" is not an audible voice. It comes from within as spiritual knowing.

stimulant--Any external element that excites activity not characteristic of man's natural state.

stomach--The stomach stands for the meditative faculty and is the spiritual essence, the living energy out of which everything is made. Through substance all the attributes of Being are expressed. It sustains and enriches any idea that is projected into it.

Divine substance is man's supply. Out of it he forms whatever he will according to his faith and understanding. By entering into the silence, acknowledging divine substance, affirming his faith in and oneness with it, man becomes conscious of substance.

Spiritual realization of divine substance enriches the soil or thought-stuff of the mind. Jesus considered divine substance the treasure field in which He could find the fulfillment of His every need. Every demonstration over mortal limitations is followed by a realization of infinite reality. When man puts away the belief in the reality of matter, there follows a realization of the presence of true substance, of which matter is a mortal concept. Hence this thought-stuff may be made active by holding an affirmation. The rich substance of the kingdom of God is pouring its plenty perpetually into my mind and affairs, and I am in all ways prospered.

success--Attainment of a desired goal. Success comes as the result of faithfulness and earnestness in the application of God's law.

When success fails to crown our efforts, we sometimes become discouraged and quit. Then we try to console ourselves with the thought that it is God's will for us to fail. Failure is not God's will, but man lays it to the charge of God to excuse his own feeling of inadequacy and defeat. God's will is health, happiness, and prosperity for every man; and to have all that is good and beautiful is to express God's will for us.

suggestion--A mental process by which one mind influences another mind, or one's subconscious mind is influenced by one's own efforts.

Suggestion and realization differ in that spiritual realization comes from consciously entering into the Truth of Being, while suggestion may be either of Truth or error. The results of suggestion are temporary; spiritual realizations abide.

sun--The realm of consciousness that has been illuminded by Spirit. "The greater light to rule the day" (Gen. 1:16).

superconscious mind--A state of consciousness based on true ideas, on an understanding and realization of spiritual Truth.

"Where there is no vision the people cast off restraint" (Prov. 29:18). Men must see beyond matter and material possessions, or civilization will perish from the earth. If the superconsciousness, or the Christ Mind, is not developed, the people will destroy one another in insane warring for the fleeting things of the world. Preaching the glories of heaven will not reach a mind that has no capacity for the enjoyment of heaven.

The connection between the superconscious mind and the conscious mind is established within--by meditation, by going into the silence, and by speaking the word.

The superconsciousness is man's only sure guide through the maze of the creative process. By trusting to the infallibility of this guide, man opens himself to the inspiration of the Almighty.

supermind--The Christ consciousness; the mind that knows all and is able to accomplish all things because it is one with the Mind of God.

superstitions--Beliefs of those who live on the mere surface of things; beliefs that certain things or occurrences are good or bad omens. Under all conditions and circumstances declare the perfect law of Divine Mind. "Thou shalt be perfect with Jehovah thy God" (Deut. 18:13).

supplication--The earnest prayer or entreaty of the mind for a way of escape from the dominance of sense.

supply--Spiritual substance. Supply often fails to flow to one whose faith is fixed in some outer source instead of in substance. Jesus understood spiritual substance and could make from it whatever He wished, whenever He wished.

Anxiety about supply can be overcome by a recognition of the omnipresence of Spirit substance and the centering of faith in it as the one source of supply.

supreme Mind--God-Mind. The universal storehouse of all perfect ideas.

supreme voice--The voice of the Spirit of truth within each man.

swaddling clothes--Bands of cloth in which it was customary to wrap newborn babies. They represent confinement to the limitations of the physical nature of this first emanation of divine life, "because there was no room for them in the inn" (outer consciousness).

sword--Represents any weapon that man may turn against his fellow man. The tongue is called a sharp sword. Unloving words pierce like a sword. We reap whatever we sow. As we do to others so is it done to us. If we sow thoughts and words of destruction we will reap them.

sword, flaming--I AM is the gate through which the thinker comes forth from the invisible to the visible, and it is through this gate that he must go to come into the presence of Spirit. "I am the way, and the truth, and the life" (John 14:6). Hence, we take words and go to God. We come into His presence through the I AM gate and we return the same way. On the inner side of the gate is the Garden of Eden, but "the Cherubim, and the flame of a sword" are there, "to keep the way of the tree of life" (Gen. 3:24).

swords into plowshares--Destructive thoughts transformed into instruments of body culture.

symbols--Represent steps in the masonry of the soul. All scriptural symbols have to do with the spiritual progress of man. In the Bible every name stands for an idea and has a meaning that gives a due to the symbol.

A symbol loses its usefulness when man clings to it as the reality and fails to see the Truth that it represents.

synagogue--Represents an aggregation of religious ideas based on Truth, thoughts that have not yet received the inspiration of the whole Truth. A synagogue also represents a fixed religious state of consciousness.

A Jewish synagogue was a little chapel, where anyone could hear the law read out of the Hebrew Scriptures; or if he was a rabbi he could read out of the law himself. A constant stream of people came and went in the synagogue, and it fifty represents the mind of man, or a phase of man's mind that is given over to religious thought. In the new birth, or regeneration, the rebuilding of man's consciousness begins in this synagogue or religious mentality.

The synagogue of Acts 17:1, 2 in which Paul "for three Sabbath days reasoned with them from the scriptures," is the established religious thought bred in us by tradition, education, and inheritance.

tabernacle--Represents the temporal body of man, as the Temple built by Solomon in Jerusalem represents the permanent body. In the wilderness of sense, man worships God in a tent, or a temporary, transitory state of mind, which makes a perishable body. Yet in this flimsy structure are all the furnishings of the great temple that is to be built. So the body of every man is the promise of an imperishable one.

tables of stone--Represent the very foundation of our being, on which are engraved the memories of all our religious experiences.

talents (Matt. 25:14-30)–Symbolize our spiritual gifts of life, love, truth, substance, intelligence, faith, power, judgment, and will. Every inherent attribute of man's being has its root in God. All the gifts of Spirit are to be used to our fullest capacity.

teacher--Jesus appointed but one teacher in His school: the Spirit of truth, the Comforter in every man. "But the Comforter, even the Holy Spirit, whom the Father will send in my name, he shall teach you all things, and bring to you remembrance all that I said unto you" (John 14:25).

telepathy--Thought transference; exchange of thought between persons without visible means of transmission. This is a limited concept of omnipresent knowing. When one becomes spiritually developed he does not send his thought to another, but realizes omnipresent knowing, and the ideas he wishes to communicate are received and understood.

Temple, Solomon's--Metaphysically, a symbol of the regenerated body of man, which when he attains it he will never leave. This enduring temple is built in the understanding of Spirit as the one and only cause of all things.

temptation--A proving, testing, or trying. The temptations in the wilderness (Matt. 4:1-11) represent the desires and ambitions of the untried and untrained forces in the subconsciousness. When in the wilderness, Jesus was tempted by the Adversary, or personality; but with His superior understanding, He withstood the deceptive promises made to Him. When the personality suggested that Jesus make matter out of substance, use His power to rule over others, or do other marvelous things to prove His mastery, He said to the satanic personality, "Get thee hence, Satan."

That the temptations in the wilderness were not physical is quite evident, because there was no mountain from which all the kingdoms of the earth could be seen, nor was there a temple in the wilderness to which the Adversary could have taken Jesus. All these, and many more, including the royal entry of Jesus into Jerusalem riding on an ass, are allegorical representations of the way in which certain states of mind are handled by the initiate.

tents--The flesh bodies of man that he puts on and off again and again. (see tabernacle)

thanksgiving--Rendering our grateful thoughts to God for His manifold blessings. "Surely goodness and loving-kindness shall follow me all the days of my life" (Psalms 23:6). We give thanks that this is Truth.

Thanksgiving will keep the heart fresh; for true thanksgiving may be likened to rain falling upon ready soil, refreshing it and increasing its productiveness.

therapy--That phase of metaphysics which treats of divine healing. We are all interested in the soul and how to save it. Those who follow Jesus go one step farther in soul therapy than the average psychoanalyst; they incorporate Spirit with soul and make it the primal source and sustainer of both soul and body. "It is the spirit that giveth life" (John 6:63).

things--Thoughts lowered in vibration to the level of sense perception. The things that appear are the formulations of man's ideas of himself and God. Back of everything is a thought. Still the senses and you will perceive the thought behind the things.

thinking--The formulating process of mind. It is a faculty of the ego, the omnipotent I AM of each one of us. The thinking faculty is the inlet and the outlet of all your ideas. It is active, zealous, impulsive, but not always wise. Its nature is to think, and think it will. If you are ignorant of your office--a prince in the house of David--and stand meekly by and let it think unsifted thoughts, your thinking faculty will prove an unruly servant. Its food is ideas--symbolized in the Gospels as fishes--and it is forever casting its net on the right, on the left, for a draught. You alone can direct where its net shall be cast. You are the one who says, "Cast the net on the right side" (John 21:6).

The thinking faculty in you makes you a free agent, because it is your creative center; in and through this one power you establish your consciousness--you build your world. Through the volition of this faculty, you can refuse to receive ideas from Christ, you can cut yourself away from the realm of original Truth, or from the illusionary universe in which you are forever unraveling tangled ends and chasing shadows. Thus we see clearly that this faculty is the rock, the foundation upon which the consciousness must be built.

Be no longer a slave to the thinking faculty; command it to be still and know. Stand at the center of your being and say "I and the Father are one" (John 10:30). "I am meek and lowly in heart" (Matt. 11:29). "All authority hath been given unto me in heaven and on earth" (Matt. 28:18). "There is no God else besides me" (Isa. 45:21).

thought--A product of thinking; a mental vibration or impulse. Each thought is an identity that has a central ego, around which all its elements revolve. Thoughts are capable of expressing themselves. Every thought clothes itself in a life form according to the character given it by the thinker. The form is simply the conclusion of the thought.

One of the axiomatic truths of metaphysics is that "thoughts are things." That the mind of man marshals its faculties and literally makes into living entities the thoughts that it entertains is also a foregone conclusion. The word things expresses poorly the active and very vital character of the thoughts to which the mind gives life, substance, and intelligence. We see many inanimate "things" around us in the material world. If we compare our creative thoughts with them we get an inferior conception of the marvelous ability of our mind in its creative capacity.

Thought is controlled by the right use of affirmation and denial--by the power of the mind to accept and reject. This power of the mind is the I AM, and it is through the avenue of expression (I AM) that thought control, dominion, and mastery are obtained. Thoughts are controlled by the mind through its power to say "yes" or "no." To "hold a thought" is to affirm or deny a certain proposition both mentally and audibly until the logic of the mind is satisfied and spiritual realization is attained.

thought atmosphere--The surrounding mental climate created by each person in accordance with the character of his thinking. Thoughts of negation build an antagonistic and discordant atmosphere. Thoughts of love and prosperity, of health and faith, create a harmonious mental atmosphere.

thought center--A collection or aggregation of ideas in the mind. Thoughts of one kind are attracted one to another, form in consciousness, group themselves in the body, and build organs through which they manifest. For example, love manifests through the heart.

thought, colony of--Like attracts like. A thought will take up its abode in our consciousness with thoughts of like character. This law of attraction continues until combined thoughts make a colony. This colony of thoughts expresses itself in the cells of the body--for good or ill.

thought power--The moving force within an idea that gives it expression. All structures are built by thought power. This power is transmitted from mind to mind and from mind to body in all living forms.

thought-stuff--The omnipresent, invisible substance ever ready to take form in accordance with one's mental pattern. The thought-stuff of the universe is more sensitive than a phonographic record; it transcribes not only all sounds, but even the slightest vibration of thought.

thought vibrations--Energies sent out by the force and power of thought. All who are in like planes of consciousness with the thinker of the thought receive these thought energies. In this way telepathic messages are sent and received. When one sends thoughts in personal consciousness, the process is laborious and dangerous. There is a law of Spirit that equalizes all forces generated by the mind. This law is in the keeping of divine Principle, and there is neither success nor safety in using thought energies without its guiding wisdom.

time--The limitation of man's consciousness of space. A day is a measure of time in the realm of effects. A sidereal day is that period in which the earth rotates once on its axis. Man divided that period into seconds, minutes, hours, and thus invented time.

Time is the measure that man gives to passing events. The only power in time is what man imparts to it. When man gets into the understanding of the Absolute, he takes his freedom from all bondage of time and declares that time shall no more enter into the substance of his mind or body or affairs.

tithe--A tenth part. In the Old Testament the tithe or tenth is mentioned as a reasonable and just return to the Lord by way of acknowledging Him as the source of supply.

tithing--Giving a tenth of one's supply to God and His work. Tithing is a tacit agreement that man is in partnership with God in the conduct of his finances. This leads to confidence and assurance that whatever is done will bring increase of some kind. "Give, and it shall be given unto you" (Luke 6:38).

Tithing, which is based on a law that cannot fail, establishes method in giving. It brings into the consciousness a sense of divine order that is manifested in one's outer life and affairs as increased efficiency and greater prosperity. It is the surest way ever found to demonstrate plenty, for it is God's own law and way of giving. "Freely ye received, freely give" (Matt. 10:8).

tolerance--Forbearance; allowing to be done without hindering. Tolerance is passive, and good as far as it goes. Love is active good will. Love takes the initiative in doing and thinking good, and is far superior to tolerance.

tomb of Joseph of Arimathea--A tomb is a resting place; Arimathea represents an aggregation of thoughts of lofty character, a high state of consciousness in man; Joseph represents a state of consciousness in which we are improving spiritually.

The tomb where Jesus was laid to rest represents an elevated, peaceful state of consciousness in which He rested the three days previous to His resurrection. The word of Truth within Jesus did not die, but was quietly spreading from point to point during this period, getting ready for the supreme test: the overcoming of the appearance of death. For us, the tomb represents a high state of consciousness in us in which we improve in character along all lines. We not only grow into a broader understanding but also we increase in vitality and substance. We are resting in God, and at the same time gathering strength for the power of greater demonstrations to follow. In this state of consciousness the word of Truth is not idle, but quietly spreading. This process continues until the whole consciousness is vitalized by the Holy Spirit.

tongues, speaking with--Symbolizes increased ability to express Truth clearly and freely.

traits, inherited--Belief in the authority of our forefathers to determine our physical and mental characteristics. A form of error thinking. "Call no man your father on the earth" (Matt. 23:9).

transcendent God--God above or beyond His universe, apart from it. God is more than His universe; He is prior to and is exalted above it, but at once He is in His universe as the very essence of it. God is both transcendent and immanent.

transfiguration--Supernatural change of appearance that takes place as one experiences the full flow of divine power through his being. A lifting up of the soul that electrifies the body, causing it to shine. An example held before every follower of the Christ, of the glory it is possible to experience through habitual uplift of life and thought.

transgression of the law--Thinking thoughts that violate the principle of mental harmony inherent in Being.

transmutation--Change in character, from one phase to another. The lifting up of mind and body, from material aspect to spiritual character.

According to modern science this whole universe of forms can be dissolved into energy, from which it may again be formed. Science does not say that the directive and formative power is man, but the Bible so teaches and especially Jesus. Jesus said that all authority was given to Him in heaven and on earth. He manifested His power in a small way by multiplying a few loaves and fishes to feed more than five thousand persons. In various other instances He demonstrated that He had an understanding of the transmutation of substance. He raised His flesh body to an energy level far higher in potential life and substance than any reached before.

transubstantiation--The doctrine that the consecration by the minister of bread and wine changes the material elements to Christ elements, without affecting their appearance. At the Last Supper Jesus taught that the bread and wine which He consecrated were His body and His blood, and He told His followers to partake of them in remembrance of Him. He did not say that these elements were symbols of His blood and body, but that they were essentially the same substance and life as His body. This also has been the teaching of the church, as interpreted by the Council of Trent: "Under each species and under each particle of each species Christ is contained whole and entire."

This doctrine has been attacked both within and without the church, the majority of ministers and laymen accepting it on faith as in some way related to the miraculous. But the discoveries of the elemental character of matter by modern science are revealing the universal unity of substance and the possibility of its transformation from one thing to another by changing the number of arrangement of the electrons in the atom.

treatment--Spiritual realization of God's Truth for oneself or another. Spiritual process, or prayer, by which man receives the healing power of God.

A treatment is a prayer of faith and understanding for healing, harmony, wisdom, prosperity, or any other good that man may desire. Its object is to raise the consciousness of the one being treated to a high spiritual consciousness through which healing is accomplished.

trees--Represent nerves, and nerves are expressions of thoughts of unity. They connect thought centers. The trees growing on both sides of the river represent the nerves radiating from the vital flow on each side of the spinal column, and connecting and unifying the whole organism.

From the center of our being there spreads into every department of mind and body, the life-giving, everbearing tree of the Spirit of God. Its fruits are intelligence to the mind, substance to the body, and life to the entire being.

tree, oak--An oak tree in itself stands for something very strong and protective; but in Hebrew it has a deeper significance than this. The word comes from the root from which is derived the word Elohim; so we are reminded of the truth that those who trust God as their defense, as their refuge, their fortress, and dwell "in the secret place of the Most High, shall abide under the shadow of the Almighty," and shall not only be kept from all evil and its results, but shall continue to grow and unfold in understanding, in spirituality, and in every good.

"tree of life" (Gen. 2:9).–The eternal, omnipresent life of God that is within man. The tree of life "in the midst of the garden" is the innate, indwelling idea of immortal life, and the fruit of that tree is the consciousness of eternal life in the body.

The "tree of life" (figuratively in the midst of the garden) manifests in the body as a reserve force. The brain is the center, the solar plexus is the subcenter, and there are innumerable minor centers throughout the organism, the spinal cord, and nervous system. A conservation of the life and substance of the organism is necessary to its spiritualization and redemption.

"tree of the knowledge of good and evil" (Gen. 2:9)–Indicates a dual state of consciousness, a belief in both good and error, which eventually drives man out of the garden (his body temple).

tree, olive--Growing both under and above water, represents the restoration of unity between the material and spiritual, or God and man.

trinity--The religious terms for the trinity are Father, Son, and Holy Spirit. The metaphysical terms are mind, idea, and expression.

Father is the source, origin, essence, root, creator of all. Son is that which proceeds from, is begotten of the Father, like Him in nature, and essentially all that the Father is. Holy Spirit is God's word in movement: the working, moving, breathing, brooding of Spirit, made known to men through revelation, inspiration, and guidance. The Holy Spirit is the Comforter who will bring all things to their remembrance.

The doctrine of the trinity is often a stumbling block, because we find it difficult to understand how three persons can be one. Three persons cannot be one, and theology will always be a mystery until theologians become metaphysicians.

God is the name of the all-encompassing Mind. Christ is the name of the all-loving Mind. Holy Spirit is the all-active manifestation. These three are one fundamental Mind in its three creative aspects.

trouble--Calamity, difficulty, disaster; the sure result of wrong thinking. All economic, social, and personal trouble can be traced back to selfishness of the sense man. When spiritual man takes control of mind substance, all trouble of every kind dissolves into thin air.

trumpets and cymbals (Ezra 3: 10)–The trumpets and cymbals in the hands of the priests and Levites are the thrills and waves of harmonious energy. They go to every part of our mind and our body when we rejoice in Spirit, when our heart is filled with gratitude, and we express ourselves in thanksgiving to the Author of our being.

Truth--The Absolute; that which accords with God as divine principle; that which is, has been, and ever will be; that which eternally is. The Truth of God is reality: "the same yesterday and to-day, yea and for ever." The verities of being are eternal and have always existed. Truth abides in fullness at the very core of man's being. As his consciousness (awareness) expands, he touches the everlasting Truth. What seems new is but the unveiling of that which always has been.

The basic principle of Truth is that the mind of each individual may be consciously unified with Divine Mind through the indwelling Christ. By affirming at-one-ment with God-Mind, we eventually realize that perfect mind which was in Christ Jesus.

Truth, road of--The straight and narrow path along which Spirit directs, and which proves so smooth and safe that one refuses to allow oneself to be misled by habit into trusting sense perception.

Truth, source of--God is a special, personal Father to all His children, and from no other source can they get absolute Truth.

truth, Spirit of--God's thought projecting into our mind ideas that will build spiritual consciousness like that of Jesus. The Spirit of truth watches every detail of our life. When we ask and by affirmation proclaim its presence, it brings new life into both mind and body and moves us to observe spiritual and physical laws that restore health.

twelve--Metaphysically, twelve always refers to spiritual fulfillment. "And Elijah took twelve stones, according to the number of the tribes of the sons of Jacob . . . And with the stones he built an altar in the name of Jehovah" (I Kings 18:31, 32). The twelve stones represent the twelve most important nerve centers in the body. All material things represent spiritual realities.

Before we can realize unfettered power we must establish permanent resolutions of purity and covenants of conformity with the higher law of obedience. Elijah repaired the altar of Jehovah that had been thrown down. Obedience seems a simple matter, but the twelve fundamental faculties enter into its perfect expression. Elijah took twelve stones and fitted them together to form the altar, each stone representing one of the sons of Jacob, who won the name Israel in recognition of his perseverance toward perfection.

Understanding--God is supreme knowing. That in man which comprehends is understanding; it knows and comprehends in wisdom. Its comparisons are not made in the realm of form, but in the realm of ideas. It knows how to accomplish things. Spiritual discernment reveals that knowledge and intelligence are auxiliary to understanding. There are two ways of getting understanding. One is by following the guidance of Spirit that dwells within, and the other is to go blindly ahead and learn by hard experience.

Intellectual understanding of Truth is a tremendous step in advance of sense consciousness, and its possession brings a temptation to use for selfish ends the wisdom and power thereby revealed.

unfoldment--Bringing out by successive development; growth. As we unfold spiritually day by day, Spirit reveals more and more good to us. (see I Cor. 2:9)

union with God--Unification of our consciousness with that of God-Mind. This is the Christ consciousness. "I and the Father are one" (John 10:30).

unity--Universal oneness of God, man, and all creation. The only real unity is in Spirit. It is found nowhere else because personality always strives for its own success and aims for the good of the personal man, instead of the good of all men.

Man makes conscious unity with God first at the center of spirituality, this center having its basis of action in the top of the head. The only way to establish unity with the Father-Mind is by prayer. God's name is I AM. Our name is I AM. Speaking this name in the silence, recognizing that it is God's name and ours, we establish conscious unity with Him.

universal--All-encompassing. There is one life force: the creative universal life, even God. This life is eternal and infinite, from everlasting to everlasting.

universal resource--Omnipresent cosmic substance and reality from which all supply flows to man by means of his spoken word.

universal Spirit--Omnipresent, omnipotent, and omniscient God.

universal substance--The omnipresent mind stuff that can be molded to man's use through his thinking; mind substance.

universal urge--The urge toward perfection. In man this urge is the spiritual seed of the Christ, which ever seeks to unfold its divine nature.

universe--The total of all that is. It was first expressed as an idea in Divine Mind and later made manifest; that is, it became visible to the five senses by means of the creative power, the Word.

unreal--That which is temporal or transient; not based on Truth. Evil is the perfect example of the unreal. As soon as divine law is applied, the unreal, evil, has no existence. In Truth, it is nothing.

upper chamber--A higher state of consciousness attained through prayer or by going into the silence. “And when they were come in, they went up into the upper chamber, where they were abiding” (Acts 1:13).

The “upper chamber” to which the apostles went for the baptism of the Holy Spirit is the high state of mind that we assume in thinking about spiritual things. It may be attained through prayer, going into the silence with true words, or in meditation.

vegetarian--One who abstains from eating animal food or products. "And God said, Behold, I have given you every herb yielding seed, which is upon the face of all the earth, and every tree, in which is the fruit of a tree yielding seed; to you it shall be for food" (Gen. 1:29)

Vegetarianism is one of the ways to real health, because it requires, in a measure, the keeping of the spiritual law

veil of the Temple--That in the body which has shut out the light of Spirit and has hindered man from consciously standing in the presence of God. The rending of the veil of the Temple pictures a letting go of the belief in the reality of material consciousness. The relinquishment of the soul to God is the final giving up of all human ambitions and aims.

verities, eternal--The truths of Being, which are without beginning and without end; facts of existence.

vessels, holy--(I Kings 8:4). The thoughts that lie back of and form the various organs of the body. The vessels that had been taken from the Temple by Nebuchadnezzar and returned by Cyrus (Ezra 16:8) represent our capacity to comprehend and our ability to measure and appreciate life, love, and Truth.

vessels of silver--Fruit of one's experience in the sense consciousness added to one's innate spiritual consciousness.

vesture of Jesus--(John 19:23). Symbolizes the consciousness of unity, which is the inner conviction of all things. (see coat without seam)

vibrations--The rate at which all forces move. One of the greatest discoveries of all ages is that of physical science which shows that all things have their source and being in vibrations. What Jesus taught so profoundly in symbols about the riches of the kingdom of the heavens has now been proved true.

The whole universe is in vibration, and that vibration is under law. Chaos would result if the law were not supreme. Each particular thing has its rate of vibration. Heat, light, and color are different rates of vibration in one field of primal energy. Different colors are caused by the different frequencies of the vibrations as they strike the eye. But what causes vibration? We answer, mind.

vibrations, thought--Energies sent out by the force and power of thought.

vine and branches--The I AM within us is the vine, our faculties are the branches, and the perfect body is the fruit. The life current as it comes from the universal source is combined in vine, branches, and fruit, and it is on this free-flowing inner force that we fix our attention when we demonstrate the power of Spirit. Material symbols are likely to be misleading unless we remember always to get the spiritual import of their I AM application.

vineyard--The fruit of the vine is a symbol of life. Jesus said, "I am the vine." The vineyard represents manifest man, or humanity which was planted in perfection, and perfection is its destiny.

virgins--The ten virgins represent the senses. The senses are five. in number but have a twofold action--five in the inner realm and five in the outer world. The way to supply oil for the lamps of the virgins, even of the foolish ones is to affirm that the life source, Spirit, from which comes the power of hearing, smelling, seeing, feeling, and tasting, is not material but spiritual. Each sense has an inner counterpart, which is connected with the one life, from which it draws its oil, or life current. There is a soul eye and a soul ear, and these on their inner side are in direct contact with Spirit. But their outer side is in touch with the intellect and through the intellect with the formed organ of sense in the body. It is on this intellectual plane that mortal mind has its citadel and causes so much trouble with the outer organs.

vision, spiritual--Seeing God as the foundation of all, the sources of all, and the substance of all. Seeing the good, the true, and the beautiful everywhere. In this manner is the eye single and vision perfected.

voice--"Faculty or power of utterance" (Webster). The power center in the throat controls all the vibratory energies of this organism. It is the open door between the formless and the formed worlds of vibrations pertaining to the expression of sound. Every word that goes forth receives its specific character from the power faculty. Therefore, the voice is the most direct avenue of expression of consciousness.

Spirit is the "still small voice" in every man that hears and blesses and uplifts. Spirit is made manifest as perfect wholeness through the illumined mind.

The art of listening to the inner voice and obeying it is well-worth developing. Then it is that the Christ of one's life calls out, "Put out into the deep, and let down your nets for a draught." When the thinking faculty is obedient and does as it is told, it is always rewarded with a multitude of new ideas (fishes).

wait on the Lord--When we listen to the voice of Spirit we are waiting on the Lord.

walk by the Spirit--Means to acknowledge the power of the Christ Spirit within mind and body as the dominating force.

watch, high--Persistent looking toward the fulfillment of divine ideals.

watchman--A spiritually developed person who sees within and without, and with the word of command challenges anything negative.

water--In its different aspects water represents weakness and negativeness, cleansing, mental potentiality, and in some cases life, or vital energy.

In one of its aspects, water represents negativeness. The individual who allows himself to become negative to the good finds himself uncertain and unstable in his mind, and often becomes so submerged in the waters of negation that his physical condition is low. Weak sympathy with error and the results of error helps to produce this condition. To be positive toward the good it is very necessary that one have right ideas of God, that one know Him as all good.

Water also represents the great mass of thoughts that conform to environment. Every thought leaves its form in the consciousness, and all the weak characterless words and expressions gather in the subconscious mind as water gathers in holes. When we get discouraged or disappointed and "give up," the undertow of life sweeps this flood of negative thought over us, and we are conscious of bodily weakness of some sort. When we know the Truth, and "brace up," however, the waters are confined to their natural channels again and our strength is restored.

From the intellectual viewpoint water represents cleansing. When John the Baptist baptized with water, he washed away the sins of an external character. His baptism did not enter into the subconsciousness. It takes something more powerful than water to purify the error conditions accumulated by the soul in its many incarnations. The presence of God through Christ is necessary to purify this part of man.

water, above and below the firmament--In every mental proposition we have an above and a below. Above the firmament are the unexpressed capacities (waters) of the conscious mind resting in faith in Divine Mind. In this realm when "God says," the word is instantly fulfilled; the mental image of the word is registered in consciousness.

Below the firmament are the expressed capacities (waters) of the subconscious mind, which may be called memory but has not power to do original thinking. To reach the subconscious realm, the word must be declared consciously, and then from this firm starting point, directed down into the subconscious realm, where the redemptive work is carried on.

water, walk on--Water (the sea) represents mental potentiality. The race thoughts have formed a sea of thought, and to walk over it safely requires that one have faith in oneself. Faith necessary to accomplish so great an undertaking comes from understanding--understanding of God and man and the law of mastery given to man.

If one is to walk on the waves of troubled thought without sinking, he must become established in the faith of Spirit through Christ.

waterpots--The "six waterpots of stone" (John 2:6,7) represent the six nerve centers in the body, which are filled with the water of life, nerve fluid.

The waterpots filled to the brim with water by the servants show the extent to which God is prepared to fulfill the transformation from natural life to spiritual life through the power of the word.

This transformation into vitalizing Spirit is accomplished by adding to every word a spiritual idea. The idea of omnipresent life will then quicken the natural life in man, and it will make conscious contact with the one life and draw it out for the benefit of the many.

way, the--The I AM in man, the open door to the kingdom of God. (see Christ and Jesus)

wealth--True wealth is a state of consciousness, the consciousness of God as man's supply. Spiritual wealth expresses itself as faith, love, wisdom, substance, joy, and so on. Material wealth expresses as worldly riches, possessions of an earthly nature.

wedding garment--Garments represent the outer clothing of the mind. The "wedding garment" (Matt. 22:11) is the role of righteousness (right-use-ness) and is symbolical of a state of consciousness in which there is special preparation for the union unique. In other words, our external thinking must be in harmony with the inner revelation before we can make complete union with the Christ.

well--Symbolizes inspiration through the intellect alone. The well of living water (John 4:10-14) in man is the fount of inspiration within his consciousness, which flows forth peacefully, majestically, vitalizing and renewing mind and body.

well-beloved--The Christ, the ideal man.

wholeness--The perfect unification and expression of man as Spirit, soul, and body. True healing means to make whole. It is brought about by regeneration.

widow--One who has lost sight of God as support. When the conscious mind has ceased to be positive, the subconscious mind becomes like a "widow." The conscious unity between the mind and the vitality of the organism has been severed, and there is lack and burden (debt). This takes place eventually in all who do not consciously take possession of the twelve faculties in the organism.

The "widow" in Luke 18:1-5 typifies a belief in lack. Lack is not good in itself, but it serves to call man's attention to the law (judge). Dependence on the judgments of the law, without consciousness of love, subjects one to hard experience and laborious expression.

Jesus portrays the power of affirmative prayer, or repeated silent demands for justice, as a widow, one bereft of worldly protection and power. Under her persistence even the ungodly judge succumbs. The unceasing prayer of faith is commanded in the Scriptures, in various places.

widow of Zarephath--The widow of Zarephath, to whom Elijah was sent for sustenance, represents love bereft of wisdom. She represents the divine feminine, while Elijah here is the divine masculine or wisdom. Separated they are both in a state of semi-starvation but when they are joined in consciousness, increase at once begins and lack ceases. "The jar of meal wasted not, neither did the cruse of oil fail" (I King 17:9-16).

wife, taking a--Represents a unification of the I AM with the affections.

wilderness--In individual consciousness the wilderness is symbolical of the multitude of undisciplined and uncultivated thoughts.

will, the--The will is the executive faculty of the mind, the determining factor in man. What man wills or decrees comes to pass in his experience. "Thou shalt also decree a thing, and it shall be established unto thee" (Job 22:28).

The will is the center in mind and body around which revolve all the activities that constitute consciousness. It is the avenue through which the I AM expresses its potentiality.

The will may be said to be the man, because it is the directive power that determines character formation. When man wills to do the will of God, he exercises his individual will in wisdom, love, and spiritual understanding; he builds spiritual character.

The use of the will is very important in making demonstrations. One must be very persistent since persistence is essential to demonstration. Truth builds the perfect body, and the will must resolutely lay hold and keep hold of the word of Truth until the word becomes flesh.

will and desire--Desire is a reaching out of the mind for satisfaction. Will is the controlling, directing faculty of mind. One may have the desire to be well and yet not have the will to be well.

will and I AM--The will is the executive faculty of the mind and carries out the edicts of the I AM. All thoughts that go in and out of man's consciousness pass the gate at which sits the will. If the will understands its office, the character and value of every thought are inquired into and a certain tribute is exacted for the benefit of the whole man.

will and wisdom--When the will of man adheres to wisdom faithfully and carries out in its work the plans that are idealized in wisdom, it creates in man a consciousness of harmony and peace. Spirit breathes into such an individual continually the inspiration and knowledge necessary to give him superior understanding.

will, divine--(see God, will of)

will, personal--The adversary in sense-conscious will. He usurps power and considers himself the rightful ruler. This erroneous belief relating to personal will is discerned and adjusted by spiritual thoughts attained through prayer.

This adversary troubles us because we strive to maintain personal freedom instead of submitting to divine guidance. Self-confidence is a virtue when founded on the Truth of Being, but when it arises from the personal consciousness it keeps man from his dominion.

wind, east--Life currents that come from within and surround the whole being; the executive power of mind clearing the way to higher states of consciousness.

wine--Symbolizes the vitality that forms the connecting link between soul and body. It represents an all-pervading, free essence that is generated from the nerve substance, or water of life. The wine of life, or vitality of the organism, must be available in large quantities before a blending of thoughts, or of soul and body (wedding), can be made successfully. When the new Christ life comes into a mind where old beliefs concerning the body have been held, the body is transformed into its innate spiritual perfection.

wings--Symbolize freedom from material limitations.

wisdom--Intuitive knowing; spiritual intuition; the voice of God within as the source of our understanding; mental action based on the Christ Truth within. Wisdom includes judgment, discrimination, intuition, and all the departments of mind that come under the head of knowing. This "knowing" capacity transcends intellectual knowledge. Spiritual discernment always places wisdom above the other faculties of the mind and reveals that knowledge and intelligence are auxiliary to understanding.

wisdom and divine understanding--These attributes come from the Spirit of Christ within us. The price that we must pay for the conscious attainment of divine wisdom and understanding is the letting go of the personal self with its limited beliefs. Paul saw the Christ waiting at the door of every soul when he wrote: "Awake, thou that sleepest, and arise from the dead, and Christ shall shine upon thee" (Eph. 5:17).

wisdom, worldly--Wisdom is the ability to use knowledge. Worldly wisdom is knowledge of worldly things, with the ability to use them.

Wise Men--The Wise Men of the East who came to visit the baby Jesus may be likened to the stored-up resources of the soul that rise to the surface when its depths are stirred by a great spiritual revelation. In scriptural symbology East always means the within.

The gold, frankincense, and myrrh that the Wise Men brought when Jesus was born are symbolical of the inner resources open to the Christ child. They may be the stored-up deeds and thoughts of previous incarnations that wisdom within (the Wise Men) carefully guards and gives to the soul as an inheritance. Thus no good thought or deed is ever lost in the divine economy.

wishing--A wish is a superficial expression of desire, and is only fleeting. The patience, perseverance, and intense eagerness necessary to spiritual growth cannot come from anything as shallow as a wish.

Wishing will give way to desire when one consecrates himself wholly to God and follows up his consecration with prayer and meditation on Truth.

wolves--Devouring thoughts. They represent fear thoughts, thoughts of lack, and all thoughts that rob one of life and substance ideas.

woman--The feminine phase of man. In Genesis 2:18-25 woman typifies love in the soul not yet developed and established in substance.

woman, Greek--Signifies the intuitive perception of Truth reflected into the intellect from the soul. She also represents the unspiritualized love that is natural to the body.

Word--The agency by which God reveals Himself in some measure to all men, but to greater degree to highly developed souls; the thought of God or the sum total of God's creative power. The Word gives order and regularity to the movement of things and is the divine dynamic, the energy and self-revelation of God.

The Word of God is immanent in man and all the universe. All original creation is carried forward by and through man's conscious recognition of this mighty One.

Man is the consummation of the Word. His spirit has within it the concentration of all that is contained within the Word. God being perfect, His idea, thought, Word, must be perfect. Jesus expresses this perfect Word of God as spiritual man. "The Word became flesh, and dwelt among us" (John 1:14).

Word, creative--The creative idea in Divine Mind, which may be expressed by man when he has fulfilled the law of expression. All words are formative, but not all words are creative. The creative Word lays hold of Spirit substance and power. When Jesus said with a loud voice to Lazarus, "Come forth," (John 11:43) He had contact with the creative Word. As spirituality increases we fulfill the law. Our word has power and is creative.

word, healing--As man is quickened with spiritual faith his word is endowed with power. It becomes so charged with spiritual energy he is enabled to heal all manner of diseases, even at a distance. "The supplication [word] of a righteous man availeth much" (James 5:16).

word, reproving--A word of authoritative command; a form of vigorous denial that reaches the error belief behind the disease. "And Jesus rebuked him, saying, Hold thy peace, and come out of him" (Mark 1:25).

words--The vehicles through which ideas make themselves manifest. Words that have in them the realization of perfect, everywhere-present, always-present divine life, and our oneness with this life, are dominant in the restoration of life and health.

When spiritual words abide in man's consciousness, the word or thought formed in intellectual and sense mind must give way to the higher principles of Being. The whole consciousness is then raised to a more spiritual plane. Affirmations of words or of Truth realized in consciousness bring the mind into just the right attitude to receive light, and power, and guidance from Spirit.

work, object of--The true object of all work is to express the powers of one's being and to benefit mankind.

work in consciousness--To erase persistent forms of manifest negations through the increased use of denials and affirmations is often necessary. Man does the works that Jesus did by entering into the same consciousness that He was in--the realization of oneness with the Father.

world, the--A state of consciousness formed through the belief in the reality of things external. It leads one to follow standards of living based on man's opinions rather than on Truth. The world is overcome by our denying that it has any power over us and affirming freedom in Christ.

world, end of--"The end of the age," as Ferrar Fenton puts it, is the point in consciousness where true thoughts are in the majority, and error thoughts have lost their hold. This is the final consummation of the regenerative process. Everything that has been stored in consciousness is brought forth and becomes of visible, practical value to man.

The end of the world prophesied in the Bible will come as a thief in the night--quietly, silently. Those who are wrapped up in the things of sense will suddenly awake to the consciousness that they have lost their all, that this too solid earth has dissolved and left them without a place of action for their material thoughts.

worship--When one worships he bestows his love on, or identifies himself with, the things of Spirit. Worship represents the efforts of man to sustain a right mental attitude toward God.

wrath of God--Some Bible authorities claim that the "wrath of God" (Rom. 1:18) might with equal propriety be translated the "blessing of God." We know that after the destruction of limited and inferior thoughts and forms of life, other and higher thoughts and forms take their place, and the change is actually a blessing in the end. So even the "wrath" that comes to our fleshly tabernacles, when we persist in holding them in material thought, is ultimately a blessing. When we are loving and nonresistant we do not suffer under the transformations that go on when the Mosaic law is being carried out. The "wrath of God" is really the working out of the law of Being for the individual who does not conform to the law but thinks and acts in opposition to it.

Y

Yahweh--The original Hebrew form of Jehovah. It means "the self-existent one" who reveals Himself to His creation and through His creation.

Yahweh revealed Himself to Jesus as the Father within; Yahweh revealed himself to Moses as "I AM THAT I AM" (Exod. 3:14).

years--The measure of passing events. They constitute what we call time. But man's bodily condition depends on his state of mind. No two persons the same age are in exactly the same bodily condition. This shows that years do not make man young or old. "For as he thinketh within himself, so is he" (Prov. 23:7).

youth--The natural estate of all men. The bouyancy and joy of youth should be cultivated enthusiastically as the years advance. Deep in the subconscious mind is the God idea of eternal youth. It may have become dormant and needs to be awakened. Deny the belief in feebleness as the foolish fallacy of the race mind. Affirm and express the wondrous dynamic life of God and you will remain forever young.

zeal--Intensity, ardor, enthusiasm; the inward fire of the soul that urges man onward, regardless of the intellectual mind of caution and conservatism.

Zeal is the mighty force that incites the winds, the tides, the storms; it urges the planet on its course, and spurs the ant to greater exertion. It is the urge behind all things. Zeal is the affirmative impulse of existence, its command is "Go forward!"

"The zeal of thy house hath eaten me up" (Psalms 69:9) means that the zeal faculty has become so active intellectually that it has consumed the vitality and left nothing for spiritual growth. One may become so zealous for the spread of Truth as to bring on nervous prostration. "Take time to be holy." Turn a portion of your zeal to do God's will; to the establishing of His kingdom within you. Do not put all your enthusiasm into teaching, preaching, healing, and helping others; help your own soul. Do not let your zeal run away with your judgement. When zeal and judgment work together great things can be accomplished.

zone, spiritual - Through His spiritual attainments Jesus formed a spiritual zone in the earth's mental atmosphere. His followers make connection with that zone when they pray in His "name." He stated this fact in John 14:2, "I go to prepare a place for you." Simon Peter said, "Lord, whither goest thou?" Jesus answered him, "Whither I go, thou canst not follow me now; but thou shall follow afterwards" (John 13:36).

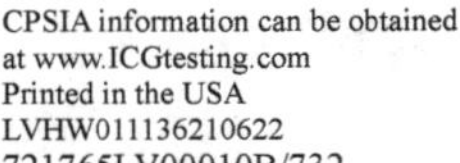

CPSIA information can be obtained
at www.ICGtesting.com
Printed in the USA
LVHW011136210622
721765LV00010B/732